THE OFFICIAL®
PRICE GUIDE TO

Royal Doulton®

Ruth M. Pollard

D1559530

Sixth Edition

HOUSE OF COLLECTIBLES
New York, New York 10022

DISCLAIMER

Products listed or shown were originally manufactured by Royal Doulton (UK) Limited, and distributed in the United States by Royal Doulton USA Inc. Ruth M. Pollard is an independent dealer who is in no way connected with Royal Doulton (UK) Limited and/or Royal Doulton USA Inc., which claim and reserve all rights under the trademark and copyright laws with respect to each of the products listed or shown. These products are listed or shown with the permission of Royal Doulton USA Inc., and the prices are those of the author and not necessarily endorsed by Royal Doulton USA Inc. Royal Doulton (UK) Limited and Royal Doulton USA Inc. have no responsibility for any of the information in this book.

The items in the cover photo are courtesy of Princess and Barry Weiss, Yesterday's, P.O. Box 296, New City, NY 10956.

Important Notice. All of the information, including valuations, in this book has been compiled from the most reliable sources, and every effort has been made to eliminate errors and questionable data. Nevertheless the possibility of error, in a work of such immense scope, always exists. The publisher will not be held responsible for losses which may occur in the purchase, sale, or other transaction of items because of information contained herein. Readers who feel they have discovered errors are invited to *write* and inform us, so they may be corrected in subsequent editions. Those seeking further information on the topics covered in this book are advised to refer to the complete line of *Official Price Guides* published by the House of Collectibles.

Published by: The House of Collectibles
201 East 50th Street
New York, New York 10022

Distributed by Ballantine Books, a division of Random House, Inc., New York and simultaneously in Canada by Random House of Canada Limited, Toronto.

Manufactured in the United States of America

Library of Congress Catalog Card Number: 84-644919

ISBN: 0-876-37763-0

10 9 8 7 6 5 4 3 2 1

To my dear and long-time friends, Cliff and Shirley Keith,
for their encouragement to continue my endeavors in the face of
much adversity during 1987.

TABLE OF CONTENTS

ACKNOWLEDGMENTS

For their contributions in pricing and identification, we acknowledge and thank Nikki Budin, Gourmet Antiques, Mansfield, Ohio; Barry Weiss of Yesterday's, New City, New York; Mrs. Helen Fortune, Ashtabula Antiques Importing Co., Ashtabula, Ohio; Major William F. Fortune, California; several specialty collectors who wish to remain anonymous; and Mr. Fred Dearden, Trenton, New Jersey, for selected black and white photos. A special thanks to Joseph Schenberg, not only for his assistance in a specialty collection but for his thoughtfulness and concern.

An Overview

MARKET REVIEW

Two years have passed since the release of the fifth edition of *The Official Price Guide to Royal Doulton*. You will note, as you use or glance through this sixth edition, that many changes have taken place; some will enhance your collecting, others I feel are harmful to the collector.

As the guide reflects, prices on the older and very scarce pieces are climbing, some substantially. The more common figurines have declined in value . . . not a great deal but enough to show that there are a number of the same pieces for sale. Most dealers sales have been very good with collectors waiting for the rarities.

Character jugs have not increased drastically and they remain a very good buy because prices are still reasonable. In 1986 and 1987 there had been many new releases. Character jugs that were previously discontinued have been re-introduced with color changes and in limited editions. This was done, no doubt, to encourage the collector to add these desirable pieces to their collections. However, in discussing this with dealers I find that most are disappointed with this approach because the prices advance so rapidly and the edition is so small that many collectors have no source of availability. Personally, I would rather see some new ideas than repeats of discontinued pieces.

The Celebrity collection was completely discontinued at the end of 1986. The Antagonist collection stands at four pieces, all with a limited edition of 9,500. The Star Crossed Lovers collection now consists of three pieces with a limited edition of 9,500. Eight new pieces have been added to the Doultonville Tobies, making a total of twenty pieces for a complete collection.

Thirty new figurines have been added to the beautiful "Reflections" collection. In 1987, the "Nicola" figurine with a new colorway as a special edition was seen at all Michael Doulton events. Three new figurines especially appealing are Happy Birthday, Happy Anniversary and Merry Christmas. Royal Doulton, on various occasions, has issued figures and other items to celebrate a proud British Heritage. In 1987 the introduction of a prestigious collection, titled Queens of the Realm, was seen. This series consists of four figures, the first being *Queen Elizabeth I* and is limited to 5,000 pieces. In mid-year 1987, Images of Fire introduced two figures from the Image of Nature Collection in that beautiful and unusual process known as Rouge Flambé. This process is so difficult that it is unique to see any new pieces introduced. Titled *Courtship* and *Gift of Life,* these should be considered by the discriminating collector.

Currently there are a number of shows in the United States pertaining mostly to discontinued items. Attendance at these functions has been excellent with both United States and foreign dealers participating. There is an ever-growing interest in Royal Doulton and, in my opinion, with the volatility of the stock market, mutual funds, etc., more people will be seeking good collectibles for their money investments, and they will become aware of the wonderful world of Royal Doulton.

INTRODUCTION

Like a royal bloodline, Royal Doulton creations of the 1970s and 1980s are as collectible as those originating prior to World War I.

Although Royal Doultons are distributed internationally, they are still uncommon compared to the works of other potteries. Royal Doultons will never be plentiful because they are not manufactured in large quantities. Thus the owner of even a single prized work has something that carries an authentic exclusiveness.

Royal Doultons have always possessed a magical quality that intensifies with time. A good portion of Britain's history is incorporated in Royal Doulton figures of kings, queens, sea captains and adventurers. Not only did the company produce figures of high society but common British citizens as well. For example, the Gardener Character Jug is a faithful creation of a laboring gardener who kept the grounds of noble estates. He was a solid part of Britain's history, perhaps ignored in the history books, but not in Royal Doulton porcelain. Royal Doultons have a timelessness because their subjects are vignettes out of history captured dramatically in the porcelain art.

The backbone behind this highly collectible ware is made up of the creative and highly skilled artists. A high standard is always required for each piece that leaves the factory. Therefore, since the 1800s, this ware has been collectible. Today in English country estates, owned by dukes and earls of the 1800s and 1900s, Royal Doulton ware is found. With this high level of perfection found in each piece, saying Royal Doulton will continue to be very collectible is an understatement. No other ceramic ware of the twentieth century, with the possible exception of Goebel Hummel figurines, is as universally sought and esteemed as Royal Doulton ware.

HISTORY

At twelve, John Doulton began his distinguished career in pottery. Little did he know that his name would survive almost two centuries and be associated with the most sought after ware in pottery history.

Though the Royal Doulton firm has roots extended into history, admiration for fine pottery had already been established before it came upon the scene. In addition to manufacturing terra-cotta or earthenware for household use, ancient civilizations also worked pottery into artistic forms. The earliest specimens were not cast from molds, but made freehand by the modeler and thus could not be precisely duplicated. They also did not possess a lustrous finish or bright enameling. They were usually left in the basic earth color (reddish) and sometimes painted with decorations. This was firmly believed to be the highest state earthenware could reach. Therefore, the western world was very surprised to find that the Chinese manufactured a far superior type of ceramic: hard, smooth, glossy, and beautifully enameled. It soon acquired the name China-ware, and became the rage of Europe. By the 1400s it was being imported in very large quantities. The difference in quality between Chinaware and Euro-pean pottery was so great that demand for the latter dwindled.

For many years, European potters tried to duplicate the imported product but the technique of making true porcelain remained a secret until the early eighteenth century when porcelain began to be produced at Meissen in Prussia.

The "secret" was the use of a special clay. Though strenuous efforts were made to keep the formula in Prussian hands, porcelain was soon manufactured in far-flung parts of the continent.

The history of Royal Doulton pottery began in the seventeenth century. The successful commercial sale of Oriental wares had prompted potters to strive for reasonably faithful imitations. One of these was John Dwight of Fulham, a small country village just outside London. Dwight wanted to manufacture por-celain. If he could not do that, he would at least manufacture something more dazzling than earthenware. After much struggle and experimentation, Dwight produced a white stoneware with a lustrous finish. It was not really porcelain, but a better imitation of it than any other Englishman had made up to that time. Bubbling with excitement and a dream of vast riches, Dwight applied to Charles II for a patent in 1671 and received it.

Dwight did prosper. He eventually was running a string of factories in Fulham and was, unquestionably, the town's leading citizen. As far as his works are concerned, their modeling was better than their finishing. Dwight restrained himself from putting out cascades of small inexpensive figures. In-stead he stayed mainly with grand concepts, producing large stoneware busts and classical statuary similar in design to bronzes and marbles. Made in limited numbers, they have become quite rare and are often found in museums.

During the following century, numerous major developments occurred in pottery making. Of the British potteries, Staffordshire became the unrivaled leader in figureware. Its figures were not usually as delicate or colorful as those of continental European makers, but had charm and originality. By the late 1700s every British pottery works was getting its inspiration from Staffordshire.

Porcelain popularity was still riding very high in England when John Doul-ton was born in 1793. The native manufacturers had received a boost from the French Revolution, which had reduced exports from France and aided sales of British ware. Doulton's place of birth was Fulham, not far from Dwight's pottery, which was still in operation. Many youths from the region were au-tomatically apprenticed to the pottery trade. John Doulton was one of them. Doulton went for apprenticeship to Dwight's in 1805 and remained there until reaching age nineteen in 1812.

Doulton, like other apprentices, braved the intense heat, the filth-riddled air and the 12-hour working days for seven or eight years to become a master. But even those who successfully completed their apprenticeship had an uncertain future. They were not automatically guaranteed a position at the factory where they served, and it was always questionable whether employment could be found elsewhere.

Doulton did not work for Dwight's after filling out his apprenticeship. He went to Lambeth, another small English village known for pottery, and was employed by the Vauxhall works. This had been a successful organization some years earlier but had met with lean times because of the owner's death. It was then being run by his widow, Martha Jones. In 1815 Doulton, then twenty-two, with three years under his belt at Vauxhall, bought a partnership in the factory for 100 pounds of sterling. The partnership gave him one-third ownership, the other two-thirds belonged to Mrs. Jones and another partner named John Watt.

Although this arrangement lasted five years because of a poor economy, Mrs. Jones withdrew from Vauxhall. Doulton and Watt decided to keep the company open.

Things improved considerably thereafter. The early 1820s was a period of significant growth for the company. Watt and Doulton proved amicable partners. Watt handled the business end while Doulton ran factory operations.

The firm's line in this era differed considerably from what we now familiarly recognize as "Doulton." A large part of the trade for potters was garden ornaments. These large creations brought a good profit.

Doulton and Watt also made Toby Jugs, commercial packing jars, and decorative flasks.

In 1826 the firm acquired new headquarters on High Street in Lambeth— not far from historic Lambeth Palace, built in the Middle Ages. Growing tourism brought many art-minded visitors to Lambeth Palace, and many stopped to see Doulton and Watt's company called Lambeth Pottery. A drawing by Thomas Wakeman, made around the time of Queen Victoria's ascent, shows the factory's exterior and a general view of the street. It was not a typical-looking factory but had the appearance of a gentleman's country estate. The building was made entirely of stone. At the front was a tall stately iron gate, leading into a sculpture garden. The gateposts were surmounted with huge likenesses of eagles, and there were various embellishments on the building itself: classical urns along the roof fronting and a sculptured coat of arms rising high over the door.

Henry Doulton, John's son, joined the staff in 1835 at age fifteen. He had been primed for a university education but saw no reason why he should not start as early as possible to learn the business he would eventually inherit. Henry was well-schooled in art and not only knew artistic porcelain but was attuned to the artistic tastes of the public. He was a go-getter who thought unceasingly of expansion. In 1877 he bought out a factory in Burslem, England, previously used by the firm Pinder, Bourne and Company. Five years later the name was changed to Doulton and Company. It was here that most of the firm's figureware was made in the late nineteenth century.

Doulton's had become one of Britain's major industrial enterprises. Its works had enormous influence, not only on other potteries of the time, but in setting styles and shaping public tastes. Doulton pottery was featured in exhibitions and placed in museums. Both wealthy American and English citizens stocked their homes with Doultons.

Because of his artistic and commercial contributions to Britain, Henry Doulton was knighted by Queen Victoria in 1887. This was the first time a potter had received such distinction.

A change in Doulton pottery occurred in the early 1900s. Instead of the emphasis on vases and ornaments, small decorative figures were introduced. Because of the strong collecting interest for eighteenth century Staffordshire figures, Doulton Art Director Charles Noke felt the public would be willing to buy fine modern figures for a lower price. Therefore, in 1913 Doulton introduced a series of small models called the HN series named after the firm's head colorist, Harry Nixon. Also in 1913, the firm's name changed to Royal Doulton inspired partially by a visit from King George V and Queen Mary to the Burslem factory.

By the end of 1913, Royal Doulton had placed forty character figurines on the market. The figures were well received by the public. Because of World War I, less than a dozen new numbers were added to the HN line in 1914, and even fewer in 1915. But the output rose in 1916 and continued to rise at the war's conclusion. Although most of the early designs were retained until 1938, they were rare due to limited distribution, lost or damaged specimens, and often low production figures.

Because of the Depression, the company knew it had to diversify. Therefore, in 1932, a line of miniature figures was introduced. At first, the series carried HN numbers, but later was given M numbers, and finally the number scheme was dropped altogether.

The company also introduced limited editions and gave greater attention to its miscellaneous wares.

After World War II, Royal Doulton sped ahead full pace surpassing anything in the company's history. Collecting enthusiasm boomed, spurred by the discontinuation of the early HN line and by the scarcity of those figures because of the tremendous destruction suffered by Britain during World War II.

In recent years, Royal Doulton has introduced several new series including Dancers of the World, Soldiers of the Revolution, and Gentle Arts Series.

SIR HENRY DOULTON[a]
by John Morton[b]

With all the international attention given to the company and its products, I find it somewhat strange that so little seems to be known of the man who more than any other was responsible for making the company an international success. For more than fifty years Henry Doulton *was* Doulton; his vision, his imagination and his genius for inspiring others established the company at the forefront of the industry and, on the wider stage, revitalised a rather moribund nineteenth century industry.

The bare facts of Henry Doulton's life read like one of those biographies that used to be held up to children as a moral lesson in the rewards that follow from a life of hard work and attention to duty. Born in 1820, he entered his father's business at the age of fifteen and for ten years worked to become a sound and practised potter and to understand every aspect of the trade.

[a]Reprinted with permission of Royal Doulton International Collectors Club, from an article appearing in the Summer 1984 edition.
[b]John Morton was instrumental in setting up the Sir Henry Doulton gallery at the pottery in Burslem. He is no way associated with the prices in this book.

Between 1846 and 1856 he was to make stoneware the virtually universal material for drainage systems and, in so doing, made a fortune. With his commercial success secured, he went on to make Doulton the leading producer of art wares of the age, gathering a great store of honours for the company and for himself. Behind this uninterrupted rise to fame and fortune lies a rich and complex personality that does not easily fit the normal image of the Victorian entrepreneur as a Mr. Hardcastle type who knew little of, and cared less for, art and culture. From his earliest childhood Henry Doulton was noted for his bookishness and his family had always assumed that this would lead him to a career in the law or the Church—the bookish professions of the age. He surprised them all by expressing a wish to follow his father into potting but never lost his love of literature which remained one of the dominant forces of his life. In particular he was a passionate, almost evangelical, lover of poets and poetry and was famous for his habit of quoting, frequently and at length, from the works of his favourites—Milton, Tennyson and, above all, Wordsworth. This devotion to literature engendered in him an idealistic view of the artist as a special, spiritual being who was in some way above the normal rules that govern mankind and deserved to be shielded from the brutalities of a harsh, materialistic world—an attitude that was to have profound implications for the development of the Lambeth and Burslem studios.

It would be a great mistake, however, to see Henry Doulton as some dewey-eyed romantic—he wasn't! Quite clearly he was a shrewd and immensely capable businessman who created an enormous industrial empire based on strict utilitarian production. He was a man of powerful imagination, however, and had the vision to perceive the immense possibilities opened up by the sanitary revolution. Having grasped the suitability of stoneware as a material for drain-pipes and conduits, he pursued this idea tirelessly in the face of great prejudice and opposition. Even the reservations of his own family had to be overcome and he was later to remark on how hard he had to work to persuade his father to become a rich man! The single-minded way in which Doulton followed through his original idea is indicative of his entire character and the definiteness of his aims is one of the dominant features of his personality. Looking over the course of his career one gains the clear impression of a man who liked to proceed on his way in clear orderly stages, never taking on new challenges until he had secured his current goal. He first mastered his trade, he then worked hard to develop new applications for the stonewares in which the pottery specialised, and it was only when his commercial success was secured that he felt able to move into the entirely new field of art wares. It is characteristic that when he was first approached by John Sparkes, head of the Lambeth School of Art, with a scheme to revive the production of decorated stonewares, he should refuse. At the time he was deeply involved with the expansion of his pipe-making business and clearly felt that his mind was fully occupied. Fortunately Sparkes did not give up and upon approaching Henry Doulton once more he was received enthusiastically. From the first experiments in 1866 it was only ten years before the whole world was buzzing with excitement about the Doulton Wares. A clear example of what he could do when he put his mind to something!

It was the combination of the apparently contradictory aspects of his personality—the idealistic lover of art and literature and the shrewd and decisive entrepreneur—that was the basis for Henry Doulton's unique contribution. I find it difficult to believe that a Mr. Hardcastle would have devoted himself so wholeheartedly to the development of the art wares, especially as they never made money, yet conversely, only supreme entrepreneurial flair could have made such a success of the venture and provided the huge investments involved. It needed an idealist to allow his artists the unheard of freedom they enjoyed, and a shrewd businessman to realise that the burst of creativity this produced would provide enormous prestige for the firm, prestige that would reflect onto the utilitarian wares upon which the whole company was based.

Henry Doulton was very much a man of his time. In the age of the entrepreneur, he was the entrepreneur supreme, and at a time when many great intellects feared that the growing industrial world was in danger of destroying the creative and spiritual aspect of men, he was concerned that art and the artist must play a central role in life. It was this duality in his character that made Henry Doulton a great rather than simply a successful man.

DESIGNERS

The success of any manufacturer of artistic porcelain depends in large measure on the designers and artists who create each design and the working models for them.

The serious collector realizes that no degree of manufacturing talent can turn a mediocre model into a public favorite when the finished work goes on sale. In a company such as Royal Doulton, a high standard is always required; and at the same time, imaginative designing that does not merely repeat what has been done in the past. Thus, experimentation is always a necessity, and designers and artists must constantly bring a high level of quality to their experimental efforts.

The following paragraphs give some brief information on noteworthy Doulton artists and designers.

GEORGE TINWORTH. George Tinworth's influence on the factory and on porcelain making in general is well recognized. Tinworth had a very successful career as an independent sculptor in Britain in addition to his work with Doulton. Born in 1843, he grew up in the dawning years of one of the more memorable classical revivals. Heroic sculptures after the Greek manner were strongly in demand when Tinworth began his career, and he received many commissions for such works. Some of his productions showing warriors, gladiators, etc., were of immense size. At the same time he also sculpted small figures of children and animals. Some of Tinworth's models were cast at Doulton's. They enjoyed great popularity, and Tinworth gained a reputation in Britain on a par with that of John Rogers in America—though the "Tinworths" were much smaller physically. A number of Tinworth's models provided inspiration for Doulton's artists. His most significant connection with the firm came through his set of *Merry Musicians,* a group of children playing various instruments.

LESLIE HARRADINE. Leslie Harradine was born in 1887 and came to Doulton as an apprentice modeler at age fifteen. His great creativity proved a driving force in the organization and resulted in many imaginative creations. Harradine was responsible for a number of the character jugs issued in the early 1900s including Sam Weller, Pickwick, Sairey Gamp, and Micawber. His personal tastes in modeling ran strongly in the direction of figureware, but the firm's trade then consisted heavily of vases and garden ornaments, so his talents were directed toward them as well. In 1912, when still very young and on the threshold of an apparently bright career, Harradine decided that factory life did not appeal to him. He bought a farm in Canada and refused all offers to return to Doulton's. However, an arrangement was worked out. For nearly forty years, Harradine modeled figures in clay and shipped them across the Atlantic for use in the Royal Doulton line. In this fashion Royal Doulton gained some of its most popular models including Polly Peachum, The Goose Girl, Contentment, and others.

RICHARD GARBE. Richard Garbe worked at Royal Doulton during the 1930s and created many of its Limited Editions of that era, such as Spirit of the Wind, Beethoven, Salome, and Lady of the Snows. He also modeled wall masks. Garbe had the important distinction of being instructor in sculpture at London's Royal College of Art. The letters "RA," often shown after his name, signify Royal Artist.

CHARLES NOKE. Charles Noke was Art Director of Doulton's for many years during the late nineteenth and early twentieth centuries. He had previously been with Worcester, a rival factory, and joined Doulton in 1889. Noke receives credit for shaping Doulton into its present form. He conceived the idea of Fancy Character Figures and instituted the HN series. Noke was extremely partial to figureware and even before the HN series he was adding figures to the Doulton line. He was originally a modeler.

MARGARET M. DAVIES. Peggy Davies, as she is known, has been responsible for designing and modeling many of Royal Doulton's post-war creations. She joined the firm in 1939 just as the war was beginning. Trade was naturally curtailed by the war, and Peggy's home was damaged by German air raids. But she continued her interest in art, and after the war became a very successful independent sculptress. Though not employed by Royal Doulton thereafter, she executed many works for the firm on a contract arrangement. Her Royal Doultons have included Lady Musicians, Figures of Williamsburg, and the much-heralded Dancers of the World, in which each piece has a low limited number of just 750 specimens.

ERIC GRIFFITHS. A sculptor of considerable skill and reputation, Eric Griffiths is noted for his masterful Soldiers of the Revolution series. His early background was in industrial sculpturing. Griffiths now serves as Head of Sculpture for Royal Doulton.

MARY NICOLL. Mary Nicoll contributed many works to the HN series during the 1960s and 1970s, until her death in 1974. Her figures were mainly "general types" rather than historical or fictional characters. They included a number of nautical types, in which she had a special interest.

A dramatic expansion in the figurine and character jug collections has taken place in the last ten years along with a number of limited edition series such as Queens of the Realm, Les Saisons Series, Gentle Arts and others. Along with these new series, new artists have come into prominence with the introduction of their designs.

Artist Robert Jefferson has responded with his beautiful Jefferson Sculptures and the limited edition Myths and Maidens Series. Robert Tabbenor, an assistant to Eric Griffiths in the design studios, joined Royal Doulton in 1973.

Peter Gee joined the Doulton organization just a short time prior to Robert Tabbenor. After serving as an apprentice for nine years, his first design, Rachel HN 2919, was introduced in 1981.

Artists Bill Harper, Adrian Hughes and Pauline Parsons work from their own studios in different parts of the country and come to Burslem, from time to time, to submit their latest designs. There are now a number of students doing their apprenticeships in clay sculpturing who, after completing their courses, may go forward to keep this form of art continuing into the next century.

PRODUCING FIGURINES

Any Royal Doulton article is a work of art. From its inception to finished product, the pieces are carefully produced by exceptionally skilled and dedicated workers. This high level of perfection is the exception rather than the rule in twentieth century pottery making. The following step-by-step process shows the manufacture of figurines.

Each item entering the Royal Doulton figurine line begins with an idea usually formed by one of the factory's artists. When working up a design, an artist must consider if a work is compatible with the products already in the line, if it can be rendered with genuine visual appeal, and if it is decorative enough to stand on its own merits. Royal Doultons need not be pretty, but must be captivating.

After deciding on a design, sketches are made showing several poses or attitudes. The sketched idea is then formed into a clay working model. The working model must be the exact size and design of the future porcelain model. To make the working model, soft non-hardening clay is used. The clay of the finished model is quite different. Its ingredients are selected to provide maximum hardness. Each ingredient is inspected to assure proper texture and quality and blended together at the factory according to rigid procedures.

When the working model is approved, a cast made from plaster of Paris is taken of it. The cast is used as the figurine's mold. After it hardens, the cast is sawed into several pieces making several small molds. Clay slip is then poured into each mold. When hardened, the molds are assembled into figures and then dried. The model is then fired in an oven heated to as high as 1,240 degrees centigrade.

Since most Royal Doulton figurines are highly translucent, the piece is dipped into a vat of liquid glaze which has an appearance of buttermilk. However, when the piece is again fired in the kiln, it emerges with a crystal-like coating. After the second firing, it is hand painted. This step in porcelain factories is called enameling. After the figures are painted, several pieces are inspected. Any defects will deem the piece unsatisfactory.

CARE AND REPAIR

A broken Royal Doulton is worth just a fraction of the normal value of a mint condition specimen because mint condition pieces are easily attainable.

Do not buy a broken Royal Doulton believing if it is repaired it will be worth the same as a mint condition specimen. Unfortunately, it will not. If a specimen breaks, repair it to serve as a filler until another piece can be purchased. If the break is particularly bad, for example if it shatters, discarding it may be wiser than having it repaired, since the expense of the repair may cost more than the broken Royal Doulton is worth.

To fix a clean break between two pieces, apply rubber cement with a brush to the areas that will be fitted together. Let it dry for a minute, then press together gently until fully dry. With a fast drying cement, also hold the pieces together until fully dry.

A professional restorer will usually apply enamel to the joined areas to conceal the break. Again, consider the cost of professional restoration before having the piece repaired. Although the break may not be noticeable, the piece is still damaged and will not retain the value of a mint condition piece.

CLEANING: Royal Doultons may require a periodical cleaning. If the surface is simply dusty, brush with a dry soft cloth. If the surface needs a thorough cleaning, immerse the piece in lukewarm water. Never use hot water which could damage the enamel. Next, soak the piece for several minutes in lukewarm soapy water. Do not use bleach or other harsh detergents, instead use a mild hand soap. After this step, rinse with lukewarm water. If the piece is extremely dirty, the same procedure is used but repeated several times.

TRADEMARKS

Generally, porcelain markings have a reputation for being confusing. Although there are questions about old Doulton marks from the 1800s, fortunately after 1913 Doulton ware is distinctly marked.

In the 1850s the familiar marking was a terse "DOULTON, LAMBETH." It gave the manufacturer's name and location as shown in illustrations 1–6.

After expansion in 1877, the backstamps referred to either the Lambeth or Burslem factories. The coronet was added at the Burslem factory in 1886. After 1891, the word "England" was added. In 1902, Royal was added to the company's name. The marking system became more detailed through the years arriving at its present form of a lion and crown. See illustration 12.

In 1913, the HN numbering system was instituted. The letters HN stood for Royal Doulton's chief colorist Harry Nixon. The plan was to have the HN prefix on every model followed by a serial number and the official name of the

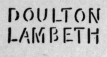

1

2

3

4

5

6

model. At first the model names were applied by hand, then later they were stamped.

Occasionally specimens turn up which bear the model name without the series number.

In addition, many pieces are hand marked "Potted by Doulton & Co." Usually pieces after 1913 carry a stamped lion and crown symbol.

Bone china products after 1928 are marked "BONE CHINA" with the artist's signature and often a number enclosed by a rectangle. Sometimes an

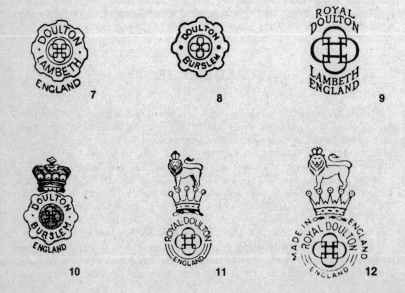

13

14

Rd. No. is shown, which is the figure's registration number at the British Patent Office.

In the 1950s and 1960s, script stamped lettering was used to give the appearance of hand lettering. This practice was discontinued.

Revisions of lettering styles naturally created a situation in which identical figures do not always bear identical markings. This is a useful aid in dating. Illustration 17 shows the current marking of "THE BALLOON MAN," the same figure pictured in illustration 18. In this case the numbering is alike but the style of lettering different.

Examples of the same figures with the same names bearing different numbers are also found. Royal Doulton changes the series number whenever it makes revisions in a figure's color scheme. Therefore, the same figure could have several different numbers. *Kate Hardcastle* exists with numbers HN 1718, HN 1719, HN 1734, HN 1919 and HN 2028. If a date appears impressed into the mold, this could signify the date of that model's introduction to the line. These dates are occasionally found on older figures only. Molds for HN 564, *Parson's Daughter,* carried a dating of 3-1-31. This work remained in the line from then until 1949. When reading these dates, it is important to remember that the British give the DAY before the MONTH. Thus, 3-1-31 is January 3, 1931.

Generally, the HN series runs in sequence and the numerical order roughly indicates the chronological order in which figures were issued. Do not assume the HN numbers follow a precise chronological order. Although recent HN models are numbered in the 2,800s, there are not 2,800 different pieces produced. Gaps have occurred in the numbering system for several reasons. Groups of numbers are reserved for pieces which will be made in the future or are never made.

The M series comprises miniature figures 4½″ tall introduced in 1932. Some of the works in this series are reduced versions of HN figures, while others were created expressly for the M series and have no HN counterpart. When Royal Doulton began this series, the M prefix was not used. The early miniatures carried HN numbers and were serialized as part of the regular HN series. The last miniatures to carry HN numbers appeared in 1949. Today, *numbering has been abandoned*

15

16

17

18

for the miniature figures; they now bear only the model name. They are readily identified by the standard Royal Doulton markings. Some of the earliest miniatures are marked "DOULTON" or "DOULTON C.," but those in current production have the same stamping as the HN figures.

Royal Doulton marks its special series and editions with unique backstamp information which identifies a particular item or series. Dickensware, which was first introduced in 1908, was marked with a brown backstamp until 1930 when it became a black backstamp until 1960. The Rouge Flambé trademarks vary. Sometimes several marks are found on one piece while others have only one marking along with the traditional Royal Doulton emblem.

HOW TO USE THIS BOOK

The HN series which comprises the majority of the Royal Doulton line is listed both numerically and alphabetically. The numerical list records the HN figures with their dates of introduction and discontinuance. In the alphabetical list, a brief description of the pieces is given. Subjects in the HN series are highly diversified, representing the works of many different artists at different time periods. This series is good for topical collecting. Basically, there are three categories: historical characters, fictional characters, and general characters. Historical characters include kings, queens and other individuals taken from

history. Fictional characters are best exemplified by the Dickens characters. General characters, which is the largest of the groups, include trades people and ladies in flowing gowns.

Following the numerical listing of the HN series is the numerical listing of the M series which contains miniature fancy and character figures. The numerical listings of both groups include all objects bearing those prefix letters including those which belong to sub-series of their own. The numerical listings are designed for quick, easy reference. More detailed information on these works is contained in the alphabetical listings.

Through the years, Royal Doulton has issued many wildlife figurines. The majority, while carrying HN prefix numbers, were grouped into a sub-series of their own. In addition to these HN figures of animals and birds, a K series or miniature animal and bird figures was also produced. The HN animal and bird figures are listed numerically followed by a numerical listing of the K animal and bird figures. These numerical listings are then followed by a priced alphabetical listing of both groups.

Following is a combined alphabetical listing of the HN and M series. The book also includes different series of limited editions, Toby jugs, plates, rouge flambé, and miscellaneous items.

PRICES. Prices shown in this book represent average retail selling prices compiled from dealers' catalogues, auction results, magazine ads, and other sources. Price ranges are given for out-of-production items while those in current production are listed at the retail price. Although extreme care has been taken to be accurate, the prices listed should be used as guidelines. Prices vary throughout the country; therefore, discovering prices higher or lower than those listed is possible, although unusual.

SUGGESTED READINGS

Atterbury, Paul and Louise Irvine. *The Doulton Story,* Stoke-on-Trent, England: Royal Doulton Tableware Limited.

Dennis, Richard. *Doulton Character Jugs,* Stoke-on-Trent, England: Royal Doulton Limited, 1986.

Dennis, Richard. *Doulton Stoneware Pottery,* London, England: Robert Stockwell Limited, 1971.

Dennis, Richard. *Limited Edition Loving-Cups and Jugs,* London, England: Richard Dennis, 1987.

Eyles, Desmond. *Doulton Lambeth Wares.* London, England: Barrie and Jenkins, 1975.

Eyles, Desmond, Richard Dennis, and Louise Irvine. *Royal Doulton Figures,* Stoke-on-Trent, England: Royal Doulton Limited, 1987.

Irvine, Louise. *Royal Doulton Series Ware,* London, England: Richard Dennis, 1980.

Lukins, Jocelyn. *Doulton Flambe Animals,* Devon, England: N.P.E. 26.

Lukins, Jocelyn. *Doulton Kingsware Whiskey Flasks,* Devon, England: N.P.E. 26.

McClinton, Katherine Morrison. *Royal Doulton Figurines and Character Jugs,* Des Moines, IA: Wallace-Homestead, 1978.

Pearson, Kevin. *The Character Jug Collectors Handbook,* London, England: Kevin Francis Publ., 1986.

Pearson, Kevin. *The Doulton Figure Collectors Handbook,* London, England: Kevin Francis Publ., 1986.

Weiss, Barry and Princess Weiss. *Royal Doulton Discontinued Jugs,* New York, NY: Barry and Princess Weiss, 1987.

Royal Doulton Listings

"HN" NUMERICAL LISTINGS OF FANCY AND CHARACTER FIGURINES

	Date	Price Range	
☐ HN 1, Darling (1st version)	1913–1928	1500.00	2000.00
☐ HN 2, Elizabeth Fry	1913–1938	3500.00	5000.00
☐ HN 3, Milking Time	1913–1938	3000.00	3500.00
☐ HN 4, Picardy Peasant (female)	1913–1938	2000.00	2500.00
☐ HN 5, Picardy Peasant (female)	1913–1938	2000.00	2500.00
☐ HN 6, Dunce	1913–1938	2750.00	3000.00
☐ HN 7, Pedlar Wolf	1913–1938	2500.00	3000.00
☐ HN 8, The Crinoline	1913–1938	1400.00	1800.00
☐ HN 9, The Crinoline	1913–1938	1400.00	1800.00
☐ HN 9A, The Crinoline	1913–1938	1400.00	1800.00
☐ HN 10, Madonna of the Square	1913–1938	1450.00	1600.00
☐ HN 10A, Madonna of the Square	1913–1938	1350.00	1500.00
☐ HN 11, Madonna of the Square	1913–1938	1450.00	1700.00
☐ HN 12, Baby	1913–1938	3500.00	4500.00
☐ HN 13, Picardy Peasant (male)	1913–1938	2000.00	2500.00
☐ HN 14, Madonna of the Square	1913–1938	1450.00	1700.00
☐ HN 15, The Sleepy Scholar	1913–1938	2500.00	3000.00
☐ HN 16, The Sleepy Scholar	1913–1938	2500.00	3000.00
☐ HN 17, Picardy Peasant (male)	1913–1938	2000.00	2500.00
☐ HN 17A, Picardy Peasant (female)	1913–1938	2000.00	2500.00
☐ HN 18, Pussy	1913–1938	5500.00	6500.00
☐ HN 19, Picardy Peasant (male)	1913–1938	2000.00	2500.00
☐ HN 20, The Coquette	1913–1938	3000.00	4000.00
☐ HN 21, The Crinoline	1913–1938	1400.00	1800.00
☐ HN 21A, The Crinoline	1913–1938	1400.00	1800.00
☐ HN 22, The Lavender Woman	1913–1938	2100.00	2300.00
☐ HN 23, The Lavender Woman	1913–1938	2100.00	2300.00
☐ HN 23A, The Lavender Woman	1913–1938	2100.00	2300.00
☐ HN 24, Sleep	1913–1938	2500.00	3000.00
☐ HN 24A, Sleep	1913–1938	2500.00	3000.00
☐ HN 25, Sleep	1913–1938	2500.00	3000.00
☐ HN 25A, Sleep	1913–1938	2500.00	3000.00
☐ HN 26, The Diligent Scholar	1913–1938	2200.00	2500.00
☐ HN 27, Madonna of the Square	1913–1938	1650.00	1800.00
☐ HN 28, Motherhood	1913–1938	2200.00	2500.00
☐ HN 29, The Sleepy Scholar	1913–1938	2500.00	3000.00
☐ HN 30, Motherhood	1913–1938	3000.00	3250.00
☐ HN 31, The Return of Persephone ...	1913–1938	4000.00	5000.00
☐ HN 32, Child and Crab	1913–1938	3000.00	3500.00
☐ HN 33, An Arab	1913–1938	1800.00	2500.00

	Date	Price Range	
☐ HN 34, Moorish Minstrel	1913–1938	2500.00	2750.00
☐ HN 35, Charley's Aunt (1st version)	1914–1938	750.00	850.00
☐ HN 36, The Sentimental Pierrot	1914–1938	2000.00	2350.00
☐ HN 37, The Coquette	1914–1938	3000.00	4000.00
☐ HN 38, The Carpet Vendor (1st version)	1914–1938	3500.00	4500.00
☐ HN 38A, The Carpet Vendor (1st version)	1914–1938	3500.00	4500.00
☐ HN 39, The Welsh Girl	1914–1938	2500.00	2750.00
☐ HN 40, A Lady of the Elizabethan Period (1st version)	1914–1938	1750.00	2000.00
☐ HN 40A, A Lady of the Elizabethan Period (1st version)	1914–1938	1750.00	2000.00
☐ HN 41, A Lady of the Georgian Period	1914–1938	1750.00	2250.00
☐ HN 42, Robert Burns	1914–1938	3500.00	4000.00
☐ HN 43, A Lady of the Time of Henry VI	1914–1938	3000.00	3500.00
☐ HN 44, A Lilac Shawl	1915–1938	1600.00	1850.00
☐ HN 44A, A Lilac Shawl	1915–1938	1600.00	1850.00
☐ HN 45, A Jester (1st version)	1915–1938	1700.00	1900.00
☐ HN 45A, A Jester (2nd version)	1915–1938	1700.00	1900.00
☐ HN 45B, A Jester (2nd version)	1915–1938	2000.00	2400.00
☐ HN 46, The Gainsborough Hat	1915–1938	1200.00	1350.00
☐ HN 46A, The Gainsborough Hat	1915–1938	1200.00	1350.00
☐ HN 47, The Gainsborough Hat	1915–1938	1200.00	1350.00
☐ HN 48, Lady of the Fan	1916–1938	1700.00	1900.00
☐ HN 48A, Lady with Rose	1916–1938	1700.00	1900.00
☐ HN 49, Under the Gooseberry Bush	1916–1938	1500.00	2000.00
☐ HN 50, A Spook	1916–1938	1350.00	1600.00
☐ HN 51, A Spook	1916–1938	1350.00	1600.00
☐ HN 51A, A Spook	1916–1938	1350.00	1600.00
☐ HN 51B, A Spook	1916–1938	1350.00	1600.00
☐ HN 52, Lady of the Fan	1916–1938	1700.00	1900.00
☐ HN 52A, Lady with Rose	1916–1938	1700.00	1900.00
☐ HN 53, Lady of the Fan	1916–1938	1700.00	1900.00
☐ HN 53A, Lady of the Fan	1916–1938	1700.00	1900.00
☐ HN 54, Lady Ermine	1916–1938	1500.00	1800.00
☐ HN 55, A Jester (2nd version)	1916–1938	2000.00	2400.00
☐ HN 56, The Land of Nod	1916–1938	2500.00	3000.00
☐ HN 56A, The Land of Nod	1916–1938	2500.00	3000.00
☐ HN 56B, The Land of Nod	1916–1938	2500.00	3000.00
☐ HN 57, The Curtsey	1916–1938	1500.00	1750.00
☐ HN 57A, The Flounced Skirt	1916–1938	1650.00	1800.00
☐ HN 57B, The Curtsey	1916–1938	1500.00	1750.00
☐ HN 58, A Spook	1916–1938	1350.00	1600.00
☐ HN 59, Upon her Cheeks she Wept ..	1916–1938	2000.00	2400.00

	Date	Price Range	
☐ HN 60, Shy Anne	1916–1938	2000.00	2500.00
☐ HN 61, Katharine	1916–1938	1500.00	1700.00
☐ HN 62, A Child's Grace	1916–1938	3000.00	3500.00
☐ HN 62A, A Child's Grace	1916–1938	3000.00	3500.00
☐ HN 63, The Little Land	1916–1938	2100.00	2500.00
☐ HN 64, Shy Anne	1916–1938	2000.00	2500.00
☐ HN 65, Shy Anne	1916–1938	2000.00	2500.00
☐ HN 66, The Flounced Skirt	1916–1938	1650.00	1800.00
☐ HN 66A, The Curtsey	1916–1938	1550.00	1700.00
☐ HN 67, The Little Land	1916–1938	2100.00	2500.00
☐ HN 68, Lady with a Rose	1916–1938	1700.00	1900.00
☐ HN 69, Pretty Lady	1916–1938	850.00	1000.00
☐ HN 70, Pretty Lady	1916–1938	850.00	1000.00
☐ HN 71, A Jester (1st version)	1917–1938	1500.00	1700.00
☐ HN 71A, A Jester (1st version)	1917–1938	1500.00	1700.00
☐ HN 72, An Orange Vendor	1917–1938	1100.00	1450.00
☐ HN 73, A Lady of the Elizabethan Period (1st version)	1917–1938	1800.00	2000.00
☐ HN 74, Katharine	1917–1938	1650.00	1800.00
☐ HN 75, Blue Beard (1st version)	1917–1938	4000.00	5000.00
☐ HN 76, Carpet Vendor (2nd version)	1917–1938	3500.00	4500.00
☐ HN 77, The Flounced Skirt	1917–1938	1650.00	1800.00
☐ HN 78, The Flounced Skirt	1917–1938	1650.00	1800.00
☐ HN 79, Shylock	1917–1938	2500.00	2750.00
☐ HN 80, Fisherwomen	1917–1938	4000.00	4500.00
☐ HN 81, A Shepherd (1st version)	1918–1938	2250.00	2500.00
☐ HN 82, The Afternoon Call	1918–1938	3000.00	3500.00
☐ HN 83, The Lady Anne	1918–1938	3000.00	3500.00
☐ HN 84, A Mandarin (1st version)	1918–1938	3000.00	3500.00
☐ HN 85, Jack Point	1918–1938	2500.00	3200.00
☐ HN 86, Out for a Walk	1918–1936	2500.00	3000.00
☐ HN 87, The Lady Anne	1918–1938	3000.00	3500.00
☐ HN 88, Spooks	1918–1938	2000.00	2500.00
☐ HN 89, Spooks	1918–1938	2000.00	2500.00
☐ HN 90, Doris Keene as Cavallini (1st version)	1918–1936	2000.00	2500.00
☐ HN 91, Jack Point	1918–1938	2000.00	2500.00
☐ HN 92, The Welsh Girl	1918–1938	2500.00	2750.00
☐ HN 93, The Lady Anne	1918–1938	3000.00	3500.00
☐ HN 94, The Young Knight	1918–1938	2750.00	3250.00
☐ HN 95, Europa and the Bull	1918–1938	4000.00	5000.00
☐ HN 96, Doris Keene as Cavallini (2nd version)	1918–1938	2500.00	3000.00
☐ HN 97, The Mermaid	1918–1938	700.00	900.00
☐ HN 98, Guy Fawkes	1918–1949	1250.00	1500.00
☐ HN 99, Jack Point	1918–1938	2000.00	2500.00

	Date	Price Range	
HN 100–HN 299 ANIMAL AND BIRD MODELS			
☐ **HN 300**, The Mermaid	1918–1936	800.00	1000.00
☐ **HN 301**, Moorish Piper Minstrel	1918–1938	3200.00	3550.00
☐ **HN 302**, Pretty Lady	1918–1938	900.00	1100.00
☐ **HN 303**, Motherhood	1918–1938	3000.00	3250.00
☐ **HN 304**, Lady with Rose	1918–1938	1700.00	1900.00
☐ **HN 305**, A Scribe	1918–1936	1000.00	1300.00
☐ **HN 306**, Milking Time	1913–1938	2750.00	3000.00
☐ **HN 307**, The Sentimental Pierrot	1918–1938	2000.00	2350.00
☐ **HN 308**, A Jester (2nd version)	1918–1938	2000.00	2400.00
☐ **HN 309**, A Lady of the Elizabethan Period (2nd version)	1918–1938	1750.00	2000.00
☐ **HN 310**, Dunce	1918–1938	2750.00	3000.00
☐ **HN 311**, Dancing Figure	1918–1938	3500.00	4000.00
☐ **HN 312**, Spring (1st version) The Seasons	1918–1938	1500.00	1800.00
☐ **HN 313**, Summer (1st version) The Seasons	1918–1938	1650.00	1800.00
☐ **HN 314**, Autumn (1st version) The Seasons	1918–1938	1500.00	1800.00
☐ **HN 315**, Winter (1st version) The Seasons	1918–1938	1500.00	1800.00
☐ **HN 316**, A Mandarin (1st version) ...	1918–1938	3000.00	3500.00
☐ **HN 317**, Shylock	1918–1938	2500.00	2750.00
☐ **HN 318**, A Mandarin (1st version) ...	1918–1938	3000.00	3500.00
☐ **HN 319**, A Gnome	1918–1938	1200.00	1500.00
☐ **HN 320**, A Jester (1st version)	1918–1938	1700.00	1900.00
☐ **HN 321**, Digger (New Zealand)	1918–1938	1500.00	2000.00
☐ **HN 322**, Digger (Australian)	1918–1938	1500.00	2000.00
☐ **HN 323**, Blighty	1918–1938	1500.00	1850.00
☐ **HN 324**, A Scribe	1918–1938	1000.00	1300.00
☐ **HN 325**, Pussy	1918–1938	7500.00	9500.00
☐ **HN 326**, Madonna of the Square	1918–1938	1650.00	1800.00
☐ **HN 327**, The Curtsey	1918–1938	1550.00	1700.00
☐ **HN 328**, Moorish Piper Minstrel	1918–1938	3200.00	3550.00
☐ **HN 329**, The Gainsborough Hat	1918–1938	1200.00	1350.00
☐ **HN 330**, Pretty Lady	1918–1938	900.00	1100.00
☐ **HN 331**, A Lady of the Georgian Period	1918–1938	1850.00	2250.00
☐ **HN 332**, Lady Ermine	1918–1938	1600.00	1900.00
☐ **HN 333**, The Flounced Skirt	1918–1938	1550.00	1700.00
☐ **HN 334**, The Curtsey	1918–1938	1450.00	1600.00
☐ **HN 335**, Lady of the Fan	1919–1938	1700.00	1900.00
☐ **HN 336**, Lady with Rose	1919–1938	1700.00	1900.00
☐ **HN 337**, The Parson's Daughter	1919–1938	800.00	900.00
☐ **HN 338**, The Parson's Daughter	1919–1938	800.00	900.00

	Date	Price Range	
☐ **HN 339,** In Grandma's Days (A Lilac Shawl)	1919–1938	1400.00	1600.00
☐ **HN 340,** In Grandma's Days (A Lilac Shawl)	1919–1938	1400.00	1600.00
☐ **HN 341,** Katherine	1919–1938	1250.00	1500.00
☐ **HN 342,** The Lavender Woman	1919–1938	2100.00	2300.00
☐ **HN 343,** An Arab	1919–1938	2000.00	2750.00
☐ **HN 344,** Henry Irving as Cardinal Wolsey	1919–1949	2000.00	2500.00
☐ **HN 345,** Doris Keene as Cavallini (2nd version)	1919–1949	2750.00	3000.00
☐ **HN 346,** Tony Weller (1st version)	1919–1938	1800.00	2000.00
☐ **HN 347,** Guy Fawkes	1919–1938	1500.00	1800.00
☐ **HN 348,** The Carpet Vendor (1st version)	1919–1938	3500.00	4500.00
☐ **HN 349,** Fisherwomen	1919–1968	2750.00	3000.00
☐ **HN 350,** The Carpet Vendor (1st version)	1919–1938	3500.00	4500.00
☐ **HN 351,** Picardy Peasant (female)	1919–1938	3000.00	3250.00
☐ **HN 352,** The Gainsborough Hat	1919–1938	1750.00	2000.00
☐ **HN 353,** Digger (Australian)	1919–1938	1600.00	2100.00
☐ **HN 354,** A Geisha (1st version)	1919–1938	2500.00	3100.00
☐ **HN 355,** Dolly	1919–1938	2500.00	3000.00
☐ **HN 356,** Sir Thomas Lovell	1919–1938	2500.00	3000.00
☐ **HN 357,** Dunce	1919–1938	2750.00	3000.00
☐ **HN 358,** An Old King	1919–1938	1600.00	1800.00
☐ **HN 359,** Fisherwomen	1919–1938	4000.00	4500.00
HN 360 NO DETAILS AVAILABLE			
☐ **HN 361,** Pretty Lady	1919–1938	900.00	1100.00
☐ **HN 362,** In Grandma's Days	1919–1938	1550.00	1700.00
☐ **HN 363,** The Curtsey	1919–1938	1600.00	1700.00
☐ **HN 364,** Moorish Minstrel	1920–1938	3200.00	3550.00
☐ **HN 365,** Double Jester	1920–1938	4000.00	5000.00
☐ **HN 366,** A Mandarin (2nd version)	1920–1938	3000.00	3500.00
☐ **HN 367,** A Jester (1st version)	1920–1938	1800.00	2000.00
☐ **HN 368,** Tony Weller (1st version)	1920–1938	1800.00	2000.00
☐ **HN 369,** Cavalier (1st version)	1920–1938	4000.00	5000.00
☐ **HN 370,** Henry VIII (1st version)	1920–1938	3500.00	4000.00
☐ **HN 371,** The Curtsey	1920–1938	1650.00	1800.00
☐ **HN 372,** Spooks	1920–1936	2000.00	2500.00
☐ **HN 373,** Boy on a Crocodile	1920–1938	5000.00	5500.00
☐ **HN 374,** Lady and Blackamoor (1st version)	1920–1936	2500.00	3000.00
☐ **HN 375,** Lady and Blackamoor (2nd version)	1920–1938	2500.00	3000.00
☐ **HN 376,** A Geisha (1st version)	1920–1938	2500.00	3100.00
☐ **HN 377,** Lady and Blackamoor (2nd version)	1920–1938	2500.00	3000.00
☐ **HN 378,** An Arab	1920–1938	2250.00	2950.00

	Date	Price Range	
☐ HN 379, Ellen Terry as Queen Catherine	1920–1949	2750.00	3000.00
☐ HN 380, A Gnome	1920–1938	1200.00	1500.00
☐ HN 381, A Gnome	1920–1938	1200.00	1500.00
☐ HN 382, A Mandarin (1st version) ...	1920–1938	3000.00	3500.00
☐ HN 383, The Gainsborough Hat	1920–1938	1150.00	1300.00
☐ HN 384, Pretty Lady	1920–1938	900.00	1100.00
☐ HN 385, St. George (1st version)	1920–1938	4500.00	5000.00
☐ HN 386, St. George (1st version)	1920–1938	4500.00	5000.00
☐ HN 387, A Geisha (1st version)	1920–1938	2500.00	3100.00
☐ HN 388, In Grandma's Days	1920–1938	1650.00	1800.00
☐ HN 389, The Little Mother (1st version)	1920–1938	2500.00	2700.00
☐ HN 390, The Little Mother (1st version)	1920–1938	2500.00	2700.00
☐ HN 391, A Princess	1920–1938	2750.00	3000.00
☐ HN 392, A Princess	1920–1938	2750.00	3000.00
☐ HN 393, Lady Without Bouquet	1920–1938	2300.00	2600.00
☐ HN 394, Lady Without Bouquet	1920–1938	2300.00	2600.00
☐ HN 395, Contentment	1920–1938	1850.00	2000.00
☐ HN 396, Contentment	1920–1938	1850.00	2000.00
☐ HN 397, Puff and Powder	1920–1938	2000.00	2200.00
☐ HN 398, Puff and Powder	1920–1938	2000.00	2200.00
☐ HN 399, Japanese Fan	1920–1938	2000.00	2500.00
☐ HN 400, Puff and Powder	1920–1938	2000.00	2200.00
☐ HN 401, Marie (1st version)	1920–1938	2500.00	2800.00
☐ HN 402, Betty (1st version)	1920–1938	2600.00	3000.00
☐ HN 403, Betty (1st version)	1920–1938	2500.00	2900.00
☐ HN 404, King Charles	1920–1951	2000.00	2200.00
☐ HN 405, Japanese Fan	1920–1938	2000.00	2500.00
☐ HN 406, The Bouquet	1920–1938	2200.00	2500.00
☐ HN 407, Omar Khayyam and the Beloved	1920–1938	4500.00	5000.00
☐ HN 408, Omar Khayyam (1st version)	1920–1938	3000.00	3500.00
☐ HN 409, Omar Khayyam (1st version)	1938–1938	3000.00	3500.00
☐ HN 410, Blue Beard (1st version)	1920–1938	4000.00	5000.00
☐ HN 411, A Lady of the Elizabethan Period (1st version)	1920–1938	2000.00	2500.00
☐ HN 412, A Jester (1st version)	1920–1938	1800.00	2000.00
☐ HN 413, The Crinoline	1920–1938	1700.00	1950.00
☐ HN 414, The Bouquet	1920–1938	2200.00	2500.00
☐ HN 415, Moorish Minstrel	1920–1938	3200.00	3550.00
☐ HN 416, Moorish Piper Minstrel	1920–1938	3200.00	3550.00
☐ HN 417, One of the Forty (1st version)	1920–1938	1250.00	1500.00

	Date	Price Range	
☐ HN 418, One of the Forty (2nd version)	1920–1938	1250.00	1500.00
☐ HN 419, Omar Khayyam and the Beloved	1920–1938	4500.00	5000.00
☐ HN 420, A Princess	1920–1938	2750.00	3000.00
☐ HN 421, Contentment	1920–1938	1500.00	1700.00
☐ HN 422, The Bouquet	1920–1938	2200.00	2500.00
☐ HN 423, One of the Forty (3rd and 8th version)	1921–1938	850.00	1050.00
☐ HN 424, Sleep	1921–1938	2500.00	3000.00
☐ HN 425, The Goosegirl	1921–1938	2750.00	3000.00
☐ HN 426, A Jester (1st version)	1921–1938	1750.00	2000.00
☐ HN 427, One of the Forty (9th version)	1921–1938	1250.00	1500.00
☐ HN 428, The Bouquet	1921–1938	2200.00	2500.00
☐ HN 429, The Bouquet	1921–1938	2200.00	2500.00
☐ HN 430, A Princess	1921–1938	2750.00	3000.00
☐ HN 431, A Princess	1921–1938	2750.00	3000.00
☐ HN 432, Puff and Powder	1921–1938	2000.00	2200.00
☐ HN 433, Puff and Powder	1921–1938	2000.00	2200.00
☐ HN 434 Marie (1st version)	1921–1938	2500.00	2800.00
☐ HN 435, Betty (1st version)	1921–1938	2200.00	2500.00
☐ HN 436, The Goosegirl	1921–1938	2500.00	3000.00
☐ HN 437, The Goosegirl	1921–1938	2500.00	3000.00
☐ HN 438, Betty (1st version)	1921–1938	2200.00	2500.00
☐ HN 439, Japanese Fan	1921–1938	2000.00	2500.00
☐ HN 440, Japanese Fan	1921–1938	2000.00	2500.00
☐ HN 441, The Parson's Daughter	1921–1938	850.00	950.00
☐ HN 442, In Grandma's Days	1921–1938	1650.00	1800.00
☐ HN 443, Out for a Walk	1921–1938	2750.00	3250.00
☐ HN 444, A Lady of the Georgian Period	1921–1938	2000.00	2500.00
☐ HN 445, Guy Fawkes	1921–1938	1500.00	1800.00
☐ HN 446, A Jester (1st version)	1921–1936	1700.00	1900.00
☐ HN 447, Lady with Shawl	1921–1936	4200.00	4700.00
☐ HN 448, The Goosegirl	1921–1936	2750.00	3000.00
☐ HN 449, Fruit Gathering	1921–1938	2750.00	3000.00
☐ HN 450, A Mandarin (3rd version)	1921–1938	3000.00	3500.00
☐ HN 451, An Old man	1921–1938	3000.00	3500.00
HN 452 NO DETAILS AVAILABLE			
☐ HN 453, The Gainsborough Hat	1921–1938	1250.00	1400.00
☐ HN 454, The Smiling Buddha	1921–1938	2500.00	3000.00
☐ HN 455, A Mandarin (2nd version)	1921–1938	3000.00	3500.00
☐ HN 456, The Welsh Girl	1921–1938	2500.00	2700.00
☐ HN 457, Crouching Nude	1921–1938	1500.00	1750.00
☐ HN 458, Lady with Shawl	1921–1938	4200.00	4700.00

	Date	Price Range	
☐ **HN 459**, Omar Khayyam and the Beloved	1921–1938	4500.00	5000.00
☐ **HN 460**, A Mandarin (3rd version) ..	1921–1938	3000.00	3500.00
☐ **HN 461**, A Mandarin (3rd version) ..	1921–1938	3000.00	3500.00
☐ **HN 462**, Woman Holding Child	1921–1938	2000.00	2200.00
☐ **HN 463**, Polly Peachum (1st version)	1921–1949	375.00	475.00
☐ **HN 464**, Captain MacHeath	1921–1949	700.00	850.00
☐ **HN 465**, Polly Peachum	1921–1949	425.00	525.00
☐ **HN 466**, Tulips	1921–1938	1700.00	1900.00
☐ **HN 467**, Doris Keane as Cavallini (1st version)	1921–1936	2000.00	2200.00
☐ **HN 468**, Contentment	1921–1938	1750.00	2000.00
☐ **HN 469**, The Little Mother (1st version)	1921–1938	2500.00	2700.00
☐ **HN 470**, Lady and Blackamoor (2nd version)	1921–1938	2500.00	3000.00
☐ **HN 471**, Katharine	1921–1938	2000.00	2500.00
☐ **HN 472**, Spring (1st version) The Seasons	1921–1938	1600.00	1900.00
☐ **HN 473**, Summer (1st version) The Seasons	1921–1938	1650.00	1900.00
☐ **HN 474**, Autumn (1st version) The Seasons	1921–1938	1600.00	1900.00
☐ **HN 475**, Winter (1st version) The Seasons	1921–1938	1600.00	1950.00
☐ **HN 476**, Fruit Gathering	1921–1938	2650.00	2800.00
☐ **HN 477**, Betty (1st version)	1921–1938	2500.00	3000.00
☐ **HN 478**, Betty (1st version)	1921–1938	2500.00	3000.00
☐ **HN 479**, The Balloon Seller	1921–1938	2000.00	2500.00
☐ **HN 480**, One of the Forty (10th version)	1921–1938	1250.00	1500.00
☐ **HN 481**, One of the Forty (11th version)	1921–1938	1250.00	1500.00
☐ **HN 482**, One of the Forty (12th version)	1921–1938	1250.00	1500.00
☐ **HN 483**, One of the Forty (11th version)	1921–1938	1250.00	1500.00
☐ **HN 484**, One of the Forty (12th version)	1921–1938	1250.00	1500.00
☐ **HN 485**, Lucy Lockett (1st version) ..	1921–1949	600.00	700.00
☐ **HN 486**, The Balloon Seller	1921–1938	1800.00	2100.00
☐ **HN 487**, Pavlova	1921–1938	4500.00	5000.00
☐ **HN 488**, Tulips	1921–1938	1700.00	1900.00
☐ **HN 489**, Polly Peachum (2nd version)	1921–1938	300.00	400.00
☐ **HN 490**, One of the Forty (1st version)	1921–1938	1100.00	1200.00

	Date	Price Range	
☐ **HN 491,** One of the Forty (11th version)	1921–1938	1250.00	1550.00
☐ **HN 492,** One of the Forty (12th version)	1921–1938	1600.00	1800.00
☐ **HN 493,** One of the Forty (10th version)	1921–1938	1250.00	1500.00
☐ **HN 494,** One of the Forty (2nd version)	1921–1938	1250.00	1500.00
☐ **HN 495,** One of the Forty (1st version)	1921–1938	1250.00	1500.00
☐ **HN 496,** One of the Forty (13th version)	1921–1938	1250.00	1500.00
☐ **HN 497,** One of the Forty (10th version)	1921–1938	1250.00	1500.00
☐ **HN 498,** One of the Forty (2nd version)	1921–1938	1250.00	1500.00
☐ **HN 499,** One of the Forty (10th version)	1921–1938	1250.00	1500.00
☐ **Hn 500,** One of the Forty (13th version)	1921–1938	1400.00	1650.00
☐ **HN 501,** One of the Forty (1st version)	1921–1938	1250.00	1500.00
☐ **HN 502,** Marie (1st version)	1921–1938	2500.00	2800.00
☐ **HN 503,** Fruit Gathering	1921–1938	2500.00	3000.00
☐ **HN 504,** Marie (1st version)	1921–1938	2500.00	2800.00
☐ **HN 505,** Marie (1st version)	1921–1938	2500.00	2800.00
☐ **HN 506,** Marie (1st version)	1921–1938	2500.00	2800.00
☐ **HN 507,** Pussy	1921–1938	7500.00	9500.00
☐ **HN 508,** An Orange Vendor	1921–1938	1100.00	1450.00
☐ **HN 509,** Lady of the Fan	1921–1938	1700.00	1900.00
☐ **HN 510,** A Child's Grace	1921–1938	3500.00	4000.00
☐ **HN 511,** Upon her Cheeks she Wept	1921–1938	2000.00	2400.00
☐ **HN 512,** A Spook	1921–1938	1350.00	1600.00
☐ **HN 513,** Picardy Peasant (female)	1921–1938	3000.00	3500.00
☐ **HN 514,** The Welsh Girl	1921–1938	2500.00	2700.00
☐ **HN 515,** Lady with Rose	1921–1938	1700.00	1900.00
☐ **HN 516,** The Welsh Girl	1921–1938	2500.00	2700.00
☐ **HN 517,** Lady with Rose	1921–1938	1700.00	1900.00
☐ **HN 518,** The Curtsey	1921–1938	1650.00	1800.00
☐ **HN 519,** The Welsh Girl	1921–1938	2500.00	2700.00
☐ **HN 520,** The Welsh Girl	1921–1938	2500.00	2700.00
☐ **HN 521,** An Orange Vendor	1921–1938	1100.00	1450.00
☐ **HN 522,** Upon her Cheeks she Wept	1921–1938	2000.00	2400.00
☐ **HN 523,** Sentinel	1921–1938	5500.00	6500.00
☐ **HN 524,** Lucy Lockett	1921–1938	600.00	700.00
☐ **HN 525,** The Flower Seller's Children	1921–1949	1300.00	1500.00
☐ **HN 526,** The Beggar (1st version)	1921–1949	800.00	1200.00

	Date	Price Range	
☐ **HN 527**, The Highwayman	1921–1949	800.00	900.00
☐ **HN 528**, One of the Forty (1st version)	1921–1938	1400.00	1650.00
☐ **HN 529**, Mr. Pickwick (1st version) ..	1922–	65.00	85.00
renumbered as miniature	1932–		
☐ **HN 530**, The Fat Boy (1st version) ...	1922–	55.00	85.00
renumbered as miniature	1932–		
☐ **HN 531**, Sam Weller	1922–1985	75.00	90.00
renumbered as miniature	1932–		
☐ **HN 532**, Mr. Micawber (1st version)	1922–	65.00	85.00
renumbered as miniature	1932–		
☐ **HN 533**, Sairey Gamp (1st version) ..	1922–1985	75.00	90.00
renumbered as miniature	1921–		
☐ **HN 534**, Fagin	1922–	55.00	85.00
renumbered as miniature	1932–		
☐ **HN 535**, Pecksniff (1st version)	1922–	65.00	85.00
renumbered as miniature	1932–		
☐ **HN 536**, Stiggins	1922–	65.00	85.00
renumbered as miniature	1932–		
☐ **HN 537**, Bill Sykes	1922–	65.00	85.00
renumbered as miniature	1932–		
☐ **HN 538**, Buz Fuz	1922–	55.00	85.00
renumbered as miniature	1932–		
☐ **HN 539**, Tiny Tim	1922–	65.00	85.00
renumbered as miniature	1932–		
☐ **HN 540**, Little Nell	1922–	55.00	85.00
renumbered as miniature	1932–		
☐ **HN 541**, Alfred Jingle	1922–	60.00	85.00
renumbered as miniature	1932–		
☐ **HN 542**, The Cobbler (1st version) ...	1922–1939	1200.00	1300.00
☐ **HN 543**, The Cobbler (1st version) ...	1922–1938	1200.00	1300.00
☐ **HN 544**, Tony Weller (2nd version) ..	1922–	65.00	85.00
renumbered as miniature	1932–		
☐ **HN 545**, Uriah Heep (1st version)	1922–	65.00	85.00
renumbered as miniature	1932–		
☐ **HN 546**, The Artful Dodger	1922–	65.00	85.00
renumbered as miniature	1932–		
☐ **HN 547**, The Curtsey	1922–1938	1450.00	1600.00
☐ **HN 548**, The Balloon Seller	1922–1938	1200.00	1500.00
☐ **HN 549**, Polly Peachum (2nd version)	1922–1949	400.00	475.00
☐ **HN 550**, Polly Peachum (1st version)	1922–1949	400.00	500.00
☐ **HN 551**, The Flower Seller's Children	1922–1949	1300.00	1500.00
☐ **HN 552**, A Jester (1st version)	1922–1938	1700.00	1900.00
☐ **HN 553**, Pecksniff (2nd version)	1923–1939	350.00	400.00
☐ **HN 554**, Uriah Heep (2nd version) ...	1923–1939	300.00	400.00
☐ **HN 555**, The Fat Boy (2nd version) ..	1923–1939	375.00	425.00

	Date	Price Range	
☐ **HN 556**, Mr. Pickwick (2nd version)	1923–1939	375.00	450.00
☐ **HN 557**, Mr. Micawber (2nd version)	1923–1939	375.00	450.00
☐ **HN 558**, Sairey Gamp (2nd version)	1923–1939	550.00	650.00
☐ **HN 559**, The Goosegirl	1923–1938	2750.00	3000.00
☐ **HN 560**, The Goosegirl	1923–1938	2750.00	3000.00
☐ **HN 561**, Fruit Gathering	1923–1938	2500.00	3000.00
☐ **HN 562**, Fruit Gathering	1923–1938	2500.00	3000.00
☐ **HN 563**, Man in Tudor Costume	1923–1938	2500.00	3500.00
☐ **HN 564**, The Parson's Daughter	1923–1949	400.00	500.00
☐ **HN 565**, Pretty Lady	1923–1938	900.00	1100.00
☐ **HN 566**, The Crinoline	1923–1938	1250.00	1400.00
☐ **HN 567**, The Bouquet	1923–1938	2500.00	3000.00
☐ **HN 568**, Shy Anne	1923–1949	2000.00	2500.00
☐ **HN 569**, The Lavender Woman	1924–1928	2000.00	2200.00
☐ **HN 570**, Woman Holding Child	1923–1938	2000.00	2200.00
☐ **HN 571**, Falstaff (1st version)	1923–1938	1200.00	1600.00
☐ **HN 572**, Contentment	1923–1938	1750.00	2000.00
☐ **HN 573**, Madonna of the Square	1913–1938	1650.00	1800.00
HN 574 NO DETAILS AVAILABLE			
☐ **HN 575**, Falstaff (1st version)	1923–1938	1200.00	1600.00
☐ **HN 576**, Madonna of the Square	1923–1938	1650.00	1800.00
☐ **HN 577**, The Chelsea Pair (female)	1923–1938	850.00	1000.00
☐ **HN 578**, The Chelsea Pair (female)	1923–1938	850.00	1000.00
☐ **HN 579**, The Chelsea Pair (male)	1923–1938	850.00	1000.00
☐ **HN 580**, The Chelsea Pair (male)	1923–1938	850.00	1000.00
☐ **HN 581**, The Perfect Pair	1923–1938	1200.00	1550.00
☐ **HN 582**, Grossmith's "Tsang Ihang" Perfume of Tibet (also called "Tibetan Lady")	1923–Unknown	700.00	800.00
☐ **HN 583**, The Balloon Seller	1923–1949	600.00	775.00
☐ **HN 584**, Lady with Rose	1923–1938	1700.00	1900.00
☐ **HN 585**, Harlequinade	1923–1938	900.00	1000.00
☐ **HN 586**, Boy with Turban	1923–1938	850.00	1000.00
☐ **HN 587**, Boy with Turban	1923–1938	850.00	1000.00
☐ **HN 588**, Girl with Yellow Frock	1923–1938	2500.00	3000.00
☐ **HN 589**, Polly Peachum (1st version)	1924–1949	400.00	500.00
☐ **HN 590**, Captain MacHeath	1924–1949	700.00	850.00
☐ **HN 591**, The Beggar (1st version)	1924–1949	600.00	750.00
☐ **HN 592**, The Highwayman	1924–1949	800.00	900.00
☐ **HN 593**, Nude on Rock	1924–1938	1350.00	1600.00
☐ **HN 594**, Madonna of the Square	1924–1938	1650.00	1800.00
☐ **HN 595**, Grief	1924–1938	1400.00	1650.00
☐ **HN 596**, Despair	1924–1938	2000.00	2500.00
☐ **HN 597**, The Bather (1st version)	1924–1938	1500.00	1850.00
☐ **HN 598**, Omar Khayyam and the Beloved	1924–1938	4500.00	5000.00

	Date	Price Range	
☐ **HN 599,** Masquerade (male, 1st version)	1924–1949	1000.00	1200.00
☐ **HN 600,** Masquerade (female, 1st version)	1924–1949	1100.00	1250.00
☐ **HN 601,** A Mandarin (3rd version) ..	1924–1938	3000.00	3500.00
HN 602 NO DETAILS AVAILABLE			
☐ **HN 603a,** Child Study	1924–1938	675.00	850.00
☐ **HN 603b,** Child Study	1924–1938	675.00	850.00
☐ **HN 604a,** Female Study	1924–1938	675.00	850.00
☐ **HN 604b,** Female Study	1924–1938	675.00	850.00
☐ **HN 605a,** Child Study	1924–1938	675.00	850.00
☐ **HN 605b,** Child Study	1924–1938	675.00	850.00
☐ **HN 606a,** Child Study	1924–1949	675.00	850.00
☐ **HN 606b,** Child Study	1924–1949	675.00	850.00
HN 607 NO DETAILS AVAILABLE			
☐ **HN 608,** Falstaff (1st version)	1924–1938	1200.00	1600.00
☐ **HN 609,** Falstaff (1st version)	1924–1938	1200.00	1600.00
☐ **HN 610,** Henry Lytton as Jack Point	1924–1949	900.00	1150.00
☐ **HN 611,** A Mandarin (3rd version) ..	1924–1938	3000.00	3500.00
☐ **HN 612,** Poke Bonnett	1924–1938	1500.00	1700.00
☐ **HN 613,** Madonna of the Square	1924–1938	1650.00	1800.00
☐ **HN 614,** Polly Peachum (1st version)	1924–1938	600.00	700.00
☐ **HN 615,** Katharine	1924–1938	1650.00	1800.00
☐ **HN 616,** A Jester (1st version)	1924–1938	1700.00	1900.00
☐ **HN 617,** A Shepherd (1st version)	1924–1938	2250.00	2500.00
☐ **HN 618,** Falstaff (2nd version)	1924–1938	1200.00	1600.00
☐ **HN 619,** Falstaff (1st version)	1924–1938	1200.00	1600.00
☐ **HN 620,** Polly Peachum (2nd version)	1924–1938	300.00	400.00
☐ **HN 621,** Pan on Rock	1924–1938	2500.00	3000.00
☐ **HN 622,** Pan on Rock	1924–1938	2500.00	3000.00
☐ **HN 623,** An Old King	1924–1938	1600.00	1800.00
☐ **HN 624,** Lady with Rose	1924–1938	1700.00	1900.00
☐ **HN 625,** A Spook	1924–1938	1350.00	1600.00
☐ **HN 626,** Lady with Shawl	1924–1938	4200.00	4700.00
☐ **HN 627,** A Jester (1st version)	1924–1938	1700.00	1900.00
☐ **HN 628,** The Crinoline	1924–1938	1350.00	1500.00
☐ **HN 629,** The Curtsey	1924–1938	1650.00	1800.00
☐ **HN 630,** A Jester (2nd version)	1924–1938	2000.00	2200.00
☐ **HN 631,** Fisherwomen	1924–1938	4000.00	4500.00
☐ **HN 632,** A Shepherd (1st version)	1924–1938	2250.00	2500.00
☐ **HN 633,** A Princess	1924–1938	2750.00	3000.00
☐ **HN 634,** A Geisha (1st version)	1924–1938	2500.00	3100.00
☐ **HN 635,** Harlequinade	1924–1938	1150.00	1300.00
☐ **HN 636,** Masquerade (male, 1st version)	1924–1938	1100.00	1300.00

	Date	Price Range	
☐ **HN 637,** Masquerade (female, 1st version)	1924–1938	1100.00	1300.00
☐ **HN 638,** Falstaff (1st version)	1924–1938	1200.00	1600.00
☐ **HN 639,** Elsie Maynard	1924–1949	875.00	1050.00
☐ **HN 640,** Charley's Aunt (1st version)	1924–1938	1100.00	1200.00
☐ **HN 641,** A Mandarin	1924–1938	3000.00	3500.00
☐ **HN 642,** Pierrette (1st version)	1924–1938	1200.00	1400.00
☐ **HN 643,** Pierrette (1st version)	1924–1938	1200.00	1400.00
☐ **HN 644,** Pierrette (1st version)	1924–1938	800.00	900.00
☐ **HN 645,** One of the Forty (12th version)	1924–1938	1250.00	1500.00
☐ **HN 646,** One of the Forty (11th version)	1924–1938	1250.00	1500.00
☐ **HN 647,** One of the Forty (2nd version)	1924–1938	1250.00	1500.00
☐ **HN 648,** One of the Forty (1st version)	1924–1938	1250.00	1500.00
☐ **HN 649,** One of the Forty (13th version)	1924–1938	1250.00	1500.00
☐ **HN 650,** Crinoline Lady (miniature)	1924–1938	800.00	1000.00
☐ **HN 651,** Crinoline Lady (miniature)	1924–1938	800.00	1000.00
☐ **HN 652,** Crinoline Lady (miniature)	1924–1938	800.00	1000.00
☐ **HN 653,** Crinoline Lady (miniature)	1924–1938	800.00	1000.00
☐ **HN 654,** Crinoline Lady (miniature)	1924–1938	800.00	1000.00
☐ **HN 655,** Crinoline Lady (miniature)	1924–1938	800.00	1000.00
☐ **HN 656,** The Mask	1924–1938	1600.00	1800.00
☐ **HN 657,** The Mask	1924–1938	1600.00	1800.00
☐ **HN 658,** Mam'selle	1924–1938	1450.00	1650.00
☐ **HN 659,** Mam'selle	1924–1938	1450.00	1650.00
☐ **HN 660,** The Welsh Girl	1924–1938	2500.00	2750.00
☐ **HN 661,** Boy with Turban	1924–1938	850.00	1000.00
☐ **HN 662,** Boy with Turban	1924–1938	850.00	1000.00
☐ **HN 663,** One of the Forty (12th version)	1924–1938	1250.00	1500.00
☐ **HN 664,** One of the Forty (10th version)	1924–1938	1400.00	1650.00
☐ **HN 665,** One of the Forty (13th version)	1924–1938	1250.00	1500.00
☐ **HN 666,** One of the Forty (2nd version)	1924–1938	1400.00	1650.00
☐ **HN 667,** One of the Forty (11th version)	1924–1938	1400.00	1650.00
☐ **HN 668,** The Welsh Girl	1924–1938	2500.00	2700.00
☐ **HN 669,** The Welsh Girl	1924–1938	2500.00	2700.00
☐ **HN 670,** The Curtsey	1924–1938	1450.00	1600.00
☐ **HN 671,** Lady Ermine	1924–1938	1650.00	1900.00
☐ **HN 672,** Tulips	1924–1938	1750.00	2000.00

	Date	Price Range	
☐ **HN 673,** Henry VIII (1st version)	1924–1938	**3500.00**	**4000.00**
☐ **HN 674,** Masquerade (female, 1st version)	1924–1938	**1100.00**	**1250.00**
☐ **HN 675,** The Gainsborough Hat	1924–1938	**1350.00**	**1500.00**
☐ **HN 676,** Pavlova	1924–1938	**4500.00**	**5000.00**
☐ **HN 677,** One of the Forty (1st version)	1924–1938	**1250.00**	**1500.00**
☐ **HN 678,** Lady with Shawl	1924–1938	**4200.00**	**4700.00**
☐ **HN 679,** Lady with Shawl	1924–1938	**4200.00**	**4700.00**
☐ **HN 680,** Polly Peachum (1st version)	1924–1949	**550.00**	**650.00**
☐ **HN 681,** The Cobbler (2nd version) ..	1924–1938	**750.00**	**850.00**
☐ **HN 682,** The Cobbler (1st version) ...	1924–1938	**1100.00**	**1200.00**
☐ **HN 683,** Masquerade (male, 1st version)	1924–1938	**1200.00**	**1400.00**
☐ **HN 684,** Tony Weller (1st version) ...	1924–1938	**1650.00**	**1800.00**
☐ **HN 685,** Contentment	1923–1938	**1900.00**	**2000.00**
☐ **HN 686,** Contentment	1924–1938	**1900.00**	**2000.00**
☐ **HN 687,** The Bather (1st version)	1924–1949	**850.00**	**1200.00**
☐ **HN 688,** A Yeoman of the Guard	1924–1938	**800.00**	**900.00**
☐ **HN 689,** A Chelsea Pensioner	1924–1938	**1250.00**	**1400.00**
☐ **HN 690,** A Lady of the Georgian Period	1925–1938	**2000.00**	**2500.00**
☐ **HN 691,** Pierrette (1st version)	1925–1938	**1250.00**	**1500.00**
☐ **HN 692,** Sleep	1925–1938	**2500.00**	**3000.00**
☐ **HN 693,** Polly Peachum (1st version)	1925–1949	**500.00**	**600.00**
☐ **HN 694,** Polly Peachum (2nd version)	1925–1949	**400.00**	**500.00**
☐ **HN 695,** Lucy Lockett (2nd version)	1925–1949	**650.00**	**750.00**
☐ **HN 696,** Lucy Lockett (2nd version)	1925–1949	**650.00**	**750.00**
☐ **HN 697,** The Balloon Seller	1925–1938	**800.00**	**900.00**
☐ **HN 698,** Polly Peachum (3rd version, miniature)	1925–1949	**375.00**	**450.00**
☐ **HN 699,** Polly Peachum (3rd version, miniature)	1925–1949	**375.00**	**450.00**
☐ **HN 700,** Pretty Lady	1925–1938	**900.00**	**1100.00**
☐ **HN 701,** The Welsh Girl	1925–1938	**2500.00**	**2700.00**
☐ **HN 702,** A Lady of the Georgian Period	1925–1938	**2000.00**	**2500.00**
☐ **HN 703,** Woman Holding Child	1925–1938	**2000.00**	**2200.00**
☐ **HN 704,** One of the Forty (2nd version)	1925–1938	**1250.00**	**1500.00**
☐ **HN 705,** The Gainsborough Hat	1925–1938	**1200.00**	**1350.00**
☐ **HN 706,** Fruit Gathering	1925–1938	**2500.00**	**3000.00**
☐ **HN 707,** Fruit Gathering	1925–1938	**3000.00**	**3500.00**
☐ **HN 708,** Shepherdess (1st version, miniature)	1925–1948	**1000.00**	**1500.00**

	Date	Price Range	
☐ **HN 709,** Shepherd (1st version, miniature)	1925–1938	1000.00	1500.00
☐ **HN 710,** Sleep	1925–1938	2500.00	3000.00
☐ **HN 711,** Harlequinade	1925–1938	1100.00	1400.00
☐ **HN 712,** One of the Forty (11th version)	1925–1938	1250.00	1500.00
☐ **HN 713,** One of the Forty (12th version)	1925–1938	1250.00	1500.00
☐ **HN 714,** One of the Forty (10th version)	1925–1938	1250.00	1500.00
☐ **HN 715,** Proposal (lady)	1925–1938	1400.00	1700.00
☐ **HN 716,** Proposal (lady)	1925–1938	1400.00	1700.00
☐ **HN 717,** Lady Clown	1925–1938	2500.00	3000.00
☐ **HN 718,** Lady Clown	1925–1938	2500.00	3000.00
☐ **HN 719,** Butterfly	1925–1938	1200.00	1400.00
☐ **HN 720,** Butterfly	1925–1938	1200.00	1400.00
☐ **HN 721,** Pierrette (1st version)	1925–1938	1100.00	1400.00
☐ **HN 722,** Mephisto	1925–1938	2500.00	3000.00
☐ **HN 723,** Mephisto	1925–1938	2500.00	3000.00
☐ **HN 724,** Mam'selle	1925–1938	1450.00	1650.00
☐ **HN 725,** The Proposal (male)	1925–1938	1450.00	1700.00
☐ **HN 726,** A Victorian Lady	1925–1938	500.00	700.00
☐ **HN 727,** A Victorian Lady	1925–1938	325.00	425.00
☐ **HN 728,** A Victorian Lady	1925–1952	325.00	425.00
☐ **HN 729,** The Mask	1925–1938	1700.00	1900.00
☐ **HN 730,** Butterfly	1925–1938	1350.00	1550.00
☐ **HN 731,** Pierrette (1st version)	1925–1938	1100.00	1400.00
☐ **HN 732,** Pierrette (1st version)	1925–1938	1100.00	1400.00
☐ **HN 733,** The Mask	1925–1938	1600.00	1800.00
☐ **HN 734,** Polly Peachum (2nd version)	1925–1949	450.00	500.00
☐ **HN 735,** Shepherdess (2nd version) ..	1925–1939	1500.00	1750.00
☐ **HN 736,** A Victorian Lady	1925–1938	600.00	800.00
HN 737 NO DETAILS AVAILABLE			
☐ **HN 738,** Lady Clown	1925–1938	2500.00	3000.00
☐ **HN 739,** A Victorian Lady	1925–1938	650.00	750.00
☐ **HN 740,** A Victorian Lady	1925–1938	600.00	800.00
☐ **HN 741,** A Geisha (1st version)	1925–1938	2500.00	3100.00
☐ **HN 742,** A Victorian Lady	1925–1938	500.00	700.00
☐ **HN 743,** Woman Holding Child	1925–1938	2050.00	2200.00
☐ **HN 744,** The Lavender Woman	1925–1938	2100.00	2300.00
☐ **HN 745,** A Victorian Lady	1925–1938	600.00	775.00
☐ **HN 746,** A Mandarin (1st version) ...	1926–1938	3000.00	3500.00
☐ **HN 747,** Tulips	1925–1938	1750.00	2000.00
☐ **HN 748,** Out for a Walk	1925–1936	3000.00	3500.00
☐ **HN 749,** London Cry, Strawberries ..	1925–1938	1300.00	1400.00
☐ **HN 750,** Shepherdess (2nd version) ..	1925–1938	1500.00	1750.00
☐ **HN 751,** Shepherd (3rd version)	1925–1938	2250.00	2500.00

	Date	Price Range	
☐ **HN 752**, London Cry, Turnips and Carrots	1925–1938	1300.00	1400.00
☐ **HN 753**, The Dandy	1925–1938	1200.00	1400.00
☐ **HN 754**, The Belle	1925–1938	1250.00	1500.00
☐ **HN 755**, Mephistopheles and Marguerite	1925–1949	1500.00	1750.00
☐ **HN 756**, The Modern Piper	1925–1938	2500.00	3000.00
☐ **HN 757**, Polly Peachum (3rd version)	1925–1949	350.00	450.00
☐ **HN 758**, Polly Peachum (3rd version)	1925–1949	350.00	450.00
☐ **HN 759**, Polly Peachum (3rd version)	1925–1949	350.00	450.00
☐ **HN 760**, Polly Peachum (3rd version miniature)	1925–1949	450.00	550.00
☐ **HN 761**, Polly Peachum (3rd version miniature)	1925–1949	350.00	400.00
☐ **HN 762**, Polly Peachum (3rd version miniature)	1925–1949	350.00	400.00
☐ **HN 763**, Pretty Lady	1925–1938	900.00	1100.00
☐ **HN 764**, Madonna of the Square	1925–1938	1650.00	1800.00
☐ **HN 765**, The Poke Bonnet	1925–1938	1500.00	1700.00
☐ **HN 766**, Irish Colleen	1925–1938	2500.00	3000.00
☐ **HN 767**, Irish Colleen	1925–1938	2500.00	3000.00
☐ **HN 768**, Harlequinade Masked	1925–1938	2250.00	2750.00
☐ **HN 769**, Harlequinade Masked	1925–1938	2250.00	2750.00
☐ **HN 770**, Lady Clown	1925–1938	2500.00	3000.00
☐ **HN 771**, London Cry, Turnips and Carrots	1925–1938	1300.00	1400.00
☐ **HN 772**, London Cry, Strawberries ..	1925–1938	1300.00	1400.00
☐ **HN 773**, The Bather (2nd version) ...	1925–1938	1800.00	2500.00
☐ **HN 774**, The Bather (2nd version) ...	1925–1938	1800.00	2500.00
☐ **HN 775**, Mephistopheles and Marguerite	1925–1949	1500.00	1750.00
☐ **HN 776**, The Belle	1925–1938	1250.00	1500.00
☐ **HN 777**, Bo-Peep (1st version)	1926–1938	1400.00	1800.00
☐ **HN 778**, Captain (1st version)	1926–1938	2000.00	2500.00
☐ **HN 779**, A Geisha (1st version)	1926–1938	2500.00	3100.00
☐ **HN 780**, Harlequinade	1926–1938	1200.00	1500.00
☐ **HN 781**, The Bather (1st version)	1826–1938	1500.00	1800.00
☐ **HN 782**, The Bather (1st version)	1926–1938	1500.00	1800.00
☐ **HN 783**, Pretty Lady	1926–1938	900.00	1100.00
☐ **HN 784**, Pierette (1st version)	1926–1938	1400.00	1600.00
☐ **HN 785**, The Mask	1926–1938	1600.00	1800.00
☐ **HN 786**, Mam'selle	1926–1938	1450.00	1650.00
☐ **HN 787**, A Mandarin (1st version) ...	1926–1938	3000.00	3500.00
☐ **HN 788**, Proposal (lady)	1926–1938	1400.00	1700.00

	Date	Price Range	
☐ HN 789, The Flower Seller	1926–1938	700.00	850.00
☐ HN 790, The Parson's Daughter	1926–1938	550.00	600.00
☐ HN 791, A Mandarin (1st version) ...	1926–1938	3000.00	3500.00
☐ HN 792, The Welsh Girl	1926–1938	2550.00	2700.00
☐ HN 793, Katharine	1926–1938	1650.00	1800.00
☐ HN 794, The Bouquet	1926–1938	2500.00	3000.00
☐ HN 795, Pierrette (2nd version, miniature)	1926–1938	800.00	1100.00
☐ HN 796, Pierrette (2nd version, miniature)	1926–1938	800.00	1100.00
☐ HN 797, Moorish Minstrel	1926–1949	3200.00	3550.00
☐ HN 798, Tete-a-Tete (1st version)	1926–1938	950.00	1200.00
☐ HN 799, Tete-a-Tete (1st version)	1926–1938	950.00	1200.00
HN 800–HN 1200 ANIMAL AND BIRD MODELS			
☐ HN 1201, Hunts Lady	1926–1938	2000.00	2500.00
☐ HN 1202, Bo-Peep (1st version)	1926–1938	1400.00	1800.00
☐ HN 1203, Butterfly	1926–1938	1550.00	1850.00
☐ HN 1204, Angela	1926–1938	1200.00	1500.00
☐ HN 1205, Miss 1926	1926–1938	2500.00	3000.00
☐ HN 1206, The Flower Seller's Children	1926–1949	400.00	500.00
☐ HN 1207, Miss 1926	1926–1938	2500.00	3000.00
☐ HN 1208, A Victorian Lady	1920–1938	600.00	800.00
☐ HN 1209, The Proposal (male)	1926–1938	1900.00	2150.00
☐ HN 1210, Boy with Turban	1926–1938	900.00	1100.00
☐ HN 1211, Quality Street	1926–1938	1000.00	1200.00
☐ HN 1212, Boy with Turban	1926–1938	900.00	1100.00
☐ HN 1213, Boy with Turban	1926–1938	900.00	1100.00
☐ HN 1214, Boy with Turban	1926–1938	900.00	1100.00
☐ HN 1215, The Pied Piper	1926–1938	1650.00	2000.00
☐ HN 1216, Falstaff (1st version)	1926–1949	1200.00	1600.00
☐ HN 1217, The Prince of Wales	1926–1938	1500.00	1700.00
☐ HN 1218, A Spook	1926–1938	1350.00	1600.00
☐ HN 1219, Negligee	1927–1938	1900.00	2250.00
☐ HN 1220, Lido Lady	1927–1938	1200.00	1450.00
☐ HN 1221, Lady Jester (1st version) ...	1927–1938	1600.00	2000.00
☐ HN 1222, Lady Jester (1st version) ...	1927–1938	1600.00	2000.00
☐ HN 1223, A Geisha (2nd version)	1927–1938	975.00	1275.00
☐ HN 1224, The Wandering Minstrel ..	1927–1938	2000.00	2400.00
☐ HN 1225, Boy with Turban	1927–1938	900.00	1100.00
☐ HN 1226, The Huntsman (1st version)	1927–1938	2000.00	2500.00
☐ HN 1227, The Bather (2nd version) ..	1927–1938	1800.00	2500.00
☐ HN 1228, Negligee	1927–1938	1900.00	2250.00
☐ HN 1229, Lido Lady	1927–1938	1200.00	1450.00
☐ HN 1230, Baba	1927–1938	800.00	950.00
☐ HN 1231, Cassim (1st version)	1927–1938	850.00	1050.00

	Date	Price Range	
☐ **HN 1232**, Cassim (1st version)	1927–1938	850.00	1250.00
☐ **HN 1233**, Susanna	1927–1938	1100.00	1200.00
☐ **HN 1234**, A Geisha (2nd version)	1927–1938	975.00	1275.00
☐ **HN 1235**, A Scribe	1927–1938	1000.00	1300.00
☐ **HN 1236**, Tete-a-Tete (2nd version)	1927–1938	900.00	1300.00
☐ **HN 1237**, Tete-a-Tete (2nd version)	1927–1938	900.00	1300.00
☐ **HN 1238**, The Bather (1st version) ...	1927–1938	1100.00	1500.00
☐ **HN 1242**, The Parson's Daughter	1927–1938	550.00	600.00
☐ **HN 1243**, Baba	1927–1938	900.00	1050.00
☐ **HN 1244**, Baba	1927–1938	800.00	950.00
☐ **HN 1245**, Baba	1927–1938	800.00	950.00
☐ **HN 1246**, Baba	1927–1938	800.00	950.00
☐ **HN 1247**, Baba	1928–1938	875.00	1000.00
☐ **HN 1248**, Baba	1927–1938	800.00	950.00
☐ **HN 1249**, Circe	1927–1938	2000.00	2200.00
☐ **HN 1250**, Circe	1927–1938	2000.00	2200.00
☐ **HN 1251**, The Cobbler	1927–1938	1100.00	1200.00
☐ **HN 1252**, Kathleen	1927–1938	675.00	775.00
☐ **HN 1253**, Kathleen	1927–1938	700.00	800.00
☐ **HN 1254**, Circe	1927–1938	2000.00	2200.00
☐ **HN 1255**, Circe	1927–1938	2000.00	2200.00
☐ **HN 1256**, Captain MacHeath	1927–1949	700.00	850.00
☐ **HN 1257**, The Highwayman	1927–1949	700.00	800.00
☐ **HN 1258**, A Victorian Lady	1927–1938	600.00	800.00
☐ **HN 1259**, The Alchemist	1927–1938	1500.00	1800.00
☐ **HN 1260**, Carnival	1927–1938	3500.00	4500.00
☐ **HN 1261**, Sea Sprite (1st version)	1927–1938	650.00	850.00
☐ **HN 1262**, Spanish Lady	1927–1938	1000.00	1250.00
☐ **HN 1263**, Lady Clown	1927–1938	2500.00	3000.00
☐ **HN 1264**, Judge and Jury	1927–1938	8000.00	9500.00
☐ **HN 1265**, Lady Fayre	1928–1938	650.00	750.00
☐ **HN 1266**, Ko-Ko	1928–1949	800.00	950.00
☐ **HN 1267**, Carmen (1st version)	1928–1938	1250.00	1350.00
☐ **HN 1268**, Yum-Yum	1928–1938	700.00	850.00
☐ **HN 1269**, Scotch Girl	1928–1938	2000.00	2500.00
☐ **HN 1270**, The Swimmer	1928–1938	1700.00	1900.00
☐ **HN 1271**, The Mask	1928–1938	1600.00	1800.00
☐ **HN 1272**, Negligee	1928–1938	1900.00	2250.00
☐ **HN 1273**, Negligee	1928–1938	1900.00	2250.00
☐ **HN 1274**, Harlequinade Masked	1928–1938	2250.00	2750.00
☐ **HN 1275**, Kathleen	1928–1938	700.00	800.00
☐ **HN 1276**, A Victorian Lady	1928–1938	650.00	850.00
☐ **HN 1277**, A Victorian Lady	1928–1938	700.00	900.00
☐ **HN 1278**, Carnival	1928–1938	3500.00	4500.00
☐ **HN 1279**, Kathleen	1928–1938	675.00	775.00
☐ **HN 1280**, Blue Bird	1928–1938	750.00	900.00

	Date	Price Range	
☐ **HN 1281**, Scotties	1928–1938	**1300.00**	**1550.00**
☐ **HN 1282**, The Alchemist	1928–1938	**1500.00**	**1800.00**
☐ **HN 1283**, The Cobbler (2nd version)	1928–1949	**750.00**	**850.00**
☐ **HN 1284**, Lady Jester (2nd version) ..	1928–1938	**2000.00**	**2250.00**
☐ **HN 1285**, Lady Jester (2nd version) ..	1928–1938	**2000.00**	**2250.00**
☐ **HN 1286**, Ko-Ko	1938–1949	**800.00**	**950.00**
☐ **HN 1287**, Yum-Yum	1928–1939	**700.00**	**850.00**
☐ **HN 1288**, Susanna	1928–1938	**1100.00**	**1200.00**
☐ **HN 1289**, Midinette (1st version)	1928–1938	**2450.00**	**2750.00**
☐ **HN 1290**, Spanish Lady	1928–1938	**1000.00**	**1250.00**
☐ **HN 1291**, Kathleen	1928–1938	**850.00**	**950.00**
☐ **HN 1292**, A Geisha (2nd version)	1928–1938	**1000.00**	**1300.00**
☐ **HN 1293**, Spanish Lady	1928–1938	**1000.00**	**1250.00**
☐ **HN 1294**, Spanish Lady	1928–1938	**1000.00**	**1250.00**
☐ **HN 1295**, A Jester (1st version)	1928–1949	**1700.00**	**1800.00**
☐ **HN 1296**, Columbine (1st version) ...	1928–1938	**1000.00**	**1200.00**
☐ **HN 1297**, Columbine (1st version) ...	1928–1938	**1000.00**	**1200.00**
☐ **HN 1298**, Sweet and Twenty (1st version)	1928–1969	**275.00**	**325.00**
☐ **HN 1299**, Susanna	1928–1938	**1100.00**	**1200.00**
☐ **HN 1300**, Carmen (1st version)	1928–1938	**1350.00**	**1450.00**
☐ **HN 1301**, Gypsy Woman with Child	1928–1938	**2500.00**	**3000.00**
☐ **HN 1302**, Gypsy Girl with Flowers ...	1928–1938	**2500.00**	**2750.00**
☐ **HN 1303**, Angela	1928–1938	**1400.00**	**1750.00**
☐ **HN 1304**, Harlequinade Masked	1928–1938	**2250.00**	**2750.00**
☐ **HN 1305**, Siesta	1928–1938	**2500.00**	**3000.00**
☐ **HN 1306**, Midinette (1st version)	1928–1938	**2450.00**	**2750.00**
☐ **HN 1307**, An Irishman	1928–1938	**2750.00**	**3350.00**
☐ **HN 1308**, The Moor	1928–1938	**1500.00**	**1750.00**
☐ **HN 1309**, Spanish Lady	1928–1938	**1000.00**	**1250.00**
☐ **HN 1310**, A Geisha (2nd version)	1929–1938	**975.00**	**1275.00**
☐ **HN 1311**, Cassim (2nd version)	1929–1938	**900.00**	**1100.00**
☐ **HN 1312**, Cassim (2nd version)	1929–1938	**900.00**	**1100.00**
☐ **HN 1313**, Sonny	1929–1938	**1100.00**	**1200.00**
☐ **HN 1314**, Sonny	1929–1938	**1100.00**	**1200.00**
☐ **HN 1315**, Old Balloon Seller	1929–	**275.00**	
☐ **HN 1316**, Toys	1929–1938	**4000.00**	**4500.00**
☐ **HN 1317**, The Snake Charmer	1929–1938	**1400.00**	**1650.00**
☐ **HN 1318**, Sweet Anne	1929–1949	**175.00**	**250.00**
☐ **HN 1319**, Darling (1st version)	1929–1959	**150.00**	**175.00**
☐ **HN 1320**, Rosamund (1st version)	1929–1938	**2200.00**	**2500.00**
☐ **HN 1321**, A Geisha (1st version)	1929–1938	**2500.00**	**3100.00**
☐ **HN 1322**, A Geisha (1st version)	1929–1938	**2500.00**	**3100.00**
☐ **HN 1323**, Contentment	1929–1938	**1900.00**	**2000.00**
☐ **HN 1324**, Fairy	1929–1938	**1500.00**	**1750.00**
☐ **HN 1325**, The Orange Seller	1929–1949	**1100.00**	**1350.00**
☐ **HN 1326**, The Swimmer	1929–1938	**1700.00**	**1900.00**

	Date	Price Range	
☐ HN 1327, Bo-Peep (1st version)	1929–1938	1700.00	1900.00
☐ HN 1328, Bo-Peep (1st version)	1929–1938	1700.00	1900.00
☐ HN 1329, The Swimmer	1929–1938	1700.00	1900.00
☐ HN 1330, Sweet Anne	1929–1949	275.00	375.00
☐ HN 1331, Sweet Anne	1929–1949	275.00	350.00
☐ HN 1332, Lady Jester (1st version) ...	1929–1938	1600.00	1900.00
☐ HN 1333, A Jester (2nd version)	1929–1949	1900.00	2000.00
☐ HN 1334, Tulips	1929–1938	1750.00	2000.00
☐ HN 1335, Folly ..../...........	1929–1938	1600.00	1850.00
☐ HN 1336, One of the Forty (11th version)	1929–1938	1250.00	1500.00
☐ HN 1337, Priscilla	1929–1938	600.00	750.00
☐ HN 1338, The Courtier	1929–1938	3000.00	3750.00
☐ HN 1339, Covent Garden	1929–1938	1500.00	1750.00
☐ HN 1340, Priscilla	1929–1949	300.00	350.00
☐ HN 1341, Marietta	1929–1949	650.00	750.00
☐ HN 1342, The Flower Seller's Children	1929–	550.00	
☐ HN 1343, Dulcinea	1929–1938	1100.00	1300.00
☐ HN 1344, Sunshine Girl	1929–1938	1750.00	2000.00
☐ HN 1345, A Victorian Lady	1929–1949	300.00	400.00
☐ HN 1346, Iona	1929–1938	2750.00	3250.00
☐ HN 1347, Moira	1929–1938	3000.00	3500.00
☐ HN 1348, Sunshine Girl	1929–1938	1750.00	2000.00
☐ HN 1349, Scotties	1929–1949	2500.00	3000.00
☐ HN 1350, One of the Forty (11th version)	1929–1949	1250.00	1500.00
☐ HN 1351, One of the Forty (1st version)	1929–1949	1250.00	1500.00
☐ HN 1352, One of the Forty (1st verson)	1929–1949	1250.00	1500.00
☐ HN 1353, One of the Forty (2nd version)	1929–1949	1250.00	1500.00
☐ HN 1354, One of the Forty (13th version)	1929–1949	1250.00	1500.00
☐ HN 1355, The Mendicant	1929–1938	750.00	900.00
☐ HN 1356, The Parson's Daughter	1929–1938	475.00	550.00
☐ HN 1357, Kathleen	1929–1938	800.00	900.00
☐ HN 1358, Rosina	1929–1938	800.00	975.00
☐ HN 1359, Two-A-Penny	1929–1938	2000.00	2500.00
☐ HN 1360, Sweet and Twenty (1st version)	1929–1938	575.00	750.00
☐ HN 1361, Mask Seller	1929–1938	1500.00	1800.00
☐ HN 1362, Pantalettes	1929–1938	325.00	400.00
☐ HN 1363, Doreen	1929–1938	900.00	1200.00
☐ HN 1364, Rosina	1929–1938	800.00	975.00
☐ HN 1365, The Mendicant	1929–1969	250.00	325.00

	Date	Price Range	
☐ HN 1366, The Moor	1930–1949	1500.00	1750.00
☐ HN 1367, Kitty	1930–1938	2500.00	3000.00
☐ HN 1368, Rose	1930–	95.00	
☐ HN 1369, Boy on Pig	1930–1938	4000.00	4500.00
☐ HN 1370, Marie (2nd version)	1930–1988	95.00	
☐ HN 1371, Darling (1st version)	1930–1938	750.00	1100.00
☐ HN 1372, Darling (1st version)	1930–1938	750.00	1100.00
☐ HN 1373, Sweet Lavender	1930–1949	375.00	475.00
☐ HN 1374, Fairy	1930–1938	1000.00	1300.00
☐ HN 1375, Fairy	1930–1938	900.00	1150.00
☐ HN 1376, Fairy	1930–1938	700.00	850.00
☐ HN 1377, Fairy		700.00	850.00
☐ HN 1378, Fairy	1930–1938	700.00	850.00
☐ HN 1379, Fairy	1930–1938	800.00	1000.00
☐ HN 1380, Fairy	1930–1938	1100.00	1400.00

HN 1381–HN 1386 FAIRIES—NOT ISSUED

	Date	Price Range	
☐ HN 1387, Rose	1930–1938	300.00	350.00
☐ HN 1388, Marie (2nd version)	1930–1938	400.00	500.00
☐ HN 1389, Doreen	1930–1938	850.00	950.00
☐ HN 1390, Doreen	1930–1938	850.00	950.00
☐ HN 1391, Pierrette (3rd version)	1930–1938	1200.00	1600.00
☐ HN 1392, Paisley Shawl (1st version)	1930–1949	400.00	500.00
☐ HN 1393, Fairy	1930–1938	950.00	1100.00
☐ HN 1394, Fairy	1930–1938	700.00	850.00
☐ HN 1395, Fairy	1930–1938	900.00	1100.00
☐ HN 1396, Fairy	1930–1938	800.00	1000.00
☐ HN 1397, Gretchen	1930–1938	800.00	1200.00
☐ HN 1398, Derrick	1930–1938	850.00	1000.00
☐ HN 1399, The Young Widow	1930–	2500.00	3000.00
☐ HN 1400, The Windmill Lady	1930–1938	2750.00	3250.00
☐ HN 1401, Chorus Girl	1930–1938	3500.00	5000.00
☐ HN 1402, Miss Demure	1930–1975	225.00	325.00
☐ HN 1403, The Old Huntsman	NOT ISSUED		
☐ HN 1404, Betty (2nd version)	1930–1938	1500.00	2000.00
☐ HN 1405, Betty (2nd version)	1930–1938	1500.00	2000.00
☐ HN 1406, The Flower Seller's Children	1930–1938	950.00	1250.00
☐ HN 1407, The Winner	1930–1938	6500.00	7500.00
☐ HN 1408, John Peel	1930–1937	3000.00	3500.00
☐ HN 1409, Hunting Squire	1930–1938	2500.00	3000.00
☐ HN 1410, Abdullah	1930–1938	1000.00	1100.00
☐ HN 1411, Charley's Aunt (2nd version)	1930–1938	1375.00	1425.00
☐ HN 1412, Pantalettes	1930–1949	350.00	400.00
☐ HN 1413, Margery	1930–1949	450.00	500.00
☐ HN 1414, Patricia	1930–1949	600.00	750.00

HN 1415 NO DETAILS AVAILABLE

	Date	Price Range	
☐ HN 1416, Rose	1930–1949	250.00	300.00
☐ HN 1417, Marie (2nd version)	1930–1949	300.00	400.00
☐ HN 1418, The Little Mother (2nd version)	1930–1938	2500.00	3000.00
☐ HN 1419, Dulcinea	1930–1938	1200.00	1500.00
☐ HN 1420, Phyllis	1930–1949	575.00	675.00
☐ HN 1421, Barbara	1930–1938	750.00	950.00
☐ HN 1422, Joan	1930–1949	400.00	500.00
☐ HN 1423, Babette	1930–1938	900.00	1200.00
☐ HN 1424, Babette	1930–1938	900.00	1200.00
☐ HN 1425, The Moor	1930–1949	1500.00	1750.00
☐ HN 1426, The Gossips	1930–1949	1650.00	1800.00
☐ HN 1427, Darby	1930–1949	325.00	400.00
☐ HN 1428, Calumet	1930–1949	1000.00	1100.00
☐ HN 1429, The Gossips	1930–1949	675.00	825.00
☐ HN 1430, Phyllis	1930–1938	700.00	800.00
☐ HN 1431, Patricia	1930–1949	550.00	650.00
☐ HN 1432, Barbara	1930–1938	750.00	950.00
☐ HN 1433, The Little Bridesmaid (1st version)	1930–1951	150.00	175.00
☐ HN 1434, The Little Bridesmaid (1st version)	1930–1949	275.00	350.00
☐ HN 1435, Betty (2nd version)	1930–1938	1500.00	2000.00
☐ HN 1436, Betty (2nd version)	1930–1938	1500.00	2000.00
☐ HN 1437, Sweet and Twenty (1st version)	1930–1938	575.00	750.00
☐ HN 1438, Sweet and Twenty (1st version)	1930–1938	575.00	750.00
☐ HN 1439, Columbine (1st version) ...	1930–1938	1000.00	1200.00
☐ HN 1440, Miss Demure	1930–1949	600.00	750.00
☐ HN 1441, Child Study	1931–1938	850.00	950.00
☐ HN 1442, Child Study	1931–1938	850.00	950.00
☐ HN 1443, Child Study	1931–1938	850.00	950.00
☐ HN 1444, Pauline	1931–1938	400.00	450.00
☐ HN 1445, Biddy	1931–1938	195.00	300.00
☐ HN 1446, Marietta	1931–1949	700.00	800.00
☐ HN 1447, Marigold	1931–1949	500.00	600.00
☐ HN 1448, Rita	1931–1938	700.00	800.00
☐ HN 1449, The Little Mistress	1931–1949	400.00	500.00
☐ HN 1450, Rita	1931–1938	700.00	800.00
☐ HN 1451, Marigold	1931–1938	600.00	700.00
☐ HN 1452, A Victorian Lady	1931–1949	300.00	400.00
☐ HN 1453, Sweet Anne	1931–1949	325.00	375.00
☐ HN 1454, Negligee	1931–1938	1900.00	2250.00
☐ HN 1455, Molly Malone	1931–1938	2000.00	2400.00
☐ HN 1456, Butterfly	1931–1938	1300.00	1500.00
☐ HN 1457, All-A-Blooming	1931–	1850.00	2100.00

	Date	Price Range	
☐ HN 1458, Monica	1931–1949	450.00	550.00
☐ HN 1459, Monica	1931–	450.00	550.00
☐ HN 1460, Paisley Shawl (1st version)	1931–1949	500.00	650.00
☐ HN 1461, Barbara	1931–1938	750.00	1000.00
☐ HN 1462, Patricia	1931–1938	600.00	750.00
☐ HN 1463, Miss Demure	1931–1949	600.00	750.00
☐ HN 1464, The Carpet Seller	1931–1969	275.00	350.00
☐ HN 1464A, The Carpet Seller	1931–	700.00	800.00
☐ HN 1465, Lady Clare	1931–1938	650.00	750.00
☐ HN 1466, All-A-Blooming	1931–1938	1450.00	1700.00
☐ HN 1467, Monica	1931–	140.00	
☐ HN 1468, Pamela	1931–1938	950.00	1150.00
☐ HN 1469, Pamela	1931–1938	750.00	850.00
☐ HN 1470, Chloe	1931–1949	255.00	300.00
☐ HN 1471, Annette	1931–1938	450.00	550.00
☐ HN 1472, Annette	1931–1949	400.00	475.00
☐ HN 1473, Dreamland	1931–1938	3000.00	3250.00
☐ HN 1474, In the Stocks (1st version)	1931–1938	2000.00	2500.00
☐ HN 1475, In the Stocks (1st version)	1931–1938	2000.00	2500.00
☐ HN 1476, Chloe	1931–1938	275.00	325.00
HN 1477 NO DETAILS AVAILABLE			
☐ HN 1478, Sylvia	1931–1938	600.00	800.00
☐ HN 1479, Chloe	1931–1949	250.00	300.00
☐ HN 1480, Newhaven Fishwife	1931–1938	3500.00	4000.00
☐ HN 1481, Dreamland	1931–1938	3000.00	3250.00
☐ HN 1482, Pearly Boy (1st version)	1931–1949	350.00	400.00
☐ HN 1483, Pearly Girl (1st version)	1931–1949	350.00	400.00
☐ HN 1484, Jennifer	1931–1949	500.00	600.00
☐ HN 1485, Greta	1931–1953	275.00	350.00
☐ HN 1486, Phyllis	1931–1949	650.00	750.00
☐ HN 1487, Suzette	1931–1950	300.00	350.00
☐ HN 1488, Gloria	1932–1938	1500.00	1700.00
☐ HN 1489, Marie (2nd version)	1932–1949	300.00	400.00
☐ HN 1490, Dorcas	1932–1938	850.00	950.00
☐ HN 1491, Dorcas	1932–1938	850.00	950.00
☐ HN 1492, Old Lavender Seller	1932–1949	875.00	1000.00
☐ HN 1493, The Potter	1932–	450.00	
☐ HN 1494, Gwendolen	1932–1938	800.00	1000.00
☐ HN 1495, Priscilla	1932–1949	700.00	800.00
☐ HN 1496, Sweet Anne	1932–1967	200.00	275.00
☐ HN 1497, Rosamund (2nd version)	1932–1938	2200.00	2500.00
☐ HN 1498, Chloe	1932–1938	450.00	550.00
☐ HN 1499, Miss Demure	1932–1938	550.00	650.00
☐ HN 1500, Biddy	1932–1938	300.00	350.00
☐ HN 1501, Priscilla	1932–1938	650.00	800.00
☐ HN 1502, Lucy Ann	1932–1951	250.00	325.00
☐ HN 1503, Gwendolen	1932–1949	800.00	1000.00

	Date	Price Range	
☐ **HN 1504**, Sweet Maid (1st version) ..	1932–1938	**1200.00**	**1500.00**
☐ **HN 1505**, Sweet Maid (1st version) ..	1932–1938	**1200.00**	**1500.00**
☐ **HN 1506**, Rose	1932–1938	**300.00**	**350.00**
☐ **HN 1507**, Pantalettes	1932–1949	**500.00**	**650.00**
☐ **HN 1508**, Helen	1932–1938	**1200.00**	**1400.00**
☐ **HN 1509**, Helen	1932–1938	**1200.00**	**1400.00**
☐ **HN 1510**, Constance	1932–1938	**1250.00**	**1500.00**
☐ **HN 1511**, Constance	1932–1938	**1250.00**	**1500.00**
☐ **HN 1512**, Kathleen	1932–1938	**800.00**	**900.00**
☐ **HN 1513**, Biddy	1932–1951	**160.00**	**225.00**
☐ **HN 1514**, Dolly Vardon	1932–1938	**1200.00**	**1400.00**
☐ **HN 1515**, Dolly Vardon	1932–1949	**1200.00**	**1400.00**
☐ **HN 1516**, Cicely	1932–1949	**1200.00**	**1400.00**
☐ **HN 1517**, Veronica (1st version)	1932–1951	**350.00**	**400.00**
☐ **HN 1518**, The Potter	1932–1949	**1000.00**	**1200.00**
☐ **HN 1519**, Veronica (1st version)	1932–1938	**550.00**	**750.00**
☐ **HN 1520**, Eugene	1932–1938	**875.00**	**975.00**
☐ **HN 1521**, Eugene	1932–1938	**875.00**	**975.00**
☐ **HN 1522**, The Potter	1932–1949	**1000.00**	**1200.00**
☐ **HN 1523**, Lisette	1932–1938	**1000.00**	**1100.00**
☐ **HN 1524**, Lisette	1932–1938	**1000.00**	**1100.00**
☐ **HN 1525**, Clarissa (1st version)	1932–1938	**500.00**	**650.00**
☐ **HN 1526**, Anthea	1932–1938	**900.00**	**1100.00**
☐ **HN 1527**, Anthea	1932–1949	**700.00**	**900.00**
☐ **HN 1528**, Bluebeard (2nd version) ...	1932–1949	**900.00**	**1000.00**
☐ **HN 1529**, A Victorian Lady	1932–1938	**600.00**	**800.00**
☐ **HN 1530**, The Little Bridesmaid	1932–1938	**400.00**	**450.00**
☐ **HN 1531**, Marie (2nd version)	1932–1938	**300.00**	**400.00**
☐ **HN 1532**, Fairy	1932–1938	**1100.00**	**1500.00**
☐ **HN 1533**, Fairy	1932–1938	**900.00**	**1100.00**
☐ **HN 1534**, Fairy	1932–1938	**900.00**	**1100.00**
☐ **HN 1535**, Fairy	1932–1938	**800.00**	**1000.00**
☐ **HN 1536**, Fairy	1932–1938	**800.00**	**1000.00**
☐ **HN 1537**, Janet (1st version)	1932–	**160.00**	
☐ **HN 1538**, Janet (1st version)	1932–1949	**650.00**	**750.00**
☐ **HN 1539**, A Saucy Nymph	1933–1949	**400.00**	**550.00**
☐ **HN 1540**, 'Little Child so Rare and Sweet'	1933–1949	**600.00**	**700.00**
☐ **HN 1541**, 'Happy Joy, Baby Boy'	1933–1949	**800.00**	**1000.00**
☐ **HN 1542**, 'Little Child so Rare and Sweet'	1933–1949	**500.00**	**600.00**
☐ **HN 1543**, 'Dancing Eyes and Sunny Hair'	1933–1949	**375.00**	**425.00**
☐ **HN 1544**, 'Do You Wonder Where Fairies Are That Folk Declare Have Vanished'	1933–1949	**750.00**	**950.00**

	Date	Price Range	
☐ HN 1545, 'Called Love, a Little Boy, Almost Naked, Wanton, Blind, Cruel Now, and Then as Kind'	1933–1949	850.00	1150.00
☐ HN 1546, 'Here a Little Child I Stand'	1933–1949	750.00	850.00
☐ HN 1547, Pearly Boy (1st version)	1933–1949	650.00	850.00
☐ HN 1548, Pearly Girl (1st version) ...	1933–1949	650.00	850.00
☐ HN 1549, Sweet and Twenty (1st version)	1933–1949	600.00	850.00
☐ HN 1550, Annette	1933–1949	400.00	475.00
☐ HN 1551, Rosamund (2nd version) ..	1933–1938	2200.00	2500.00
☐ HN 1552, Pinkie	1933–1938	800.00	950.00
☐ HN 1553, Pinkie	1933–1938	800.00	950.00
☐ HN 1554, Charley's Aunt (2nd version)	1933–1938	1350.00	1500.00
☐ HN 1555, Marigold	1933–1949	500.00	600.00
☐ HN 1556, Rosina	1933–1938	775.00	950.00
☐ HN 1557, Lady Fayre	1933–1938	1100.00	1350.00
☐ HN 1558, Dorcas	1933–1952	350.00	450.00
☐ HN 1559, Priscilla	1933–1949	650.00	800.00
☐ HN 1560, Miss Demure	1933–1949	600.00	750.00
☐ HN 1561, Willy-Won't He	1933–1949	500.00	600.00
☐ HN 1562, Gretchen	1933–1938	900.00	1250.00
☐ HN 1563, Sweet and Twenty (1st version)	1933–1938	600.00	850.00
☐ HN 1564, Pamela	1933–1938	950.00	1150.00
☐ HN 1565, Lucy Ann	1933–1938	500.00	675.00
☐ HN 1566, Estelle	1933–1938	800.00	900.00
☐ HN 1567, Patricia	1933–1949	950.00	1150.00
☐ HN 1568, Charmain	1933–1938	775.00	875.00
☐ HN 1569, Charmain	1933–1938	775.00	875.00
☐ HN 1570, Gwendolen	1933–1949	800.00	950.00
☐ HN 1571, Old Lavender Seller	1933–1949	1100.00	1350.00
☐ HN 1572, Helen	1933–1938	1200.00	1400.00
☐ HN 1573, Rhoda	1933–1949	600.00	800.00
☐ HN 1574, Rhoda	1933–1938	600.00	800.00
☐ HN 1575, Daisy	1933–1949	450.00	650.00
☐ HN 1576, Tildy	1933–1938	850.00	950.00
☐ HN 1577, Suzette	1933–1949	650.00	750.00
☐ HN 1578, The Hinged Parasol	1933–1949	550.00	700.00
☐ HN 1579, The Hinged Parasol	1933–1949	550.00	700.00
☐ HN 1580, Rosebud (1st version)	1933–1938	750.00	950.00
☐ HN 1581, Rosebud (1st version)	1933–1938	750.00	950.00
☐ HN 1582, Marion	1933–1938	1400.00	1600.00
☐ HN 1583, Marion	1933–1938	1400.00	1600.00
☐ HN 1584, Willy-Won't He	1933–1949	350.00	450.00
☐ HN 1585, Suzette	1933–1938	650.00	750.00
☐ HN 1586, Camille	1933–1949	775.00	900.00

	Date	Price Range	
☐ HN 1587, Fleurette	1933–1949	500.00	650.00
☐ HN 1588, The Bride (1st version)	1933–1938	750.00	1000.00
☐ HN 1589, Sweet and Twenty (2nd version)	1933–1949	250.00	325.00
HN 1590–HN 1597 WALL MASKS			
☐ HN 1598, Clothilde	1933–1949	700.00	800.00
☐ HN 1599, Clothilde	1933–1949	700.00	800.00
☐ HN 1600, The Bride (1st version)	1933–1949	750.00	1000.00
HN 1601–HN 1603 WALL MASKS			
☐ HN 1604, The Emir	1933–1949	800.00	1000.00
☐ HN 1605, The Emir	1933–1949	800.00	1000.00
☐ HN 1606, Falstaff (1st version)	1933–1949	1200.00	1500.00
☐ HN 1607, Cerise	1933–1949	450.00	500.00
HN 1608–HN 1609 WALL MASKS			
☐ HN 1610, Sweet and Twenty (2nd version)	1933–1938	200.00	300.00
HN 1611–HN 1614 WALL MASKS			
☐ HN 1615, Bookend, Micawber	Unknown	2000.00	2500.00
☐ HN 1616, Bookend, Tony Weller	Unknown	2000.00	2500.00
☐ HN 1617, Primroses	1934–1949	775.00	875.00
☐ HN 1618, Maisie	1934–1949	550.00	650.00
☐ HN 1619, Maisie	1934–1949	375.00	475.00
☐ HN 1620, Rosabell	1934–1938	1300.00	1550.00
☐ HN 1621, Irene	1934–1951	325.00	375.00
☐ HN 1622, Evelyn	1934–1949	1000.00	1250.00
☐ HN 1623, Bookend, Pickwick		2000.00	2500.00
HN 1624 NO DETAILS AVAILABLE			
☐ HN 1625, Bookend, Sairey Gamp		2000.00	2500.00
☐ HN 1626, Bonnie Lassie	1934–1953	275.00	375.00
☐ HN 1627, Curly Knob	1934–1949	550.00	650.00
☐ HN 1628, Margot	1934–1938	850.00	1000.00
☐ HN 1629, Grizel	1934–1938	1300.00	1500.00
HN 1630 WALL MASK			
☐ HN 1631, Sweet Anne	1934–1938	300.00	400.00
☐ HN 1632, A Gentlewoman	1934–1949	750.00	850.00
☐ HN 1633, Clemency	1934–1938	875.00	1000.00
☐ HN 1634, Clemency	1934–1949	650.00	775.00
☐ HN 1635, Marie (2nd version)	1934–1949	400.00	500.00
☐ HN 1636, Margot	1934–1938	850.00	1000.00
☐ HN 1637, Evelyn	1934–1938	1050.00	1200.00
☐ HN 1638, Ladybird	1934–1949	1500.00	2000.00
☐ HN 1639, Dainty May	1934–1949	400.00	450.00
☐ HN 1640, Ladybird	1934–1938	1500.00	2000.00
☐ HN 1641, The Little Mother (2nd version)	1934–1949	2500.00	3000.00
☐ HN 1642, Granny's Shawl	1934–1949	450.00	550.00
☐ HN 1643, Clemency	1934–1938	650.00	775.00

	Date	Price Range	
☐ HN 1644, Herminia	1934–1938	1200.00	1500.00
☐ HN 1645, Aileen	1934–1938	1150.00	1350.00
☐ HN 1646, Herminia	1934–1938	1200.00	1500.00
☐ HN 1647, Granny's Shawl	1934–1949	425.00	475.00
☐ HN 1648, Camille	1934–1949	775.00	900.00
☐ HN 1649, Sweet and Twenty (1st version)	1934–1949	575.00	750.00
☐ HN 1650, Veronica (1st version)	1934–1949	550.00	750.00
☐ HN 1651, Charmain	1934–1938	1150.00	1300.00
☐ HN 1652, Janet (1st version)	1934–1949	375.00	400.00
☐ HN 1653, Margot	1934–1938	850.00	1000.00
☐ HN 1654, Rose	1934–1938	300.00	350.00
☐ HN 1655, Marie (2nd version)	1934–1938	500.00	600.00
☐ HN 1656, Dainty May	1934–1949	450.00	550.00
☐ HN 1657, The Moor	1934–1949	1500.00	1750.00
HN 1658–HN 1661 WALL MASKS			
☐ HN 1662, Delicia	1934–1938	900.00	1000.00
☐ HN 1663, Delicia	1934–1938	900.00	1000.00
☐ HN 1664, Aileen	1934–1938	1150.00	1350.00
☐ HN 1665, Miss Winsome	1934–1949	800.00	950.00
☐ HN 1666, Miss Winsome	1934–1938	900.00	1100.00
☐ HN 1667, Blossom	1934–1949	1500.00	1750.00
☐ HN 1668, Sibell	1934–1949	1000.00	1250.00
☐ HN 1669, Anthea	1934–1938	1000.00	1250.00
☐ HN 1670, Gillian	1934–1949	700.00	800.00
HN 1671–HN 1676 WALL MASKS			
☐ HN 1677, Tinkle Bell	1935–1988	110.00	
☐ HN 1678, Dinky Doo	1934–	95.00	
☐ HN 1679, Babie	1935–	110.00	
☐ HN 1680, Tootles	1935–1975	75.00	125.00
☐ HN 1681, Delicia	1935–1938	1250.00	1400.00
☐ HN 1682, Teresa	1935–1949	1000.00	1200.00
☐ HN 1683, Teresa	1935–1938	1400.00	1600.00
☐ HN 1684, Lisette	1935–1938	1200.00	1500.00
☐ HN 1685, Cynthia	1935–1949	750.00	900.00
☐ HN 1686, Cynthia	1935–1949	750.00	900.00
☐ HN 1687, Clarissa (1st version)	1935–1949	600.00	750.00
☐ HN 1688, Rhoda	1935–1949	650.00	850.00
☐ HN 1689, Calumet	1935–1949	750.00	850.00
☐ HN 1690, June	1935–1949	450.00	550.00
☐ HN 1691, June	1935–1949	400.00	475.00
☐ HN 1692, Sonia	1935–1949	1100.00	1200.00
☐ HN 1693, Virginia	1935–1949	800.00	1000.00
☐ HN 1694, Virginia	1935–1949	800.00	1000.00
☐ HN 1695, Sibell	1935–1949	900.00	1000.00
☐ HN 1696, Suzette	1935–1949	650.00	750.00
☐ HN 1697, Irene	1935–1949	750.00	850.00

	Date	Price Range	
☐HN 1698, Phyllis	1935–1949	750.00	850.00
☐HN 1699, Marietta	1935–1949	700.00	800.00
☐HN 1700, Gloria	1935–1938	1700.00	2000.00
☐HN 1701, Sweet Anne	1935–1938	300.00	400.00
☐HN 1702, A Jester (1st version)	1935–1949	1000.00	1200.00
☐HN 1703, Charley's Aunt (3rd version)	1935–1938	1400.00	1600.00
☐HN 1704, Herminia	1935–1938	1200.00	1500.00
☐HN 1705, The Cobbler (3rd version)	1935–1949	850.00	950.00
☐HN 1706, The Cobbler (3rd version)	1935–1949	225.00	300.00
☐HN 1707, Paisley Shawl (1st version)	1935–1949	700.00	850.00
☐HN 1708, The Bather (1st version) ...	1935–1938	1800.00	2250.00
☐HN 1709, Pantalettes	1935–1938	950.00	1150.00
☐HN 1710, Camilla	1935–1949	850.00	1050.00
☐HN 1711, Camilla	1935–1949	850.00	1050.00
☐HN 1712, Daffy Down Dilly	1935–1975	250.00	325.00
☐HN 1713, Daffy Down Dilly	1935–1949	1000.00	1250.00
☐HN 1714, Millicent	1935–1949	1450.00	1650.00
☐HN 1715, Millicent	1935–1949	1450.00	1650.00
☐HN 1716, Diana	1935–1949	400.00	450.00
☐HN 1717, Diana	1935–1949	400.00	450.00
☐HN 1718, Kate Hardcastle	1935–1949	700.00	800.00
☐HN 1719, Kate Hardcastle	1935–1949	550.00	650.00
☐HN 1720, Frangcon	1935–1949	900.00	1200.00
☐HN 1721, Frangcon	1935–1949	900.00	1200.00
☐HN 1722, The Coming of Spring	1935–1949	2500.00	3000.00
☐HN 1723, The Coming of Spring	1935–1949	2500.00	3000.00
☐HN 1724, Ruby	1935–1949	550.00	750.00
☐HN 1725, Ruby	1935–1949	550.00	750.00
☐HN 1726, Celia	1935–1949	1000.00	1300.00
☐HN 1727, Celia	1935–1949	1000.00	1300.00
☐HN 1728, The New Bonnet	1935–1949	950.00	1250.00
☐HN 1729, Vera	1935–1938	1200.00	1600.00
☐HN 1730, Vera	1935–1938	1200.00	1600.00
☐HN 1731, Daydreams	1935–	195.00	
☐HN 1732, Daydreams	1935–1949	750.00	950.00
HN 1733 WALL MASK			
☐HN 1734, Kate Hardcastle	1935–1949	1200.00	1400.00
☐HN 1735, Sibell	1935–1949	1000.00	1250.00
☐HN 1736, Camille	1935–1949	950.00	1150.00
☐HN 1737, Janet (1st version)	1935–1949	600.00	750.00
☐HN 1738, Sonia	1938–1949	1200.00	1500.00
☐HN 1739, Paisley Shawl (1st version)	1935–1949	650.00	850.00
☐HN 1740, Gladys	1935–1949	900.00	1100.00
☐HN 1741, Gladys	1935–1938	900.00	1100.00
☐HN 1742, Sir Walter Raleigh	1935–1949	1200.00	1500.00
☐HN 1743, Mirabel	1935–1949	1250.00	1500.00

	Date	Price Range	
☐ HN 1744, Mirabel	1935–1949	1100.00	1250.00
☐ HN 1745, The Rustic Swain	1935–1949	2250.00	2500.00
☐ HN 1746, The Rustic Swain	1935–1949	2250.00	2500.00
☐ HN 1747, Afternoon Tea	1935–1982	275.00	350.00
☐ HN 1748, Afternoon Tea	1935–1949	1200.00	1500.00
☐ HN 1749, Pierrette (3rd version)	1936–1949	1200.00	1600.00
☐ HN 1750, Folly	1936–1949	1500.00	1750.00
☐ HN 1751, Sir Walter Raleigh	1936–1949	1200.00	1500.00
☐ HN 1752, Regency	1936–1949	1600.00	1900.00
☐ HN 1753, Eleanore	1936–1949	1350.00	1500.00
☐ HN 1754, Eleanore	1936–1949	1350.00	1500.00
☐ HN 1755, The Court Shoemaker	1936–1949	2100.00	2500.00
☐ HN 1756, Lizana	1936–1949	700.00	875.00
☐ HN 1757, Romany Sue	1936–1949	900.00	1050.00
☐ HN 1758, Romany Sue	1936–1949	900.00	1050.00
☐ HN 1759, The Orange Lady	1936–1975	250.00	300.00
☐ HN 1760, Four O'Clock	1936–1949	900.00	1100.00
☐ HN 1761, Lizana	1936–1938	850.00	950.00
☐ HN 1762, The Bride (1st version)	1936–1949	750.00	1000.00
☐ HN 1763, Windflower (1st version)	1936–1949	400.00	475.00
☐ HN 1764, Windflower (1st version)	1936–1949	550.00	700.00
☐ HN 1765, Chloe	1936–1950	250.00	300.00
☐ HN 1766, Nana	1936–1949	475.00	600.00
☐ HN 1767, Nana	1936–1949	475.00	600.00
☐ HN 1768, Ivy	1936–1949	75.00	100.00
☐ HN 1769, Ivy	1936–1938	600.00	700.00
☐ HN 1770, Maureen	1936–1959	275.00	325.00
☐ HN 1771, Maureen	1936–1949	650.00	750.00
☐ HN 1722, Delight	1936–1967	175.00	225.00
☐ HN 1773, Delight	1936–1949	450.00	550.00
☐ HN 1774, Spring (2nd version) (Limited Edition, Figurines)	1933–	5000.00	6000.00
☐ HN 1775, Salome (Limited Edition, Figurines)	1933–	6500.00	8000.00
☐ HN 1776, West Wind (Limited Edition, Figurines)	1933–	4500.00	5000.00
☐ HN 1777, Spirit of the Wind (Limited Edition, Miscellaneous)	1933–	6500.00	8000.00
☐ HN 1778, Beethoven (Limited Edition, Figurines)	1933–	6000.00	6500.00
☐ HN 1779, Bird Model (Macaw by R. Garbe)	Unknown		
☐ HN 1780, Lady of the Snows (withdrawn date not available)	1933–	4000.00	4500.00

HN 1781–HN 1786 WALL MASKS
HN 1787–HN 1790 NO DETAILS AVAILABLE

	Date	Price Range	
☐ HN 1791, Old Balloon Seller and Bull-dog	1932–1938	2000.00	2500.00
☐ HN 1792, Henry VIII (2nd version) (Limited Edition, Figurines)	1933–1939	3500.00	4000.00
☐ HN 1793, This Little Pig	1936–	110.00	
☐ HN 1794, This Little Pig	1936–1949	450.00	550.00
☐ HN 1795, M'Lady's Maid	1936–1949	2000.00	2200.00
☐ HN 1796, Hazel	1936–1949	600.00	750.00
☐ HN 1797, Hazel	1936–1949	600.00	750.00
☐ HN 1798, Lily	1936–1949	100.00	125.00
☐ HN 1799, Lily	1936–1949	300.00	375.00
☐ HN 1800, St. George (1st version)	1934–1950	3000.00	3500.00
☐ HN 1801, An Old King	1937–1954	1600.00	1800.00
☐ HN 1802, Estelle	1937–1949	800.00	900.00
☐ HN 1803, Aileen	1937–1949	1100.00	1350.00
☐ HN 1804, Granny	1937–1949	1300.00	1500.00
☐ HN 1805, To Bed	1937–1959	150.00	200.00
☐ HN 1806, To Bed	1937–1949	350.00	400.00
☐ HN 1807, Spring Flowers	1937–1959	300.00	350.00
☐ HN 1808, Cissie	1937–1951	450.00	550.00
☐ HN 1809, Cissie	1937–	140.00	
☐ HN 1810, Bo-Peep (2nd version)	1937–1949	500.00	650.00
☐ HN 1811, Bo-Peep (2nd version)	1937–	140.00	
☐ HN 1812, Forget-me-not	1937–1949	600.00	700.00
☐ HN 1813, Forget-me-not	1937–1949	600.00	700.00
☐ HN 1814, The Squire	1937–1949	2500.00	3000.00
☐ HN 1815, The Huntsman (2nd version)	1937–1949	3000.00	3500.00
HN 1816–HN 1817 WALL MASKS			
☐ HN 1818, Miranda	1937–1949	1300.00	1500.00
☐ HN 1819, Miranda	1937–1949	1300.00	1500.00
☐ HN 1820, Reflections	1937–1938	1500.00	1700.00
☐ HN 1821, Reflections	1937–1938	1500.00	1700.00
☐ HN 1822, M'Lady's Maid	1937–1949	2200.00	2500.00
HN 1823–1824 WALL MASKS			
☐ HN 1825, Spirit of the Wind	1937–1949	3500.00	4000.00
☐ HN 1826, West Wind	1937–1949	5000.00	6500.00
☐ HN 1827, Spring (2nd version)	1937–1949	2500.00	3000.00
☐ HN 1828, Salome	1937–1949	4500.00	5000.00
☐ HN 1830, Lady of the Snows	1937–1949	4000.00	4500.00
☐ HN 1831, The Cloud	1937–1949	4000.00	4500.00
☐ HN 1832, Granny	1937–1949	1300.00	1500.00
☐ HN 1833, Top o' the Hill	1937–1971	200.00	250.00
☐ HN 1834, Top o' the Hill	1937–	230.00	
☐ HN 1835, Verena	1938–1949	1200.00	1500.00
☐ HN 1836, Vanessa	1938–1949	775.00	900.00
☐ HN 1837, Mariquita	1938–1949	2200.00	2500.00
☐ HN 1838, Vanessa	1938–1949	775.00	900.00

	Date	Price Range	
☐ **HN 1839,** Christine (1st version)	1938–1949	700.00	850.00
☐ **HN 1840,** Christine (1st version)	1938–1949	700.00	850.00
☐ **HN 1841,** The Bride (1st version)	1938–1949 ·	1250.00	1750.00
☐ **HN 1842,** Babie	1938–1949	350.00	450.00
☐ **HN 1843,** Biddy Penny Farthing	1938–	275.00	
☐ **HN 1844,** Odds and Ends	1938–1949	850.00	1050.00
☐ **HN 1845,** Modena	1938–1949	2000.00	2250.00
☐ **HN 1846,** Modena	1938–1949	1500.00	1800.00
☐ **HN 1847,** Reflections	1938–1949	1100.00	1250.00
☐ **HN 1848,** Reflections	1938–1949	1100.00	1250.00
☐ **HN 1849,** Top o' the Hill	1938–1975	200.00	250.00
☐ **HN 1850,** Antoinette (1st version)	1938–1949	1100.00	1500.00
☐ **HN 1851,** Antoinette (1st version)	1938–1949	1200.00	1600.00
☐ **HN 1852,** The Mirror	1938–1949	2500.00	3000.00
☐ **HN 1853,** The Mirror	1938–1949	2500.00	3000.00
☐ **HN 1854,** Verena	1938–1949	1200.00	1500.00
☐ **HN 1855,** Memories	1938–1949	450.00	550.00
☐ **HN 1856,** Memories	1938–1949	500.00	600.00
☐ **HN 1857,** Memories	1938–1949	450.00	550.00
☐ **HN 1858,** Dawn	1938–1949	1350.00	1500.00
☐ **HN 1858,** Dawn with Headdress	1938–1949	2200.00	2500.00
☐ **HN 1859,** Tildy	1938–1949	950.00	1100.00
☐ **HN 1860,** Millicent	1938–1949	1850.00	2100.00
☐ **HN 1861,** Kate Hardcastle	1938–1949	850.00	1000.00
☐ **HN 1862,** Jasmine	1938–1949	800.00	950.00
☐ **HN 1863,** Jasmine	1938–1949	900.00	1000.00
☐ **HN 1864,** Sweet and Fair	1938–1949	900.00	1200.00
☐ **HN 1865,** Sweet and Fair	1938–1949	900.00	1200.00
☐ **HN 1866,** Wedding Morn	1938–1949	1800.00	2100.00
☐ **HN 1867,** Wedding Morn	1938–1949	2250.00	2500.00
☐ **HN 1868,** Serena	1938–1949	1100.00	1200.00
☐ **HN 1869,** Dryad of the Pines	1938–1949	4500.00	5500.00
☐ **HN 1870,** Little Lady Make Believe	1938–1949	450.00	550.00
☐ **HN 1871,** Annabella	1938–1949	550.00	750.00
☐ **HN 1872,** Annabella	1938–1949	550.00	750.00
☐ **HN 1873,** Granny's Heritage	1938–1949	1150.00	1350.00
☐ **HN 1874,** Granny's Heritage	1938–1949	700.00	950.00
☐ **HN 1875,** Annabella	1938–1949	600.00	850.00
☐ **HN 1876,** Jasmine	1938–1949	800.00	950.00
☐ **HN 1877,** Jean	1938–1949	550.00	650.00
☐ **HN 1878,** Jean	1938–1949	400.00	450.00
☐ **HN 1879,** Bon Jour	1938–1949	800.00	1000.00
☐ **HN 1880,** The Lambeth Walk	1938–1949 ·	2500.00	3000.00
☐ **HN 1881,** The Lambeth Walk	1938–1949	2500.00	3000.00
☐ **HN 1882,** Nell Gwynn	1938–1949	975.00	1250.00
☐ **HN 1883,** Prudence	1938–1949	950.00	1150.00
☐ **HN 1884,** Prudence	1938–1949	950.00	1150.00

	Date	Price Range	
☐HN 1885, Nadine	1938–1949	1000.00	1250.00
☐HN 1886, Nadine	1938–1949	1000.00	1250.00
☐HN 1887, Nell Gwynn	1938–1949	975.00	1250.00
☐HN 1888, Bon Jour	1938–1949	750.00	950.00
☐HN 1889, Goody Two Shoes	1938–1949	450.00	550.00
☐HN 1890, Lambing Time	1938–1980	150.00	200.00
☐HN 1891, Pecksniff (2nd version)	1938–1952	325.00	400.00
☐HN 1892, Uriah Heep (2nd version)	1938–1952	275.00	325.00
☐HN 1893, Fat Boy (2nd version)	1938–1952	300.00	400.00
☐HN 1894, Mr. Pickwick (2nd version)	1938–1952	350.00	400.00
☐HN 1895, Mr. Micawber (2nd version)	1938–1952	375.00	450.00
☐HN 1896, Sairey Gamp (2nd version)	1938–1952	300.00	375.00
☐HN 1897, Miss Fortune	1938–1949	800.00	1000.00
☐HN 1898, Miss Fortune	1938–1949	800.00	1000.00
☐HN 1899, Midsummer Noon	1939–1949	650.00	750.00
☐HN 1900, Midsummer Noon	1939–1949	1500.00	1800.00
☐HN 1901, Penelope	1939–1975	275.00	375.00
☐HN 1902, Penelope	1939–1949	1000.00	1400.00
☐HN 1903, Rhythm	1939–1949	2000.00	2500.00
☐HN 1904, Rhythm	1939–1949	2000.00	2500.00
☐HN 1905, Goody Two Shoes	1939–1949	450.00	550.00
☐HN 1906, Lydia	1939–1949	700.00	850.00
☐HN 1907, Lydia	1939–1949	700.00	850.00
☐HN 1908, Lydia	1939–	160.00	
☐HN 1909, Honey	1939–1949	350.00	450.00
☐HN 1910, Honey	1939–1949	750.00	950.00
☐HN 1911, Autumn Breezes	1939–1976	175.00	250.00
☐HN 1912, Old Balloon Seller and Bulldog	1939–1949	2250.00	2750.00
☐HN 1913, Autumn Breezes	1939–1971	195.00	275.00
☐HN 1914, Paisley Shawl (2nd version)	1939–1949	300.00	350.00
☐HN 1915, Veronica (2nd version)	1939–1949	400.00	450.00
☐HN 1916, Janet (2nd version)	1939–1949	275.00	325.00
☐HN 1917, Meryll	1939–1949	3500.00	4000.00
☐HN 1918, Sweet Suzy	1939–1949	800.00	950.00
☐HN 1919, Kate Hardcastle	1939–1949	850.00	1000.00
☐HN 1920, Windflower (2nd version)	1939–1949	2250.00	2750.00
☐HN 1921, Roseanna	1940–1949	1400.00	1700.00
☐HN 1922, Spring Morning	1940–1973	175.00	225.00
☐HN 1923, Spring Morning	1940–1949	650.00	750.00
☐HN 1924, Fiona (1st version)	1940–1949	750.00	900.00
☐HN 1925, Fiona (1st version)	1940–1949	750.00	900.00
☐HN 1926, Roseanna	1940–1959	300.00	350.00

	Date	Price Range	
☐ HN 1927, The Awakening (very rare)	1940–1949	4500.00	5500.00
☐ HN 1928, Marguerite	1940–1959	325.00	400.00
☐ HN 1929, Marguerite	1940–1949	650.00	750.00
☐ HN 1930, Marguerite	1940–1949	800.00	900.00
☐ HN 1931, Meriel	1940–1949	1550.00	1850.00
☐ HN 1932, Meriel	1940–1949	1550.00	1850.00
☐ HN 1933, Fiona (1st version)	1940–1949	850.00	1100.00
☐ HN 1934, Autumn Breezes	1940–	230.00	
☐ HN 1935, Sweeting	1940–1973	125.00	175.00
☐ HN 1936, Miss Muffet	1940–1967	175.00	225.00
☐ HN 1937, Miss Muffet	1940–1952	250.00	325.00
☐ HN 1938, Sweeting	1940–1949	600.00	675.00
☐ HN 1939, Windflower (2nd version)	1940–1949	2000.00	2500.00
☐ HN 1940, Toinette	1940–1949	1450.00	1750.00
☐ HN 1941, Peggy	1940–1949	125.00	175.00
☐ HN 1942, Pyjams	1940–1949	700.00	800.00
☐ HN 1943, Veronica	1940–1949	550.00	700.00
☐ HN 1944, Daydreams	1940–1949	850.00	1000.00
☐ HN 1945, Spring Flowers	1940–1949	800.00	1000.00
☐ HN 1946, Marguerite	1940–1949	700.00	800.00
☐ HN 1947, June	1940–1949	600.00	700.00
☐ HN 1948, Lady Charmain	1940–1973	200.00	260.00
☐ HN 1949, Lady Charmain	1940–1975	225.00	275.00
☐ HN 1950, Claribel	1940–1949	600.00	800.00
☐ HN 1951, Claribel	1940–1949	600.00	800.00
☐ HN 1952, Irene	1940–1950	900.00	1000.00
☐ HN 1953, Orange Lady	1940–1975	275.00	325.00
☐ HN 1954, The Balloon Man	1940–	275.00	
☐ HN 1955, Lavinia	1940–1979	100.00	125.00
☐ HN 1956, Chloe	1940–1949	600.00	750.00
☐ HN 1957, The New Bonnet	1940–1949	1500.00	1750.00
☐ HN 1958, Lady April	1940–1959	300.00	400.00
☐ HN 1959, The Choice	1941–1949	1650.00	2000.00
☐ HN 1960, The Choice	1941–1949	1650.00	2000.00
☐ HN 1961, Daisy	1941–1949	500.00	650.00
☐ HN 1962, Genevieve	1941–1975	200.00	260.00
☐ HN 1963, Honey	1941–1949	1250.00	1450.00
☐ HN 1964, Janet (2nd version)	1941–1949	275.00	350.00
☐ HN 1965, Lady April	1941–1949	750.00	850.00
☐ HN 1966, Orange Vendor	1941–1949	950.00	1100.00
☐ HN 1967, Lady Betty	1941–1951	300.00	350.00
☐ HN 1968, Madonna of the Square	1941–1949	850.00	950.00
☐ HN 1969, Madonna of the Square	1941–1949	850.00	950.00
☐ HN 1970, Milady	1941–1949	975.00	1150.00
☐ HN 1971, Springtime	1941–1949	1200.00	1300.00
☐ HN 1972, Regency Beau	1941–1949	1100.00	1300.00

	Date	Price Range	
☐ HN 1973, The Corinthian	1941–1949	1100.00	1300.00
☐ HN 1974, Forty Winks	1945–1973	225.00	275.00
☐ HN 1975, The Shepherd (4th version)	1945–1975	150.00	200.00
☐ HN 1976, Easter Day	1945–1951	400.00	475.00
☐ HN 1977, Her Ladyship	1945–1959	275.00	350.00
☐ HN 1978, Bedtime	1945–	80.00	
☐ HN 1979, Gollywog	1945–1959	450.00	550.00
☐ HN 1980, Gwynneth	1945–1952	275.00	325.00
☐ HN 1981, The Ermine Coat	1945–1967	225.00	300.00
☐ HN 1982, Sabbath Morn	1945–1959	250.00	325.00
☐ HN 1983, Rosebud (2nd version)	1945–1952	400.00	500.00
☐ HN 1984, The Patchwork Quilt	1945–1959	275.00	350.00
☐ HN 1985, Darling (2nd version)	1946–	80.00	
☐ HN 1986, Diana	1946–1975	125.00	175.00
☐ HN 1987, Paisley Shawl (1st version)	1946–1959	225.00	325.00
☐ HN 1988, Paisley Shawl (2nd version)	1946–1975	150.00	225.00
☐ HN 1989, Margaret	1947–1959	300.00	400.00
☐ HN 1990, Mary Jane	1947–1959	400.00	450.00
☐ HN 1991, Market Day (Country Lass)	1947–1955	275.00	350.00
☐ HN 1991, Country Lass	1975–1981	150.00	200.00
☐ HN 1992, Christmas Morn	1947–	195.00	
☐ HN 1993, Griselda	1947–1953	425.00	500.00
☐ HN 1994, Karen	1947–1955	450.00	500.00
☐ HN 1995, Olivia	1947–1951	550.00	650.00
☐ HN 1996, Prue	1947–1955	300.00	350.00
☐ HN 1997, Belle o' the Ball	1947–1979	300.00	350.00
☐ HN 1998, Collinette	1947–1949	500.00	600.00
☐ HN 1999, Collinette	1947–1949	500.00	600.00
☐ HN 2000, Jacqueline	1947–1951	450.00	650.00
☐ HN 2001, Jacqueline	1947–1951	450.00	650.00
☐ HN 2002, Bess	1947–1969	275.00	350.00
☐ HN 2003, Bess	1947–1950	400.00	500.00
☐ HN 2004, A'Courting	1947–1953	550.00	650.00
☐ HN 2005, Henrietta Maria	1948–1953	450.00	550.00
☐ HN 2006, The Lady Anne Nevill	1948–1953	700.00	800.00
☐ HN 2007, Mrs. Fitzherbert	1948–1953	650.00	750.00
☐ HN 2008, Philippa of Hainault	1948–1953	600.00	700.00
☐ HN 2009, Eleanor of Provence	1948–1953	550.00	675.00
☐ HN 2010, The Young Miss Nightingale	1948–1953	450.00	550.00
☐ HN 2011, Matilda	1948–1953	450.00	550.00
☐ HN 2012, Margaret of Anjou	1948–1953	500.00	600.00
☐ HN 2013, Angelina	1948–1951	850.00	1100.00
☐ HN 2014, Jane	1948–1951	1200.00	1500.00

	Date	Price Range	
☐ **HN 2015,** Sir Walter Raleigh	1948–1955	700.00	800.00
☐ **HN 2016,** A Jester (1st version)	1949–	295.00	
☐ **HN 2017,** Silks and Ribbons	1949–	195.00	
☐ **HN 2018,** Parson's Daughter	1949–1953	350.00	400.00
☐ **HN 2019,** Minuet	1949–1971	250.00	350.00
☐ **HN 2020,** Deidre	1949–1955	375.00	450.00
☐ **HN 2021,** Blithe Morning	1949–1971	150.00	175.00
☐ **HN 2022,** Janice	1949–1955	500.00	600.00
☐ **HN 2023,** Joan	1949–1959	350.00	425.00
☐ **HN 2024,** Darby	1949–1959	225.00	325.00
☐ **HN 2025,** Gossips	1949–1967	375.00	425.00
☐ **HN 2026,** Suzette	1949–1959	250.00	350.00
☐ **HN 2027,** June	1949–1952	400.00	500.00
☐ **HN 2028,** Kate Hardcastle	1949–1952	500.00	600.00
☐ **HN 2029,** Windflower (1st version) ...	1949–1952	425.00	500.00
☐ **HN 2030,** Memories	1949–1959	450.00	550.00
☐ **HN 2031,** Granny's Heritage	1949–1969	375.00	425.00
☐ **HN 2032,** Jean	1949–1959	250.00	325.00
☐ **HN 2033,** Midsummer Noon	1949–1955	650.00	750.00
☐ **HN 2034,** Madonna of the Square	1949–1951	800.00	900.00
☐ **HN 2035,** Pearly Boy (2nd version) ..	1949–1959	175.00	225.00
☐ **HN 2036,** Pearly Girl (2nd Version)	1949–1959	175.00	225.00
☐ **HN 2037,** Goody Two Shoes	1949–	140.00	
☐ **HN 2038,** Peggy	1949–1979	85.00	100.00
☐ **HN 2039,** Easter Day	1949–1969	275.00	325.00
☐ **HN 2040,** Gollywog	1949–1959	250.00	300.00
☐ **HN 2041,** The Broken Lance	1949–1975	450.00	550.00
☐ **HN 2042,** Owd Willum	1949–1973	225.00	275.00
☐ **HN 2043,** The Poacher	1949–1959	225.00	275.00
☐ **HN 2044,** Mary Mary	1949–1973	125.00	150.00
☐ **HN 2045,** She Loves Me Not	1949–1962	175.00	225.00
☐ **HN 2046,** He Loves Me	1949–1962	200.00	225.00
☐ **HN 2047,** Once Upon a Time	1949–1955	400.00	475.00
☐ **HN 2048,** Mary Had a Little Lamb ..	1949–1988	140.00	
☐ **HN 2049,** Curly Locks	1949–1953	400.00	475.00
☐ **HN 2050,** Wee Willie Winkie	1949–1953	375.00	450.00
☐ **HN 2051,** St. George (2nd version) ...	1950–1985	400.00	500.00
☐ **HN 2052,** Grandma	1950–1959	300.00	350.00
☐ **HN 2053,** The Gaffer	1950–1959	450.00	525.00
☐ **HN 2054,** Falstaff (2nd version)	1950–	195.00	
☐ **HN 2055,** The Leisure Hour	1950–1965	425.00	475.00
☐ **HN 2056,** Susan	1950–1959	325.00	400.00
☐ **HN 2057,** The Jersey Milkmaid	1950–1959	275.00	325.00
☐ **HN 2057,** The Milkmaid	1975–1981	150.00	200.00
☐ **HN 2058,** Hermione	1950–1952	1200.00	1500.00
☐ **HN 2059,** The Bedtime Story	1950–	295.00	
☐ **HN 2060,** Jack	1950–1971	125.00	175.00

	Date	Price Range	
☐ HN 2061, Jill	1950–1971	125.00	175.00
☐ HN 2062, Little Boy Blue	1950–1973	100.00	125.00
☐ HN 2063, Little Jack Horner	1950–1953	400.00	450.00
☐ HN 2064, My Pretty Maid	1950–1954	450.00	550.00
☐ HN 2065, Blithe Morning	1950–1973	150.00	175.00
☐ HN 2066, Minuet	1950–1955	1000.00	1250.00
☐ HN 2067, St. George (1st version)	1950–1976	2500.00	3000.00
☐ HN 2068, Calumet	1950–1953	550.00	650.00
☐ HN 2069, Farmer's Wife	1951–1955	500.00	600.00
☐ HN 2070, Bridget	1951–1973	300.00	350.00
☐ HN 2071, Bernice	1951–1953	850.00	950.00
☐ HN 2072, The Rocking Horse	1951–1953	1750.00	2000.00
☐ HN 2073, Vivienne	1951–1967	250.00	325.00
☐ HN 2074, Marianne	1951–1953	650.00	750.00
☐ HN 2075, French Peasant	1951–1955	600.00	700.00
☐ HN 2076, Promenade	1951–1953	1500.00	1850.00
☐ HN 2077, Rowena	1951–1955	600.00	750.00
☐ HN 2078, Elfreda	1951–1955	775.00	975.00
☐ HN 2079, Damaris	1951–1952	1400.00	1550.00
☐ HN 2080, Jack Point (Prestige Series)	1952–	2200.00	
☐ HN 2081, Princess Badoura (Prestige Series)	1952–	23,000.00	
☐ HN 2082, The Moor (Prestige Series)	1952–	1900.00	
HN 2083 NO DETAILS AVAILABLE			
☐ HN 2084, King Charles I (Prestige Series)	1952–	1900.00	
☐ HN 2085, Spring (3rd version)	1952–1959	300.00	400.00
☐ HN 2086, Summer (2nd version)	1952–1959	400.00	500.00
☐ HN 2087, Autumn (2nd version)	1952–1959	475.00	550.00
☐ HN 2088, Winter (2nd version)	1952–1959	375.00	450.00
☐ HN 2089, Judith	1952–1959	300.00	350.00
☐ HN 2090, Midinette (2nd version)	1952–1965	275.00	325.00
☐ HN 2091, Rosemary	1952–1959	400.00	500.00
☐ HN 2092, Sweet Maid (2nd version)	1952–1955	500.00	550.00
☐ HN 2093, Georgiana	1952–1955	1100.00	1300.00
☐ HN 2094, Uncle Ned	1952–1965	375.00	475.00
☐ HN 2095, Ibrahim	1952–1955	650.00	775.00
☐ HN 2096, The Fat Boy (3rd version)	1952–1967	300.00	350.00
☐ HN 2097, Mr. Micawber (3rd version)	1952–1967	325.00	375.00
☐ HN 2098, Pecksniff (3rd version)	1952–1967	275.00	350.00
☐ HN 2099, Mr. Pickwick (3rd version)	1952–1967	325.00	375.00
☐ HN 2100, Sairey Gamp (3rd version)	1952–1967	325.00	425.00
☐ HN 2101, Uriah Heep (3rd version)	1952–1967	275.00	325.00

	Date	Price Range	
☐ HN 2102, Pied Piper	1953–1976	275.00	350.00
☐ HN 2103, Mask Seller	1953–	250.00	
☐ HN 2104, Abdulah	1953–1962	500.00	600.00
☐ HN 2105, Bluebeard (2nd version) ...	1953–	550.00	
☐ HN 2106, Linda	1953–1976	100.00	150.00
☐ HN 2107, Valerie	1953–	140.00	
☐ HN 2108, Baby Bunting	1953–1959	200.00	300.00
☐ HN 2109, Wendy	1953–	110.00	
☐ HN 2110, Christmas Time	1953–1967	350.00	375.00
☐ HN 2111, Betsy	1953–1959	325.00	375.00
☐ HN 2112, Carolyn	1953–1965	300.00	400.00
☐ HN 2113, Maytime	1953–1967	225.00	325.00
☐ HN 2114, Sleepyhead	1953–1955	1000.00	1250.00
☐ HN 2115, Coppelia	1953–1959	550.00	650.00
☐ HN 2116, Ballerina	1953–1973	275.00	350.00
☐ HN 2117, The Skater	1953–1971	325.00	385.00
☐ HN 2118, Good King Wenceslas	1953–1976	300.00	425.00
☐ HN 2119, Town Crier	1953–1976	250.00	325.00
☐ HN 2120, Dinky Do	1983–	95.00	
☐ HN 2121, Babie	1983–	110.00	
☐ HN 2122, Yoeman of the Guard	1954–1959	650.00	750.00
☐ HN 2123, Rose	1983–	95.00	
HN 2124 NOT ISSUED			
☐ HN 2125, This Little Pig	1985–	60.00	
HN 2126–HN 2127 NOT ISSUED			
☐ HN 2128, River Boy	1962–1975	150.00	200.00
HN 2129–HN 2131 NOT ISSUED			
☐ HN 2132, The Suitor	1962–1971	375.00	450.00
☐ HN 2133, Faraway	1958–1962	350.00	400.00
☐ HN 2134, An Old King	1954–	625.00	
☐ HN 2135, Gay Morning	1954–1967	275.00	325.00
☐ HN 2136, Delphine	1954–1967	250.00	325.00
☐ HN 2137, Lilac Time	1954–1969	275.00	350.00
☐ HN 2138, La Sylphide	1956–1965	400.00	500.00
☐ HN 2139, Giselle	1954–1969	350.00	425.00
☐ HN 2140, Giselle, Forest Glade	1954–1965	350.00	425.00
☐ HN 2141, Choir Boy	1954–1975	90.00	125.00
☐ HN 2142, Rag Doll	1954–1986	85.00	100.00
☐ HN 2143, Friar Tuck	1954–1965	450.00	600.00
☐ HN 2144, The Jovial Monk	1954–1967	175.00	250.00
☐ HN 2145, Wardrobe Mistress	1954–1967	425.00	500.00
☐ HN 2146, The Tinsmith	1962–1967	500.00	575.00
☐ HN 2147, Autumn Breezes	1955–1971	300.00	400.00
☐ HN 2148, The Bridesmaid (2nd version)	1955–1959	250.00	300.00
☐ HN 2149, Love Letter	1958–1976	250.00	350.00
☐ HN 2150, Willy Won't He	1955–1959	375.00	450.00

	Date	Price Range	
☐ HN 2151, Mother's Help	1962–1969	200.00	250.00
☐ HN 2152, Adrienne	1964–1976	145.00	175.00
☐ HN 2153, The One That Got Away	1955–1959	450.00	550.00
☐ HN 2154, A Child from Williamsburg	1964–1983	100.00	125.00
HN 2155 NOT ISSUED			
☐ HN 2156, The Polka	1955–1969	250.00	325.00
☐ HN 2157, A Gypsy Dance (1st version)	1955–1957	500.00	600.00
☐ HN 2158, Alice	1960–1980	125.00	150.00
☐ HN 2159, Fortune Teller	1955–1967	450.00	550.00
☐ HN 2160, The Apple Maid	1957–1962	350.00	450.00
☐ HN 2161, The Hornpipe	1955–1962	650.00	750.00
☐ HN 2162, The Foaming Quart	1955–	230.00	
☐ HN 2163, In the Stocks (2nd version)	1955–1959	600.00	700.00
HN 2164 NOT ISSUED			
☐ HN 2165, Janice	1955–1965	475.00	525.00
☐ HN 2166, The Bride (2nd version)	1956–1976	150.00	225.00
☐ HN 2167, Home Again	1956–	160.00	
☐ HN 2168, Esmeralda	1956–1959	400.00	475.00
☐ HN 2169, Dimity	1956–1959	325.00	400.00
☐ HN 2170, Invitation	1956–1975	125.00	160.00
☐ HN 2171, The Fiddler	1956–1962	700.00	850.00
☐ HN 2172, Jolly Sailor	1956–1965	500.00	600.00
☐ HN 2173, The Organ Grinder	1956–1965	650.00	750.00
☐ HN 2174, The Tailor	1956–1959	500.00	600.00
☐ HN 2175, The Beggar (2nd version)	1956–1962	550.00	750.00
HN 2176 NOT ISSUED			
☐ HN 2177, My Teddy	1962–1967	450.00	650.00
☐ HN 2178, Enchantment	1957–1982	125.00	175.00
☐ HN 2179, Noelle	1957–1967	425.00	475.00
HN 2180 NOT ISSUED			
☐ HN 2181, Summer's Day	1957–1962	375.00	450.00
HN 2182 NOT ISSUED			
☐ HN 2183, Boy from Williamsburg	1969–1983	125.00	175.00
☐ HN 2184, Sunday Morning	1963–1969	265.00	325.00
☐ HN 2185, Columbine (2nd version)	1957–1969	225.00	275.00
☐ HN 2186, Harlequin	1957–1969	225.00	275.00
HN 2187–HN 2190 NOT ISSUED			
☐ HN 2191, Sea Sprite (2nd version)	1958–1962	475.00	525.00
☐ HN 2192, Wood Nymph	1958–1962	175.00	250.00
☐ HN 2193, Fair Lady	1963–	195.00	
HN 2194–HN 2195 NOT ISSUED			
☐ HN 2196, The Bridesmaid (3rd version)	1960–1976	100.00	150.00
HN 2197–HN 2201 NOT ISSUED			

	Date	Price Range	
☐ HN 2202, Melody	1957–1962	200.00	275.00
☐ HN 2203, Teenager	1957–1962	225.00	275.00
☐ HN 2204, Long John Silver	1957–1965	425.00	485.00
☐ HN 2205, Master Sweep	1957–1962	550.00	650.00
☐ HN 2206, Sunday Best	1979–1984	200.00	300.00
☐ HN 2207, Stayed at Home	1958–1969	150.00	200.00
☐ HN 2208, Silversmith of Williamsburg	1960–1983	150.00	225.00
☐ HN 2209, Hostess of Williamsburg	1960–1983	150.00	225.00
☐ HN 2210, Debutante	1963–1967	300.00	375.00
☐ HN 2211, Fair Maiden	1967–	140.00	
☐ HN 2212, Rendezvous	1962–1971	325.00	400.00
☐ HN 2213, Contemplation (White)	1983–1986	75.00	100.00
☐ HN 2214, Bunny	1960–1975	150.00	200.00
☐ HN 2215, Sweet April	1965–1967	325.00	400.00
☐ HN 2116, Pirouette	1959–1967	250.00	300.00
☐ HN 2117, Old King Cole	1963–1967	650.00	800.00
☐ HN 2218, Cookie	1958–1975	125.00	175.00
HN 2219 NOT ISSUED			
☐ HN 2220, Winsome	1960–1985	140.00	175.00
☐ HN 2221, Nanny	1958–	250.00	
☐ HN 2222, Camelia	1960–1971	250.00	350.00
☐ HN 2223, Schoolmarm	1958–1980	165.00	250.00
☐ HN 2224, Make Believe	1985–1988	95.00	
☐ HN 2225, Make Believe	1962–1988	140.00	
☐ HN 2226, The Cellist	1960–1967	375.00	450.00
☐ HN 2227, Gentleman from Williamsburg	1960–1983	150.00	200.00
☐ HN 2228, Lady from Williamsburg	1960–1983	150.00	225.00
☐ HN 2229, Southern Belle	1958–	275.00	
☐ HN 2230, A Gypsy Dance (2nd version)	1959–1971	225.00	300.00
☐ HN 2231, Sweet Sixteen	1958–1965	175.00	225.00
HN 2232 NOT ISSUED			
☐ HN 2233, Royal Governor's Cook	1960–1983	375.00	425.00
☐ HN 2234, Michelle	1967–	195.00	
☐ HN 2235, Dancing Years	1965–1971	300.00	400.00
☐ HN 2236, Affection	1962–	140.00	
☐ HN 2237, Celeste	1959–1971	250.00	300.00
☐ HN 2238, My Pet	1962–1975	150.00	175.00
☐ HN 2239, Wigmaker of Williamsburg	1960–1983	150.00	200.00
☐ HN 2240, Blacksmith of Williamsburg	1960–1983	160.00	225.00
☐ HN 2241, Contemplation (Black)	1983–1986	75.00	100.00
☐ HN 2242, First Steps	1959–1965	450.00	550.00
☐ HN 2243, Treasure Island	1962–1975	150.00	200.00
☐ HN 2244, Newsboy	1959–1965	550.00	650.00
☐ HN 2245, The Basket Weaver	1959–1962	475.00	525.00

	Date	Price Range	
☐ HN 2246, Cradle Song	1959–1962	400.00	500.00
☐ HN 2247, Omar Khayyam (2nd version)	1965–1983	145.00	175.00
☐ HN 2248, Tall Story	1968–1975	185.00	225.00
☐ HN 2249, The Favourite	1960–	230.00	
☐ HN 2250, The Toymaker	1959–1973	375.00	450.00
☐ HN 2251, Masquerade (2nd version)	1960–1965	325.00	350.00
HN 2252 NOT ISSUED			
☐ HN 2253, The Puppetmaker	1962–1973	425.00	475.00
☐ HN 2254, Shore Leave	1965–1979	175.00	225.00
☐ HN 2255, Teatime	1972–	230.00	
☐ HN 2256, Twilight	1971–1976	125.00	175.00
☐ HN 2257, Sea Harvest	1969–1976	175.00	250.00
☐ HN 2258, A Good Catch	1966–1986	175.00	225.00
☐ HN 2259, Masquerade (2nd version)	1960–1965	300.00	350.00
☐ HN 2260, The Captain (2nd version)	1965–1982	250.00	350.00
☐ HN 2261, Marriage of Art and Industry (Limited Edition, Figurines)	1958–	9000.00	10,000.00
☐ HN 2262, Lights Out	1965–1969	200.00	250.00
☐ HN 2263, Seashore	1961–1965	300.00	425.00
☐ HN 2264, Elegance	1961–1985	150.00	175.00
☐ HN 2265, Sara	1980–	295.00	
☐ HN 2266, Ballad Seller	1968–1973	250.00	350.00
☐ HN 2267, Rhapsody	1961–1973	200.00	250.00
☐ HN 2268, Daphne	1963–1975	160.00	200.00
☐ HN 2269, Leading Lady	1965–1976	150.00	200.00
☐ HN 2270, Pillow Fight	1965–1969	200.00	250.00
☐ HN 2271, Melanie	1965–1980	125.00	150.00
☐ HN 2272, Repose	1972–1979	175.00	225.00
☐ HN 2273, Denise	1964–1971	275.00	325.00
☐ HN 2274, Golden Days	1964–1973	125.00	175.00
☐ HN 2275, Sandra	1969–	195.00	
☐ HN 2276, Heart to Heart	1961–1971	350.00	400.00
HN 2277 NOT ISSUED			
☐ HN 2278, Judith	1986–	195.00	
☐ HN 2279, The Clockmaker	1961–1975	275.00	325.00
☐ HN 2280, The Mayor	1963–1971	475.00	575.00
☐ HN 2281, The Professor	1965–1980	175.00	225.00
☐ HN 2282, The Coachman	1963–1971	475.00	550.00
☐ HN 2283, Dreamweaver	1972–1976	250.00	300.00
☐ HN 2284, The Craftsman	1961–1965	400.00	500.00
HN 2285–HN 2286 NOT ISSUED			
☐ HN 2287, Symphony	1961–1965	300.00	350.00
HN 2288–HN 2303 NOT ISSUED			
☐ HN 2304, Adrienne	1964–	195.00	
☐ HN 2305, Dulcie	1981–1984	175.00	225.00

	Date	Price Range	
☐ **HN 2306**, Reverie	1964–1981	250.00	300.00
☐ **HN 2307**, Coralie	1964–1988	195.00	
☐ **HN 2308**, Picnic	1965–	140.00	
☐ **HN 2309**, Buttercup	1964–	185.00	
☐ **HN 2310**, Lisa	1969–1982	175.00	225.00
☐ **HN 2311**, Lorna	1965–1985	150.00	200.00
☐ **HN 2312**, Soiree	1967–1984	130.00	175.00
HN 2313 NOT ISSUED			
☐ **HN 2314**, Old Mother Hubbard	1964–1975	300.00	375.00
☐ **HN 2315**, Last Waltz	1967–	250.00	
HN 2316 NOT ISSUED			
☐ **HN 2317**, The Lobster Man	1964–	230.00	
☐ **HN 2318**, Grace	1966–1980	125.00	175.00
☐ **HN 2319**, The Bachelor	1964–1975	300.00	375.00
☐ **HN 2320**, Tuppence a Bag	1969–	230.00	
☐ **HN 2321**, Family Album	1966–1973	375.00	425.00
☐ **HN 2322**, The Cup of Tea	1964–1983	125.00	150.00
☐ **HN 2323**, The Lobster Man	1987–	230.00	
☐ **HN 2324**, Matador and Bull (Prestige Series)	1964–	17,500.00	
☐ **HN 2325**, The Master	1967–	230.00	
☐ **HN 2326**, Antoinette (2nd version) ...	1967–1979	125.00	175.00
☐ **HN 2327**, Katrina	1965–1969	325.00	375.00
☐ **HN 2328**, Queen of Sheba	1982–	975.00	1150.00
☐ **HN 2329**, Lynne	1971–	230.00	
☐ **HN 2330**, Meditation	1971–1983	200.00	300.00
☐ **HN 2331**, Cello (Limited Edition, Lady Musicians)	1970–	1100.00	1200.00
☐ **HN 2332**, Monte Carlo (Limited Edition, Sweet and Twenty Figures)	1984–	250.00	
☐ **HN 2333**, Jacqueline	1983–	195.00	
☐ **HN 2334**, Fragrance	1966–	230.00	
☐ **HN 2335**, Hilary	1967–1980	120.00	160.00
☐ **HN 2336**, Alison	1966–	195.00	
☐ **HN 2337**, Loretta	1966–1980	120.00	150.00
☐ **HN 2338**, Penny	1968–	95.00	
☐ **HN 2339**, My Love	1969–	250.00	
☐ **HN 2340**, Belle (2nd version)	1968–1988	95.00	
☐ **HN 2341**, Cherie	1966–	140.00	
☐ **HN 2342**, Lucrezia Borgia (Limited Edition, Femme Fatale Series)	1985–	975.00	1150.00
☐ **HN 2343**, Premiere	1969–1979	125.00	175.00
☐ **HN 2344**, Deauville (Limited Edition, Sweet and Twenty Figures)	1984–	250.00	
☐ **HN 2345**, Clarissa (2nd version)	1968–1981	150.00	175.00
☐ **HN 2346**, Kathy (Kate Greenaway) ..	1981–1987	80.00	100.00
☐ **HN 2347**, Nina	1969–1976	175.00	225.00

	Date	Price Range	
☐ **HN 2348**, Geraldine	1972–1976	**140.00**	**185.00**
☐ **HN 2349**, Flora	1966–1973	**275.00**	**325.00**
HN 2350–HN 2351 NOT ISSUED			
☐ **HN 2352**, A Stitch In Time	1966–1980	**125.00**	**175.00**
HN 2353–HN 2355 NOT ISSUED			
☐ **HN 2356**, Ascot	1968–	**250.00**	
HN 2357–HN 2358 NOT ISSUED			
☐ **HN 2359**, The Detective	1977–1983	**200.00**	**300.00**
HN 2360 NOT ISSUED			
☐ **HN 2361**, The Laird	1969–	**250.00**	
☐ **HN 2362**, The Wayfarer	1970–1976	**150.00**	**200.00**
HN 2363–HN 2367 NOT ISSUED			
☐ **HN 2368**, Fleur	1968–	**250.00**	
☐ **HN 2369**, Fleur	1984–1986	**175.00**	**225.00**
☐ **HN 2370**, Sir Edward	1979–		
☐ **HN 2371**, Sir Ralph	1979–		
☐ **HN 2372**, Sir Thomas	1979–		
☐ **HN 2373**, Joanne	1982–	**130.00**	
☐ **HN 2374**, Mary	1984–1986	**95.00**	**115.00**
☐ **HN 2375**, The Viking	1973–1976	**325.00**	**375.00**
☐ **HN 2376**, Indian Brave (Limited Edition, Figurines)	1967–	**6500.00**	**8000.00**
☐ **HN 2377**, Georgina (Kate Greenaway)	1981–1986	**90.00**	**125.00**
☐ **HN 2378**, Simone	1971–1981	**150.00**	**200.00**
☐ **HN 2379**, Ninette	1971–	**250.00**	
☐ **HN 2380**, Sweet Dreams	1971–	**195.00**	
☐ **HN 2381**, Kirsty	1971–	**250.00**	
☐ **HN 2382**, Secret Thoughts	1971–1988	**295.00**	
☐ **HN 2383**, Breton Dancer (Limited Edition, Dancers of the World)	1981–	**850.00**	
☐ **HN 2384**, West Indian Dancer (Limited Edition, Dancers of the World) ...	1981–	**700.00**	**750.00**
☐ **HN 2385**, Debbie	1969–1982	**100.00**	**125.00**
☐ **HN 2386**, Prince Phillip (Limited Edition, Figurines)	1981–	**450.00**	**500.00**
☐ **HN 2387**, Helen of Troy (Limited Edition, Femme Fatale Series)	1981–	**975.00**	**1150.00**
☐ **HN 2388**, Karen	1982–	**275.00**	
☐ **HN 2389**, Angela	1982–1986	**95.00**	**115.00**
☐ **HN 2390**, Spinning (Limited Edition, Gentle Arts Series)	1985–	**1250.00**	
☐ **HN 2391**, TZ 'U-HSI Empress Dowager (Limited Edition, Femme Fatale Series)	1983–	**975.00**	**1150.00**
☐ **HN 2392**, Jennifer	1982–	**215.00**	
☐ **HN 2393**, Rosalind	1970–1975	**150.00**	**200.00**
☐ **HN 2394**, Lisa	1983–	**185.00**	

	Date	Price Range	
HN 2395 NOT ISSUED			
☐ **HN 2396,** Wistful	1979–	**450.00**	
☐ **HN 2397,** Margaret	1982–	**130.00**	
☐ **HN 2398,** Alexandra	1970–1976	**150.00**	**200.00**
☐ **HN 2399,** Buttercup	1983–	**185.00**	
☐ **HN 2400,** Debbie	1983–	**110.00**	
☐ **HN 2401,** Sandra	1984–	**195.00**	
HN 2402–HN 2407 NOT ISSUED			
☐ **HN 2408,** A Penny's Worth	1986–	**195.00**	
HN 2409 NOT ISSUED			
☐ **HN 2410,** Lesley	1986–	**250.00**	
HN 2411–HN 2416 NOT ISSUED			
☐ **HN 2417,** The Boatman	1971–1987	**175.00**	**250.00**
HN 2418–HN 2420 NOT ISSUED			
☐ **HN 2421,** Charlotte	1972–1986	**150.00**	**200.00**
☐ **HN 2422,** Francine	1972–1980	**65.00**	**100.00**
☐ **HN 2423,** Charlotte	1986–	**230.00**	
☐ **HN 2424,** Penny	1983–	**95.00**	
☐ **HN 2425,** Southern Belle	1984–	**215.00**	
☐ **HN 2426,** Tranquility (Image Series) (Black)	1980–1986	**75.00**	**100.00**
☐ **HN 2427,** Virginals (Limited Edition, Lady Musicians)	1971–	**1500.00**	**2000.00**
☐ **HN 2428,** The Palio (Limited Edition, Miscellaneous)	1971–	**6500.00**	**8000.00**
☐ **HN 2429,** Elyse	1972–	**250.00**	
☐ **HN 2430,** Romance	1972–1980	**150.00**	**200.00**
☐ **HN 2431,** Lute (Limited Edition, Lady Musicians)	1972–	**850.00**	**1000.00**
☐ **HN 2432,** Violin (Limited Edition, Lady Musicians)	1972–	**1000.00**	**1200.00**
☐ **HN 2433,** Peace (Image Series, Black)	1980–1985	**50.00**	**75.00**
☐ **HN 2434,** Fair Maiden	1983–	**140.00**	
☐ **HN 2435,** Queen of the Ice	1983–1986	**125.00**	**175.00**
☐ **HN 2436,** Scottish Highland Dancer (Limited Edition, Dancers of the World)	1978–	**900.00**	**1100.00**
☐ **HN 2437,** Queen of the Dawn	1983–1986	**125.00**	
☐ **HN 2438,** Sonata	1983–1985	**125.00**	
☐ **HN 2439,** Phillippine Dancer (Limited Edition, Dancers of the World)	1978–	**850.00**	**1000.00**
☐ **HN 2440,** Cynthia	1984–	**170.00**	
☐ **HN 2441,** Pauline	1984–	**275.00**	
☐ **HN 2442,** Sailor's Holiday	1972–1979	**200.00**	**250.00**
☐ **HN 2443,** The Judge, Matte Finish ..	1972–1976	**150.00**	**200.00**
☐ **HN 2444,** Bon Appetit	1972–1976	**200.00**	**275.00**
☐ **HN 2445,** Parisian	1972–1975	**150.00**	**200.00**

	Date	Price Range	
☐ HN 2446, Thanksgiving	1972–1976	225.00	275.00
HN 2447–HN 2454 NOT ISSUED			
☐ HN 2455, The Seafarer	1972–1976	175.00	225.00
HN 2456–HN 2460 NOT ISSUED			
☐ HN 2461, Janine	1971–	230.00	
HN 2462 NOT ISSUED			
☐ HN 2463, Olga	1972–1975	175.00	200.00
HN 2464–HN 2465 NOT ISSUED			
☐ HN 2466, Eve	1984–	800.00	850.00
☐ HN 2467, Melissa	1981–	230.00	
☐ HN 2468, Diana (Litho Lady Series)	1986–	170.00	
☐ HN 2469, Tranquility (Image Series)	1980–1986	75.00	100.00
☐ HN 2470, Peace (Image Series)	1980–	75.00	
☐ HN 2471, Victoria	1973–	230.00	
☐ HN 2472, Wistful (Time Limited Edition)	1985–	200.00	250.00
☐ HN 2473, At Ease	1973–1979	165.00	200.00
☐ HN 2474, Elyse	1987–	195.00	
☐ HN 2475, Vanity	1973–	140.00	
☐ HN 2476, Mandy	1982–	95.00	
☐ HN 2477, Denise	1986–	130.00	
☐ HN 2478, Kelly	1985–	160.00	
☐ HN 2479, Pamela	1986–	130.00	
☐ HN 2480, Adele	1987–	170.00	
☐ HN 2481, Maureen	1987–	170.00	
☐ HN 2482, Harp (Limited Edition, Lady Musicians)	1973–	1400.00	1675.00
☐ HN 2483, Flute (Limited Edition, Lady Musicians)	1973–	975.00	1075.00
☐ HN 2484, Past Glory	1973–1979	175.00	225.00
☐ HN 2485, Lunchtime	1973–1980	200.00	250.00
HN 2486 NOT ISSUED			
☐ HN 2487, Beachcomber	1973–1976	200.00	250.00
HN 2488–HN 2491 NOT ISSUED			
☐ HN 2492, The Huntsman (3rd version)	1974–1979	170.00	220.00
HN 2493 NOT ISSUED			
☐ HN 2494, Old Meg	1974–1976	300.00	375.00
HN 2495–HN 2498 NOT ISSUED			
☐ HN 2499, Helmsman	1974–1986	250.00	300.00
HN 2500–HN 2670 ANIMAL MODELS			
☐ HN 2502, Queen Elizabeth II (Limited Edition)	1973–	1900.00	2300.00
☐ HN 2520, Farmers Boy w/Boy	1938–1960	2000.00	2500.00
☐ HN 2520, Farmers Boy w/Girl	Unknown	4000.00	4500.00
☐ HN 2542, Boudoir (Haute Ensemble)	1974–1979	400.00	475.00
☐ HN 2543, Eliza (Haute Ensemble)	1974–1979	200.00	300.00

	Date	Price Range	
☐ **HN 2544,** A la Mode (Haute Ensemble)	1974–1979	175.00	225.00
☐ **HN 2545,** Carmen (Haute Ensemble) (2nd version)	1974–1979	350.00	400.00
☐ **HN 2546,** Buddies	1973–1976	175.00	250.00
☐ **HN 2547,** Royal Canadian Mounted Police	1973–	250.00	350.00
☐ **HN 2554,** Masque	1973–1982	200.00	275.00
☐ **HN 2555,** 1873 Mountie (Limited Edition 1500)	1973–	1250.00	1500.00
☐ **HN 2671,** Good Morning	1974–1976	325.00	375.00
HN 2672–HN 2676 NOT ISSUED			
☐ **HN 2677,** Taking Things Easy	1975–1987	225.00	275.00
☐ **HN 2678,** Carpenter	1986–	215.00	
☐ **HN 2679,** Drummer Boy	1976–1981	300.00	375.00
☐ **HN 2680,** Taking Things Easy (White)	1987–	215.00	
HN 2681–HN 2682 NOT ISSUED			
☐ **HN 2683,** Stop Press	1977–1980	125.00	175.00
HN 2684–HN 2693 NOT ISSUED			
☐ **HN 2694,** Fiona (2nd version)	1974–1980	140.00	180.00
HN 2695–HN 2697 NOT ISSUED			
☐ **HN 2698,** Sunday Best	1985–	160.00	
☐ **HN 2699,** Cymbals (Limited Editions, Lady Musicians)	1974–	500.00	600.00
☐ **HN 2700,** Chitarrone (Limited Editions, Lady Musicians)	1974–	750.00	900.00
HN 2701 NOT ISSUED			
☐ **HN 2702,** Shirley	1985–	160.00	
HN 2703 NOT ISSUED			
☐ **HN 2704,** Pensive Moments	1974–1981	150.00	225.00
☐ **HN 2705,** Julia	1975–	195.00	
☐ **HN 2706,** Julia	1985–	160.00	
HN 2707–HN 2708 NOT ISSUED			
☐ **HN 2709,** Regal Lady	1975–1983	125.00	175.00
☐ **HN 2710,** Jean	1984–1986	95.00	115.00
HN 2711 NOT ISSUED			
☐ **HN 2712,** Mantilla	1974–1979	300.00	350.00
☐ **HN 2713,** Tenderness (White)	1983–	110.00	
☐ **HN 2714,** Tenderness (Black)	1983–1985	75.00	100.00
☐ **HN 2715,** Patricia	1982–1985	95.00	115.00
☐ **HN 2716,** Cavalier (2nd version)	1976–1982	200.00	300.00
☐ **HN 2717,** Private, 2nd South Carolina Regiment, 1781 (Limited Edition, Soldiers)	1975–	1000.00	1200.00
☐ **HN 2718,** Lady Pamela	1974–1980	150.00	200.00
☐ **HN 2719,** Laurianne	1974–1979	150.00	200.00

	Date	Price Range	
☐**HN 2720,** Family (Image Series, White)	1980–	140.00	
☐**HN 2721,** Family (Image Series, Black)	1980–1985	95.00	125.00
☐**HN 2722,** Veneta	1974–1980	125.00	150.00
☐**HN 2723,** Grand Manner	1975–1981	175.00	250.00
☐**HN 2724,** Clarinda	1975–1980	150.00	200.00
☐**HN 2725,** Santa Claus	1982–	295.00	
☐**HN 2726,** The Centurion	1982–1984	175.00	250.00
☐**HN 2727,** Little Miss Muffett	1984–1987	95.00	
☐**HN 2728,** Rest Awhile	1981–1985	175.00	200.00
☐**HN 2729,** Song of the Sea	1983–	230.00	
HN 2730 NOT ISSUED			
☐**HN 2731,** Thanks Doc	1975–	295.00	
☐**HN 2732,** Thank You	1983–1986	150.00	175.00
☐**HN 2733,** Officer of the Line	1983–1986	150.00	200.00
☐**HN 2734,** Sweet Seventeen	1975–	250.00	
☐**HN 2735,** Young Love	1975–	950.00	
☐**HN 2736,** Tracy	1983–	130.00	
☐**HN 2737,** Harlequin	1982–	895.00	
☐**HN 2738,** Columbine	1982–	895.00	
☐**HN 2739,** Ann	1984–1985	95.00	115.00
☐**HN 2740,** Becky	1987–	—	
☐**HN 2741,** Sally	1987–	195.00	
☐**HN 2742,** Sheila	1984–	185.00	
☐**HN 2743,** Meg	1987–	195.00	
☐**HN 2744,** Modesty	1987–	130.00	
☐**HN 2745,** Florence	1987–	195.00	
☐**HN 2746,** May	1987–	215.00	
☐**HN 2747,** First Love	1987–	120.00	
☐**HN 2748,** Wedding Day	1987–	140.00	
HN 2749–HN 2751 NOT ISSUED			
☐**HN 2752,** Major, 3rd New Jersey Regiment, 1776 (Limited Edition, Soldiers)	1975–	1750.00	2100.00
☐**HN 2753,** Serenade	1983–1985	95.00	
☐**HN 2754,** Private, 3rd North Carolina Regiment, 1778 (Limited Edition, Soldiers)	1976–	950.00	1250.00
☐**HN 2755,** Captain, 2nd New York Regiment, 1775 (Limited Edition, Soldiers)	1976–	900.00	1100.00
☐**HN 2756,** Musicale	1983–1985	125.00	
☐**HN 2757,** Lyric	1983–1985	95.00	
☐**HN 2758,** Linda	1984–	130.00	
☐**HN 2759,** Private, Rhode Island Regiment, 1781 (Limited Edition, Soldiers)	1977–	750.00	900.00

	Date	Price Range	
☐ **HN 2760**, Private, Massachusetts Regiment, 1778 (Limited Edition, Soldiers)	1977–	750.00	900.00
☐ **HN 2761**, Private, Delaware Regiment, 1776 (Limited Edition, Soldiers)	1977–	750.00	900.00
☐ **HN 2762**, Lovers (Image Series, White)	1980–	140.00	
☐ **HN 2763**, Lovers (Image Series, Black)	1980–1985	95.00	125.00
☐ **HN 2764**, The Lifeboat Man	1987–	230.00	
☐ **HN 2765**, Punch & Judy Man	1981–	395.00	
HN 2766–HN 2767 NOT ISSUED			
☐ **HN 2768**, Pretty Polly	1984–1986	150.00	175.00
HN 2769 NOT ISSUED			
☐ **HN 2770**, New Companions	1982–1985	175.00	225.00
HN 2771–HN 2772 NOT ISSUED			
☐ **HN 2773**, Robin Hood	1985–	215.00	
HN 2774–HN 2778 NOT ISSUED			
☐ **HN 2779**, Private, 1st Georgia Regiment, 1777 (Limited Edition, Soldiers)	1975–	900.00	1000.00
☐ **HN 2780**, Corporal, 1st New Hampshire Regiment, 1778 (Limited Edition, Soldiers)	1975–	900.00	1100.00
HN 2781 NOT ISSUED			
☐ **HN 2782**, Blacksmith	1987–	185.00	
☐ **HN 2783**, Good Friends	1985–	185.00	
HN 2784–HN 2787 NOT ISSUED			
☐ **HN 2788**, Marjorie	1980–1984	150.00	200.00
☐ **HN 2789**, Kate	1978–	185.00	
HN 2790 NOT ISSUED			
☐ **HN 2791**, Elaine	1980–	250.00	
☐ **HN 2792**, Christine (2nd version)	1978–	275.00	
☐ **HN 2793**, Clare	1980–1984	175.00	250.00
HN 2794 NOT ISSUED			
☐ **HN 2795**, French Horn (Limited Editions, Lady Musicians)	1976–	500.00	600.00
☐ **HN 2796**, Hurdy Gurdy (Limited Editions, Lady Musicians)	1975–	500.00	600.00
☐ **HN 2797**, Viola d'Amore (Limited Editions, Lady Musicians)	1976–	500.00	600.00
☐ **HN 2798**, Dulcimer (Limited Edition, Lady Musicians)	1975–	550.00	650.00
☐ **HN 2799**, Ruth (Kate Greenaway) ...	1976–1982	95.00	125.00
☐ **HN 2800**, Carrie (Kate Greenaway) ..	1976–1981	100.00	125.00
☐ **HN 2801**, Lori (Kate Greenaway)	1976–1987	100.00	
☐ **HN 2802**, Anna (Kate Greenaway) ...	1976–1987	100.00	125.00
☐ **HN 2803**, First Dance	1977–	230.00	

	Date	Price Range	
☐ **HN 2804,** Nicola (Limited Edition 1,500, Red)	1987–	195.00	250.00
☐ **HN 2805,** Rebecca	1980–	450.00	
☐ **HN 2806,** Jane	1983–1986	100.00	150.00
☐ **HN 2807,** Stephanie	1977–1982	135.00	175.00
☐ **HN 2808,** Balinese Dancer	1982–	650.00	750.00
☐ **HN 2809,** North American Indian Dancer	1982–	650.00	750.00
☐ **HN 2810,** Solitude	1977–1983	150.00	200.00
☐ **HN 2811,** Stephanie	1983–	230.00	
HN 2812–HN 2813 NOT ISSUED			
☐ **HN 2814,** Eventide	1977–	230.00	
☐ **HN 2815,** Sergeant, 6th Maryland Regiment, 1777 (Limited Edition, Soldiers)	1976–	800.00	975.00
☐ **HN 2816,** Votes for Women	1978–1981	200.00	250.00
HN 2817 NOT ISSUED			
☐ **HN 2818,** Balloon Girl	1982–	185.00	
HN 2819–HN 2823 NOT ISSUED			
☐ **HN 2824,** Harmony	1978–1984	150.00	200.00
☐ **HN 2825,** Lady and the Unicorn	1982–	2500.00	
☐ **HN 2826,** Leda and the Swan	1983–	2500.00	
☐ **HN 2827,** Juno and the Peacock	1984–	1250.00	
☐ **HN 2828,** Europa and the Bull (Limited Edition, Myths and Maidens Series)	1985–	2500.00	
☐ **HN 2829,** Diana the Huntress (Limited Edition, Myths and Maidens Series)	1986–	2500.00	
☐ **HN 2830,** Indian Temple Dancer (Limited Edition, Dancers of the World)	1977–	1200.00	1400.00
☐ **HN 2831,** Spanish Flamenco Dancer (Limited Edition, Dancers of the World)	1977–	1500.00	1800.00
☐ **HN 2832,** Fair Lady	1977–	195.00	
☐ **HN 2833,** Sophie (Kate Greenaway)	1977–1987	100.00	
☐ **HN 2834,** Emma (Kate Greenaway)	1977–1982	100.00	125.00
☐ **HN 2835,** Fair Lady	1977–	195.00	
☐ **HN 2836,** Polish Dancer (Limited Edition, Dancers of the World)	1980–	850.00	950.00
☐ **HN 2837,** Awakening (Image Series, Black)	1980–1986	50.00	75.00
☐ **HN 2838,** Sympathy (Image Series, Black)	1980–1986	75.00	100.00
☐ **HN 2839,** Nicola	1978–	350.00	
☐ **HN 2840,** Chinese Dancer (Limited Edition, Dancers of the World)	1980–	750.00	850.00

	Date	Price Range	
☐ **HN 2841,** Mother & Daughter (Image Series)	1980–	140.00	
☐ **HN 2842,** Innocence	1979–1983	120.00	160.00
☐ **HN 2843,** Mother & Daughter (Image Series, Black)	1980–1985	95.00	125.00
☐ **HN 2844,** Sergeant, Virginia 1st Regiment Continental Light Dragoons, 1777 (Limited Edition, Soldiers)	1978–	2500.00	3200.00
☐ **HN 2845,** Private, Connecticut Regiment, 1777 (Limited Edition, Soldiers)	1978–	750.00	900.00
☐ **HN 2846,** Private, Pennsylvania Rifle Battalion, 1776 (Limited Edition, Soldiers)	1978–	750.00	900.00
HN 2847–HN 2850 NOT ISSUED			
☐ **HN 2851,** Christmas Parcels	1978–1982	250.00	350.00
HN 2852–HN 2854 NOT ISSUED			
☐ **HN 2855,** Embroidering	1980–	295.00	
☐ **HN 2856,** St. George (3rd version) (Prestige Series)	1978–	10,000.00	
HN 2857 NOT ISSUED			
☐ **HN 2858,** The Doctor	1979–	295.00	
HN 2859–HN 2860 NOT ISSUED			
☐ **HN 2861,** George Washington at Prayer (Limited Edition, Soldiers)	1977–	2000.00	2500.00
☐ **HN 2862,** First Waltz	1979–1983	175.00	240.00
☐ **HN 2863,** Lucy (Kate Greenaway) ...	1980–1984	90.00	115.00
☐ **HN 2864,** Tom (Kate Greenaway)	1978–1981	95.00	110.00
☐ **HN 2865,** Tess (Kate Greenaway)	1978–1983	95.00	125.00
☐ **HN 2866,** Mexican Dancer (Limited Edition, Dancers of the World)	1979–	550.00	650.00
☐ **HN 2867,** Kurdish Dancer (Limited Edition, Dancers of the World)	1979–	800.00	900.00
☐ **HN 2868,** Cleopatra and Slave (Limited Edition, Femme Fatale Series)	1979–	1100.00	1300.00
☐ **HN 2869,** Louise (Kate Greenaway)	1980–1985	100.00	125.00
☐ **HN 2870,** Beth (Kate Greenaway)	1980–1983	100.00	150.00
☐ **HN 2871,** Beat You To It	1980–1987	395.00	
☐ **HN 2872,** The Young Master	1980–	475.00	
☐ **HN 2873,** Bride (4th version)	1980–	250.00	
☐ **HN 2874,** Bridesmaid (4th version) ...	1980–	140.00	
☐ **HN 2875,** Awakening (Image Series)	1980–	75.00	
☐ **HN 2876,** Sympathy (Image Series) ..	1980–1986	75.00	100.00
☐ **HN 2877,** The Wizard	1979–	295.00	
☐ **HN 2878,** Her Majesty Queen Elizabeth II	1983–	495.00	
☐ **HN 2879,** Gamekeeper	1984–	185.00	
HN 2880 NOT ISSUED			

	Date	Price Range	
☐ **HN 2881,** Lord Olivier as Richard III	1985–	**750.00**	
☐ **HN 2882,** Queen Mother (Limited Edition, Figurines)	1980–	**1200.00**	**1400.00**
☐ **HN 2883,** H.R.H. The Prince of Wales.	1982–	**600.00**	**750.00**
HN 2884 NOT ISSUED			
☐ **HN 2885,** Lady Diana Spencer	1982–	**650.00**	**900.00**
HN 2886–HN 2887 NOT ISSUED			
☐ **HN 2888,** His Holiness Pope John Paul II	1982–	**185.00**	
☐ **HN 2889,** Captain Cook	1980–1984	**375.00**	**425.00**
☐ **HN 2890,** The Clown	1979–	**395.00**	
☐ **HN 2891,** Newsvendor (Limited Edition, 2,500)	1986–	**250.00**	**300.00**
☐ **HN 2892,** The Chief	1979–	**275.00**	
HN 2893 NOT ISSUED			
☐ **HN 2894,** Balloon Clown	1986–	**195.00**	
☐ **HN 2895,** Morning M'aam	1986–	**185.00**	
☐ **HN 2896,** Good Day Sir	1986–	**195.00**	
HN 2897 NOT ISSUED			
☐ **HN 2898,** Ko-Ko (2nd version)	1980–1985	**600.00**	**750.00**
☐ **HN 2899,** Yum-Yum (2nd version) ...	1980–1985	**750.00**	
☐ **HN 2900,** Ruth the Pirate Maid	1981–1985	**750.00**	
☐ **HN 2901,** The Pirate King	1981–1985	**750.00**	
☐ **HN 2902,** Elsie Maynard	1982–1985	**750.00**	
☐ **HN 2903,** Colonel Fairfax	1982–1985	**750.00**	
HN 2904–HN 2905 NOT ISSUED			
☐ **HN 2906,** Paula	1980–1986	**150.00**	**200.00**
☐ **HN 2907,** The Piper	1980–	**350.00**	
☐ **HN 2908,** Ajax (Limited Edition, Ships Figurehead)	1980–1983	**750.00**	
☐ **HN 2909,** Benmore (Limited Edition, Ships Figurehead)	1980–1983	**950.00**	
☐ **HN 2910,** Lalla Rookh (Limited Edition, Ships Figurehead)	1981–1983	**750.00**	
☐ **HN 2911,** Gandolf (J.R.R. Tolkien Series)	1980–1983	**100.00**	**125.00**
☐ **HN 2912,** Frado (J.R.R. Tolkien Series)	1980–1983	**60.00**	**75.00**
☐ **HN 2913,** Gollum (J.R.R. Tolkien Series)	1980–1983	**75.00**	**100.00**
☐ **HN 2914,** Bilbo (J.R.R. Tolkien Series)	1980–1983	**60.00**	**75.00**
☐ **HN 2915,** Galadrial (J.R.R. Tolkien Series)	1981–1983	**60.00**	**75.00**
☐ **HN 2916,** Aragorn (J.R.R. Tolkien Series)	1980–1983	**60.00**	**75.00**

	Date	Price Range	
☐ **HN 2917**, Legolas (J.R.R. Tolkien Series)	1981–1983	60.00	75.00
☐ **HN 2918**, Boromir (J.R.R. Tolkien Series)	1981–1983	95.00	125.00
☐ **HN 2919**, Rachel	1981–1984	150.00	200.00
☐ **HN 2920**, Yearning (White)	1983–1986	75.00	100.00
☐ **HN 2921**, Yearning (Black)	1983–1986	75.00	100.00
☐ **HN 2922**, Gimli (J.R.R. Tolkien Series)	1981–1983	60.00	75.00
☐ **HN 2923**, Barliman Butterbur	1982–1983	85.00	125.00
☐ **HN 2924**, Tom Bombadil	1982–1983	175.00	225.00
☐ **HN 2925**, Samwise	1982–1983	100.00	125.00
☐ **HN 2926**, Tom Sawyer	1982–	50.00	75.00
☐ **HN 2927**, Huckleberry Finn	1982–	50.00	75.00
☐ **HN 2928**, Nelson (Limited Edition, Ships Figureheads)	1981–1983	950.00	
☐ **HN 2929**, Chieftain (Limited Edition, Ships Figureheads)	1982–	950.00	
☐ **HN 2930**, Pocahontas (Limited Edition, Ships Figureheads)	1982–	950.00	
☐ **HN 2931**, Mary Queen of Scots (Limited Edition, Ships Figureheads)	1983–	1500.00	
☐ **HN 2932**, Hibernia (Limifed Edition, Ships Figureheads)	1983–	1150.00	
☐ **HN 2933**, Kathleen	1984–	260.00	
☐ **HN 2934**, Balloon Boy	1984–	140.00	
☐ **HN 2935**, Balloon Lady	1984–	170.00	
☐ **HN 2936**, Rachel	1985–	230.00	
☐ **HN 2937**, Gail	1986–	230.00	
☐ **HN 2938**, Isadora	1986–	195.00	
☐ **HN 2939**, Donna	1986–	130.00	
☐ **HN 2940**, All Aboard	1982–1986	175.00	200.00
☐ **HN 2941**, Tom Brown	1983–	50.00	75.00
☐ **HN 2942**, Prized Possessions (Collectors Club figurine)	1982–	550.00	650.00
☐ **HN 2943**, The China Repairer	1983–	275.00	
☐ **HN 2944**, Rag Doll Seller	1983–	195.00	
☐ **HN 2945**, Pride and Joy	1984–	300.00	350.00
☐ **HN 2946**, Elizabeth	1982–1986	175.00	225.00
HN 2947–HN 2951 NOT ISSUED			
☐ **HN 2952**, Susan	1982–	275.00	
☐ **HN 2953**, Sleepy Darling (Collectors Club figurine)	1981–	200.00	250.00
☐ **HN 2954**, Samantha	1982–1984	95.00	115.00
☐ **HN 2955**, Nancy	1982–	130.00	
☐ **HN 2956**, Heather	1982–	130.00	
☐ **HN 2957**, Edith	1982–1985	95.00	125.00

	Date	Price Range	
☐ HN 2958, Amy	1982–	100.00	
☐ HN 2959, Save Some For Me	1983–	75.00	100.00
☐ HN 2960, Laura	1983–	195.00	
☐ HN 2961, Carol	1982–	130.00	
☐ HN 2962, Barbara	1982–1984	95.00	115.00
☐ HN 2963, It Won't Hurt	1982–	75.00	100.00
☐ HN 2964, Dressing Up	1982–	75.00	100.00
☐ HN 2965, Pollyanna	1982–	50.00	75.00
☐ HN 2966, And So To Bed	1983–	75.00	100.00
☐ HN 2967, Please Keep Still	1983–	75.00	100.00
HN 2968–HN 2969 NOT ISSUED			
☐ HN 2970, And One For You	1982–	75.00	100.00
☐ HN 2971, As Good As New	1982–	75.00	100.00
☐ HN 2972, Little Lord Fauntleroy	1982–	50.00	75.00
HN 2973 NOT ISSUED			
☐ HN 2974, Carolyn	1983–1986	150.00	175.00
☐ HN 2975, Heidi	1983–	50.00	75.00
☐ HN 2976, I'm Nearly Ready	1984–	75.00	100.00
☐ HN 2977, Magic Dragon	1983–1986	75.00	
☐ HN 2978, Magpie Ring	1983–1986	95.00	
☐ HN 2979, Fairyspell	1983–1986	65.00	
☐ HN 2980, Just One More	1984–1985	75.00	100.00
☐ HN 2981, Stick 'Em Up	1984–1985	75.00	100.00
HN 2982–HN 2987 NOT ISSUED			
☐ HN 2988, Auctioneer (Collectors Club Figure)	1986–	200.00	250.00
☐ HN 2989, The Genie	1983–	140.00	
☐ HN 2990, Shepherdess	1987–	170.00	
HN 2991–HN 2993 NOT ISSUED			
☐ HN 2994, Helen	1985–	70.00	
☐ HN 2995, Julie	1985–	80.00	
☐ HN 2996, Amanda	1986–	80.00	
☐ HN 2997, Chic	1987–	150.00	
HN 2998–HN 3001 NOT ISSUED			
☐ HN 3002, Marilyn	1986–	170.00	
☐ HN 3003, Lilian in Summer (Danbury Mint Time-limited Series)	1986–	300.00	400.00
☐ HN 3004, Emily in Autumn (Danbury Mint Time-limited Series)	1986–	300.00	400.00
☐ HN 3005, Sarah in Winter (Danbury Mint Time-limited Series)	1986–	300.00	400.00
☐ HN 3006, Catherine in Spring (Danbury Mint Time-limited Series)	1986–	300.00	400.00
☐ HN 3011, Kathleen (Michael Doulton Special Event)	1986–	200.00	250.00
☐ HN 3012, Painting (Gentle Arts Series)	1987–	1250.00	

	Date	Price Range	
☐ HN 3013, James	1983–	100.00	
☐ HN 3014, Nell	1983–	100.00	
HN 3015 NOT ISSUED			
☐ HN 3016, Graduate, girl	1984–	170.00	
☐ HN 3017, Graduate, boy	1984–	170.00	
☐ HN 3018, Sisters, White	1984–	125.00	
☐ HN 3019, Sisters, Black	1984–1985	95.00	125.00
☐ HN 3020, Ellen	1984–	100.00	
☐ HN 3021, Polly Put the Kettle On	1984–	95.00	
HN 3022–HN 3023 NOT ISSUED			
☐ HN 3024, April Showers	1983–1986	75.00	
☐ HN 3025, Rumplestiltskin	1983–1986	125.00	
☐ HN 3026, Carefree, White	1985–	110.00	
☐ HN 3027, Windswept	1985–	130.00	
☐ HN 3028, Panorama	1985–	140.00	
☐ HN 3029, Carefree, Black	1985–1986	75.00	100.00
☐ HN 3030, Little Bo Peep	1984–	95.00	
☐ HN 3031, Wee Willie Winkie	1984–	95.00	
☐ HN 3032, Tom, Tom the Piper's Son	1984–	95.00	
☐ HN 3033, Springtime (Collectors Club figurine)	1983–	300.00	400.00
☐ HN 3034, Little Jack Horner	1984–	95.00	
☐ HN 3035, Little Boy Blue	1984–	95.00	
☐ HN 3036, Kerry	1986–	80.00	
☐ HN 3037, Miranda	1987–	215.00	
☐ HN 3038, Yvonne	1987–	185.00	
☐ HN 3039 Reflection	1987–	170.00	
HN 3040 NOT ISSUED			
☐ HN 3041, The Lawyer	1985–	160.00	
☐ HN 3042, Gillian	1985–	185.00	
☐ HN 3043, Lynsey	1985–	80.00	
☐ HN 3044, Catherine	1985–	80.00	
☐ HN 3045, Demure	1985–	140.00	
☐ HN 3046, Debut	1985–	160.00	
☐ HN 3047, Sharon	1984–	140.00	
☐ HN 3048, Tapestry (Gentle Arts Series, Limited Edition of 750)	1986–	1250.00	
☐ HN 3049, Writing (Gentle Arts Series)	1986–	1250.00	
☐ HN 3050, Susan	1986–	215.00	
☐ HN 3051, Country Girl	1987–	110.00	
☐ HN 3052, A Winter's Walk	1987–	185.00	
HN 3053–HN 3056 NOT ISSUED			
☐ HN 3057, Sir Winston Churchill	1985–	185.00	
☐ HN 3058, Andrea	1985–	80.00	
☐ HN 3059, Sophistication	1987–	140.00	
☐ HN 3060, Wintertime	1985–	200.00	250.00
HN 3061–HN 3065 NOT ISSUED			

	Date	Price Range
☐ HN 3066, Printemps (Les Saisons Series)	1987–	795.00
HN 3067–HN 3069 NOT ISSUED		
☐ HN 3070, Cocktails	1985–	170.00
☐ HN 3071, Flirtation	1985–	170.00
☐ HN 3072, Promenade	1985–	170.00
☐ HN 3073, Strolling	1985–	195.00
☐ HN 3074, Paradise	1985–	160.00
☐ HN 3075, Tango	1985–	170.00
☐ HN 3076, Bolero	1985–	185.00
☐ HN 3077, Windflower	1986–	140.00
☐ HN 3078, Dancing Delight	1986–	140.00
☐ HN 3079, Sleeping Beauty	1987–	195.00
☐ HN 3080, Allure	1985–	130.00
HN 3081–HN 3082 NOT ISSUED		
☐ HN 3083, Sheikh	1987–	140.00
HN 3084 NOT ISSUED		
☐ HN 3085, Summer Rose	1987–	140.00
HN 3086–HN 3088 NOT ISSUED		
☐ HN 3089, Grace Darling	1987–	—
☐ HN 3090, Charisma	1986–	140.00
☐ HN 3091, Summer Darling	1986–	185.00
☐ HN 3092, Cherry Blossom	1986–	160.00
☐ HN 3093, Morning Glory	1986–	140.00
☐ HN 3094, Sweet Perfume	1986–	140.00
☐ HN 3095, Happy Birthday	1987–	215.00
☐ HN 3096, Merry Christmas	1987–	215.00
☐ HN 3097, Happy Anniversary	1987–	215.00
☐ HN 3098, Dorothy	1987–	295.00
☐ HN 3099, Queen Elizabeth I (Queens of the Realm Series)	1987–	450.00
☐ HN 3100, Kathleen	1986 only	200.00 250.00
HN 3101–HN 3104 NOT ISSUED		
☐ HN 3105, The Love Letter (Jefferson Quartet)	1986–	130.00
☐ HN 3106, Secret Moment (Jefferson Quartet)	1986–	140.00
☐ HN 3107, Daybreak (Jefferson Quartet)	1986–	140.00
☐ HN 3108, Enchanting Evening (Jefferson Quartet)	1986–	140.00
☐ HN 3109, Pensive	1986–	130.00
☐ HN 3110, Enigma	1986–	140.00
HN 3111–HN 3114 NOT ISSUED		
☐ HN 3115, Idle Hours	1986–	150.00
☐ HN 3116, Park Parade	1987–	170.00

	Date	Price Range
☐ HN 3117, Indian Maiden	1987–	160.00
HN 3118–HN 3124 NOT ISSUED		
☐ HN 3125, Queen Victoria	1988–	450.00
☐ HN 3126, Storytime	1987–	175.00
☐ HN 3127, Playmates	1987–	175.00
☐ HN 3128, Tomorrow's Dreams	1987–	185.00
☐ HN 3129, Thankful	1987–	75.00
☐ HN 3130, Sisterly Love	1987–	140.00
HN 3131 NOT ISSUED		
☐ HN 3132, Good Pals	1987–	140.00
☐ HN 3133, Dreaming	1987–	110.00
☐ HN 3134, Ballet Class	1987–	175.00
HN 3135–HN 3136 NOT ISSUED		
☐ HN 3137, Summertime (Collector Club figure)	1987–	140.00
HN 3138–HN 3144 NOT ISSUED		
☐ HN 3145, Rose Arbour	1987–	160.00
HN 3146–HN 3154 NOT ISSUED		
☐ HN 3155, Water Maiden	1987–	140.00
☐ HN 3156, Bathing Beauty	1987–	140.00
☐ HN 3157, Free Spirit	1987–	110.00

"M" NUMERICAL LISTINGS OF MINIATURE FANCY AND CHARACTER FIGURINES

	Date	Price Range	
☐ **M1,** Victorian Lady	1932–1945	**275.00**	**350.00**
☐ **M2,** Victorian Lady	1932–1945	**275.00**	**350.00**
☐ **M3,** Paisley Shawl	1932–1938	**325.00**	**425.00**
☐ **M4,** Paisley Shawl	1932–1945	**325.00**	**400.00**
☐ **M5,** Sweet Anne	1932–1945	**250.00**	**300.00**
☐ **M6,** Sweet Anne	1932–1945	**325.00**	**425.00**
☐ **M7,** Patricia ....\..................	1932–1945	**275.00**	**350.00**
☐ **M8,** Patricia	1932–1938	**275.00**	**350.00**
☐ **M9,** Chloe	1932–1945	**275.00**	**325.00**
☐ **M10,** Chloe	1932–1945	**300.00**	**350.00**
☐ **M11,** Bridesmaid	1932–1938	**250.00**	**350.00**
☐ **M12,** Bridesmaid	1932–1945	**250.00**	**350.00**
☐ **M13,** Priscilla	1932–1938	**400.00**	**450.00**
☐ **M14,** Priscilla	1932–1945	**400.00**	**450.00**
☐ **M15,** Pantalettes	1932–1945	**275.00**	**375.00**
☐ **M16,** Pantalettes	1932–1945	**300.00**	**425.00**
☐ **M17,** Shepherd	1932–1938	**1200.00**	**1700.00**
☐ **M18,** Shepherdess	1932–1938	**1200.00**	**1600.00**
☐ **M19,** Shepherd	1932–1938	**1300.00**	**1700.00**
☐ **M20,** Shepherdess	1932–1938	**1200.00**	**1700.00**
☐ **M21,** Polly Peachum	1932–1945	**300.00**	**375.00**
☐ **M22,** Polly Peachum	1932–1938	**400.00**	**475.00**
☐ **M23,** Polly Peachum	1932–1938	**400.00**	**475.00**
☐ **M24,** Priscilla	1932–1945	**350.00**	**400.00**
☐ **M25,** Victorian Lady	1932–1945	**275.00**	**350.00**
☐ **M26,** Paisley Shawl	1932–1945	**325.00**	**400.00**
☐ **M27,** Sweet Anne	1932–1945	**250.00**	**300.00**
☐ **M28,** Patricia	1932–1945	**275.00**	**350.00**
☐ **M29,** Chloe	1932–1945	**300.00**	**350.00**
☐ **M30,** Bridesmaid	1932–1945	**250.00**	**350.00**
☐ **M31,** Pantalettes	1932–1945	**300.00**	**425.00**
☐ **M32,** Rosamund	1932–1945	**550.00**	**700.00**
☐ **M33,** Rosamund	1932–1945	**450.00**	**550.00**
☐ **M34,** Denise	1933–1945	**500.00**	**600.00**
☐ **M35,** Denise	1933–1945	**500.00**	**600.00**
☐ **M36,** Norma	1933–1945	**600.00**	**850.00**
☐ **M37,** Norma	1933–1945	**600.00**	**850.00**
☐ **M38,** Robin	1933–1945	**500.00**	**650.00**
☐ **M39,** Robin	1933–1945	**600.00**	**650.00**
☐ **M40,** Erminie	1933–1945	**550.00**	**650.00**

	Date	Price Range	
☐ **M41**, Mr. Pickwick	1932–1983	55.00	65.00
☐ **M42**, Mr. Micawber	1932–1983	55.00	65.00
☐ **M43**, Mr. Pecksniff	1932–1983	55.00	65.00
☐ **M44**, Fat Boy	1932–1983	55.00	85.00
☐ **M45**, Uriah Heep	1932–1983	55.00	65.00
☐ **M46**, Sairey Gamp	1932–1983	55.00	75.00
☐ **M47**, Tony Weller	1932–1983	55.00	75.00
☐ **M48**, Sam Weller	1932–1983	55.00	75.00
☐ **M49**, Fagin	1932–1983	55.00	85.00
☐ **M50**, Stiggins	1932–1983	55.00	75.00
☐ **M51**, Little Nell	1932–1983	55.00	85.00
☐ **M52**, Alfred Jingle	1932–1983	45.00	55.00
☐ **M53**, Buz Fuz	1932–1983	55.00	85.00
☐ **M54**, Bill Sykes	1932–1983	50.00	75.00
☐ **M55**, Artful Dodger	1932–1983	45.00	55.00
☐ **M56**, Tiny Tim	1932–1983	55.00	75.00

M57–M62 DICKENS NAPKIN RINGS
M63 NOT ISSUED

	Date	Price Range	
☐ **M64**, Veronica	1934–1949	475.00	600.00
☐ **M65**, June	1935–1949	400.00	575.00
☐ **M66**, Monica	1935–1949	550.00	750.00
☐ **M67**, Dainty May	1935–1949	350.00	450.00
☐ **M68**, Mirabel	1936–1949	600.00	750.00
☐ **M69**, Janet	1936–1949	400.00	500.00
☐ **M70**, Veronica	1936–1949	475.00	600.00
☐ **M71**, June	1936–1949	400.00	575.00
☐ **M72**, Monica	1936–1949	550.00	750.00
☐ **M73**, Dainty May	1936–1949	350.00	450.00
☐ **M74**, Mirabel	1936–1949	600.00	750.00
☐ **M75**, Janet	1936–1949	400.00	450.00
☐ **M76**, Bumble	1939–1982	55.00	85.00
☐ **M77**, Captain Cuttle	1939–1983	55.00	85.00
☐ **M78**, Windflower	1939–1949	600.00	850.00
☐ **M79**, Windflower	1939–1949	600.00	850.00
☐ **M80**, Goody Two Shoes	1939–1949	700.00	850.00
☐ **M81**, Goody Two Shoes	1939–1949	700.00	850.00
☐ **M82**, Bo-Peep	1939–1949	550.00	650.00
☐ **M83**, Bo-Peep	1939–1949	550.00	650.00
☐ **M84**, Maureen	1939–1949	700.00	800.00
☐ **M85**, Maureen	1939–1949	700.00	800.00
☐ **M86**, Mrs. Bardell	1949–1983	55.00	85.00
☐ **M87**, Scrooge	1949–1983	55.00	70.00
☐ **M88**, David Copperfield	1949–1983	55.00	85.00
☐ **M89**, Oliver Twist	1949–1983	55.00	85.00
☐ **M90**, Dick Swiveller	1949–1983	55.00	85.00
☐ **M91**, Trotty Veck	1949–1985	55.00	75.00

"HN" NUMERICAL LISTINGS OF
ANIMAL AND BIRD MODELS

- [ ] **HN 100,** Fox in Red Frock Coat
- [ ] **HN 101,** Hare in Red Coat
- [ ] **HN 102,** Hare in White Coat
- [ ] **HN 103,** Double Penguins
- [ ] **HN 104,** Single Penguin
- [ ] **HN 105,** Collie (Sable)
- [ ] **HN 106,** Collie (White & Sable)
- [ ] **HN 107,** Hare, crouching
- [ ] **HN 108,** Rabbit
- [ ] **HN 109,** Cat (White)
- [ ] **HN 110,** Titanian Bowl, jade
- [ ] **HN 111,** Cockerel on Stand
- [ ] **HN 112,** Alsatian (Pale gray)
- [ ] **HN 113,** Penguin
- [ ] **HN 114,** Drake (Malachite head)
- [ ] **HN 115,** Drake (Blue head)
- [ ] **HN 116,** Drake (Bright colors overall)
- [ ] **HN 117,** Two Foxes
- [ ] **HN 118,** Monkey
- [ ] **HN 119,** Polar Bear, sitting on green cube
- [ ] **HN 120,** Cat (White)
- [ ] **HN 121,** Polar Bear, sitting
- [ ] **HN 122,** Two Turtle Doves
- [ ] **HN 123,** Pelican
- [ ] **HN 124,** Cockerel, sitting
- [ ] **HN 125,** Guinea Fowl
- [ ] **HN 126,** Hare, crouching
- [ ] **HN 127,** Pekinese
- [ ] **HN 128,** Puppy
- [ ] **HN 129,** Bulldog, sitting
- [ ] **HN 130,** Fox
- [ ] **HN 131,** Kingfisher on Rock
- [ ] **HN 132,** Drake on Rock
- [ ] **HN 133,** Double Penguins
- [ ] **HN 134,** Single Penguin
- [ ] **HN 135,** Raven on Rock
- [ ] **HN 136,** Robin on Rock
- [ ] **HN 137,** Blue Tit on Rock
- [ ] **HN 138,** Squirrel
- [ ] **HN 139,** Falcon on Rock
- [ ] **HN 140,** Ape
- [ ] **HN 141,** Rhinoceros
- [ ] **HN 142,** Hare, crouching
- [ ] **HN 143,** Chaffinch on its back
- [ ] **HN 144,** Wren
- [ ] **HN 145,** Small Yellow Bird on Rock, beak open
- [ ] **HN 145A,** Small Yellow Bird on Rock, beak closed
- [ ] **HN 146,** 'Old Bill' Bulldog with Helmet and Haversack
- [ ] **HN 147,** Fox on Rock
- [ ] **HN 148,** Two Drakes
- [ ] **HN 149,** Swallow on Rock
- [ ] **HN 150,** Duck
- [ ] **HN 151,** Rabbit
- [ ] **HN 152,** Kingfisher on Rock
- [ ] **HN 153,** 'Old Bill' Bulldog with Tammy and Haversack
- [ ] **HN 154,** Character Cat
- [ ] **HN 155,** Owl
- [ ] **HN 156,** Monkey, listening
- [ ] **HN 157,** Cockerel
- [ ] **HN 158,** Toucan
- [ ] **HN 159,** Toucan
- [ ] **HN 160,** Owl and Young
- [ ] **HN 161,** Four Thrush Chicks
- [ ] **HN 162,** Butterfly (Blue and gold)
- [ ] **HN 163,** Budgerigar
- [ ] **HN 164,** Cockerel, crowing
- [ ] **HN 165,** Kingfisher
- [ ] **HN 166,** Foxhound, seated
- [ ] **HN 167,** Tern Duck
- [ ] **HN 168,** Tern Drake
- [ ] **HN 169,** Owl
- [ ] **HN 170,** Brown Bear, Titanian ware
- [ ] **HN 171,** Four Baby Birds
- [ ] **HN 172,** Buffalo
- [ ] **HN 173,** 'Wise Old Owl' in Red Cloak and Ermine Collar

- ☐ **HN 175,** Great Crested Grebe
- ☐ **HN 176,** Bloodhound
- ☐ **HN 177,** Powder Bowl with Small Ape Figure Seated on Lid
- ☐ **HN 178,** Cockerel, crouching
- ☐ **HN 179,** Two Foxes
- ☐ **HN 180,** Cockerel, crouching
- ☐ **HN 181,** Elephant
- ☐ **HN 182,** Character Monkey (Green jacket)
- ☐ **HN 183,** Character Monkey (Blue jacket)
- ☐ **HN 184,** Cockerel, crowing
- ☐ **HN 185,** Parrot on rock
- ☐ **HN 186,** Elephant
- ☐ **HN 187,** Character Owl (Check shawl, ermine collar)
- ☐ **HN 188,** Duckling (Yellow and brown)
- ☐ **HN 189,** Duckling (Black and yellow)
- ☐ **HN 190,** Duckling (Green and blue)
- ☐ **HN 191,** Parrot, baby (Blue and purple)
- ☐ **HN 192,** Parrot, baby (Red and orange)
- ☐ **HN 193,** Tortoise
- ☐ **HN 194,** Terrier Puppy
- ☐ **HN 195,** Tern Duck
- ☐ **HN 196,** Toucan
- ☐ **HN 197,** Bird on Rock
- ☐ **HN 198,** Penguin and Young
- ☐ **HN 199,** Budgerigar on Stand (Green and yellow)
- ☐ **HN 200,** Parrot, baby (Decorated in enamel flowers)
- ☐ **HN 201,** Tabby Cat and Mouse
- ☐ **HN 202,** Black Cat and Mouse
- ☐ **HN 203,** Tortoiseshell Cat on Pillar
- ☐ **HN 204,** Tortoiseshell Cat
- ☐ **HN 205,** Two Ducklings (Black and white)
- ☐ **HN 206,** Two Ducklings (Brown and white)
- ☐ **HN 207,** Character Mouse
- ☐ **HN 208,** Character Toucan
- ☐ **HN 209,** Two Rabbits
- ☐ **HN 210,** Black and White Cat
- ☐ **HN 211,** Black-headed Gull
- ☐ **HN 212,** Black-headed Gull
- ☐ **HN 213,** Two Pigs
- ☐ **HN 214,** Bird and Four Chicks (Black, pink and brown)
- ☐ **HN 215,** Bird and Four Chicks (Gray, blue and lemon)
- ☐ **HN 216,** Bird and Four Chicks (Green, blue and lemon)
- ☐ **HN 217,** Two Rabbits (Brown patches on faces)
- ☐ **HN 218,** Two Rabbits (Brown and black patches on faces)
- ☐ **HN 219,** Two Rabbits (Brown, black, and yellow patches on faces)
- ☐ **HN 220,** Bird on rock
- ☐ **HN 221,** Cat (Back and white)
- ☐ **HN 222,** Owl in boat
- ☐ **HN 223,** Lion, sitting
- ☐ **HN 224,** Kingfisher on rock
- ☐ **HN 225,** Tiger, lying
- ☐ **HN 226,** Character Mouse (Blue coat)
- ☐ **HN 227,** Tabby Cat, asleep
- ☐ **HN 228,** Character Mouse (Yellow coat)
- ☐ **HN 229,** Teal Duck
- ☐ **HN 231,** Foxhound
- ☐ **HN 232,** Puppy with Bone
- ☐ **HN 233,** Kitten
- ☐ **HN 234,** Two Cats
- ☐ **HN 235,** Duckling
- ☐ **HN 236,** Two Baby Birds
- ☐ **HN 237,** Character Mouse with Basket of Babies
- ☐ **HN 238,** Two Pigs
- ☐ **HN 239,** Two Ducks
- ☐ **HN 240,** Bird on Rock
- ☐ **HN 241,** Eagle (Brown and gold)
- ☐ **HN 242,** Eagle (Lighter color, white head and neck)
- ☐ **HN 243,** Piggy Bowl
- ☐ **HN 244,** Cat and Mouse (Cat black and white)
- ☐ **HN 245,** Cat and Mouse (Cat all black)
- ☐ **HN 246,** Character Pig

- ☐ **HN 247,** Guinea Fowl
- ☐ **HN 248,** Drake, large size
- ☐ **HN 249,** Mallard Drake, large size
- ☐ **HN 250,** Heron
- ☐ **HN 251,** Heron
- ☐ **HN 252,** Drake, large size
- ☐ **HN 253,** Small Ape, sitting
- ☐ **HN 254,** Two small Apes
- ☐ **HN 255-HN 266,** Miniature Character Penguins and Puffins
- ☐ **HN 267,** Cockerel, sitting
- ☐ **HN 268,** Kingfisher
- ☐ **HN 269,** Blue Bird on Rock
- ☐ **HN 270,** Brown Bear, sitting up
- ☐ **HN 271,** Duck
- ☐ **HN 272,** Bird with Three Chicks
- ☐ **HN 273,** Rabbit
- ☐ **HN 274,** Green Bird
- ☐ **HN 275,** Two Orange Birds
- ☐ **HN 276,** Rabbit
- ☐ **HN 277,** Wren
- ☐ **HN 278,** Two Green Birds
- ☐ **HN 279,** Green Bird on Rock
- ☐ **HN 280,** Three Chicks
- ☐ **HN 281,** Yellow Bird on Rock
- ☐ **HN 282,** Blue Bird
- ☐ **HN 283-HN 293,** Miniature Character Penguins and Puffins
- ☐ **HN 294,** Toucan, large size (Black and white, red beak)
- ☐ **HN 295,** Toucan, large size (Black and green, brown beak)
- ☐ **HN 295A,** Toucan, large size (Black and green, brown beak)
- ☐ **HN 296,** Penguin
- ☐ **HN 297,** Penguin and Young
- ☐ **HN 298,** Duck, sitting
- ☐ **HN 299,** Drake, lying
- ☐ **HN 800,** Pig, asleep
- ☐ **HN 801,** Pig asleep, larger version
- ☐ **HN 802,** Two Pigs
- ☐ **HN 803,** Rabbit
- ☐ **HN 804,** Miniature Pup, playing (Pale orange)
- ☐ **HN 805,** Miniature Pup, playing (Malachite and purple)
- ☐ **HN 806,** Miniature Drake (White)
- ☐ **HN 807,** Miniature Drake (Malachite and purple)
- ☐ **HN 808-HN 812,** Miniature Character Pups
- ☐ **HN 813,** Miniature White Bird
- ☐ **HN 814,** Miniature Character Pup
- ☐ **HN 815,** Miniature Character Pup
- ☐ **HN 818,** Character Cat 'Lucky' (Black and white)
- ☐ **HN 819,** Miniature Cat 'Lucky' (White)
- ☐ **HN 820-HN 825,** Miniature Kittens
- ☐ **HN 826,** Character Pup
- ☐ **HN 827,** Character Cat (Tortoiseshell)
- ☐ **HN 828,** Character Cat (Tabby)
- ☐ **HN 829,** Character Cat (Black and white)
- ☐ **HN 830,** NO RECORD
- ☐ **HN 831,** Beagle Puppy
- ☐ **HN 832,** Pekinese Puppy, sitting
- ☐ **HN 833,** Pekinese Puppy, standing
- ☐ **HN 834,** Pekinese Puppy on Stand (Black and brown)
- ☐ **HN 835,** Pekinese Puppy on Stand (Lighter brown)
- ☐ **HN 836,** Pekinese Puppy on Stand (Light color)
- ☐ **HN 837,** Chow on Stand (Brown)
- ☐ **HN 838,** Chow on Stand (Lighter brown)
- ☐ **HN 839,** Chow on Stand (White and gray)
- ☐ **HN 840-HN 845,** Character Ducks
- ☐ **HN 846,** Toucan
- ☐ **HN 847,** Yellow Bird
- ☐ **HN 849,** Duck and Ladybird
- ☐ **HN 850,** Duck, standing on rocks
- ☐ **HN 851,** Bird on Tree Stump
- ☐ **HN 852,** Penguin, standing on rocks

- [ ] **HN 853,** Small Mallard Drake on Rocks
- [ ] **HN 854,** Budgerigar
- [ ] **HN 855,** Small Bird on Tree Stump
- [ ] **HN 856,** Penguin on Rocks
- [ ] **HN 858,** Kingfisher on Rock
- [ ] **HN 859,** Tortoise on Rocks
- [ ] **HN 860,** Small Bird on Tree Stump
- [ ] **HN 861,** Polar Bear
- [ ] **HN 862A,** Kingfisher on Stand, with Primroses
- [ ] **HN 862B,** Kingfisher on Stand, with Kingcups
- [ ] **HN 863,** Ducks, quacking
- [ ] **HN 864,** Ducks, quacking
- [ ] **HN 865,** Ducks, quacking
- [ ] **HN 866,** Fox, sitting

HN 867-HN 874

- [ ] **HN 875,** Kingfisher on Tree Stump
- [ ] **HN 876,** Tiger on Rock
- [ ] **HN 877,** Baby Parrot
- [ ] **HN 878,** Cockerel (White)
- [ ] **HN 879,** Cockerel (Blue and green)
- [ ] **HN 880,** Cockerel (Brown and orange)
- [ ] **HN 881,** Bulldog, sitting
- [ ] **HN 882,** Penguin, large size
- [ ] **HN 883,** Two Monkeys
- [ ] **HN 884,** Cockatoo (Blue and orange)
- [ ] **HN 885,** Cockatoo (Pink, purple and orange)
- [ ] **HN 886,** Cockatoo (Red, blue and orange)
- [ ] **HN 888,** Cockatoo (Pale blue and yellow)
- [ ] **HN 889,** Dog, seated greyhound (Black and white)
- [ ] **HN 890,** Dog, seated greyhound (Brown)
- [ ] **HN 891,** Elephant, large size (Silver gray)
- [ ] **HN 892,** Character Pigs, in clown costume
- [ ] **HN 893,** Character Pigs, in clown costume
- [ ] **HN 894,** Character Pigs, in clown costume
- [ ] **HN 895,** Character Pigs, in clown costume
- [ ] **HN 896,** Character Pigs, in clown costume
- [ ] **HN 897,** Character Pigs, in clown costume
- [ ] **HN 898,** Alsatian's Head
- [ ] **HN 899,** Alsatian, sitting
- [ ] **HN 900,** Fox Terrier (White and brown)
- [ ] **HN 901,** Fox Terrier (White and black)
- [ ] **HN 902,** Character Pigs
- [ ] **HN 903,** Character Pigs
- [ ] **HN 904,** Terrier Puppy
- [ ] **HN 905,** Small Frog
- [ ] **HN 906,** Spaniel Puppy (Black and white)
- [ ] **HN 907,** Spaniel Puppy (Brown and white)
- [ ] **HN 908,** Spaniel Puppy's Head
- [ ] **HN 909,** Fox Terrier, standing
- [ ] **HN 910,** Fox Terrier, sitting
- [ ] **HN 911,** Tiger, lying
- [ ] **HN 912,** Tiger, sitting
- [ ] **HN 913-HN 918,** Toucan Head, on round bowl-like bodies
- [ ] **HN 919,** Leopard, sitting
- [ ] **HN 920,** Two Foxes (Brown)
- [ ] **HN 921,** Alsatian, sitting, large size
- [ ] **HN 922,** Character Hare
- [ ] **HN 923,** Fox Terrier, standing
- [ ] **HN 924,** Fox Terrier, sitting, large size
- [ ] **HN 925,** Two Foxes (Gray and brown)
- [ ] **HN 926,** Two Foxes (Miniature model)
- [ ] **HN 927,** Two Pekinese Dogs
- [ ] **HN 928,** Large Toucan Bowl
- [ ] **HN 929,** Miniature Terrier Pup, sitting
- [ ] **HN 930,** Miniature Alsatian, sitting

☐ **HN 931,** Miniature Terrier Pup
☐ **HN 932,** Miniature Scotch Terrier
☐ **HN 933,** Miniature Scotch Terrier
☐ **HN 934,** Miniature Scotch Terrier
☐ **HN 935,** Pip, Squeak and Wilfred Ashtray
☐ **HN 936,** Teal, swimming
☐ **HN 937,** Alsatian on Stand
☐ **HN 938,** Alsatian on Stand, sitting
☐ **HN 939,** Large and Small Brown Bears
☐ **HN 940,** Large and Small Brown Bears (Light brown)
☐ **HN 941,** Elephant, large size (Black)
☐ **HN 942,** Terrier
☐ **HN 943,** Terrier
☐ **HN 944,** Fox Terrier
☐ **HN 945,** Fox Terrier
☐ **HN 946,** Penguin Chick
☐ **HN 947,** Penguin Chick
☐ **HN 948,** Bulldog, large size (Brown)
☐ **HN 949,** Baby Elephant
☐ **HN 950,** Baby Elephant
☐ **HN 951,** Baby Elephant
☐ **HN 952,** Baby Elephant
☐ **HN 953,** Terrier Pup (Brown and black)
☐ **HN 954,** Terrier Pup (Darker brown and black)
☐ **HN 955,** Brown Bear, standing
☐ **HN 956,** Mallard Drake, large size
☐ **HN 957,** Spaniel (Liver and white)
☐ **HN 958,** Spaniel (Black and white)
☐ **HN 960,** Character Ape with Book, eyes open
☐ **HN 961,** Character Ape with Book, eyes closed
☐ **HN 962,** Terrier's Head
☐ **HN 963,** Fox, sitting

☐ **HN 964,** Scotch Terrier, large size (Black)
☐ **HN 965,** Scotch Terrier, large size (Brown)
☐ **HN 966,** Elephant, large size (Brown and gray)
☐ **HN 967,** Tabby Cat
☐ **HN 968,** Pig (Black and white)
☐ **HN 969,** Two Rabbits
☐ **HN 970,** Dachshund
☐ **HN 971,** 'Lucky' Cat Ashtray
☐ **HN 972,** Character Ape in Dunce's cap, reading book
☐ **HN 973,** Character Duck (Orange)
☐ **HN 974,** Character Duck (Lemon yellow)
☐ **HN 975,** Collie (Silver gray)
☐ **HN 976,** Collie (Brown)
☐ **HN 977,** Duck
☐ **HN 978,** Fox, lying
☐ **HN 979,** Hare, lying
☐ **HN 980,** Scotch Terrier (Black)
☐ **HN 981,** Scotch Terrier (Light gray and brown)
☐ **HN 982,** Sealyham Terrier (Black patches on face)
☐ **HN 983,** Sealyham Terrier (Brown patches on face)
☐ **HN 984,** Hare, lying (White)
☐ **HN 985,** Hare, lying (Gray)
☐ **HN 986,** Alsatian Sitting on Lid of Lustre Bowl
☐ **HN 987,** Bulldog Sitting on Lid of Lustre Bowl
☐ **HN 988,** Airedale Terrier (Brown)
☐ **HN 989,** Sealyham Terrier (Gray)
☐ **HN 990,** Tiger, crouching
☐ **HN 991,** Tiger, crouching (Smaller model)
☐ **HN 992,** Sealyham Terrier (Black)
☐ **HN 993,** Cat Asleep on Cushion
☐ **HN 994,** Fox on pedestal
☐ **HN 995,** Pekinese (Brown)
☐ **HN 996,** Airedale Terrier (Black, blue and brown)

- ☐ **HN 997,** Terrier, seated (Black and brown)
- ☐ **HN 998,** Penguin and Baby
- ☐ **HN 999,** Persian Cat (Black and white)
- ☐ **HN 1000,** Cocker Spaniel, large size (black)
- ☐ **HN 1001,** Cocker Spaniel and Pheasant, large size
- ☐ **HN 1002,** Cocker Spaniel (Liver and white)
- ☐ **HN 1003,** Pekinese (Dark coloring)
- ☐ **HN 1004,** Blue Tit on Bough with Blossom
- ☐ **HN 1005,** Thrush on Bough with Blossom
- ☐ **HN 1007,** Ch. 'Charley Startler' Rough-haired Terrier, large size
- ☐ **HN 1008,** Ch. 'Albourne Arthur' Scottish Terrier, large size
- ☐ **HN 1009,** Hare and Two Leverets
- ☐ **HN 1010,** Ch. 'Biddie of Ifield' Pekinese, large size
- ☐ **HN 1011,** Ch. 'Biddie of Ifield' Pekinese, medium size
- ☐ **HN 1012,** Ch. 'Biddie of Ifield' Pekinese, small size
- ☐ **HN 1013,** Ch. 'Charley Hunter' Fox Terrier, medium size
- ☐ **HN 1014,** Ch. 'Charley Hunter' Fox Terrier, small size
- ☐ **HN 1015,** Ch. 'Albourne Arthur' Scottish Terrier, medium size
- ☐ **HN 1016,** Ch. 'Albourne Arthur' Scottish Terrier, small size
- ☐ **HN 1017,** Scottish Terrier, sitting (Black)
- ☐ **HN 1018,** Scottish Terrier, sitting (Black)
- ☐ **HN 1019,** Scottish Terrier, sitting (Black)
- ☐ **HN 1020,** Ch. 'Lucky Star of Ware' Cocker Spaniel, medium size
- ☐ **HN 1021,** Ch. 'Lucky Star of Ware' Cocker Spaniel, small size
- ☐ **HN 1022,** Ch. 'Cotsfold Topsail' Airedale Terrier, large size
- ☐ **HN 1023,** Ch. 'Cotsfold Topsail' Airedale Terrier, medium size
- ☐ **HN 1024,** Ch. 'Cotsfold Topsail' Airedale Terrier, small size
- ☐ **HN 1025,** Ch. 'Tring Rattler' Foxhound, large size
- ☐ **HN 1026,** Ch. 'Tring Rattler' Foxhound, medium size
- ☐ **HN 1027,** Ch. 'Tring Rattler' Foxhound, small size
- ☐ **HN 1028,** Cocker Spaniel and Pheasant, medium size
- ☐ **HN 1029,** Cocker Spaniel and Pheasant, small size
- ☐ **HN 1030,** Ch. 'Scotia Stylist' Sealyham, large size
- ☐ **HN 1031,** Ch. 'Scotia Stylist' Sealyham, medium size
- ☐ **HN 1032,** Ch. 'Scotia Stylist' Sealyham, small size
- ☐ **HN 1033,** Ch. 'Charming Eyes' Cairn, large size
- ☐ **HN 1034,** Ch. 'Charming Eyes' Cairn, medium size
- ☐ **HN 1035,** Ch. 'Charming Eyes' Cairn, small size
- ☐ **HN 1036,** Cocker Spaniel, medium size (Liver and white)
- ☐ **HN 1037,** Cocker Spaniel, small size (Liver and white)
- ☐ **HN 1038,** Scottish Terrier, begging
- ☐ **HN 1039,** Pekinese, sitting, large size
- ☐ **HN 1040,** Pekinese, sitting, small size
- ☐ **HN 1041,** Sealyham, lying, large size
- ☐ **HN 1042,** Bulldog, large size (Brindle)
- ☐ **HN 1043,** Bulldog, medium size (Brindle)
- ☐ **HN 1044,** Bulldog, small size (Brindle)
- ☐ **HN 1045,** Bulldog, large size (Brown and white)

☐ **HN 1046,** Bulldog, medium size (Brown and white)

☐ **HN 1047,** Bulldog, small size (Brown and white)

☐ **HN 1048,** West Highland White Terrier, large size

☐ **HN 1049,** Ch. 'Maesydd Mustard' English Setter, large size

☐ **HN 1050,** Ch. 'Maesydd Mustard' English Setter, medium size

☐ **HN 1051,** Ch. 'Maesydd Mustard' English Setter, small size

☐ **HN 1052,** Sealyham, lying, medium size

☐ **HN 1053,** Sealyham, lying, small size

☐ **HN 1054,** Irish Setter, large size

☐ **HN 1055,** Irish Setter, medium size

☐ **HN 1056,** Irish Setter, small size

☐ **HN 1057,** Ch. 'Ashstead Applause' Collie, large size

☐ **HN 1058,** Ch. 'Ashstead Applause' Collie, medium size

☐ **HN 1059,** Ch. 'Ashstead Applause' Collie, small size

☐ **HN 1062,** Cocker Spaniel and Pheasant (Black and white), small size

☐ **HN 1063,** Cocker Spaniel and Hare, medium size (Liver and white)

☐ **HN 1064,** Cocker Spaniel and Hare, small size (Liver and white)

☐ **HN 1065,** Greyhound, large size (Brown)

☐ **HN 1066,** Greyhound, medium size (Brown)

☐ **HN 1067,** Greyhound, small size (Brown)

☐ **HN 1068,** Smooth-haired Fox Terrier, large size

☐ **HN 1069,** Smooth-haired Fox Terrier, medium size

☐ **HN 1070,** Smooth-haired Fox Terrier, small size

☐ **HN 1071,** Hare, lying

☐ **HN 1072,** Bulldog, large size (White)

☐ **HN 1073,** Bulldog, medium size (White)

☐ **HN 1074,** Bulldog, small size (White)

☐ **HN 1075,** Greyhound, large size (Black and white)

☐ **HN 1076,** Greyhound, medium size (Black and white)

☐ **HN 1077,** Greyhound, small size (Black and white)

☐ **HN 1078,** Cocker Spaniel, small size (Black and white)

☐ **HN 1079,** Gordon Setter, large size

☐ **HN 1080,** Gordon Setter, medium size

☐ **HN 1081,** Gordon Setter, small size

☐ **HN 1082,** Tiger, stalking, large size

☐ **HN 1083,** Tiger, stalking, medium size

☐ **HN 1084,** Tiger, stalking, medium size

☐ **HN 1084,** Tiger, stalking, small size

☐ **HN 1085,** Lion, large size

☐ **HN 1086,** Lion, medium size

☐ **HN 1087–HN 1093A,** Ashtray

☐ **HN 1094,** Leopard

☐ **HN 1095–1095A,** Ashtray

☐ **HN 1096,** Character Fox with Stolen Goose (Green cloak and hat)

☐ **HN 1097,** Character Dog, running with ball

☐ **HN 1098,** Character Dog

☐ **HN 1099,** Character Dog, yawning

☐ **HN 1100,** Character Dog

☐ **HN 1101,** Character Dog, lying

☐ **HN 1102,** Character Fox with Stolen Goose (Red cloak and hat)

☐ **HN 1103,** Character Dog, with ball

- ☐ **HN 1104,** Cairn, large size (Black)
- ☐ **HN 1105,** Cairn, medium size (Black)
- ☐ **HN 1106,** Cairn, small size (Black)
- ☐ **HN 1107,** Cairn, large size (Black, earthenware)
- ☐ **HN 1108,** Cocker Spaniel, large size (Black and white)
- ☐ **HN 1109,** Cocker Spaniel, medium size (Black and white)
- ☐ **HN 1111,** Ch. 'Goworth Victor' Dalmatian, large size
- ☐ **HN 1112,** Lion, large size
- ☐ **HN 1113,** Ch. 'Goworth Victor' Dalmatian, medium size
- ☐ **HN 1114,** Ch. 'Goworth Victor' Dalmatian, small size
- ☐ **HN 1115,** Ch. 'Benign of Picardy' Alsatian, large size
- ☐ **HN 1116,** Ch. 'Benign of Picardy' Alsatian, medium size
- ☐ **HN 1117,** Ch. 'Benign of Picardy' Alsatian, small size
- ☐ **HN 1118,** Tiger on Rock, large size (Earthenware)
- ☐ **HN 1119,** Lion on Rock, large size (Earthenware)
- ☐ **HN 1120,** Fighting Elephant, large size (Earthenware)
- ☐ **HN 1121,** Elephant, large size
- ☐ **HN 1122,** Elephant, large size
- ☐ **HN 1123,** Elephant, medium size
- ☐ **HN 1124,** Elephant, large size
- ☐ **HN 1125,** Lion on Alabaster Base
- ☐ **HN 1126,** Tiger on Alabaster Base
- ☐ **HN 1127,** Ch. 'Shrewd Saint' Dachshund, large size
- ☐ **HN 1128,** Ch. 'Shrewd Saint' Dachshund, medium size
- ☐ **HN 1129,** Ch. 'Shrewd Saint' Dachshund, small size
- ☐ **HN 1130,** Fox, large size
- ☐ **HN 1131,** Staffordshire Bull Terrier, large size
- ☐ **HN 1132,** Staffordshire Bull Terrier, medium size
- ☐ **HN 1133,** Staffordshire Bull Terrier, small size
- ☐ **HN 1134,** Cocker Spaniel, large size (Liver and white)
- ☐ **HN 1135,** Cocker Spaniel, medium size (Liver and white)
- ☐ **HN 1136,** Cocker Spaniel, small size (Liver and white)
- ☐ **HN 1137,** Cocker Spaniel and Pheasant, large size (Black and white)
- ☐ **HN 1138,** Cocker Spaniel and Pheasant, medium size (Black and white)
- ☐ **HN 1139,** Dachshund, large size
- ☐ **HN 1140,** Dachshund, medium size
- ☐ **HN 1141,** Dachshund, small size
- ☐ **HN 1142,** Ch. 'Bokus Brock' Bull Terrier, large size
- ☐ **HN 1143,** Ch. 'Bokus Brock' Bull Terrier, medium size
- ☐ **HN 1144,** Ch. 'Bokus Brock' Bull Terrier, small size
- ☐ **HN 1145,** Moufflon, standing (Green matte)
- ☐ **HN 1146,** Calf, sleeping (Green matte)
- ☐ **HN 1147,** Calf, standing (Green matte)
- ☐ **HN 1148,** Buffalo (Green matte)
- ☐ **HN 1149,** Donkey, small size (Green matte)
- ☐ **HN 1150,** Young Doe (Green matte)
- ☐ **HN 1151,** Swiss Goat (Green matte)
- ☐ **HN 1152,** Horse (Green matte)
- ☐ **HN 1153,** Moufflon, lying (Green matte)
- ☐ **HN 1154,** Jumping Goat (Green matte)
- ☐ **HN 1155,** Donkey, large size (Green matte)
- ☐ **HN 1156,** Suspicious Doe (Green matte)
- ☐ **HN 1157,** Antelope (Green matte)

- ☐ **HN 1158,** Character Dog with Plate
- ☐ **HN 1159,** Character Dog with Bone
- ☐ **HN 1160,** Moufflon, standing (Cream matte)
- ☐ **HN 1161,** Calf, sleeping (Cream matte)
- ☐ **HN 1162,** Calf, standing (Cream matte)
- ☐ **HN 1163,** Buffalo (Cream matte)
- ☐ **HN 1164,** Donkey, small size (Cream matte)
- ☐ **HN 1165,** Young Doe (Cream matte)
- ☐ **HN 1166,** Swiss Goat (Cream matte)
- ☐ **HN 1167,** Horse (Cream matte)
- ☐ **HN 1168,** Moufflon, lying (Cream matte)
- ☐ **HN 1169,** Jumping Goat (Cream matte)
- ☐ **HN 1170,** Donkey, large size (Cream matte)
- ☐ **HN 1171,** Suspicious Dog (Cream matte)
- ☐ **HN 1172,** Antelope (Cream matte)
- ☐ **HN 1173,** Calf, sleeping (Natural colors)
- ☐ **HN 1174,** Calf, standing (Natural colors)
- ☐ **HN 1175,** Buffalo (Natural colors)
- ☐ **HN 1176,** Donkey, small size (Natural colors)
- ☐ **HN 1177,** Young Doe (Natural colors)
- ☐ **HN 1178,** Swiss Goat (Natural colors)
- ☐ **HN 1179,** Moufflon, standing (Natural colors)
- ☐ **HN 1180,** Horse (Natural colors)
- ☐ **HN 1181,** Moufflon, lying (Natural colors)
- ☐ **HN 1182,** Jumping Goat (Natural colors)
- ☐ **HN 1183,** Donkey, large size (Natural colors)
- ☐ **HN 1184,** Suspicious Doe (Natural colors)
- ☐ **HN 1185,** Antelope (Natural colors)
- ☐ **HN 1186,** Cocker Spaniel, large size (Golden brown)
- ☐ **HN 1187,** Cocker Spaniel, medium size (Golden brown)
- ☐ **HN 1188,** Cocker Spaniel, small size (Golden brown)
- ☐ **HN 1189,** King Penguin
- ☐ **HN 1190,** Penguin
- ☐ **HN 1191,** Mallard
- ☐ **HN 1192,** Duck
- ☐ **HN 1193,** Tern
- ☐ **HN 1194,** Tern
- ☐ **HN 1195,** Seagull
- ☐ **HN 1196,** Seagull
- ☐ **HN 1197,** Gannet
- ☐ **HN 1198,** Drake
- ☐ **HN 1199,** Penguin
- ☐ **HN 2500,** Cerval
- ☐ **HN 2501,** Lynx
- ☐ **HN 2502,** Deer (Green)
- ☐ **HN 2503,** Deer (White)
- ☐ **HN 2504,** Lamb (Green)
- ☐ **HN 2505,** Lamb (White)
- ☐ **HN 2506,** Asiatic Elephant
- ☐ **HN 2507,** Zebra
- ☐ **HN 2508,** Character Dog
- ☐ **HN 2509,** Sealyham
- ☐ **HN 2510,** Character Dog
- ☐ **HN 2511,** Character Dog
- ☐ **HN 2512,** Ch. 'Chosen Dan of Notts' Smooth-haired Terrier, large size
- ☐ **HN 2513,** Ch. 'Chosen Dan of Notts' Smooth-haired Terrier, medium size
- ☐ **HN 2514,** Ch. 'Chosen Dan of Notts' Smooth-haired Terrier, small size
- ☐ **HN 2515,** Ch. 'Dry Toast' Springer Spaniel, large size
- ☐ **HN 2516,** Ch. 'Dry Toast' Springer Spaniel, medium size
- ☐ **HN 2517,** Ch. 'Dry Toast' Springer Spaniel, small size

☐ **HN 2518,** 'Pride of the Shires,' mare and foal (Brown)

☐ **HN 2519,** 'The Gude Gray Mare,' with foal, large size

☐ **HN 2520,** The Farmer's Boy on Dappled Shire

☐ **HN 2521,** 'The Dapple Gray' (Girl on shire pony)

☐ **HN 2522,** 'The Chestnut Mare' with Foal, large size

☐ **HN 2523,** 'Pride of the Shires' Mare and Foal (Dapple gray)

☐ **HN 2524,** American Foxhound, large size

☐ **HN 2525,** American Foxhound, medium size

☐ **HN 2526,** American Foxhound, small size

☐ **HN 2527,** Fox, sitting

☐ **HN 2528,** 'Pride of the Shires' Replacing 2518

☐ **HN 2529,** English Setter and Pheasant

☐ **HN 2530,** 'Merely a Minor,' large size (Brown)

☐ **HN 2531,** 'Merely a Minor,' large size (Gray)

☐ **HN 2532,** 'The Gude Gray Mare' with foal, medium size

☐ **HN 2533,** 'The Chestnut Mare' with foal, small size

☐ **HN 2534,** 'Pride of the Shires' Mare and Foal, small size (Brown)

☐ **HN 2535,** Tiger on Rock

☐ **HN 2536,** 'Pride of the Shires' Mare and Foal, small size (Gray)

☐ **HN 2537,** 'Merely a Minor,' medium size (Brown)

☐ **HN 2538,** 'Merely a Minor,' medium size (Gray)

☐ **HN 2539,** Persian Cat (White)

☐ **HN 2540,** Kingfisher

☐ **HN 2541,** Kingfisher

☐ **HN 2542,** Baltimore Oriole

☐ **HN 2543,** Blue Bird

☐ **HN 2544,** Mallard

☐ **HN 2545,** Pheasant

☐ **HN 2546,** Yellow Throated Warbler

☐ **HN 2547,** Budgerigars, pair

☐ **HN 2548,** Golden Crested Wren

☐ **HN 2549,** Robin

☐ **HN 2550,** Chaffinch

☐ **HN 2551,** Bullfinch

☐ **HN 2552,** Young Thrushes, pair

☐ **HN 2553,** Young Robins, group

☐ **HN 2554,** Cardinal Bird

☐ **HN 2555,** Drake Mallard

☐ **HN 2556,** Mallard

☐ **HN 2557,** Welsh Corgi, large size

☐ **HN 2558,** Welsh Corgi, medium size

☐ **HN 2559,** Welsh Corgi, small size

☐ **HN 2560,** Great Dane, large size

☐ **HN 2561,** Great Dane, medium size

☐ **HN 2562,** Great Dane, small size

☐ **HN 2563,** 'Pride of the Shires,' no foal, large size (Brown)

☐ **HN 2564,** 'Pride of the Shires,' no foal, medium size (Brown)

☐ **HN 2565,** 'The Chestnut Mare,' no foal, large size

☐ **HN 2566,** 'The Chestnut Mare,' no foal, small size

☐ **HN 2567,** 'Merely a Minor' small size (Gray)

☐ **HN 2568,** 'The Gude Gray Mare,' no foal, large size

☐ **HN 2569,** 'The Gude Gray Mare,' no foal, medium size

☐ **HN 2570,** 'The Gude Gray Mare,' no foal, small size

☐ **HN 2571,** 'Merely a Minor,' small size (Brown)

☐ **HN 2572,** Drake Mallard, small size

☐ **HN 2573,** Kingfisher, small size

☐ **HN 2574,** Seagull, small size

☐ **HN 2575,** Swan

☐ **HN 2576,** Pheasant, small size

☐ **HN 2577,** Peacock

☐ **HN 2578,** Horse without Boy (Dapple gray)

- ☐ **HN 2579,** Kitten lying on Back (Brown)
- ☐ **HN 2580,** Kitten, sitting licking hind paw (Brown)
- ☐ **HN 2581,** Kitten, sleeping (Brown)
- ☐ **HN 2582,** Kitten, sitting on haunches (Tan)
- ☐ **HN 2583,** Kitten, sitting licking front paw (Tan)
- ☐ **HN 2584,** Kitten, sitting surprised (Tan)
- ☐ **HN 2585,** Puppy in basket, lying (Cocker)
- ☐ **HN 2586,** Puppy in basket (Cocker)
- ☐ **HN 2587,** Puppy in basket (Terrier)
- ☐ **HN 2588,** Puppies in basket, three terriers
- ☐ **HN 2589,** Puppy, begging (Cairn)
- ☐ **HN 2590,** Cocker Spaniels, sleeping, pair
- ☐ **HN 2591,** Drake Mallard
- ☐ **HN 2592,** Hare
- ☐ **HN 2593,** Hare
- ☐ **HN 2594,** Hare, lying, small size
- ☐ **HN 2595,** Lambs
- ☐ **HN 2596,** Lambs
- ☐ **HN 2597,** Lambs
- ☐ **HN 2598,** Lambs
- ☐ **HN 2599,** English Setter and Pheasant
- ☐ **HN 2600,** Cocker Spaniel and Pheasant, small size
- ☐ **HN 2601,** American Great Dane, large size
- ☐ **HN 2602,** American Great Dane, medium size
- ☐ **HN 2603,** American Great Dane, small size
- ☐ **HN 2604,** Peacock Butterfly
- ☐ **HN 2605,** Camberwell Beauty Butterfly
- ☐ **HN 2606,** Swallowtail Butterfly
- ☐ **HN 2607,** Red Admiral Butterfly
- ☐ **HN 2608,** Copper Butterfly
- ☐ **HN 2609,** Tortoiseshell Butterfly
- ☐ **HN 2610,** Hen Pheasant
- ☐ **HN 2611,** Chaffinch
- ☐ **HN 2612,** Baltimore Oriole
- ☐ **HN 2613,** Golden Crested Wren
- ☐ **HN 2614,** Blue Bird
- ☐ **HN 2615,** Cardinal Bird
- ☐ **HN 2616,** Bullfinch
- ☐ **HN 2617,** Robin
- ☐ **HN 2618,** Yellow Throated Warbler
- ☐ **HN 2619,** Grouse
- ☐ **HN 2620,** English Setter, large size (Liver and white)
- ☐ **HN 2621,** English Setter, medium size (Liver and white)
- ☐ **HN 2622,** English Setter, small size (Liver and white)
- ☐ **HN 2623,** Horse without Boy (Brown)
- ☐ **HN 2624,** Pointer
- ☐ **HN 2625,** Poodle, large size
- ☐ **HN 2626,** Poodle, medium size
- ☐ **HN 2627,** Poodle, small size
- ☐ **HN 2628,** Chow, large size
- ☐ **HN 2629,** Chow, medium size
- ☐ **HN 2630,** Chow, small size
- ☐ **HN 2631,** French Poodle
- ☐ **HN 2632,** Cock Pheasant
- ☐ **HN 2633,** Penguin, large size
- ☐ **HN 2634,** Pheasant, large size
- ☐ **HN 2635,** Mallard, large size
- ☐ **HN 2636,** Indian Rummer Drake
- ☐ **HN 2637,** Polar Bear
- ☐ **HN 2638,** Leopard on Rock
- ☐ **HN 2639,** Tiger on Rock
- ☐ **HN 2640,** Fighter Elephant
- ☐ **HN 2641,** Lion on Rock
- ☐ **HN 2642,** Squirrel
- ☐ **HN 2643,** Ch. 'Warlord of Mazelaine,' Boxer
- ☐ **HN 2644,** Elephant
- ☐ **HN 2645,** Doberman Pinscher
- ☐ **HN 2646,** Tiger
- ☐ **HN 2647,** Drake
- ☐ **HN 2648,** Character Piglets
- ☐ **HN 2649,** Character Piglets
- ☐ **HN 2650,** Character Piglets
- ☐ **HN 2651,** Character Piglets
- ☐ **HN 2652,** Character Piglets

☐ **HN 2653,** Character Piglets

☐ **HN 2654,** Character Dog with Slipper

☐ **HN 2655,** Siamese Cat, sitting (Chatcull Range)

☐ **HN 2656,** Pine Martin (Chatcull Range)

☐ **HN 2657,** Langur Monkey (Chatcull Range)

☐ **HN 2658,** White-tailed Deer (Chatcull Range)

☐ **HN 2659,** Brown Bear (Chatcull Range)

☐ **HN 2660,** Siamese Cat, standing (Chatcull Range)

☐ **HN 2661,** Mountain Sheep (Chatcull Range)

☐ **HN 2662,** Siamese Cat, lying (Chatcull Range)

☐ **HN 2663,** River Hog (Chatcull Range)

☐ **HN 2664,** Nyala Antelope (Chatcull Range)

☐ **HN 2665,** Llama (Chatcull Range)

☐ **HN 2666,** Badger (Chatcull Range)

☐ **HN 2667,** Ch. 'Bumblikite of Mansergh' Black Labrador (Chatcull Range)

☐ **HN 2668,** Puffins (Jefferson Sculptures)

☐ **HN 2669,** Snowy Owl (Jefferson Sculptures)

☐ **HN 2670,** Snowy Owl (Jefferson Sculptures)

☐ **HN 3500,** Black Throat Loon (Jefferson Sculptures)

☐ **HN 3501,** White Winged Crossbills (Jefferson Sculptures)

☐ **HN 3502,** King Eider (Jefferson Sculptures)

☐ **HN 3503,** Roseate Terns (Jefferson Sculptures)

☐ **HN 3504,** Golden-Crowned Kinglet (Jefferson Sculptures)

☐ **HN 3505,** Winter Wren (Jefferson Sculptures)

☐ **HN 3506,** Colorado Chipmunks (Jefferson Sculptures)

☐ **HN 3507,** Harbor Seals (Jefferson Sculptures)

☐ **HN 3508,** Snowshoe Hares (Jefferson Sculptures)

☐ **HN 3509,** Downy Woodpecker (Jefferson Sculptures)

☑ **HN 3510,** Fledgling Bluebird (Jefferson Sculptures)

☐ **HN 3511,** Chipping Sparrow (Jefferson Sculptures)

☐ **HN 3522,** The Leap

☐ **HN 3523,** Capricorn

☐ **HN 3524,** The Gift of Life

☐ **HN 3525,** Courtship

☐ **HN 3526,** Shadowplay

☐ **HN 3527,** Going Home

☐ **HN 3528,** Freedom

☐ **HN 3529,** Bright Water

☐ **HN 3530,** Clearwater

☐ **HN 3531,** Nestling Down Swan

☐ **HN 3532,** The Homecoming

☐ **HN 3533,** Patience

☐ **HN 3534,** Playful

☐ **HN 3535,** Courtship, rouge flambé

☐ **HN 3536,** The Gift of Life, rouge flambé

☐ **HN 6406,** Bulldog, Union Jack, large

☐ **HN 6407,** Bulldog, Union Jack, small

☐ **HN 6448,** Huntsman Fox (Jefferson Sculptures)

"K" NUMERICAL LISTINGS OF MINIATURE ANIMALS AND BIRD MODELS

☐ **K1,** Bulldog
☐ **K2,** Bull Pup
☐ **K3,** Sealyham
☐ **K4,** Sealyham
☐ **K5,** Airedale
☐ **K6,** Pekinese
☐ **K7,** Foxhound
☐ **K8,** Terrier
☐ **K9,** Cocker Spaniel
☐ **K10,** Scottish Terrier
☐ **K11,** Cairn
☐ **K12,** Cat
☐ **K13,** Alsatian
☐ **K14,** Bull Terrier
☐ **K15,** Chow Chow
☐ **K16,** Welsh Corgi
☐ **K17,** Dachshund
☐ **K18,** Scottish Terrier
☐ **K19,** St. Bernard
☐ **K20,** Penguins

☐ **K21,** Penguin
☐ **K22,** Penguins
☐ **K23,** Penguin
☐ **K24,** Penguin
☐ **K25,** Penguins
☐ **K26,** Mallard
☐ **K27,** Yellow-Throated Warbler
☐ **K28,** Cardinal Bird
☐ **K29,** Baltimore Oriole
☐ **K30,** Blue Bird
☐ **K31,** Bull Finch
☐ **K32,** Budgerigar
☐ **K33,** Golden Crested Wren
☐ **K34,** Magpie
☐ **K35,** Jay
☐ **K36,** Goldfinch
☐ **K37,** Hare, lying
☐ **K38,** Hare, sitting, ears down
☐ **K39,** Hare, sitting, ears up

ANIMAL AND BIRD MODELS

The following alphabetical listings include all the Royal Doulton Animal and Bird figurines in the HN and K series (the HN being full-sized figures and the K miniatures). Keep in mind when using these listings that titles were often similar or identical on a number of different figures. These can be distinguished by description (as given) or by the difference in serial numbers. Similarity in figures is not necessarily an indication of similarity in value.

Several animal figures, particularly dogs, are known to be in collections although they were not production models, such as three sizes of cows and three sizes of regular white poodles. Also several of the "Champion Dog Series" were produced in Flambé, but not for production. There were approximately twenty-five or more dog models done in Flambé. Royal Doulton also issued several items incorporating the K Series dogs, such as calendars, pen holders, and ashtrays. While few head plaques are listed in Royal Doulton references, it is felt that a full dozen were produced.

Royal Doulton character dogs, sundry animals, and birds are no longer being produced, except for the Images of Nature Series.

The difference in pricing (in "Character Dog" series) is due to the popularity of the breed with collectors. HN 2511 and HN 1100 are both considered by fanciers to be bull terriers. Most of the others are nondescript terriers, except for the Sealyhams.

The author has included, in this edition, the date that a number of the dog models were discontinued. About half the "Champion Series" including all large-size models were discontinued by 1959. If a collector has any additional information on the discontinuance of any animal and bird models, the author would be pleased to hear from him.

		Price Range	
☐ **Airedale**, lying, disc. 1959	K 5	125.00	140.00
☐ **Airedale**, 'Cotsford Topsail,' large, disc. 1960	HN 1022	400.00	500.00
☐ **Airedale**, 'Cotsford Topsail,' medium, disc. 1984	HN 1023	150.00	225.00
☐ **Airedale**, 'Cotsford Topsail,' small, disc. 1969	HN 1024	150.00	175.00
☐ **Airedale Terrier**	HN 988	500.00	600.00
☐ **Airedale Terrier**	HN 996	500.00	600.00
☐ **Alsatian**, disc. 1977	K 13	60.00	70.00
☐ **Alsatian**, pale gray	HN 112	400.00	500.00
☐ **Alsatian**, Head	HN 898	400.00	500.00
☐ **Alsatian**, sitting, large	HN 921	500.00	600.00
☐ **Alsatian**, 'Benign of Picardy,' large, disc. 1960	HN 1115	350.00	400.00
☐ **Alsatian**, 'Benign of Picardy,' medium, disc. 1984	HN 1116	125.00	150.00

		Price Range	
☐ **Alsatian**, 'Benign of Picardy,' small, disc. 1969	HN 1117	100.00	125.00
☐ **Alsatian**, sitting	HN 899	400.00	500.00
☐ **Alsatian**, on stand	HN 937	200.00	300.00
☐ **Alsatian**, on stand, sitting	HN 938	200.00	300.00
☐ **Alsatian**, sitting, miniature	HN 930	250.00	300.00
☐ **Alsatian**, sitting on lid of Lustre Bowl	HN 986	300.00	350.00
☐ **American Foxhound**, large, disc. 1955	HN 2524	375.00	450.00
☐ **American Foxhound**, medium, disc. 1960	HN 2525	275.00	325.00
☐ **American Foxhound**, small	HN 2526	200.00	250.00
☐ **American Great Dane**, large	HN 2601	600.00	700.00
☐ **American Great Dane**, medium	HN 2602	300.00	350.00
☐ **American Great Dane**, small	HN 2603	275.00	325.00
☐ **Antelope**, cream matte	HN 1172	450.00	550.00
☐ **Antelope**, natural	HN 1185	450.00	550.00
☐ **Antelope**, green matte	HN 1157	450.00	550.00
☐ **Ape**	HN 140	300.00	400.00
☐ **Ape**, sitting	HN 253	200.00	250.00
☐ **Ape**, character, with book, eyes open	HN 960	400.00	500.00
☐ **Ape**, character, with book, eyes closed	HN 961	400.00	500.00
☐ **Ape**, character, in Dunce's cap, reading book	HN 972	1500.00	1700.00
☐ **Apes**, two small	HN 254	300.00	350.00
☐ **Baby Birds**, two	HN 236	100.00	150.00
☐ **Badger** (Chatcull Range)	HN 2666	250.00	300.00
☐ **Baltimore Oriole**	HN 2542	300.00	450.00
☐ **Baltimore Oriole**	K 29	75.00	100.00
☐ **Baltimore Oriole**	HN 2612	150.00	200.00
☐ **Beagle**, puppy	HN 831	500.00	600.00
☐ **Bird**, white, miniature	HN 813	125.00	150.00
☐ **Bird**, on rock	HN 240	125.00	150.00
☐ **Bird**, on rock	HN 197	125.00	150.00
☐ **Bird**, on rock	HN 220	100.00	150.00
☐ **Bird**, with three chicks	HN 272	150.00	200.00
☐ **Bird**, with four chicks, green, blue and lemon	HN 216	150.00	200.00
☐ **Bird**, with four chicks, blue, pink and brown	HN 214	150.00	200.00
☐ **Bird**, with four chicks, gray, blue and lemon	HN 215	150.00	200.00
☐ **Bird**, on tree stump, small	HN 855	150.00	200.00
☐ **Bird**, on tree stump, small	HN 860	150.00	200.00
☐ **Bird**, on tree stump	HN 851	150.00	200.00
☐ **Birds**, two, orange	HN 275	150.00	200.00
☐ **Black-headed Gull**	HN 211	175.00	225.00
☐ **Black-headed Gull**	HN 212	175.00	225.00

Price Range

☐ **Black Labrador,** 'Bumblikite of Mansergh,' disc. 1984	HN 2667	65.00	75.00
☐ **Bloodhound**	HN 176	500.00	600.00
☐ **Blue Bird**	HN 2614	150.00	200.00
☐ **Blue Bird**	K 30	75.00	100.00
☐ **Blue Bird**	HN 282	125.00	150.00
☐ **Blue Bird**	HN 2543	125.00	150.00
☐ **Blue Bird,** on rock	HN 269	125.00	150.00
☐ **Blue Tit,** on rock	HN 137	200.00	250.00
☐ **Blue Tit,** on bough with blossom	HN 1004	150.00	200.00
☐ **Boxer,** Ch. 'Warlord of Mazelaine,' disc. 1984	HN 2643	65.00	75.00
☐ **Brown Bear,** Titanian ware	HN 170	400.00	500.00
☐ **Brown Bear,** standing	HN 955	250.00	300.00
☐ **Brown Bears,** large and small	HN 939	400.00	500.00
☐ **Brown Bears,** large and small, light brown	HN 940	400.00	500.00
☐ **Budgerigars,** pair	HN 2547	125.00	150.00
☐ **Budgerigar**	HN 854	150.00	200.00
☐ **Budgerigar**	K 32	75.00	100.00
☐ **Budgerigar**	HN 163	150.00	200.00
☐ **Budgerigar,** on stand, green and yellow	HN 199	200.00	250.00
☐ **Buffalo**	HN 172	750.00	850.00
☐ **Buffalo,** natural	HN 1175	500.00	600.00
☐ **Buffalo,** green matte	HN 1148	500.00	600.00
☐ **Buffalo,** cream	HN 1163	500.00	600.00
☐ **Bulldog,** pup, disc. 1977	K 2	70.00	80.00
☐ **Bulldog,** disc. 1977	K 1	70.00	80.00
☐ **Bulldog,** brown, large	HN 948	600.00	700.00
☐ **Bulldog,** sitting on lid of Lustre Bowl	HN 987	400.00	500.00
☐ **Bulldog,** sitting	HN 129	500.00	600.00
☐ **Bulldog,** sitting	HN 881	500.00	600.00
☐ **Bulldog,** brindle, large, disc. 1960	HN 1042	525.00	575.00
☐ **Bulldog,** brindle, medium, disc. 1960	HN 1043	300.00	350.00
☐ **Bulldog,** brindle, small, disc. 1969	HN 1044	175.00	225.00
☐ **Bulldog,** brown and white, large, disc. 1960	HN 1045	525.00	575.00
☐ **Bulldog,** brown and white, medium, disc. 1960	HN 1046	250.00	350.00
☐ **Bulldog,** brown and white, small, disc. 1984	HN 1047	150.00	250.00
☐ **Bulldog,** 'Old Bill' with helmet and haversack	HN 146	500.00	600.00
☐ **Bulldog,** 'Old Bill' with tammy and haversack	HN 153	500.00	600.00

Bulldog, Brindle, HN 1042, 525.00–575.00

		Price Range	
☐ **Bulldog**, Union Jack, large	HN 6406	475.00	525.00
☐ **Bulldog**, Union Jack, medium	—	250.00	350.00
☐ **Bulldog**, Union Jack, small	HN 6407	175.00	225.00
☐ **Bulldog**, Union Jack w/Derby, large	HN	1750.00	2000.00
☐ **Bulldog**, Union Jack w/Derby, small	HN	1200.00	1500.00
☐ **Bulldog**, Union Jack w/cap, large	HN	1000.00	1250.00
☐ **Bulldog**, Union Jack w/cap, small	HN	850.00	950.00
☐ **Bulldog**, white, large, disc. 1960	HN 1072	675.00	775.00
☐ **Bulldog**, white, medium, disc. 1960 ..	HN 1073	350.00	450.00
☐ **Bulldog**, white, small, disc. 1984	HN 1074	200.00	275.00
☐ **Bull Finch**	K 31	75.00	100.00
☐ **Bull Finch**	HN 2616	125.00	175.00
☐ **Bull Finch**	HN 2551	125.00	175.00
☐ **Bull Terrier**, 'Bokus Brock,' large	HN 1142	1200.00	1400.00

		Price Range	
☐ **Bull Terrier,** 'Bokus Brock,' medium, disc. 1960	HN 1143	700.00	800.00
☐ **Bull Terrier,** 'Bokus Brock,' small	HN 1144	600.00	700.00
☐ **Bull Terrier,** Staffordshire, white, large	HN 1131	1200.00	1400.00
☐ **Bull Terrier,** Staffordshire, white, medium	HN 1132	350.00	450.00
☐ **Bull Terrier,** Staffordshire, white, small	HN 1133	600.00	700.00
☐ **Bull Terrier,** Staffordshire, white, lying	K 14	150.00	200.00
☐ **Butterfly,** blue and gold	HN 162	150.00	200.00
☐ **Butterfly,** Peacock	HN 2604	200.00	300.00
☐ **Butterfly,** Camberwell Beauty	HN 2605	200.00	300.00
☐ **Butterfly,** Swallowtail	HN 2606	200.00	300.00
☐ **Butterfly,** Red Admiral	HN 2607	200.00	300.00
☐ **Butterfly,** Copper	HN 2608	200.00	300.00
☐ **Butterfly,** Tortoiseshell	HN 2609	200.00	300.00
☐ **Cairn,** disc. 1977	K 11	50.00	60.00
☐ **Cairn,** black, large	HN 1104	450.00	500.00
☐ **Cairn,** black, large, earthenware	HN 1107	450.00	500.00
☐ **Cairn,** black, medium	HN 1105	200.00	250.00
☐ **Cairn,** black, small	HN 1106	115.00	140.00
☐ **Cairn,** 'Charming Eyes,' large, disc. 1955	HN 1033	450.00	500.00
☐ **Cairn,** 'Charming Eyes,' medium, disc. 1960	HN 1034	200.00	250.00
☐ **Cairn,** 'Charming Eyes,' small, disc. 1984	HN 1035	100.00	125.00
☐ **Calf,** sleeping, green matte	HN 1146	400.00	500.00
☐ **Calf,** standing, green matte	HN 1147	400.00	500.00
☐ **Calf,** sleeping, cream matte	HN 1161	400.00	500.00
☐ **Calf,** standing, cream matte	HN 1162	400.00	500.00
☐ **Calf,** sleeping, natural	HN 1173	400.00	500.00
☐ **Calf,** standing, natural	HN 1174	400.00	500.00
☐ **Cardinal Bird**	K 28	75.00	100.00
☐ **Cardinal Bird**	HN 2554	150.00	200.00
☐ **Cardinal Bird**	HN 2615	150.00	200.00
☐ **Cat**	K 12	80.00	90.00
☐ **Cat,** Persian, black and white	HN 999	200.00	250.00
☐ **Cat,** Persian, white	HN 2539	150.00	175.00
☐ **Cat,** Siamese, standing (Chatcull Range)	HN 2660	60.00	70.00
☐ **Cat,** Siamese, sitting (Chatcull Range)	HN 2655	60.00	70.00
☐ **Cat,** Siamese, lying (Chatcull Range)	HN 2662	60.00	70.00
☐ **Cat,** Tortoiseshell	HN 204	600.00	700.00
☐ **Cat,** two	HN 234	350.00	400.00
☐ **Cat**	HN 109	250.00	350.00
☐ **Cat,** white	HN 120	300.00	400.00

		Price Range	
□ Cat, Tabby	HN 967	350.00	450.00
□ Cat, Tabby, asleep	HN 227	400.00	500.00
□ Cat, black and white	HN 210	300.00	400.00
□ Cat, black and white	HN 221	350.00	450.00
□ Cat, 'Lucky,' miniature, white	HN 819	225.00	275.00
□ Cat, 'Lucky,' black and white	HN 818	225.00	275.00
□ Cat, 'Lucky,' ashtray	HN 971	200.00	300.00
□ Cat, on pillar, tortoiseshell	HN 203	600.00	700.00
□ Cat, tortoiseshell	HN 204	600.00	700.00
□ Cat and Mouse, cat black and white	HN 244	500.00	600.00
□ Cat and Mouse, cat black	HN 245	500.00	600.00
□ Cat and Mouse, cat black	HN 202	650.00	750.00
□ Cat and Mouse, cat tabby	HN 201	650.00	750.00
□ Cat, asleep on cushion	HN 993	800.00	900.00
□ Cerval	HN 2500	150.00	250.00
□ Chaffinch	HN 2611	125.00	175.00
□ Chaffinch, on its back	HN 143	125.00	150.00
□ Chaffinch	HN 2550	125.00	175.00
□ Character Cat, tortoiseshell	HN 827	225.00	275.00
□ Character Cat, tabby	HN 828	225.00	275.00
□ Character Cat, black and white	HN 829	225.00	275.00
□ Character Cat	HN 154	250.00	350.00
□ Character Dog, running with ball, disc. 1984	HN 1097	35.00	50.00
□ Character Dog, Sealyham, lying on back, disc. 1959	HN 1098	125.00	150.00
□ Character Dog, yawning, disc. 1984 ..	HN 1099	35.00	50.00
□ Character Dog, Bull Terrier, walking, disc. 1959	HN 1100	125.00	150.00
□ Character Dog, lying down, disc. 1959	HN 1101	125.00	150.00
□ Character Dog, with ball, disc. 1984 ...	HN 1103	35.00	50.00
□ Character Dog, with plate, disc. 1984	HN 1158	35.00	50.00
□ Character Dog, with bone, disc. 1984	HN 1159	35.00	50.00
□ Character Dog, Sealyham sitting, disc. 1959	HN 2508	125.00	150.00
□ Character Dog, Sealyham standing, disc. 1959	HN 2509	125.00	150.00
□ Character Dog, running, disc. 1959 ..	HN 2510	125.00	175.00
□ Character Dog, standing, disc. 1959	HN 2511	130.00	160.00
□ Character Dog, with slipper, disc. 1984	HN 2654	35.00	50.00
□ Character Fox, with stolen Goose, green cloak and hat	HN 1096	750.00	850.00
□ Character Fox, with stolen Goose, red cloak and hat	HN 1102	700.00	800.00
□ Character Hare	HN 922	150.00	200.00
□ Character Monkey, green jacket	HN 182	350.00	400.00
□ Character Monkey, blue jacket	HN 183	350.00	400.00
□ Character Mouse	HN 207	300.00	350.00

		Price Range	
☐ **Character Mouse,** blue coat	HN 226	350.00	400.00
☐ **Character Mouse,** yellow coat	HN 228	350.00	400.00
☐ **Character Mouse,** with basket of babies	HN 237	375.00	425.00
☐ **Character Pig**	HN 246	200.00	250.00
☐ **Character Pigs,** in Clown costume	HN 892	350.00	450.00
☐ **Character Pigs,** in Clown costume	HN 893	350.00	450.00
☐ **Character Pigs,** in Clown costume	HN 894	350.00	450.00
☐ **Character Pigs,** in Clown costume	HN 895	350.00	450.00
☐ **Character Pigs,** in Clown costume	HN 896	350.00	450.00
☐ **Character Pigs,** in Clown costume	HN 897	350.00	450.00
☐ **Character Pigs**	HN 902	150.00	200.00
☐ **Character Pigs**	HN 903	150.00	200.00
☐ **Character Toucan**	HN 208	125.00	150.00
☐ **Chestnut Mare with Foal,** large	HN 2522	400.00	500.00
☐ **Chicks,** three	HN 280	150.00	200.00
☐ **Chow Chow,** disc. 1977	K 15	50.00	60.00
☐ **Chow,** large	HN 2628	500.00	600.00
☐ **Chow,** medium	HN 2629	250.00	300.00
☐ **Chow,** small	HN 2630	250.00	300.00
☐ **Chow,** on stand, lighter brown	HN 838	400.00	450.00
☐ **Chow,** on stand, brown	HN 837	400.00	450.00
☐ **Chow,** on stand, white and gray	HN 839	400.00	450.00
☐ **Cock Pheasant**	HN 2632	425.00	500.00
☐ **Cockatoo,** black and orange	HN 884	150.00	200.00
☐ **Cockatoo,** pink, purple, and orange ..	HN 885	150.00	200.00
☐ **Cockatoo,** red, blue, and orange	HN 886	150.00	200.00
☐ **Cockatoo,** pale blue and yellow	HN 888	150.00	200.00
☐ **Cockerel,** white	HN 878	150.00	200.00
☐ **Cockerel,** blue and green	HN 879	150.00	200.00
☐ **Cockerel,** brown and orange	HN 880	150.00	200.00
☐ **Cockerel,** sitting	HN 267	125.00	175.00
☐ **Cockerel,** crowing	HN 164	125.00	175.00
☐ **Cockerel,** crowing	HN 184	125.00	175.00
☐ **Cockerel,** crouching	HN 178	150.00	200.00
☐ **Cockerel,** crouching	HN 180	150.00	200.00
☐ **Cockerel,** on stand	HN 111	125.00	175.00
☐ **Cockerel,** on stand	HN 157	125.00	175.00
☐ **Cocker Spaniel**	K 9	50.00	60.00
☐ **Cocker Spaniel,** black and white, large, disc. 1960	HN 1108	250.00	300.00
☐ **Cocker Spaniel,** black and white, medium, disc. 1984	HN 1109	60.00	70.00
☐ **Cocker Spaniel,** black and white, small, disc. 1969	HN 1078	100.00	125.00
☐ **Cocker Spaniel,** golden brown, large, disc. 1960	HN 1186	300.00	400.00

Price Range

☐ **Cocker Spaniel,** golden brown, medium, disc. 1984	HN 1187	60.00	70.00
☐ **Cocker Spaniel,** golden brown, small, disc. 1969	HN 1188	115.00	140.00
☐ **Cocker Spaniel,** liver and white, large, disc. 1960	HN 1002	300.00	350.00
☐ **Cocker Spaniel,** liver and white, large	HN 1134	350.00	400.00
☐ **Cocker Spaniel,** liver and white, medium	HN 1135	60.00	70.00
☐ **Cocker Spaniel,** liver and white, small	HN 1136	100.00	135.00
☐ **Cocker Spaniel,** liver and white, small, disc. 1969	HN 1037	75.00	100.00
☐ **Cocker Spaniel,** liver and white, medium, disc. 1984	HN 1036	75.00	100.00
☐ **Cocker Spaniel,** 'Lucky Star of Ware,' large, disc. 1960	HN 1000	300.00	350.00
☐ **Cocker Spaniel,** 'Lucky Star of Ware,' medium, disc. 1984	HN 1020	60.00	70.00
☐ **Cocker Spaniel,** 'Lucky Star of Ware,' small, disc. 1969	HN 1021	115.00	140.00
☐ **Cocker Spaniels,** sleeping (pair)	HN 2590	50.00	75.00
☐ **Cocker Spaniel and Hare,** liver and white, medium	HN 1063	250.00	350.00
☐ **Cocker Spaniel andHare,** liver and white, small	HN 1064	200.00	250.00
☐ **Cocker Spaniel and Pheasant,** large, liver and white, disc. 1969	HN 1001	325.00	375.00
☐ **Cocker Spaniel and Pheasant,** large, black and white, disc. 1969	HN 1137	350.00	400.00
☐ **Cocker Spaniel and Pheasant,** medium, liver and white, disc. 1984	HN 1028	100.00	125.00
☐ **Cocker Spaniel and Pheasant,** medium, black and white, disc. 1984	HN 1138	100.00	125.00
☐ **Cocker Spaniel and Pheasant,** small, liver and white, disc. 1969	HN 1029	150.00	200.00
☐ **Cocker Spaniel and Pheasant,** small, black and white, disc. 1969	HN 1062	125.00	150.00
☐ **Cocker Spaniel and Pheasant,** small	HN 2600	125.00	150.00
☐ **Cockerel,** sitting	HN 124	150.00	200.00
☐ **Collie,** 'Ashstead Applause,' large, disc. 1960	HN 1057	350.00	450.00
☐ **Collie,** 'Ashstead Applause,' medium, disc. 1984	HN 1058	75.00	125.00
☐ **Collie,** 'Ashstead Applause,' small, disc. 1969	HN 1059	100.00	125.00
☐ **Collie,** brown	HN 976	450.00	550.00
☐ **Collie,** silver gray	HN 975	450.00	550.00

Cocker Spaniel and Pheasant, HN 1028, 100.00–125.00

		Price Range	
☐ Collie, sable	HN 105	400.00	600.00
☐ Collie, sable and white	HN 106	450.00	600.00
☐ Dachshund, disc. 1977	K 17	50.00	60.00
☐ Dachshund	HN 970	300.00	400.00
☐ Dachshund, disc. 1955	HN 1139	350.00	400.00
☐ Dachshund, disc. 1969	HN 1140	200.00	250.00
☐ Dachshund, disc. 1969	HN 1141	135.00	165.00
☐ Dachshund, 'Shrewd Saint,' large, disc. 1955	HN 1127	350.00	400.00
☐ Dachshund, 'Shrewd Saint,' medium, disc. 1984	HM 1128	70.00	80.00
☐ Dachshund, 'Shrewd Saint,' small, disc. 1969	HN 1129	140.00	175.00
☐ Dalmatian, 'Goworth Victor,' large, disc. 1955	HN 1111	375.00	450.00
☐ Dalmatian, 'Goworth Victor,' medium, disc. 1984	HN 1113	70.00	80.00

Collie, HN 1057, 350.00–450.00

		Price Range	
☐ **Dalmatian**, 'Goworth Victor,' small, disc. 1969	HN 1114	135.00	165.00
☐ **Deer**, green	HN 2502	150.00	250.00
☐ **Deer**, white	HN 2503	150.00	250.00
☐ **Doberman Pinscher**, Ch. 'Rancho Dobe's Storm,' disc. 1984	HN 2645	80.00	100.00
☐ **Donkey**, small, green matte	HN 1149	400.00	500.00
☐ **Donkey**, large, green matte	HN 1155	400.00	500.00
☐ **Donkey**, large, natural	HN 1183	400.00	500.00
☐ **Donkey**, small, cream matte	HN 1164	400.00	500.00
☐ **Donkey**, small, natural	HN 1176	400.00	500.00
☐ **Donkey**, large, cream matte	HN 1170	400.00	500.00
☐ **Double Doves**	HN 122	500.00	600.00
☐ **Drake**, Mallard, large	HN 249	200.00	300.00
☐ **Drake**, Mallard, small	HN 2572	100.00	150.00
☐ **Drake**, Mallard, large	HN 956	200.00	250.00
☐ **Drake**, Mallard	HN 2591	125.00	150.00
☐ **Drake**, Mallard	K 26	50.00	75.00
☐ **Drake**, Mallard	HN 2555	125.00	175.00

Doberman Pinscher, HN 2645, 80.00–100.00

		Price Range	
☐ **Drake,** Mallard on rocks, small	HN 853	175.00	250.00
☐ **Drake,** miniature, malachite and purple	HN 807	100.00	150.00
☐ **Drake,** miniature, white	HN 806	150.00	200.00
☐ **Drake,** large	HN 252	150.00	200.00
☐ **Drake**	HN 1198	150.00	200.00
☐ **Drake**	HN 2647	125.00	175.00
☐ **Drake,** large	HN 248	200.00	250.00
☐ **Drake,** lying	HN 299	125.00	175.00
☐ **Drake,** on rock	HN 132	125.00	175.00
☐ **Drake,** malachite head	HN 114	125.00	175.00
☐ **Drake,** blue head	HN 115	125.00	175.00
☐ **Drake,** bright colors overall	HN 116	125.00	175.00
☐ **Drakes,** two	HN 148	150.00	200.00
☐ **Duck**	HN 150	125.00	175.00
☐ **Duck**	HN 271	125.00	175.00
☐ **Duck**	HN 977	150.00	200.00
☐ **Duck**	HN 1192	150.00	200.00
☐ **Duck,** sitting	HN 298	125.00	175.00

		Price Range	
☐ **Duck and Ladybird**	HN 849	175.00	225.00
☐ **Duck,** standing on rock	HN 850	150.00	200.00
☐ **Duck,** Character, orange	HN 973	150.00	200.00
☐ **Duck,** Character, lemon yellow	HN 974	150.00	200.00
☐ **Ducks,** two	HN 239	150.00	200.00
☐ **Ducks,** quacking	HN 863–		
	HN 865	150.00	200.00
☐ **Ducks,** Character	HN 840–		
	HN 845	125.00	150.00
☐ **Duckling,** yellow and brown	HN 188	100.00	150.00
☐ **Duckling,** blue and yellow	HN 189	100.00	150.00
☐ **Duckling,** green and blue	HN 190	100.00	150.00
☐ **Duckling**	HN 235	125.00	150.00
☐ **Ducklings,** two, black and white	HN 205	150.00	200.00
☐ **Ducklings,** two, brown and white	HN 206	150.00	200.00
☐ **Eagle,** brown and gold	HN 241	500.00	600.00
☐ **Eagle,** lighter color, white head and neck	HN 242	500.00	600.00
☐ **Elephant**	HN 181	275.00	325.00
☐ **Elephant**	HN 180	350.00	450.00
☐ **Elephant**	HN 1121–		
	HN 1122	500.00	600.00
☐ **Elephant,** large	HN 1124	500.00	600.00
☐ **Elephant,** medium	HN 1123	400.00	500.00
☐ **Elephant,** fighting, large, earthenware	HN 1120	1000.00	1500.00
☐ **Elephant,** fighting	HN 2640	1900.00	
☐ **Elephant,** baby	HN 949	350.00	450.00
☐ **Elephant,** baby	HN 950–		
	HN 952	300.00	400.00
☐ **Elephant,** large, black	HN 941	450.00	550.00
☐ **Elephant,** large, brown, and gray	HN 966	400.00	500.00
☐ **Elephant,** Asiatic	HN 2506	300.00	400.00
☐ **Elephant**	HN 2644	80.00	95.00
☐ **Elephant,** trunk up	HN 891	500.00	600.00
☐ **Elephant,** fighting ....:......	HN 2640	1450.00	1600.00
☐ **English St. Bernard,** sitting	HN 231	500.00	600.00
☐ **English Setter,** liver and white, large	HN 2620	400.00	450.00
☐ **English Setter,** liver and white, medium	HN 2621	200.00	250.00
☐ **English Setter,** liver and white, small	HN 2622	150.00	175.00
☐ **English Setter,** 'Maesydd Mustard,' large, disc. 1960	HN 1049	350.00	450.00
☐ **English Setter,** 'Maesydd Mustard,' medium, disc. 1984	HN 1050	75.00	100.00
☐ **English Setter,** 'Maesydd Mustard,' small, disc. 1969	HN 1051	125.00	150.00

Foxhound, K 7, 60.00–75.00

		Price Range	
☐ **English Setter and Pheasant,** on base, large, disc. 1984	HN 2529	375.00	395.00
☐ **English Setter and Pheasant**	HN 2599	300.00	400.00
☐ **Falcon,** on rock	HN 139	250.00	350.00
☐ **Fox**	HN 130	175.00	225.00
☐ **Fox,** large	HN 1130	400.00	500.00
☐ **Fox,** sitting	HN 963	200.00	300.00
☐ **Fox,** sitting	HN 2527	275.00	375.00
☐ **Fox,** lying	HN 978	150.00	200.00
☐ **Fox,** sitting	HN 2634	1200.00	
☐ **Fox,** on pedestal	HN 994	200.00	300.00
☐ **Fox,** on rock	HN 147	200.00	300.00
☐ **Fox,** red frock coat	HN 100	1000.00	1350.00
☐ **Fox,** sitting	HN 866	400.00	500.00
☐ **Foxes,** two	HN 117	150.00	250.00
☐ **Foxes,** two	HN 179	200.00	250.00
☐ **Foxes,** two, brown	HN 920	300.00	400.00
☐ **Foxes,** two, gray and brown	HN 925	300.00	400.00
☐ **Foxes,** two, miniature	HN 926	300.00	400.00
☐ **Four Thrush Chicks**	HN 161	150.00	200.00
☐ **Four Baby Birds**	HN 171	200.00	250.00
☐ **Foxhound,** disc. 1977	K 7	60.00	75.00
☐ **Foxhound,** seated	HN 166	450.00	550.00

	Date	Price Range	
☐ Foxhound, 'English Tring Rattler,' large, disc. 1955	HN 1025	400.00	450.00
☐ Foxhound, 'English Tring Rattler,' medium, disc. 1960	HN 1026	250.00	300.00
☐ Foxhound, 'English Tring Rattler,' small, disc. 1956	HN 1027	215.00	240.00
☐ Fox Terrier, white and brown	HN 900	350.00	450.00
☐ Fox Terrier, white and black	HN 901	350.00	450.00
☐ Fox Terrier	HN 942	300.00	450.00
☐ Fox Terrier	HN 943	300.00	450.00
☐ Fox Terrier	HN 944	300.00	450.00
☐ Fox Terrier, startler	HN 945	300.00	450.00
☐ Fox Terrier, standing	HN 909	300.00	400.00
☐ Fox Terrier, sitting	HN 910	300.00	400.00
☐ Fox Terrier, standing	HN 923	300.00	400.00
☐ Fox Terrier, sitting, large	HN 924	300.00	400.00
☐ Fox Terrier, Ch. 'Crackley Startler,' large	HN 1007	400.00	500.00
☐ Fox Terrier, Ch. 'Crackley,' medium	HN 1013	200.00	250.00
☐ Fox Terrier, Ch. 'Crackley Startler,' small	HN 1014	175.00	225.00
☐ Fox Terrier, smooth-haired, large	HN 1068	450.00	550.00
☐ Fox Terrier, smooth-haired, medium, disc. 1960	HN 1069	250.00	300.00
☐ Fox Terrier, smooth-haired, small	HN 1070	185.00	225.00
☐ Fox Terrier, Ch. 'Chosen Dan of Notts,' smooth, large	HN 2512	400.00	500.00
☐ Fox Terrier, Ch. 'Chosen Dan of Notts,' smooth, medium, disc. 1960	HN 2513	250.00	300.00
☐ Fox Terrier, Ch. 'Chosen Dan of Notts,' smooth, small	HN 2514	200.00	250.00
☐ French Poodle, medium, disc. 1984	HN 2631	75.00	100.00
☐ Frog, small	HN 905	350.00	450.00
☐ Gannet	HN 1197	150.00	200.00
☐ Gordon Setter, large, disc. 1955	HN 1079	800.00	1000.00
☐ Gordon Setter, medium, disc. 1955	HN 1080	400.00	500.00
☐ Gordon Setter, small, disc. 1960	HN 1081	250.00	350.00
☐ Great Crested Grebe	HN 175	350.00	450.00
☐ Great Dane, Ch. 'Rebeller of Ouborough,' large	HN 2560	500.00	600.00
☐ Great Dane, Ch. 'Rebeller of Ouborough,' medium, disc. 1960	HN 2561	300.00	350.00
☐ Great Dane, Ch. 'Rebeller of Ouborough,' small	HN 2662	250.00	300.00
☐ Great Dane, American, large, disc. 1955	HN 2601	600.00	700.00

Price Range

☐ **Great Dane**, American, medium, disc. 1960	HN 2602	300.00	350.00
☐ **Great Dane**, American, small	HN 2603	275.00	325.00
☐ **Green Bird**	HN 274	100.00	150.00
☐ **Green Bird,** on rock	HN 279	125.00	175.00
☐ **Green Bird,** two	HN 178	150.00	200.00
☐ **Greyhound,** brown, brindle, large, disc. 1955	HN 1065	550.00	650.00
☐ **Greyhound,** brown, brindle, medium, disc. 1955	HN 1066	400.00	450.00
☐ **Greyhound,** brown, brindle, small, disc. 1960	HN 1067	200.00	250.00
☐ **Greyhound,** black and white, large, disc. 1956	HN 1075	550.00	650.00
☐ **Greyhound,** black and white, medium, disc. 1955	HN 1076	400.00	450.00
☐ **Greyhound,** black and white, small, disc. 1955	HN 1077	200.00	250.00
☐ **Greyhound,** black and white, seated	HN 889	700.00	900.00
☐ **Greyhound,** brown, seated	HN 890	700.00	900.00
☐ **Grouse**	HN 2619	125.00	175.00
☐ **Gude Gray Mare,** no foal, large	HN 2568	500.00	600.00
☐ **Gude Gray Mare,** no foal, medium	HN 2569	400.00	450.00
☐ **Gude Gray Mare,** no foal, small	HN 2570	300.00	400.00
☐ **Gude Gray Mare,** with foal, large	HN 2519	500.00	550.00
☐ **Gude Gray Mare,** with foal, medium	HN 2532	300.00	350.00
☐ **Gude Gray Mare,** with foal, small	HN 2533	350.00	450.00
☐ **Guinea Fowl**	HN 125	150.00	200.00
☐ **Guinea Fowl**	HN 247	300.00	350.00
☐ **Hare,** lying	K 37	50.00	60.00
☐ **Hare,** lying, small	HN 2594	100.00	150.00
☐ **Hare,** sitting, ears down	K 38	100.00	150.00
☐ **Hare,** sitting, ears up	K 39	100.00	150.00
☐ **Hare**	HN 2592– HN 2593	40.00	60.00
☐ **Hare,** lying, small	HN 2594	35.00	50.00
☐ **Hare,** lying	HN 979	150.00	200.00
☐ **Hare,** lying, white	HN 984	175.00	225.00
☐ **Hare,** lying, gray	HN 985	175.00	225.00
☐ **Hare,** lying	HN 1071	100.00	150.00
☐ **Hare,** crouching	HN 107	150.00	200.00
☐ **Hare,** crouching	HN 142	150.00	200.00
☐ **Hare,** crouching	HN 126	125.00	175.00
☐ **Hare,** in red coat	HN 101	450.00	550.00
☐ **Hare,** in white coat	HN 102	450.00	550.00
☐ **Hare and Two Leverets**	HN 1009	300.00	350.00
☐ **Heron**	HN 250	175.00	225.00
☐ **Heron**	HN 251	175.00	225.00

	Date	Price Range	
☐ Horse, green matte	HN 1152	450.00	550.00
☐ Horse, natural	HN 1180	450.00	550.00
☐ Horse, without boy, dapple gray	HN 2578	250.00	300.00
☐ Huntsman Fox	HN 6448	75.00	100.00
☐ Indian Rummer Drake	HN 2636	125.00	175.00
☐ Irish Setter, large, disc. 1960	HN 1054	400.00	500.00
☐ Irish Setter, medium, disc. 1984	HN 1055	135.00	150.00
☐ Irish Setter, small, disc. 1969	HN 1056	125.00	150.00
☐ Jumping Goat, green matte	HN 1154	400.00	500.00
☐ Jumping Goat, cream matte	HN 1169	400.00	500.00
☐ Jumping Goat, natural	HN 1182	400.00	500.00
☐ Kingfisher, small	HN 2573	75.00	100.00
☐ Kingfisher	HN 268	125.00	150.00
☐ Kingfisher	HN 131	125.00	150.00
☐ Kingfisher	HN 165	125.00	150.00
☐ Kingfisher	HN 2540–		
	HN 2541	125.00	150.00
☐ Kingfisher	HN 2573	125.00	150.00
☐ Kingfisher, on rock	HN 152	125.00	150.00
☐ Kingfisher, on rock	HN 224	150.00	200.00
☐ Kingfisher, on rock	HN 858	150.00	200.00
☐ Kingfisher, on tree stump	HN 875	175.00	225.00
☐ Kingfisher, on stand with primroses	HN 862A	200.00	250.00
☐ Kingfisher, on stand with Kingcups	HN 862B	200.00	250.00
☐ Kitten	HN 233	300.00	350.00
☐ Kitten, lying on back, brown	HN 2579	40.00	60.00
☐ Kitten, sitting licking hind paw	HN 2580	40.00	60.00
☐ Kitten, sleeping	HN 2581	40.00	60.00
☐ Kitten, sitting licking front paw	HN 2583	40.00	60.00
☐ Kitten, sitting, surprised	HN 2584	40.00	60.00
☐ Kittens, miniature	HN 820–		
	HN 825	200.00	250.00
☐ Lamb, green	HN 2504	150.00	200.00
☐ Lamb, white	HN 2505	150.00	200.00
☐ Lambs	HN 2595–		
	HN 2598	150.00	200.00
☐ Langur Monkey (Chatcull Range)	HN 2657	150.00	200.00
☐ Leopard, on Rock	HN 2638	1800.00	2300.00
☐ Lion, on Rock	HN 2641	1800.00	2300.00
☐ Llama (Chatcull Range)	HN 2665	150.00	200.00
☐ Leopard	HN 1094	400.00	500.00
☐ Leopard, on rock	HN 919	400.00	500.00
☐ Lion, large	HN 1085	500.00	600.00
☐ Lion, large	HN 1112	700.00	800.00
☐ Lion, medium	HN 1086	400.00	500.00
☐ Lion, sitting	HN 223	800.00	900.00
☐ Lion, on rock, large, earthenware	HN 1119	700.00	800.00
☐ Lion, on alabaster base	HN 1125	500.00	600.00

		Price Range	
☐ Llama (Chatcull Range)	HN 2665	175.00	225.00
☐ Lynx	HN 2501	200.00	250.00
☐ Magpie	K 34	75.00	100.00
☐ Mallard	HN 2556	200.00	225.00
☐ Mallard	HN 2544	125.00	150.00
☐ Mallard	HN 2556	125.00	150.00
☐ Mallard, large	HN 2635	125.00	150.00
☐ Mallard	HN 1191	200.00	250.00
☐ Merely a Minor, gray, small	HN 2567	300.00	350.00
☐ Merely a Minor, brown, small	HN 2571	250.00	300.00
☐ Merely a Minor, gray, medium	HN 2538	400.00	450.00
☐ Merely a Minor, gray, large	HN 2531	500.00	600.00
☐ Monkey	HN 118	150.00	200.00
☐ Monkey, listening	HN 156	200.00	250.00
☐ Monkeys, two	HN 883	275.00	325.00
☐ Moufflon, standing, green	HN 1145	450.00	500.00
☐ Moufflon, standing, cream matte	HN 1160	450.00	500.00
☐ Moufflon, lying, cream matte	HN 1168	450.00	500.00
☐ Moufflon, lying, green matte	HN 1153	450.00	500.00
☐ Moufllon, lying, natural	HN 1181	450.00	500.00
☐ Moufflon, standing, natural	HN 1179	450.00	500.00
☐ Mountain Sheep (Chatcull Range)	HN 2661	200.00	250.00
☐ Owl, character, check shawl, ermine collar	HN 187	1000.00	1500.00
☐ Owl, 'Wise Old,' red cloak, ermine collar	HN 173	1500.00	2000.00
☐ Owl	HN 155	200.00	250.00
☐ Owl	HN 169	200.00	250.00
☐ Owl and Young	HN 160	300.00	350.00
☐ Owl, in boat	HN 222	400.00	500.00
☐ Parrot, on rock	HN 185	250.00	300.00
☐ Parrot, baby	HN 877	150.00	200.00
☐ Parrot, baby, blue and purple	HN 191	150.00	200.00
☐ Parrot, baby, red and orange	HN 192	150.00	200.00
☐ Parrot, baby, decorated on enamel flowers	HN 200	300.00	350.00
☐ Peacock	HN 2577	150.00	175.00
☐ Pekinese, disc. 1977	K 6	50.00	60.00
☐ Pekinese, 'Biddee of Ifield,' extra large	HN 1010	425.00	475.00
☐ Pekinese, 'Biddee of Ifield,' large, disc. 1955	HN 1011	200.00	250.00
☐ Pekinese, 'Biddie of Ifield,' small, disc. 1984	HN 1012	60.00	80.00
☐ Pekinese, sitting, large	HN 1039	350.00	400.00
☐ Pekinese, sitting, small	HN 1040	250.00	275.00
☐ Pekinese, dark coloring	HN 1003	250.00	300.00
☐ Pekinese Puppy, sitting	HN 832	400.00	500.00
☐ Pekinese, brown	HN 995	300.00	350.00

		Price Range	
☐ Pekinese	HN 127	250.00	300.00
☐ Pekinese, two	HN 927	350.00	400.00
☐ Pelican	HN 123	125.00	150.00
☐ Penguin	HN 1199	175.00	225.00
☐ Penguin	HN 1190	300.00	400.00
☐ Penguin Chick	HN 946	275.00	325.00
☐ Penguin Chick	HN 947	275.00	325.00
☐ Penguin and Baby	HN 998	250.00	300.00
☐ Penguin, on rocks	HN 856	150.00	200.00
☐ Penguin, standing on rocks	HN 852	175.00	225.00
☐ Penguin	HN 296	150.00	200.00
☐ Penguin, King	HN 1189	350.00	450.00
☐ Penguin and Young	HN 297	200.00	250.00
☐ Penguin, with Young	HN 198	400.00	450.00
☐ Penguins, double	HN 103	300.00	400.00
☐ Penguins, double	HN 133	200.00	300.00
☐ Penguin, single	HN 104	200.00	300.00
☐ Penguin, single	HN 113	125.00	175.00
☐ Penguin, single	HN 134	150.00	200.00
☐ Penguin, large	HN 882	300.00	400.00
☐ Penguin, large	HN 2633	400.00	500.00
☐ Penguins and Puffins, character, miniature	HN 356– HN 266	150.00	200.00
☐ Penguins and Puffins, character, miniature	HN 283– HN 293	175.00	225.00
☐ Penguins	K 20	150.00	200.00
☐ Penguins	K 21	100.00	150.00
☐ Penguins	K 22	150.00	200.00
☐ Penguins	K 23	100.00	150.00
☐ Penguins	K 24	100.00	150.00
☐ Penguins	K 25	150.00	200.00
☐ Pheasant	HN 2545	200.00	275.00
☐ Pheasant, small	HN 2576	150.00	175.00
☐ Pheasant, large	HN 2634	125.00	150.00
☐ Pheasant, cock	HN 2632	550.00	
☐ Pheasant, hen	HN 2610	150.00	200.00
☐ Pig, asleep	HN 800	200.00	300.00
☐ Pig, asleep, large	HN 801	250.00	350.00
☐ Pig, black and white	HN 968	300.00	350.00
☐ Piggy Bowl	HN 243	250.00	300.00
☐ Piglets, character	HN 2648	150.00	200.00
☐ Piglets, character	HN 2649	150.00	200.00
☐ Piglets, character	HN 2650	150.00	200.00
☐ Piglets, character	HN 2651	150.00	200.00
☐ Piglets, character	HN 2652	150.00	200.00
☐ Piglets, character	HN 2653	150.00	200.00

		Price Range	
☐ **Pigs,** pair	HN 802	250.00	350.00
☐ **Pigs,** two	HN 213	175.00	225.00
☐ **Pigs,** two	HN 238	200.00	250.00
☐ **Pip, Squeak, and Wilfred Ashtray**	HN 935	550.00	650.00
☐ **Pointer,** on base, large	HN 2624	250.00	300.00
☐ **Polar Bear**	HN 861	250.00	300.00
☐ **Polar Bear**	HN 2637	250.00	350.00
☐ **Polar Bear,** sitting	HN 121	200.00	250.00
☐ **Polar Bear,** sitting on a green cube	HN 119	200.00	250.00
☐ **Polar Bear,** sitting on green cube	HN 119	300.00	500.00
☐ **Poodle,** large	HN 2625	1000.00	1500.00
☐ **Poodle,** medium	HN 2626	125.00	150.00
☐ **Poodle,** small	HN 2627	450.00	500.00
☐ **'Pride of Shires,'** mare and foal, gray, large	HN 2523	400.00	500.00
☐ **'Pride of Shires,'** mare and foal, gray, small	HN 2536	200.00	250.00
☐ **'Pride of Shires,'** mare, no foal, brown, large	HN 2528	400.00	500.00
☐ **'Pride of Shires,'** mare, no foal, brown, medium	HN 2564	250.00	300.00
☐ **Pup,** character	HN 826	200.00	250.00
☐ **Pup,** character, miniature	HN 814– HN 815	200.00	225.00
☐ **Pup,** miniature, playing, pale orange	HN 804	400.00	500.00
☐ **Pup,** miniature, playing, malachite and purple	HN 805	400.00	500.00
☐ **Pups,** character, miniature	HN 808– HN 812	200.00	225.00
☐ **Puppy**	HN 128	250.00	350.00
☐ **Puppy,** with bone	HN 232	400.00	500.00
☐ **Puppies in Basket,** three terriers	HN 2588	45.00	55.00
☐ **Puppy**	HN 128	300.00	500.00
☐ **Puppy,** begging, Cairn	HN 2589	45.00	55.00
☐ **Puppy,** in basket, cocker	HN 2586	45.00	55.00
☐ **Puppy,** in basket, lying, cocker	HN 2585	45.00	55.00
☐ **Puppy,** in basket, terrier	HN 2587	45.00	55.00
☐ **Rabbit**	HN 273	150.00	200.00
☐ **Rabbit**	HN 108	125.00	150.00
☐ **Rabbit**	HN 276	200.00	250.00
☐ **Rabbit**	HN 151	100.00	150.00
☐ **Rabbits,** two, brown patches on faces	HN 217	150.00	200.00
☐ **Rabbits,** two, black patches on faces	HN 218	150.00	200.00
☐ **Rabbits,** two, yellow on faces	HN 219	150.00	200.00
☐ **Raven,** on rock	HN 135	150.00	200.00
☐ **Robin,** on rock	HN 136	150.00	200.00
☐ **Robin**	HN 2617	125.00	150.00

	Date	Price Range	
☐ Robin	HN 2549	125.00	150.00
☐ Rhinoceros	HN 141	600.00	800.00
☐ River Hog (Chatcull Range)	HN 2663	200.00	250.00
☐ Scottish Terrier, begging, disc. 1977	K 10	50.00	60.00
☐ Scottish Terrier, seated, disc. 1977	K 18	50.00	60.00
☐ Scottish Terrier, Ch. 'Albourne Arthur,' large, disc. 1955	HN 1008	400.00	500.00
☐ Scottish Terrier, Ch. 'Albourne Arthur,' medium, disc. 1960	HN 1015	300.00	350.00
☐ Scottish Terrier, Ch. 'Albourne Arthur,' small, disc. 1984	HN 1016	50.00	75.00
☐ Scottish Terrier, sitting, black	HN 1017	400.00	500.00
☐ Scottish Terrier, sitting, black	HN 1018	250.00	300.00
☐ Scottish Terrier, sitting, black	HN 1019	250.00	300.00
☐ Scottish Terrier, begging	HN 1038	400.00	450.00
☐ Scottish Terrier, light gray and brown	HN 981	400.00	500.00
☐ Scotch Terrier, large, black	HN 964	450.00	550.00
☐ Scotch Terrier, black	HN 980	300.00	400.00
☐ Scotch Terrier, large, brown	HN 965	450.00	550.00
☐ Scotch Terrier, miniature	HN 932– HN 934	275.00	325.00
☐ Seagull	HN 1196	150.00	200.00
☐ Seagull, small	HN 2574	125.00	175.00
☐ Sealyham, begging, disc. 1977	K 3	50.00	60.00
☐ Sealyham, sleeping, disc. 1959	K 4	120.00	135.00
☐ Sealyham, character sitting	HN 2508	125.00	150.00
☐ Sealyham, character dog standing	HN 2509	200.00	250.00
☐ Sealyham, lying, large	HN 1041	300.00	400.00
☐ Sealyham, lying, medium	HN 1052	200.00	300.00
☐ Sealyham, lying, small	HN 1053	150.00	200.00
☐ Sealyham, 'Scotia Stylist,' large, disc. 1956	HN 1030	600.00	700.00
☐ Sealyham, 'Scotia Stylist,' medium, disc. 1955	HN 1031	225.00	275.00
☐ Sealyham, 'Scotia Stylist,' small, disc. 1960	HN 1032	140.00	190.00
☐ Sealyham, terrier, black patches on face	HN 982	350.00	450.00
☐ Sealyham, terrier, brown patches on face	HN 983	350.00	450.00
☐ Sealyham, terrier	HN 992	300.00	400.00
☐ Sealyham, terrier, gray	HN 989	300.00	400.00
☐ Spaniel, liver and white	HN 957	250.00	300.00
☐ Spaniel, brown and white	HN 958	250.00	300.00
☐ Spaniel Puppy, black and white	HN 906	300.00	350.00
☐ Spaniel Puppy, brown and white	HN 907	300.00	350.00
☐ Spaniel Puppy's Head	HN 908	325.00	375.00

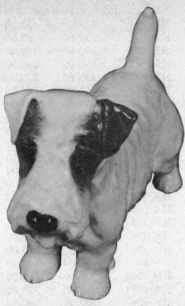

Sealyham, HN 1030, large, discontinued 1956, 600.00–700.00

		Price Range	
☐ Springer Spaniel, 'Dry Toast,' large, disc. 1955	HN 2515	325.00	375.00
☐ Springer Spaniel, 'Dry Toast,' medium	HN 2516	200.00	250.00
☐ Springer Spaniel, 'Dry Toast,' small	HN 2517	100.00	125.00
☐ St. Bernard, lying, disc. 1977	K 19	50.00	60.00
☐ Squirrel	HN 138	250.00	300.00
☐ Squirrel	HN 2642	400.00	500.00
☐ Swallow, on rock	HN 149	150.00	200.00
☐ Swan	HN 2575	150.00	200.00
☐ Swiss Goat, green matte	HN 1151	450.00	550.00
☐ Swiss Goat, cream matte	HN 1166	450.00	550.00
☐ Swiss Goat, natural	HN 1178	450.00	550.00
☐ Suspicious Doe, green matte	HN 1156	450.00	550.00
☐ Suspicious Doe, cream matte	HN 1171	450.00	550.00
☐ Teal Duck	HN 229	200.00	300.00
☐ Teal, swimming	HN 936	175.00	225.00
☐ Teal Duck	HN 229	125.00	150.00
☐ Tern Duck	HN 167	200.00	300.00
☐ Tern	HN 1193– HN 1194	150.00	200.00
☐ Tern Duck	HN 167	125.00	150.00
☐ Tern Duck	HN 168	125.00	150.00

		Price Range	
☐ **Tern Duck**	HN 195	125.00	150.00
☐ **Terrier**, disc. 1977	K 8	50.00	60.00
☐ **Terrier**, seated, black and brown	HN 997	350.00	450.00
☐ **Terrier's Head**	HN 962	500.00	600.00
☐ **Terrier Pup**, brown and black	HN 953	250.00	300.00
☐ **Terrier Pup**, darker brown and black	HN 954	250.00	300.00
☐ **Terrier Pup**, miniature	HN 931	250.00	300.00
☐ **Terrier Pup**, miniature, sitting	HN 929	250.00	300.00
☐ **Terrier Puppy**	HN 194	450.00	550.00
☐ **Terrier Puppy**	HN 904	300.00	350.00
☐ **Thrush on Bough**, with Blossom	HN 1005	150.00	200.00
☐ **Tiger**	HN 2646		1500.00
☐ **Tiger**, lying	HN 911	500.00	650.00
☐ **Tiger**, sitting	HN 912	500.00	650.00
☐ **Tiger**, on rock	HN 2639		2300.00
☐ **Tiger**, lying	HN 225	400.00	500.00
☐ **Tiger**, crouching	HN 990	400.00	500.00
☐ **Tiger**, crouching (smaller model)	HN 991	375.00	425.00
☐ **Tiger**, stalking, large	HN 1082	400.00	500.00
☐ **Tiger**, stalking, medium	HN 1083	300.00	400.00
☐ **Tiger**, stalking, small	HN 1084	275.00	325.00
☐ **Tiger**, on rock	HN 876	400.00	500.00
☐ **Tiger**, on rock	HN 2535	1000.00	1200.00
☐ **Tiger**, on rock, large, earthenware	HN 1118	700.00	800.00
☐ **Tiger**, on alabaster base	HN 1126	500.00	600.00
☐ **Titanian Bowl**, jade	HN 110	150.00	200.00
☐ **Tortoise**	HN 193	400.00	500.00
☐ **Tortoise**, on rocks	HN 859	225.00	250.00
☐ **Toucan**	HN 158	300.00	400.00
☐ **Toucan**	HN 159	300.00	400.00
☐ **Toucan**	HN 196	150.00	200.00
☐ **Toucan**	HN 846	150.00	200.00
☐ **Toucan**, black and white, red beak, large	HN 294	200.00	250.00
☐ **Toucan**, black, green, brown beak, large	HN 295	200.00	250.00
☐ **Toucan**, black, green, brown beak	HN 295A	200.00	250.00
☐ **Toucan Bowl**, large	HN 928	275.00	325.00
☐ **Welsh Corgi**, disc. 1977	K 16	50.00	60.00
☐ **Welsh Corgi**, Ch. 'Spring Robin,' large, disc. 1955	HN 2557	450.00	500.00
☐ **Welsh Corgi**, Ch. 'Spring Robin,' medium, disc. 1969	HN 2558	250.00	300.00
☐ **Welsh Corgi**, Ch. 'Spring Robin,' small, disc. 1984	HN 1559	50.00	75.00
☐ **West Highland White Terrier**, large	HN 1048	500.00	600.00
☐ **Wren**	HN 144	125.00	150.00

		Price Range	
☐ Wren	HN 277	125.00	150.00
☐ Wren, Golden Crested	HN 2548	125.00	175.00
☐ Wren, Golden Crested	HN 2613	125.00	175.00
☐ Wren, Golden Crested	K 33	75.00	100.00
☐ Yellow Bird	HN 847	125.00	150.00
☐ Yellow Bird, on rock	HN 281	125.00	150.00
☐ Yellow Bird, on rock, beak closed	HN 145A	100.00	125.00
☐ Yellow Bird, on rock, beak open	HN 145	200.00	250.00
☐ Yellow Throated Warbler	K 27	50.00	75.00
☐ Yellow Throated Warbler	HN 2548	125.00	150.00
☐ Young Doe, green matte	HN 1150	450.00	550.00
☐ Young Doe, cream matte	HN 1165	450.00	550.00
☐ Young Doe, natural	HN 1177	450.00	550.00
☐ Young Robins	HN 2553	125.00	150.00
☐ Young Thrushes, pair	HN 2552	125.00	150.00
☐ Zebra	HN 2507	150.00	200.00

CHATCULL RANGE OF ANIMALS

This is a series bearing standard HN prefix numbers, which originated in 1940. The designer of these appealing portrayals was Joseph Ledger, whose estate was known as "Chatcull Hall"—thus the title for the series. These were not limited editions but the majority are now out of production and are becoming harder to find. Prices are likely to rise more sharply across-the-board when the entire Chatculls series is out of production.

		Price Range	
☐ Badger	HN 2666	250.00	300.00
☐ Brown Bear	HN 2659	175.00	225.00
☐ Langur Monkey	HN 2657	150.00	200.00
☐ Llama	HN 2665	150.00	200.00
☐ Mountain Sheep	HN 2661	200.00	250.00
☐ Nyala Antelope	HN 2664	150.00	200.00
☐ Pine Martin	HN 2656	450.00	525.00
☐ River Hog	HN 2663	200.00	250.00
☐ Siamese Cat, lying	HN 2662	75.00	100.00
☐ Siamese Cat, sitting	HN 2655	75.00	100.00
☐ Siamese Cat, standing	HN 2660	75.00	100.00
☐ White-tailed Deer	HN 2658	200.00	225.00

IMAGES OF NATURE

An exciting new approach has been introduced in the Animal and Bird Models. These figures present a streamlined and modernistic style, each conveying an animal in action. This new Image Collection was introduced in 1982.

Going Home, HN 3527, 75.00

	Date	Price Range

THE LEAP
HN 3522
☐ Dolphin rising from the water, designer A. Hughes 110.00

GOING HOME
HN 3527
☐ A pair of flying geese, designer A. Hughes 75.00

CAPRICORN
HN 3523
☐ Mountain goat poised on a precipice, designer A. Hughes 75.00

THE GIFT OF LIFE
HN 3524
☐ A mare with her newborn foal, designer R. Willis 475.00

	Date	Price Range	

COURTSHIP
HN 3525
☐ Dramatic mating display of two terns, designer R. Willis .... | | 600.00 | |

SHADOWPLAY
HN 3526
☐ A playful cat sitting erect, designer R. Willis .... | | 110.00 | |

FREEDOM
HN 3528
☐ A pair of otters at play, designer Robert Jefferson .... | 1982–1986 | 200.00 | 300.00 |

BRIGHTWATER
HN 3529
☐ Single otter, designer Robert Jefferson | 1982–1986 | 100.00 | 200.00 |

CLEARWATER
HN 3530
☐ Single otter, designer Robert Jefferson | 1982–1986 | 100.00 | 200.00 |

NESTLING DOWN
HN 3531
☐ Two swans, male swans' wings outspread to protect female who is curled up and resting, designer A. Hughes .. | 1986– | 475.00 | |

THE HOMECOMING
HN 3532
☐ Two beautiful white doves mounted on a wooden base. One is resting on an olive branch. The other is just arriving with wings outspread, designer R. Willis .... | 1986– | 475.00 | |

PATIENCE
HN 3533
☐ A tall and very distinctive rendition of that stately bird "the heron," height 12¼", designer P. Gee .... | 1987– | 110.00 | |

PLAYFUL
HN 3534
☐ Two lion cubs in a friendly scuffle, height 7½", designer A. Hughes ...... | 1987– | 140.00 | |

The Homecoming, HN 3532, 475.00

IMAGES OF FIRE

A distinctive and new concept of two Images of Nature figures recreated in Rouge Flambé, creating a mottled, splash, and veined effect.

	Date	Price Range
COURTSHIP **HN 3535** ☐ Dramatic mating display of two terns, height 15″, designer R. Willis	1987–	1300.00

The Gift of Love, HN 3536, 900.00

	Date	Price Range
THE GIFT OF LOVE **HN 3536** □ A mare with her newborn foal, height 9″, designer R. Willis	1987–	975.00

JEFFERSON SCULPTURES

The following wildlife sculptures were created by Robert Jefferson. Beautiful renditions of nature, most were produced in limited edition; however, a few models were unlimited. First limited edition was released in 1974.

		Date	Price
☐ Black-Throated Loon, Limited edition of 150	HN 3500	1974–	2350.00
☐ Chipping Sparrow, Limited edition of 200	HN 3511	1976–	950.00
☐ Colorado Chipmunks, Limited edition of 75	HN 3506	1974–	7500.00
☐ Downy Woodpecker, Edition unlimited	HN 3509	1975–	525.00
☐ Fledgling Bluebird, Limited edition of 250	HN 3510	1976–	600.00
☐ Golden-Crowned Kinglet, Edition unlimited	HN 3504	1974–	525.00
☐ Harbor Seals, Limited edition of 75 ..	HN 3507	1975–	1600.00
☐ Huntsman Fox, Edition unlimited	HN 6448	—	50.00
☐ King Elder, Limited edition of 150 ...	HN 3502	1974–	1800.00
☐ Puffins, Limited edition of 250	HN 2668	1974–	1600.00
☐ Roseate Terns, Limited edition of 150	HN 3503	1974–	2500.00
☐ Snowshoe Hares, Limited edition of 75	HN 3508	1975–	2750.00
☐ Snowy Owl, Female, Limited edition of 150	HN 2670	1974–	2150.00
☐ Snowy Owl, Male, Limited edition of 150	HN 2669	1974–	1750.00
☐ White-Winged Cross Bills, Limited edition of 250	HN 3501	1974–	1450.00
☐ Winter Wren, Edition unlimited	HN 3505	1974–	375.00

FANCY AND CHARACTER FIGURINES

The following *alphabetical* listing gives series numbers, dates, descriptions, and current retail selling prices for figures in the HN series. Descriptions indicate the color schemes found on the majority of the specimens on each model. Color variations do exist on many models. While some collectors take a special interest in "off-color" models, the market on them is not widespread enough to establish firm values.

	Date	Price Range	
ABDULLAH			
HN 1410			
☐ Dark skinned figure seated on blue cushions, green turban, height 5¾", designer L. Harradine	1930–1938	1000.00	1100.00
HN 2104			
☐ Dark skinned figure seated on black base that has blue rug with red, green, black squares, large cushion of yellow and green, gray trousers, black coat, orange shirt, red waistband, orange and red turban with green feather, height 6", designer L. Harradine	1953–1962	500.00	600.00
A'COURTING			
HN 2004			
☐ Boy and girl figure on light green base, boy's costume is shaded blues, jacket dark blue with gold buttons, hat black; girl's costume is red dress with white collar, white apron in hand, white head cap with blue ribbon, height 7¼", designer L. Harradine	1947–1953	550.00	650.00
ADELE			
HN 2480			
☐ Adaptation of white Vanity Fair Margaret. Dressed in white with delicately painted flowers around her skirt, brown hair and wearing a Gainsborough-type hat with beautiful, blue ribbons, height 8", designer P. Davies	1987–	170.00	

Abdullah, HN 2104, 1000.00–1100.00

	Date	Price Range	
ADRIENNE			
HN 2152			
□ Gown of purple with yellow scarf, height 7½″, designer M. Davies	1964–1976	145.00	175.00
HN 2304			
□ Gown of blue with very light green scarf, height 7½″, designer M. Davies	1964–	195.00	
AFFECTION			
HN 2236			
□ Small girl in gown of purple with white trim, seated on bench of green holding small white kitten, height 4¾″, designer M. Davies	1962–	140.00	

AFTERNOON CALL, The
(Sometimes referred to as Lady With
Ermine Muff)

Adele, HN 2480, 160.00

	Date	Price Range	

HN 82

☐ Lady seated on beige couch, cream gown with green designs, coat of blue with white fur trim and muff, green hat with blue feather, height 6¾″, designer E.W. Light 1918–1938 3000.00 3500.00

AFTERNOON TEA
HN 1747

☐ Two ladies seated on sofa, one gown is pink, bonnet of green with blue ribbons; the other gown is white skirt with blue and yellow flower design, jacket is light blue, bonnet is white with red ribbons, height 5¾″, designer P. Railston 1935–1982 275.00 350.00

HN 1748

☐ Green dress, height 5¼″, designer P. Railston 1935–1949 1200.00 1500.00

	Date	Price Range	

AILEEN
HN 1645

☐ Seated figure in green dress, shawl is light blue with red and blue flowers, white necklace, red shoes, height 6″, designer L. Harradine 1934–1938 1150.00 1350.00

HN 1664

☐ Pink skirt, height 6″, designer L. Harradine 1934–1938 1150.00 1350.00

HN 1803

☐ Cream dress, blue shawl, height 6″, designer L. Harradine 1937–1949 1100.00 1350.00

A LA MODE
HN 2544

☐ Tall figure with red hair, green dress with a darker green design, height 12½″, designer E.J. Griffiths 1974–1979 175.00 225.00

ALCHEMIST, The
HN 1259

☐ Mottled robe, red hat, height 11½″, designer L. Harradine 1927–1938 1500.00 1800.00

HN 1282

☐ Dark brown robe with multicolored sleeves and red scarf, dark brown hat, holding small object in one hand, height 11¼″, designer L. Harradine 1928–1938 1500.00 1800.00

ALEXANDRA
HN 2398

☐ Green dress with white flowers and flowing yellow cape, height 7¾″, designer M. Davies 1970–1976 150.00 200.00

ALFRED JINGLE
HN 541

☐ This was discontinued in 1932, renumbered in 1932 and still produced.
☐ A character from Dickens' ''Pickwick Papers,'' height 3¾″, designer L. Harradine 1922–1932 60.00 85.00

☐ **M-52** Renumbered as a miniature, height 3¾″, designer L. Harradine ... 1932–1983 45.00 55.00

ALICE
HN 2158

☐ Blue dress, white ribbon in blonde hair, open book on lap, height 5″, designer M. Davies 1960–1980 125.00 150.00

	Date	Price Range	

ALISON
HN 2336
☐ White skirt with small red and green design, blue overdress, height 7½″, designer M. Davies 1966– **195.00**

ALL ABOARD
HN 2940
☐ Depicts an old sea captain, standing on a gray base. Alongside is a clock and a sign telling departure time of deep sea trips. Man's outfit is a blue turtleneck sweater over beige trousers, black boots, height 9¼″, designer R. Tabbenor 1982–1986 **175.00** **200.00**

ALL-A-BLOOMING
HN 1457
☐ Blue dress, height 6½″, designer L. Harradine .... 1931– Unknown **1850.00** **2100.00**
HN 1466
☐ Lady seated on brown wicker stand, yellow/green basket of flowers beside her, skirt red, apron white, shawl dark blue with shades of yellow and green, hat is shades of blue with green feathers, height 6½″, designer L. Harradine 1931–1938 **1450.00** **1700.00**

AMY
HN 2958
☐ One of the charming Kate Greenaway figures. Young figure in very pale blue dress with darker blue ruffles on bottom, dark blue ribbon at waist. Dark hair with white cap. Figure is holding a doll in red dress, yellow hair, height 6″, designer P. Parsons 1982–1987 **100.00**

ANGELA
HN 1204
☐ Figure on light colored pedestal, costume of shaded reds and blue, red shoes, holding large fan behind head of dark blue and red, height 7¼″, designer L. Harradine 1926–1938 **1200.00** **1500.00**
HN 1303
☐ Blue fan and spotted costume, height 7¼″, designer L. Harradine 1928–1938 **1400.00** **1750.00**

Angela, HN 1204, 1200.00–1500.00

	Date	Price Range	
ANGELINA			
HN 2013			
☐ Red dress trimmed in white, holding green hat with blue ribbon, height 6¾", designer L. Harradine	1948–1951	850.00	1100.00
ANNA (Kate Greenaway)			
HN 2802			
☐ Small girl, purple dress, white apron and bonnet, holding flower in one hand, on white base, height 5¾", designer M. Davies	1976–1982	100.00	125.00
ANNABELLA			
HN 1871			
☐ Small figure in curtsy position, orange skirt with green bodice, holding basket			

Annette, HN 1550, 400.00–475.00

	Date	Price Range	
of flowers on arm, hat matches skirt, height 5¼″, designer L. Harradine ...	1938–1949	**550.00**	**750.00**
HN 1872			
☐ Green skirt and blue bodice, height 5¼″, designer L. Harradine	1938–1949	**550.00**	**750.00**
HN 1875			
☐ Red dress, height 4¾″, designer L. Harradine	1938–1949	**600.00**	**850.00**

ANNETTE
HN 1471
☐ Dutch figure in blue gown with white apron, white Dutch cap, carrying light colored basket with red fruit, light wooden shoes, height 6¼″, designer L.

Harradine	1931–1938	**450.00**	**550.00**

	Date	Price Range	

HN 1472

☐ Gown of green, apron shaded green, red and cream, red basket, height 6″, designer L. Harradine 1931–1949   400.00   475.00

HN 1550

☐ Green skirt, apron with light stripes, red blouse, height 6¼″, designer L. Harradine 1933–1949   400.00   475.00

ANTHEA
HN 1526

☐ Green dress with white designs, blue shawl with red flowers, green hat with red feather, carrying parasol, height 6½″, designer L. Harradine 1932–1938   900.00   1100.00

HN 1527

☐ Gown of shaded blues and reds with cream, shawl white with red and black designs, blue hat with light feather, height 6½″, designer L. Harradine ... 1932–1949   700.00   900.00

HN 1669

☐ Skirt of cream, jacket red, shawl green, hat green, height 6½″, designer L. Harradine 1934–1938   1000.00   1250.00

ANTOINETTE
HN 1850

☐ Black base and pedestal, gown is red with green trim, hat green with black ribbons (1st version), height 8¼″, designer L. Harradine 1938–1949   1100.00   1500.00

HN 1851

☐ Base black, pedestal blue and cream, gown shaded blue and red with blue overdress, blue hat with green ribbons (1st version), height 8¼″, designer L. Harradine 1938–1949   1200.00   1600.00

HN 2326

☐ White gown with gold design and trim, gold shoe, seated figure (2nd version), height 6¼″, designer M. Davies 1967–1979   125.00   175.00

A PENNY'S WORTH
HN 2408

☐ An older lady filling a cone with candy; jars of colorful candy sitting on a table and colorful boxes of candy underneath the table, height 7″, designer M. Nicoll 1986–   195.00

A Penny's Worth, HN 2408, 180.00

	Date	Price Range	

APPLE MAID, The
HN 2160
☐ Figure seated on brown wicker chair, black skirt, green blouse, white apron, white head covering, brown basket with apples, height 6½″, designer L. Harradine 1957–1962 **350.00** **450.00**

ARAB/MOOR
HN 33
☐ Green costume, blue cloak, height 15¾″, designer C.J. Noke 1913–1938 **1800.00** **2500.00**

	Date	Price Range	

HN 343

□ Striped yellow and purple costume, height 16½″, designer C.J. Noke 1919–1938 2000.00 2750.00

HN 378

□ Costume of patchwork colors of green, brown, yellow hooded cloak of dark blue, multicolored base, height 16½″, designer C.J. Noke 1920–1930 2250.00 2950.00

ARTFUL DODGER, The
HN 546

□ A character from Dickens' "Oliver Twist," height 3¾″, designer L. Harradine 1922– 65.00 85.00

□ **M-55** Renumbered as a miniature, height 4¼″, designer L. Harradine ... 1932–1983 45.00 55.00

ASCOT
HN 2356

□ Seated lady on brown chair, green dress, green hat with blue trim, yellow boa, light blue parasol, height 5¾″, designer M. Davies 1968– 250.00

AT EASE
HN 2473

□ Lady seated on green and brown chaise lounge, dark hair, pale green gown trimmed in brown, height 6″, designer M. Davies 1973–1979 165.00 200.00

AUCTIONEER
HN 2988

See Royal Doulton International Collector Club section.

AUTUMN
HN 314

□ Blue/gray base, pink gown, autumn colored flowers in arm (1st version), height 7¼″, designer unknown 1918–1938 1500.00 1800.00

HN 474

□ Patterned robe (1st version), height 7½″, designer unknown 1921–1938 1600.00 1900.00

HN 2087

□ Green and yellow base, gown of red, blue and white apron, small white cap with blue ribbons, brown broom (2nd version), height 7¼″, designer M. Davies 1952–1959 475.00 550.00

Autumn, HN 314, 1500.00–1800.00

	Date	Price Range	

AUTUMN BREEZES
HN 1911
☐ Pink and pale blue skirt, green bodice and hat, white muff. Earlier mold has two feet, height 7½", designer L. Harradine 1939–1976 **175.00** **250.00**

HN 1913
☐ Green skirt, dark blue bodice, blue hat with black apron, white muff, height 7½", designer L. Harradine 1939–1971 **195.00** **275.00**

HN 1934
☐ Red skirt and bodice, white hat, height 7½", designer L. Harradine 1940– **230.00**

HN 2147
☐ White skirt, black bodice, white hat and

	Date	Price Range	
muff, height 7½", designer L. Harradine	1955–1971	300.00	400.00

AWAKENING, The
HN 1927
☐ Nude figure on light colored base with a full length of light material draped down front, height unknown, designer L. Harradine (very rare) ....

	1940–1949	4500.00	5500.00

BABA
HN 1230
☐ Small seated figure with striped yellow and purple trousers and cone shaped hat, height 3¼", designer L. Harradine ....

	1927–1938	800.00	950.00

HN 1243
☐ Orange trousers, height 3¼", designer L. Harradine ....

	1927–1938	900.00	1050.00

HN 1244
☐ Yellow trousers with green stripes, height 3¼", designer L. Harradine ...

	1927–1938	800.00	950.00

HN 1245
☐ White trousers with blue/black markings, height 3¼", designer L. Harradine ....

	1927–1938	800.00	950.00

HN 1246
☐ Green trousers, height 3¼", designer L. Harradine ....

	1927–1938	800.00	950.00

HN 1247
☐ White trousers with black spots, height 3¼", designer L. Harradine ....

	1928–1938	875.00	1000.00

HN 1248
☐ Green striped trousers, white striped sleeves, red waistband, white cone shaped hat, height 3¼", designer L. Harradine ....

	1927–1938	800.00	950.00

BABETTE
HN 1423
☐ Small figure in bathing costume on base with open parasol, blue and white costume, height 5", designer L. Harradine ....

	1930–1938	900.00	1200.00

HN 1424
☐ Yellow costume with red stripes, height 5", designer L. Harradine ....

	1930–1938	900.00	1200.00

	Date	Price Range

BABIE
HN 1679
☐ Small figure in gown of green and cream, blue bonnet with red feather, carrying red parasol, height 4¾″, designer L. Harradine **1935–** **110.00**

HN 1842
☐ Pink dress, green hat and umbrella, height 4¾″, designer L. Harradine ... **1938–1949** **350.00** **450.00**

HN 2121
☐ Dress is shades of pinks decorated with white summer flowers. Bonnet is pink with gold ribbon, gold parasol, height 4¾″, designer L. Harradine **1983–** **110.00**

BABY
HN 12
☐ Small child figure on base, wrapped entirely in blue/gray robe, height unknown, designer C.J. Noke **1913–1938** **3500.00** **4500.00**

BABY BUNTING
HN 2108
☐ White child figure with brown covering arms and head, head cover has ears, height 5¼″, designer M. Davies **1953–1959** **200.00** **300.00**

BACHELOR, The
HN 2319
☐ Character figure seated in dark brown chair with foot stool darning blue sock, wears brown trousers, black vest, white shirt, brown tie, blue socks, brown shoes, height 7″, designer M. Nicoll **1964–1975** **300.00** **375.00**

BALLAD SELLER
HN 2266
☐ Skirt and bonnet of pink, bodice white with gold, holding white sheet with printing in one hand, rolled white sheet in other, height 7½″, designer M. Davies **1968–1973** **250.00** **350.00**

BALLERINA
HN 2116
☐ White dress with shades of blue and red, red ribbon at waist, red ballet shoes on dark base, blue ribbon and flower trim on gown, height 7¼″, designer M. Davies **1953–1973** **275.00** **350.00**

Ballerina, HN 2116, 275.00–350.00

	Date	Price Range

BALLOON BOY
HN 2934
☐ Base resembles cobble street, boy dressed in dark pants, white shirt, green jacket and beige cap, holding a bunch of gaily colored balloons, height 7 1/2 ", designer P. Gee 1984– **140.00**

BALLOON CLOWN
HN 2894
☐ White clown wearing white suit with blue pompoms holding a rope with colorful balloons, and rope is attached at bottom to a heavy weight, height 9 1/4 ", designer W.K. Harper 1986– **195.00**

	Date	Price Range	

BALLOON GIRL
HN 2618

☐ Seated blonde girl dressed in gray skirt, yellow blouse, red scarf tied around neck, green shawl with red fringe, hat is black with beige ribbon, colorful balloons in her hand, height 6½″, designer W.K. Harper 1982– 185.00

BALLOON LADY
HN 2935

☐ Dressed in a burnt ochre skirt and white buttoned apron, white blouse, purple shawl with heavy fringe, black hat with green feather, holding a colorful bunch of balloons, height 8¼″, designer P. Gee 1984– 170.00

BALLOON MAN, The
HN 1954

☐ Character figure seated on brown box, green trousers, black shoes, black coat, brown vest, white shirt, brown hat, holding multicolored balloons, with red knapsack, height 7¼″, designer L. Harradine 1940– 275.00

BALLOON SELLER, The
HN 479

☐ Blue dress, white spots, height 9″, designer L. Harradine 1921–1938 2000.00 2500.00

HN 486

☐ Blue dress, no hat, height 9″, designer L. Harradine 1921–1938 1800.00 2100.00

HN 548

☐ Black shawl, blue dress, height 9″, designer L. Harradine 1922–1938 1200.00 1500.00

HN 583

☐ White skirt with small green design, green shawl with red fringe, red blouse, black hat with green feather, baby in orange and red, balloons multicolored, height 9″, designer L. Harradine 1923–1949 600.00 775.00

HN 697

☐ Striped red shawl, blue dress, height 9″, designer L. Harradine 1925–1938 800.00 900.00

Balloon Man, HN 1954, 275.00

	Date	Price Range	

BARBARA
HN 1421
☐ Brown base, gown of cream with red and blue flower design, blue and red shawl with black designs, blue and red bonnet, holding small envelope in one hand and small round red and yellow purse, height 7¾", designer L. Harradine ....

| | 1930–1938 | 750.00 | 950.00 |

HN 1432
☐ Black base, gown of shaded blue, red, green, multicolored shawl and bonnet, small purse, height 7¾", designer L. Harradine ....

| | 1930–1938 | 750.00 | 950.00 |

Balloon Seller, HN 583, 600.00–775.00

	Date	Price Range	

HN 1461
☐ Green dress, height 7¾″, designer L. Harradine 1931–1938 **750.00 1000.00**

BASKET WEAVER, The
HN 2245
☐ Seated figure in light green gown with white trim, light-colored basket on lap and at side, height 5¾″, designer M. Nicoll 1959–1962 **475.00 525.00**

BATHER, The
HN 597
☐ Mottled gray robe, blue base (1st version), height 7¾″, designer L. Harradine 1924–1938 **1500.00 1850.00**

The Bather, HN 774, 1800.00–2500.00

	Date	Price Range	
HN 687			
☐ Royal blue base, also royal blue lining of purple robe which has blue designs, nude white figure with greenish shoes (1st version), height 7¾″, designer L. Harradine	1924–1949	850.00	1200.00
HN 773			
☐ Pink robe, blue and black markings (2nd version), height 7½″, designer L. Harradine	1925–1938	1800.00	2500.00
HN 774			
☐ Nude white figure on black base with purple robe that has red lining, black spots (2nd version), height 7¾″, designer L. Harradine	1925–1938	1800.00	2500.00

	Date	Price Range	

HN 781
☐ Blue and green robe (1st version), height 7¾″, designer L. Harradine ... 1925–1938 1500.00 1800.00

HN 782
☐ Mottled purple robe, black lining (1st version), height 7¾″, designer L. Harradine 1926–1938 1500.00 1800.00

HN 1227
☐ Flowered pink robe (2nd version), height 7½″, designer L. Harradine ... 1927–1938 1800.00 2500.00

HN 1238
☐ Brown base, white nude figure, black robe with gold design, lining of robe is red (1st version), height 7¾″, designer L. Harradine 1927–1938 1100.00 1500.00

HN 1708
☐ Light green base, figure has black bathing suit, black shoes, robe of red with black and green shadings, blue lining (1st version), height 7¾″, designer L. Harradine 1935–1938 1800.00 2250.00

BEACHCOMBER
HN 2487
☐ Light colored base, barefooted character figure, gray pants, lavender shirt, green scarf, gray hat, holding shell, matte finish, height 6¼″, designer M. Nicoll 1973–1976 200.00 250.00

BEAT YOU TO IT
HN 2871
☐ Blue base, light tan wicker chair, brown dog in chair with blue cushions, girl's gown is white with shaded red and yellow sleeves, tiny flower design at hem line, height 6½″, designer M. Davies 1980–1987 395.00

BECKY
HN 2740
☐ Figure stands on a base with wind blowing gown of white, yellow, green, showing white pantaloons. Her white bonnet is held on with bright red ribbons tied gracefully under her chin. Available only in the United Kingdom, height 8″, designer D. Tootle, price unavailable .... 1987– —

Bedtime, HN 1978, 80.00

	Date	Price Range

BEDTIME
HN 1978
☐ Small girl in white nightgown on black base, height 5¾", designer L. Harradine 1945–   80.00

BEDTIME STORY, The
HN 2059
☐ Three figures, lady's gown is red; girl's gown is white skirt with blue design, blue bodice; boy dressed in tan trousers, blue jacket, height 4¾", designer L. Harradine 1950–   295.00

	Date	Price Range	

BEGGAR, The
HN 526

☐ A character from "The Beggar's Opera," with blue trousers, red sash and dark gray cloak (1st version), height 6½", designer L. Harradine ... 1921–1949 800.00 1200.00

HN 591

☐ Different glaze finish (1st version), height 6¾", designer L. Harradine ... 1924–1949 600.00 750.00

HN 2175

☐ Taller version but with brown trousers, red sash and darker gray cloak (2nd version), height 6¾", designer L. Harradine 1956–1962 550.00 750.00

BELLE, The
HN 754

☐ Eighteenth century style gown of multicolors, trimmed in green, blue bonnet with red ribbons, red shoes, on green and black base, height 6½", designer L. Harradine 1925–1938 1250.00 1500.00

HN 776

☐ No color detail available, height 6½", designer L. Harradine 1925–1938 1250.00 1500.00

BELLE
HN 2340

☐ Small female figure in green tiered dress, trimmed in white (2nd version), height 4½", designer M. Davies 1968–1988 95.00

BELLE O' THE BALL
HN 1997

☐ Shaded yellow, red, blue gown with red overdress, small hat, holding masking in one hand, seated on couch of brown and light yellow with shaded blue and red, pillow multicolored 1947–1979 300.00 350.00

BERNICE
HN 2071

☐ Dress is shaded colors of red with red cloak, black hat with blue feather, height 7¾", designer M. Davies 1951–1953 850.00 950.00

BESS
HN 2002

☐ White dress with colored flowers, red cloak, height 7¼", designer L. Harradine 1947–1969 275.00 350.00

	Date	Price Range	

HN 2003

☐ Pink dress with blue cloak with red lining, height 7¼″, designer L. Harradine 1947–1950 400.00 500.00

BETH (Kate Greenaway)
HN 2870

☐ Small figure on white base, light lavender dress and white apron with green trim, holding single flower, white bonnet with green ribbon, height 5¾″, designer M. Davies 1980–1983 100.00 150.00

BETSY
HN 2111

☐ Gown of shaded blues and reds, white apron with blue flower design trimmed in green, white cap, height 7″, designer L. Harradine 1953–1959 325.00 375.00

BETTY
HN 402

☐ Full pink gown with black collar, tall hat of black with gold feather and trim (1st version), height unknown, designer L. Harradine 1920–1938 2600.00 3000.00

HN 403

☐ Green skirt, blue, yellow and white border (1st version), height unknown, designer L. Harradine 1920–1938 2500.00 2900.00

HN 435

☐ Blue skirt with yellow spots (1st version), height unknown, designer L. Harradine 1921–1938 2200.00 2500.00

HN 438

☐ Green skirt (1st version), height unknown, designer L. Harradine 1921–1938 2200.00 2500.00

HN 477

☐ Spotted green skirt (1st version), height unknown, designer L. Harradine 1921–1938 2500.00 3000.00

HN 478

☐ White spotted skirt (1st version), height unknown, designer L. Harradine 1921–1938 2500.00 3000.00

HN 1404

☐ Small girl with white dog at feet, gown of white with shaded reds trimmed in blue, with tiny blue figure on dress (2nd version), height 4½″, designer L. Harradine 1930–1938 1500.00 2000.00

	Date	Price Range	

HN 1405
☐ Green dress (2nd version), height 4½″,
designer L. Harradine 1930–1938 **1500.00** **2000.00**

HN 1435
☐ Mottled multicolored dress (2nd version), height 4½″, designer L. Harradine 1930–1938 **1500.00** **2000.00**

HN 1436
☐ Patterned green dress (2nd version), height 4½″, designer L. Harradine ... 1930–1938 **1500.00** **2000.00**

BIDDY
HN 1445
☐ Green tiered gown with blue shawl, blue bonnet, holding a green parasol, height 5½″, designer L. Harradine ... 1931–1938 **195.00** **300.00**

HN 1500
☐ Yellow dress, height 5½″, designer L. Harradine 1932–1938 **300.00** **350.00**

HN 1513
☐ Shaded gown of red with blue shawl, blue bonnet, holding shaded blue and yellow parasol, height 5½″, designer L. Harradine 1932–1951 **160.00** **225.00**

BIDDY PENNY FARTHING
HN 1843
☐ Older lady figure in very light blue skirt, lavender bodice with gold design, dark gray shawl with lavender fringe, holding balloon and basket of flowers, height 9″, designer L. Harradine 1938– **275.00**

BILL SYKES
HN 537
☐ A character from Dickens' "Oliver Twist," height 3¾″, designer L. Harradine 1922– **65.00** **85.00**
☐ **M-54** Made as a miniature, height 4¼″, designer L. Harradine 1932– **50.00** **75.00**

BLACKSMITH
HN 2782
☐ Figure standing by an anvil which is resting on an old tree stump, wearing a leather apron tied with a rope; he is holding a pair of tongs and hammer, height 9″, designer W.K. Harper 1987– **185.00**

Biddy, HN 1513, 160.00–225.00

	Date	Price Range	
BLACKSMITH OF WILLIAMSBURG **HN 2240** ☐ Blue trousers, black boots with light top, brown apron and cap, white shirt, gray anvil also on white base, height 6¾″, designer M. Davies	1960–	160.00	225.00
BLIGHTY **HN 323** ☐ Mottled green and brown costume of British soldier, on same colored base, height 11¼″, designer E.W. Light	1918–1938	1500.00	1850.00
BLITHE MORNING **HN 2021** ☐ Pink skirt with blue bodice, red shawl, green hat, height 7¼″, designer L. Harradine	1949–1971	150.00	175.00

Blacksmith, HN 2782, 185.00

	Date	Price Range	
HN 2065			
☐ Red dress, green and yellow shawl, pale colored hat, height 7¼″, designer L. Harradine	1950–1973	150.00	175.00
BLOSSOM			
HN 1667			
☐ Seated lady in light green gown with multicolored shawl, small girl standing in between knees of lady, in gown of shaded blue, white collar, basket of multicolored flowers at lady's side, height 6¾″, designer L. Harradine ...	1934–1949	1500.00	1750.00

Blithe Morning, HN 2021, 150.00–175.00

	Date	Price Range	
BLUE BEARD			
HN 75			
☐ Costume of white with blue trim, cloak blue with yellow lining (1st version), height unknown, designer E.W. Light	1917–1938	4000.00	5000.00
HN 410			
☐ Blue costume (1st version), height unknown, designer E.W. Light	1920–1938	4000.00	5000.00
HN 1528			
☐ Red costume with multicolored robe and turban (2nd version), height 11 ½″, designer L. Harradine	1932–1949	900.00	1000.00

	Date	Price Range	

HN 2105
☐ Yellow, green and orange costume with dark blue robe (2nd version), height 11″, designer L. Harradine 1953–ㅤ550.00

BLUE BIRD
HN 1280
☐ Small kneeling white figure on red and cream colored base, holding dark colored bird on one hand, height 4¾″, designer L. Harradine 1928–1938ㅤ750.00ㅤ900.00

BOATMAN, The
HN 2417
☐ Character figure seated on gray chest, white life preserver at side, black boots, green trousers, yellow slicker, yellow hat, painting on white preserver, height 6½″, designer M. Nicoll 1971–1987ㅤ175.00ㅤ250.00

BON APPETIT
HN 2444
☐ Character figure on green and yellow base which has small bonfire and tan wicker basket on it, brown costume with long blue coat, blue hat, yellow shirt, brown tie, frying fish in black skillet, matte finish, height 6″, designer M. Nicoll 1972–1976ㅤ200.00ㅤ275.00

BON JOUR
HN 1879
☐ Green tiered gown with white trim, red shawl with black designs, red bonnet with dark ribbons, height 6¾″, designer L. Harradine 1938–1949ㅤ800.00ㅤ1000.00

HN 1888
☐ Red gown trimmed in white, shawl red with darker design, black bonnet with green ribbons, height 6¾″, designer L. Harradine 1938–1949ㅤ750.00ㅤ950.00

BONNIE LASSIE
HN 1626
☐ Seated figure in cream colored gown, red shawl with black stripes, hat to match, black shoes, light colored basket of flowers at feet, pail with flowers, height 5¼″, designer L. Harradine ... 1934–1953ㅤ275.00ㅤ375.00

Bo-Peep, HN 1811, 140.00

	Date	Price Range	
BO-PEEP			
HN 777			
☐ Gown of purple with green design, black hat with red ribbon, black staff, black base with small lamb (1st version), height 6¾", designer L. Harradine	1926–1938	**1400.00**	**1800.00**
HN 1202			
☐ Skirt is purple with green, pink and black trim (1st version), height 6¾", designer L. Harradine	1926–1938	**1400.00**	**1800.00**
HN 1327			
☐ Flowered multicolored costume (1st version), height 6¾", designer L. Harradine	1929–1938	**1700.00**	**1900.00**

	Date	Price Range	

HN 1328

☐ Cream skirt with black and blue small squares, overlay is red with black designs; bodice is dark with green squares; bonnet light with dark ribbon; staff is brown, base black with small lamb (1st version), height 6¾″, designer L. Harradine 1929–1938 1700.00 1900.00

HN 1810

☐ White, blue and red shirt, blue overlay, blue bonnet with red ribbon, holding staff in both hands (2nd version), height 5″, designer L. Harradine 1937–1949 500.00 650.00

HN 1811

☐ Red skirt with dark red overlay, green bonnet with green ribbons, staff light green (2nd version), height 5″, designer L. Harradine 1937– 140.00

☐ **M-82** Made as a miniature, red gown, height 4″, designer L. Harradine 1939–1949 550.00 650.00

☐ **M-83** Gown of blue, height 4″, designer L. Harradine 1939–1949 550.00 650.00

BOUDOIR
HN 2542

☐ Tall figure in grayest blue with white design gown, height 12¼″, designer E.J. Griffiths 1974–1979 400.00 475.00

BOUQUET, The
HN 406

☐ No record of coloring, height 9″, designer G. Lambert 1920–1938 2200.00 2500.00

HN 414

☐ Pink and yellow shawl, height 9″, designer G. Lambert 1920–1938 2200.00 2500.00

HN 422

☐ Yellow and pink striped skirt, height 9″, designer G. Lambert 1920–1938 2200.00 2500.00

HN 428

☐ Blue gown, shawl striped, height 9″, designer G. Lambert 1921–1938 2200.00 2500.00

HN 429

☐ Multicolored gown, with green designed shawl, colored flowers, height 9″, designer G. Lambert 1921–1938 2200.00 2500.00

HN 567

☐ Shaded design pink dress with white

	Date	Price Range	

shawl with designs of red and green, colored flowers, height 9″, designer G. Lambert 1923–1938 2500.00 3000.00

HN 794

☐ Blue shawl with red and green spots, height 9″, designer G. Lambert 1926–1938 2500.00 3000.00

BOY FROM WILLIAMSBURG
HN 2183

☐ Dark blue trousers and coat with gold trim, red long vest, white cravat, black hat, holding brown and white object, brown stamp behind figure, height 5½″, designer M. Davies 1969–1983 125.00 175.00

BOY ON A CROCODILE
HN 373

☐ Small white figure seated on crocodile, height 5″, designer C.J. Noke 1920–1938 5000.00 5500.00

BOY ON PIG
HN 1369

☐ Small white figure seated on multicolored pig, height 4″, designer C.J. Noke 1930–1938 4000.00 4500.00

BOY WITH TURBAN
HN 586

☐ Small seated Arab figure with blue and green costume, height 3¾″, designer L. Harradine 1923–1938 850.00 1000.00

HN 587

☐ Green trousers and red shirt, height 3¾″, designer L. Harradine 1923–1938 850.00 1000.00

HN 661

☐ Blue costume, height 3¾″, designer L. Harradine 1924–1938 850.00 1000.00

HN 662

☐ Costume of black and white checks, height 3¾″, designer L. Harradine ... 1924–1938 850.00 1000.00

HN 1210

☐ Black and red turban, white pants with large red dots, height 3¾″, designer L. Harradine 1926–1938 900.00 1100.00

HN 1212

☐ Blue and green trousers, multicolored turban and shirt, height 3¾″, designer L. Harradine 1926–1938 900.00 1100.00

Boy with Turban, HN 587, 850.00–1000.00

	Date	Price Range	

HN 1213
☐ White costume with black squares, height 3¾″, designer L. Harradine ... 1926–1938 900.00 1100.00

HN 1214
☐ White costume with black and green markings, height 3¾″, designer L. Harradine 1926–1938 900.00 1100.00

HN 1225
☐ Yellow trousers with blue spots, height 3¾″, designer L. Harradine 1927–1938 900.00 1100.00

BRIDE
HN 1588
☐ White bridal gown and veil, holding lilies in arm (1st version), height 8¾″, designer L. Harradine 1933–1938 750.00 1000.00

HN 1600
☐ Flowers are roses (1st version), height 8¾″, designer L. Harradine 1933–1949 750.00 1000.00

HN 1762
☐ Cream dress (1st version), height 8¾″, designer L. Harradine 1936–1949 750.00 1000.00

Bride, HN 1588, 750.00–1000.00

	Date	Price Range	
HN 1841			
☐ Blue dress (1st version), height 9½", designer L. Harradine	1938–1949	**1250.00**	**1750.00**
HN 2166			
☐ Full bridal gown, holding flower bouquet in hand (2nd version), height 8", designer M. Davies	1956–1976	**175.00**	**250.00**
HN 2873			
☐ Empire style gown of white trimmed in gold, holding single flower (4th version), height 8", designer M. Davies	1980–	**250.00**	
BRIDESMAID, The Little			
HN 1433			
☐ Multicolored tiered gown, holding bouquet with green ribbon, flowered band in hair (1st version), height 5¼", designer L. Harradine	1930–1951	**150.00**	**175.00**
HN 1434			
☐ Green and yellow gown, blue band in hair (1st version), height 5", designer L. Harradine	1930–1949	**275.00**	**350.00**

	Date	Price Range	

HN 1530

☐ Yellow and green dress, height 5″, designer L. Harradine .... | 1932–1938 | 400.00 | 450.00

☐ **M-11** Made as a miniature, pink and lilac dress, height 3¾″, designer L. Harradine .... | 1932–1938 | 250.00 | 350.00

☐ **M-12** Multicolored gown, height 3¾″, designer L. Harradine .... | 1932–1938 | 250.00 | 350.00

☐ **M-30** Red and lavender gown, height 3¾″, designer L. Harradine .... | 1932–1945 | 250.00 | 350.00

HN 2148

☐ Off white full gown with blue sash, holding flowers in right arm (2nd version), height 5½″, designer M. Davies | 1955–1959 | 250.00 | 300.00

HN 2196

☐ Full skirted light blue gown with raised design of white, small red ribbons on white collar, small brimmed head piece, holding small flowers in hand (3rd version), height 5¼″, designer M. Davies | 1960–1976 | 100.00 | 150.00

HN 2874

☐ White gown and cap trimmed in gold, holding very small bouquet in hand (4th version), height 5¼″, designer M. Davies .... | 1980– | 140.00 |

BRIDGET
HN 2070

☐ Older lady, green dress with yellow design, orange shawl and hand bag, black hat with red ribbon, height 8¾″, designer M. Davies .... | 1951–1973 | 300.00 | 350.00

BROKEN LANCE, The
HN 2041

☐ Green base with design, horse is white with blue cloth cover that has darker blue and yellow designs, red lining, gray suit of armor, red and dark blue headdress, red and gold shield, brown and light red lance, height 8¾″, designer M. Davies .... | 1949–1975 | 450.00 | 550.00

BUDDIES
HN 2546

☐ Black and green base, seated boy in brown shorts, blue shirt, brown and black dog, matte finish, height 6″, designer E.J. Griffiths .... | 1973–1976 | 175.00 | 250.00

Bridget, HN 2070, 300.00–350.00

	Date	Price Range	

BUMBLE
Issued only as a miniature
☐ **M-76** Red vest, black pants, green cape with yellow trim, black tri-cornered hat with yellow trim, black stand, height 4″, designer L. Harradine 1939–1982   55.00   85.00

BUNNY
HN 2214
☐ Small girl, green and pink gown, holding bunny, height 5″, designer M. Davies 1960–1975   150.00   200.00

BUTTERCUP
HN 2309
☐ Gown of shaded yellow, green bodice,

Butterfly, HN 720, 1200.00-1400.00

	Date	Price Range	
hand on green hat, height 7″, designer M. Davies	1964–	**185.00**	
HN 2399			
☐ Gown and hat scarlet, sleeves and bow of gown lemon yellow, height 7½″, designer M. Davies	1983–	**185.00**	
BUTTERFLY **HN 719**			
☐ Butterfly costumed figure on black pedestal type base, wings are multicolored, pink and black dress, height 6½″, designer L. Harradine	1925–1938	**1200.00**	**1400.00**
HN 720			
☐ Red wings, white dress with black checks, height 6½″, designer L. Harradine	1925–1938	**1200.00**	**1400.00**

	Date	Price Range	

HN 730
☐ Yellow dress, blue and black wings, height 6½″, designer L. Harradine ... 1925–1938 1350.00 1550.00

HN 1203
☐ Gold wings, height 6½″, designer L. Harradine 1926–1938 1550.00 1850.00

HN 1456
☐ Wings in shades of lavender and pink, dress shades of green, height 6½″, designer L. Harradine 1931–1938 1300.00 1500.00

BUZ FUZ
HN 538
☐ A character from Dickens' "Pickwick Papers," height 3¾″, designer L. Harradine 1922– 55.00 85.00
☐ **M-53** Renumbered as a miniature, height 4″, designer L. Harradine 1932–1983 55.00 85.00

'CALLED LOVE, A LITTLE BOY . . .'
HN 1545
☐ Small naked child crouching on base, holding red and blue bucket, height 3½″, designer unknown 1933–1949 850.00 1150.00

CALUMET
HN 1428
☐ Base is multicolored striped blanket, Indian costume is light brown, robe is stripes of green, yellow, red, and tan; bowl on base has red and green stripe, height 6″, designer C.J. Noke 1930–1949 1000.00 1100.00

HN 1689
☐ Base is green blanket with patch of blue, red, and green; Indian costume is darker brown, robe is green with yellow, blue bowl, height 6½″, designer C.J. Noke 1935–1949 750.00 850.00

HN 2068
☐ HN 1689 with minor glaze differences, height 6¼″, designer C.J. Noke 1950–1953 550.00 650.00

CAMELLIA
HN 2222
☐ Pink gown with very light blue scarf and bow in hair, height 7¾″, designer M. Davies 1960–1971 250.00 350.00

Calumet, HN 1689, 750.00–850.00

	Date	Price Range	
CAMILLA			
HN 1710			
☐ Eighteenth century style gown of red and white with red lines, dark hair with green bow, on light colored base, height 7″, designer L. Harradine	1935–1949	850.00	1050.00
HN 1711			
☐ Light hair, light red gown with darker red design, green overdress with white designs, height 7″, designer L. Harradine	1935–1949	850.00	1050.00
CAMILLE			
HN 1586			
☐ Eighteenth century style gown of very light red with overdress of darker red, black hat with light red trim, holding mirror, height 6½″, designer L. Harradine	1933–1949	775.00	900.00

Camille, HN 1586, 775.00–900.00

	Date	Price Range	

HN 1648

☐ Light red gown with overdress of cream skirt with red flower design, green bodice with red bows, green hat with red trim, height 6½″, designer L. Harradine 1934–1949 775.00 900.00

HN 1736

☐ Red and white costume, height 6½″, designer L. Harradine 1935–1949 950.00 1150.00

CAPTAIN

HN 778

☐ Black pedestal style base, red long coat with gold trim, white trousers and long vest with gold buttons, black boots, black hat with white and gold trim, white cravat, black strap holding sword (1st version), height 7″, designer L. Harradine 1926–1938 2000.00 2500.00

	Date	Price Range	

HN 2260

☐ White trousers and stockings, black shoes with gold trim, black coat and hat with white and gold trim; hand on map lies on brown stand, book and paper on bottom of stand (2nd version), height 9½", designer M. Nicoll 1965–1982   250.00   350.00

CAPTAIN COOK
HN 2889

☐ Navy uniform of white trousers, black coat with yellow trim and white buttons, seated on stool with base of light brown, maps in drawer on base, map on lap, black bag leaning against yellow pedestal, height 8", designer W.K. Harper 1980–1984   375.00   425.00

CAPTAIN CUTTLE
Issued only as a miniature

☐ **M-77** Yellow vest, light yellow pants, red tie, black coat, light brown hat with black band, black stand, height 4", designer L. Harradine 1939–   55.00   85.00

CAPTAIN MacHEATH
HN 464

☐ A character of "The Beggar's Opera," red coated figure on black material, height 7", designer L. Harradine 1921–1949   700.00   850.00

HN 590

☐ Yellow cravat only difference, height 7", designer L. Harradine 1924–1949   700.00   850.00

HN 1256

☐ Earthenware, height 7", designer L. Harradine 1927–1949   700.00   850.00

CARMEN
HN 1267

☐ Dark haired figure with red dress, red and black shawl, red shoes, on base, holding tambourine (1st version), height 7", designer L. Harradine 1928–1938   1250.00   1350.00

HN 1300

☐ Blue and yellow gown, green shoes, green base (1st version), height 7", designer L. Harradine 1928–1938   1350.00   1450.00

HN 2545

☐ Tall figure with black hair, blue and

	Date	Price Range	

black gown, light blue bodice (2nd version), height 11½″, designer E.J. Griffiths 1974–1979 350.00 400.00

CARNIVAL
HN 1260
☐ Half nude figure with pink tights on black base, height 8¼″, designer L. Harradine 1927–1938 3500.00 4500.00
HN 1278
☐ Half nude figure with blue tights, black and gold waist band, holding long cloth, which is yellow and purple, behind head, on black base, height 8½″, designer L. Harradine 1928–1938 3500.00 4500.00

CAROLYN
HN 2112
☐ White gown with flowers, green cummerbund and gloves, holding black hat and white handkerchief, height 7″, designer L. Harradine 1953–1959 300.00 400.00
HN 2974
☐ Two tone green gown, frilled white cuffs and trim; low neckline accented by yellow rose, (2nd version), height 5½″, designer A. Hughes 1983–1986 150.00 175.00

CARPENTER
HN 2678
☐ Depicts older, gray-haired man wearing white apron, working over a bench which has a detailed study of hammers, screwdrivers, saw, vise and plane, height 8″, designer M. Nicoll 1986– 215.00

CARPET SELLER, The
HN 1464A
☐ Blue robed figure with black and multicolored rug on black base, hand open, height 9″, designer L. Harradine 1931– 700.00 800.00
HN 1464
☐ Same figure with same coloring except hand closed, height 9¼″, designer L. Harradine 1931–1969 275.00 350.00

CARPET VENDOR, The
HN 38
☐ Kneeling figure on green base, holding one end of unrolled blue striped carpet,

Carpenter, HN 2678, 190.00

	Date	Price Range	
costume of blue trousers, yellow and red shirt trimmed in white, dark blue and red turban (1st version), height unknown, designer C.J. Noke	1914–1938	3500.00	4500.00
HN 38A			
☐ Persian style carpet (1st version), height unknown, designer C.J. Noke	1914–1938	3500.00	4500.00
HN 76			
☐ Kneeling figure on blue and black checked cushion, blue costume with orange trim, turban green, orange rug in front of figure (2nd version), height 5½″, designer C.J. Noke	1917–1938	3500.00	4500.00
HN 348			
☐ Blue and green costume with checkered base (1st version), height unknown, designer C.J. Noke	1919–1938	3500.00	4500.00
HN 350			
☐ Blue costume, green and brown floral			

The Carpet Seller, HN 1464, 275.00–350.00

	Date	Price Range	
carpet (1st version), height 5½″, designer C.J. Noke	1919–1938	3500.00	4500.00

CARRIE (Kate Greenaway)
HN 2800
☐ Small girl with blue coat, white hat with blue and red ribbons, holding single flower in one hand, on white base, height 6″, designer M. Davies .... | 1976–1981 | 100.00 | 125.00

CASSIM
HN 1231
☐ Small seated Arab figure, with blue trousers, multicolored vest and blue

The Carpet Vendor, HN 76, 3500.00–4500.00

	Date	Price Range	
cone shaped hat (1st version), height 3″, designer L. Harradine	1927–1938	850.00	1050.00
HN 1232			
☐ White and orange striped trousers, dark colored vest with red hat (1st version), height 3″, designer L. Harradine	1927–1938	850.00	1050.00
HN 1311			
☐ HN 1231 mounted on lidded pink bowl (2nd version), height 3¾″, designer L. Harradine	1929–1938	900.00	1100.00
HN 1312			
☐ Mounted on blue bowl (2nd version), height 3¾″, designer L. Harradine ...	1929–1938	900.00	1100.00

CAVALIER
HN 369
☐ Blue trousers, white stockings, black shoes with blue bows, dark blue coat, light green waistcoat with white collar,

	Date	Price Range	

yellow feather on hat, base (1st version), height unknown, designer unknown 1920–1938 4000.00 5000.00

HN 2716

☐ Black trousers, boots, vest and hat, white shirt, dark cape with red lining (2nd version), height 9¾", designer E.J. Griffiths. 1976–1982 200.00 300.00

CELESTE
HN 2237

☐ Gown of shaded greens with dark ribbon at waist, sleeves and shoulder, height 6¾", designer M. Davies. 1958–1971 250.00 300.00

CELIA
HN 1727

☐ Tall figure with pale pink nightgown, height 11½", designer L. Harradine. 1935–1949 1000.00 1300.00

HN1727

☐ Pale green night gown, height 11½", designer L. Harradine. 1935–1949 1000.00 1300.00

CELLIST, The
HN 2226

☐ Black suit, white shirt, black bow tie, playing brown cello seated on brown stool, blue and purple books under cello, height 8", designer M. Davies. 1960–1967 375.00 450.00

CENTURION, The
HN 2726

☐ Depicts a warrior perhaps from the old Roman Empire in his armor, sword in hand and shield of light and dark brown standing at his feet. Figure on gray base, height 9½", designer W.K. Harper. 1982–1984 175.00 250.00

CERISE
HN 1607

☐ Small figure in light red figured gown with darker sash, holding fruit basket, height 5¼", designer L. Harradine. .. 1933–1949 450.00 500.00

CHARITY
HN 3087

☐ Child figure with long, blond hair dressed in a gown of shades of yellow

	Date	Price Range	

to gold, holding teddy bear in arms with purple blanket wrapped around her waist and the teddy bear. Limited edition of 9,500 commissioned by Lawley's of England, height 8½", designer E. Griffiths. .... | 1987– | 225.00 | 300.00 |

CHARLEY'S AUNT
HN 35
□ Black and white gowned figure on base which has the inscription 'W.S. Penley as Charley's Aunt' (1st version), height 7", designer A. Toft. .... | 1914–1938 | 750.00 | 850.00 |

HN 640
□ Green dress, mauve spotted (1st version), height 7", designer A. Toft. .... | 1924–1938 | 1100.00 | 1200.00 |

HN 1411
□ Seated figure with dark dress and white lace shawl (2nd version), height 8", designer H. Fenton. .... | 1930–1938 | 1375.00 | 1425.00 |

HN 1554
□ Purple dress (2nd version), height 8", designer H. Fenton. .... | 1933–1938 | 1350.00 | 1500.00 |

HN 1703
□ Not mounted on base, lilac and white dress with dark ribbons on bonnet (3rd version), height 6", designer A. Toft. | 1935–1938 | 1400.00 | 1600.00 |

CHARLOTTE
HN 2421
□ Purple gown with gold design at hem line, holding small light tan dog, seated on yellow chair, height 6½", designer J. Bromley. .... | 1972–1986 | 150.00 | 200.00 |

HN 2423
□ New color version. Seated figure holding small dog, wearing pale blue dress with pink petticoat. Hair is silver with white ribbon, height 6¾", designer J. Bromley. .... | 1986– | 230.00 | |

CHARMIAN
HN 1568
□ White gown with shaded red overdress, holding small dark fan, height 6½", designer L. Harradine. .... | 1933–1938 | 775.00 | 875.00 |

HN 1569
□ Green gown with red and blue overdress, height 6½", designer L. Harradine. .... | 1933–1938 | 775.00 | 875.00 |

	Date	Price Range	

HN 1651

☐ Red bodice, green skirt, height 6½", designer L. Harradine. 1934–1938 1150.00 1300.00

CHELSEA PAIR (Female)
HN 577

☐ Eighteenth century styled figure seated on tree on green base, white gown with blue flower design, red bonnet with blue ribbons, height 6", designer L. Harradine. 1923–1938 850.00 1000.00

HN 578

☐ Red blouse, height 6", designer L. Harradine. 1923–1938 850.00 1000.00

CHELSEA PAIR (Male)
HN 579

☐ Eighteenth century style figure seated on tree, reddish-brown coat, black trousers, black hat, green base, height 6", designer L. Harradine. 1923–1938 850.00 1000.00

HN 580

☐ Blue flowers instead of white, height 6", designer L. Harradine. 1923–1938 850.00 1000.00

CHELSEA PENSIONER
HN 689

☐ Red coated seated figure with black trousers, hat, cane and pipe on brown base, height 5¾", designer L. Harradine. 1924–1938 1250.00 1400.00

CHERIE
HN 2341

☐ Small figure wearing blue gown with white cuffs holding yellow gloves in hands, blue hat with light blue feather and yellow ribbon bow, height 5½", designer M. Davies. 1966– 140.00

CHIEF, The
HN 2892

☐ Seated figure on green and brown base, light brown costume with blue trim on front, green cloth with design of red, blue and orange on lap, blue, black and white feathered headdress, band of blue with yellow design, moccasins of white tops with brown and blue design,

Child on Crab, HN 32, 3000.00–3500.00

	Date	Price Range	
brown peace pipe in hands, height 7″, designer W.K. Harper.	1979–1988	275.00	

CHILD FROM WILLIAMSBURG
HN 2154
☐ Small girl figure in blue gown, holding flower, height 5¾″, designer M. Davies. ....

	1964–1983	100.00	125.00

CHILD ON CRAB
HN 32
☐ Green and brown crab, child wears pale blue robe, height 5¼″, designer C.J. Noke. ....

	1913–1938	3000.00	3500.00

CHILD'S GRACE, A
HN 62
☐ HN 62A except there is additional black patterning over the green coat, height

	Date	Price Range	
6¾", designer L. Perugini.	1916–1938	3000.00	3500.00
HN 62A			
□ Small girl figure with hands clasped on pedestal which contains printed poem, green dress with orange underlay, height 6¾", designer L. Perugini.	1916–1938	3000.00	3500.00
HN 510			
□ Checkered dress, green base, height 6¾", designer L. Perugini.	1921–1938	3500.00	4000.00

CHILD STUDY

	Date	Price Range	
HN 603A			
□ White child's nude figure seated on rock with base which has flowers, height 4¾", designer L. Harradine.	1924–1938	675.00	850.00
HN 603B			
□ Kingcup flowers around base, height 4¾", designer L. Harradine.	1924–1938	675.00	850.00
HN 605A			
□ Standing white nude child's figure on pedestal and base covered with flowers, height 5¾", designer L. Harradine. ..	1924–1938	675.00	850.00
HN 605B			
□ Different flowers, height 5¾", designer L. Harradine.	1924–1938	675.00	850.00
HN 606A			
□ White nude child's figure standing on rock bending over to look at flowers on base, height 5", designer L. Harradine.	1924–1938	675.00	850.00
HN 606B			
□ Kingcups on base, height 5", designer L. Harradine.	1924–1938	675.00	850.00
HN 1441			
□ Seated white nude child's figure with blonde hair, multicolored rock, with applied flowers on base, height 5", designer L. Harradine.	1931–1938	850.00	950.00
HN 1442			
□ Standing white nude child's figure with blonde hair, multicolored rock, with applied flowers on base, height 6¼", designer L. Harradine.	1931–1938	850.00	950.00
HN 1443			
□ Figure 1540, with applied flowers on base, height 5", designer L. Harradine.	1931–1938	850.00	950.00

Chloe, HN 1476, 275.00–325.00

	Date	Price Range

CHINA REPAIRER, The
HN 2943
☐ Man seated at his work bench working on a broken horse. Gray hair, blue shirt, white apron, height 6¾″, designer R. Tabbenor. ....

1983–1988	275.00	

CHLOE
HN 1470
☐ Red and cream tiered gown, blue bonnet with ribbons, height 5¾″, designer L. Harradine. ....

1931–1949	255.00	300.00

☐ **M-29** Made as a miniature, red/cream, height 3″, designer L. Harradine. ....

1932–1945	300.00	350.00

HN 1476
☐ Blue gown with pink bonnet with ribbons, height 5¾″, designer L. Harradine. ....

1931–1938	275.00	325.00

	Date	Price Range	

HN 1479

☐ Blue gown with red bonnet and ribbons, height 5¾″, designer L. Harradine. 1931–1949 250.00 300.00

HN 1498

☐ Yellow and green, height 5¾″, designer L. Harradine. 1932–1938 450.00 550.00

HN 1765

☐ Blue gown with blue ribbon on bonnet, height 6″, designer L. Harradine. 1936–1950 250.00 300.00

☐ **M-10** Made as a miniature, blue, height 3″, designer L. Harradine. 1932–1945 300.00 350.00

HN 1956

☐ HN 1470 except red skirt and green ribbon, height 6″, designer L. Harradine. 1940–1949 600.00 750.00

☐ **M-9** Made as a miniature, pink, height 3″, designer L. Harradine. 1932–1945 275.00 325.00

CHOICE, The
HN 1959

☐ Red gowned lady trying on bonnet, with box at foot, height 7″, designer L. Harradine. 1941–1949 1650.00 2000.00

HN 1960

☐ Red and blue gown, height 7″, designer L. Harradine. 1941–1949 1650.00 2000.00

CHOIR BOY
HN 2141

☐ Red and white choir robe, height 4⅞″, designer M. Davies. 1954–1975 90.00 125.00

CHORUS GIRL
HN 1401

☐ Red, yellow, and black costume, figure on pedestal, height and designer unknown. Rare. 1930–1938 3500.00 5000.00

CHRISTINE
HN 1839

☐ Lilac tiered dress with blue shawl, bonnet trimmed with flowers (1st version), height 7¾″, designer L. Harradine. .. 1938–1949 700.00 850.00

HN 1840

☐ Red dress with blue figured shawl (1st version), height 7¾″, designer L. Harradine. 1938–1949 700.00 850.00

	Date	Price Range	

HN 2792

☐ Light cream gown with shades of very light red and yellow, with multicolored flowers over skirt (2nd version), height 7¾", designer M. Davies. .... — 1978– — 350.00

CHRISTMAS MORN
HN 1992

☐ Red coat with jacket trimmed in white fur, with muff, height 7¼", designer M. Davies. .... — 1947– — 195.00

CHRISTMAS PARCELS
HN 2851

☐ Dark green cloak with yellow trim, figure holding one Christmas parcel of purple and red, many parcels around foot, small basket, green Christmas tree, height 8⅝", designer W.K. Harper. .... — 1978–1982 — 250.00 — 350.00

CHRISTMAS TIME
HN 2110

☐ Red cloak trimmed with white around bottom, holding small parcels in hand, black bonnet, height 6⅞", designer M. Davies. .... — 1953–1967 — 350.00 — 375.00

CICELY
HN 1516

☐ Light blue skirt with darker blue jacket, figure seated on small couch, height 5½", designer L. Harradine. .... — 1932–1949 — 1200.00 — 1400.00

CIRCE
HN 1249

☐ White nude figure of woman on base, with multicolored robe hanging from one arm, height 7½", designer L. Harradine. .... — 1927–1938 — 2000.00 — 2200.00

HN 1250

☐ Orange and black robe, height 7½", designer L. Harradine. .... — 1927–1938 — 2000.00 — 2200.00

HN 1254

☐ Orange and red robe, height 7½", designer L. Harradine. .... — 1927–1938 — 2000.00 — 2200.00

HN 1255

☐ Blue robe, height 7½", designer L. Harradine. .... — 1927–1938 — 2000.00 — 2200.00

Christmas Time, HN 2110, 350.00–375.00

	Date	Price Range	

CISSIE
HN 1808
☐ Small figure with green dress, holding basket of flowers on arms, height 5″, designer L. Harradine. .... 1937–1951 | **450.00** | **550.00**

HN 1809
☐ Shaded red dress with blue bonnet and green ribbons, height 5″, designer L. Harradine. .... 1937– | **140.00** |

CLARE
HN 2793
☐ Shaded blue gown with multicolored flower design, yellow shawl and bonnet with red ribbon, height 7½″, designer M. Davies. .... 1980–1984 | **175.00** | **250.00**

Cissie, HN 1809, 140.00

	Date	Price Range	

CLARIBEL
HN 1950
☐ Small figure with blue skirt, white cap with green ribbon, height 4¾″, designer L. Harradine. .... | 1940–1949 | **600.00** | **800.00** |

HN 1951
☐ Red and shaded blue dress, blue ribbon on cap, height 4¾″, designer L. Harradine. .... | 1940–1949 | **600.00** | **800.00** |

CLARINDA
HN 2724
☐ Blue and green gown with light blue designs, darker blue and green overdress, figure on green base with blue and white bird on green pedestal at side, height 8½″, designer W.K. Harper. .... | 1975–1980 | **150.00** | **200.00** |

Claribel, HN 1951, 600.00–800.00

	Date	Price Range	
CLARISSA			
HN 1525			
☐ Green gown with red shawl, holding open parasol (1st version), height 10″, designer L. Harradine.	1932–1938	500.00	650.00
HN 1687			
☐ Pale blue gown, green shawl (1st version), height 10″, designer L. Harradine.	1935–1949	600.00	750.00
HN 2345			
☐ Green gown with white sleeves, figure holding basket with two hands (2nd version), height 8″, designer M. Davies. ..	1968–1981	150.00	175.00

CLEMENCY
HN 1633
☐ White, two tiered dress with flower

	Date	Price Range	

design, blue jacket, green bonnet with red ribbons, height 7″, designer L. Harradine. .... — 1934–1938 — 875.00 — 1000.00

HN 1634

☐ White dress trimmed in red, multicolored jacket, height 7″, designer L. Harradine. .... — 1934–1949 — 650.00 — 775.00

HN 1643

☐ White gown trimmed in green, red jacket, height 7″, designer L. Harradine. .... — 1934–1938 — 650.00 — 775.00

CLOCKMAKER, The
HN 2279

☐ Character figure in green coat, green shirt, lighter green apron, blue shirt, brown tie, black shoes, looking at clock piece, clock is brown and green setting on dark stand, height 7¼″, designer M. Nicoli. .... — 1961–1975 — 275.00 — 325.00

CLOTHILDE
HN 1598

☐ Pale pink gown with red robe, height 7¼″, designer L. Harradine. .... — 1933–1949 — 700.00 — 800.00

HN 1599

☐ Pale blue gown with multi-flowered top and sleeves with blue robe with red lining, height 7¼″, designer L. Harradine. .... — 1933–1949 — 700.00 — 800.00

CLOUD, The
HN 1831

☐ Flowing white robed figure with long golden hair, height 23″, designer R. Garbe. .... — 1937–1949 — 4000.00 — 4500.00

CLOWN, The
HN 2890

☐ Clown on brown and yellow base, blue trousers, gold coat, spotted yellow tie, dark hat with flower, gray bucket also on base, height 8¾″, designer W.K. Harper. ..... — 1979–1988 — 395.00

COACHMAN, The
HN 2282

☐ Character figure seated in brown chair, long purple coat, green coat and trousers, purple coat has blue lining, black tall hat with green trim, holding blue

Clothilde, HN 1598, 700.00–800.00

	Date	Price Range	
tankard, height 7″, designer M. Nicoll.	1963–1971	475.00	550.00

COBBLER, The
HN 542
☐ Green costumed, round turban, seated on brown base (1st version), height 7½″, designer C.J. Noke. ....

| | 1922–1939 | 1100.00 | 1200.00 |

HN 543
☐ Specially fired (1st version), height 7½″, designer C.J. Noke. ....

| | 1922–1938 | 1200.00 | 1300.00 |

HN 681
☐ Larger figure on black base, with green costume, red shirt and cone-shaped

The Cobbler, Second Version, HN 1283, 750.00–850.00

	Date	Price Range	
turban (2nd version), height 8½″, designer C.J. Noke.	1924–1938	750.00	850.00
HN 682			
□ Red shirt with green robe (1st version), height 7½″, designer C.J. Noke.	1924–1938	1100.00	1200.00
HN 1251			
□ Black trousers and red shirt, height 8½″, designer C.J. Noke.	1927–1938	1100.00	1200.00
HN 1283			
□ Green costume with yellow and red shirt (2nd version), height 8½″, designer C.J. Noke.	1928–1949	750.00	850.00

	Date	Price Range	

HN 1705
☐ Multicolored costume with blue shirt on colored base (3rd version), height 8″, designer C.J. Noke. 1935–1949 850.00 950.00

HN 1706
☐ Brown costume with green striped shirt (3rd version), height 8″, designer C.J. Noke. 1935–1969 225.00 300.00

COLLINETTE
HN 1998
☐ White gown with long blue cloak, height 7¼″, designer L. Harradine. .. 1947–1969 500.00 600.00

HN 1999
☐ Red cloak, height 7¼″, designer L. Harradine. 1947–1949 500.00 600.00

COLUMBINE
HN 1296
☐ A tutu style costume on figure seated on cream colored pedestal, red and blue striped costume (1st version), height 6″, designer L. Harradine. 1928–1938 1000.00 1200.00

HN 1297
☐ Costume not striped, white base (1st version), height 6″, designer L. Harradine. 1928–1938 1000.00 1200.00

HN 1439
☐ Costume multicolored floral design, light green base (1st version), height 6″, designer L. Harradine 1930–1938 1000.00 1200.00

HN 2185
☐ Standing figure on white base, light pink dress with blue design, small crown on head, holding tambourine (2nd version), height 7″, designer M. Davies. 1957–1969 225.00 275.00

COMING OF SPRING, The
HN 1722
☐ Pink costume on barefoot figure, flower ringed base, holding light colored robe above head, height 12½″, designer L. Harradine. 1935–1949 2500.00 3000.00

HN 1723
☐ Light green costume, height 12½″, designer L. Harradine. 1935–1949 2500.00 3000.00

The Coming of Spring, HN 1723, 2500.00–3000.00

	Date	Price Range	

CONSTANCE
HN 1510

☐ Purple and yellow four tiered gown, holding small purse, height unknown, designer L. Harradine. .... | 1932–1938 | **1250.00** | **1500.00**

HN 1511

☐ Pale pink gown, holding red handbag, height unknown, designer L. Harradine. .... | 1932–1938 | **1250.00** | **1500.00**

CONTENTMENT
HN 395

☐ Woman seated in chair with small child in arms, yellow skirt with pink stripes, blue patterned blouse, height 7 ¼ ″, designer L. Harradine. .... | 1920–1938 | **1850.00** | **2000.00**

	Date	Price Range	

HN 396

☐ Yellow and pink striped chair, height 7¼″, designer L. Harradine. 1920–1938 1850.00 2000.00

HN 421

☐ Gown of light blue patterned with darker blue, light yellow blouse with colored circle pattern, height 7¼″, designer L. Harradine. 1920–1938 1500.00 1700.00

HN 468

☐ Green spotted dress, height 7¼″, designer L. Harradine. 1921–1938 1750.00 2000.00

HN 572

☐ Spotted cream skirt with spotted pink blouse, height 7¼″, designer L. Harradine. 1923–1938 1750.00 2000.00

HN 685

☐ Black and white floral dress, height 7¼″, designer L. Harradine. 1923–1938 1900.00 2000.00

HN 686

☐ Black and white striped chair, height 7¼″, designer L. Harradine. 1924–1938 1900.00 2000.00

HN 1323

☐ Shades of blue and red skirt, with red blouse, blue chair, height 7¼″, designer L. Harradine. 1929–1938 1900.00 2000.00

COOKIE
HN 2218

☐ Small figure, red dress, white apron, holding a small object in each hand, height 4¾″, designer M. Davies. 1958–1975 125.00 175.00

COPPELIA
HN 2115

☐ Ballet figure, red, blue, white costume, standing on toes on base that has books on it, height 7¼″, designer M. Davies. 1953–1959 550.00 650.00

COQUETTE, The
HN 20

☐ Red haired, bare footed figure on base, green gown holding fan, height 9¼″, designer W. White. 1913–1938 3000.00 4000.00

HN 37

☐ Green costume with flower sprays, height 9¼″, designer W. White. 1914–1938 3000.00 4000.00

The Corinthian, HN 1973, 1100.00–1300.00

	Date	Price Range

CORALIE
HN 2307
☐ Yellow gown with white and brown dots
  under gown and cuffs, height 7 ⅛″, de-
  signer M. Davies. 1964–1988 **195.00**

CORINTHIAN, The
HN 1973
☐ Male figure on base, cream trousers,
  blue coat, white vest with multicolored
  design, black cloak with red lining,
  black hat, holding cane, height 7 ¾″,
  designer H. Fenton. 1941–1949 **1100.00** **1300.00**

COUNTRY LASS
HN 1991
☐ Figure on base, blue dress, white
  apron, white kerchief on head, goose in

	Date	Price Range	

arm, basket on the other arm, brown shawl. Also see Market Day, height 7⅜″, designer L. Harradine. 1975–1981 150.00 200.00

COURT SHOEMAKER, The
HN 1755
☐ Two figures, eighteenth century style, costume of man is red, woman's gown is shaded blue, trying on red shoes, height 6¾″, designer L. Harradine. .. 1936–1949 2100.00 2500.00

COURTIER, The
HN 1338
☐ Male figure seated in red and gold chair on base, red and white costume, black base, height 4½″, designer L. Harradine. 1929–1938 3000.00 3750.00

COVENT GARDEN
HN 1339
☐ Figure wearing green dress with shaded red and blue apron, green hat, holding basket on head and carrying basket in other hand, height 9″, designer L. Harradine. 1929–1938 1500.00 1750.00

CRADLE SONG
HN 2246
☐ Seated lady rocking cradle, green dress, dark hair, baby in brown cradle, height 5½″, designer M. Davies. 1959–1962 400.00 500.00

CRAFTSMAN, The
HN 2284
☐ Character figure on one knee, in blue shirt, tan apron, black shoes, white stockings, tools in pocket, working on brown and cream colored chair, height 6″, designer M. Nicoll. 1961–1965 400.00 500.00

CRINOLINE, The
HN 8
☐ Figure is wearing a wide hooped gown of shaded blue, flowers at neck and in hand, height 6¼″, designer G. Lambert. 1913–1938 1400.00 1800.00
HN 9
☐ Pale green skirt with flower sprays, height 6¼″, designer G. Lambert. 1913–1939 1400.00 1800.00

	Date	Price Range	

HN 9A

☐ No flower sprays on skirt, height 6¼", designer G. Lambert. .... 1913–1938 · 1400.00 · 1800.00

HN 21

☐ Yellow skirt with rosebuds, height 6¼", designer G. Lambert. .... 1913–1938 · 1400.00 · 1800.00

HN 21A

☐ No rosebuds on skirt, height 6¼", designer G. Lambert. .... 1913–1938 · 1400.00 · 1800.00

HN 413

☐ Cream skirt with blue trim, blue ribbons on flowers, height 6¼", designer G. Lambert. .... 1920–1938 · 1700.00 · 1950.00

HN 566

☐ Cream skirt with green spots, green blouse, height 6¼", designer G. Lambert. .... 1923–1938 · 1250.00 · 1400.00

HN 628

☐ Bodice of yellow and blue checks, height 6¼", designer G. Lambert. .... 1924–1938 · 1350.00 · 1500.00

CRINOLINE LADY (Miniature)

HN 650

☐ Small eighteenth century style figure with wide hooped gown, white with red rosebuds trim, light green overlay, green bodice, height 3", designer unknown. .. 1924–1938 · 800.00 · 1000.00

HN 651

☐ White gown with orange trim and green design, black bodice, height 3", designer unknown. .... 1924–1938 · 800.00 · 1000.00

HN 652

☐ Purple dress, height 3", designer unknown. .... 1924–1938 · 800.00 · 1000.00

HN 653

☐ Gray and white striped dress, height 3", designer unknown. .... 1924–1938 · 800.00 · 1000.00

HN 654

☐ Orange and green mottled dress, height 3", designer unknown. .... 1924–1938 · 800.00 · 1000.00

HN 655

☐ Blue dress, height 3", designer unknown. .... 1924–1938 · 800.00 · 1000.00

CROUCHING NUDE

HN 457

☐ Crouching white figure on green base, height 5½", designer unknown. .... 1921–1938 · 1500.00 · 1750.00

	Date	Price Range	

CUP OF TEA, The
HN 2322
☐ Older lady figure seated in chair, feet on stool holding cup and saucer, black dress, gray sweater, height 7½″, designer M. Nicoll. 1964–1983 125.00 150.00

CURLY KNOB
HN 1627
☐ Seated figure on box style base holding baby in arms; blue costume with red and blue striped shawl, basket of flowers in front of figure, height 6¼″, designer L. Harradine. 1934–1938 550.00 650.00

CURLY LOCKS
HN 2049
☐ Small female figure seated on base, red dress with blue designs, golden curly locks, height 4½″, designer M. Davies 1939–1953 400.00 475.00

CURTSEY, The
HN 57
☐ Figure making curtsy, orange lustre dress, height 11″, designer E.W. Light. 1916–1938 1500.00 1750.00
HN 57B
☐ Lilac dress, height 11″, designer E.W. Light. 1916–1938 1500.00 1750.00
HN 66A
☐ Lilac dress, this could possibly be renumbered version of 57B, height 11″, designer E.W. Light. 1916–1938 1550.00 1700.00
HN 327
☐ Dark blue dress, height 11″, designer E.W. Light. 1918–1938 1550.00 1700.00
HN 334
☐ Lilac dress with brown design and green trim, height 11″, designer E.W. Light. 1918–1938 1450.00 1600.00
HN 363
☐ Lilac and peach costume, height 11″, designer E.W. Light. 1919–1938 1600.00 1700.00
HN 371
☐ Yellow dress, height 11″, designer E.W. Light. 1920–1938 1650.00 1800.00

	Date	Price Range	

HN 518
☐ Lilac skirt with orange spots, height 11″, designer E.W. Light. 1921–1938 **1650.00** **1800.00**

HN 547
☐ Blue bodice, green and yellow skirt, height 11″, designer E.W. Light. 1922–1938 **1450.00** **1600.00**

HN 629
☐ Green dress with black trimmings, height 11″, designer E.W. Light. 1924–1938 **1650.00** **1800.00**

HN 670
☐ Pink and yellow spotted dress, height 11″, designer E.W. Light. 1924–1938 **1450.00** **1600.00**

CYNTHIA
HN 1685
☐ Seated figure with pink and blue gown, holding flowers, height 5¾″, designer L. Harradine. 1935–1949 **750.00** **900.00**

HN 1686
☐ Red gown with multicolored cloak, green ribbons on bonnet, height 5¾″, designer L. Harradine. 1935–1949 **750.00** **900.00**

HN 2440
☐ Dressed in swirling gown of green and white, dark haired figure with her head held high and her hands lifting her gown as if she were ready to dance, height unknown, designer M. Davies. 1984– **170.00**

DAFFY DOWN DILLY
HN 1712
☐ Green gown and bonnet, height 8″, designer L. Harradine. 1935–1975 **250.00** **325.00**

HN 1713
☐ Shaded blue gown with white apron, bonnet with red trim, holding flat baskets of flowers under each arm, height 8″, designer L. Harradine. 1935–1949 **1000.00** **1250.00**

DAINTY MAY
HN 1639
☐ Eighteenth century figure with red and green gown, small green hat, holding small bouquet, height 6″, designer L. Harradine. 1934–1949 **400.00** **450.00**

HN 1656
☐ Blue and white gown with flowers, small blue hat, height 6″, designer L. Harradine. 1934–1949 **450.00** **550.00**

	Date	Price Range	

☐ **M-67** Made as a miniature, blue and white gown, dark hat, height 4″, designer L. Harradine. 1935–1949 350.00 450.00

☐ **M-73** Red and green gown, green hat, height 4″, designer L. Harradine. 1935–1949 350.00 450.00

DAISY
HN 1575
☐ Small figure with blue gown, white floral design, height 3½″, designer L. Harradine. 1933–1949 450.00 650.00

HN 1961
☐ Pink dress, height 3½″, designer L. Harradine. 1941–1949 500.00 650.00

DAMARIS
HN 2079
☐ Blue and white gown, long red and blue cloak trimmed with white fur, white and dark blue head piece, height 7½″, designer M. Davies. 1951–1952 1400.00 1550.00

'DANCING EYES AND SUNNY HAIR'
HN 1543
☐ Small dark haired white female seated on shaded blue rock, height 5″, designer unknown. 1933–1949 375.00 425.00

DANCING FIGURE
HN 311
☐ Pink flowing gown, holding tambourine in hand, height 17¾″, designer unknown. 1918–1938 3500.00 4000.00

DANCING YEARS
HN 2235
☐ Blue and pink costume, blue ribbon in hair, figure in deep curtsy position, height 7″, designer M. Davies. 1965–1971 300.00 400.00

DANDY, The
HN 753
☐ Eighteenth century style costume of male, white trousers, black boots, red coat, red and black hat, leaning against tree, height 6¾″, designer L. Harradine. 1925–1938 1200.00 1400.00

The Dandy, HN 753, 1200.00–1400.00

	Date	Price Range	

DAPHNE
HN 2268
☐ Pink gowned figure on white base, height 8½″, designer M. Davies. ..... | 1963–1975 | **160.00** | **200.00**

DARBY
HN 1427
☐ Gray haired male seated in high backed blue-green chair, black trousers, blue jacket, red patterned long coat, black shoes, white stockings, height 5½″, designer L. Harradine. .... | 1930–1949 | **325.00** | **400.00**

HN 2024
☐ Minor glaze differences, height 5½″, designer L. Harradine. .... | 1949–1959 | **225.00** | **325.00**

	Date	Price Range	

DARLING
HN 1
☐ Blonde haired figure in white nightshirt on white base (1st version), height 8½", designer C. Vyse. .... | 1913–1928 | 1500.00 | 2000.00
HN 1319
☐ Black base (1st version), height 7½", designer C. Vyse. .... | 1929–1959 | 150.00 | 175.00
HN 1371
☐ Green nightshirt (1st version), height 7½", designer C. Vyse. .... | 1930–1938 | 750.00 | 1100.00
HN 1372
☐ Pink nightshirt (2nd version), height 7½", designer C. Vyse. .... | 1930–1938 | 750.00 | 1100.00
HN 1985
☐ Small figure in white nightshirt on black base (2nd version), height 5¼", designer C. Vyse. .... | 1946– | 80.00 |

DAVID COPPERFIELD
Issued only as a miniature
☐ **M-88** White collar, yellow vest, tan pants, brown hat in hand, black jacket and black stand, height 4¼", designer L. Harradine. .... | 1949–1983 | 55.00 | 85.00

DAWN
HN 1858
☐ White nude figure on blue base, holding blue material down front. Earlier version of this figure had a headdress making it 10¼" in height; without, figure is approximately 9¾", designer L. Harradine. .... | 1938–1949 | 1350.00 | 1500.00
☐ With headdress .... | | 2200.00 | 2500.00

DAYDREAMS
HN 1731
☐ Figure seated on bench, cream gown with red bodice and blue trim, light red bonnet, holding small bouquet, height 5½", designer L. Harradine. .... | 1935– | 195.00 |
HN 1732
☐ Pale blue dress with pink trim, height 5½", designer L. Harradine. .... | 1935–1949 | 750.00 | 950.00
HN 1944
☐ Red dress with white trim, figure holding larger bouquet, height 5½", designer L. Harradine. .... | 1940–1949 | 850.00 | 1000.00

	Date	Price Range	

DEAUVILLE
HN 2344
☐ Figure in the Sweet and Twenty Series. Designed to capture the era of the 1920s and 1930s, this figure depicts a girl playing tennis. Dressed in short, white skirt with yellow sweater, she is holding a tennis racket in one hand and a ball in the other. Limited edition of 1,500, height 8¼", designer M. Davies. 1982– 250.00

DEBBIE
HN 2385
☐ Small figure in dark blue overgown, white with green design undergown, height 5¾", designer M. Davies. 1969–1982 100.00 125.00
HN 2400
☐ Yellow gown, rose overdress with frilled sleeves of half length. Blond hair, height 6", designer M. Davies. 1983– 110.00

DEBUTANTE
HN 2210
☐ Bowing figure in blue dress with high blue headdress, height 5", designer M. Davies. 1963–1967 300.00 375.00

DEIDRE
HN 2020
☐ Blue and red gown, blue bonnet with red lining, height 7", designer L. Harradine. 1949–1955 375.00 450.00

DELICIA
HN 1662
☐ Pink, shaded blue and white gown, small ribbon tied hat has small bouquet on wrist, height 5¾", designer L. Harradine. 1934–1938 900.00 1000.00
HN 1663
☐ Flowered purple, green and yellow skirt, height 5¾", designer L. Harradine. 1934–1938 900.00 1000.00
HN 1681
☐ Green and purple dress, height 5¾", designer L. Harradine. 1935–1938 1250.00 1400.00

DELIGHT
HN 1772
☐ Red gowned figure on black base, small

Delphine, HN 2136, 250.00–325.00

	Date	Price Range	
white cap, trimmed with blue ribbons, height 6¾″, designer L. Harradine. ..	1936–1967	175.00	225.00

HN 1773

☐ Blue gown with red bow, height 6¾″, designer L. Harradine. 1936–1949   450.00   550.00

DELPHINE
HN 2136

☐ Light lavender gown with blue coat that has cream lining, fur stole, bonnet with flower trim, height 7¼″, designer M. Davies. 1954–1967   250.00   325.00

DENISE
HN 2273

☐ Red gown with white trim, bonnet with

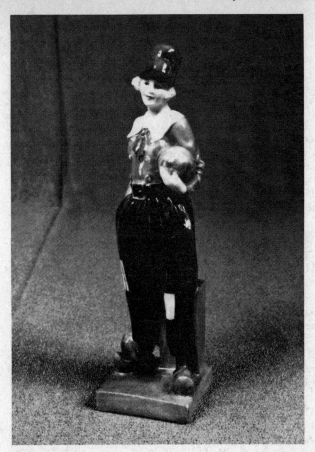

Derrick, HN 1398, 850.00–1000.00

	Date	Price Range	
blue ribbons, height 7¼", designer M. Davies.	1964–1971	275.00	325.00
☐ **M-34** Made as a miniature, pale green dress, rose overskirt, blue bodice and cap, height 4½", designer unknown.	1933–1945	500.00	600.00
☐ **M-35** No color detail available, height 4½", designer unknown.	1933–1945	500.00	600.00

DERRICK
HN 1398

	Date	Price Range	
☐ Dutch boy on base, blue trousers, white and light blue shirt, yellow buttons, red hat, height 8", designer L. Harradine.	1930–1938	850.00	1000.00

	Date	Price Range	

DESPAIR
HN 596
☐ Small figure all wrapped in cobalt blue cape, features are light blue, height 4½", designer unknown. 1924–1938   2000.00   2500.00

DETECTIVE, The
HN 2359
☐ Green and black base, character figure in long brown coat with cape, double billed brown cap, white shirt, black tie, brown trousers, black shoes, holding magnifying glass and white object, height 9¼", designer E.J. Griffiths. .. 1977–1983   200.00   300.00

DIANA
HN 1716
☐ Small figure in blue skirt, pink blouse, holding small bouquet, height 5¾", designer L. Harradine. 1935–1949   400.00   450.00
HN 1717
☐ Green and white dress, white gloves, dark ribbons height 5¾", designer L. Harradine. 1935–1949   400.00   450.00
HN 1986
☐ Shaded red dress, red bonnet, height 5¾", designer L. Harradine. 1946–1975   125.00   175.00
HN 2468
☐ Figure in the Crinoline Ladies Series. She is depicted moving gracefully with one slipper showing. Her gown is white, decorated with the floral table design "Marlow" by Minton. Silver hair is featured in a pompadour style, height 8", designer P. Davies. 1987–   170.00

DICK SWIVELLER
Issued only as a miniature.
☐ **M-90** Brown hat, yellow vest, and pants, dark brown coat, cane and stand, height 4¼", designer unknown. 1949–   55.00   85.00

DIGGER (New Zealand)
HN 321
☐ Green mottled figure of a soldier on base, height 11¼", designer E.W. Light. 1918–1938   1500.00   2000.00

	Date	Price Range	

DIGGER (Australian)
HN 322
☐ Brown soldier figure on base, height 11¼″, designer E.W. Light. 1918–1938 1500.00 2000.00
HN 353
☐ This figure painted naturalistically, height 11¾″, designer E.W. Light. ... 1919–1938 1600.00 2100.00

DILIGENT SCHOLAR, The
HN 26
☐ Seated figure on green base, green trousers, light shirt, multicolored coat, holding slate, height 7″, designer W. White. 1913–1938 2200.00 2500.00

DIMITY
HN 2169
☐ Two tiered white gown with lavender and green flowers, green bodice, lavender sleeves, height 5¾″, designer L. Harradine. 1956–1959 325.00 400.00

DINKY DOO
HN 1678
☐ Small figure in shaded blue gown, white cap, height 4¾″, designer L. Harradine. 1934– 95.00
HN 2120
☐ Figure is in curtsy position. Gown has red bodice with shades of pink in her skirt (2nd Version), height 4¾″, designer L. Harradine. 1983– 95.00

DOCTOR, The
HN 2858
☐ Black coat, blue trousers and vest, seated in chair with doctor's bag at side, height 7½″, designer W.K. Harper. 1979– 295.00

DOLLY
HN 355
☐ Figure in shaded blue and white gown, holding doll, height 7¼″, designer C.J. Noke. 1919–1938 2500.00 3000.00

DOLLY VARDON
HN 1514
☐ White gown with floral flower figures, red patterned cloak with light lining, white muff, green basket at feet, height 8½″, designer L. Harradine. 1932–1938 1200.00 1400.00

Dolly Vardon, HN 1515, 1200.00–1400.00

	Date	Price Range	

HN 1515

☐White and shaded blue gown, multi-colored cloak with light green lining, brown basket at feet, height 8½″, designer L. Harradine. 1932–1949 1200.00 1400.00

DORÇAS
HN 1490

☐Light colored gown with darker over-blouse, Dutch style bonnet with dark ribbons, holding bowl of flowers, height 7″, designer L. Harradine. 1932–1938 850.00 950.00

HN 1491

☐Shaded green gown with darker blouse, height 7″, designer L. Harradine. 1932–1938 850.00 950.00

HN 1558

☐Shaded red gown with designed red

	Date	Price Range	
over blouse, height 7″, designer L. Harradine.	1933–1952	**350.00**	**450.00**

DOREEN
HN 1363
☐ Figure in curtsy position wearing pink gown, height 5¼″, designer L. Harradine. 1929–1938 **900.00** **1200.00**

HN 1389
☐ Green gown trimmed in white, dark haired figure, height 5¼″, designer L. Harradine. 1930–1938 **850.00** **950.00**

HN 1390
☐ Shaded blue gown with white trim, light haired, height 5¼″, designer L. Harradine. 1929–1938 **850.00** **950.00**

DORIS KEENE as Cavallini
HN 90
☐ Black hair, black full gown with silver jewelry (1st version), height 11″, designer C.J. Noke. 1918–1936 **2000.00** **2250.00**

HN 96
☐ Black gown, white fur coat and muff, small hat (2nd version), height 10½″, designer C.J. Noke. 1918–1932 **2500.00** **3000.00**

HN 345
☐ Dark fur collar, striped muff (2nd version), height 10½″, designer C.J. Noke. 1919–1949 **2750.00** **3000.00**

HN 467
☐ Gold jewelry (1st version), height 11″, designer C.J. Noke. 1921–1936 **2000.00** **2200.00**

DOROTHY
HN 3098
☐ Figure seated on a stool making lace, gray dress with large, white collar, black cat at her feet, height 7″, designer P. Parsons. 1987– **295.00**

'DO YOU WONDER . . .'
HN 1544
☐ Small blonde figure wearing blue sun suit on light base, height 5″, designer unknown 1933–1949 **750.00** **950.00**

	Date	Price Range	

DOUBLE JESTER
HN 365
☐ Multicolored Jester costume, standing on base, holds pole which has two faced bust, height unknown, designer C.J. Noke .... | 1920–1938 | **4000.00** | **5000.00**

DREAMLAND
HN 1473
☐ Figure lying on multicolored sofa, costume of several colors, throw on back of couch is also multicolored, height 4¾″, designer L. Harradine .... | 1931–1938 | **3000.00** | **3250.00**

HN 1481
☐ Darker sofa, yellow and red costume, height 4⅓″, designer L. Harradine ... | 1931–1938 | **3000.00** | **3250.00**

DREAMWEAVER
HN 2283
☐ Bearded figure seated on base which contains small animals playing pipes, green trousers, dark blue shirt, wearing sandals, this figure has matte finish, height 8¾″, designer M. Nicoll .... | 1972–1976 | **250.00** | **300.00**

DRUMMER BOY
HN 2679
☐ Brown base, soldier uniform of blue trousers, red and white jacket, black tall hat with white and gold trim, gray knapsack, black boots, sitting on drum of red, white and blue, height 8½″, designer M. Nicoll .... | 1976–1981 | **375.00** | **450.00**

DRYAD OF THE PINES
HN 1869
☐ White nude figure with flowing gold hair, standing on gold colored rock on base, height 23″, designer R. Garbe | 1938–1949 | **4500.00** | **5500.00**

DULCIE
HN 2305
☐ Full white skirt, white bodice with red, yellow, and white designs, trimmed in blue, royal blue overshirt, height 7¼″, designer M. Davies .... | 1981–1984 | **175.00** | **225.00**

DULCINEA
HN 1343
☐ Figure seated on multicolored chaise

	Date	Price Range	

lounge, of red and black costume, black
Spanish style hat, height 5¼", de-
signer L. Harradine .... | 1929–1938 | 1100.00 | 1300.00

HN 1419
☐ Red and pink dress with green shoes,
height 5¼", designer L. Harradine ... | 1930–1938 | 1200.00 | 1500.00

DUNCE
HN 6
☐ Cloaked figure on base wearing dunce
cap, height 10½", designer C.J. Noke | 1913–1938 | 2750.00 | 3000.00

HN 310
☐ Black and white patterned costume,
green base, height 10½", designer C.J.
Noke .... | 1918–1938 | 2750.00 | 3000.00

HN 357
☐ Gray costume with black pattern,
height 10½", designer C.J. Noke ..... | 1919–1938 | 2750.00 | 3000.00

EASTER DAY
HN 1976
☐ Full skirted pale lavender flowered
gown, dark bodice, height 7½", de-
signer M. Davies .... | 1945–1951 | 400.00 | 475.00

HN 2039
☐ Gown with multicolored flowers around
bottom, black bonnet with blue ribbons
and green lining, height 7½", designer
M. Davies .... | 1949–1969 | 275.00 | 325.00

EDITH
HN 2957
☐ One of the charming Kate Greenaway
collection. Small figure with green
dress, white underskirt, white apron
held up containing red flowers, blonde
hair, white bonnet, height 5¾", de-
signer P. Parsons .... | 1982–1985 | 95.00 | 125.00

ELAINE
HN 2791
☐ Blue ball gown, holding fan, height
7½", designer M. Davies .... | 1980– | 250.00 |

ELEANORE
HN 1753
☐ Figure leaning against post, green and
pink skirt with blue bodice, wearing
small bonnet on side of head, height
7", designer L. Harradine .... | 1936–1949 | 1350.00 | 1500.00

Easter Day, HN 1976, 400.00–475.00

	Date	Price Range	
HN 1754			
☐ White gown with blue and red flowers, shaded red bodice, blue bonnet with blue ribbons, height 7″, designer L. Harradine	1936–1949	**1350.00**	**1500.00**
ELEANOR OF PROVENCE			
HN 2009			
☐ Queen figure, dark blue and red gown, red cloak, and white covering on head, height 9½″, designer M. Davies	1948–1953	550.00	675.00
ELEGANCE			
HN 2264			
☐ Shaded green gown trimmed in white and green, green cloak, blue ribbon in hair, height 7½″, designer M. Davies	1961–1985	150.00	175.00

	Date	Price Range	

ELFREDA
HN 2078
☐ Patterned red and blue ball gown, carrying white fan, feathers trimmed in black, height 7¼", designer L. Harradine 1951–1955 775.00 975.00

ELIZA
HN 2543
☐ Tall figure (11¾"), brown costume, black flat hat, carrying basket of flowers on arm, holding bouquet in hand, designer E.J. Griffiths 1974–1979 200.00 300.00

ELIZABETH
HN 2946
☐ A regal lady in her gown of shaded green with gold ruffle showing layers of white skirt underneath. Gold shawl adorns her shoulders. Carrying a very light green parasol. Red hair underneath a bonnet of yellow, height 8", designer B. Franks 1982–1986 175.00 225.00

ELIZABETH FRY
HN 2
☐ Shaded light blue costume, head covering in same color, in light green base, height 17", designer C. Vyse 1913–1938 3500.00 5000.00
HN 2A
☐ Blue base, height 17", designer C. Vyse 1913–1938 3500.00 5000.00

ELLEN
HN 3020
☐ Child sitting on a floor cushion rocking her doll, dressed in a white pinafore with puffed sleeves and wearing a white cap, height unknown, designer unknown 1984–1987 100.00

ELLEN TERRY as Queen
Catherine
HN 379
☐ Shaded blue gown trimmed in black, white and green on black base, head gear of blue, yellow and white, height 12½", designer C.J. Noke 1920–1949 2750.00 3000.00

Elizabeth Fry, HN 2, 3500.00–5000.00

	Date	Price Range	

ELSIE MAYNARD
HN 639

☐ Multicolored costume, white stockings, black shoes on black base, holding tambourine in hand above head, height 7″, designer C.J. Noke 1924–1949 **875.00** **1050.00**

ELYSE
HN 2429

☐ Seated figure, blue gown, flowers in hair, holding white hat with red ribbons, height 6¾″, designer M. Davies 1972– **250.00**

	Date	Price Range	

HN 2474

☐ New color version, dark green with fuchsia-colored slippers and white hat with fuchsia ribbons, height 6¾″, designer P. Davies 1987–ㅤ195.00

EMBROIDERING
HN 2855

☐ Older figure seated in chair, blue gown, green apron, with embroidery on lap, sewing basket at side, height 7¼″, designer W.K. Harper 1980–ㅤ295.00

EMIR
HN 1604

☐ Cream colored robe with red and green patterned scarf, height 7½″, designer C.J. Noke 1933–1949ㅤ800.00ㅤ1000.00

HN 1605

☐ Cream robe with shades of yellow, multicolored striped scarf, height 7½″, designer C.J. Noke 1933–1949ㅤ800.00ㅤ1000.00

EMMA (Kate Greenaway)
HN 2834

☐ Small figure, red dress, white apron trimmed with red flowers, holding green flowers in hands on white base, height 5¾″, designer M. Davies 1977–1981ㅤ100.00ㅤ125.00

ENCHANTMENT
HN 2178

☐ Shaded blue gown with white and yellow sleeves, gown has dark blue designs, height 7¾″, designer M. Davies 1957–1982ㅤ125.00ㅤ175.00

ERMINE COAT, The
HN 1981

☐ Red gown with white fur coat and muff, red stole with light blue and green designs, height 6¾″, designer L. Harradine 1945–1967ㅤ225.00ㅤ300.00

ERMINIE
Issued only as a miniature.

☐ **M-40** Pink skirt with white cape, pink shoes on white stand, height 4″, designer unknown 1933–1945ㅤ550.00ㅤ650.00

ESMERALDA
HN 2168

☐ Cream gown with blue design, red

	Date	Price Range	
shawl, dark blue parasol, holding small bird on hand, height 5¼", designer M. Davies	1956–1959	400.00	475.00

ESTELLE
HN 1566
☐ Light colored gown with shaded blues, blue bonnet, blue muff, blue shoes, height 8", designer L. Harradine 1933–1938   800.00   900.00
HN 1802
☐ Pink dress, height 8", designer L. Harradine 1937–1949   800.00   900.00

EUGENE
HN 1520
☐ Seated figure in shaded green and pink gown, holding fan, height 5¾", designer L. Harradine 1932–1938   875.00   975.00
HN 1521
☐ Shaded red and white gown, height 5¾", designer L. Harradine 1932–1938   875.00   975.00

EUROPA AND THE BULL
HN 95
☐ Lady seated on bull, naturalistically painted, height 9¾", designer H. Tittensor 1918–1938   4000.00   5000.00

EVELYN
HN 1622
☐ Cream colored gown with red bodice, red bonnet with shaded blue feathers, holding parasol across lap, height 6", designer L. Harradine 1934–1949   1000.00   1250.00
HN 1637
☐ Blue bodice, green hat, red parasol, height 6", designer L. Harradine. 1934–1938   1050.00   1200.00

EVENTIDE
HN 2814
☐ Seated old lady figure in blue dress with white apron, patchwork quilt on lap, height 7¾", designer W.K. Harper .. 1977–   230.00

FAGIN
HN 534
☐ A character from Dickens' ''Oliver Twist,'' height 4", designer L. Harradine 1922–   55.00   85.00

	Date	Price Range	

☐ **M-49** Renumbered as a miniature, height 4″, designer L. Harradine ..... | 1932–1983 | **55.00** | **85.00**

FAIR LADY
HN 2193
☐ Green gown, yellow sleeves, bonnet hanging on arm, height 7¾″, designer M. Davies .... | 1963– | **195.00** |

HN 2832
☐ Red gown, green sleeves, dark hair, height 7¾″, designer M. Davies ...... | 1977– | **195.00** |

HN 2835
☐ Orange gown with multicolored designs on white sleeves, height 7¾″, designer M. Davies .... | 1977– | **195.00** |

FAIR MAIDEN
HN 2211
☐ Small figure, green dress, yellow sleeves, bonnet hanging on right wrist, height 5¼″, designer M. Davies ...... | 1967– | **140.00** |

HN 2434
☐ Scarlet gown with green puffed sleeves and a multi-layered petticoat. Green hat trimmed in gold, gold coif in her dark brown hair, height 5¼″, designer M. Davies .... | 1983– | **140.00** |

FAIRY
HN 1324
☐ Nude white child figure seated on pedestal style base with multicolored wings, height unknown, designer L. Harradine .... | 1929–1938 | **1500.00** | **1750.00**

HN 1374
☐ Nude white figure seated on toad stool, which is on green base surrounded by yellow flowers, height 4″, designer L. Harradine .... | 1930–1938 | **1000.00** | **1300.00**

HN 1375
☐ Fairy type figure lying on base covered with flowers, height 3″, designer L. Harradine .... | 1930–1938 | **900.00** | **1150.00**

HN 1376
☐ No mushroom, height 2½″, designer L. Harradine .... | 1930–1938 | **700.00** | **850.00**

HN 1377
☐ Believed not to have been issued but has surfaced priced at. .... | | **700.00** | **850.00**

	Date	Price Range	

HN 1378

☐ Small white kneeling figure on green base with orange flowers, height 2½", designer L. Harradine 1930–1938 700.00 850.00

HN 1379

☐ Small white kneeling figure on green base, has blue and white flowers around figure, height 2½", designer L. Harradine 1930–1938 800.00 1000.00

HN 1380

☐ Dark mottled mushroom, height 4", designer L. Harradine 1930–1938 1100.00 1400.00

HN 1393

☐ Small white figure seated on green base covered with yellow flowers and green leaves, height 2½", designer L. Harradine 1930–1938 950.00 1100.00

HN 1394

☐ Yellow flowers, height 2½", designer L. Harradine 1930–1938 700.00 850.00

HN 1395

☐ Blue flowers, height 3", designer L. Harradine 1930–1938 900.00 1100.00

HN 1396

☐ Small white kneeling figure on green base with blue and white flowers on base and on arm, height 2½", designer L. Harradine 1930–1938 800.00 1000.00

HN 1532

☐ Nude white figure seated on toad stool, which is on green base surrounded by multicolored flowers, height 4", designer L. Harradine 1932–1938 1100.00 1500.00

HN 1533

☐ Multicolored flowers, height 3", designer L. Harradine 1932–1938 900.00 1100.00

HN 1534

☐ Large yellow flowers, height 2½", designer L. Harradine 1932–1938 900.00 1100.00

HN 1535

☐ Yellow and blue flowers, height 2½", designer L. Harradine 1932–1938 800.00 1000.00

HN 1536

☐ Light green base, height 2½", designer L. Harradine 1932–1938 800.00 1000.00

	Date	Price Range	

FAITH
HN 3082
☐ Child figure dressed in a light pink nightgown under a dark pink robe, long blond hair; child is holding a teddy bear. Limited edition of 9,500 commissioned by Lawley's of England, height 8½″, designer E. Griffiths .... | 1986– | 225.00 | 300.00

FALSTAFF
HN 571
☐ Rotund figure in shades of brown costume on base, base has wicker stand covered with green and black striped cover, dark hat with orange feather (1st version), height 7″, designer C.J. Noke | 1923–1938 | 1200.00 | 1600.00

HN 575
☐ Brown coat, yellow spotted cloth over base (1st version), height 7″, designer C.J. Noke .... | 1923–1938 | 1200.00 | 1600.00

HN 608
☐ Red coat with red cloth over base (1st version), height 7″, designer C.J. Noke | 1924–1938 | 1200.00 | 1600.00

HN 609
☐ Green coat with green cloth over base (1st version), height 7″, designer C.J. Noke .... | 1924–1938 | 1200.00 | 1600.00

HN 618
☐ Black color, spotted lilac cloth on green base (2nd version), height 7″, designer C.J. Noke .... | 1924–1938 | 1200.00 | 1600.00

HN 619
☐ Brown coat with green collar, yellow cloth over base (1st version), height 7″, designer C.J. Noke .... | 1924–1938 | 1200.00 | 1600.00

HN 638
☐ Red coat, spotted cream cloth over base (1st version), height 7″, designer C.J. Noke .... | 1924–1938 | 1200.00 | 1600.00

HN 1216
☐ With multicolored costume (1st version), height 7″, designer C.J. Noke | 1926–1949 | 1200.00 | 1600.00

HN 1606
☐ Red costume, brown boots, black hat with red feathers, green cloth with red design on base (1st version), height 7″, designer C.J. Noke .... | 1933–1949 | 1200.00 | 1500.00

	Date	Price Range	

HN 2054

☐ Red jacket, brown boots, gloves and collar, no hat, cream colored cloth on orange colored base (2nd version), height 7″, designer C.J. Noke 1950– 195.00

FAMILY ALBUM
HN 2321

☐ Older lady seated in chair with album in lap, blue skirt, lavender blouse and cap, blue and black striped shawl, height 6¼″, designer M. Nicoll 1966–1973 375.00 425.00

FARAWAY
HN 2133

☐ Girl figure lying on tummy on pillow, reading book, white dress, blue bodice and shoes, height 2½″, designer M. Davies 1958–1962 350.00 400.00

FARMER'S BOY
HN 2520

☐ Boy figure seated on large horse, mounted on base, height 8¾″, designer W.M. Chance 1938–1960 2000.00 2500.00

FARMER'S BOY
NO HN

☐ Girl figure seated on large horse, mounted on base (sometimes known as Monaveen) 4000.00 4500.00

FARMER'S WIFE
HN 2069

☐ Green skirt, red blouse with green collar, white bonnet, skirt has chicken feed in it, base has two chickens on it, height 9″, designer L. Harradine 1951–1955 500.00 600.00

FAT BOY, The
HN 530

☐ A character from Dickens' "Pickwick Papers" (1st version), height 3½″, designer L. Harradine 1922– 55.00 85.00

☐ **M-44** Renumbered as a miniature, height 4¼″, designer L. Harradine ... 1932–1983 55.00 85.00

HN 555

☐ Larger version of character, white trousers, blue coat with white buttons, white neck scarf and cloth over hand,

	Date	Price Range	

on same base (2nd version), height 7″,
designer L. Harradine 1923–1952 **375.00** **425.00**

HN 1893

☐ Very minor color changes (2nd version), height 7″, designer L. Harradine 1938–1952 **300.00** **400.00**

HN 2096

☐ White trousers, blue coat, yellow and black dotted scarf, white cloth with red trim on arm, on dark green base (3rd version), height 7¼″, designer L. Harradine 1952–1967 **300.00** **350.00**

FAVOURITE, The
HN 2249

☐ Older lady figure with cream pitcher and saucer in hands, blue gown with white apron, brown cat at feet, height 7¼″, designer M. Nicoll 1960– **230.00**

FEMALE STUDY
HN 604A

☐ White, nude lady figure kneeling on pedestal that is on a base, with primroses around the base, height 5¾″, designer L. Harradine 1924–1938 **675.00** **850.00**

HN 604B

☐ Same as 604A, except flowers around the base are not primroses but another variety, height 5¾″, designer L. Harradine 1924–1938 **675.00** **850.00**

FIDDLER, The
HN 2171

☐ Eighteenth century figure, dancing and playing fiddle on brown base, light yellow trousers, jacket has yellow and green stripes, black hat with feather, height 8¾″, designer M. Nicoll 1956–1962 **700.00** **850.00**

FIONA
HN 1924

☐ Shaded red gown with purple jacket trimmed in black and white, small black bonnet, seated on green couch with multicolored design (1st version), height 5¾″, designer L. Harradine ... 1940–1949 **750.00** **900.00**

HN 1925

☐ Green skirt (1st version), height 5¾″, designer L. Harradine 1940–1949 **750.00** **900.00**

The Fiddler, HN 2171, 700.00–850.00

	Date	Price Range	
HN 1933			
☐ Multicolored gown, red hat, shaded blue couch (1st version), height 5¾", designer L. Harradine	1940–1949	850.00	1100.00
HN 2694			
☐ Standing figure with blue and red skirt, white bodice and sleeves with small lavender designs (2nd version), height 7½", designer M. Davies	1974–1980	140.00	180.00
FIRST DANCE			
HN 2803			
☐ White gown with flower trim, green bodice, holding multi-flowered fan, height 7¼", designer M. Davies	1977–	230.00	

	Date	Price Range	

FIRST STEPS
HN 2242

☐ Blue gown with beige sleeves and white collar, figure holding hands of small figure, wearing blue trousers with beige skirt, height 6¾", designer M. Davies — 1959–1965 — 450.00 — 550.00

FIRST WALTZ
HN 2862

☐ Ball gown of red with blue and green designs, light blue sleeves, holding large white feather fan, height 7½", designer M. Davies .... — 1979–1983 — 175.00 — 240.00

FISHERWOMEN
HN 80

☐ Three figures on brown base, first figure with green shawl, height unknown, designer unknown .... — 1917–1938 — 4000.00 — 4500.00

HN 349

☐ Central figure has yellow shawl, height unknown, designer unknown .... — 1919–1968 — 2750.00 — 3000.00

HN 359

☐ Central figure has red with black stripes in shawl, height unknown, designer unknown .... — 1919–1938 — 4000.00 — 4500.00

HN 631

☐ Central figure has green shawl, height unknown, designer unknown .... — 1924–1938 — 4000.00 — 4500.00

FLEUR
HN 2368

☐ Green gown with gold design at hemline, darker green jacket with gold dots, holding single flower in upraised hand, light green drape from top of bodice back, height 7½", designer J. Bromley — 1968– — 250.00

HN 2369

☐ Orange dress, pale blue jacket trimmed in white, height 7½", designer John Bromley .... — 1984–1986 — 175.00 — 250.00

FLEURETTE
HN 1587

☐ White gown with red designs, red overlay, holding fan, height 6½", designer L. Harradine .... — 1933–1949 — 500.00 — 650.00

	Date	Price Range	

FLORA
HN 2349

☐ Older lady figure in dark brown dress with white apron, flowers in pot and under stool, height 7¾", designer M. Nicoll 1966–1973   275.00   325.00

FLORENCE
HN 2745

☐ Figure on ivory-colored base. She is strolling along, dressed in purple with darker bodice. Hat is white, trimmed in purple; she is holding a white muff, height 8", designer D. Tootle 1987–   195.00

FLOUNCED SKIRT, The
HN 57A

☐ Many tiered orange dress, figure wearing jewelry, height 9¾", designer E.W. Light 1916–1938   1650.00   1800.00

HN 66

☐ Lilac dress, height 9¾", designer E.W. Light 1916–1938   1650.00   1800.00

HN 77

☐ Lemon yellow dress with black trimmings, height 9¾", designer E.W. Light 1917–1938   1650.00   1800.00

HN 78

☐ Flowered yellow dress, height 9¾", designer E.W. Light 1917–1938   1650.00   1800.00

HN 333

☐ Mottled brown tone dress, height 9¾", designer E.W. Light 1918–1938   1550.00   1700.00

FLOWER SELLER, The
HN 789

☐ Yellow dress with green designs, red blouse, green shawl, green feathers on black hat, holding wrapped baby in one arm and a basket of flowers on other arm, height 8¾", designer L. Harradine 1926–1938   700.00   850.00

FLOWER SELLER'S CHILDREN, The
HN 525

☐ Boy and girl seated on stone bench with basket of flowers, green costume on boy, blue costume on girl, height 8¼", designer L. Harradine 1921–1949   1300.00   1500.00

The Flower Seller, HN 789, 700.00–850.00

	Date	Price Range	
HN 551			
☐ Costume of boy blue, girl's checkered orange and yellow, height 8¼″, designer L. Harradine	1922–1949	**1300.00**	**1500.00**
HN 1206			
☐ Costume of girl multicolored, boy's in shaded blues, cloth of dark blue, most flowers dark blue, height 8¼″, designer L. Harradine	1926–1949	400.00	500.00
HN 1342			
☐ Boy's costume shades of blue and red, girl's red with black design, robe shades of red and blue, height 8¼″, designer L. Harradine	1929–	550.00	

	Date	Price Range	

HN 1406

☐ Yellow costume, dark blue cloth over basket, height 8¼″, designer L. Harradine ....

1930–1938   950.00   1250.00

FOAMING QUART, The
HN 2162

☐ Rotund figure seated in dark gray and white chair, purple trousers, purple and red tunic with yellow collar, green gloves and long boots, purple hat with beige trim, blue and gray beard and hair, light blue tankard, height 5¾″, designer M. Davies ....

1955–   230.00

FOLLY
HN 1335

☐ Short red costume, green collar, dark blue sash, light green dunce type hat, holding several small round objects of red, yellow and white, height 9″, designer L. Harradine ....

1929–1938   1600.00   1850.00

HN 1750

☐ Earthenware, with brown hat, white muff, dark dress, height 9½″, designer L. Harradine ....

1936–1949   1500.00   1750.00

FORGET-ME-NOT
HN 1812

☐ Red haired figure seated on bench style base, pink dress, green ribbons, holding small round purse, height 6″, designer L. Harradine ....

1937–1949   600.00   700.00

HN 1813

☐ Red dress, dark blue bonnet with ribbons, height 6″, designer L. Harradine ....

1937–1949   600.00   700.00

FORTUNE TELLER
HN 2159

☐ Gypsy figure seated on wicker stand, at small table with green and black cover, crystal ball and cards on table, red dress with green shawl, height 6½″, designer L. Harradine ....

1955–1967   450.00   550.00

FORTY WINKS
HN 1974

☐ Elderly lady seated in tall backed red and yellow chair, dark skirt, white

Fortune Teller, HN 2159, 450.00–550.00

	Date	Price Range	
apron, red blouse, dark shawl, cat at feet, height 6¾″, designer H. Fenton	1945–1973	225.00	275.00

FOUR O'CLOCK
HN 1760

☐ Shaded blue gown with white trim, multicolored bonnet, holding tea cup and saucer, height 6″, designer L. Harradine 1936–1949   900.00   1100.00

FRAGRANCE
HN 2334

☐ Blue gown with white circular designs and white trim, height 7⅜″, designer M. Davies 1966–   230.00

FRANCINE
HN 2422

☐ Small dark haired figure with green

	Date	Price Range	

dress and yellow sleeves, blue waist ribbon, holding brown bird on arm, height 5¼″, designer J. Bromley .... 1972–1980 · 65.00 100.00

FRANGCON
HN 1720
☐ Multicolored flowered gown with black hat and shoes, on base trimmed in black, height 7½″, designer L. Harradine 1935–1949 900.00 1200.00

HN 1721
☐ Green dress, green hat and shoes, base trimmed in brown, height 7½″, designer L. Harradine 1935–1949 900.00 1200.00

FRENCH PEASANT
HN 2075
☐ Light red skirt with red designs, shaded blue blouse, white headdress with red ribbons, on multicolored base, height 9½″, designer L. Harradine 1951–1955 600.00 700.00

FRIAR TUCK
HN 2143
☐ Brown monk's robe, holding sword and shield, on brown base, height 7½″, designer M. Davies 1954–1967 450.00 600.00

FRUIT GATHERING
HN 449
☐ Blue striped blouse, blue skirt, figure holding basket, has dog on base with figure, height 7¾″, designer L. Harradine 1921–1938 2750.00 3000.00

HN 476
☐ Green check blouse, blue check skirt, height 7¾″, designer L. Harradine ... 1921–1938 2650.00 2800.00

HN 503
☐ Brown and blue checkered dress, height 7¾″, designer L. Harradine 1921–1938 2500.00 3000.00

HN 561
☐ Yellow designed skirt, green blouse, bonnet same as skirt, height 7¾″, designer L. Harradine 1923–1938 2500.00 3000.00

HN 562
☐ Pink blouse with spotted skirt, height 7¾″, designer L. Harradine 1923–1938 2500.00 3000.00

Friar Tuck, HN 2143, 450.00–600.00

	Date	Price Range	

HN 706
☐ Purple blouse with yellow skirt, height
7¾″, designer L. Harradine 1925–1938 2500.00 3000.00
HN 707
☐ Red blouse, spotted skirt, height 7¾″,
designer L. Harradine 1925–1938 3000.00 3500.00

GAFFER, The
HN 2053
☐ Elderly male figure with white beard on
base, green trousers, dark coat, red
vest, brown hat, holding staff and red
and white dotted kerchief, height 7¾″,
designer L. Harradine 1950–1959 450.00 525.00

The Gaffer, HN 2053, 450.00–525.00

	Date	Price Range	
GAINESBOROUGH HAT, The			
HN 46			
☐ Lilac dress, wearing huge black and white hat, height 8¾″, designer H. Tittensor	1915–1938	**1200.00**	**1350.00**
HN 46A			
☐ Black patterned collar was added to costume, height 8¾″, designer H. Tittensor	1915–1938	**1200.00**	**1350.00**
HN 47			
☐ Green dress, height 8¾″, designer H. Tittensor	1915–1938	**1200.00**	**1350.00**

	Date	Price Range	

HN 329
- ☐ Patterned blue dress, height 8¾", designer H. Tittensor 1918–1938 1200.00 1350.00

HN 352
- ☐ Yellow dress and purple hat, height 8¾", designer H. Tittensor 1919–1938 1750.00 2000.00

HN 383
- ☐ Striped dress, height 8¾", designer H. Tittensor 1920–1938 1150.00 1300.00

HN 453
- ☐ Red, blue and green costume, height 8¾", designer H. Tittensor 1921–1938 1250.00 1400.00

HN 675
- ☐ Cream gown with red and yellow design, black hat, height 8¾", designer H. Tittensor 1924–1938 1350.00 1500.00

HN 705
- ☐ Shaded blue gown with red and yellow designs, height 8¾", designer H. Tittensor 1925–1938 1200.00 1350.00

GAMEKEEPER, The
HN 2879
- ☐ Figure kneeling on ground (base) dressed in gray colored trousers, dark green jacket, cream colored polo neck sweater, dog sitting beside him is black, gamekeeper is holding a gun, height unknown, designer E. Griffiths 1984– 185.00

GAY MORNING
HN 2135
- ☐ Cream colored skirt, with very light red bodice, large white sleeves trimmed in blue, blue and red scarf in hand, height 7", designer M. Davies 1954–1967 275.00 325.00

GEISHA, A
HN 354
- ☐ Japanese style figure, yellow kimono, pink cuffs, blue flowered waistband, holding fan (1st version), height 10¾", designer H. Tittensor 1919–1938 2500.00 3100.00

HN 376
- ☐ Blue and yellow mottled kimono (1st version), height 10¾", designer H. Tittensor 1920–1938 2500.00 3100.00

	Date	Price Range	

HN 387
☐ Blue kimono, yellow cuffs (1st version), height 10¾″, designer H. Tittensor .. 1920–1938 — 2500.00 — 3100.00

HN 634
☐ Black and white kimono (1st version), height 10¾″, designer H. Tittensor .. 1924–1938 — 2500.00 — 3100.00

HN 741
☐ Dark multicolored kimono, black trim (1st version), height 10¾″, designer H. Tittensor .... 1925–1938 — 2500.00 — 3100.00

HN 779
☐ Red kimono with black spots (1st version), height 10¾″, designer H. Tittensor .... 1926–1938 — 2500.00 — 3100.00

HN 1223
☐ Seated Japanese style figure playing instrument on base, red and black striped costume, flowers in hair (2nd version), height 6¾″, designer C.J. Noke .... 1927–1938 — 975.00 — 1275.00

HN 1234
☐ Multicolored costume (2nd version), height 6¾″, designer C.J. Noke .... 1927–1938 — 975.00 — 1275.00

HN 1292
☐ Orange kimono, blue and green collar (2nd version), height 6¾″, designer C.J. Noke .... 1928–1938 — 1000.00 — 1300.00

HN 1310
☐ Multicolored spotted kimono (2nd version), height 6¾″, designer C.J. Noke 1929–1938 — 975.00 — 1275.00

HN 1321
☐ HN 779 with green kimono (1st version), height 10¾″, designer H. Tittensor .... 1929–1938 — 2500.00 — 3100.00

HN 1322
☐ Pink kimono, with blue markings (1st version), height 10¾″, designer H. Tittensor .... 1929–1938 — 2500.00 — 3100.00

GENEVIEVE
HN 1962
☐ Full red gown with blue and pink ribbons, white muff, black ribbon on dark blue hat with green lining, height 7″, designer L. Harradine .... 1941–1975 — 200.00 — 260.00

GENIE, The
HN 2989
☐ Rising from a lamp, this figure has a dark blue cloak around his bare torso.

	Date	Price Range	

Head bald except for a black topknot. Arms are folded, height 9¾", designer R. Tabbenor 1983– 140.00

GENTLEMEN FROM WILLIAMSBURG
HN 2227
☐ Green costume, white stockings, black shoes, black hat, seated figure on wooden bench, height 6¼", designer M. Davies 1960–1983 150.00 200.00

GENTLEWOMAN, A
HN 1632
☐ Older woman in lavender gown holding green parasol and bonnet, height 7½", designer L. Harradine 1934–1949 750.00 850.00

GEORGIANA
HN 2093
☐ Eighteenth century ball gown in red, blue and pale yellow, headdress of red and blues, height 8¼", designer M. Davies 1952–1955 1100.00 1300.00

GEORGINA (Kate Greenaway)
HN 2377
☐ White base, shaded yellow gown, red cloak, white bonnet with blue ribbons, holding hoop and stick, height 5¾", designer M. Davies 1981–1986 90.00 125.00

GERALDINE
HN 2348
☐ Brown gown with white flowers on bottom edge, white collar, brown ribbon in hair, matte finish, height 7½", designer M. Davies 1972–1976 140.00 185.00

GILLIAN
HN 1670
☐ Shaded red gown, green bonnet and ribbons, white shawl with multicolored design, height 7¾", designer L. Harradine 1934–1949 700.00 800.00
HN 3042
☐ Young lady with gown of green, accented with white sleeves, carrying a fan, silvery hair, height 6¼", designer R. Tabbenor 1985– 185.00

Giselle, The Forest Glade, HN 2140, 350.00–425.00

	Date	Price Range	

GIRL WITH YELLOW FROCK
HN 588
☐ Young girl in yellow frock on green base, height 6¼″, designer unknown — 1923–1938 — 2500.00 — 3000.00

GISELLE
HN 2139
☐ Seated ballet dancer on wooden bench on shaded green base, light blue costume with white trim, blue headdress, height 6¼″, designer M. Davies ...... 1954–1969 — 350.00 — 425.00

GISELLE, THE FOREST GLADE
HN 2140
☐ Ballet figure standing on toes on base of shaded greens, white costume, holding blue cloth by one hand, height 7¼″, designer M. Davies .... 1954–1967 — 350.00 — 425.00

	Date	Price Range	

GLADYS
HN 1740
☐ Figure only of head, shoulders and arms leaning on green base, green gown, height 5″, designer L. Harradine .... | 1935–1949 | 900.00 | 1100.00

HN 1741
☐ Pink dress, height 5″, designer L. Harradine .... | 1935–1938 | 900.00 | 1100.00

GLORIA
HN 1488
☐ Shaded blue gown and cloak, fur trimmed sleeves, blue hat with red feather, red purse, height 7″, designer L. Harradine .... | 1932–1938 | 1500.00 | 1700.00

HN 1700
☐ Light green skirt, green blouse with black designs, black jacket, cloak multicolored, black hat, height 7″, designer L. Harradine .... | 1935–1938 | 1700.00 | 2000.00

GNOME, A
HN 319
☐ Seated elf type figure with pale blue costume, height 6¼″, designer H. Tittensor .... | 1918–1938 | 1200.00 | 1500.00

HN 380
☐ Purple costume, height 6¼″, designer H. Tittensor .... | 1920–1938 | 1200.00 | 1500.00

HN 381
☐ Purple and green costume, green face, hands and arms green, height 6¼″, designer H. Tittensor .... | 1920–1938 | 1200.00 | 1500.00

GOLDEN DAYS
HN 2274
☐ Small girl and dog on dark brown and green base, yellow gown with blue trim, white and brown dog, height 4″, designer M. Davies .... | 1964–1973 | 125.00 | 175.00

GOLLYWOG
HN 1979
☐ Small boy figure in white coveralls with animal designs, on base, holding doll, height 5¼″, designer L. Harradine ... | 1945–1959 | 450.00 | 550.00

HN 2040
☐ Light blue coveralls, green hat, height 5¼″, designer L. Harradine .... | 1949–1959 | 250.00 | 300.00

Gollywog, HN 1979, 450.00–550.00

	Date	Price Range	

GOOD CATCH, A
HN 2258
☐ Man in dark brown suit, on base with fish in hand, net and hamper on base, height 7″, designer M. Nicoll 1966–1986 **175.00** **225.00**

GOOD DAY SIR
HN 2896
☐ Figure is poised as if speaking to someone. Gown is deep purple; blond hair shows underneath a hat of dark blue to purple trimmed in white. She is wearing white gloves and carrying two parcels wrapped with pretty ribbon with a hat box at her feet, height 8½″, designer W.K. Harper 1986– **195.00**

	Date	Price Range

GOOD FRIENDS
HN 2783
☐ Old lady dressed in a long blue dress with black apron, white bonnet, holding a saucer with nuts she is feeding to a friendly squirrel, height 9″, designer B. Harper ....

| | 1985– | 185.00 |

GOOD KING WENCESLAS
HN 2118
☐ Costume of shaded oranges, dark cloak, holding lantern in one hand, on light brown base, height 9″, designer M. Davies ....

| | 1953–1976 | 300.00 | 425.00 |

GOOD MORNING
HN 2671
☐ Lady feeding birds, bird house on tree stump, gown white with floral design edge, light red blouse, matte finish, height 8″, designer M. Nicoll ....

| | 1974–1976 | 325.00 | 375.00 |

GOODY TWO SHOES
HN 1889
☐ Small figure in green dress with white trim, white cap, height 4¾″, designer L. Harradine ....

| | 1938–1949 | 450.00 | 550.00 |

HN 1905
☐ Pink skirt with red overdress, height 4¾″, designer L. Harradine ....

| | 1939–1949 | 450.00 | 550.00 |

HN 2037
☐ Red dress with white trim, red shoes, white cap, height 5¼″, designer L. Harradine ....

| | 1949– | 140.00 |

☐ **M-80** Made as a miniature, blue skirt, height 4″, designer L. Harradine .....

| | 1939–1949 | 700.00 | 850.00 |

☐ **M-81** Cream skirt with mottled overlay, height 4″, designer L. Harradine

| | 1939–1949 | 700.00 | 850.00 |

GOOSEGIRL, The
HN 425
☐ Figure on dark base with goose, blue skirt, striped blue blouse, holding basket, height unknown, designer L. Harradine ....

| | 1921–1938 | 2750.00 | 3000.00 |

HN 436
☐ Green skirt with blue spots, spotted blouse, height unknown, designer L. Harradine ....

| | 1921–1938 | 2500.00 | 3000.00 |

	Date	Price Range	

HN 437
☐ Checkered brown and blue dress, height unknown, designer L. Harradine 1921–1938 2500.00 3000.00

HN 448
☐ Blue striped blouse, blue hat, height unknown, designer L. Harradine 1921–1938 2750.00 3000.00

HN 559
☐ Spotted pink dress, height unknown, designer L. Harradine 1923–1938 2750.00 3000.00

HN 560
☐ Red striped skirt, red blouse, white apron, white with designed rings head kerchief, height unknown, designer L. Harradine 1923–1938 2750.00 3000.00

GOSSIPS, The
HN 1426
☐ Two ladies seated on brown sofa, one costume of shaded blues, with blue ribbon on bonnet, other costume of white with shaded reds, dark hair with small hat, height 5¾", designer L. Harradine 1930–1949 1650.00 1800.00

HN 1429
☐ Red sofa, one gown of red with bonnet, other is white with floral design, small red hat, height 5¾", designer L. Harradine 1930–1949 675.00 825.00

HN 2025
☐ Minor glaze differences, height 5¾", designer L. Harradine 1949–1967 375.00 425.00

GRACE
HN 2318
☐ Green skirt, dark green jacket with fur trim, small fur hat and muff, figure is skating, height 7⅞", designer M. Nicoll 1966–1980 125.00 175.00

GRACE DARLING
HN 3089
☐ Lady figure standing on a brown base, resembling a portion of the wharf, looking out to sea for survivors of one of England's worst storms, which occurred on September 6, 1838. Beautiful

	Date	Price Range	

figure dressed in long skirt of dark blue to almost black, and gold blouse highlighted with black buttons, a red cape is flowing over her shoulders. Issued in a limited edition of 9,500 to support the Royal National Lifeboat Institution, available in the United Kingdom only, height 9″, designer E. Griffiths 1987– **225.00** **300.00**

GRADUATE
HN 3016
□ Young lady wearing the classic black gown and hat, height unknown, designer unknown 1984– **170.00**

HN 3017
□ Young man wearing a black gown over a gray pinstriped suit and cap, height unknown, designer unknown 1984– **170.00**

GRANDMA
HN 2052
□ White skirt, red jacket, multicolored, carrying basket on arm, walking stick in other hand. There are some known color variations of this number, height 6¾″, designer L. Harradine 1950–1959 **300.00** **350.00**

GRAND MANNER
HN 2723
□ Yellow, blue and red gown with white flower design, with hat to match, dark green ribbon on dress, height 7¾″, designer W.K. Harper 1975–1981 **175.00** **250.00**

GRANNY
HN 1804
□ Seated figure on chair, gray dress, purple and brown checkered shawl, small tea table at side, height 7″, designer L. Harradine 1937–1949 **1300.00** **1500.00**

HN 1832
□ Yellow dress with green trim on edge, red and blue shawl, height 7″, designer L. Harradine 1937–1949 **1300.00** **1500.00**

GRANNY'S HERITAGE
HN 1873
□ Seated older lady with child in front, flower baskets on each side, red flowered shawl on granny, green dress on

Granny's Heritage, HN 2031, 375.00–425.00

	Date	Price Range	
child, height 6¼″, designer L. Harradine	1938–1949	1150.00	1350.00
HN 1874			
☐ Granny in blue shawl, green skirt, height 6¼″, designer L. Harradine ...	1938–1949	700.00	950.00
HN 2031			
☐ Granny in green skirt with mottled blue shawl, child in shaded blue dress, height 6¼″, designer L. Harradine ...	1949–1969	375.00	425.00

GRANNY'S SHAWL

HN 1642

	Date	Price Range	
☐ White dress, blue cloak with red ribbons, bonnet with green ribbons, holding basket of flowers, height 6″, designer L. Harradine	1934–1949	450.00	550.00

HN 1647

☐ White dress, red cloak, bonnet with

	Date	Price Range	

dark green ribbons, height 6", designer L. Harradine 1934–1949 **425.00** **475.00**

GRETA
HN 1485
☐ Small figure on base, white gown with blue tinge, red scarf, holding basket in front of her with both hands, height 5½", designer L. Harradine 1931–1953 **275.00** **350.00**

GRETCHEN
HN 1397
☐ Dutch girl on base, blue gown with white apron, white bonnet with green trim, holding jug, height 7¾", designer L. Harradine 1930–1938 **800.00** **1200.00**

HN 1562
☐ Dark hair, multicolored skirt, red blouse, height 7¾", designer L. Harradine 1933–1938 **900.00** **1250.00**

GRIEF
HN 595
☐ Small seated figure wrapped completely in blue robe, dark hair, has only toes peeking from robe, height 2", designer unknown 1924–1938 **1400.00** **1650.00**

GRIZEL
HN 1629
☐ Pink tiered skirt with multicolored blouse, green hat and green shoes, small bit of pantalettes showing, height 6¾", designer L. Harradine 1934–1938 **1300.00** **1500.00**

GRISELDA
HN 1993
☐ Cream colored gown with lavender overlay, trimmed in white, green bonnet with red ribbons, height 5¾", designer L. Harradine 1947–1953 **425.00** **500.00**

GROSSMITH'S 'TSANG IHANG' PERFUME OF TIBET
HN 582
☐ Chinese lady on black base with printing, yellow costume with red flowers, trimmed in blue, wearing white jewelry

	Date	Price Range	

(see classification Tibetian Lady), height 11½″, designer unknown .... **1923– Unknown** **700.00** **800.00**

GUY FAWKES
HN 98
☐ Black costume covered with red cloak, black hat, carrying lantern, height 10½″, designer C.J. Noke **1918–1949** **1250.00** **1500.00**
HN 347
☐ Brown cloak, height 10½″, designer C.J. Noke **1919–1938** **1500.00** **1800.00**
HN 445
☐ Green cloak, height 10½″, designer C.J. Noke **1921–1938** **1500.00** **1800.00**

GWENDOLEN
HN 1494
☐ Seated dark haired figure, tiered green and pink gown, green shoes, holding small floral bouquet on lap, height 6″, designer L. Harradine **1932–1938** **800.00** **1000.00**
HN 1503
☐ Shaded yellow and orange gown, height 6″, designer L. Harradine **1932–1949** **800.00** **1000.00**
HN 1570
☐ Pink gown, height 6″, designer L. Harradine **1933–1949** **800.00** **950.00**

GWYNNETH
HN 1980
☐ Red gown trimmed with white, small white head cap, height 7″, designer L. Harradine **1945–1952** **275.00** **325.00**

GYPSY DANCE, A
HN 2157
☐ White and shaded blue gown, bare footed, free hand not attached to dress (1st version), height 7″, designer M. Davies **1955–1957** **500.00** **600.00**
HN 2230
☐ White and shaded purple gown, hand is attached to gown (2nd version), height 7″, designer M. Davies **1959–1971** **225.00** **300.00**

GYPSY WOMAN WITH CHILD
HN 1301
☐ Blue skirt, red blouse, green shawl,

Happy Birthday, HN 3095, 215.00

	Date	Price Range	
holding wrapped baby in one arm, red tied scarf in other hand, height unknown, designer unknown	1928–1938	2500.00	3000.00

GYPSY GIRL WITH FLOWERS
HN 1302

☐ Striped green skirt, red blouse, holding flowers, height unknown, designer unknown ....

	Date	Price Range	
	1928–1938	2500.00	2750.00

HAPPY ANNIVERSARY
HN 3097

☐ One of the Special Occasion figures. Silver-haired lady sitting on a stool ready to open a gift that is on her lap. Gown is blue, with a lace collar and leafy flounce at bottom, height 6½″, designer P. Parsons ....

	Date	Price Range
	1987–	215.00

HAPPY BIRTHDAY
HN 3095

☐ One of the Special Occasion figures. Lady with white pinafore over a yellow dress; light brown hair. Figure is

	Date	Price Range	
reaching for a package that is resting on a small table with a red cover, height 7 ½ ″, designer P. Parsons	1987–	215.00	

'HAPPY JOY, BABY BOY'
HN 1541
☐ Small white figure standing on multi-colored rock, holding small very light green robe, height 6 ¼ ″, designer unknown ....

	1933–1949	800.00	1000.00

HARLEQUIN
HN 2186
☐ Light blue trousers with darker blue design, blue jacket with darker blue and white checks, white stockings, blue hat with white trim, on base, height 7 ¼ ″, designer M. Davies ....

	1957–1969	225.00	275.00

HARLEQUINADE
HN 585
☐ Costume of black, yellow, green, purple checks, trimmed in white, black hat, black shoes, dark stockings, standing on pedestal style base, height 6 ½ ″, designer L. Harradine ....

	1923–1938	900.00	1000.00

HN 635
☐ Gold costume, height 6 ½ ″, designer L. Harradine ....

	1924–1938	1150.00	1300.00

HN 711
☐ Black and white costume, height 6 ½ ″, designer L. Harradine ....

	1925–1938	1100.00	1400.00

HN 780
☐ Pink dress with blue, black and orange markings, height 6 ½ ″, designer L. Harradine ....

	1926–1938	1200.00	1500.00

HARLEQUINADE MASKED
HN 768
☐ Black, red and green checkered costume, figure standing on black pedestal style base, height 6 ½ ″, designer L. Harradine ....

	1925–1938	2250.00	2750.00

HN 769
☐ Blue, red and yellow checkered costume, height 6 ½ ″, designer L. Harradine ....

	1925–1938	2250.00	2750.00

HN 1274
☐ Red and black checkered costume with red hat, height 6 ½ ″, designer L. Harradine ....

	1928–1938	2250.00	2750.00

Hazel, HN 1797, 600.00–730.00

	Date	Price Range	
HN 1304			
☐ Spotted black costume, height 6½″, designer L. Harradine	1928–1938	2250.00	2750.00
HARMONY			
HN 2824			
☐ Figure holding small white bird in hand, blue and gray gown, height 8″, designer R. Jefferson	1978–1984	150.00	200.00
HAZEL			
HN 1796			
☐ Small figure in green tiered dress, green bonnet, holding small round purse, height 5¼″, designer L. Harradine ...	1936–1949	600.00	750.00
HN 1797			
☐ Shaded red dress, trimmed with small floral design, blue and red shawl, small blue purse, height 5¼″, designer L. Harradine	1936–1949	600.00	750.00

	Date	Price Range	

HEART TO HEART
HN 2276

☐ Two figures each seated in yellow chairs, one dressed in lavender gown trimmed in white, the other in white with blue designs and blue shawl, the figures are facing each other, height 5½", designer M. Davies 1961–1971 350.00 400.00

HELEN
HN 1508

☐ Green gown with red floral design trimmed in white, bonnet with red ribbons, black shoes on base, open parasol, height 8", designer L. Harradine 1932–1938 1200.00 1400.00

HN 1509

☐ White gown with red floral design, red shoes, height 8", designer L. Harradine 1932–1938 1200.00 1400.00

HN 1572

☐ Red gown, shaded red bonnet with blue ribbons, height 8", designer L. Harradine 1933–1938 1200.00 1400.00

HELMSMAN
HN 2499

☐ Foul weather costume, black hat, figure standing on base before helm with hands on wheel, height 8½", designer M. Nicoll 1974–1986 250.00 300.00

HE LOVES ME
HN 2046

☐ Small blonde girl standing on yellow rock, red and blue sun dress, holding single flower in hands, height 5½", designer L. Harradine 1949–1962 200.00 225.00

HENRIETTA MARIA
HN 2005

☐ Red and yellow gown with light blue designs, holding small round red and white fan, height 9½", designer M. Davies 1948–1953 450.00 550.00

HENRY VIII
HN 370

☐ Purple, brown, yellow and green robes,

	Date	Price Range	

standing on base (1st version), height
unknown, designer C.J. Noke 1920–1938 **3500.00** **4000.00**

HN 673

☐ Brown and lilac robes (1st version),
height unknown, designer C.J. Noke 1924–1938 **3500.00** **4000.00**

HENRY IRVING AS CARDINAL WOLSEY
HN 344

☐ Figure with red costume and red hat on
black base, height 13¼″, designer C.J.
Noke 1919–1949 **2000.00** **2500.00**

HENRY LYTTON AS JACK POINT
HN 610

☐ Figure in clown costume of blue with
red and black stripes, green stockings
and shoes, on black base, height 6½″,
designer C.J. Noke 1924–1949 **900.00** **1150.00**

'HERE A LITTLE CHILD I STAND'
HN 1546

☐ Small child standing on multicolored
rock, light blue gown, height 6¼″, de-
signer unknown 1933–1949 **750.00** **850.00**

HER LADYSHIP
HN 1977

☐ Light green gown with green floral design, paisley shawl, pale green bonnet
with green ribbons, white fur muff,
height 7¼″, designer L. Harradine ... 1945–1959 **275.00** **350.00**

HERMINIA
HN 1644

☐ White gown and shawl with red and
green floral design, light green bonnet
with green ribbons, small red purse,
height 6½″, designer L. Harradine ... 1934–1938 **1200.00** **1500.00**

HN 1646

☐ Red dress, white stripes, height 6½″,
designer L. Harradine 1934–1938 **1200.00** **1500.00**

HN 1704

☐ Red gown, mottled green shawl and
purse, green bonnet with red ribbons,
height 6½″, designer L. Harradine ... 1935–1938 **1200.00** **1500.00**

Herminia, HN 1644, 1200.00–1500.00

	Date	Price Range	
HERMIONE **HN 2058** ☐ Cream and shaded blue gown with red trim, large red hat with feathers and ribbons, black ribbon around neck, height 7½″, designer M. Davies	1950–1952	1200.00	1500.00
HIGHWAYMAN, The **HN 527** ☐ A character from "The Beggar's Opera," red coat with dark overcoat, black hat with red trim, black stockings and shoes, drawing pistol, figure on black base, height 6½″, designer L. Harradine	1921–1949	800.00	900.00
HN 592 ☐ Different glaze finish, height 6½″, designer L. Harradine	1924–1949	800.00	900.00

The Hinged Parasol, HN 1578, 550.00–700.00

	Date	Price Range	
HN 1257			
☐ Earthenware, height 6½″, designer L. Harradine	1927–1949	700.00	800.00
HILARY			
HN 2335			
☐ Blue gown with white designs, trimmed in white and blue, holding yellow and white hat, height 7¼″, designer unknown	1967–1980	120.00	160.00
HINGED PARASOL, The			
HN 1578			
☐ Tiered cream and red gown with large blue dots, green hat, shoes and parasol, height 6½″, designer L. Harradine ...	1933–1949	550.00	700.00
HN 1579			
☐ Red and blue gown, red shoes, parasol			

	Date	Price Range	

and hat, height 6½″, designer L. Harradine 1933–1949 550.00 700.00

HIS HOLINESS POPE JOHN PAUL II
HN 2888

☐ Beautiful likeness of His Holiness inspired by his visit to the United Kingdom, height 10″, designer E.J. Griffiths 1982– 185.00

HOME AGAIN
HN 2167

☐ Small girl in red gown with white dog on base, small green hat, green shoes and ribbons, height 3½″, designer M. Davies 1956– 160.00

HONEY
HN 1909

☐ Pink dress with red jacket, blue shawl with white dots, blue bonnet with green ribbons, holding small round purse in one hand, small bouquet in other, height 7″, designer L. Harradine 1939–1949 350.00 450.00

HN 1910

☐ Blue dress with darker blue jacket, white shawl with blue designs, bonnet has black ribbons, holding larger bouquet of flowers, height 7″, designer L. Harradine 1939–1949 750.00 950.00

HN 1963

☐ Red and blue hat strings and shawl, height 7″, designer L. Harradine 1941–1949 1250.00 1450.00

HOPE
HN 3061

☐ Child figure dressed in a full nightgown with various shades of white to medium-gray, trimmed in chartreuse, holding a teddy bear in one hand; figure has red hair. Limited edition of 9,500 commissioned by Lawley's of England, height 8¼″, designer S. Mitchell 1984– 225.00 300.00

HORNPIPE, The
HN 2161

☐ Figure of sailor in dancing position on base, striped trousers, blue and white

	Date	Price Range	

jacket, white shirt, black hat, height
9¼″, designer M. Nicoll 1955–1962 650.00 750.00

HOSTESS OF WILLIAMSBURG
HN 2209
☐ Pink gown with trim of white and blue
ribbons, holding closed fan in hand,
height 7¼″, designer M. Davies 1960–1983 150.00 225.00

HUNTING SQUIRE
HN 1409
☐ Figure seated on blue and white horse
mounted on black base, red jacket,
white trousers, black boots, black hat,
height 9¾″, designer unknown 1930–1938 2500.00 3000.00

HUNTS LADY
HN 1201
☐ Riding costume of white trousers, blue
and gray coat, brown boots and hat,
white shirt, standing on brown base,
height 8¼″, designer L. Harradine ... 1926–1938 2000.00 2500.00

HUNTSMAN, The
HN 1226
☐ Riding costume of red jacket, white
trousers, black boots and hat, holding
riding crop, standing on brown base
(1st version), height 8¾″, designer L.
Harradine 1927–1938 2000.00 2500.00
HN 1815
☐ Seated figure on brown horse mounted
on black base, red jacket, white trousers, black boots and hat, blowing horn,
earthenware (2nd version), height
9½″, designer unknown 1937–1949 3000.00 3500.00
HN 2492
☐ Seated figure on wooden bench with
dog at side, yellow trousers, gray jacket,
black riding cap, black boots with
brown trim (3rd version), height 7½″,
designer M. Nicoll 1974–1980 170.00 220.00

IBRAHIM
HN 2095
☐ Shaded light red robe with cream col-
ored scarf, height 7¾″, designer C.J.
Noke 1952–1955 650.00 775.00

Ibrahim, HN 2095, 650.00–775.00

	Date	Price Range	
IN GRANDMA'S DAY			
HN 339			
□ See classification "LILAC SHAWL, A," height 8¾", designer C.J. Noke	1919–1938	1400.00	1600.00
HN 340			
□ See classification "LILAC SHAWL, A," height 8¾", designer C.J. Noke	1919–1938	1400.00	1600.00
HN 362			
□ See classification "LILAC SHAWL, A," height 8¾", designer C.J. Noke	1919–1938	1550.00	1700.00
HN 388			
□ See classification "LILAC SHAWL, A," height 8¾", designer C.J. Noke	1920–1938	1650.00	1800.00
HN 442			
□ See classification "LILAC SHAWL, A," height 8¾", designer C.J. Noke	1921–1938	1650.00	1800.00

	Date	Price Range	

IN THE STOCKS
HN 1474
☐ This figure also known as LOVE IN THE STOCKS and LOVE LOCKED IN—Small white angel in stocks, girl seated beside stocks in red dress, holding bonnet by ribbons (1st version), height 5¼″, designer L. Harradine ... | 1931–1938 | 2000.00 | 2500.00

HN 1475
☐ Green gown and green slippers, blue ribbons (1st version), height 5¼″, designer L. Harradine .... | 1931–1938 | 2000.00 | 2500.00

HN 2163
☐ Character figure in brown stocks on brown base, red costume with black hat (2nd version), height 5″, designer M. Nicoll .... | 1955–1959 | 600.00 | 700.00

INNOCENCE
HN 2842
☐ Dark haired figure in red gown with black ribbon straps, height 7½″, designer E.J. Griffiths .... | 1979–1983 | 120.00 | 160.00

INVITATION
HN 2170
☐ Pink gown with shoulder trim of blue ribbon and white flowers, holding open fan of blue, red and white, height 5½″, designer M. Davies .... | 1956–1975 | 125.00 | 160.00

IONA
HN 1346
☐ Lady and German Shepherd dog on black base, blue costume trimmed in purple, red and green, tall green hat with purple feather, height 7½″, designer L. Harradine .... | 1929–1938 | 2750.00 | 3250.00

IRENE
HN 1621
☐ Tiered light yellow gown, with red bodice, light red bonnet with green ribbon, holding small flower, height varies from 6½ to 7″, designer L. Harradine | 1934–1951 | 325.00 | 375.00

HN 1697
☐ Red gown, green bonnet, bouquet of yellow roses, height varies from 6½ to 7″, designer L. Harradine .... | 1935–1949 | 750.00 | 850.00

	Date	Price Range	

HN 1952

☐ Red and blue gown, blue bonnet, multi-colored flowers in bouquet, height varies from 6½ to 7″, designer L. Harradine   1940–1950   **900.00**   **1000.00**

IRISH COLLEEN
HN 766

☐ Figure standing on black base, short black skirt with white stripes, red jacket, black vest, tall black hat with red floral trim, height 6½″, designer L. Harradine 1925–1938   **2500.00**   **3000.00**

HN 767

☐ Black, red and green striped skirt, black jacket, red vest, red shoes, height 6½″, designer L. Harradine 1925–1938   **2500.00**   **3000.00**

IRISHMAN, AN
HN 1307

☐ Figure standing on shaded blue base, green coat, red vest, brown striped trousers, green hat, height 6¾″, designer H. Fenton 1928–1938   **2750.00**   **3350.00**

ISADORA
HN 2938

☐ Figure is posed as in a dance movement. Gown is orchid with shades of purple and lavender, highlighted by a red ribbon, blond hair, height 8″, designer P. Gee 1986–   **195.00**

IVY
HN 1768

☐ Small figure in blue gown, red bonnet with white feather and green ribbon, holding small round purse, white pantalettes showing slightly, height 4¾″, designer L. Harradine 1936–1979   **75.00**   **100.00**

HN 1769

☐ Color details not recorded, made for a brief period, height 4¾″, designer L. Harradine 1936–1938   **600.00**   **700.00**

JACK
HN 2060

☐ Small boy figure on green and yellow base, holding pail, black trousers, blue coat, white shirt, red sash, black shoes, height 5½″, designer L. Harradine ... 1950–1971   **125.00**   **175.00**

	Date	Price Range	

JACK POINT
HN 85

☐ Jester type figure standing on green base, red checkered costume, holding small pouch, hand under chin, height 16¼″, designer C.J. Noke 1918–1938 2500.00 3200.00

HN 91

☐ Green, black and purple checkered costume, very light colored base, height 16¼″, designer C.J. Noke 1918–1938 2000.00 2500.00

HN 99

☐ Heraldic tunic, height 16¼″, designer C.J. Noke 1918–1938 2000.00 2500.00

HN 2080

☐ Costume of red, purple, green with gold lion and leaf trim, has instrument slung over shoulder, base is light beige, designer C.J. Noke 1962– 2200.00

JACQUELINE
HN 2000

☐ Blue and gray gown with white apron, flower trimmed sleeves, height 7½″, designer L. Harradine 1947–1951 450.00 650.00

HN 2001

☐ Red gown with white apron, darker flowers on sleeves, height 7½″, designer L. Harradine 1947–1951 450.00 650.00

HN 2333

☐ Light gray gown with yellow band and flower at the waist, height 7½″, designer M. Davies 1983– 195.00

JAMES
HN 3013

☐ Young male figure in gray knee length breeches, wearing a white smock, black shoes, wide hat with black bow, reddish brown hair, holding a puppy, height 6″, designer P. Parsons 1983–1987 100.00

JANE
HN 2014

☐ Red skirt, red overlay with blue dots, trimmed in white, white cap with blue ribbons, holding water jug and glass in hands, height 6¼″, designer L. Harradine 1948–1951 1200.00 1500.00

Janet, HN 1537, 150.00

	Date	Price Range	
HN 2806			
☐ Pastel yellow gown, black ribbon at the waist, holding an umbrella reflecting many colors, blonde hair, height 8″, designer M. Davies	1983–1986	100.00	150.00
JANET			
HN 1537			
☐ Red and white gown, white bonnet with green ribbons, carrying flat basket of flowers (1st version), height 6½″, designer L. Harradine	1932–	160.00	
HN 1538			
☐ Red and blue gown, white bonnet with green ribbon (1st version), height 6½″, designer L. Harradine	1932–1949	650.00	750.00

	Date	Price Range	

HN 1652
☐ Pink skirt with floral pattern, red bodice (1st version), height 6½″, designer L. Harradine 1934–1949 **375.00** **400.00**

HN 1737
☐ Green gown, red shoe (1st version), height 6½″, designer L. Harradine ... 1935–1949 **600.00** **750.00**

HN 1916
☐ Small figure with red skirt, blue bodice, red shoes (2nd version), height 5¼″, designer L. Harradine 1939–1949 **275.00** **325.00**

HN 1964
☐ Pink dress (2nd version), height 5¼″, designer L. Harradine 1936–1949 **275.00** **350.00**

☐ **M-69** Made as a miniature, green dress, height 4″, designer L. Harradine 1936–1949 **400.00** **500.00**

☐ **M-75** Red and blue dress, height 4″, designer L. Harradine 1936–1949 **400.00** **450.00**

JANICE
HN 2022
☐ Green and orange Regal gown, small green headdress, jewels at neck, holding small book in hand, height 7¼″, designer M. Davies 1949–1955 **500.00** **600.00**

HN 2165
☐ Dark green and white gown, blonde hair, height 7¼″, designer M. Davies 1955–1965 **475.00** **525.00**

JANINE
HN 2461
☐ Green and white gown with green designs, height 7⅞″, designer J. Bromley 1971– **230.00**

JAPANESE FAN
HN 399
☐ Japanese lady seated, gown of purple with multicolored jacket, holding round fan, also made as a lidded bowl, height 4¾″, designer H. Tittensor 1920–1938 **2000.00** **2500.00**

HN 405
☐ Pale yellow costume, height 4¾″, designer H. Tittensor 1920–1938 **2000.00** **2500.00**

HN 439
☐ Blue costume, green spots, height 4¼″, designer H. Tittensor 1921–1938 **2000.00** **2500.00**

	Date	Price Range	

HN 440

☐ Yellow costume, orange spots, height
4 ¼ ", designer H. Tittensor .... | 1921–1938 | 2000.00 | 2500.00

JASMINE
HN 1862

☐ Green gown with multicolored, flowered jacket, strand of long beads on
front, head covering of same material
as jacket, height 7 ½ ", designer L.
Harradine .... | 1938–1949 | 800.00 | 950.00

HN 1863

☐ White gown with multicolored, flowered jacket, beige with green border on
jacket, light colored beads, head covering is flowered to match jacket, height
7 ½ ", designer L. Harradine .... | 1938–1949 | 900.00 | 1000.00

HN 1876

☐ Flowered blue coat with pink trim,
height 7 ½ ", designer L. Harradine ... | 1938–1949 | 800.00 | 950.00

JEAN
HN 1877

☐ Shaded light red gown with blue cloak
with ribbon of green, holding basket of
flowers on one arm, height 7 ½ ", de-
signer L. Harradine .... | 1938–1949 | 550.00 | 650.00

HN 1878

☐ Green dress with red shawl, height
7 ½ ", designer L. Harradine .... | 1938–1949 | 400.00 | 450.00

HN 2032

☐ Green dress with accents of darker
green, red cloak with black ribbons,
flowers yellow in basket, height 7 ½ ",
designer L. Harradine .... | 1949–1959 | 250.00 | 325.00

JENNIFER
HN 1484

☐ Light yellow gown with yellow flower
design, multi-yellow flowered jacket,
dark blue cloak, green bonnet, height
6 ½ ", designer L. Harradine .... | 1931–1949 | 500.00 | 600.00

HN 2392

☐ Beautiful figure of young girl in blue
gown with yellow sash, cream sleeves,
long blonde hair, height 7 ", designer
M. Davies .... | 1982– | 215.00 |

	Date	Price Range	

JERSEY MILKMAID, The
HN 2057

☐ Green skirt, brown blouse, blue and white apron trimmed in brown, blue and white farm bonnet, carrying brown jug. In 1975 re-issued same number titled "THE MILKMAID," see proper classification, there are known color variations of this number (dress and jug), height 6½", designer L. Harradine ... | 1950–1959 | 275.00 | 325.00 |

JESTER, A
HN 45

☐ Figure seated on light pedestal base, black and white checkered costume, holding one leg (1st version), height 10", designer C.J. Noke .... | 1915–1938 | 1700.00 | 1900.00 |

HN 45A

☐ Costume of green and white checks, legs crossed, one hand to face (2nd version), height 10", designer C.J. Noke | 1915–1938 | 1700.00 | 1900.00 |

HN 45B

☐ Brown and white checkered costume (2nd version), height 10", designer C.J. Noke .... | 1915–1938 | 2000.00 | 2400.00 |

HN 55

☐ Black and lilac costume (2nd version), height 10", designer C.J. Noke .... | 1916–1938 | 2000.00 | 2400.00 |

HN 71

☐ Black and green costume with black and green checks and orange balls (1st version), height 10", designer C.J. Noke .... | 1917–1938 | 1500.00 | 1700.00 |

HN 71A

☐ No color details available (1st version), height 10", designer C.J. Noke .... | 1917–1938 | 1500.00 | 1700.00 |

HN 308

☐ A note below HN 308 in the figure design book says, 'same as 55' (2nd version), height 10", designer C.J. Noke | 1918–1938 | 2000.00 | 2400.00 |

HN 320

☐ HN 45, green and black costume (1st version), height 10", designer C.J. Noke .... | 1918–1938 | 1700.00 | 1900.00 |

HN 367

☐ Green and shaded red costume, seated on black pedestal (1st version), height 10", designer C.J. Noke .... | 1920–1938 | 1800.00 | 2000.00 |

	Date	Price Range	

HN 412
☐ Green and red striped tights (1st version), height 10″, designer C.J. Noke — 1920–1938 — 1800.00 — 2000.00

HN 426
☐ Costume of pink markings, black tights (1st version), height 10″, designer C.J. Noke .... 1921–1938 — 1750.00 — 2000.00

HN 446
☐ Green sleeves, blue pedestal (1st version), height 10″, designer C.J. Noke — 1921–1938 — 1700.00 — 1900.00

HN 552
☐ Black and red costume (1st version), height 10″, designer C.J. Noke .... 1922–1938 — 1700.00 — 1900.00

HN 616
☐ Quartered heraldic tunic (1st version), height 10″, designer C.J. Noke .... 1924–1938 — 1700.00 — 1900.00

HN 627
☐ Brown checkered costume (1st version), height 10″, designer C.J. Noke — 1924–1938 — 1700.00 — 1900.00

HN 630
☐ HN 45A, brown striped tights (2nd version), height 10″, designer C.J. Noke .... 1924–1938 — 2000.00 — 2200.00

HN 1295
☐ Brown costume, brown and orange stripes, seated on black pedestal (1st version), height 10″, designer C.J. Noke .... 1928–1949 — 1700.00 — 1800.00

HN 1333
☐ Blue tunic with yellow and black stripes (2nd version), height 10″, designer C.J. Noke .... 1929–1949 — 1900.00 — 2000.00

HN 1702
☐ HN 2016, with minor variations (1st version), height 10″, designer C.J. Noke .... 1935–1949 — 1000.00 — 1200.00

HN 2016
☐ Shaded brown costume, one leg with darker stripes, costume trimmed in orange with orange balls, pedestal is gray with darker base (1st version), height 10″, designer C.J. Noke .... 1949– — 295.00

JILL
HN 2061
☐ Small girl figure on yellow and green base, red dress with white apron, white

	Date	Price Range	

bonnet with green ribbons, height
5½″, designer L. Harradine .... | 1950–1971 | 125.00 | 175.00

JOAN
HN 1422
☐ Older lady figure seated in blue and
green back chair, blue dress, black
shawl, holding red yarn in hands, small
foot stool, height 5½″, designer L.
Harradine .... | 1930–1949 | 400.00 | 500.00

HN 2023
☐ Minor glaze differences, height 5¾″,
designer L. Harradine .... | 1949–1959 | 350.00 | 425.00

JOHN PEEL
HN 1408
☐ Figure seated on brown horse mounted
on black base, red coat, white trousers,
black hat and boots, blowing horn.
Later re-issued with the new title, THE
HUNTSMAN, height 9¼″, designer
unknown .... | 1930–1937 | 3000.00 | 3500.00

JOLLY SAILOR
HN 2172
☐ Seated character figure of sailor, black
trousers, white and blue striped shirt,
straw colored hat, playing instrument,
height 6½″, designer M. Nicoll .... | 1956–1965 | 500.00 | 600.00

JOVIAL MONK, The
HN 2144
☐ Brown robe with rope style belt, carrying basket in one hand, height 7¾″,
designer M. Davies .... | 1954–1976 | 175.00 | 250.00

JUDGE, The
HN 2443
☐ Red and white costume, seated in
brown high back chair, white wig, black
shoes, holding papers in hand, height
6½″, designer M. Nicoll .... | 1972– | 250.00 |

☐ In 1976 this figure was changed from a
matte to a glazed finish, height 6½″,
designer M. Nicoll .... | 1976 | 150.00 | 200.00

JUDGE AND JURY
HN 1264
☐ Judge figure in red and white costume,
little dog chained to chair, three small

Jolly Sailor, HN 2172, 500.00–600.00

	Date	Price Range	
children in witness stand, another child outside of stand, all on black base, height 6″, designer J.G. Hughes	1927–1938	8000.00	9500.00

JUDITH
HN 2089
☐ Red dress with blue vest which has a darker blue design and blue trim on sleeves, blue shoes, height 6⅞″, designer L. Harradine 1952–1959   300.00   350.00

HN 2278
☐ Blond-haired figure with beautiful, yellow gown trimmed at waist with emerald ribbons. Emerald green Juliet

	Date	Price Range	

cap, seated on a brown, stone pillar, height 6¾″, designer M. Nicoll 1987– **195.00**

JULIA
HN 2705
☐ Brown gown with white trim, brown hat with yellow ribbons, carrying yellow parasol, height 7⅝″, designer M. Davies 1975– **195.00**

HN 2706
☐ Gown of pink and turquoise, bonnet and veil the same colors, height 7⅝″, designer M. Davies 1985– **160.00**

JUNE
HN 1690
☐ Green and white gown, green bonnet with black ribbons, carrying flowers in one arm, holding parasol in other, height 7½″, designer L. Harradine ... 1935–1949 **450.00** **550.00**

HN 1691
☐ Cream gown with light shades of green and yellow, front panel has flower designs, red bonnet, parasol has green trim, shawl black, height 7½″, designer L. Harradine 1935–1949 **400.00** **475.00**

HN 1947
☐ Shaded red and blue gown trimmed with white, bonnet same trimmed with blue ribbons, parasol dark, height 7½″, designer L. Harradine 1940–1949 **600.00** **700.00**

HN 2027
☐ Minor glaze changes, height 7½″, designer L. Harradine 1949–1952 **400.00** **500.00**

☐ **M-65** Made as a miniature figure, shaded red gown with dark trim, height 4″, designer L. Harradine 1935–1949 **400.00** **575.00**

☐ **M-71** Shaded blue gown with red trim, height 4″, designer L. Harradine 1936–1949 **400.00** **575.00**

KAREN
HN 1994
☐ Figure in Edwardian riding costume of red and white, green hat with feather, holding riding crop, on brown base, height 8″, designer L. Harradine 1947–1955 **450.00** **500.00**

HN 2388
☐ Red gown with white bodice, black

Karen, HN 1994, 450.00–500.00

	Date	Price Range	
waistband, dark hair (2nd version), height 8″, designer M. Davies	1982–	275.00	

KATE
HN 2789
☐ White gown with multicolored flower design around bottom, white headband, height 7½″, designer M. Davies | 1978–1987 | 155.00 | 195.00

KATE HARDCASTLE
HN 1718
☐ Eighteenth century style pink and green gown, pink bonnet with green ribbons, green gloves, leaning on light colored pedestal on base, height 8″, designer L. Harradine .... | 1935–1949 | 700.00 | 800.00

	Date	Price Range	

HN 1719

☐ Red and green gown, green bonnet with red ribbons, red gloves, leaning on dark pedestal with light base, height 8¼", designer L. Harradine .... | 1935–1949 | 550.00 | 650.00

HN 1734

☐ Green and white gown with green designs, light yellow bonnet with green ribbons, green gloves, dark pedestal on light base, height 8¼", designer L. Harradine .... | 1935–1949 | 1200.00 | 1400.00

HN 1861

☐ Red gown with shaded blue and green overlay, black bonnet with blue ribbons, red gloves, green colored pedestal on light base, height 8¼", designer L. Harradine .... | 1938–1949 | 850.00 | 1000.00

HN 1919

☐ Red overskirt, green dress, black base, height 8¼", designer L. Harradine ... | 1939–1949 | 850.00 | 1000.00

HN 2028

☐ HN 1719, with minor glaze difference, height 8¼", designer L. Harradine ... | 1949–1952 | 500.00 | 600.00

KATHERINE
HN 61

☐ Full covering gown of green with white collar, green hat with white brim, height 5¾", designer C.J. Noke .... | 1916–1938 | 1500.00 | 1700.00

HN 74

☐ Pale blue dress with green spots, height 5¾", designer C.J. Noke .... | 1917–1938 | 1650.00 | 1800.00

HN 341

☐ Red gown, height 5¾", designer C.J. Noke .... | 1919–1938 | 1250.00 | 1500.00

HN 471

☐ Spotted blouse and dress, height 5¾", designer C.J. Noke .... | 1921–1938 | 2000.00 | 2500.00

HN 615

☐ Pink skirt with green spots, height 5¾", designer C.J. Noke .... | 1924–1938 | 1650.00 | 1800.00

HN 793

☐ Lilac dress with green spots, height 5¾", designer C.J. Noke .... | 1926–1938 | 1650.00 | 1800.00

KATHLEEN
HN 1252

☐ Shaded blue skirt, red jacket, red and

Kathleen, HN 1252, 675.00–775.00

	Date	Price Range	
blue shawl, black ribbon in hair, holding black bonnet in one hand, height 7½″, designer L. Harradine	1927–1938	675.00	775.00
HN 1253			
☐ Red skirt, multicolored jacket, dark blue and black shawl, height 7½″, designer L. Harradine	1927–1938	700.00	800.00
HN 1275			
☐ HN 1252, flowered black shawl, height 7½″, designer L. Harradine	1928–1938	700.00	800.00
HN 1279			
☐ Mottled red skirt and jacket, red shawl, height 7½″, designer L. Harradine ...	1928–1938	675.00	775.00
HN 1291			
☐ Red shawl with mottled yellow dress, height 7½″, designer L. Harradine ...	1928–1938	850.00	950.00

	Date	Price Range	

HN 1357
☐ Pink, orange and yellow mottled skirt, height 7½″, designer L. Harradine ... | 1929–1938 | 800.00 | 900.00

HN 1512
☐ Pale lilac dress, blue hat, height 7½″, designer L. Harradine .... | 1932–1938 | 800.00 | 900.00

HN 2933
☐ This figure is seated, multicolored gown, she is wearing a dark green large hat, holding an artist palette leaning forward as if to paint, height 6½″, designer Sharon Keenan .... | 1984–1987 | 225.00 | 275.00

HN 3100
☐ This variation of Kathleen is in lavender and pinks. Issued as a special piece for Michael Doulton events. Height 6½″, designer Sharon Keenan .... | 1986 only | 235.00 | 295.00

KATHY (Kate Greenaway)
HN 2346
☐ This figure is seated on green stool, wearing white gown with red sash, white bonnet with light blue ribbon, red shoes, holding small light blue flower in one hand, height 4¾″, designer M. Davies .... | 1981–1987 | 80.00 | 100.00

KATRINA
HN 2327
☐ Red gown trimmed with white collar, high comb in hair, both hands on head, height 7½″, designer M. Davies ...... | 1965–1969 | 325.00 | 375.00

KELLY
HN 2478
☐ Young lady dressed in beautiful white ball gown decorated with blue flowers, a string of pearls highlight her dark hair, height 7½″, designer M. Davies | 1985– | 160.00 |

KING CHARLES
HN 404
☐ Deep navy blue costume, deep navy blue cloak, navy blue with light blue feather hat, deep navy stockings, black shoes, black walking stick on pink base, height 16¾″, designers C.J. Noke and H. Tittensor .... | 1920–1951 | 2000.00 | 2200.00

HN 2084, see Prestige Figures

	Date	Price Range	

KIRSTY
HN 2381
☐ Yellow gown with shades of brown with design around rim of skirt, white trim on sleeves, white collar with ribbon, height 7¾", designer M. Davies 1971– 250.00

KITTY
HN 1367
☐ Lady seated with foot on footstool, white gown and yellow with darker thin stripes of blue, holding dark kitten in hands, has small white cap with red ribbon on head, height 4", designer unknown 1930–1938 2500.00 3000.00

KO-KO
HN 1266
☐ Japanese figure with black and yellow costume, standing on green and yellow base, holding fan, height 5", designer L. Harradine 1928–1949 800.00 950.00
HN 1286
☐ Red and blue costume standing on dark base, height 5", designer L. Harradine 1938–1949 800.00 950.00
HN 2898
☐ Japanese figure with black hair on light brown base, orange, blue, green, black and red costume, holding scroll, with large ax-like weapon on stand (2nd version), height 11½", designer W.K. Harper 1980–1985 600.00 750.00

LADY ANNE, The
HN 83
☐ Yellow gown with dark trim, one foot on stool, has high head covering of net and flowers, height unknown, designer E.W. Light 1918–1938 3000.00 3500.00
HN 87
☐ Green gown, red shoes, height unknown, designer E.W. Light 1918–1938 3000.00 3500.00
HN 93
☐ Blue gown, height unknown, designer E.W. Light 1918–1938 3000.00 3500.00

Lady April, HN 1958, 300.00–400.00

	Date	Price Range	

LADY ANNE NEVILL, The
HN 2006
☐ Purple gown with white fur trim, gold belt and jewels, very high and wide head covering of white, height 9¾", designer M. Davies .... 1948–1953 · 700.00 · 800.00

LADY APRIL
HN 1958
☐ Red gown, purple, blue and red cloak with green straps, red bonnet with red and black trim, holding small bouquet in one arm, green gloves, height 7", designer L. Harradine .... 1940–1959 · 300.00 · 400.00

HN 1965
☐ Green dress, height 7", designer L. Harradine .... 1941–1949 · 750.00 · 850.00

	Date	Price Range	

LADY BETTY
HN 1967
☐ Red gown with blue ruffle trim collar, blue bonnet with cream feather and black ribbons, holding flower basket, height 6½″, designer L. Harradine ... 1941–1951   300.00   350.00

LADYBIRD
HN 1638
☐ Young girl in pink ballet costume, standing on toes on base, spray of flowers in hair, height 7¾″, designer L. Harradine 1924–1949   1500.00   2000.00
HN 1640
☐ Light blue costume and ballet shoes, height 7¾″, designer L. Harradine ... 1934–1938   1500.00   2000.00

LADY AND BLACKAMOOR
HN 374
☐ Large full skirted gown of blue and green patterns with blue bodice, holding fan in one hand, high hair style with small black figure behind her, with blue costume and yellow turban (1st version), height unknown, designer H. Tittensor 1920–1938   2500.00   3000.00
HN 375
☐ Light colored skirt with designs of flowers and leaves with purple trim, black bodice trimmed in pink (2nd version), height unknown, designer H. Tittensor 1920–1938   2500.00   3000.00
HN 377
☐ Pink and green dress (2nd version), height unknown, designer H. Tittensor 1920–1938   2500.00   3000.00
HN 470
☐ Green and lilac dress (2nd version), height unknown, design H. Tittensor 1921–1938   2500.00   3000.00

LADY CHARMIAN
HN 1948
☐ Green gown, mottled red shawl, green bonnet, holding single flower in one hand and basket of flowers with other, height 8″, designer L. Harradine 1940–1973   200.00   260.00
HN 1949
☐ Red gown, green shawl, red bonnet

	Date	Price Range	

with black ribbons, height 8″, designer
L. Harradine 1940–1975   225.00   275.00

LADY CLARE
HN 1465
☐ Red and blue tiered gown with blue
and red shawl, holding small purse and
parasol, light bonnet with red ribbons,
height 7¾″, designer L. Harradine ... 1931–1938   650.00   750.00

LADY CLOWN
HN 717
☐ White costume with red and green
stripes and black blocks, dunce style
hat, red shoes, standing on one foot on
black base, height 7½″, designer L.
Harradine 1925–1938   2500.00   3000.00
HN 718
☐ White costume, red stripes, black spots,
height 7½″, designer L. Harradine ... 1925–1938   2500.00   3000.00
HN 738
☐ Black and white trousers, red spots,
height 7½″, designer L. Harradine ... 1925–1938   2500.00   3000.00
HN 770
☐ Costume painted with green masks and
streamers, height 7½″, designer L.
Harradine 1925–1938   2500.00   3000.00
HN 1263
☐ Multicolored trousers, one leg blue, the
other one with red stripes, height 7½″,
designer L. Harradine 1927–1938   2500.00   3000.00

LADY ERMINE
HN 54
☐ Light green gown, blue coat with fur
trim, muff of fur, green hat with yellow
ribbon and feather, height 8½″, de-
signer C.J. Noke 1916–1938   1500.00   1800.00
HN 332
☐ Red coat and hat, green and yellow
patterned skirt, height 8½″, designer
C.J. Noke 1918–1938   1600.00   1900.00
HN 671
☐ Green coat, yellow skirt, height 8½″,
designer C.J. Noke 1924–1938   1650.00   1900.00

LADY FAYRE
HN 1265
☐ Blue and red gown and bodice, blond

	Date	Price Range	

hair, red shoes, in curtsy position, height 5¾″, designer L. Harradine ... 1928–1938 650.00 750.00

HN 1557

☐ Pink gown, height 5¾″, designer L. Harradine 1933–1938 1100.00 1350.00

LADY FROM WILLIAMSBURG
HN 2228

☐ Figure seated on bench, green gown with yellow ribbon trim, small white covering on head, holding bonnet in hands, height 6″, designer M. Davies 1960–1983 150.00 225.00

LADY JESTER
HN 1221

☐ Costume of checkered pink and black skirt, standing on pedestal style base (1st version), height 7″, designer L. Harradine 1927–1938 1600.00 2000.00

HN 1222

☐ Checkered black and white costume with shoes (1st version), height 7″, designer L. Harradine 1927–1938 1600.00 2000.00

HN 1284

☐ Seated figure with legs crossed, costume of red tights, dark blue vest with checkered red and black sleeves, holding jester doll with black and white costume (2nd version), height 4¼″, designer L. Harradine 1928–1938 2000.00 2250.00

HN 1285

☐ Blue costume with red stripes on tights, red vest with very light red sleeves, holds jester doll in white, black and blue costume (2nd version), height 4¼″, designer L. Harradine 1928–1938 2000.00 2250.00

HN 1332

☐ Red costume, blue and black scalloped pattern on skirt (1st version), height 7″, designer L. Harradine 1929–1938 1600.00 1900.00

LADY OF THE ELIZABETHAN PERIOD
HN 40

☐ Very full gown of brown and patterned orange, high wide white collar, headdress dark and has a long hanging cloth

Lady of the Elizabethan Period, HN 411, 2000.00–2500.00

	Date	Price Range	
(1st version), height 9½″, designer E.W. Light	1914–1938	**1750.00**	**2000.00**
HN 40A			
☐ No pattern on dress (1st version), height 9½″, designer E.W. Light	1914–1938	**1750.00**	**2000.00**
HN 73			
☐ Dark blue-green costume (1st version), height 9½″, designer E.W. Light	1917–1938	**1800.00**	**2000.00**
HN 309			
☐ Green patterned costume, with white patterned and raised green dots, gown trimmed in blue, headdress dark (2nd version), height 9½″, designer E.W. Light	1918–1938	**1750.00**	**2000.00**

	Date	Price Range	

HN 411

☐ Costume of purple patterned with mottled colors in sleeves and underskirt, wide white collar (1st version), height 9½″, designer E.W. Light 1920–1938   2000.00   2250.00

LADY OF THE FAN
HN 48

☐ Lilac dress, black shoes, feather in hair, holding fan, figure in bowing position, height 9½″, designer E.W. Light 1916–1938   1700.00   1900.00

HN 52

☐ Shaded yellow gown, height 9½″, designer E.W. Light 1916–1938   1700.00   1900.00

HN 53

☐ Dark blue dress, height 9½″, designer E.W. Light 1916–1938   1700.00   1900.00

HN 53A

☐ Green and blue dress, height 9½″, designer E.W. Light 1916–1938   1700.00   1900.00

HN 335

☐ Blue dress with brown patterning, height 9½″, designer E.W. Light 1919–1938   1700.00   1900.00

HN 509

☐ Green, lilac and blue spotted dress, height 9½″, designer E.W. Light 1921–1938   1700.00   1900.00

LADY OF THE GEORGIAN PERIOD
HN 41

☐ Red and white gown which has shaded blue and dark bows, has large white turban style headdress trimmed with dark blue ribbons, height 10¼″, designer E.W. Light 1914–1938   1750.00   2250.00

HN 331

☐ Patterned brown and yellow gown, dark brown headdress with red ribbons, height 10¼″, designer E.W. Light 1918–1938   1850.00   2250.00

HN 444

☐ Green-blue spotted dress, height 10¼″, designer E.W. Light 1921–1938   2000.00   2500.00

HN 690

☐ Color design not available, height 10¼″, designer E.W. Light 1925–1938   2000.00   2500.00

	Date	Price Range	

HN 702
☐ Striped pink skirt, green overdress, height 10¼", designer E.W. Light .... | 1925–1938 | 2000.00 | 2500.00

LADY OF THE SNOWS
HN 1780
☐ No further information available, height unknown, designer R. Garbe .. | 1933– | 4000.00 | 4500.00
HN 1830
☐ Tinted model, height unknown, designer R. Garbe .... | 1937–1949 | 4000.00 | 4500.00

LADY OF THE TIME OF HENRY VI
HN 43
☐ Yellow gown with green overdress trimmed in fur, green head covering, height 9¼", designer E.W. Light ..... | 1914–1938 | 3000.00 | 3500.00

LADY PAMELA
HN 2718
☐ Lavender gown with lighter lavender overlay, dark lavender bonnet with still darker ribbon trim, holding mirror, height 8", designer D. V. Tootle ...... | 1974–1980 | 150.00 | 200.00

LADY WITH ROSE
HN 48A
☐ White gown with dark ribbon style trim on ruffles and orange lining, black waistband, holding red rose, height 9½", designer E.W. Light .... | 1916–1938 | 1700.00 | 1900.00
HN 52A
☐ Yellow dress, height 9½", designer E.W. Light .... | 1916–1938 | 1700.00 | 1900.00
HN 68
☐ Green and yellow dress, height 9½", designer E.W. Light .... | 1916–1938 | 1700.00 | 1900.00
HN 304
☐ Gray-lilac dress with brown patterning, height 9½", designer E.W. Light ..... | 1918–1938 | 1700.00 | 1900.00
HN 336
☐ Multicolored dress with brown patterning, height 9½", designer E.W. Light .... | 1919–1938 | 1700.00 | 1900.00
HN 515
☐ Striped lilac and green dress, height 9½", designer E.W. Light .... | 1921–1938 | 1700.00 | 1900.00

	Date	Price Range	

HN 517
☐ Lilac dress with orange spots, height 9½″, designer E.W. Light 1921–1938 1700.00 1900.00

HN 584
☐ Green and pink dress, height 9½″, designer E.W. Light 1923–1938 1700.00 1900.00

HN 624
☐ Green-blue skirt, pink and black cuffs, height 9½″, designer E.W. Light 1924–1938 1700.00 1900.00

LADY WITHOUT BOUQUET
HN 393
☐ Light red gown with blue and white ring designs, blue bodice with gold trim, large blue stole with purple lining with blue and white ring design, height 9″, designer G. Lambert 1920–1938 2300.00 2600.00

HN 394
☐ Blue and yellow costume, height 9″, designer G. Lambert 1920–1938 2300.00 2600.00

LADY WITH SHAWL
HN 447
☐ Figure on mottled blue base, white and blue striped gown, dark blue waistband with white round designs, white shawl with blue and gold ring designs, height 13¼″, designer L. Harradine 1921–1938 4200.00 4700.00

HN 458
☐ Multicolored shawl, pink dress, height 13¼″, designer L. Harradine 1921–1938 4200.00 4700.00

HN 626
☐ Yellow shawl with pink spots, white dress with green spots, height 13¼″, designer L. Harradine 1924–1938 4200.00 4700.00

HN 678
☐ Black and white shawl, yellow and white dress, height 13¼″, designer L. Harradine 1924–1938 4200.00 4700.00

HN 679
☐ Black, yellow and blue shawl, black and white dress, height 13¼″, designer L. Harradine 1924–1938 4200.00 4700.00

LAIRD, The
HN 2361
☐ Character figure in Scottish costume, green and black striped skirt, dark green and beige jacket, brown tam,

	Date	Price Range	

brown shoes and green stockings, holding staff, greenish tan shawl over shoulder, height 8⅛″, designer M. Nicoll   1969–   250.00

LAMBETH WALK, The
HN 1880
☐ Blue dress, height 10″, designer L. Harradine   1938–1949   2500.00   3000.00
HN 1881
☐ Shaded red dress with red flower design on bottom, large blue hat with red trim, red shoe, light colored base, height 10″, designer L. Harradine   1938–1949   2500.00   3000.00

LAMBING TIME
HN 1890
☐ Character figure on brown base, brown trousers with long yellow and brown coat, brown hat and small scarf, holding a lamp under each arm, height 8½″, designer L. Harradine   1938–1980   150.00   200.00

LAND OF NOD, The
HN 56
☐ HN 56A, ivory nightshirt, height 9¾″, designer H. Tittensor   1916–1938   2500.00   3000.00
HN 56A
☐ Small figure in very light blue nightshirt, holding candle with brown and white owl on light base with printing, height 9¾″, designer H. Tittensor   1916–1938   2500.00   3000.00
HN 56B
☐ Pale gray nightshirt and red candlestick, height 9¾″, designer H. Tittensor   1916–1938   2500.00   3000.00

LAST WALTZ
HN 2315
☐ White gown with gold designs, dark yellow overlay trimmed in green, holding dance program book and pencil, height 8″, designer M. Davies   1967–   250.00

LA SYLPHIDE
HN 2138
☐ White gown with light blue trim, ribbon around head, hands crossed, light blue ballet slippers on green and yellow base, height 7¼″, designer M. Davies   1956–1965   400.00   500.00

	Date	Price Range	

LAURA
HN 2960
□ Seated figure with blue and white gown decorated on the bodice and overskirt with orange flowers, blonde hair, height 7¼″, designer P. Parsons ....

| | 1983– | 195.00 | |

LAURIANNE
HN 2719
□ Seated lady with blue and white gown, dark blue overdress, with book on lap, height 6½″, designer D. V. Tootle ...

| | 1974–1979 | 150.00 | 200.00 |

LAVENDER WOMAN, The
HN 22
□ Light blue dress and shawl, holding wrapped infant in one arm and brown basket with flowers in other arm, on light blue base, height 8¼″, designer P. Stabler ....

| | 1913–1938 | 2100.00 | 2300.00 |

HN 23
□ Green dress, height 8¼″, designer P. Stabler ....

| | 1913–1938 | 2100.00 | 2300.00 |

HN 23A
□ Blue and green dress, height 8¼″, designer P. Stabler ....

| | 1913–1938 | 2100.00 | 2300.00 |

HN 342
□ Patterned dress and lilac shawl, height 8¼″, designer P. Stabler ....

| | 1919–1938 | 2100.0 | 2300.00 |

HN 569
□ Blue gown with large red spots, red shawl with shaded blue stripes, on brown base, height 8¼″, designer P. Stabler ....

| | 1924–1938 | 2000.00 | 2200.00 |

HN 744
□ Spotted dress and striped shawl, height 8¼″, designer P. Stabler ....

| | 1925–1938 | 2100.00 | 2300.00 |

LAVINIA
HN 1955
□ Small figure with red gown trimmed with white, white ruffled cap with blue ribbon trim, carrying basket on arm and small object in other hand, height 5″, designer L. Harradine ....

| | 1940–1978 | 100.00 | 125.00 |

LAWYER, The
HN 3041
□ Elderly gentleman wearing a typical

	Date	Price Range	

black robe trimmed with gray over a gray striped suit, wearing a gray wig, resting one arm on a pillar, height 9″, designer P. Parsons 1985– 160.00

LEADING LADY
HN 2269
□ Pale yellow gown with lavender over-dress, red bow on bodice, yellow ribbon in hair, lavender shoe, holding brown and white object in uplifted hand, height 7¾″, designer M. Davies 1965–1976 150.00 200.00

LEISURE HOUR, The
HN 2055
□ Lady seated in very high backed brown chair on brown base, gown of pale orange with overdress of patterned green and white with red trim, holding large red backed open book on lap, height 6¾″, designer M. Davies 1950–1965 425.00 475.00

LESLEY
HN 2410
□ Lovely figure dressed in shades of peach to flaming red, with basket of colorful flowers in her hand. Dark brown curly hair, height 8″, designer M. Nicoll ... 1986– 250.00

LIDO LADY
HN 1220
□ Pajama clad figure seated on pedestal style base, holding very small brown dog, blue costume with red and dark blue designs, height 6¾″, designer L. Harradine 1927–1938 1200.00 1450.00

HN 1229
□ Flowered pink costume, height 6¾″, designer L. Harradine 1927–1938 1200.00 1450.00

LIFEBOAT MAN, The
HN 2764
□ Figure standing on brown base, dressed in yellow oilskins, wearing a life jacket and carrying a telescope, height 9½″, designer W.K. Harper 1987– 230.00

LIGHTS OUT
HN 2262
□ Small boy figure in pajama costume,

Lido Lady, HN 1220, 1200.00–1450.00

	Date	Price Range	
blue trousers, white top with gold dots, white pillow with red stripes on white base, height 5″, designer M. Davies ..	1965–1969	200.00	250.00

LILAC SHAWL, A
HN 44
☐ Cream colored tiered gown with dark ribbon trim, lilac shawl with red rose figure design, light colored bonnet with yellow ribbons, height 8¾″, designer C.J. Noke ....

| | 1915–1938 | 1600.00 | 1850.00 |

HN 44A
☐ Roses on shawl replaced by printed pattern, height 8¾″, designer C.J. Noke ....

| | 1915–1938 | 1600.00 | 1850.00 |

	Date	Price Range	

HN 339
☐ This figure is now called IN GRAND-MA'S DAY. Yellow gown with brown trim, dark patterned brown shawl, dark bonnet with red rose trim and with blue ribbon with darker dots and fringe, height 8¾″, designer C.J. Noke 1919–1938   1400.00   1600.00

HN 340
☐ Yellow and lilac costume, height 8¾″, designer C.J. Noke 1919–1938   1400.00   1600.00

HN 362
☐ Green, red, yellow striped skirt, height 8¾″, designer C.J. Noke 1919–1938   1550.00   1700.00

HN 388
☐ Patterned blue costume, height 8¾″, designer C.J. Noke 1920–1938   1650.00   1800.00

HN 442
☐ White spotted skirt, green shawl, height 8¾″, designer C.J. Noke 1921–1938   1650.00   1800.00

HN 612
☐ This figure is now called THE POKE BONNET. Dark yellow gown with dark blue circle design, blue and green patterned shawl, dark blue bonnet with red flower trim, red ribbons with blue and white stripes and small dark dots, height 8¾″, designer C.J. Noke 1924–1938   1500.00   1700.00

HN 765
☐ Mottled dark green, blue and purple skirt, height 8¾″, designer C. J. Noke   1925–1938   1500.00   1700.00

LILAC TIME
HN 2137
☐ Red costume with hat which has lilac trim, figure holding bouquet of lilacs in arm, height 7½″, designer M. Davies   1954–1969   275.00   350.00

LILY
HN 1798
☐ Small figure with shaded red gown, white shawl with red and blue designs, cream bonnet with blue ribbons, pantalettes showing slightly, height 5″, designer L. Harradine 1936–1949   100.00   125.00

HN 1799
☐ Blue shawl, with green dress, height 5″, designer L. Harradine 1936–1949   300.00   375.00

	Date	Price Range	

LINDA
HN 2106

☐ Small figure seated on white bench, red cloak, with blue ribbon trim, basket on bench also, height 4¾", designer L. Harradine 1953–1976   100.00   150.00

LISA
HN 2310

☐ Dark blue skirt with large white trim at bottom, white bodice and sleeves with small dark blue dots, matte finish, height 7½", designer M. Davies 1969–1982   175.00   225.00

HN 2394

☐ Pink and blue gown, lilac slippers, dark hair (2nd version), height 7½", designer M. Davies 1983–   185.00

LISETTE
HN 1523

☐ Small figure with cream tiered skirt, red bodice, holding open fan, red ribbon in hair, height 5¼", designer L. Harradine 1932–1938   1000.00   1100.00

HN 1524

☐ Red and blue gown with blue bows as trim, height 5¼", designer L. Harradine 1932–1938   1000.00   1100.00

HN 1684

☐ Pink dress with green trim, height 5¼", designer L. Harradine 1935–1938   1300.00   1500.00

LITTLE BOY BLUE
HN 2062

☐ Small boy figure on yellow and green base, light blue trousers, long dark coat with white collar and red bow, black shoes, horn strapped over shoulder, height 5½", designer L. Harradine ... 1950–1973   100.00   125.00

'LITTLE CHILD SO RARE AND SWEET'
HN 1540

☐ Small white nude blonde haired figure on multicolored rock, figure is bending as if looking for something, height 5", designer unknown 1933–1949   600.00   700.00

	Date	Price Range	

HN 1542

☐ Small white nude figure seated on shaded blue rock, figure has dark hair, height 5″, designer unknown 1933–1949 500.00 600.00

LITTLE JACK HORNER
HN 2063

☐ Small figure seated on bench style base of shaded blue and yellows, red jacket with black buttons, holding pie on lap, has plum in hand at mouth, height 4½″, designer L. Harradine 1950–1953 400.00 450.00

LITTLE LADY MAKE BELIEVE
HN 1870

☐ Small figure seated on bench style base, blue dress, red cloak with blue, green bonnet with blue ribbons, holding small parasol in both hands, height 6″, designer L. Harradine 1938–1949 450.00 550.00

LITTLE LAND, The
HN 63

☐ Green and yellow costume, height 7½″, designer H. Tittensor 1916–1938 2100.00 2500.00

HN 67

☐ Light colored gray gown with a black trim and small round raised white dots, seated on green base which contains little fairies and elves, height 7½″, designer H. Tittensor 1916–1938 2100.00 2500.00

LITTLE MISTRESS, The
HN 1449

☐ Light green gown, shawl of shaded blue with green trim and red stripes and darker blue fringe, red bonnet with red ribbons, carrying basket, height 6″, designer L. Harradine 1931–1949 400.00 500.00

LITTLE MOTHER, The
HN 389

☐ Figure in pink nightdress, standing on brown pillow, holding small black animal, fair hair (1st version), height unknown, designer H. Tittensor 1920–1938 2500.00 2700.00

HN 390

☐ Dark hair (1st version), height unknown, designer H. Tittensor 1920–1938 2500.00 2700.00

The Little Land, HN 67, 2100.00–2500.00

	Date	Price Range	
HN 469			
☐ Cream nightdress, brown hair (1st version), height unknown, designer H. Tittensor	1921–1938	2500.00	2700.00
HN 1399, see Young Widow			
HN 1418			
☐ Young girl and small boy seated on block, girl's costume of mottled dark blue, red and light blues, multicolored shawl, boy's costume striped red and blue, girl holding bouquet of flowers and large brown basket with flowers in front of figures (2nd version), height unknown, designer H. Tittensor	1930–1938	2500.00	3000.00
HN 1641			
☐ Green shawl, pale skirt and basket is of a lighter color (2nd version), height unknown, designer H. Tittensor	1934–1949	2500.00	3000.00

	Date	Price Range	

LITTLE NELL
HN 540
☐ A character from Dickens' "The Old Curiosity Shop," height 4″, designer L. Harradine 1922– 55.00 85.00
☐ **M 51** Renumbered as a miniature, height 4¼″, designer L. Harradine ... 1932–1983 55.00 85.00

LIZANA
HN 1756
☐ Shaded red gown, shawl of multicolored flowers, second shawl is very long and patterned greens, Spanish comb in hair, height 8½″, designer L. Harradine 1936–1949 700.00 875.00
HN 1761
☐ Green dress, leopard-skin cloak, height 8½″, designer L. Harradine 1936–1938 850.00 950.00

LOBSTER MAN, The
HN 2317
☐ Character figure seated on green base with brown lobster basket, brown trousers, dark blue sweater, black cap, black boots with white tops, has lobster in hand, pipe in mouth, height 6⅞″, designer M. Nicoll 1964– 230.00

LOBSTER MAN, The (White)
HN 2323
☐ Figure sitting on a lobster pot, black trousers and boots, white turtleneck sweater, white cap with black bill, white pipe in mouth. Large basket at his feet, height 7½″, designer M. Nicoll 1987– 230.00

LONDON CRY, STRAWBERRIES
HN 749
☐ Lady and small girl figures on brown base, lady's skirt is red, white apron, red belt, white bonnet, girl's skirt is dark color, red blouse, white bonnet, each is carrying basket of light color, with large basket on base at their feet, height 6¾″, designer L. Harradine ... 1925–1938 1300.00 1400.00
HN 772
☐ Both gowns are multicolored, baskets are of darker brown, base is of a lighter

The Lobster Man, HN 2317, 230.00

	Date	Price Range	

brown, height 6¾″, designer L. Harradine 1925–1938 1300.00 1400.00

LONDON CRY, TURNIPS AND CARROTS
HN 752
☐ Lady and small boy figures on brown base, lady's skirt purple and red with lightly colored apron, boy's brown trousers, jacket and hat, with light shirt, both are holding vegetables with basket on base, height 6¾″, designer L. Harradine 1925–1938 1300.00 1400.00
HN 771
☐ Lady's dress of shaded blues and reds, boy's lighter brown suit and hat, basket

Long John Silver, HN 2204, 425.00–485.00

	Date	Price Range	
on base is darker brown, cream base, height 6¾″, designer L. Harradine ...	1925–1938	1300.00	1400.00

LONG JOHN SILVER
HN 2204
☐ Black, gold and white Pirate costume, on red and green base, parrot is green, red and light brown, height 9″, designer M. Nicoll .... | 1957–1965 | 425.00 | 485.00 |

LORETTA
HN 2337
☐ Purple gown with yellow shawl, green

	Date	Price Range	

and white feathers in hair, height 7¾″, designer M. Davies 1966–1980 **120.00** **150.00**

LORI (Kate Greenaway)
HN 2801
☐ Small girl on white base, white gown with red sash and red flowers around bottom, large brim hat of white with red ribbon trim, holding single flower, height 5⅞″, designer M. Davies 1976–1987 **100.00**

LORNA
HN 2311
☐ Green gown trimmed in yellow, yellow stole, holding small blue and white fan, long blue gloves, height 8⅜″, designer M. Davies 1965–1985 **150.00** **200.00**

LOUISE (Kate Greenaway)
HN 2869
☐ Small figure, brown gown with white crossed collar, black bonnet with yellow ribbon, single flower in both hands, height 6″, designer M. Davies 1979–1985 **100.00** **125.00**

LOVE LETTER
HN 2149
☐ Two figures seated on couch with small red table at side, one gown is red and white with gold design, black shoes, small white head covering, other gown is shaded blues with black trim, light blue pillow on couch, one figure holding small white paper, height 5″, designer M. Davies 1958–1976 **250.00** **350.00**

LUCY (Kate Greenaway)
HN 2863
☐ Small figure on white base, holding single flower in hands, skirt of light blue and white, vest of dark blue, white and blue blouse, tall blue hat with white and blue ribbon, height 6″, designer M. Davies 1980–1984 **90.00** **115.00**

LUCY ANN
HN 1502
☐ Shaded red gown with blue ribbon, holding up skirt which is filled with

	Date	Price Range	

flowers, height 5¼″, designer L. Harradine 1932–1951 250.00 325.00

HN 1565
☐ Pale green dress, height 5¼″, designer L. Harradine 1933–1938 500.00 675.00

LUCY LOCKETT
HN 485
☐ Very wide skirted green gown with red gloves and small red purse, long strand of dark beads, on black base, has hands crossed. A character from "The Beggar's Opera" (1st version), height 6″, designer L. Harradine 1921–1949 600.00 700.00

HN 524
☐ HN 695, yellow dress, wine gloves and purse (2nd version), height 6″, designer L. Harradine 1921–1949 600.00 700.00

HN 695
☐ Orange gown with red gloves and purse, also beads, this figure has one hand in waist and one hand in front (2nd version), height 6″, designer L. Harradine 1925–1949 650.00 750.00

HN 696
☐ Powder blue costume (2nd version), height 6″, designer L. Harradine 1925–1949 650.00 750.00

LUNCHTIME
HN 2485
☐ Male figure seated on brown bench on base, one squirrel also on base and bench, green suit with light brown overcoat, hat and scarf same color as suit, holding open paperbag, feeding one squirrel, height 8″, designer M. Nicoll 1973–1980 200.00 250.00

LYDIA
HN 1906
☐ Figure seated with flowers in back on each side, gown of orange and pink overdress, pale pink flowered underskirt, holding open book in one hand, height 4¼″, designer L. Harradine ... 1939–1949 700.00 850.00

HN 1907
☐ Green gown, green bonnet with black ribbon, height 4¼″, designer L. Harradine 1939–1949 700.00 850.00

	Date	Price Range	

HN 1908

☐ Red gown and bonnet, height 4⅛″, designer L. Harradine 1939– 160.00

LYNNE
HN 2329

☐ Yellow and green gown with white designs on bottom, yellow and green ribbon in hair, height 7″, designer M. Davies 1971– 230.00

MADONNA OF THE SQUARE
HN 10

☐ Lilac costume, height 7″, designer P. Stabler 1913–1938 1450.00 1600.00

HN 10A

☐ Seated lady, blue costume that covers her entirely, only face and hand shows, infant in lap also wrapped n blue, small basket at feet filled with multicolored flowers, height 7″, designer P. Stabler 1913–1938 1350.00 1500.00

HN 11

☐ Gray costume, height 7″, designer P. Stabler 1913–1938 1450.00 1700.00

HN 14

☐ Renumbered version of HN 10A, height 7″, designer P. Stabler 1913–1938 1450.00 1700.00

HN 27

☐ Mottled green and blue costume, height 7″, designer P. Stabler 1913–1938 1650.00 1800.00

HN 326

☐ Gray and blue costume, earthenware, height 7″, designer P. Stabler 1918–1938 1650.00 1800.00

HN 573

☐ Orange skirt and cubist-style shawl, height 7″, designer P. Stabler 1913–1938 1650.00 1800.00

HN 576

☐ Green skirt and patterned black shawl, height 7″, designer P. Stabler 1923–1938 1650.00 1800.00

HN 594

☐ Green skirt and patterned brown shawl, height 7″, designer P. Stabler 1924–1938 1650.00 1800.00

HN 613

☐ Striped pink skirt and spotted orange shawl, height 7″, designer P. Stabler 1924–1938 1650.00 1800.00

HN 764

☐ Blue and purple striped shawl, yellow skirt, height 7″, designer P. Stabler .. 1925–1938 1650.00 1800.00

	Date	Price Range	

HN 1968
☐ Pale green costume, height 7″, designer P. Stabler 1941–1949 850.00 950.00

HN 1969
☐ Lilac costume, height 7″, designer P. Stabler 1941–1949 850.00 950.00

HN 2034
☐ Shaded green and blue costume, height 7″, designer P. Stabler 1949–1951 800.00 900.00

MAISIE
HN 1618
☐ Tiered pale green skirt, shaded blue blouse, red bonnet, white pantalettes showing, on base, height 6¼″, designer L. Harradine 1934–1949 550.00 650.00

HN 1619
☐ Shaded red gown, dark hair, dark base, height 6¼″, designer L. Harradine ... 1934–1949 375.00 475.00

MAKE BELIEVE
HN 2224
☐ Same as HN 2225 except it is an all white figure, height 5¾″, designer M. Nicoll 1985–1988 95.00

HN 2225
☐ Small figure in very light blue gown; holding very large yellow hat with flower trim, green shoes on one side, red purse on other side, height 5¾″, designer M. Nicoll 1962–1988 140.00

MAM'SELLE
HN 658
☐ Black and white costume with black triangular hat, black shoes, standing on black pedestal style base, height 7″, designer L. Harradine 1924–1938 1450.00 1650.00

HN 659
☐ Dark blue and red costume, hat matches costume, height 7″, designer L. Harradine 1924–1938 1450.00 1650.00

HN 724
☐ Red hat, yellow trimmed dress, height 7″, designer L. Harradine 1925–1938 1450.00 1650.00

HN 786
☐ Red skirt with black square, top is black with gold stripe, height 7″, designer L. Harradine 1926–1938 1450.00 1650.00

	Date	Price Range	

MANDARIN, A
HN 84
☐ HN 318, mauve shirt, green cloak (1st version), height 10¼", designer C.J. Noke 1918–1938 3000.00 3500.00

HN 316
☐ Rotund Chinese figure, black and gold costume, yellow tunic with green dragon and gold flower design (1st version), height 10¼", designer C.J. Noke 1918–1938 3000.00 3500.00

HN 318
☐ Rotund Chinese figure with black costume with gold designs, gold tunic with raised pattern design of dragon and other designs (1st version), height 10¼", designer C.J. Noke 1918–1938 3000.00 3500.00

HN 366
☐ Small seated Chinese male on a pedestal, yellow and blue costume (2nd version), height 8¼", designer C.J. Noke 1920–1938 3000.00 3500.00

HN 382
☐ Blue and yellow costume (1st version), height 10¼", designer C.J. Noke 1920–1938 3000.00 3500.00

HN 450
☐ Red costume with black designs in circle of deeper red trimmed in green, also has red and black design, red, black and green cap (3rd version), height unknown, designer C.J. Noke 1921–1938 3000.00 3500.00

HN 455
☐ Green costume (2nd version), height 8¼", designer C.J. Noke 1921–1938 3000.00 3500.00

HN 460
☐ Blue costume (3rd version), height unknown, designer C.J. Noke 1921–1938 3000.00 3500.00

HN 461
☐ Red costume (3rd version), height unknown, designer C.J. Noke 1921–1938 3000.00 3500.00

HN 601
☐ Blue costume (3rd version), height unknown, designer C.J. Noke 1924–1938 3000.00 3500.00

HN 611
☐ Yellow patterned tunic (3rd version), height 10¼", designer C.J. Noke 1924–1938 3000.00 3500.00

	Date	Price Range	

HN 641
□ HN 366, onyx style coloring (2nd version), height 8¼″, designer C. J. Noke — 1924–1938 — 3000.00 — 3500.00

HN 746
□ Black costume with green dragons (1st version), height 10¼″, designer C.J. Noke .... — 1925–1938 — 3000.00 — 3500.00

HN 787
□ Pink and orange tunic decorated with black flowers (1st version), height 10¼″, designer C.J. Noke .... — 1926–1938 — 3000.00 — 3500.00

HN 791
□ Yellow tunic with green and red markings (1st version), height 10¼″, designer C.J. Noke .... — 1926–1938 — 3000.00 — 3500.00

MANDY
HN 2476
□ Young girl in a cream colored off the shoulder gown with short bouffant sleeves, dark hair, holding a yellow lantern, height 4½″, designer M. Davies — 1982– — 95.00

MAN IN TUDOR COSTUME
HN 563
□ Gold, green, and purple costume on black base, height 3¾″, designer unknown .... — 1923–1938 — 2500.00 — 3500.00

MANTILLA
HN 2712
□ Tall figure in red Spanish style costume with black and red shawl, high comb in hair, height 11¾″, designer E.J. Griffiths .... — 1974–1979 — 300.00 — 350.00

MARGARET
HN 1989
□ Green gown with mottled red, blue and yellow overdress, green hat with red ribbon, height 7¼″, designer L. Harradine .... — 1947–1959 — 300.00 — 400.00

MARGARET OF ANJOU
HN 2012
□ Mottled green and yellow gown trimmed in white with wide and high bluish white head covering, height 9¼″, designer M. Davies .... — 1948–1953 — 500.00 — 600.00

	Date	Price Range	

MARGARET THATCHER
HN 2886
□ A bust of the first woman party leader in British politics, on a base, height 4½″, designer E. Griffiths 1983–

MARGERY
HN 1413
□ Red and patterned black gown trimmed in white with various colors, green bonnet with black ribbons, height 10¾″, designer L. Harradine 1930–1949 450.00 500.00

MARGOT
HN 1628
□ Full skirted gown of shaded blues, large brim blue hat with red ribbons, carrying small basket of flowers, height 5¾″, designer L. Harradine 1934–1938 850.00 1000.00
HN 1636
□ Red bodice, pink and yellow skirt, height 5¾″, designer L. Harradine ... 1934–1938 850.00 1000.00
HN 1653
□ White skirt with blue flower design, red bodice, red hat, height 5¾″, designer L. Harradine 1934–1938 850.00 1000.00

MARGUERITE
HN 1928
□ HN 1946, pink dress, height 8″, designer L. Harradine 1940–1959 325.00 400.00
HN 1929
□ Pink fading to yellow at bottom of dress, height 8″, designer L. Harradine 1940–1949 650.00 750.00
HN 1930
□ Blue dress with purple stripes, height 8″, designer L. Harradine 1940–1949 800.00 900.00
HN 1946
□ Red gown with white and green trim on bodice, black bonnet with green lining and green feather trim, holding small bouquet of flowers to face, height 8″, designer L. Harradine 1940–1949 700.00 800.00

MARIANNE
HN 2074
□ Red skirt with darker red jacket trimmed in white, black hat trimmed

	Date	Price Range	
in white, holding riding crop, height 7¼", designer L. Harradine	1951–1953	650.00	750.00

MARIE
HN 401
□ White skirt with purple designs trimmed in gold, purple and pink overlay, pink bodice trimmed with white (1st version), height unknown, designer L. Harradine 1920–1938 2500.00 2800.00

HN 434
□ Yellow skirt with orange stripes (1st version), height unknown, designer L. Harradine 1921–1938 2500.00 2800.00

HN 502
□ White dress, red and blue bodice (1st version), height unknown, designer L. Harradine 1921–1938 2500.00 2800.00

HN 504
□ Green and blue dress, red spots (1st version), height unknown, designer L. Harradine 1921–1938 2500.00 2800.00

HN 505
□ Spotted blue bodice, green and lilac skirt (1st version), height unknown, designer L. Harradine 1921–1938 2500.00 2800.00

HN 506
□ Blue and green striped bodice, spotted lilac skirt (1st version), height unknown, designer L. Harradine 1921–1938 2500.00 2800.00

HN 1370
□ Small figure in full shaded purple gown (2nd version), height 4½", designer L. Harradine 1930–1988 95.00

HN 1388
□ Red and blue flowered dress (2nd version), height 4½", designer L. Harradine 1930–1938 400.00 500.00

HN 1417
□ Orange dress (2nd version), height 4½", designer L. Harradine 1930–1949 300.00 400.00

HN 1489
□ Shaded green dress (2nd version), height 4½", designer L. Harradine ... 1932–1949 300.00 400.00

HN 1531
□ Yellow and green dress (2nd version), height 4½", designer L. Harradine ... 1932–1938 300.00 400.00

	Date	Price Range	

HN 1635
☐ Flowered pink skirt (2nd version), height 4½″, designer L. Harradine ... 1934–1949 400.00 500.00

HN 1655
☐ Pink bodice, flower white shirt (2nd version), height 4½″, designer L. Harradine 1934–1938 500.00 600.00

MARIETTA
HN 1341
☐ Stylish bat costume of black and red on red base, height 8″, designer L. Harradine 1929–1949 650.00 750.00

HN 1446
☐ Shaded blue and red costume, green cloak with green lining, height 8″, designer L. Harradine 1931–1949 700.00 800.00

HN 1699
☐ Green costume, red cloak with blue lining, height 8″, designer L. Harradine 1935–1949 700.00 800.00

MARIGOLD
HN 1447
☐ Shaded blue gown, green bonnet with green ribbons, height 6″, designer L. Harradine 1931–1949 500.00 600.00

HN 1451
☐ Yellow dress, height 6″, designer L. Harradine 1931–1938 600.00 700.00

HN 1555
☐ Costume is red skirt with light blue jacket, blue bonnet with darker blue ribbons, height 6″, designer L. Harradine 1931–1951 500.00 600.00

MARILYN
HN 3002
☐ Gown is white with sprays of flowers adapted from the Royal Crown Darby pattern "Posie." Red hair with white ribbon; she is delicately holding a fan in one hand and gently lifting skirt with the other hand, height 7¼″, designer P. Gee 1986– 170.00

	Date	Price Range	

MARION
HN 1582
☐ Green bonnet, pink skirt, height 6½″, designer L. Harradine 1933–1938   1400.00   1600.00

HN 1583
☐ Figure seated in cream chair, blue skirt, dark blue blouse, multicolored shawl, shaded blue and red bonnet with red ribbons, height 6½″, designer L. Harradine 1933–1938   1400.00   1600.00

MARIQUITA
HN 1837
☐ Red and shaded blue skirt, red bodice and sleeves trimmed with white, blue hat, holding open fan in one hand, height 8″, designer L. Harradine 1938–1949   2200.00   2500.00

MARJORIE
HN 2788
☐ Figure in seated position, white gown with blue trim, blue bodice, height 5¼″, designer M. Davies 1980–1984   150.00   200.00

MARKET DAY
HN 1991
☐ Blue skirt, white apron, shaded blue and red shawl, white head covering, goose under one arm and basket of flowers under other. Reissued as Country Lass, height 7¼″, designer L. Harradine 1947–1955   275.00   350.00

MARY HAD A LITTLE LAMB
HN 2048
☐ Small figure in seated position in shaded blue and red gown trimmed in white, blue ribbon in hair, small lamb on lap with blue ribbon, height 3⅝″, designer M. Davies 1949–1988   140.00

MARY JANE
HN 1990
☐ Light red dress with flower design, shaded blue apron, small white cap with black ribbon, height 7½″, designer L. Harradine 1947–1959   400.00   450.00

MARY MARY
HN 2044
☐ Small girl figure on yellow-green base,

	Date	Price Range	

pink skirt, red blouse, blue sash, holds watering can, height 5″, designer L. Harradine 1949–1973 125.00 150.00

MASK, The
HN 656
☐ Blue and purple costume, height 6¾″, designer L. Harradine 1924–1938 1600.00 1800.00
HN 657
☐ White costume with black trim and black spots, on black base, holding mask, small black cap, height 6¾″, designer L. Harradine 1924–1938 1600.00 1800.00
HN 729
☐ Red costume with black squares and black collar, height 6¾″, designer L. Harradine 1925–1938 1700.00 1900.00
HN 733
☐ White costume with black squares, height 6¾″, designer L. Harradine ... 1925–1938 1600.00 1800.00
HN 785
☐ Blue costume, pink striped skirt, height 6¾″, designer L. Harradine 1926–1938 1600.00 1800.00
HN 1271
☐ Black and red costume with spots of blue, green, and yellow, height 6¾″, designer L. Harradine 1928–1938 1600.00 1800.00

MASK SELLER
HN 1361
☐ Character figure in black cloak, red hat with green feather, green stockings and shoes on gray and green base, holds white masks on red carrier, holds flute in hands, height 8¾″, designer L. Harradine 1929–1938 1500.00 1800.00
HN 2103
☐ Green cloak, black hat, brown stockings and shoes on brown base, masks of different colors, flute is larger, lantern panes are colored, height 8¾″, designer L. Harradine 1953– 250.00

MASQUE
HN 2554
☐ Dark blue with black shadings, cloak covers figure, has mask on long handle. Note: Second figure has hand up to

Masquerade, HN 600, 1100.00–1250.00

	Date	Price Range	
mask with dark blue cloak, discontinued, height 8⅞″, designer D. V. Tootle	1973–1982	275.00	350.00

MASQUERADE
HN 599
☐ Male figure standing on brown base with brown bush, eighteenth-century style costume of red coat, brown trousers, white stockings, brown shoes and hat (1st version), height 6¾″, designer L. Harradine

	1924–1949	1000.00	1200.00

HN 600
☐ Female figure standing on brown base with bush, holding basket of fruit, white eighteenth-century style costume with

	Date	Price Range	

red designs, white hair (1st version), height varies from 6″ to 6¾″, designer L. Harradine 1924–1949 1100.00 1250.00

HN 636

☐ Male, gold costume (1st version), height 6¾″, designer L. Harradine ... 1924–1938 1100.00 1300.00

HN 637

☐ Female, everything gold (1st version), height varies from 6″ to 6¾″, designer L. Harradine 1924–1938 1100.00 1300.00

HN 674

☐ Female, orange and yellow checkered dress (1st version), height varies from 6″ to 6¾″, designer L. Harradine 1924–1938 1100.00 1250.00

HN 683

☐ Male, green coat (1st version), height 6¾″, designer L. Harradine 1924–1938 1200.00 1400.00

HN 2251

☐ Eighteenth-century style figure on white base, blue and white costume with green designs, tiny blue head cap (2nd version), height 8½″, designer M. Davies 1960–1965 325.00 350.00

HN 2259

☐ Red dress with white, no gold design (2nd version), height 8½″, designer M. Davies 1960–1965 300.00 350.00

MASTER, The
HN 2325

☐ Character figure seated on rock with dog and staff, brown trousers and shoes, green coat, light tan hat lying beside figure, height 5⅝″, designer M. Davies 1967– 230.00

MASTER SWEEP
HN 2205

☐ Boy figure with black trousers, dark green coat, black hat and shoes, orange scarf, standing on dark base, has brown bag in one hand, chimney brush in other, height 8½″, designer M. Nicoll 1957–1962 550.00 650.00

MATILDA
HN 2011

☐ Purple and red gown, long red cloak, gold rope belt, holding open book, dark

	Date	Price Range	

braided hair, height 9¼", designer M.
Davies .... | 1948–1953 | 450.00 | 550.00

MAUREEN
HN 1770
☐ Light red gown, black gloves, black hat
with white and black tip feathers, holding black riding crop, height 7½", de-
signer L. Harradine .... | 1936–1959 | 275.00 | 325.00

HN 1771
☐ Shaded blue dress, green bonnet with
white feather, green gloves, holding
brown riding crop, height 8", designer
L. Harradine .... | 1936–1959 | 650.00 | 750.00

☐ M-84 Made as a miniature, shaded orange gown, height 4", designer L.
Harradine .... | 1939–1949 | 700.00 | 800.00

☐ M-85 Light blue skirt, red and blue
jacket, height 4", designer L. Harra-
dine .... | 1939–1949 | 700.00 | 800.00

MAY
HN 2746
☐ Figure on a stone base walking against
a very cold wind. Dressed in green with
a blue-hooded cape, lined in green,
height 8", designer D. Tootle .... | 1987– | 215.00 |

MAYOR, The
HN 2280
☐ Red and white costume, black hat with
white trim, black shoes with buckle
trim, gold chain around chest, height
8¼", designer M. Nicoll .... | 1963–1971 | 475.00 | 575.00

MAYTIME
HN 2113
☐ Shaded red gown, light blue and green
scarf, bonnet with red ribbons, dark
hair, height 6¾", designer L. Harra-
dine .... | 1953–1967 | 225.00 | 325.00

MEDITATION
HN 2330
☐ Lady seated at skirted writing table of
white with shaded green which contains yellow candleholder, yellow ink
bottle and open book, brown gown with
cream that contains orange designs,

	Date	Price Range	
white hair, height 5¾″, designer M. Davies	1971–1983	200.00	300.00

MEG
HN 2743
☐ Figure stands on white base, dressed in multilayered gown with shades of pink, purple, yellow, blue, and cream. Below gown are matching pantaloons. Long, light brown hair covered by a bonnet with colors matching gown; she is holding a small basket, height 8½″, designer D. Tootle 1987– 195.00

MELANIE
HN 2271
☐ Blue gown with yellow collar, hair tied with pink ribbon, holding small wrapped bouquet in hand, height 7⅞″, designer M. Davies 1965–1980 125.00 150.00

MELISSA
HN 2467
☐ White undergown and cuffs, shaded red and purple overdress, one hand raised to blonde hair, height 6¾″, designer M. Davies 1981– 230.00

MELODY
HN 2202
☐ Lady seated, gown of light orange, skirt with green bodice trimmed in white, playing white instrument held on lap, height 6¼″, designer M. Davies 1957–1962 200.00 275.00

MEMORIES
HN 1855
☐ Green bodice and hat, red skirt, height 6″, designer L. Harradine 1938–1949 450.00 550.00
HN 1856
☐ Lady seated leaning against brown tree stump, pale blue gown with darker blue designs, blue bodice trimmed in white, bonnet with black ribbons, holding green open book on knee, height 6″, designer L. Harradine 1938–1949 500.00 600.00
HN 1857
☐ Red bodice with red and lilac skirt, height 6″, designer L. Harradine 1938–1949 450.00 550.00

	Date	Price Range	

HN 2030
☐ Shaded red skirt, green bodice, bonnet with green ribbons, height 6″, designer L. Harradine .... | 1949–1959 | 450.00 | 550.00

MENDICANT, The
HN 1355
☐ Shaded brown, black and green costume, orange, green and brown turban, seated on base of reddish bricks with multicolored cloth, holding tambourine, height 8¼″, designer L. Harradine .... | 1929–1938 | 750.00 | 900.00
HN 1365
☐ Minor glaze differences, height 8¼″, designer L. Harradine .... | 1929–1969 | 250.00 | 325.00

MEPHISTO
HN 722
☐ Black blouse, height 6½″, designer L. Harradine .... | 1925–1938 | 2500.00 | 3000.00
HN 723
☐ Masquerade type costume of red with black stripes on skirt, red jacket, red cap with black lining, wide white collar, small triangular hat of red and black, on black pedestal style base, height 6½″, designer L. Harradine ... | 1925–1938 | 2500.00 | 3000.00

MEPHISTOPHELES AND MARGUERITE
HN 755
☐ Two-sided figure with black base, one side lady in orange dress, purple cloak; other side male figure in red outfit wit red cloak, height 7¾″, designer C.J. Noke .... | 1925–1949 | 1500.00 | 1750.00
HN 775
☐ Two figures on black base, the lady in white costume with gold designs, red cloak with white lining, red shoes; reverse side is male figure in red with black stripes and red cloak with black lining, height 7¾″, designer C.J. Noke | 1925–1949 | 1500.00 | 1750.00

MERIEL
HN 1931
☐ Pink gown with wide white collar, bon-

The Mermaid, HN 97, 700.00–900.00

	Date	Price Range	
net with trim of black, seated on bench, height 7 1/4″, designer L. Harradine ...	1940–1949	1550.00	1850.00
HN 1932			
☐ Green gown, height 7 1/4″, designer L. Harradine	1940–1949	1550.00	1850.00
MERMAID, The			
HN 97			
☐ Mermaid seated on brown and yellow rock, green and blue fish tail, upper torso white, red beads and red decoration in hair, height 7″, designer H. Tittensor	1918–1936	700.00	900.00

	Date	Price Range	

HN 300
☐ Red berries in hair, with darker base, height 7″, designer H. Tittensor ...... 1918–1936 | 800.00 | 1000.00

MERRY CHRISTMAS
HN 3096
☐ One of the Special Occasion figures. Gown is holly green over white under-skirt. Figure is reading a card which is held in one hand and, in the other hand, she carries a Christmas package, height 8½″, designer P. Parsons ...... 1987– | 215.00

MERYLL
HN 1917
☐ Red jacket and green skirt. This figure was renamed shortly after its introduc-tion, height 6¾″, designer L. Harra-dine .... 1939–1940 | 3500.00 | 4000.00

MICHELLE
HN 2234
☐ Gown of green with white design on edge, undergown of light red, also sleeves of light red, height 6⅞″, de-signer M. Davies .... 1967– | 195.00

MIDINETTE
HN 1289
☐ Short skirt of light red with flower de-sign, mottled red jacket, red shoes on light base, carrying two hat boxes, one is white with yellow stripes and yellow and brown dots, the other is yellow, dark blue, black and white stripes (1st version), height 9″, designer L. Har-radine .... 1928–1938 | 2450.00 | 2750.00

HN 1306
☐ Green skirt, red jacket, black base, one hat box is white with green and gold stripes, the other is white with red and green stripes (1st version), height 9″, designer L. Harradine .... 1928–1938 | 2450.00 | 2750.00

HN 2090
☐ Light blue skirt and jacket, hat with red feather, white hat box with blue design and red ribbon, full length skirt, this figure is not on a base (2nd version), height 7¼″, designer L. Harradine ... 1952–1965 | 275.00 | 325.00

Midinette, HN 1289, 2450.00–2750.00

	Date	Price Range	
MIDSUMMER NOON			
HN 1899			
☐ Figure seated on bench, beige skirt, red, white, and blue bodice, on bench is basket of flowers and shawl with green border, height 4½″, designer L. Harradine	1939–1949	650.00	750.00
HN 1900			
☐ Blue dress, height 4½″, designer L. Harradine	1939–1949	1500.00	1800.00
HN 2033			
☐ Only minor color differences, height 4½″, designer L. Harradine	1949–1955	650.00	750.00

	Date	Price Range	

MILADY
HN 1970
☐ Shaded red gown with white collar with
black ribbon, black gloves, black hat
with feather trim, holding riding crop,
height 6½″, designer L. Harradine ... | 1941–1949 | 975.00 | 1150.00

MILKING TIME
HN 3
☐ Light blue gown with white apron,
standing on round base with brown and
white goat, figure holding jug on arm,
height unknown, designer P. Stabler .. | 1913–1938 | 3000.00 | 3500.00

HN 306
☐ Pale costume with black printed markings,
height unknown, designer P. Stabler ...... | 1913–1938 | 2750.00 | 3000.00

MILKMAID, The
HN 2057
☐ Green skirt, brown blouse, blue and
white apron trimmed in brown, white
farm bonnet, carrying brown jug,
height 6½″, designer L. Harradine ... | 1975–1981 | 150.00 | 200.00

MILLICENT
HN 1714
☐ Red and white gown with blue designs
and stripes, red shawl, blue bonnet with
green ribbons, holding small round
purse, height 8″, designer L. Harradine | 1935–1949 | 1450.00 | 1650.00

HN 1715
☐ Flowered shawl and purple dress,
height 8″, designer L. Harradine ..... | 1935–1949 | 1450.00 | 1650.00

HN 1860
☐ No details of color available, height 8″,
designer L. Harradine .... | 1938–1949 | 1850.00 | 2100.00

MINUET
HN 2019
☐ White gown with blue and gold de-
signs, light blue shoes, height 7¼″, de-
signer M. Davies .... | 1949–1971 | 250.00 | 350.00

HN 2066
☐ Red and blue gown, height 7¼″, de-
signer M. Davies .... | 1950–1955 | 1000.00 | 1250.00

MIRABEL
HN 1743
☐ Cream and shaded blue gown and
cloak, cloak has red edge trim, green

	Date	Price Range	

hat, red open parasol, height 7¾″, designer L. Harradine 1935–1949   **1250.00**   **1500.00**

HN 1744

☐ Shaded red gown with red flowers and cream colored stripes, red cloak, light green bonnet, open parasol, height 7¾″, designer L. Harradine 1935–1949   **1150.00**   **1250.00**

☐ **M-68** Introduced as a miniature, red gown with green cloak, black bonnet, green parasol, height 4″, designer L. Harradine 1936–1949   **600.00**   **750.00**

☐ **M-74** Green dress, height 4″, designer L. Harradine 1936–1949   **600.00**   **750.00**

MIRANDA
HN 1818

☐ Red skirt, with blue mottled bodice and overskirt, trimmed with green, small wrapped head covering of green with black ribbon, holding open fan in one hand, on black base, height 8½″, designer L. Harradine 1937–1949   **1300.00**   **1500.00**

HN 1819

☐ Green skirt, height 8½″, designer L. Harradine 1937–1949   **1300.00**   **1500.00**

HN 3037

☐ Figure wearing full-skirted, white gown shaded with lemon. Gown has a fuchsia bodice with a very low neckline, showing jeweled necklace. She is holding white handkerchief in one hand, raised toward her face. Hair is dark brown, height 8¼″, designer A. Hughes 1987–   **215.00**

MIRROR, The
HN 1852

☐ Slender figure in red and blue gown with white collar that has blue and red flowers, holding small mirror, height 7½″, designer L. Harradine 1938–1949   **2500.00**   **3000.00**

HN 1853

☐ Blue costume, height 7½″, designer L. Harradine 1938–1949   **2500.00**   **3000.00**

MISS DEMURE
HN 1402

☐ Pink gown with blue shawl that has yellow and green stripe, light green bonnet with darker green ribbons, open red

	Date	Price Range	
parasol with white fringe, height 7″, designer L. Harradine	1930–1975	**225.00**	**325.00**

HN 1440
☐ Blue gown with dark blue shawl, blue bonnet with darker blue ribbons, open red parasol with reddish white trim, height 7″, designer L. Harradine .....

	Date	Price Range	
	1930–1949	**600.00**	**750.00**

HN 1463
☐ Green dress, height 7″, designer L. Harradine ....

	1931–1949	**600.00**	**750.00**

HN 1499
☐ Yellow bonnet, pink dress, height 7″, designer L. Harradine ....

	1932–1938	**550.00**	**650.00**

HN 1560
☐ Cream and shaded blue gown, shaded red and blue shawl, red bonnet with dark blue ribbons, open multicolored parasol, height 7″, designer L. Harradine ....

	1933–1949	**600.00**	**750.00**

MISS 1926
HN 1205
☐ Figure standing on brown pedestal style base, with dark fur coat with white fur trim, height 7¼″, designer L. Harradine ....

	1926–1938	**2500.00**	**3000.00**

HN 1207
☐ Black fur collar, height 7¼″, designer L. Harradine ....

	1926–1938	**2500.00**	**3000.00**

MISS FORTUNE
HN 1897
☐ Red skirt, shawl of white with blue and green designs, blue bonnet with red ribbons, on base that has basket of flowers and single yellow flower on it, height 5¾″, designer L. Harradine ...

	1938–1949	**800.00**	**1000.00**

HN 1898
☐ Green and yellow shawl, mauve dress, height 5¾″, designer L. Harradine ...

	1938–1949	**800.00**	**1000.00**

MISS MUFFET
HN 1936
☐ Small figure in white gown, red long coat with white fur trim, white fur muff, white open parasol, red cap with black ribbons, height 5½″, designer L. Harradine ....

	1940–1967	**175.00**	**225.00**

Miss Muffet, HN 1936, 175.00–225.00

	Date	Price Range	

HN 1937

☐ Very light red gown, green long coat with white fur trim, green cap with red ribbons, parasol, height 5½", designer L. Harradine 1940–1952 250.00 325.00

MISS WINSOME
HN 1665

☐ Shaded purple gown, white shawl with red flower design, green bonnet, small green round purse, height 6¾", designer L. Harradine 1934–1949 800.00 950.00

HN 1666

☐ Green gown, shawl multicolored, red bonnet with green ribbons, small red purse, height 6¾", designer L. Harradine 1934–1938 900.00 1100.00

M'LADY'S MAID
HN 1795

☐ Red gown with very small white apron,

	Date	Price Range	

white trim on sleeves, small white cap with ribbon trim, gold rope with key attached, carrying small tray with objects on it, height 9″, designer L. Harradine 1936–1949 2000.00 2200.00

HN 1822
☐ Multicolored dress, height 9″, designer L. Harradine 1937–1949 2200.00 2500.00

MODENA
HN 1845
☐ Blue dress, height 7¼″, designer L. Harradine 1938–1949 2000.00 2250.00

HN 1846
☐ Full red skirt with green bows, green bodice with red rose trim, white shawl with green and red design, shawl covers comb in hair, red rose in hair, height 7¼″, designer L. Harradine ... 1938–1949 1500.00 1800.00

MODERN PIPER, The
HN 756
☐ Costume of pink tights with blue diamond design and gold jacket mottled red and blue, green and blue cloak, gold pipe on green and yellow base with four tiny figures, height 8½″, designer L. Harradine 1925–1938 2500.00 3000.00

MODESTY
HN 2744
☐ Young figure on light, lime-green base, dressed in white undergarment, blond hair is covered with dust cap, height 8¼″, designer D. Tootle 1987– 130.00

MOIRA
HN 1347
☐ Figure of lady with dog on pedestal style base, woman's costume of blue, green, yellow, and black, vest also multicolored, green and blue striped hat, green gloves, dark brown and white dog, height 6½″, designer L. Harradine 1929–1938 3000.00 3500.00

MOLLY MALONE
HN 1455
☐ Skirt with white apron with blue tint, overdress is of red and darker blue,

The Modern Piper, HN 756, 2500.00–3000.00

	Date	Price Range	
dark bodice with multicolored collar, multicolored kerchief on head, the base contains figure, brown wheelbarrow and basket, height 7″, designer L. Harradine	1931–1938	2000.00	2400.00

MONICA
HN 1458
☐ Small seated figure, white gown with multicolored flower designs, black bonnet with green ribbons, holds red basket of flowers, height 4″, designer L. Harradine ....

	1931–1949	450.00	550.00

	Date	Price Range	

HN 1459
☐ Lilac dress, height 4″, designer L. Harradine ....

1931– Unknown 450.00 550.00

HN 1467
☐ White and shaded blue gown with a very faint flower design, red bodice, red and blue sleeves, red bonnet with blue ribbon, basket is light color, red flowers, height 4″, designer L. Harradine

1931– 140.00

☐ **M-66** Introduced as a miniature, height 3″, designer L. Harradine ....

1935–1949 550.00 750.00

☐ **M-72** White gown with large blue spots, blue bodice, pink bonnet with black ribbons, basket has yellow and red flowers, height 3″, designer L. Harradine ....

1936–1949 550.00 750.00

MONTE CARLO
HN 2332
☐ Figure in the Sweet and Twenty Series. Designed to capture the era of the 1920s and 1930s, this figure depicts a red-haired girl dressed in a sleeveless, green gown with a multicolored cape draped around her legs. Limited edition of 1,500, height 8¼″, designer M. Davies ....

1982– 250.00

MOOR, The
HN 1308
☐ Patterned blue costume with mottled red cloak, height 16½″, designer C.J. Noke ....

1929–1938 1500.00 1750.00

HN 1366
☐ Red costume with multicolored patterning, height 16½″, designer C. J. Noke ....

1930–1949 1500.00 1750.00

HN 1425
☐ Dark multicolored costume, height 16½″, designer C.J. Noke ....

1930–1949 1500.00 1750.00

HN 1657
☐ Striped waistband, black cloak, height 16½″, designer C.J. Noke ....

1934–1949 1500.00 1750.00

MOORISH MINSTREL
HN 34
☐ Brown figure on brown pedestal, dark blue costume, small brown hat and

	Date	Price Range	
shoes, holding brown instrument, height 13½", designer C.J. Noke	1913–1938	2500.00	2750.00
HN 364			
☐ Blue, green and orange striped costume, height 13½", designer C.J. Noke	1920–1938	3200.00	3550.00
HN 415			
☐ Green and yellow striped costume, height 13½", designer C.J. Noke	1920–1938	3200.00	3550.00
HN 797			
☐ Purple costume, height 13½", designer C.J. Noke	1926–1949	3200.00	3550.00

MOORISH PIPER MINSTREL
HN 301

	Date	Price Range	
☐ Dark figure on dark brown base, purple costume with orange scarf around neck, dunce shaped orange and brown hat, light colored pipe, height 13½", designer C.J. Noke	1918–1938	3200.00	3550.00
HN 328			
☐ Green and brown striped robe, height 13½", designer C.J. Noke	1918–1938	3200.00	3550.00
HN 416			
☐ Green and yellow striped robe, height 13½", designer C.J. Noke	1920–1938	3200.00	3550.00

MORNING MA'AM
HN 2895

	Date	Price Range	
☐ Figure of a soldier in a gray military uniform, with a sword and scabbard at his side. Hand is raised in a salute; figure is supported by a small, brown stone pillar, height 9", designer W.K. Harper	1986	185.00	

MOTHERHOOD
HN 28

	Date	Price Range	
☐ Gray costume, height unknown, designer P. Stabler	1913–1938	2200.00	2500.00
HN 30			
☐ Figure seated on bench that is on base, white gown with blue designs and dots, white apron with blue designs and blue trim, holding small nude child figure, height unknown, designer P. Stabler ..	1913–1938	3000.00	3250.00
HN 303			
☐ White dress with black patterning, height unknown, designer P. Stabler ..	1918–1938	3000.00	3250.00

	Date	Price Range	

MOTHER'S HELP
HN 2151

☐ Small figure in brown gown with white bib apron, white sleeves and collar, white head covering, height 5″, designer M. Davies .... | 1962–1969 | 200.00 | 250.00

MR. MICAWBER
HN 532

☐ Character from Dickens' "David Copperfield" (1st version), height 3½″, designer L. Harradine .... | 1922– | 65.00 | 85.00

☐ **M-42** Renumbered as a miniature, height 4″, designer L. Harradine ..... | 1932–1983 | 55.00 | 65.00

HN 557

☐ Larger figure standing on brown base with green bush, black trousers, brown coat, yellow vest, white shirt with black bow tie (2nd version), height 7″, designer L. Harradine .... | 1923–1939 | 375.00 | 450.00

HN 1895

☐ Very minor color changes (2nd version), height 7″, designer L. Harradine .... | 1938–1952 | 375.00 | 450.00

HN 2097

☐ Figure standing on small black base, light brown trousers, black coat, brown and yellow vest, white shirt, red bow tie (3rd version), height 7½″, designer L. Harradine .... | 1952–1967 | 325.00 | 375.00

MR. PICKWICK
HN 529

☐ Character from Dickens' "Pickwick Papers" (1st version), height 3¾″, designer L. Harradine .... | 1922– | 65.00 | 85.00

☐ **M-41** Renumbered as a miniature, height 4″, designer L. Harradine ..... | 1932–1983 | 55.00 | 65.00

HN 556

☐ Figure standing on brown base with bush, yellow trousers, blue coat, tan vest, white cravat, black hat in hand, black boots (2nd version), height 7″, designer L. Harradine .... | 1923–1939 | 375.00 | 450.00

HN 1894

☐ Very minor color changes (2nd version), height 7″, designer L. Harradine .... | 1938–1942 | 350.00 | 400.00

	Date	Price Range	

HN 2099

☐ Figure on green base, light brown trousers, black coat, brown and orange vest, white cravat, brown hat, yellow spats (3rd version), height 7½″, designer L. Harradine 1952–1967   325.00   375.00

MRS. BARDELL
Issued only as a miniature
☐ **M-86** White dress, white hood with black trim, very light pink shawl, black stand, height 4¼″, designer L. Harradine 1949–   55.00   85.00

MRS. FITZHERBERT
HN 2007

☐ White gown with blue bow trim, mottled yellow, blue and orange overdress, red bodice, head covering of white with blue ribbon trim, holding red and white open fan, height 9″, designer M. Davies 1948–1953   650.00   750.00

MY LOVE
HN 2339

☐ White gown with gold trim and gold design in part of gown, gold shoes, holding single red rose, dark hair, height 6¼″, designer M. Davies 1969–   250.00

MY PET
HN 2238

☐ Small figure seated on cushion, blue and white skirt, blouse with blue trim, holding small brown dog in one arm and open book in other, brown shoes, height 3″, designer M. Davies 1962–1975   150.00   175.00

IN PRETTY MAID
HN 2064

☐ Small figure on yellow and green base, shaded blue gown with white collar, dark blue waistband with red trim, holding milking stool, bucket on base, height 5½″, designer L. Harradine 1950–1954   450.00   550.00

MY TEDDY
HN 2177

☐ Small figure seated on white base, shaded green gown with white collar,

Nana, HN 1766, 475.00–600.00

	Date	Price Range	
holding brown teddy bear and small mirror, height 3¼″, designer M. Davies	1962–1967	450.00	650.00

NADINE
HN 1885
☐ Light blue gown with green sash, multicolor shawl, green bonnet, blue shoes, height 7¾″, designer L. Harradine | 1938–1949 | 1000.00 | 1250.00

HN 1886
☐ Orange and red gown with blue sash, red shawl with blue and green trim, blue bonnet, height 7¾″, designer L. Harradine | 1938–1949 | 1000.00 | 1250.00

NANA
HN 1766
☐ Small figure in light red and white gown, tiny hat on side of head is blue

	Date	Price Range	
with red trim, open fan in hand, height 4¾", designer L. Harradine	1936–1949	475.00	600.00

HN 1767
□ Shaded blue and green gown, green hat with red trim, height 4¾", designer L. Harradine 1936–1949   475.00   600.00

NANNY
HN 2221
□ Older figure seated in gray rocker with brown teddy bear on lap, blue and green gown with white apron and headcap, toys on base, also basket, height 5⅝", designer M. Davies 1958–   250.00

NEGLIGEE
HN 1219
□ Figure kneeling on brown and orange cushion base, short gown of shaded blues, blue ribbon in hair, height 5", designer L. Harradine 1927–1938   1900.00   2250.00

HN 1228
□ Red, blue, and black cushion, blue gown, red ribbon in hair, height 5", designer L. Harradine 1927–1938   1900.00   2250.00

HN 1272
□ Mottled red and yellow negligee, height 5", designer L. Harradine 1928–1938   1900.00   2250.00

HN 1273
□ White negligee, height 5", designer L. Harradine 1928–1938   1900.00   2250.00

HN 1454
□ Red cushion with multicolored design, shaded pink gown, pink ribbon in hair, height 5", designer L. Harradine 1931–1938   1900.00   2250.00

NELL
HN 3014
□ Seated figure in white pinafore over a pink dress. Seated in blue cart, bright yellow wheels. Light brown hair, height 4", designer P. Parsons 1983–1987   100.00

NELL GWYNN
HN 1882
□ Blue skirt, red overlay, red bodice, white shawl, white apron, white sleeves with blue trim, green bonnet with red feather and red ribbons, blue shoes,

	Date	Price Range	

standing on base that is shaded blue, pedestal has white cloth with basket, height 6¾″, designer L. Harradine ...   1938–1949   975.00   1250.00

HN 1887
☐ Red skirt, green bodice and overlay, red bonnet with blue feather and ribbons, black shoes, base cream, height 6¾″, designer L. Harradine   1938–1949   975.00   1250.00

NEW BONNET, The
HN 1728
☐ Red full gown with very wide white collar, red shoes, small white cap on head, holding green bonnet with yellow rose trim and red ribbons, standing on base of light green, height 7″, designer L. Harradine   1935–1949   950.00   1250.00

HN 1957
☐ Red gown with shaded blues at hemline, white collar, red and white cap, green bonnet with black ribbon trim and red flower, blue shoes, black base, height 7″, designer L. Harradine   1940–1949   1500.00   1750.00

NEW COMPANIONS
HN 2770
☐ Gray and black skirt, white apron, blue shawl, black hat with pink ribbons, black and white puppy in beige basket, height 7¾″, designer W.K. Harper ..   1982–1985   175.00   225.00

NEW HAVEN FISHWIFE
HN 1480
☐ Skirt of red and white stripes, black and white striped apron, white blouse with red and blue designs, brown cloak, white head-covering with design, carrying brown basket with strap around head, on base of light brown with another basket, height 7¾″, designer H. Fenton   1931–1938   3500.00   4000.00

NEWSBOY
HN 2244
☐ Boy figure on green base, brown trousers, black coat, green scarf, black and green striped cap, holding newspaper placard and folded newspapers—Note: A limited edition of 250 was also produced for Stoke-on-Trent's local

	Date	Price Range	

paper, *The Evening Sentinel*; figure had the word *Sentinel* printed on newsboy's placard, height 8½", designer M. Davies 1959–1965   550.00   650.00

NEWSVENDOR, The
HN 2891
☐ Gentleman sitting on a cornerstone. Figure is on a gray base. Dressed in gray pants, brown top coat and dark brown hat. Holding a newspaper in one hand, sign explaining the latest news in the other. Issued in a limited edition of 2,500 to commemorate the 150th Anniversary of the Newspaper Society, 1836–1986, height 8¼", designer W.K. Harper 1986–   250.00   300.00

NICOLA
HN 2804
☐ New colorway introduced in 1987, available only at events featuring Michael Doulton. Dressed in coral and blue with coral ribbon in her light auburn hair, height 7½", designer M. Davies 1987–   250.00   300.00
HN 2839
☐ Shaded blue and red gown with white, yellow and green flower design, white trim, dark bow on hair curls, holding bird in hand, height 7⅛", designer M. Davies 1978–   350.00

NINA
HN 2347
☐ Blue gown with white design at hemline, white collar, with white ribbon in hair, this figure has a matte finish, height 7½", designer M. Davies 1969–1976   175.00   225.00

NINETTE
HN 2379
☐ Yellow gown with white trim and golden design, flower in hair, height 8", designer M. Davies 1971–   250.00

NOELLE
HN 2179
☐ White gown with black stripes, long red

Nina, HN 2347, 175.00–225.00

	Date	Price Range	
jacket with hood trimmed in white fur, white muff, height 6¾″, designer M. Davies	1957–1967	425.00	475.00

NORMA
Issued only as a miniature

	Date	Price Range	
☐ **M-36** No color details available, height 4½″, designer unknown	1933–1945	600.00	850.00
☐ **M-37** Red and blue print dress, blue sleeves, green and blue shawl, green and red hat, height 4½″, designer unknown	1933–1945	600.00	850.00

Noelle, HN 2179, 425.00–475.00

	Date	Price Range	

NUDE ON ROCK
HN 593

☐ White nude figure lying on blue and white rock, height unknown, designer unknown 1924–1938 1350.00 1600.00

ODDS AND ENDS
HN 1844

☐ Green skirt with black, red and yellow stripes, yellow bibbed apron, red blouse, green shawl, black hat with colored feathers, holding potted plants in one arm, height 7¾″, designer L. Harradine 1924–1938 850.00 1050.00

OFFICER OF THE LINE
HN 2733

☐ Depicts a soldier of the Napoleon era. High boots, light waistcoat and pants,

	Date	Price Range	

coat red with matching sash, hair powdered white to gray, black tricorn hat, height 9″, designer W. K. Harper ...: — 1983–1986 — 150.00 — 200.00

OLD BALLOON SELLER
HN 1315
☐ Older figure seated holding many different colored balloons, green skirt, white apron, red blouse, green shawl with red fringe, hat multicolored, basket at side, height 7″, designer L. Harradine .... — 1929– — 275.00

OLD BALLOON SELLER AND BULLDOG
HN 1791
☐ Same figure as Old Balloon Seller with the addition of bulldog, all mounted on mahogany stand, height 7″, designer L. Harradine .... — 1932–1938 — 2000.00 — 2500.00
HN 1912
☐ No details available, height 7″, designer L. Harradine .... — 1939–1949 — 2250.00 — 2750.00

OLD HUNTSMAN, The
HN 1403
☐ Not issued ....

OLD KING, AN
HN 358
☐ HN 2134, green shirt, purple robe, height 9¾″, designer C.J. Noke .... — 1919–1938 — 1600.00 — 1800.00
HN 623
☐ Gray, red and green robes, height 9¾″, designer C.J. Noke .... — 1924–1938 — 1600.00 — 1800.00
HN 1801
☐ No detail available, height 9¾″, designer C.J. Noke .... — 1937–1954 — 1600.00 — 1800.00
HN 2134
☐ Figure seated in brown chair on brown base, green robe with purple overrobe trimmed in a green design, red scarf, gold crown, holding sword, height 10¾″, designer C.J. Noke .... — 1954– — 625.00

OLD KING COLE
HN 2217
☐ Figure seated in light colored chair, brown and beige costume with robe trimmed in white fur, brown and gold

	Date	Price Range	

crown, small stool at feet, holding goblet, height 6¾", designer M. Davies   1963–1967   650.00   800.00

OLD LAVENDER SELLER
HN 1492

☐ Older figure seated, very dark green gown with white apron, red and yellow striped shawl with green squares, basket on one arm and small basket at side, black hat with flowers, height 6", designer L. Harradine   1932–1949   875.00   1000.00

HN 1571

☐ Patterned orange cap, height 6", designer L. Harradine   1933–1949   1100.00   1350.00

OLD MAN, AN
HN 451

☐ A seated figure covered completely by blue, green and brown robe, height unknown, designer unknown   1921–1938   3000.00   3500.00

OLD MEG
HN 2494

☐ Blue and gray gown, white and blue apron, shawl of patterned purple, green hat with blue and white scarf, red shoes, base looks like stones with brown basket, height 8", designer M. Nicoll   1974–1976   300.00   375.00

OLD MOTHER HUBBARD
HN 2314

☐ Dark green gown with lighter green trim, white apron with dark green dots, green headcap, holds bone in hand for brown and white dog, height 8", designer M. Nicoll   1964–1975   300.00   375.00

OLGA
HN 2463

☐ Yellow underskirt with blue overgrown, holds single red rose, yellow ribbon in light brown hair, height 8¼", designer J. Bromley   1972–1975   175.00   225.00

OLIVER TWIST
Issued only as a miniature

☐ **M-89** White shirt, red tie, black jacket, tan pants, black stand, height 4¼", designer L. Harradine   1949–1983   55.00   85.00

Omar Khayyam, HN 2247, 145.00–175.00

	Date	Price Range	

OLIVIA
HN 1995
☐ Light green gown with cape of red with
blue trim, holding white lilies in one
arm, height 7½″, designer L. Harra-
dine 1947–1951 **550.00** **650.00**

OMAR KHAYYAM AND THE
BELOVED
HN 407
☐ Colors were unrecorded, height 10″,
designer C.J. Noke 1920–1938 **4500.00** **5000.00**
HN 419
☐ Two figures standing together, blue
costume with dark blue robe with green

	Date	Price Range	

dot trim, green and blue turban, her
costume is gown of shaded blues with
yellow dots, robe and head trim have
orange designs and orange dots, she
holds jug, height 10″, designer C.J.
Noke .... | 1920–1938 | 4500.00 | 5000.00

HN 459
☐ Multicolored costumes, height 10″, de-
signer C.J. Noke .... | 1921–1938 | 4500.00 | 5000.00

HN 598
☐ Lady has striped pink cloak, striped
blue dress, height 10″, designer C. J.
Noke .... | 1924–1938 | 4500.00 | 5000.00

OMAR KHAYYAM
HN 408
☐ Seated figure, blue and black robes with
brown (1st version), height 6″, de-
signer C.J. Noke .... | 1920–1938 | 3000.00 | 3500.00

HN 409
☐ Black robe, yellow trousers (1st version),
height 6″, designer C.J. Noke .... | | 3000.00 | 3500.00

HN 2247
☐ Brown costume with robe of orange and
brown, orange turban, holding gray jug
and red open book (2nd version), height
6¼″, designer M. Nicoll .... | 1965–1983 | 145.00 | 175.00

ONCE UPON A TIME
HN 2047
☐ Small figure of little girl seated on tan
bench, on a yellow-green base, red
dress with white dots and blue trim,
blue shoes, open book on bench, height
4¼″, designer L. Harradine .... | 1949–1955 | 400.00 | 475.00

ONE OF THE FORTY
All of the ''One of the Forty'' models
were designed by H. Tittensor, their
height ranging from 2¾″ to 7″.
HN 417
☐ HN 528, green and blue robes (1st ver-
sion), height 5″, designer H. Tittensor | 1920–1938 | 1250.00 | 1500.00

HN 418
☐ HN 494, striped green robes (2nd ver-
sion) .... | 1920–1938 | 1250.00 | 1500.00

One of the Forty, HN 666, 1400.00–1650.00

	Date	Price Range	

HN 423

☐ These figures were very small and produced in a variety of color finishes (3rd version) 1921–1938   **850.00**   **1050.00**

HN 427

☐ Brown costume, brown and green turban, holding green bag in one arm (9th version) 1921–1938   **1250.00**   **1500.00**

HN 480

☐ Yellow trousers with black stripes, mottled dark green robe, high blue hat, mottled green bag (10th version), height 7″ 1921–1938   **1250.00**   **1500.00**

	Date	Price Range	

HN 481
☐ HN 491, dark spotted robes (11th version) 1921–1938   1250.00   1500.00

HN 482
☐ HN 492, spotted waistband (12th version) 1921–1938   1250.00   1500.00

HN 483
☐ HN 491, brown hat, green striped robes (11th version) 1921–1938   1250.00   1500.00

HN 484
☐ HN 492, mottled green robes (12th version) 1921–1938   1250.00   1500.00

HN 490
☐ HN 528, blue and brown checkered coat (1st version), height 5″ 1921–1938   1250.00   1500.00

HN 491
☐ Blue costume with white robe, blue hat, white bag which he holds under one arm and holds closed with other hand (11th version) 1921–1938   1250.00   1500.00

HN 492
☐ White costume with yellow band and yellow turban, white bag he holds with one hand, bag is open (12th version) 1921–1938   1600.00   1800.00

HN 493
☐ HN 480, blue hat and waistband (10th version) 1921–1938   1250.00   1500.00

HN 494
☐ White costume with blue waistband and blue turban, holds white bag over shoulder with one hand, white bag at feet also (2nd version) 1921–1938   1250.00   1500.00

HN 495
☐ HN 528, blue hat and waistband (1st version), height 5″ 1921–1938   1250.00   1500.00

HN 496
☐ HN 665, yellow hat and vase (13th version) 1921–1938   1250.00   1500.00

HN 497
☐ HN 480, brown hat, checkered trousers (10th version) 1921–1938   1250.00   1500.00

HN 498
☐ HN 494, dark striped coat, pale striped trousers (2nd version) 1921–1938   1250.00   1500.00

HN 499
☐ HN 480, cream costume, green hat (10th version) 1921–1938   1250.00   1500.00

	Date	Price Range	

HN 500

☐ HN 665, checkered coat and red hat (13th version) 1921–1938 1400.00 1650.00

HN 501

☐ HN 528, green striped coat (1st version), height 5″ 1921–1938 1250.00 1500.00

HN 528

☐ Brown costume, brown and purple robe, green waistband with red and yellow dots, green turban with red and yellow squares one hand on open bag at feet, other hand holds necklace, second bag open in front of him (1st version) 1921–1938 1400.00 1650.00

HN 645

☐ HN 492, blue, black, and white robes (12th version) 1924–1938 1250.00 1500.00

HN 646

☐ HN 491, blue, black, and white robes (2nd version) 1924–1938 1250.00 1500.00

HN 647

☐ HN 494, blue, black, and white robes (2nd version) 1924–1938 1250.00 1500.00

HN 648

☐ HN 528, blue, black, and white robes (1st version) 1924–1938 1250.00 1500.00

HN 649

☐ HN 665, blue, black, and white robes (13th version) 1924–1938 1250.00 1500.00

HN 663

☐ HN 492, checkered red robes (12th version) 1924–1938 1250.00 1500.00

HN 664

☐ HN 480, patterned yellow robes (10th version) 1924–1938 1400.00 1650.00

HN 665

☐ Orange robe with red and black stripes and black and green dots, turban of same color, holding black bag and green jug or bottle (13th version) 1924–1938 1250.00 1500.00

HN 666

☐ HN 494, checkered yellow robes (2nd version) 1924–1938 1400.00 1650.00

HN 667

☐ HN 491, checkered yellow robes (11th version) 1924–1938 1400.00 1650.00

	Date	Price Range	

HN 677
☐ HN 528, orange, green and red striped
coat (1st version) 1924–1938 1250.00 1500.00

HN 704
☐ HN 494, checkered red robe (2nd version) 1925–1938 1250.00 1500.00

HN 712
☐ HN 491, checkered red robes (11th version) 1925–1938 1250.00 1500.00

HN 713
☐ HN 492, checkered red robes (12th version) 1925–1938 1250.00 1500.00

HN 714
☐ HN 480, patterned red robes (10th version) 1925–1938 1250.00 1500.00

HN 1336
☐ HN 491, mottled red, orange and blue robes (11th version) 1929–1938 1250.00 1500.00

HN 1350
☐ HN 491, multicolored robes (11th version) 1929–1949 1250.00 1500.00

HN 1351
☐ HN 528, no color detail available (1st version) 1929–1939 1250.00 1500.00

HN 1352
☐ HN 528, multicolored robes (1st version) 1929–1949 1250.00 1500.00

HN 1353
☐ HN 494, multicolored robes (2nd version) 1929–1949 1250.00 1500.00

HN 1354
☐ HN 665, multicolored robes (13th version) 1929–1949 1250.00 1500.00

ONE THAT GOT AWAY, The
HN 2153
☐ Fisherman's costume of brown coat, green trousers, brown hat, black boots, on base of yellow and green, fishing basket of brown also on base, height 6¼", designer M. Davies 1955–1959 450.00 550.00

ORANGE LADY, The
HN 1759
☐ Older lady in gown of pink, with shawl of black and red, black hat with red trim, two brown baskets with oranges, height 8¾", designer L. Harradine ... 1936–1975 250.00 300.00

	Date	Price Range	

HN 1953

☐ Light green gown, black and green shawl, height 8¾", designer L. Harradine 1940–1975 275.00 325.00

ORANGE SELLER, The
HN 1325

☐ Shaded green and blue gown, shaded red and blue blouse and apron, green head covering with red trim, holding brown basket of oranges, height 7", designer L. Harradine 1929–1949 1100.00 1350.00

ORANGE VENDOR, AN
HN 72

☐ Light green costume, dark green robe and hood, face and hands are lighter color, smaller brown basket of oranges, earthenware, height 6¼", designer C.J. Noke 1941–1949 1100.00 1450.00

HN 508

☐ Purple coat, height 6¼", designer C.J. Noke 1921–1938 1100.00 1450.00

HN 521

☐ Pale blue costume, black collar, purple hood, height 6¼", designer C.J. Noke 1921–1938 1100.00 1450.00

HN 1966

☐ Dark seated male figure in shaded red and blue costume, darker blue and red robe, shaded blue and red hood, large basket of oranges in front of figure, height 6¼", designer C.J. Noke 1917–1938 950.00 1100.00

ORGAN GRINDER, The
HN 2173

☐ Yellow and brown trousers, green coat, blue and red scarf, brown hat, on brown base, brown organ grinder instrument, monkey in red coat with yellow trim, blue trousers, height 8¾", designer M. Nicoll 1956–1965 650.00 750.00

OUT FOR A WALK
HN 86

☐ Pink and gray dress, height unknown, designer H. Tittensor 1918–1936 2500.00 3000.00

HN 443

☐ Checkered skirt, green coat with white fur trim, white muff, green hat with

The Organ Grinder, HN 2173, 650.00–750.00

	Date	Price Range	
feather trim, height unknown, designer H. Tittensor	1921–1936	2750.00	3250.00
HN 748			
☐ Dark multicolored dress, white muff, height unknown, designer H. Tittensor	1925–1936	3000.00	3500.00

OWD WILLUM
HN 2042

☐ Character figure seated on green and gray stones, dark green trousers, brown leg coverings, green coat, brown hat with darker brown band, very light tan vest, red tie, large white and blue mug in one hand, red bag with white dots also on base, height 6¾", designer L. Harradine ....

	1949–1959	225.00	275.00

Paisley Shawl, Second Version, HN 1914, 300.00–350.00

	Date	Price Range

PAISLEY SHAWL
HN 1392

☐ White gown with shaded green and yellow flower designs, red paisley design shawl, light red bonnet with darker red lining with feather trim, carrying parasol (1st version), height 9″, designer L. Harradine 1930–1949 **400.00** **500.00**

HN 1460

☐ Light green gown, darker green shawl with pink trim, dark green bonnet with red feather and ribbon trim, light red

	Date	Price Range	

parasol (1st version), height 9″, designer L. Harradine 1931–1949   500.00   650.00

HN 1707
☐ HN 1392, purple shawl, green hat (1st version), height 9″, designer L. Harradine 1935–1949   700.00   850.00

HN 1739
☐ Shaded green gown, red shawl with paisley designs of darker green and black, bonnet has green feather and ribbons as trim, dark blue parasol (1st version), height 9″, designer L. Harradine 1935–1949   650.00   850.00

HN 1914
☐ Small figure, green gown, red paisley design shawl, green bonnet with black trim and blue ribbons, white feather, white parasol with black, green, and red trim (2nd version), height 9″, designer L. Harradine 1939–1949   300.00   350.00

HN 1987
☐ Light cream colored gown, black on red paisley design shawl, black bonnet with red lining, blue feather and ribbons, blue parasol (1st version), height 8½″, designer L. Harradine 1946–1959   225.00   325.00

HN 1988
☐ HN 1914, cream and light red skirt, black bonnet (2nd version), height 6¼″, designer L. Harradine 1946–1975   150.00   225.00
☐ **M-3** Made as a miniature, blue gown, mottled blue shawl, light blue bonnet and parasol, height 4″, designer L. Harradine 1932–1938   325.00   425.00
☐ **M-4** Green gown, dark green shawl, black bonnet with red feather and ribbons, height 4″, designer L. Harradine 1932–1945   325.00   400.00
☐ **M-26** Cream and green gown, red shawl, black and red bonnet, red parasol, height 4″, designer L. Harradine 1932–1945   325.00   400.00

PAMELA
HN 1468
☐ Dark blue tiered gown with red sash, holding long stemmed flowers in one arm, height 8″, designer L. Harradine 1931–1938   950.00   1150.00

HN 1469
☐ Shaded cream, red, and green tiered

	Date	Price Range	

gown with red sash, height 8″, designer L. Harradine .... | 1931–1938 | 750.00 | 850.00

HN 1564

☐ Cream and red tiered gown, red and blue sash, height 8″, designer L. Harradine .... | 1933–1938 | 950.00 | 1150.00

PAN ON ROCK
HN 621

☐ White nude figure of Pan seated on dark brown base, height unknown, designer unknown .... | 1924–1938 | 2500.00 | 3000.00

HN 622

☐ Black base, height unknown, designer unknown .... | 1924–1938 | 2500.00 | 3000.00

PANTALETTES
HN 1362

☐ Green skirt with reddish blue jacket, white pantalettes, light green bonnet with red trim and ribbons, black shoes, height 7¾″, designer L. Harradine ... | 1929–1938 | 325.00 | 400.00

HN 1412

☐ Pink skirt, blue jacket trimmed in yellow and green, light green bonnet with darker green trim and ribbons, white pantalettes, red and black shoes, height 7¾″, designer L. Harradine .... | 1930–1949 | 350.00 | 400.00

HN 1507

☐ HN 1362, yellow dress, height 7¾″, designer L. Harradine .... | 1932–1949 | 500.00 | 650.00

HN 1709

☐ Red gown, red bonnet with very light blue trim and ribbons, red shoes, white pantalettes, height 7¾″, designer L. Harradine .... | 1935–1938 | 950.00 | 1150.00

☐ **M-15** Made as a miniature, light blue skirt, darker blue bodice, red bonnet with blue trim, height 3¾″, designer L. Harradine .... | 1932–1945 | 275.00 | 375.00

☐ **M-16** Light red skirt, darker red bodice, black bonnet with red trim, height 3¾″, designer L. Harradine .... | 1932–1945 | 300.00 | 425.00

☐ **M-31** Green skirt with darker green bodice, light bonnet with red trim, height 3¾″, designer L. Harradine ... | 1932–1945 | 300.00 | 425.00

The Parson's Daughter, HN 564, 400.00–500.00

	Date	Price Range	

PARISIAN
HN 2445
☐Gray trousers, blue jacket, brown shoes, brown tam, holding newspaper in hand, with brown fox at feet, height 8″, designer M. Nicoll 1972–1975 150.00 200.00

PARSON'S DAUGHTER
HN 337
☐HN 564, lilac dress with brown floral pattern, height 10″, designer H. Tittensor 1919–1938 800.00 900.00
HN 338
☐Patterned blue dress, red bonnet and

	Date	Price Range	

shawl, height 10″, designer H. Titten-
sor .... | 1919–1938 | 800.00 | 900.00

HN 441
☐ Yellow dress with orange spots, height
10″, designer H. Tittensor .... | 1921–1938 | 850.00 | 950.00

HN 564
☐ This figure is 10″ in height, yellow
skirt with red, blue, green and black
blocks, red shawl and bonnet with black
ribbon trim, large yellow sleeves, de-
signer H. Tittensor .... | 1923–1949 | 400.00 | 500.00

HN 790
☐ Patchwork skirt, dark multicolored
shawl, height 10″, designer H. Titten-
sor .... | 1926–1938 | 550.00 | 600.00

HN 1242
☐ Patchwork skirt, lilac shawl with yellow
lining, height 10″, designer H. Titten-
sor .... | 1927–1938 | 550.00 | 600.00

HN 1356
☐ White skirt with stripes of red, blue and
black at hemline, upper portion has orange spots, large green sleeves, red
shawl and bonnet with black ribbon
trim, large yellow sleeves, height 9¼″,
designer H. Tittensor .... | 1929–1938 | 475.00 | 550.00

HN 2018
☐ Darker patchwork skirt, purple hat and
cloak, height 9¾″, designer H. Titten-
sor .... | 1949–1953 | 350.00 | 400.00

PAST GLORY
HN 2484
☐ Older male figure seated on brown and
gray trunk, black trousers, red long
coat, black cap with yellow trim, holding yellow bugle, height 7½″, designer
M. Nicoll .... | 1973–1979 | 175.00 | 225.00

PATCHWORK QUILT, The
HN 1984
☐ Seated figure in brown skirt, green
blouse, white scarf and head covering,
holding multicolored quilt on lap,
height 6″, designer L. Harradine ..... | 1945–1959 | 275.00 | 350.00

PATRICIA
HN 1414
☐ Yellow gown with green sleeves and

	Date	Price Range	

belt, black bonnet with green trim and ribbons with black tassels, height 8½", designer L. Harradine .... 1930–1949 | 600.00 | 750.00

HN 1431

☐ Shaded blue and red gown, blue sleeves, black belt, light colored bonnet with dark blue ribbons and yellow tassels, height 8½", designer L. Harradine .... 1930–1949 | 550.00 | 650.00

HN 1462

☐ Green gown with darker green top, shaded blue and green sleeves, pink bonnet with blue trim and ribbons and tassels, blue belt, height 8½", designer L. Harradine .... 1931–1938 | 600.00 | 750.00

HN 1567

☐ Red gown with light green belt, shaded red and blue bonnet, height 8½", designer L. Harradine .... 1933–1949 | 950.00 | 1150.00

☐ **M-7** Made as a miniature, cream and light green gown, red bodice and sleeves, light green bonnet, height 4", designer L. Harradine .... 1932–1945 | 275.00 | 350.00

☐ **M-8** Green, yellow, and red gown, black bonnet and ribbons, height 4", designer L. Harradine .... 1932–1938 | 275.00 | 350.00

☐ **M-28** Shaded blue gown with dark blue sleeves, light bonnet with black trim, height 4", designer L. Harradine ..... 1932–1945 | 275.00 | 350.00

PAULA
HN 2906

☐ Yellow gown with green trim, green shoes, holding small brown box in one hand, height 7", designer P. Parsons 1980–1986 | 150.00 | 200.00

PAULINE
HN 1444

☐ Mottled blue gown with green ribbon at bodice, green bonnet with darker green trim, height 6", designer L. Harradine .... 1931–1938 | 400.00 | 450.00

HN 2441

☐ This figure is relaxing on a couch with her elbow on the arm of the couch, her gown is tiered in shades of blue, pink

	Date	Price Range	

and ochre which drapes to the floor with the tip of her shoe peeking out under the gown, height unknown, designer M. Davies .... — 1984– — 275.00

PAVLOVA
HN 487
☐ Small figure in ballet position on brown base, white ballet costume with very light coloring, white headdress, height 4 ¼", designer C.J. Noke .... 1921–1938 — 4500.00 — 5000.00

HN 676
☐ Green base, height 4 ¼", designer C.J. Noke .... 1924–1938 — 4500.00 — 5000.00

PEARLY BOY
HN 1482
☐ Small figure of boy on cream colored base, brown trousers, brown coat, red vest, green scarf with black dots, black cap with white trim (1st version), height 5 ½", designer L. Harradine .... 1931–1949 — 350.00 — 400.00

HN 1547
☐ Green jacket, purple trousers (1st version), height 5 ½", designer L. Harradine .... 1933–1949 — 650.00 — 850.00

HN 2035
☐ Brown and red trousers, red and brown jacket, red vest, neck scarf with black dots, black hat with white trim, standing on reddish tint base (2nd version), height 5 ½", designer L. Harradine ... 1949–1959 — 175.00 — 225.00

PEARLY GIRL
HN 1483
☐ Small girl on light colored base with pedestal, red and green skirt, brown, red and green jacket, large brown hat with red and green feathers (1st version), height 5 ½", designer L. Harradine .... 1931–1949 — 350.00 — 400.00

HN 1548
☐ Purple bodice, green skirt (1st version), height 5 ½", designer L. Harradine ... 1933–1949 — 650.00 — 850.00

HN 2036
☐ Red and brown skirt, red, brown and green jacket, green scarf with black dots, dark hat with red and green

	Date	Price Range	
feathers, black shoes, white stockings, on light colored base (2nd version), height 5½″, designer L. Harradine ...	1949–1959	**175.00**	**225.00**

PECKSNIFF
HN 535

	Date	Price Range	
☐A character of Dickens' "Martin Chuzzlewit" (1st version), height 3¾″, designer L. Harradine	1922–	**65.00**	**85.00**
☐**M-43** Renumbered as a miniature, height 4¼″, designer L. Harradine ...	1932–	**55.00**	**65.00**

HN 553

	Date	Price Range	
☐Black trousers, long black coat, yellow vest, white cravat, brown base with green bush (2nd version), height 7″, designer L. Harradine	1923–1939	**350.00**	**400.00**

HN 1891

	Date	Price Range	
☐Very minor color changes (2nd version), height 7″, designer L. Harradine	1938–1952	**325.00**	**400.00**

HN 2098

	Date	Price Range	
☐Green base, brown trousers, black coat, orange vest, white cravat with blue tint, gold watch with chain (3rd version), height 7″, designer L. Harradine	1952–1967	**275.00**	**350.00**

PEDLAR WOLF
HN 7

	Date	Price Range	
☐Figure of wolf completely covered by gray and white robe, height 5½″, designer C.J. Noke	1913–1938	**2500.00**	**3000.00**

PEGGY
HN 1941

	Date	Price Range	
☐HN 2038, minor glaze differences, height 5″, designer L. Harradine	1940–1949	**125.00**	**175.00**

HN 2038

	Date	Price Range	
☐Red gown, darker red overdress trimmed in white, white head covering with ribbon, height 5″, designer L. Harradine	1949–1979	**100.00**	**125.00**

PENELOPE
HN 1901

	Date	Price Range	
☐Figure seated on multicolored bench, red gown with blue bows, trimmed in white, white head covering with blue ribbon, small basket on bench, holding embroidering hoop, etc., in one hand, height 7″, designer L. Harradine	1939–1975	**275.00**	**375.00**

Penelope, HN 1901, 275.00–375.00

	Date	Price Range	
HN 1902			
☐ Green petticoat, blue bodice, mauve and blue striped skirt, height 7″, designer L. Harradine	1939–1949	**1000.00**	**1400.00**
PENNY			
HN 2338			
☐ Small figure in white gown with green overdress, height 4½″, designer M. Davies	1968–	**95.00**	
HN 2424			
☐ Beautiful blond figure with delicate yellow undergown, rich yellow bodice and overgown, gown has layered frilled sleeves (2nd version), height 4¾″, designer M. Davies	1983–	**95.00**	

	Date	Price Range	

PENSIVE MOMENTS
HN 2704
☐ Figure seated with large open parasol behind, blue gown with white and black designs on hemline, light colored hat with black ribbon trim and white flower lying on skirt, lavender and yellow parasol, height 4⅞", designer M. Davies

1975–1981 · 150.00 · 225.00

PERFECT PAIR, The
HN 581
☐ Two eighteenth century figures on single brown base, man's costume is black pants, long red coat trimmed in black, black shoes, white stockings, lady's costume is pink gown trimmed in lavender, red shoes, height 7", designer L. Harradine ....

1923–1938 · 1200.00 · 1550.00

PHILIPPA OF HAINAULT
HN 2008
☐ Mottled red and blue gown, red sleeves with white fur trim, green belt with red designs, height 9¾", designer M. Davies ....

1948–1953 · 600.00 · 700.00

PHYLLIS
HN 1420
☐ Eighteenth century style gown of shaded reds and greens, white overlay with red and green designs, lavender shawl with spots of darker purples, light colored hat with floral trim, single red flower in hand, basket of flowers on light colored base, height 9", designer L. Harradine ....

1930–1949 · 575.00 · 675.00

HN 1430
☐ Dark blue shawl, striped pink skirt, height 9", designer L. Harradine .....

1930–1938 · 700.00 · 800.00

HN 1486
☐ Blue shawl, spotted pink overskirt, pink base, height 9", designer L. Harradine

1931–1949 · 650.00 · 750.00

HN 1698
☐ Blue and green gown with darker green overskirt, white shawl with red and black floral designs, green hat with red flower trim, green and brown flower

Phyllis, HN 1420, 575.00–675.00

	Date	Price Range	
basket, light green base, height 9″, designer L. Harradine	1935–1949	750.00	850.00

PICARDY PEASANT (Female)
HN 4
☐ HN 351, white hat and blue skirt, height 9½″, designer P. Stabler ..:.... 1913–1938 2000.00 2500.00

HN 5
☐ Dove gray costume, height 9½″, designer P. Stabler 1913–1938 2000.00 2500.00

HN 17A
☐ Green hat and green costume, height 9½″, designer P. Stabler 1913–1938 2000.00 2500.00

HN 351
☐ Blue striped skirt, lighter blue blouse

	Date	Price Range	

with trim of blue and pink, white apron with blue stripes, light blue hat with darker blue dots, seated on light pedestal type base, height 9½", designer P. Stabler 1919–1938 3000.00 3250.00

HN 513

☐ Blue blouse, spotted skirt, height 9½", designer P. Stabler 1921–1938 3000.00 3500.00

PICARDY PEASANT (Male)
HN 13

☐ Blue costume with lighter blue apron, white cap, seated on blue pedestal style base, height 9½", designer P. Stabler 1913–1938 2000.00 2500.00

HN 17

☐ Green hat and green trousers, height 9½", designer P. Stabler 1912–1939 2000.00 2500.00

HN 19

☐ Green costume, height 9½", designer P. Stabler 1913–1938 2000.00 2500.00

PICNIC
HN 2308

☐ Small female figure seated on green and yellow base, yellow gown with white trim, blue scarf, brown shoes, brown basket, white cloth and white cups on base, height 3¾", designer M. Davies 1965–1988 140.00

PIED PIPER, The
HN 1215

☐ Dark brown base, costume of red leggings, red cloak with yellow lining, red hat, black costume, height 8¾", designer L. Harradine 1926–1938 1650.00 2000.00

HN 2102

☐ Light brown base, beige costume, black cloak with red lining, blue hat and shoes, height 8½", designer L. Harradine 1953–1976 275.00 350.00

PIERRETTE
HN 642

☐ Blue dress (1st version), height 7¼", designer L. Harradine 1924–1938 1200.00 1400.00

HN 643

☐ Black pedestal style base, red tights, black costume with white and red squares, black bodice, red sleeves,

Pierrette, HN 1749, 1200.00–1600.00

	Date	Price Range	
white and red collar, white hat with black balls (1st version), height 7¼″, designer L. Harradine	1924–1938	1200.00	1400.00
HN 644			
☐ White tights, white costume with a few black squares, collar with black trim, white hat with black balls (1st version), height 7¼″, designer L. Harradine ...	1924–1938	800.00	900.00
HN 691			
☐ HN 643, gold costume (1st version), height 7¼″, designer L. Harradine ...	1925–1938	1250.00	1500.00
HN 721			
☐ Black and white striped skirt (1st version), height 7¼″, designer L. Harradine	1925–1938	1100.00	1400.00

	Date	Price Range	

HN 731
☐ Spotted black and white skirt (1st version), height 7¼", designer L. Harradine 1925–1938   1100.00   1400.00

HN 732
☐ Black and white dress with petalled border (1st version), height 7¼", designer L. Harradine 1925–1938   1100.00   1400.00

HN 784
☐ Jazzy markings on pink costume with black muff (1st version), height 7¼", designer L. Harradine 1926–1938   1400.00   1600.00

HN 795
☐ This figure is a miniature—pink roses on skirt, also made in color schemes not recorded in pattern books (2nd version), height 3½", designer L. Harradine 1926–1938   800.00   1100.00

HN 796
☐ Also miniature—white skirt with silver spots (2nd version), height 3½", designer L. Harradine 1926–1938   800.00   1100.00

HN 1391
☐ Black pedestal style base, red costume with tiny black, green and yellow blocks, white collar with red and green trim, black hat with yellow balls; this figure is holding a black half mask (3rd version), height 8½", designer L. Harradine 1930–1938   1200.00   1600.00

HN 1749
☐ HN 643, pink and blue costume with playing card patterns (3rd version), height 8½", designer L. Harradine ... 1936–1949   1200.00   1600.00

PILLOW FIGHT
HN 2270
☐ Small girl figure in pink nightgown with tiny design and white collar, holding white pillow over shoulder, height 5¼", designer M. Davies 1965–1969   200.00   250.00

PINKIE
HN 1552
☐ Small figure on light pedestal style base, shaded red with tiered blue gown and red sash, white pantalettes, white hat with blue ribbon trim, holding small

	Date	Price Range	

bouquet of blue flowers, height 5″, designer L. Harradine 1933–1938   **800.00**   **950.00**

HN 1553

□ Yellow and blue dress, height 5″, designer L. Harradine 1933–1938   **800.00**   **950.00**

PIPER, The
HN 2907

□ Scottish figure seated on green stone-like base, blue skirt with black stripes, white shirt, brown vest, dark blue tam, green stockings, brown shoes, brown, black and white bagpipe, height 8″, designer M. Abberley 1980–   **350.00**

PIRATE KING, The
HN 2901

□ Character seated on black and white pirate flag on light tan base, costume of green shirt, white lace ruff, blue boots and blue braided jacket with plumed captain's hat, his belt holds dagger and pistol, height 10″, designer W.K. Harper 1981–   **750.00**

PIROUETTE
HN 2216

□ Cream gown with blue tint, red trim at waist and shoulder, height 5¾″, designer M. Davies 1959–1967   **250.00**   **300.00**

POACHER, The
HN 2043

□ Character figure kneeling on one knee, brown trousers, blue and black coat, brown and orange vest and hat, red scarf with white dots, height 6″, designer L. Harradine 1949–1959   **225.00**   **275.00**

POKE BONNET
HN 612

□ See classification "LILAC SHAWL, A," height 9½″, designer C.J. Noke   1924–1938   **1500.00**   **1700.00**

HN 765

□ See classification "LILAC SHAWL, A," height 9½″, designer C.J. Noke   1925–1938   **1500.00**   **1700.00**

POLKA, The
HN 2156

□ Pink gown with white trim and yellow rose, height 7½″, designer M. Davies   1955–1969   **250.00**   **325.00**

The Poacher, HN 2043, 225.00–275.00

	Date	Price Range	

POLLY PEACHUM
HN 463

☐ Character from "The Beggar's Opera," black base, white gown with blue ribbon trim, white cap with blue ribbon (1st version), height 6¼", designer L. Harradine ....

| | 1921–1949 | 375.00 | 475.00 |

HN 465

☐ Red dress (1st version), height 6½", designer L. Harradine ....

| | 1921–1949 | 425.00 | 525.00 |

HN 489

☐ Figure in curtsy position, light green gown with white cap and green ribbon trim (2nd version), height 4¼", designer L. Harradine ....

| | 1921–1938 | 300.00 | 400.00 |

	Date	Price Range	

HN 549
☐ Red gown (2nd version), height 4¼″,
designer L. Harradine .... | 1922–1949 | 400.00 | 475.00

HN 550
☐ Pink gown (1st version), height 6½″,
designer L. Harradine .... | 1922–1949 | 400.00 | 500.00

HN 589
☐ HN 463, pink dress, yellow underskirt
(1st version), height 6½″, designer L.
Harradine .... | 1924–1949 | 400.00 | 500.00

HN 614
☐ Pale pink dress, blue bows (1st version), height 6½″, designer L. Harra-
dine .... | 1924–1949 | 600.00 | 700.00

HN 620
☐ HN 489, rose dress, cream underskirt
(2nd version), height 4¼″, designer L.
Harradine .... | 1924–1938 | 300.00 | 400.00

HN 680
☐ HN 463, white dress with black, yellow and blue spots (1st version), height
6½″, designer L. Harradine .... | 1924–1949 | 550.00 | 650.00

HN 693
☐ Deep rose pink dress with green bows
(1st version), height 6½″, designer L.
Harradine .... | 1925–1949 | 500.00 | 600.00

HN 694
☐ HN 489, deep rose pink dress, green
bows (2nd version), height 4¼″, de-
signer L. Harradine .... | 1925–1949 | 400.00 | 500.00

HN 698
☐ Figure is miniature in curtsy position,
pink gown (3rd version), height 2¼″,
designer L. Harradine .... | 1925–1949 | 375.00 | 450.00

HN 699
☐ Blue dress (3rd version), height 2¼″,
designer L. Harradine .... | 1925–1949 | 375.00 | 450.00

HN 734
☐ HN 489, black bodice, white skirt,
black spots (2nd version), height 4¼″,
designer L. Harradine .... | 1925–1949 | 450.00 | 500.00

HN 757
☐ HN 698, red bodice, spotted skirt,
holding colored streamers (3rd version), height 2¼″, designer L. Harra-
dine .... | 1925–1949 | 350.00 | 450.00

	Date	Price Range	

HN 758

☐ Pink skirt with orange stripes (3rd version), height 2¼", designer L. Harradine 1925–1949 350.00 450.00

HN 759

☐ Yellow and white skirt with black spots (3rd version), height 2¼", designer L. Harradine 1925–1949 350.00 450.00

HN 760

☐ Mottled multicolored skirt (3rd version), height 2¼", designer L. Harradine 1925–1949 450.00 550.00

HN 761

☐ Blue and purple skirt (3rd version), height 2¼", designer L. Harradine ... 1925–1949 350.00 400.00

HN 762

☐ Pink roses on skirt (3rd version), height 2¼", designer L. Harradine 1925–1949 350.00 400.00

☐ **M-21** Miniature figures in curtsy position, deep red gown, height 2¼", designer L. Harradine 1932–1945 300.00 375.00

☐ **M-22** Blue spotted gown, height 2¼", designer L. Harradine 1932–1938 400.00 475.00

☐ **M-23** White gown with red and green stripes with red overlay with red and blue dots, height 2¼", designer L. Harradine 1932–1938 400.00 475.00

POPE JOHN PAUL II
HN 2888

☐ See classification, His Holiness, Pope John Paul II. ....

POTTER, The
HN 1493

☐ Character figure seated on purple rug on brown base, dark brown and red robe and hood, multicolored jugs and jars on base, height 7", designer C.J. Noke 1932– 450.00

HN 1518

☐ Green cloak, height 7", designer C.J. Noke 1932–1949 1000.00 1200.00

HN 1522

☐ Dark blue and green cloak, height 7", designer C.J. Noke 1932–1949 1000.00 1200.00

	Date	Price Range	

PREMIERE
HN 2343
☐ Blue and white gown, dark green cloak with white design on edge and yellow lining, black opera glasses, height 7½″, designer M. Davies .... 1969–1979 | 125.00 | 175.00

PRETTY LADY
HN 69
☐ HN 70, flowered blue dress, height 9½″, designer H. Tittensor .... 1916–1938 | 850.00 | 1000.00
HN 70
☐ Pale gray gown with raised white dots, height 9½″, designer H. Tittensor .... 1916–1938 | 850.00 | 1000.00
HN 302
☐ Patterned lilac dress, height 9½″, designer H. Tittensor .... 1918–1938 | 900.00 | 1100.00
HN 330
☐ Patterned blue dress, height 9½″, designer H. Tittensor .... 1918–1938 | 900.00 | 1100.00
HN 361
☐ Blue and green dress, height 9½″, designer H. Tittensor .... 1919–1938 | 900.00 | 1100.00
HN 384
☐ Red dress with striped skirt, height 9½″, designer H. Tittensor .... 1920–1938 | 900.00 | 1100.00
HN 565
☐ Orange dress, white sleeves with green spots, height 9½″, designer H. Tittensor 1923–1938 | 900.00 | 1100.00
HN 700
☐ Yellow dress with black spots, height 9½″, designer H. Tittensor .... 1925–1938 | 900.00 | 1100.00
HN 763
☐ Orange gown with blue sleeves and black design, white waistband with red spots and stripes, orange ribbon in hair, height 9½″, designer H. Tittensor .... 1925–1938 | 900.00 | 1100.00
HN 783
☐ HN 70, blue dress, height 9½″, designer H. Tittensor .... 1926–1938 | 900.00 | 1100.00

PRETTY POLLY
HN 2768
☐ Deep pink dress over which is draped a gray cloth, she is shelling peas; turning, she offers one to a colorful parrot perched on her chair, height 6″, designer B. Harper .... 1984–1986 | 150.00 | 175.00

	Date	Price Range	

PRIMROSES
HN 1617
☐ Character figure seated with brown basket at her side, red dress, white apron, dark mottled shawl with orange fringe, black hat with floral trim and black ribbons, height 6½", designer L. Harradine ....

| | 1935–1949 | 775.00 | 875.00 |

PRINCE OF WALES, The
HN 1217
☐ Riding costume of white trousers, black and red boots, red jacket, yellow vest, white cravat, black hat, dark brown base, height 7½", designer L. Harradine ....

| | 1926–1938 | 1500.00 | 1700.00 |

PRINCESS, A
HN 391
☐ Purple skirt with green and yellow designs, green blouse, green cloak with orange round designs, has yellow lining, black rope belt, height unknown, designer unknown ....

| | 1920–1938 | 2750.00 | 3000.00 |

HN 392
☐ Multicolored costume, striped skirt, height unknown, designer unknown ...

| | 1920–1938 | 2750.00 | 3000.00 |

HN 420
☐ Pink and green striped skirt, blue cloak, height unknown, designer unknown ...

| | 1920–1938 | 2750.00 | 3000.00 |

HN 430
☐ Green floral dress, blue and green striped cloak, height unknown, designer unknown ....

| | 1921–1938 | 2750.00 | 3000.00 |

HN 431
☐ Pink dress, blue-green cloak, height unknown, designer unknown ....

| | 1921–1938 | 2750.00 | 3000.00 |

HN 633
☐ Black and white dress, height unknown, designer unknown ....

| | 1924–1938 | 2750.00 | 3000.00 |

PRISCILLA
HN 1337
☐ Tiered gown of shaded reds, yellows, and blues, pantalettes and parasol of same color, darker mottled hat and jacket, black base, height 8", designer L. Harradine ....

| | 1929–1938 | 600.00 | 750.00 |

	Date	Price Range	

HN 1340
☐ Red tiered gown with dark blue collar, blue bonnet and parasol with dark blue trim, red shoes, black base, height 8″, designer L. Harradine .... 1929–1949 · 300.00 · 350.00

HN 1495
☐ Shaded blue gown with pink collar, green bonnet and parasol, white pantalettes, height 8″, designer L. Harradine .... 1932–1949 · 700.00 · 800.00

HN 1501
☐ Shaded yellow gown, green bonnet and parasol, light red shoes, black base, height 8″, designer L. Harradine ..... 1932–1938 · 650.00 · 800.00

HN 1559
☐ HN 1337, pink and yellow skirt, height 8″, designer L. Harradine .... 1932–1959 · 650.00 · 800.00
☐ **M-13** Made as a miniature, green and yellow gown, height 3¾″, designer L. Harradine .... 1932–1938 · 400.00 · 450.00
☐ **M-14** Shaded blue gown, height 3¾″, designer L. Harradine .... 1932–1945 · 400.00 · 550.00
☐ **M-24** Red gown with green bonnet, height 3¾″, designer L. Harradine ... 1932–1945 · 350.00 · 400.00

PROFESSOR, The
HN 2281
☐ Character figure seated on brown chair, brown suit, black robe with wine lining, white shirt with black bow tie, holding open book, books stacked beside chair, glasses on head and also on knee, height 7¼″, designer M. Nicoll · 1965–1980 · 175.00 · 225.00

PROMENADE
HN 2076
☐ Two figures on black base, lady has shaded red skirt with blue overskirt trimmed in black, high head piece of white and blue; male has red shoes, white stockings, long white coat with red, blue and black designs, multicolored long vest, red sash, black curly hair, height 8″, designer M. Davies .. 1951–1953 · 1500.00 · 1850.00

PROPOSAL (Female)
HN 715
☐ Lady seated on brown and cream loveseat on black base, red gown with

	Date	Price Range	

shades of black, white cap with red and black ribbon, height 5¾″, designer unknown 1925–1938 1400.00 1700.00

HN 716

☐ White gown with a few black squares, white cap with black, height 5¾″, designer unknown 1925–1938 1400.00 1700.00

HN 78

☐ Pink gown, height 5¾″, designer unknown 1926–1938 1400.00 1700.00

PROPOSAL (Male)
HN 725

☐ Male on knee on black base, black shoes, white stockings, black trousers, black and white checkered long vest, red coat with black and white trim, white with black trim at wrist and neck, holding black hat with red feathers, dark curly hair, height 5½″, designer unknown 1925–1938 1450.00 1700.00

HN 1209

☐ Blue coat, flowered pink waistcoat, height 5½″, designer unknown 1926–1938 1900.00 2150.00

PRUDENCE
HN 1883

☐ Seated figure in shaded blue gown with lining of dark blue with red design, white collar and small white close bonnet, height 6¾″, designer L. Harradine 1938–1949 950.00 1150.00

HN 1884

☐ Shaded red gown with lining of white with blue designs, height 6¾″, designer L. Harradine 1938–1949 950.00 1150.00

PRUE
HN 1996

☐ Red gown with white apron and collar, dark red waistband, white cap with blue ribbon, carrying basket with fruit, height 6¾″, designer L. Harradine ... 1947–1955 300.00 350.00

PUFF AND POWDER
HN 397

☐ HN 398, yellow skirt, brown bodice, height unknown, designer L. Harradine 1920–1938 2000.00 2200.00

Prue, HN 1996, 300.00–350.00

	Date	Price Range	
HN 398			
☐ Lavender gown with black and white designs, purple bodice, yellow overskirt with black and white designs, height unknown, designer L. Harradine	1920–1938	2000.00	2200.00
HN 400			
☐ Green and blue bodice, yellow skirt, height unknown, designer L. Harradine	1920–1938	2000.00	2200.00
HN 432			
☐ Lilac skirt with orange spots, height unknown, designer L. Harradine	1921–1938	2000.00	2200.00
HN 433			
☐ Yellow skirt with blue spots, height unknown, designer L. Harradine	1921–1938	2000.00	2200.00

PUNCH AND JUDY MAN
HN 2765
☐ Light tan base, of elderly man in

Puff and Powder, HN 400, 2000.00–2200.00

	Date	Price Range
yellow trousers, green sweater, black shoes, puppets are male with red, yellow and black costumes; lady's costume blue dress, green shawl and white hat, height 9″, designer W. K. Harper	1981–	395.00

PUPPETMAKER, The
HN 2253
☐ Brown trousers, green vest, white shirt, small cap of brown and tan; boy puppet costume of red and green, and girl puppet dress of green with overdress of light and dark blue, height 8″, designer M. Nicoll 1962–1973 425.00 475.00

	Date	Price Range	

PUSSY
HN 18
□ Barefooted girl seated holding black cat in lap, light blue gown, height 7½″, designer F.C. Stone 1913–1938 5500.00 6500.00

HN 325
□ White dress with black patterning, height 7½″, designer F.C. Stone 1918–1938 7500.00 9500.00

HN 507
□ Spotted blue dress, height 7½″, designer F.C. Stone 1921–1938 7500.00 9500.00

PYJAMS
HN 1942
□ Small figure on white base wearing light red pajamas trimmed in white and blue stripe, holding blue ball, height 5¼″, designer L. Harradine 1940–1949 700.00 800.00

QUALITY STREET
HN 1211
□ Red gown with long blue and red scarf, light colored bonnet with red feathers and red ribbons, height 7¼″, designer unknown 1926–1938 1000.00 1200.00

RACHEL
HN 2919
□ Green gown, yellow ochre hooded coat trimmed with brown fur, height 7½″, designer P. Gee 1981–1984 150.00 200.00

HN 2936
□ Young lady wearing red cloak trimmed with gray fur over a pale lemon colored gown, height 7½″, designer P. Gee .. 1985– 230.00

RAG DOLL
HN 2142
□ Small figure in blue gown with bibbed white apron, white cap, holding doll wrapped in red, height 4¾″, designer M. Davies 1954–1986 85.00 100.00

RAG DOLL SELLER
HN 2944
□ Old lady sitting on a light brown basket selling her rag dolls, light gray skirt, light blue blouse covered with a green shawl, her gray hair is covered with a

	Date	Price Range	
white bonnet trimmed in black, height 7¼", designer R. Tabbenor	1983–	190.00	

REBECCA
HN 2805
□ Pink gown with floral design at hemline, blue overskirt with dark blue trim, pink ribbon in hair, holding single red flower, height 7¼", designer M. Davies 1980– 450.00

REFLECTIONS
HN 1820
□ HN 1821, red dress, lilac sofa, height 5", designer L. Harradine 1937–1938 1500.00 1700.00
HN 1821
□ Orange and green sofa, green gown with white trim, large white cap with red trim, multicolored pillow on sofa, height 5", designer L. Harradine 1937–1938 1500.00 1700.00
HN 1847
□ Green sofa, shaded red gown with white trim, red bonnet with blue ribbons, blue shoes, light green pillow on sofa, height 5", designer L. Harradine 1938–1949 1100.00 1250.00
HN 1848
□ Green skirt, height 5", designer L. Harradine 1938–1949 1100.00 1250.00

REGAL LADY
HN 2709
□ Cream skirt with yellow shadings, gold trim on hemline, dark blue overdress, height 7⅝", designer M. Davies 1975–1983 125.00 175.00

REGENCY
HN 1752
□ Shaded green skirt with red, green and purple stripes at hemline, long purple jacket with green and red trim, white cravat, green triangular hat with red trim, holding white and brown riding crop, height 8", designer L. Harradine 1936–1949 1600.00 1900.00

REGENCY BEAU
HN 1972
□ Eighteenth century costume of red with black buttons, green cloak, black triangular hat, black shoes, white with black trim at wrist and neck, white

Regency Beau, HN 1972, 1100.00–1300.00

	Date	Price Range	
stockings, on light colored base, height 8″, designer H. Fenton	1941–1949	1100.00	1300.00

RENDEZVOUS
HN 2212
☐ Light green gown with shaded red overdress, figure standing beside white pedestal with red roses on top, height 7¼″, designer M. Davies .... | 1962–1971 | 325.00 | 400.00

REPOSE
HN 2272
☐ Green and brown chaise lounge, barefoot figure in rose gown with blue trim, green ribbon in hair, holding small book, height 5¼″, designer M. Davies | 1972–1979 | 175.00 | 225.00

	Date	Price Range	

REST AWHILE
HN 2728
☐ Older lady figure seated on brown stile on green base, gray and blue gown with white apron, purple jacket, gray and blue bonnet with red flowers and gray and blue ribbons, holding brown basket with a green and white striped cover, height 8″, designer W.K. Harper 1981–1985   175.00   200.00

RETURN OF PERSEPHONE, The
HN 31
☐ Large, two figures on one base (16″), one costumed in gray robes, second in cream colored gown, green base with bush on one end, height 16″, designer C. Vyse 1913–1938   4000.00   5000.00

REVERIE
HN 2306
☐ Figure seated on brown and white chaise lounge, peach and yellow gown with white trim, holding open book on lap, one gray and one purple pillow, height 6½″, designer M. Davies 1964–1981   250.00   300.00

RHAPSODY
HN 2267
☐ Blue and green gown, long yellow scarf, small white fan in one hand, height 6¾″, designer M. Davies 1961–1973   200.00   250.00

RHODA
HN 1573
☐ Muted yellow and blue skirt, red bodice, shawl with colors of green, yellow and red trimmed in dark red and blue, green bonnet with green feather and purple ribbons, height 10¼″, designer L. Harradine 1933–1949   600.00   800.00
HN 1574
☐ Purple gown with red bow trim, red shawl with shaded greens, green bonnet with light green feather and purple ribbons, height 10¼″, designer L. Harradine 1933–1938   600.00   800.00
HN 1688
☐ Orange gown with purple bodice, red

	Date	Price Range	

shawl with large green and black flower design with green fringe, black bonnet with green feather and dark ribbons, height 10¼″, designer L. Harradine — 1935–1949 — 650.00 — 850.00

RHYTHM
HN 1903
☐ HN 1904, pink dress, height 6¾″, designer L. Harradine .... 1939–1949 — 2000.00 — 2500.00
HN 1904
☐ Blue gown, blue overskirt with dark blue and gold floral designs, height 6¾″, designer L. Harradine .... 1939–1949 — 2000.00 — 2500.00

RITA
HN 1448
☐ HN 1450, yellow and pink dress, height 7″, designer L. Harradine .... 1931–1938 — 700.00 — 800.00
HN 1450
☐ Blue patterned tiered gown with brown shawl, brown bonnet with green ribbons, green, white and yellow parasol, height 7″, designer L. Harradine ..... 1931–1938 — 700.00 — 800.00

RIVER BOY
HN 2128
☐ Small figure of boy kneeling on green base, dark blue trousers, very light green shirt, cream colored hat, holding black frying pan over fire, height 4″, designer M. Davies .... 1962–1975 — 150.00 — 200.00

ROBERT BURNS
HN 42
☐ Scottish figure on black base, brown trousers, green coat, orange vest, white cravat, brown tam with green ball trim, yellow scarf with brown stripes, height 18″, designer E. W. Light .... 1914–1938 — 3500.00 — 4000.00

ROBIN
Girl on hands and knees
Issued only as a miniature
☐ **M-38** Red shirt with blue collar, blue shorts on green sand, height 2½″, designer unknown .... 1933–1945 — 500.00 — 650.00
☐ **M-39** Blue shirt with red collar, green shorts on tan stand, height 2½″, designer unknown .... 1933–1945 — 500.00 — 650.00

The Rocking Horse, HN 2072, 1750.00–2000.00

	Date	Price Range
ROBIN HOOD **HN 2773** ☐ Figure seated on a tree stump about to take a drink from his jug; costume is brown, green and beige, his foot rests on a chest presumably full of gold, height 8″, designer B. Harper	1985–	215.00
ROCKING HORSE, The **HN 2072** ☐ Rocking horse on brown base, light blue-gray horse with red cloth and red straps, cream rocking base with red and yellow trim, boy figure in blue pants, lighter blue shirt, black shoes, height 7″, designer L. Harradine	1951–1953	1750.00 2000.00

ROMANCE
HN 2430
☐ Figure seated in green chair, yellow

	Date	Price Range	

gown with brown trim at hemline, black shoe, holding open book on lap, height 5¼", designer M. Davies ...... — 1972–1979 — 150.00 — 200.00

ROMANY SUE
HN 1757
☐ Green gown with pink and white striped apron, red and blue shawl with green fringe, black hat with blue and red feather, carrying basket of vegetables and flowers on each arm, height 9½", designer L. Harradine .... — 1936–1949 — 900.00 — 1050.00

HN 1758
☐ Lavender gown with apron, also lavender with darker stripe, cream colored shawl with blue designs and green fringe, dark green hat with blue and red feather, two darker brown baskets, height 9½", designer L. Harradine ... — 1936–1949 — 900.00 — 1050.00

ROSABELL
HN 1620
☐ Seated figure with muted blue and red skirt, red bodice, red hat with blue and red feather, multicolored shawl, height 6¾", designer L. Harradine .... — 1934–1938 — 1300.00 — 1550.00

ROSALIND
HN 2393
☐ Dark blue gown with white floral design and large white cuffs, dark hair, holding white fan in one hand, flower in other, height 5½", designer M. Davies .... — 1970–1975 — 150.00 — 200.00

ROSAMUND
HN 1320
☐ Shaded green skirt, light red jacket, long purple-white, green, and red scarf, tall green crown hat with black feather and red band (1st version), height 7½", designer L. Harradine .... — 1929–1938 — 2200.00 — 2500.00

HN 1497
☐ Red full skirted gown with lighter red trim, green hat, long necklace with cross, small bouquet of flowers in hand (2nd version), height 8½", designer L. Harradine .... — 1932–1938 — 2200.00 — 2500.00

Rosamund, HN 1551, 2200.00–2500.00

	Date	Price Range	
HN 1551			
☐ Blue gown trimmed in lighter blue, shaded red and blue hat, white necklace and cross, height 8½″, designer L. Harradine	1932–1938	**2200.00**	**2500.00**
☐ **M-32** Made as a miniature, shaded yellow and blue gown and hat, height 4¼″, designer L. Harradine	1932–1945	**550.00**	**700.00**
☐ **M-33** Shaded red and blue gown, red hat, height 4¼″, designer L. Harradine	1932–1945	**450.00**	**550.00**
ROSE			
HN 1368			
☐ Small figure in tiered red gown, height 4⅝″, designer L. Harradine	1930–	**95.00**	

	Date	Price Range	

HN 1387
☐ Flowered blue and pink dress, orange roses, height 4½″, designer L. Harradine 1930–1938 300.00 350.00

HN 1416
☐ Tiered shaded blue gown, height 4½″, designer L. Harradine 1930–1949 250.00 300.00

HN 1506
☐ Yellow dress, height 4½″, designer L. Harradine 1932–1938 300.00 350.00

HN 1654
☐ Green bodice, floral skirt, height 4½″, designer L. Harradine 1934–1938 300.00 350.00

HN 2123
☐ Mauve gown with layers of flounces, height 4½″, designer L. Harradine ... 1983– 95.00

ROSEANNA
HN 1921
☐ HN 1926, green dress, height 8″, designer L. Harradine 1940–1949 1400.00 1700.00

HN 1926
☐ Shaded red gown with blue and red hemline, blue and green bow trim on bodice, dark bows in hair, standing with hands on bowl of flowers on pedestal, height 8″, designer L. Harradine 1940–1959 300.00 350.00

ROSEBUD
HN 1580
☐ Very small figure, seated, in wide ruffled and pleated gown of pink (1st version), height 3″, designer L. Harradine 1933–1938 750.00 950.00

HN 1581
☐ Pale dress with flower sprays (1st version), height 3″, designer L. Harradine 1933–1938 750.00 950.00

HN 1983
☐ This is larger figure, shaded red gown with light green cross design as trim, darker red shawl, green bonnet with white trim, carrying small basket of flowers with flowers in other arm (2nd version), height 7½″, designer L. Harradine 1945–1952 400.00 500.00

ROSEMARY
HN 2091
☐ Red gown with blue shawl and red

Roseanna, HN 1926, 300.00–350.00

	Date	Price Range	
designs, dark blue bonnet with white scarf, carrying basket of flowers, height 7″, designer L. Harradine	1952–1959	400.00	500.00

ROSINA
HN 1358
☐ Seated figure, red gown and red cape with white fur trim, red bonnet with purple ribbons, height 5½″, designer L. Harradine 1929–1938   800.00   975.00

HN 1364
☐ Purple gown and cape with wide red stripe and dark dots as trim, red

Rosebud, HN 1580, 750.00–950.00

	Date	Price Range	
bonnet with purple trim and red ribbons, height 5½″, designer L. Harradine ...	1929–1938	800.00	975.00

HN 1556
☐ Cream gown with shaded blues and reds, shaded red and blue bonnet with red trim and ribbons, height 5½″, designer L. Harradine ....

	1933–1938	775.00	950.00

ROWENA
HN 2077
☐ Shaded green and red underskirt, red overskirt, dark red overlay with blue and black designs, brown muff, green bonnet with shaded blue ribbons, height 7½″, designer L. Harradine ...

	1951–1955	600.00	750.00

ROYAL GOVERNOR'S COOK
HN 2233
☐ Seated colored figure, dark blue gown with white apron and crossed white scarf, white head covering, holding pink bowl on lap, height 6″, designer M. Davies ....

	1960–1983	375.00	425.00

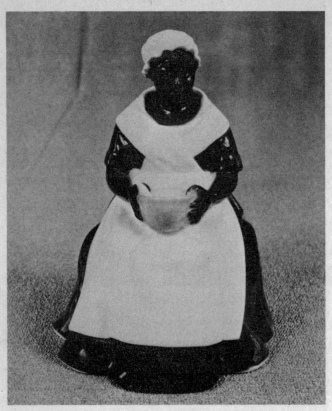

Royal Governor's Cook, HN 2333, 375.00–425.00

	Date	Price Range	

RUBY
HN 1724

☐ Shaded red and white tiered gown, dark flowers on blue ribbons in hair, holding small bouquet in hand, height 5¼″, designer L. Harradine 1935–1949   550.00   750.00

HN 1725

☐ Shaded blue tiered gown, red flowers on red ribbon in hair, height 5¼″, designer L. Harradine 1935–1949   550.00   750.00

RUSTIC SWAIN, The
HN 1745

☐ Two figures on brown couch, lady's white gown with red and blue floral

	Date	Price Range	

design, green overlay, green bonnet and
shoes, man's costume of brown and
white, dark brown hat, brown shoes,
red and white striped pillow on couch,
height 5¼", designer L. Harradine ... 1935–1949 | **2250.00** | **2500.00**

HN 1746

☐ Man's costume of green, height 5¼",
designer L. Harradine .... 1935–1949 | **2250.00** | **2500.00**

RUTH (Kate Greenaway)
HN 2799

☐ Green gown with red and yellow flowers at hemline, white waistband and
collar, large white cap with red ribbon,
holding single flower in one hand, on
white base, height 6⅛", designer M.
Davies .... 1976–1982 | **95.00** | **125.00**

RUTH THE PIRATE MAID
HN 2900

☐ Costume of brown striped skirt, blue
blouse with gold and black trim, white
apron, black captain's hat with gold
trim and white skull and cross bones,
on mottled brown base, height 11¾",
designer W.K. Harper. .... 1981– | **750.00**

SABBATH MORN
HN 1982

☐ Red gown, mottled green and yellow
shawl and parasol, red bonnet with
green and white trim and blue ribbons,
height 7¼", designer L. Harradine ... 1945–1959 | **250.00** | **325.00**

SAILOR'S HOLIDAY
HN 2442

☐ Kneeling character figure on dark
brown and purple base, purple trousers, yellow coat, green sweater, black
cap, black tie, light purple shirt, holding small blue, tan, and white sailboat,
height 6¼", designer M. Nicoll .... 1972–1979 | **200.00** | **250.00**

SAIREY GAMP
HN 533

☐ This figure is miniature—A character
from Dickens' "Martin Chuzzlewit"
(1st version), height 4", designer L.
Harradine .... 1922–1985 | **75.00** | **90.00**

☐ **M-46** Renumbered as a miniature.

	Date	Price Range	

Light green gown, black cloak, white and pink head cap with black ribbons, red small round cloth with black dots in one hand, height 4″, designer L. Harradine **1932–1983** **55.00** **75.00**

HN 558

☐ Large figure, dressed in black on black base, black bonnet with white trim, blue round cloth bag with white dots, green and blue umbrella (2nd version), height 7″, designer L. Harradine **1923–1939** **550.00** **650.00**

HN 1896

☐ Very minor color changes (2nd version), height 7″, designer L. Harradine **1938–1952** **300.00** **375.00**

HN 2100

☐ Light green gown, dark green cloak, black bonnet with white trim, red round cloth bag with white dots, black umbrella, black shoes, on black base (3rd version), height 7¼″, designer L. Harradine **1952–1967** **325.00** **425.00**

SALLY
HN 2741

☐ Figure is sitting on tree stump, wearing bright red cap over a gown of white with shades of blue to purple. Bonnet and shoes are green, brown hair, height 5½″, designer D. Tootle **1987–** **195.00**

SALOME
HN 1828

☐ Tinted finish, height unknown, designer R. Garbe **1937–1949** **4500.00** **5000.00**

SAM WELLER
HN 531

☐ A character in Dickens' "Pickwick Papers" (1st version), height 4″, designer L. Harradine **1922–1985** **75.00** **90.00**

☐ **M-48** Renumbered as a miniature, brown trousers, yellow vest with red stripes, red neck scarf, black hat, seated on black base, height 4″, designer L. Harradine **1932–1983** **55.00** **75.00**

	Date	Price Range

SANDRA
HN 2275

☐ Tan gown, white trim and petticoat with brown dots, brown hat to match gown, height 7¾", designer M. Davies 1969– 195.00

HN 2401

☐ Apple-green dress, white petticoat showing, deep green hat, height 7¾", designer M. Davies 1984– 195.00

SANTA CLAUS
HN 2725

☐ Character figure in brilliant red suit with white fur, black boots, holding aloft a teddy bear in one hand and a sack of toys in the other, height 9½", designer W.K. Harper 1982– 295.00

SARA
HN 2265

☐ White gown with red bodice and overskirt, white collar with blue floral design, height 7½", designer M. Davies 1981– 295.00

SAUCY NYMPH, A
HN 1539

☐ Small white nude figure seated on mottled green, red, brown base, height 4½", designer unknown 1933–1949 400.00 550.00

SCHOOLMARM
HN 2223

☐ Character figure seated at brown bench type desk, gray gown, purple shawl, white headcap with black ribbon, desk has red and gray inkwell, white dunce hat beside desk, white, black, orange and brown world globe under desk, height 6¾", designer M. Davies 1958–1980 165.00 250.00

SCOTCH GIRL
HN 1269

☐ Red costume with dark brown and black stripes, dark brown jacket with white trim, red stockings with black stripes, on black pedestal style base, height 7½", designer L. Harradine ... 1928–1938 2000.00 2500.00

Scotties, HN 1281, 1300.00–1550.00

	Date	Price Range	
SCOTTIES			
HN 1281			
☐ Figure seated on cream colored bench, red dress, red shoes, one black scottie on bench, the other at side of bench, height 5¼″, designer L. Harradine ...	1928–1938	1300.00	1550.00
HN 1349			
☐ Pale multicolored costume, white dogs, height 5¼″, designer L. Harradine ...	1929–1949	2500.00	3000.00
SCRIBE, A			
HN 305			
☐ Figure seated on blue and gold cushion, green robes, yellow costume, blue turban, light purple shoes, height 6″, designer C.J. Noke	1918–1936	1000.00	1300.00
HN 324			
☐ Dark green and orange cushion, shades of brown costume and robes, green and			

	Date	Price Range	

blue turban, green shoes, height 6″,
designer C.J. Noke 1918–1938 **1000.00** **1300.00**

HN 1235

☐ Brown coat, blue hat, height 6″, de-
signer C.J. Noke 1927–1938 **1000.00** **1300.00**

SCROOGE
Issued only as a miniature

☐ **M-87** White cap, brown coat, black
money bag in hands, tan shoes, black
stand, height 4″, designer L. Harra-
dine 1949–1983 **55.00** **70.00**

SEAFARER, The
HN 2455

☐ Character figure seated on light blue
pedestal on blue base, blue trousers,
black boots with red trim, yellow zip-
pered sweater, blue shirt, black cap,
base has bird on it, height 8½″, de-
signer M. Nicoll 1972–1976 **200.00** **250.00**

SEA HARVEST
HN 2257

☐ Blue coat, brown trousers, black boots,
black rain hat, holding large brown net,
height 7½″, designer M. Nicoll 1969–1976 **175.00** **250.00**

SEASHORE
HN 2263

☐ Small boy figure in red swim trunks,
on light brown base, height 3½″, de-
signer M. Davies 1961–1965 **300.00** **425.00**

SEA SPRITE
HN 1261

☐ Small white nude figure standing on
black rock style base with long red and
black scarf behind figure (1st version),
height 5″, designer L. Harradine 1927–1938 **650.00** **850.00**

HN 2191

☐ Barefooted figure in blue and white
shell, pink gown (2nd version), height
7″, designer M. Davies 1958–1962 **475.00** **525.00**

SECRET THOUGHTS
HN 2382

☐ Seated figure, shaded green and yellow
gown, blue bow in hair, holding two
pink roses, leaning on cream colored

Sea Sprite, HN 2191, 475.00–525.00

	Date	Price Range	
pedestal, height 6¼″, designer M. Davies	1971–1988	295.00	

SENTIMENTAL PIERROT, The
HN 36
☐ HN 307, dove gray costume, height 13½″, designer C.J. Noke ....

	1914–1938	2000.00	2350.00

HN 307
☐ Seated male figure in black and white costume, height 13½″, designer C.J. Noke ....

	1918–1938	2000.00	2350.00

SENTINEL
HN 523
☐ Figure in knight's costume on black base, gray and red costume, shield

	Date	Price Range	

has three golden lions' heads, height 17½″, designer unknown 1921–1938 5500.00 6500.00

SERENA
HN 1868
☐ Red gown with blue ruffle trim, light red undergown with design of red, yellow and blue, red shoes, height 11″, designer L. Harradine 1938–1949 1100.00 1200.00

SHARON
HN 3047
☐ Child figure dressed in light blue with pink sash, plum colored hat with ribbons tied under her chin, black fingerless gloves, height 4¾″, designer P. Parsons 1984– 140.00

SHE LOVES ME NOT
HN 2045
☐ Small boy figure on yellow and green base, blue suit with white straps, barefooted, red hair, height 5½″, designer L. Harradine 1949–1962 175.00 225.00

SHEILA
HN 2742
☐ Light blue gown with floral bottomed skirt, four layers of petticoat showing, a pink rose in hands, touching hair, height unknown, designer S. Keenan 1984– 185.00

SHEPHERD, A
HN 81
☐ Black base, blue and gray trousers, brown coat, brown hat with light colored scarf tied around it, holding lantern in one hand and small lamb in other arm, earthenware (1st version), height 13¼″, designer C.J. Noke 1918–1938 2250.00 2500.00
HN 617
☐ China body and purple-blue trousers and coat (1st version), height 13¼″, designer C.J. Noke 1924–1938 2250.00 2500.00
HN 632
☐ China body and white smock, blue trousers (1st version), height 13¼″, designer C.J. Noke 1924–1938 2250.00 2500.00
HN 709
☐ This is a miniature figure, green jacket,

	Date	Price Range	

red cloak and black trousers (2nd version), height 3½", designer unknown ... 1925–1938 1000.00 1500.00

HN 751

☐ Yellow and brown base, costume of black trousers, green coat, red cloak, white shirt, black hat, black cane, single flower in hand (3rd version), height 7", designer unknown 1925–1938 2250.00 2500.00

HN 1975

☐ Green base, brown trousers, long tan coat, red scarf, brown hat, carrying lantern and staff (4th version), height 8½", designer H. Fenton 1945–1975 175.00 250.00

☐ **M-17** Made as a miniature, in the style of HN 751, brown trousers, blue coat, red cloak, height 3¾", designer unknown 1932–1938 1200.00 1700.00

☐ **M-19** Brown trousers, blue coat and blue cloak, height 3¾", designer unknown 1932–1938 1200.00 1700.00

SHEPHERDESS
HN 708

☐ This is a miniature, on yellow and brown base, red overskirt with yellow and pink striped skirt (1st version), height 3½", designer unknown 1925–1948 1000.00 1500.00

☐ **M-18** Made as a miniature, green bodice, pink overskirt, height 3½", designer unknown 1932–1938 1200.00 1600.00

☐ **M-20** Yellow bodice, flowered dress, height 3¾", designer unknown 1932–1938 1300.00 1700.00

HN 735

☐ Yellow and green base, black shoes with red bows, multicolored skirt with purple overlay, yellow trim on sleeves, dark bow in hair (2nd version), height 7", designer unknown 1925–1938 1500.00 1750.00

HN 750

☐ Pink bodice, yellow skirt (2nd version), height 7", designer unknown 1925–1938 1500.00 1750.00

SHIRLEY
HN 2702

☐ Young lady with swirling white skirt embellished with pink roses, sleeveless white top with pink roses, auburn hair, height 7¼", designer M. Davies 1985– 160.00

	Date	Price Range	

SHORE LEAVE
HN 2254
□ Character figure seated on gray stone-
line wall, black suit, black cap, gray
sweater, green parrot on shoulder, bag
between feet, wicker basket at side,
height 8″, designer M. Nicoll .... | 1965–1979 | 175.00 | 225.00

SHY ANNE
HN 60
□ HN 64, floral blue dress, height 7¾″,
designer L. Perugini .... | 1916–1938 | 2000.00 | 2500.00
HN 64
□ Light colored base, girl figure in white
dress with raised white design, large
white bow in hair, says "Shy Anne"
on base, height 7¾″, designer L. Pe-
rugini .... | 1916–1938 | 2000.00 | 2500.00
HN 65
□ Spotted blue dress with dark blue hem,
height 7¾″, designer L. Perugini ..... | 1916–1938 | 2000.00 | 2500.00
HN 568
□ Black base, shaded green dress with
darker dots, yellow ribbon around
waist, dark blue bow with pink squares
in hair, pink and dark blue striped
stockings, height 7¾″, designer L. Pe-
rugini .... | 1923–1938 | 2000.00 | 2500.00

SHYLOCK
HN 79
□ HN 317, multicolored cloak, yellow
sleeves, height unknown, designer C.J.
Noke .... | 1917–1938 | 2500.00 | 2750.00
HN 317
□ Shaded blue and purple robes, headcap
of same, height unknown, designer C.J.
Noke .... | 1918–1938 | 2500.00 | 2750.00

SIBELL
HN 1668
□ Eighteenth century gown of light green
with blue bow trim, red overskirt with
white trim, black hat with red trim,
height 6½″, designer L. Harradine ... | 1934–1949 | 1000.00 | 1250.00
HN 1695
□ Green gown with blue bows, orange
overskirt with multicolored designs,
height 6½″, designer L. Harradine ... | 1935–1949 | 900.00 | 1000.00

Sibell, HN 1695, 900.00–1000.00

	Date	Price Range	

HN 1735
☐ HN 1668, blue and green gown, height 6½″, designer L. Harradine 1935–1949 **1000.00** **1250.00**

SIESTA
HN 1305
☐ White nude figure lying on dark red couch, shaded reds and blues in cloth covering couch, height 4¾″, designer L. Harradine 1928–1938 **2500.00** **3000.00**

SILKS AND RIBBONS
HN 2017
☐ Character figure seated on wooden bench, dark green dress, dark green shawl with black stripes, black bonnet with red ribbons, box of different

	Date	Price Range	

colored ribbons on lap, white apron, brown wicker basket, height 6″, designer L. Harradine .... | 1949– | 195.00 |

SILVERSMITH OF WILLIAMSBURG
HN 2208
☐ White base with brown pedestal which contains gray object, brown trousers, long blue vest, white shirt, brown headcovering, black shoes, white stockings, height 6¼″, designer M. Davies | 1960–1983 | 150.00 | 225.00

SIMONE
HN 2378
☐ Shaded green gown with white cuffs and black trim around top, blue and yellow ribbons in hair, holding small fan in one hand, height 7¼″, designer M. Davies .... | 1971–1981 | 150.00 | 200.00

SIR JOHN A. MacDONALD
HN 2860
☐ This figure depicts the gentleman who was appointed the first prime minister of Canada. Commissioned in 1987 to celebrate the centenary of the Dominion of Canada General Insurance Company; will be more widely available in 1988, height 9¼″, designer W.K. Harper, price undetermined .... | 1987– | —

SIR THOMAS LOVELL
HN 356
☐ Brown base, brown and red costume, green sleeves with yellow and red design, brown hat with orange feather, brown stockings and black shoes, height 7¾″, designer C.J. Noke .... | 1919–1938 | 2500.00 | 3000.00

SIR WALTER RALEIGH
HN 1742
☐ Black base, red stockings, red and white costume, purple vest, dark green cloak, black hat, height 10½″, designer L. Harradine .... | 1935–1949 | 1200.00 | 1500.00
HN 1751
☐ Earthenware model, with minor glaze differences, height 11½″, designer L. Harradine .... | 1936–1949 | 1200.00 | 1500.00

	Date	Price Range	

HN 2015
☐ Green base, brown stockings, orange costume with brown designs and stripes, black cloak with blue and red, black hat, height 11½″, designer L. Harradine 1948–1955 700.00 800.00

SIR WINSTON CHURCHILL
HN 3057
☐ See Miscellaneous Figurines 1985– 185.00

SKATER, The
HN 2117
☐ Red skirt, white jacket with brown collar, brown sash, light yellow bonnet with blue ribbons, brown muff on cords, height 7¼″, designer M. Davies 1953–1971 325.00 385.00

SKETCH GIRL, The
☐ This figure carries no HN number. Apparently designed from a girl figure shown on a magazine titled "Sketch." Standing on a black base, her dress is a bright red with a white blouse showing under red jacket. Bonnet white and black with red feather. She is holding a tray containing a devil, jockey, ballerina, soldier and a cupid, height 7″, designer L. Harradine 2750.00 3250.00

SLEEP
HN 24
☐ Light blue gown and hood, holding naked baby to shoulder on light blue base, height 8″, designer P. Stabler 1913–1938 2500.00 3000.00
HN 24A
☐ Dark blue dress, height 8″, designer P. Stabler 1913–1938 2500.00 3000.00
HN 25
☐ Blue-green dress, height 8″, designer P. Stabler 1913–1938 2500.00 3000.00
HN 25A
☐ Fewer firings, height 8″, designer P. Stabler 1913–1938 2500.00 3000.00

HN 424
☐ HN 24, smaller figure with blue dress, height 8″, designer P. Stabler 1921–1938 2500.00 3000.00

	Date	Price Range	

HN 692
☐ Smaller figure with gold dress, height
 8″, designer P. Stabler .... | 1925–1938 | 2500.00 | 3000.00

HN 710
☐ Smaller figure with matte vellum finish,
 height 8″, designer P. Stabler .... | 1925–1938 | 2500.00 | 3000.00

SLEEPING BEAUTY
HN 3079
☐ Young lady asleep on a chaise lounge,
 lying gracefully on a white pillow,
 wearing a pale green negligee. Black
 hair, height 4½″, 8½″ long, designer
 A. Hughes .... | 1987– | 195.00 |

SLEEPYHEAD
HN 2114
☐ Red, orange, yellow, and blue over-
 stuffed chair; girl in white dress with
 black trim, brown teddy bear, black
 and white dunce hat, blue cushion,
 height 5″, designer M. Davies .... | 1953–1955 | 1000.00 | 1250.00

SLEEPY SCHOLAR, The
HN 15
☐ HN 16, blue costume, height 6¾″, de-
 signer W. White .... | 1913–1938 | 2500.00 | 3000.00

HN 16
☐ Seated figure on blue and gray basket
 on light green base, shaded yellow and
 green dress with narrow green trim on
 hemline, black shoes with gold trim,
 height 6¾″, designer W. White .... | 1913–1938 | 2500.00 | 3000.00

HN 29
☐ Brown costume, height 6¾″, designer
 W. White .... | 1913–1938 | 2500.00 | 3000.00

SMILING BUDDHA, The
HN 454
☐ Rotund blue and green seated figure,
 patterned blue costume, very tiny Chinese figure on one knee, height 6¼″,
 designer C.J. Noke .... | 1921–1938 | 2500.00 | 3000.00

SNAKE CHARMER, The
HN 1317
☐ Seated figure on multicolored base that
 has small snake on it, black, green, and
 red costume, brown figure, green turban with black and red, brown and red

	Date	Price Range	

basket, yellow and brown pipe, height 4″, designer unknown .... 1929–1938 — 1400.00 — 1650.00

SOIREE
HN 2312
☐White gown with gold design at hemline, green overskirt, holding small white fan in one hand, height 7½″, designer M. Davies .... 1967–1984 — 130.00 — 175.00

SOLITUDE
HN 2810
☐Figure seated on brown and yellow chaise lounge, white gown mottled yellow, green, blue halfway up skirt, multicolored pillow, holding open book on pillow, height 5½″, designer M. Davies .... 1977–1983 — 150.00 — 200.00

SONG OF THE SEA
HN 2729
☐Depicts a weather-beaten man with blue turtleneck sweater, denim trousers, black boots with white socks. Man seated on fishbasket, holding shell in his hand. Boy at his feet has green short trousers, light blue shirt, height 7¼″, designer W. K. Harper .... 1983– — 230.00

SONIA
HN 1692
☐Figure seated on arm of brown and green chair, white tiered gown with red bodice and sleeves, small red hat with white trim, red shoes, small black purse and flowers on chair, height 6¼″, designer L. Harradine .... 1935–1949 — 1100.00 — 1200.00
HN 1738
☐Green dress, height 6½″, designer L. Harradine .... 1935–1949 — 1200.00 — 1500.00

SONNY
HN 1313
☐Seated barefoot figure in red costume, top has white dots, height 3½″, designer L. Harradine .... 1929–1938 — 1100.00 — 1200.00

Southern Belle, HN 2229, 225.00

	Date	Price Range	
HN 1314			
☐ Blue costume, height 3½″, designer L. Harradine	1929–1938	**1100.00**	**1200.00**
SOPHIE (Kate Greenaway)			
HN 2833			
☐ Small figure on white base, mauve coat with white fur trim, white fur muff, large light red bonnet, holding single flower, height 6″, designer M. Davies	1977–1987	**100.00**	
SOUTHERN BELLE			
HN 2229			
☐ Shaded yellow gown, red overskirt with blue bow, trim on sleeves, blue shoes, height 7½″, designer M. Davies	1958–	**275.00**	
HN 2425			
☐ Light blue blouse and pink bodice over a white petticoat with slight shading of			

	Date	Price Range	
pink, white bodice with pink ribbons, gold brooch accents gown, height 7½" designer M. Davies	1984–	215.00	

SPANISH LADY
HN 1262
☐ Brown base, patterned purple gown with large red rose design, patterned purple bodice with small red design, brown, blue and black mantilla, dark gray necklace, height 8½", designer L. Harradine ....

| | 1927–1938 | 1000.00 | 1250.00 |

HN 1290
☐ Yellow dress, height 8¼", designer L. Harradine ....

| | 1928–1939 | 1000.00 | 1250.00 |

HN 1293
☐ Patterned purple skirt with large yellow rose design, small red design bodice, brown and blue mantilla, green necklace, height 8¼", designer L. Harradine ....

| | 1928–1938 | 1000.00 | 1250.00 |

HN 1294
☐ Tiered red gown, brown, green and black mantilla, white necklace, light brown base, height 8¼", designer L. Harradine ....

| | 1928–1938 | 1000.00 | 1250.00 |

HN 1309
☐ HN 1262, black bodice, multicolored skirt, height 8¼", designer L. Harradine ....

| | 1929–1938 | 1000.00 | 1250.00 |

SPIRIT OF THE WIND
☐ Entire figure and base is green, beginning at the head a very light green, lower torso and gown a darker green, base and flowers of another green, height unknown, designer R. Garbe ..

| | 1937–1938 | 3500.00 | 4000.00 |

SPOOK, A
HN 50
☐ Figure wrapped entirely in blue robe, black cap, height 7", designer H. Tittensor ....

| | 1916–1938 | 1350.00 | 1600.00 |

HN 51
☐ Green robe with red cap, height 7", designer H. Tittensor ... .

| | 1916–1938 | 1350.00 | 1600.00 |

HN 51A
☐ Black cap, height 7", designer H. Tittensor ....

| | 1916–1938 | 1350.00 | 1600.00 |

	Date	Price Range	

HN 51B

☐ Blue cloak, height 7″, designer H. Tittensor 1916–1938   1350.00   1600.00

HN 58

☐ Color not recorded, height 7″, designer H. Tittensor 1916–1938   1350.00   1600.00

HN 512

☐ Spotted blue costume, height 7″, designer H. Tittensor 1921–1938   1350.00   1600.00

HN 625

☐ Yellow robe, height 7″, designer H. Tittensor 1924–1938   1350.00   1600.00

HN 1218

☐ Multicolored costume, blue cap, height 7″, designer H. Tittensor 1926–1938   1350.00   1600.00

SPOOKS

HN 88

☐ Two figures wrapped in shaded blue robes, dark blue caps, height 7″, designer H. Tittensor 1918–1936   2000.00   2500.00

HN 89

☐ Red caps, height 7″, designer H. Tittensor 1918–1936   2000.00   2500.00

HN 372

☐ Patterned green costume, brown caps, height 7″, designer H. Tittensor 1920–1936   2000.00   2500.00

SPRING

HN 312

☐ Blue and gray base, long narrow yellow gown, holds small bird in hands (1st version), height 7½″, designer unknown 1918–1938   1500.00   1800.00

HN 472

☐ Patterned robes (1st version), height 7½″, designer unknown 1921–1938   1600.00   1900.00

HN 1827

☐ White base, barefooted figure in very light yellow robe with gold flowers held with both hands (2nd version), height 21″, designer R. Garbe 1937–1949   2500.00   3000.00

HN 2085

☐ Cream and green base, shaded blue and red gown, dark blue bodice, white blouse, tiny blue and red cap, small white lamb on base (3rd version), height 7¾″, designer M. Davies 1952–1959   300.00   400.00

	Date	Price Range	

SPRING FLOWERS
HN 1807
☐ Light green gown, shaded blue over-skirt, white apron and white collar, blue bonnet with green lining and dark ribbons, holding flower in one hand and small basket of flowers in other arm, light colored basket of flowers on light colored base, height 7¼", designer L. Harradine 1937–1959   300.00   350.00

HN 1945
☐ Green skirt, pink overskirt, height 7¼", designer L. Harradine 1940–1949   800.00   1000.00

SPRING MORNING
HN 1922
☐ Light blue gown, long pink coat, blue and green scarf, bonnet has white feather and dark blue ribbons, height 7½", designer L. Harradine 1940–1973   175.00   225.00

HN 1923
☐ Green gown, long red coat, green and yellow scarf, bonnet blue with white feather and darker blue ribbons, height 7½", designer L. Harradine 1940–1949   650.00   750.00

SPRINGTIME
HN 1971
☐ Small girl figure in blue gown, peach coat, green bonnet, hanging head, green ribbons, holding single flower in hand, height 6", designer L. Harradine 1941–1949   1200.00   1300.00

SQUIRE, The
HN 1814
☐ Figure seated on blue and white horse mounted on black base, red jacket, white trousers, black boots, black hat, earthenware, height 9¾", designer unknown 1937–1949   2500.00   3000.00

ST. GEORGE
HN 385
☐ HN 386, blue-green multicolored costume (1st version), height 16", designer S. Thorogood 1920–1938   4500.00   5000.00

HN 386
☐ Dark colored horse and base, cloth over

St. George, HN 2067, 2500.00–3000.00

	Date	Price Range	

horse is white with dark blue, yellow and red designs, blue and gray armor, white shield with blue design, dark haired figure (1st version), height 16″, designer S. Thorogood 1920–1938 **4500.00** **5000.00**

HN 1800

☐ White horse with white robe, green overlay with crosses as a design. Knight has blue and gray armor, dark hair, red robe with gold lion and purple border (1st version), height 16″, designer S. Thorogood 1934–1950 **3000.00** **3500.00**

HN 2051

☐ Yellow and green base, white horse with gold straps, figure has green and blue armor with white overskirt with

	Date	Price Range	

red cross, green dragon also on base (2nd version), height 7½", designer M. Davies 1950–1985 400.00 500.00

HN 2067

☐ Multicolored base, light colored horse with cloth of purple with gold lions and red lining, figure has gray and blue armor with shield of white with red stripes, figure has blonde hair (1st version), height 15¾", designer S. Thorogood 1950–1976 2500.00 3000.00

HN 2856, See Prestige Figures.

STAYED AT HOME
HN 2207

☐ Green gown with darker green collar, white apron, holding white pig in arms, green head ribbon, height 5", designer M. Davies 1958–1969 150.00 200.00

STEPHANIE
HN 2807

☐ Yellow gown with brown trim near hemline, white trim on sleeves, height 7¼", designer M. Davies 1977–1882 135.00 175.00

HN 2811

☐ Crimson red and off-white gown, dark brown hair, height 7½", designer M. Davies 1983– 230.00

STIGGINS
HN 536

☐ A character of Dicken's "Pickwick Papers," 3¾", designer L. Harradine .. 1922– 65.00 85.00

☐ **M-50** Renumbered as a miniature, height 4", designer L. Harradine 1932–1983 55.00 75.00

STITCH IN TIME, A
HN 2352

☐ Character figure seated in brown rocking chair, with brown and red footstool, dark gray gown, brown shawl, green suit for child on lap, colored threads on chair arm, height 6¼", designer M. Nicoll 1966–1980 125.00 175.00

STOP PRESS
HN 2683

☐ Character figure seated on wooden box, blue trousers, brown coat, beige vest,

	Date	Price Range

light green hat with dark band, reading newspaper and eating roll, newspapers on stand next to figure, height 7½", designer M. Nicoll 1977–1980 125.00 175.00

SUITOR, The
HN 2132
☐ Two figures, male kneeling has beige trousers, dark brown coat, yellow vest, white cravat, female has cream colored gown with overskirt of shaded blues, height 7¼", designer M. Davies 1962–1971 375.00 450.00

SUMMER
HN 313
☐ Long light green slender gown, bouquet of flowers in left arm, on blue and gray base (1st version), height 7½", designer unknown 1918–1938 1650.00 1800.00
HN 473
☐ Patterned gown (1st version), height 7½", designer unknown 1921–1938 1650.00 1900.00
HN 2086
☐ Green and yellow base with brown wooden fence, red gown with blue designs, blue waistband, blue shoes, white scarf (2nd version), height 7¼", designer M. Davies 1952–1959 400.00 500.00

SUMMER'S DAY
HN 2181
☐ Seated figure on white wicker trunk, white gown with gold designs, white bonnet with gold trim beside trunk, height 5¾", designer M. Davies 1957–1962 375.00 450.00

SUNDAY BEST
HN 2206
☐ Yellow gown with large white and red floral design in skirt, yellow bonnet with red ribbons and flowers, height 7½", designer M. Davies 1979–1984 200.00 300.00
HN 2698
☐ This figure re-introduced in a peach gown with green bonnet decorated with pink roses, height 7½", designer M. Davies 1985– 160.00

	Date	Price Range	

SUNDAY MORNING
HN 2184

☐ Red cloak, dark red yoke with yellow bow trim and sleeves, bonnet with dark red ribbons, and black and white feather, height 7½″, designer M. Davies 1963–1969   265.00   325.00

SUNSHINE GIRL
HN 1344

☐ Green and yellow base with red and white towel, figure seated on towel wears green and black bathing suit, green bathing cap with black dots, black and red open parasol, height 5″, designer L. Harradine 1929–1938   1750.00   2000.00

HN 1348

☐ Black and orange costume, height 5″, designer L. Harradine 1929–1938   1750.00   2000.00

SUSAN
HN 2056

☐ Blue skirt, darker blue blouse with white collar, light red apron with small blue design, little white cap, height 7″, designer L. Harradine 1950–1959   325.00   400.00

HN 2952

☐ Young lady with blonde hair, gold gown with pale blue overdress, black jacket with blue belt, holding a white kitten aloft (2nd version), height 8½″, designer P. Parsons 1982–   275.00

HN 3050

☐ New colorway. Gown is bright orange with shades of blue, lemon, and pink. Bodice is bright red, height 8½″, designer P. Parsons 1986–   215.00

SUSANNA
HN 1233

☐ White nude figure on red colored base, long red robe hanging down back from hands, has white designs, height 6½″, designer L. Harradine 1927–1938   1100.00   1200.00

HN 1288

☐ Yellow and green base, white nude figure with red and blue robe hanging down back, height 6″, designer L. Harradine 1928–1938   1100.00   1200.00

Susan, HN 2056, 325.00–400.00

	Date	Price Range	

HN 1299

☐HN 1233, black, red and blue robe,
height 6″, designer L. Harradine 1928–1938 1100.00 1200.00

SUZETTE
HN 1487

☐Light green gown with patterned red
overgown, solid blue and red bodice,
green and blue headcap with green ribbons, blue and white apron, height
7½″, designer L. Harradine 1931–1950 300.00 350.00

HN 1577

☐Light red gown with patterned blue
overgown, blue and red bodice, white
apron, light red headcap with red

	Date	Price Range	

ribbons, height 7½″, designer L. Harradine 1933–1949 650.00 750.00

HN 1585

☐ HN 1487, green and yellow dress, height 7½″, designer L. Harradine ... 1933–1938 650.00 750.00

HN 1696

☐ Blue gown with small red floral designs, blue shoes, small blue headcap with dark blue ribbons, height 7½″, designer L. Harradine 1935–1949 650.00 750.00

HN 2026

☐ HN 1487, minor color differences, height 7¼″, designer L. Harradine ... 1949–1959 250.00 350.00

SWEET ANNE
HN 1318

☐ Shaded blue and green skirt, dark blue jacket with black trim, dark blue bonnet with dark red ribbons, height 7½″, designer L. Harradine 1929–1949 175.00 250.00

HN 1330

☐ Shaded red skirt, shaded blue and green jacket, red bonnet and ribbons, height 7¼″, designer L. Harradine 1929–1949 275.00 375.00

HN 1331

☐ Shaded yellow and blue skirt, red jacket with purple trim, red bonnet with purple ribbons, height 7¼″, designer L. Harradine 1929–1949 275.00 350.00

HN 1453

☐ Light green skirt, shaded blue jacket with darker blue trim, blue bonnet with purple ribbons, height 7″, designer L. Harradine 1931–1949 325.00 375.00

HN 1496

☐ Red skirt with patterned red jacket, shaded red and blue bonnet and ribbons, height 7″, designer L. Harradine 1932–1967 200.00 275.00

HN 1631

☐ HN 1318, green bonnet, red jacket, pink and yellow skirt, height 7″, designer L. Harradine 1934–1938 300.00 400.00

HN 1701

☐ Floral yellow and pink dress, blue trim, height 7″, designer L. Harradine 1935–1938 300.00 400.00

☐ **M-5** Made as a miniature, cream gown

	Date	Price Range	

with red shading, shaded red and blue jacket, bonnet same with dark ribbons, height 4″, designer L. Harradine 1932–1945 250.00 300.00

☐ **M-6** Light blue designed gown, dark blue jacket and bonnet, height 4″, designer L. Harradine 1932–1945 225.00 300.00

☐ **M-27** Cream gown with shaded blues, red jacket with blue trim, red bonnet with blue ribbons, height 4″, designer L. Harradine 1932–1945 250.00 300.00

SWEET AND FAIR
HN 1864
☐ HN 1865, blue shawl with pink dress, height 7½″, designer L. Harradine ... 1938–1949 900.00 1200.00

HN 1865
☐ Figure is seated on brown chair, light green skirt, dark green bodice, sleeves have blue trim, white shawl draped on chair back with multicolored flowers, open book in hand, height 7¼″, designer L. Harradine 1938–1949 900.00 1200.00

SWEET AND TWENTY
HN 1298
☐ Figure seated on small shaded blue couch, red gown, black bonnet with multicolored ribbons, holding open fan, height 5¾″, designer L. Harradine ... 1928–1969 275.00 325.00

HN 1360
☐ Blue couch, shaded red and blue gown, dark blue bonnet with shaded red and blue ribbons, height 6″, designer L. Harradine 1929–1938 575.00 750.00

HN 1437
☐ HN 1298, dark sofa, shaded red dress, height 6″, designer L. Harradine 1930–1938 575.00 750.00

HN 1438
☐ Mottled multicolored dress, height 6″, designer L. Harradine 1930–1938 575.00 750.00

HN 1549
☐ Light multicolored couch, gown is dark multicolored in skirt and lighter at waist and bodice, light multicolored bonnet, height 6″, designer L. Harradine 1933–1949 600.00 850.00

HN 1563
☐ HN 1298, black sofa, pale pink dress, height 6″, designer L. Harradine 1933–1938 600.00 850.00

Sweet and Twenty, HN 1298, 275.00–325.00

	Date	Price Range	
HN 1589			
☐ Small figure, light green couch, red and blue gown, blue and red bonnet with blue ribbon, height 6″, designer L. Harradine	1933–1949	250.00	325.00
HN 1610			
☐ Small figure, blue and green couch, red gown, black bonnet with yellow ribbon, height 3½″, designer L. Harradine	1933–1938	200.00	300.00
HN 1649			
☐ HN 1298, orange couch, white gown with small red designs, green bodice, green bonnet with shaded red ribbons, height 6″, designer L. Harradine	1934–1949	575.00	750.00

SWEET APRIL
HN 2215
☐ Light red gown with blue and red

	Date	Price Range	

collar, blue hat with green bow on top, height 7¼″, designer L. Harradine ... 1965–1969 **325.00** **400.00**

SWEET DREAMS
HN 2380
☐ Character figure seated in cream colored chair with green skirt, head on brown pillow, foot on purple stool, green gown with white bibbed apron with red design, green shoes, holding small child on lap in blue and red sleeper, height 5″, designer M. Davies 1971– **195.00**

SWEETING
HN 1935
☐ Red and shaded blue gown, blue bow in hair, height 6″, designer L. Harradine 1940–1973 **125.00** **175.00**
HN 1938
☐ Multicolored skirt, blue bodice, red bow in hair, height 6″, designer L. Harradine 1940–1949 **600.00** **675.00**

SWEET LAVENDER
HN 1373
☐ Black base, cream skirt with red stripes, green blouse, black, red and light green shawl, green hat with black feather and trim, brown basket, small baby in arm is dressed in red, red necklace, lavender in basket, height 9″, designer L. Harradine 1930–1949 **375.00** **475.00**

SWEET MAID
HN 1504
☐ Blue gown, dark blue cape, shaded red and blue bonnet with red ribbons, small round red purse, height 8″, designer L. Harradine 1932–1938 **1200.00** **1500.00**
HN 1505
☐ Shaded red and blue gown, dark red and blue cape, red bonnet with green ribbons, small green purse (1st version), height 8″, designer L. Harradine 1932–1938 **1200.00** **1500.00**
HN 2092
☐ Light lavender gown, white headdress with white veil with small design and

Sweet Maid, HN 2092, 500.00–550.00

	Date	Price Range	
purple ribbons, holding small round bouquet of flowers in hands, height 7″, designer L. Harradine	1952–1955	500.00	550.00

SWEET SEVENTEEN
HN 2734
☐ White gown with narrow gold trim, height 7 ½″, designer D.V. Tootle .... | 1975– | 250.00 |

SWEET SIXTEEN
HN 2231
☐ White base, light blue skirt, white blouse with small black design, black belt, black shoes, red bow in blonde hair, height 7 ¼″, designer M. Davies | 1958–1965 | 175.00 | 225.00 |

SWEET SUZY
HN 1918
☐ Light green gown, light red overdress with dark green trim, black bonnet with

The Swimmer, HN 1270, 1700.00–1900.00

	Date	Price Range	
green ribbon trim, height 6½″, designer L. Harradine	1939–1949	800.00	950.00

SWIMMER, The
HN 1270
☐ Black base, black swimsuit with red, green, and purple spots, red bathing shoes with spots, red robe with black design, height 7¼″, designer L. Harradine ....

	Date	Price Range	
	1928–1938	1700.00	1900.00

HN 1326
☐ Lilac and orange costume, height 7½″, designer L. Harradine ....

| | 1929–1938 | 1700.00 | 1900.00 |

HN 1329
☐ Pink costume, height 7½″, designer L. Harradine ....

| | 1929–1938 | 1700.00 | 1900.00 |

The Tailor, HN 2174, 500.00–600.00

	Date	Price Range	

SYLVIA
HN 1478
☐ Mottled orange and brown gown, blue, gray, and brown jacket, yellow bonnet with brown feather, shaded red and cream scarf, small round orange and brown purse, height 10½″, designer L. Harradine 1931–1938 600.00 800.00

SYMPHONY
HN 2287
☐ Light green skirt, brown bodice with light green bow, holding brown, blue and gray mandolin type instrument on lap, height 5¼″, designer D.B. Lovegrove 1961–1965 300.00 350.00

TAILOR
HN 2174
☐ Seated character figure, red trousers, cream shirt, orange vest, purple coat

	Date	Price Range	

with orange buttons, bolts of different colored cloth at side, height 5″, designer M. Nicoll 1956–1959   500.00   600.00

TAKING THINGS EASY
HN 2677
☐ Male figure seated in brown wicker chair, white trousers and shoes, blue coat, gray hat with light trim, newspapers on lap, also black rimmed glasses, height 6¾″, designer M. Nicoll 1975–1987   225.00   275.00

HN 2680
☐ New colorway of this figure. Gentleman asleep is now dressed in a creamy white suit with pale blue sweater, white hat, newspaper on lap. Sitting in wicker chair, height 7½″, designer M. Nicoll   1987–   215.00

TALL STORY
HN 2248
☐ Character figure seated on wooden bench, dark gray trousers, darker gray jacket, black cap with yellow trim, black boots with white cuff, tackle box beside bench, height 6½″, designer M. Nicoll 1968–1975   185.00   225.00

TEATIME
HN 2255
☐ Brown gown with dark reddish-brown jacket, beige blouse, holding white teapot and cup and saucer with blue design, height 7¼″, designer M. Nicoll   1972–   230.00

TEENAGER
HN 2203
☐ Slender white dress with red cape, height 7¼″, designer M. Davies 1957–1962   225.00   275.00

TERESA
HN 1682
☐ Lady seated on brown and multicolor loveseat, red gown with red shoes and small white cap with green ribbon, the base is black with small brown table with flowers on table and base, height 5¾″, designer L. Harradine 1935–1949   1000.00   1200.00

	Date	Price Range	

HN 1683

☐ Pale blue dress, height 5¾", designer
L. Harradine 1935–1938   1400.00   1600.00

TESS (Kate Greenaway)
HN 2865

☐ Small figure on white base, green gown
with red floral trim at hemline, red
waistband and single red flower in
hand, height 5¾", designer M. Davies   1978–1983   95.00   125.00

TETE-A-TETE
HN 798

☐ HN 799, lady's gown is pink with
shades of very light blue and white
stripes, blue and red bows on bodice.
Male costume is brownish-orange with
a white and green cravat, black hat with
orange design, purple and yellow designed couch with brown, bright blue
pillow with dark red and gold design,
all on black base (1st version), height
5¾", designer L. Harradine 1926–1938   950.00   1200.00

HN 799

☐ Two figures on black base, brown
couch; lady's gown is lavender with red
pattern, purple overskirt; male has costume of red with white, black hat with
red trim (1st version), height 5¾", de-
signer L. Harradine 1926–1938   950.00   1200.00

HN 1236

☐ Color and design same but in miniature size (2nd version), height 3", de-
signer C.J. Noke 1927–1938   900.00   1300.00

HN 1237

☐ Pink dress (2nd version), height 3",
designer C.J. Noke 1927–1938   900.00   1300.00

THANKS DOC
HN 2731

☐ Brown trousers, long white coat, white
shirt, dark tie, brown and white dog
sitting on brown stand, white towel on
side, height 8¾", designer W.K.
Harper 1975–   295.00

THANK YOU
HN 2732

☐ Old lady standing at cottage gate

Thanksgiving, HN 2446, 225.00–275.00

	Date	Price Range	
waving goodbye to someone who has given her a bouquet of bluebells. Gray hair, long brown skirt, white blouse with pink flowers, wearing cameo brooch, height 8¼″, designer W.K. Harper	1983–1986	150.00	175.00

THANKSGIVING
HN 2446
☐ Light brown base, character figure in blue overalls, red shirt, light colored hat, turkey also on base, matte finish, height 8″, designer M. Nicoll .... | 1972–1976 | **225.00** | **275.00** |

THIS LITTLE PIG
HN 1793
☐ Small seated figure wrapped completely in red robe with small design of blue, height 4″, designer L. Harradine ..... | 1936– | **110.00** | |

	Date	Price Range	

HN 1794

☐ Small figure wrapped completely in blue with green robe, height 4″, designer L. Harradine 1936–1949 450.00 550.00

HN 2125

☐ Same as HN 1793 except it is an all white figure, height 4″, designer L. Harradine 1985– 60.00

TIBETIAN LADY
HN 582

☐ Formal name is "Grossmith's 'Tsang lhang' Perfume of Tibet, see that classification, height 11½″, designer unknown .... 1923– Unknown 700.00 800.00

TILDY
HN 1576

☐ Seated figure in tiered shaded colored gown, red bodice trimmed with blue bows, shaded blue bonnet with darker blue ribbons, light blue shoes, white pantalettes, height 5″, designer L. Harradine 1933–1938 850.00 950.00

HN 1859

☐ No details of color available, height 5½″, designer L. Harradine 1938–1949 950.00 1100.00

TINKLE BELL
HN 1677

☐ Small figure in shaded red gown with darker red bodice, small white cap with red ribbons, small light colored basket on one arm, height 4¾″, designer L. Harradine 1935–1988 110.00

TINSMITH
HN 2146

☐ Character figure seated, brown trousers, mottled brown stockings, light brown shirt, green vest, white cravat, working on blue and gray material, tools in front of green and gray stump, height 6½″, designer M. Nicoll 1962–1967 500.00 575.00

TINY TIM
HN 539

☐ A character from Dickens' "Christmas Carol," height 3½″, designer L. Harradine 1922– 65.00 85.00

Toinette, HN 1940, 1450.00–1750.00

	Date	Price Range	
☐ **M-56** Renumbered as a miniature, height 3¾″, designer L. Harradine ...	1932–1983	55.00	75.00

TO BED
HN 1805
☐ Small figure on light blue colored base, pulling light green shirt over head, light green shorts, barefooted, height 6″, designer L. Harradine 1937–1959   150.00   200.00

HN 1806
☐ Green base, light blue and red shirt and shorts, height 6″, designer L. Harradine 1937–1949   350.00   400.00

TOINETTE
HN 1940
☐ Full tiered red gown with darker red jacket, black stole trimmed with white fur, green bonnet, open parasol in one

	Date	Price Range	

hand, flowers in other, height 6¾",
designer L. Harradine 1940–1949 **1450.00** **1750.00**

TOM (Kate Greenaway)
HN 2864
☐ Small male figure on white base, blue
trousers, cream colored shirt with red
designs and white collar, holding single
flower in one hand and white and yellow toy horse with other hand, height
5¾", designer M. Davies 1978–1981 **95.00** **110.00**

TONY WELLER
HN 346
☐ HN 684, green coat, blue rug, brown
base (1st version), height 10½", de-
signer C.J. Noke 1919–1938 **1800.00** **2000.00**
HN 368
☐ Blue coat, brown blanket (1st version),
height 10½", designer C.J. Noke 1920–1938 **1800.00** **2000.00**
HN 544
☐ Miniature figure, green coat, dark
brown suit, red vest, white shirt, yellow
cravat with dark spots, black hat (2nd
version), height 3½", designer L. Har-
radine 1922– **65.00** **85.00**
☐ M-47 Renumbered as a miniature,
height 4", designer L. Harradine 1932–1983 **55.00** **75.00**
HN 684
☐ Black base, long green coat, orange un-
dercoat with black buttons, red rug with
black stripes, black hat, orange scarf
with black dots (1st version), height
10½", designer L. Harradine 1924–1938 **1650.00** **1800.00**

TOOTLES
HN 1680
☐ Small figure, shaded red skirt with blue
stripes, red bodice, green apron with
green stripes, white bonnet with green
ribbons, height 4¾", designer L. Har-
radine 1935–1975 **75.00** **125.00**

TOP O' THE HILL
HN 1833
☐ Green skirt, shaded blue jacket, dark
blue large brim hat, blue and green
scarf with red designs, height 7", de-
signer L. Harradine 1937–1971 **200.00** **250.00**

The Town Crier, HN 2119, 250.00–325.00

	Date	Price Range	
HN 1834			
☐ Red gown, red hat with light green lining, mottled yellow and green scarf, height 7″, designer L. Harradine	1937–	230.00	
HN 1849			
☐ Dark pink gown, black hat with blue ribbon and lining, striped red and blue scarf, height 7¼″, designer L. Harradine	1938–1975	200.00	250.00

TOWN CRIER
HN 2119
☐ Brown base, yellow trousers, red coat

	Date	Price Range	

trimmed in yellow, black cloak with red coloring, green patterned vest, black hat trimmed in yellow, black boots with red tops, ringing bell and holding white papers, height 8½", designer M. Davies 1953–1976 250.00 325.00

TOYMAKER, The
HN 2250
☐ Character figure seated in dark gray rocker holding red engine, brown trousers, blue and green shirt, gray vest, green shoes, tools and toys at sides of rocker, height 6", designer M. Nicoll 1959–1973 375.00 450.00

TOYS
HN 1316
☐ Green skirt, white apron with blue stripes, red jacket, yellow scarf with green dots and red fringe, black hat with green feathers, holding small black tray with three male dolls, height unknown, designer L. Harradine 1929–1938 4000.00 4500.00

TREASURE ISLAND
HN 2243
☐ Small barefooted boy seated on white base, purple shorts, light brown shirt, holding open book on lap, book shows printing, height 4¾", designer M. Davies 1962–1975 150.00 200.00

TROTTY VECK
Issued only as a miniature.
☐ M-91 Orange vest, white apron, brown hat, black coat and stand, height 4¼", designer L. Harradine 1949–1985 55.00 75.00

TULIPS
HN 466
☐ HN 747, green dress, height 9½", designer unknown 1921–1938 1700.00 1900.00
HN 488
☐ Ivory dress, height 9½", designer unknown 1921–1938 1700.00 1900.00
HN 672
☐ Green shawl and cream dress, height 9½", designer unknown 1924–1938 1750.00 2000.00
HN 747
☐ Purple dress with small black designs,

	Date	Price Range	

green shawl with red thin stripes, holding bouquet of flowers in one hand, height 9½″, designer unknown 1925–1938   1750.00   2000.00

HN 1334
□ Pink and blue shawl and green dress, height 9½″, designer unknown 1929–1938   1750.00   2000.00

TUPPENCE A BAG
HN 2320
□ Seated character figure on blue and green bricks, basket beside figure, green gown, blue shawl, black brimmed hat, one bird on shoulder and one on basket handle, height 5½″, designer M. Nicoll 1968–   230.00

TWILIGHT
HN 2256
□ Character figure seated in brown rocker with purple pad and purple footstool, knitting with black kitten playing with yarn, dark green gown, black shawl, small white headcap, height 5″, designer M. Nicoll 1971–1976   125.00   175.00

TWO-A-PENNY
HN 1359
□ Green and yellow shaded skirt, red jacket with black collar and buttons, yellow shawl with green stripes, black hat with green and black feathers, white apron, holding black tray with green and black objects, height 8¼″, designer L. Harradine 1929–1938   2000.00   2500.00

UNCLE NED
HN 2094
□ Character figure seated in brown and beige chair, green trousers, long brown coat and leggings, yellow and green scarf, holding blue mug, black and white dog sitting at feet, height 6¾″, designer H. Fenton 1952–1965   375.00   475.00

UNDER THE GOOSEBERRY BUSH
HN 49
□ Small nude child lying on bed of flowers with black, green and brown bush

Uncle Ned, HN 2094, 375.00–475.00

	Date	Price Range	
over figure, height 3½″, designer C.J. Noke	1916–1938	1500.00	2000.00

'UPON HER CHEEKS SHE WEPT'

HN 59

☐ Figure of young girl, shaded blue dress, green and white checkered headband, barefooted, standing on light colored base which has flowers, printing on front of base, height 9″, designer L. Perugini 1916–1938 2000.00 2400.00

HN 511

☐ Lilac dress with large spots, height 9″, designer L. Perugini 1921–1938 2000.00 2400.00

	Date	Price Range	

HN 522
☐ Lilac dress with small spots, height 9″,
designer L. Perugini .... | 1921–1938 | **2000.00** | **2400.00**

URIAH HEEP
HN 545
☐ A character from Dickens' "David
Copperfield" (1st version), height 4″,
designer L. Harradine .... | 1922– | **65.00** | **85.00**
☐ **M-45** Renumbered as a miniature,
height 4″, designer L. Harradine ..... | 1932–1983 | **55.00** | **65.00**
HN 554
☐ Black base, complete black suit with
white cravat, a stack of books also on
base, red hair (2nd version), height
7¼″, designer L. Harradine .... | 1923–1939 | **300.00** | **400.00**
HN 1892
☐ Very minor color changes (2nd ver-
sion), height 7″, designer L. Harra-
dine .... | 1938–1952 | **275.00** | **325.00**
HN 2101
☐ Green base, green trousers, black coat,
yellow vest, white shirt, white and blue
scarf with blue dots, red hair, books on
base are browns and blacks (3rd version), height 7½″, designer L. Harra-
dine .... | 1952–1967 | **275.00** | **325.00**

VALERIE
HN 2107
☐ Small figure, light red gown with white
apron, darker red overskirt, white
headcap with blue ribbons, holding single yellow flower with green leaves,
height 4¾″, designer M. Davies ...... | 1953– | **140.00** |

VANESSA
HN 1836
☐ Green skirt, dark blue bodice with
green and white trim, green bonnet
with red ribbons, height 7½″, designer
L. Harradine .... | 1938–1949 | **775.00** | **900.00**
HN 1838
☐ Red skirt with green bodice with red
and white trim, green bonnet with red
lining, height 7½″, designer L. Har-
radine .... | 1938–1949 | **775.00** | **900.00**

	Date	Price Range	

VANITY
HN 2475
☐ Small figure, red gown with white waistband, white bow in dark hair, holding small yellow mirror, height 5¼″, designer M. Davies 1973– 140.00

VENETA
HN 2722
☐ White gown with yellow and black design, green overdress, holding small white bird in hands, height 8″, designer W.K. Harper 1974–1980 125.00 150.00

VERA
HN 1729
☐ Head and shoulders only on cream colored base, pink dress, height 4¼″, designer L. Harradine 1935–1938 1200.00 1600.00
HN 1730
☐ Green dress, height 4¼″, designer L. Harradine 1935–1938 1200.00 1600.00

VERENA
HN 1835
☐ Green gown, orange overdress with yellow floral design, white ruffles on sleeves, green hat with white and black feathers, height 8¼″, designer L. Harradine 1938–1949 1200.00 1500.00
HN 1854
☐ Green dress, height 8¼″, designer L. Harradine 1938–1949 1200.00 1500.00

VERONICA
HN 1517
☐ Tiered gown of shaded red with green ribbon trim, dark red bodice with green ribbon trim, large shaded blue and red brim hat with feathers of green, white and shaded red (1st version), height 8″, designer L. Harradine 1932–1951 350.00 400.00
HN 1519
☐ Shaded blue and cream gown, shaded red hat with cream and red feathers (1st version), height 8″, designer L. Harradine 1932–1938 550.00 750.00
HN 1650
☐ HN 1517, green dress (1st version), height 8″, designer L. Harradine 1934–1949 550.00 750.00

	Date	Price Range	

HN 1915

☐ Smaller version with shaded red gown and green ribbon trim, dark red bodice with blue ribbon trim, green hat with blue ribbon and blue and white feathers (2nd version), height 5¾", designer L. Harradine 1939–1949   400.00   450.00

☐ **M-64** Made as a miniature, shaded red gown, dark red bodice with green ribbons, blue hat, height 4¼", designer L. Harradine 1934–1949   475.00   600.00

☐ **M-70** Green gown, height 4¼", designer L. Harradine 1936–1949   475.00   600.00

HN 1943

☐ Pink dress and blue hat (1st version), height 8", designer L. Harradine 1940–1949   550.00   700.00

VICTORIA
HN 2471

☐ Large full red gown with white and green flower design, gown trimmed in white, holding open white fan, height 6½", designer M. Davies 1973–   210.00

VICTORIAN LADY, A
HN 726

☐ Tiered patterned purple, cream, red and black gown, very dark plain color shawl, black bonnet with light lining and red ribbons and red feather trim, height 7½", designer L. Harradine ... 1925–1938   500.00   700.00

HN 727

☐ Shaded yellow gown, red shawl, black bonnet with light red lining and red feather with red ribbons, height 7½", designer L. Harradine 1925–1938   325.00   425.00

HN 728

☐ Shaded red gown, shaded blue and red shawl, blue and red bonnet with feather and ribbons to match, height 7¾", designer L. Harradine 1925–1952   325.00   425.00

HN 736

☐ Purple gown with patterned white trim, red shawl, black bonnet with red feather and ribbons, height 7¾", designer L. Harradine 1925–1938   600.00   800.00

	Date	Price Range	

HN 739
☐ HN 726, mottled red, blue and yellow skirt, yellow scarf, height 7¾", designer L. Harradine 1925–1938 650.00 750.00

HN 740
☐ Shaded red gown, red shawl with black, red and blue spots, black bonnet with red feather and ribbons, height 7¾", designer L. Harradine 1925–1938 600.00 800.00

HN 742
☐ HN 726, black with white checkered shawl, white dress with blue spots, height 7¾", designer L. Harradine ... 1925–1938 500.00 700.00

HN 745
☐ Patterned dress with pink roses, height 7¾", designer L. Harradine 1925–1938 600.00 775.00

HN 1208
☐ Cream and green gown, shaded dark red shawl, dark bonnet with red feather and dark ribbons, height 7¾", designer L. Harradine 1926–1938 600.00 800.00

HN 1258
☐ HN 726, mottled purple shawl, mottled blue dress, height 7¾", designer L. Harradine 1927–1938 600.00 800.00

HN 1276
☐ Cream and green gown with large red spots, solid red bodice, purple shawl, dark bonnet with red feather and red ribbons, height 7½", designer L. Harradine 1928–1938 650.00 850.00

HN 1277
☐ HN 726, red shawl, yellow and blue tiered dress, height 7¾", designer L. Harradine 1928–1938 700.00 900.00

HN 1345
☐ Shaded green and blue gown, shaded lavender and red shawl, dark bonnet with red feather and ribbons, height 7¾", designer L. Harradine 1929–1949 300.00 400.00

HN 1452
☐ HN 726, green dress and shawl, height 7¾", designer L. Harradine 1931–1949 300.00 400.00

HN 1529
☐ Shaded green and red gown, shaded green shawl, light colored bonnet with shaded red ribbons and feather, height 7¾", designer L. Harradine 1932–1938 600.00 800.00
☐ **M-1** Made as a miniature, red and

The Viking, HN 2375, 325.00–375.00

	Date	Price Range	
cream gown, green shawl, blue and red bonnet with feather and ribbons to match, height 3¾″, designer L. Harradine	1932–1945	**275.00**	**350.00**
☐ **M-2** Blue gown, purple shawl, green bonnet with red feather and ribbons, height 3¾″, designer L. Harradine ...	1932–1945	**275.00**	**350.00**
☐ **M-25** Shaded red gown, shaded blue and red shawl, shaded red and blue bonnet with dark ribbons and feather, height 3¾″, designer L. Harradine ...	1932–1945	**275.00**	**350.00**

VIKING, The
HN 2375
☐ Beige and light blue base, costume is

	Date	Price Range	

blue shirt, brown fur-like color cape, red belt and red straps on legs, light green leggings, helmet of blue and gray with white and black horns, height 8¾", designer J. Bromley 1973–1976 325.00 375.00

VIRGINIA
HN 1693
☐ Light colored base, yellow gown with floral design and light red bows, red underskirt, red shoes, small red scarf around neck, height 7½", designer L. Harradine 1935–1949 800.00 1000.00
HN 1694
☐ Green gown with small red bows on bodice, white undergown with green dots, green shoes, red scarf around neck and held by each hand, light colored base, height 7½", designer L. Harradine 1935–1949 800.00 1000.00

VIVIENNE
HN 2073
☐ Full red gown with white at sleeves, black hat with white and pink feathers with blue ribbons, height 7¾", designer L. Harradine 1951–1967 250.00 325.00

VOTES FOR WOMEN
HN 2816
☐ White base, green gown, long brown coat, black hat tied with white scarf, holding white placard with black printing, height 9¾", designer W.K. Harper 1978–1981 200.00 250.00

WANDERING MINSTREL, The
HN 1224
☐ Checkered black and red costume, black stockings, red shoes, jester type black, red and green hat, holding small black and shaded red instrument, also small head on stick seated on green and white brick wall, height 7", designer L. Harradine 1927–1938 2000.00 2400.00

WARDROBE MISTRESS
HN 2145
☐ Character figure seated, black gown and white overdress, beside her are

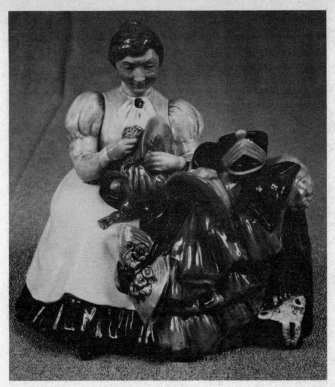

Wardrobe Mistress, HN 2145, 425.00–500.00

	Date	Price Range	
black and yellow hats, blue and red gown, height 5¾″, designer M. Davies	1954–1967	425.00	500.00

WAYFARER, The
HN 2362
☐ Character figure seated on brown base, blue and gray trousers, green jacket, red vest, checkered black and white cap, holding white bottle and white pipe, height 5½″, designer M. Nicoll

| | 1970–1978 | 150.00 | 200.00 |

WEDDING MORN
HN 1866
☐ HN 1867, cream dress, height 10½″, designer L. Harradine ....

| | 1938–1949 | 1800.00 | 2100.00 |

HN 1867
☐ Red gown with white veil and long

	Date	Price Range	

white train, holding white lilies, height 10½″, designer L. Harradine 1938–1949   2250.00   2500.00

WEE WILLIE WINKIE
HN 2050
☐ Small figure on light blue and red base, long blue nightshirt, carrying brown, red and yellow lantern, height 5¼″, designer M. Davies 1949–1953   375.00   450.00

WELSH GIRL, The
HN 39
☐ Light brown base with MYFANWY JONES printed on base, purple skirt with red floral design, red blouse with white tie collar, white apron, black cape with cream lining, broad brim black hat, height 12″, designer E.W. Light   1914–1938   2500.00   2750.00
HN 92
☐ Blue and gray costume, height 12″, designer E.W. Light 1918–1938   2500.00   2750.00
HN 456
☐ Green blouse and brown skirt, height 12″, designer E.W. Light 1921–1938   2500.00   2700.00
HN 514
☐ Green skirt, spotted apron, height 12″, designer E.W. Light 1921–1938   2500.00   2700.00
HN 516
☐ Checkered lilac dress, black spotted cloak, height 12″, designer E.W. Light   1921–1938   2500.00   2700.00
HN 519
☐ Blue skirt, checkered lilac skirt, height 12″, designer E.W. Light 1921–1938   2500.00   2700.00
HN 520
☐ Spotted lilac dress, height 12″, designer E.W. Light 1921–1938   2500.00   2700.00
HN 660
☐ Spotted white costume, blue-lined cloak, height 12″, designer E.W. Light   1924–1938   2500.00   2750.00
HN 668
☐ Checkered yellow costume, pink lined cloak, height 12″, designer E.W. Light   1924–1938   2500.00   2700.00
HN 669
☐ Spotted yellow costume, checkered green lined cloak, height 12″, designer E.W. Light 1924–1938   2500.00   2700.00
HN 701
☐ Striped costume, checkered blue lined

	Date	Price Range	

cloak, height 12″, designer E.W.
Light 1925–1938 **2500.00** **2700.00**

HN 792
☐ Pink checkered costume, blue cloak,
height 12″, designer E.W. Light 1926–1938 **2550.00** **2700.00**

WENDY
HN 2109
☐ Small figure in blue gown with shades
of red, blue bonnet with dark pink ribbons, light colored basket with flowers
in one hand, height 5″, designer L.
Harradine 1953– **110.00**

WEST WIND
HN 1826
☐ Tinted finish, height 14½″, designer
R. Garbe 1937–1949 **5000.00** **6500.00**

WIGMAKER OF
WILLIAMSBURG
HN 2239
☐ White base, has brown pedestal with
head form on it, costume of brown
trousers, white stockings, black shoes,
cream colored coat with black trim,
white shirt, height 7½″, designer M.
Davies 1960–1983 **150.00** **200.00**

WILLY-WON'T HE
HN 1561
☐ HN 1584, blue jacket and pink trou-
sers, height 6″, designer L. Harradine 1933–1949 **500.00** **600.00**

HN 1584
☐ Two figures, Dutch costumes, boy's
blue and brown trousers, red shirt, blue
cap, girl's costume, blue dress, white
apron and collar, white Dutch cap, both
wearing wooden shoes, height 6″, de-
signer L. Harradine 1933–1949 **350.00** **450.00**

HN 2150
☐ Minor glaze changes, height 5½″, de-
signer L. Harradine 1955–1959 **375.00** **450.00**

WINDFLOWER
HN 1763
☐ Pale yellow skirt with red floral design,
red blouse, shaded red and blue hat

Windflower, First Version, HN 1763, 400.00–475.00

	Date	Price Range	
with black ribbon, on green base (1st version), height 7¼″, designer L. Harradine	1936–1949	400.00	475.00
HN 1764			
☐ White skirt with blue floral design, blue blouse, shaded blue and red hat with green ribbon, green base (1st version), height 7¼″, designer L. Harradine ...	1936–1949	550.00	700.00
HN 1920			
☐ Multicolored skirt, red bodice, black base (2nd version), height 11″, designer L. Harradine	1939–1949	2250.00	2750.00
HN 1939			
☐ Floral pink skirt, blue hat and gloves (2nd version), height 11″, designer L. Harradine	1940–1949	2000.00	2500.00
☐ **M-78** Made as a miniature, light colored base, white skirt with red floral			

	Date	Price Range	

designs, red blouse, blue hat, height 4″, designer L. Harradine 1939–1949 **600.00** **850.00**

☐ **M-79** Green skirt, height 4″, designer L. Harradine 1939–1949 **600.00** **850.00**

HN 2029

☐ Light red skirt with red floral designs, red blouse, green hat with black ribbon, base is blue and green (1st version), height 7¼″, designer L. Harradine 1949–1952 **425.00** **500.00**

WINDMILL LADY, The
HN 1400

☐ Character figure seated on brown base, green skirt, black jacket, checkered red, yellow and green shawl, black hat, dark brown basket with green cloth at side, brown and white dog on other side, holding a ring of multicolored toy windmills, height 8½″, designer L. Harradine 1930–1938 **2750.00** **3250.00**

WINNER, The
HN 1407

☐ Green base with white fence, gray and white horse, rider in white trousers, dark red jacket with purple and white sleeves, purple cap, height 6¾″, designer unknown 1930–1938 **6500.00** **7500.00**

WINSOME
HN 2220

☐ Red gown, holding white bonnet with white ribbons over one arm, height 8″, designer M. Davies 1960–1985 **140.00** **175.00**

WINTER
HN 315

☐ Light colored base, figure completely wrapped in shaded blue robe (1st version), height 7½″, designer unknown 1918–1938 **1500.00** **1800.00**

HN 475

☐ Patterned robe (1st version), height 7½″, designer unknown 1921–1938 **1600.00** **1950.00**

HN 2088

☐ Blue and gray base, shaded blue skirt, shaded green jacket, dark green cloak with red lining, hood trimmed in brown fur, holding brown lantern (2nd version), height 6¼″, designer M. Davies 1952–1959 **375.00** **450.00**

	Date	Price Range	

WISTFUL
HN 2396

☐ Cream gown with light yellow shading with red floral design at hemline, red overdress with shaded blue and green design, white sleeves with green and yellow shading, holding purple mask in one hand, height 6½", designer M. Davies 1979–1985 450.00

HN 2472

☐ Re-issued for a limited time only for Michael Doulton events in 1985. Dressed in gentle tones, white skirt, blue and yellow border, the overdress is blue, height 6¼", designer M. Davies .... 1985 only 200.00 250.00

WIZARD, The
HN 2877

☐ Blue robe with beige colored rope belt, black coned hat with white designs, open book in hand, black cat at feet, brown and white owl on shoulder, height 9¾", designer A. Maslankowski 1979– 295.00

WOMAN HOLDING CHILD
HN 462

☐ Green dress, white apron and blanket, height 9¼", designer unknown 1921–1938 2000.00 2200.00

HN 570

☐ Pink and green striped skirt, pink and red striped blanket, height 9¼", designer unknown 1923–1938 2000.00 2200.00

HN 703

☐ Purple cloak, black and red checkered skirt, height 9¼", designer unknown 1925–1938 2000.00 2200.00

HN 743

☐ Blue and yellow striped apron, height 9¼", designer unknown 1925–1938 2050.00 2200.00

WOOD NYMPH
HN 2192

☐ White base with gray stripes and leaf design, blue and green costume with white waist straps, same color ribbon in hair, barefooted figure, height 7¼", designer M. Davies 1958–1962 175.00 250.00

	Date	Price Range	

YEOMAN OF THE GUARD, A
HN 688
☐ Brown and green base that has brown chest, figure seated, orange and red costume with stripes of gold and black, white ruffled collar, white design on front of jacket, black shoes with red and white trim, height 5¾", designer L. Harradine 1924–1938   800.00   900.00

HN 2122
☐ Very minor glaze differences, height 5¾", designer L. Harradine 1954–1959   650.00   750.00

YOUNG KNIGHT, The
HN 94
☐ Young man kneeling, hands holding a scepter, purple to maroon color gown, dark brown robe, armor headdress at his knees. Figurine is on a black base, height 9½", designer C.J. Noke 1918–1936   4000.00   5000.00

YOUNG LOVE
HN 2735
☐ Two figures on white base with gold trim, girl's gown is white with light shades of green, red floral design skirt, shaded green bodice, male's costume is gray trousers, white stockings, black shoes, purple long coat, blue vest, height 10", designer D.V. Tootle 1975–   950.00

YOUNG MASTER
HN 2872
☐ Shaded green base, young man with blue trousers, purple jacket trimmed in black, white shirt, holding yellow and black violin, tan dog at his feet, a sheet of music and books also on base, height 7", designer M. Davies 1980–   475.00

YOUNG MISS NIGHTINGALE, The
HN 2010
☐ Yellow and green gown with green overdress, red long jacket, green and yellow hat with red feathers, carrying parasol and round bag, height 9¼", designer M. Davies 1948–1953   450.00   550.00

Yum-Yum, HN 1268, 700.00–850.00

	Date	Price Range	

YOUNG WIDOW, The
HN 1399
☐ Quickly withdrawn and renamed 'THE
LITTLE MOTHER.' See that classi-
fication, height 8″, designer L. Har-
radine 1930– **2500.00** **3000.00**

YUM-YUM
HN 1268
☐ Chinese figure on yellow and green
base, shaded red and cream costume,
large black and red fan behind head,
height 5″, designer L. Harradine 1928–1938 **700.00** **850.00**

HN 1287
☐ Shaded brown base, shaded red, yellow
and blue costume, large dark blue and
red fan, height 5″, designer L. Har-
radine 1928–1939 **700.00** **850.00**

Yvonne, HN 3038, 160.00

	Date	Price Range
HN 2899		
☐ Round light colored base, green and yellow costume with blue and gold waistband, white flowers in black hair, holding white fan in one hand (2nd version), height 10¾″, designer W.K. Harper ...	1980–	750.00
YVONNE		
HN 3038		
☐ Gown, shades of pale blue to turquoise. Beautiful blond hair trimmed with a turquoise ribbon, height 9″, designer A. Hughes	1987–	185.00

COLLECTIONS FEATURING
CHILDHOOD THEMES

CHARACTERS FROM CHILDREN'S LITERATURE

This exciting new series, which began in 1982, features favorite characters from children's literature. Each figure has been designed from the storybook original. Each is hand-made and hand-decorated, thus no two are exactly the same. The entire series has now been discontinued.

	Date	Price Range	
HEIDI			
HN 2975			
☐ Height 4½″, designer A. Hughes	1983–1985	50.00	75.00
HUCKLEBERRY FINN			
HN 2927			
☐ Height 7″, designer D. Littleton	1982–1985	50.00	75.00
LITTLE LORD FAUNTLEROY			
HN 2972			
☐ Height 6¼″, designer A. Hughes	1982–1985	50.00	75.00
POLLYANNA			
HN 2965			
☐ Height 6¾″, designer P. Parsons	1982–1985	50.00	75.00
TOM BROWN			
HN 2941			
☐ Height 7″, designer R. Tabbenor	1983–1985	50.00	75.00
TOM SAWYER			
HN 2926			
☐ Height 5¼″, designer D. Littleton	1982–1985	50.00	75.00

CHILDHOOD DAYS SERIES

An exciting figure collection introduced in 1982. As the title suggests, these pieces capture the memorable moments of childhood. They are hand-made and hand-decorated. The entire series was discontinued at the end of 1985.

AND ONE FOR YOU
HN 2970

☐ Teddy bear sitting on a table with little
  girl bent over trying to feed him from
  the bowl which sits alongside the teddy

	Date	Price Range	

bear, height 6½", designer A. Hughes 1982–1985 75.00 100.00

AND SO TO BED
HN 2966
☐ Little girl with black hair clad in nightgown, clutching her teddy bear, ready for bed, height 7½", designer P. Parsons 1983–1985 75.00 100.00

AS GOOD AS NEW
HN 2971
☐ Dog in doghouse sitting on a white base; little boy sitting on top of doghouse with paint brush and bucket in hand painting the doghouse to make it "look as good as new," height 6½", designer A. Hughes 1982–1985 75.00 100.00

DRESSING UP
HN 2964
☐ Young lady in mother's dress that is white with blue trim, high heel black slippers, carrying gold purse, her light brown hair showing under a white hat trimmed in blue ribbons, height 7½", designer P. Parsons 1982–1985 75.00 100.00

I'M NEARLY READY
HN 2976
☐ Smartly groomed young man in black pants and white shirt tuning the strings of his violin in preparation for his debut, height 7½", designer A. Hughes 1984–1985 75.00 100.00

IT WON'T HURT
HN 2963
☐ Little girl in nurse outfit tending to a dog which is sitting on top of a brown woven basket. Both characters on a white base, height 7½", designer P. Parsons 1982–1985 75.00 100.00

JUST ONE MORE
HN 2980
☐ Little boy in bathing trunks building sandcastles, height 7", designer A. Hughes 1984–1985 75.00 100.00

	Date	Price Range	

PLEASE KEEP STILL
HN 2967
☐ Little boy on his knees bathing his dog; dog is standing in a tub patiently waiting for the boy to finish, height 4½", designer A. Hughes 1983–1985   **75.00**   **100.00**

SAVE SOME FOR ME
HN 2959
☐ Little girl mixing cake in bowl while cat at her feet watches patiently, height 7¼", designer P. Parsons 1983–1985   **75.00**   **100.00**

STICK 'EM UP
HN 2981
☐ Little boy in cowboy outfit, his hands on the twin holster at his hips, height 7", designer A. Hughes 1984–1985   **75.00**   **100.00**

NURSERY RHYME FIGURINES

This collection was introduced in 1984. Each figure is created from century-old nursery rhyme characters.

LITTLE BO PEEP
HN 3030
☐ Height 8", designer A. Hughes 1984–1987   **95.00**

LITTLE BOY BLUE
HN 3035
☐ Height 7¾", designer A. Hughes 1984–1987   **95.00**

LITTLE JACK HORNER
HN 3034
☐ Height 7", designer A. Hughes 1984–1987   **95.00**

LITTLE MISS MUFFET
HN 2727
☐ Height 6¼", designer W.K. Harper 1984–1987   **95.00**

POLLY PUT THE KETTLE ON
HN 3021
☐ Height 8", designer P. Parsons 1984–1987   **95.00**

TOM, TOM THE PIPER'S SON
HN 3032
☐ Height 7", designer A. Hughes 1984–1987   **95.00**

WEE WILLIE WINKIE
HN 3031
☐ Height 7¾", designer A. Hughes 1984–1987   **95.00**

COLLECTIONS FEATURING SPECIAL THEMES

ENCHANTMENT COLLECTION

A series of subjects all presented in beautiful ivory bone china, each trimmed with burnished gold. These were fashioned after the first figures ever made at Burslem in what was called, at that time, "vellum" figures.

The collection was introduced in 1983.

	Date	Price Range	
APRIL SHOWER **HN 3024** ☐ Designer R. Jefferson, height 4¾″	1983–1986	**75.00**	
FAIRYSPELL **HN 2979** ☐ Designer A. Hughes, height 5¼″	1983–1986	**65.00**	
LYRIC **HN 2757** ☐ Designer E. Griffiths, height 6¼″	1983–1985	**95.00**	
MAGIC DRAGON **HN 2977** ☐ Designer A. Hughes, height 4¾″	1983–1986	**75.00**	
MAGPIE RING **HN 2978** ☐ Designer A. Hughes, height 8″	1983–1986	**95.00**	
MUSICALE **HN 2756** ☐ Designer E. Griffiths, height 9″	1983–1985	**125.00**	
QUEEN OF THE DAWN **HN 2437** ☐ Designer M. Davies, height 8½″	1983–1986	**125.00**	
QUEEN OF THE ICE **HN 2435** ☐ Designer M. Davies, height 8″	1983–1986	**125.00**	**175.00**
RUMPLESTILTSKIN **HN 3025** ☐ Designer R. Jefferson, height 8″	1983–1986	**125.00**	
SERENADE **HN 2753** ☐ Designer E. Griffiths, height 9″	1983–1985	**95.00**	

	Date	Price Range

SONATA
HN 2438

☐ Designer M. Davies, height 6½″ 1983–1985   **95.00**

GILBERT & SULLIVAN SERIES

KO-KO
HN 2898

☐ Japanese figure from "The Mikado." Black hair on light brown base, costume of orange, blue, green, black, red, holding scroll, with large ax-like weapon on stand (2nd version), height 11½″, designer W.K. Harper 1980–1985   **650.00**   **750.00**

YUM-YUM
HN 2899

☐ Japanese figure from "The Mikado." Round light colored base, costume of green and yellow with waistband of blue and gold, white flowers in black hair, holding white fan in one hand (2nd version), height 10¾″, designer W.K. Harper 1980–1985   **650.00**   **750.00**

RUTH, THE PIRATE MAID
HN 2900

☐ Figure from "The Pirates of Penzance." Costume of brown, striped skirt, blue blouse with gold and black trim, white apron, black captain's hat with trim of gold and white skull and crossbones on mottled brown base, height 11¾″, designer W.K. Harper   1981–1985   **750.00**

THE PIRATE KING
HN 2901

☐ Figure from "The Pirates of Penzance." Character seated on black and white pirate flag on light tan base, costume of green shirt, white lace ruff, blue boots and blue braided jacket with plumed captain's hat, his belt holds dagger and pistol, height 10″, designer W.K. Harper 1981–1985   **750.00**

	Date	Price Range

ELSIE MAYNARD
HN 2902

☐ Figure from "The Yeomen of the Guard." Dancing girl with flowing red hair topped with a cap of blue, green skirt with white blouse, holding a tambourine aloft, height 11¼", designer W.K. Harper ....

1982–1985   **750.00**

COLONEL FAIRFAX
HN 2903

☐ Figure from "The Yeomen of the Guard." Man in traditional Beefeater uniform standing on base of mottled grays, height 11½", designer W.K. Harper ....

1982–1985   **750.00**

IMAGES

This series of modernistic figures, a fresh step taken by Royal Doulton in 1980, combines old and new. "Images" features designs that are unmistakably twentieth century, but in a concept that dates to the eighteenth century. In Georgian England, it was popular to exhibit black basalt or white marble busts and other sculptures in fashionable homes. The "Images" series recalls this tradition as each piece is available in both black basalt (matte finish) or white bone china, suggesting marble. Subjects are inspired by the works of sculptors Henry Moore and Barbara Hepworth. All-black, basalt figures were discontinued mid–year 1987.

AWAKENING
☐ **HN 2837** Black 1980–1986 **50.00** **75.00**
☐ **HN 2875** White 1980– **75.00**

CAREFREE
☐ **HN 3029** Black 1985–1986 **75.00** **100.00**
☐ **HN 3026** White 1985– **110.00**

CONTEMPLATION
☐ **HN 2241** Black 1983–1986 **75.00** **100.00**
☐ **HN 2213** White 1983–1986 **75.00** **100.00**

FAMILY
☐ **HN 2721** Black 1980–1985 **95.00** **125.00**
☐ **HN 2720** White 1980– **140.00**

FIRST LOVE
☐ **HN 2747** White 1987– **120.00**

	Date	Price Range	
FREE SPIRIT			
☐ HN 3157 White	1987–	110.00	
MOTHER AND DAUGHTER			
☐ HN 2843 Black	1980–1985	95.00	125.00
☐ HN 2841 White	1980–	140.00	
PEACE			
☐ HN 2433 Black	1980–1985	50.00	75.00
☐ HN 2470 White	1980–	75.00	
SISTERS			
☐ HN 3019 Black	1984–1985	95.00	125.00
☐ HN 3018 White	1984–	125.00	
SYMPATHY			
☐ HN 2838 Black	1980–1986	75.00	100.00
☐ HN 2876 White	1980–1986	75.00	100.00
TENDERNESS			
☐ HN 2714 Black	1983–1985	75.00	100.00
☐ HN 2713 White	1983–	110.00	
THANKFUL			
☐ HN 3129 White	1987–	75.00	
TRANQUILITY			
☐ HN 2426 Black	1980–1986	75.00	100.00
☐ HN 2469 White	1980–1986	75.00	100.00
WEDDING DAY			
☐ HN 2748 White	1987–	140.00	
YEARNING			
☐ HN 2921 Black	1983–1986	75.00	100.00
☐ HN 2920 White	1983–1986	75.00	100.00

IMAGES OF NATURE AND IMAGES OF FIRE

Can be found under Animal and Bird Models

MIDDLE EARTH FIGURINES (J.R.R. TOLKIEN SERIES)

Inspired by the great work of J.R.R. Tolkien's fiction "The Lord of the Rings" and created by the artists of Royal Doulton is this series of figures featuring new lands and new creatures. All are created from the vivid characters envisioned in the mind of Tolkien and portrayed in this book.

The entire line of Middle Earth figurines was discontinued as of March 31, 1984.

Wedding Day, HN 2748, 125.00

	Date	Price Range	
ARAGORN			
☐ HN 2916 Tan Costume	1980–1983	60.00	75.00
BARLIMAN BUTTERBUR			
☐ HN 2923	1982–1983	85.00	125.00
BILBO			
☐ HN 2914 Brown shorts, tan vest	1980–1983	60.00	75.00
BOROMIR			
☐ HN 2918	1981–1983	95.00	125.00
FRODO			
☐ HN 2912 Dark blue shorts and vest ..	1980–1983	60.00	75.00
GALADRIAL			
☐ HN 2915 Ivory dress	1981–1983	60.00	75.00
GANDALF			
☐ HN 2911 Blue cloak	1980–1983	100.00	125.00
GIMLI			
☐ HN 2922	1981–1983	60.00	75.00

Tom Bombadil, HN 2924, 175.00–225.00

	Date	Price Range	
GOLLUM			
☐HN 2913 Green	1980–1983	75.00	100.00
LEGOLAS			
☐HN 2917	1981–1983	60.00	75.00
SAMWISE			
☐HN 2925	1982–1983	100.00	125.00
TOM BOMBADIL			
☐HN 2924	1982–1983	175.00	225.00

PRESTIGE FIGURES

These are large-size figures, in some cases extremely large (Matador and Bull measures a huge 28″). While not actually limited editions, it is obvious that the Prestige Figures, because of their high retail prices, are produced in smaller edition sizes than the regular HN pieces. The concept for this series dates to 1952. Additions have been made to it only occasionally. Apparently, the feeling among directors of the factory was that wealthy collectors might welcome deluxe figures. In general the series has been well received. It would be difficult to predict the prices that might be reached by Princess Badoura and Matador and Bull (the two most spectacular Prestige Figures) if they were taken out of production.

	Date	Price Range

COLUMBINE
HN 2738
☐ Subject from the famous "Commedia dell'Arte." Swirling gown of pink, floral bodice, on a rococo style base of white with gold trim, height 12½", designer D. Tootle 1982–   895.00

ELEPHANT
HN 2640
☐ Fighting, 12" 1900.00

FOX
HN 2634
☐ Sitting, 10⅜" 1200.00

HARLEQUIN
HN 2737
☐ Subject from the famous "Commedia dell'Arte." Brightly colored checkered suit, on a rococo style base of white with gold trim, height 12½", designer D. Tootle 1982–   895.00

JACK POINT
HN 2080
☐ Costume of red, purple, green with gold lion and leaf trim, has instrument slung over shoulder, base light beige .. 1952–   2200.00

KING CHARLES
HN 2084
☐ Figure is on light beige base, 17" 1952–   1900.00

LEOPARD ON ROCK
HN 2638
☐ 9" 2300.00

LION ON ROCK
HN 2641
☐ 12" 2300.00

MATADOR AND BULL
HN 2324
☐ Bull is dark gray with brown shadings, matador costume of green and yellow, cape is blue/red with pale yellow lining, 28" 1964–   17,500.00

	Date	Price Range

THE MOOR
HN 2082

☐ Red with shaded greens costume with multicolored waistband, deep brown cloak with shades of dark green, on dark brown base, 17½″ 1952–   1900.00

PHEASANT
HN 2632

☐ Cock 550.00

PRINCESS BADOURA
HN 2081

☐ This is a 20″ figure, on black base, large elephant is dark gray with coverings of reds, blues, golds and brown, lady is seated in gold colored chair with pink gown and gold head piece and necklace, male figure is seated on head of elephant, costume of blue and gold with green trousers 1952–   23,000.00

ST. GEORGE AND THE DRAGON
HN 2856

☐ Blue/gray base with dragon head and brown tree trunk, horse is white with cloth of cream with gold designs, red lining, figure in blue/gray armor and helmet with white feather, 16″ 1978–   10,000.00

TIGER
HN 2646

☐ 1500.00

TIGER ON ROCK
HN 2639

☐ 12″ 2300.00

REFLECTIONS

This new series of figurines was introduced in late 1985. As their names imply, they will remind you, in their beauty and grace, of the Art Deco style. Each figure in the Reflections group is eloquently styled and painted in soft pastels, with delicate brushstrokes of soft beige to create fresh skin tones. It is a very beautiful and different series. Broadening the line considerably in 1986 and 1987, Royal Doulton has added shaded pastel colors of taupe, rose, and blue to the new figures to complement the flow of the figures, reflecting more the Art Deco style.

	Date	Price Range

A WINTER'S WALK
☐ **HN 3052**, height 12¼″, designer A. Hughes 1987– **185.00**

ALLURE
☐ **HN 3080**, height 12¼″, designer E. Griffiths 1985– **130.00**

BALLET CLASSES
☐ **HN 3134**, height 6″, designer P. Parsons 1987– **175.00**

BATHING BEAUTY
☐ **HN 3156**, height 9½″, designer A. Hughes 1987– **140.00**

BOLERO
☐ **HN 3076**, height 13½″, designer A. Hughes 1986– **185.00**

CHARISMA
☐ **HN 3090**, height 12½″, designer P. Parsons 1986– **140.00**

CHERRY BLOSSOM
☐ **HN 3092**, height 12¼″, designer P. Parsons 1986– **160.00**

CHIC
☐ **HN 2997**, height 13″, designer R. Tabbenor 1987– **150.00**

COCKTAILS
☐ **HN 3070**, height 12¾″, designer A. Hughes 1985– **170.00**

COUNTRY GIRL
☐ **HN 3051**, height 7¾″, designer A. Hughes 1987– **110.00**

DANCING DELIGHT
☐ **HN 3078**, height 12¾″, designer A. Hughes 1986– **140.00**

DAYBREAK
☐ **HN 3107**, height 11¾″, designer R. Jefferson 1986– **140.00**

DEBUT
☐ **HN 3046**, height 12¼″, designer P. Parsons 1985– **160.00**

Chic, HN 2997, 150.00

	Date	Price Range
DEMURE		
☐ **HN 3045**, height 12½″, designer P. Parsons	1985–	**140.00**
DREAMING		
☐ **HN 3133**, height 9″, designer P. Parsons	1987–	**110.00**
ENCHANTING EVENING		
☐ **HN 3108**, height 11¾″, designer R. Jefferson	1986–	**140.00**
ENIGMA		
☐ **HN 3110**, height 12¾″, designer R. Jefferson	1986–	**140.00**
FLIRTATION		
☐ **HN 3071**, height 10″, designer A. Hughes	1985–	**170.00**
GOOD PALS		
☐ **HN 3132**, height 6¼″, designer P. Parsons	1987–	**140.00**

Dreaming, HN 3133, 110.00

	Date	Price Range
IDLE HOURS		
☐ **HN 3115**, height 12¼″, designer A. Maslankowski	1986–	**150.00**
INDIAN MAIDEN		
☐ **HN 3117**, height 12″, designer A. Maslankowski	1987–	**160.00**
MORNING GLORY		
☐ **HN 3093**, height 12¾″, designer P. Parsons	1986–	**140.00**
PANORAMA		
☐ **HN 3028**, height 12¼″, designer R. Jefferson	1987–	**140.00**
PARADISE		
☐ **HN 3074**, height 13½″, designer A. Hughes	1987–	**160.00**

	Date	Price Range
PARK PARADE		
☐ **HN 3116**, height 11¾″, designer A. Maslankowski	1987–	170.00
PENSIVE		
☐ **HN 3109**, height 13″, designer R. Jefferson	1986–	130.00
PLAYMATES		
☐ **HN 3127**, height 8½″, designer P. Parsons	1987–	175.00
PROMENADE		
☐ **HN 3072**, height 13″, designer A. Hughes	1985–	170.00
REFLECTION		
☐ **HN 3039**, height 8″, designer A. Hughes	1987–	170.00
ROSE ARBOUR		
☐ **HN 3145**, height 12″, designer D. Brindley	1987–	160.00
SECRET MOMENT		
☐ **HN 3106**, height 12¼″, designer R. Jefferson	1986–	140.00
SHEIKH		
☐ **HN 3083**, height 10¼″, E. Griffiths	1987–	140.00
SHEPHERDESS		
☐ **HN 2990**, height 8½″, designer R. Tabbenor	1987–	170.00
SISTERLY LOVE		
☐ **HN 3130**, height 8½″, designer P. Parsons	1987–	140.00
SOPHISTICATION		
☐ **HN 3059**, height 11½″, designer A. Hughes	1987–	140.00
STORY TIME		
☐ **HN 3126**, height 6″, designer P. Parsons	1987–	175.00
STROLLING		
☐ **HN 3073**, height 13½″, designer A. Hughes	1985–	195.00
SUMMER ROSE		
☐ **HN 3085**, height 8½″, designer E. Griffiths	1987–	140.00

Shepherdess, HN 2990, 170.00

	Date	Price Range
SUMMER'S DARLING		
☐ **HN 3091**, height 11¼", designer P. Parsons	1986–	**185.00**
SWEET PERFUME		
☐ **HN 3094**, height 13", designer P. Parsons	1986–	**140.00**
TANGO		
☐ **HN 3075**, height 13", designer A. Hughes	1985–	**170.00**

	Date	Price Range

THE LOVE LETTER
☐ **HN 3105**, height 12″, designer R. Jefferson 1985–   130.00

TOMORROW'S DREAMS
☐ **HN 3128**, height 6½″, designer P. Parsons 1987–   185.00

WATER MAIDEN
☐ **HN 3155**, height 12″, designer A. Hughes 1987–   140.00

WINDFLOWER
☐ **HN 3077**, height 12¼″, designer A. Hughes 1986–   140.00

WINDSWEPT
☐ **HN 3027**, height 12″, designer R. Jefferson 1985–   130.00

The figures Daybreak, The Love Letter, Secret Moment and Enchanting Evening, each designed by R. Jefferson, are known as *The Jefferson Quartet.*

ROYAL DOULTON INTERNATIONAL COLLECTORS CLUB

In 1979 the Royal Doulton International Collectors Club was created, offering collectors of Royal Doulton items the opportunity of receiving newsletters, from the company, four times a year containing facts, articles on interesting items, new issues and announcements of shows and other special interest events. The club has offered, each year, special items available to club members only. The following is a listing of those items.

ALBERT SAGGER, THE POTTER
D 6745
☐ From the Doultonville Collection of Tobies 1986–   40.00   60.00

AUCTIONEER
HN 2988
☐ Depicts a gentleman at the auction block taking bids on the character jug ''Red-haired Clown,'' height 9″, designer R. Tabbenor 1986–   200.00   250.00

COLLECTOR BUNNYKINS
☐ Bunnykins has become such an established collectible that this item was

Dog of Fo, International Collector Club Issue 1982, 175.00–200.00

	Date	Price Range	
added to the exclusive Royal Doulton Collector Club pieces, height 4¼″	1987–	40.00	
DOG OF FO			
☐ Flambé piece	1982–	175.00	200.00
JOHN DOULTON CHARACTER JUG			
☐ Small, hands on handle at two o'clock	1979–	100.00	150.00
☐ Small, hands on handle at eight o'clock	1979 only	**RARE**	
LOVING CUP D 6696			
☐ Pottery in the Past	1983–	375.00	475.00
PRIDE AND JOY HN 2945			
☐...	1984–	300.00	350.00
PRIZED POSSESSION HN 2942			
☐...	1982–	500.00	600.00

Prized Possession, HN 2942, International Collector Club Issue 1982, 450.00–550.00

	Date	Price Range	
SIR HENRY DOULTON			
D 6703			
☐ Small, designer E. Griffiths	1984–	100.00	125.00
SLEEPY DARLING			
HN 2953			
☐..	1981–	200.00	250.00
SPRINGTIME			
HN 3033			
☐ Four Seasons, first in a set of four	1983–	300.00	400.00
SUMMERTIME			
HN 3137			
☐ Four Seasons, third in a set of four ...	1987–	140.00	
TOP O' THE HILL			
☐ Collector Plate	1985–	65.00	75.00

	Date	Price Range	

WINTERTIME
HN 3060
☐ Four Seasons, second in a set of four,
height 8½", designer A. Hughes ...... | 1985– | 200.00 | 250.00

HAMPSHIRE CRICKETER JUG
D 6739
☐ Jug was commissioned by the Hampshire Cricket Club to celebrate one hundred years of County Cricket at Southampton. Limited edition of 5,000, height 5" .... | 1985– | 75.00 | 100.00

VANITY FAIR SERIES

This collection of figurines was introduced in 1982, and is becoming extremely popular. Vanity Fair ladies are individually hand-made and hand-decorated so each is an original, each different from the other. Subtle matte skin tones are complemented by highly glazed white clothes, most with a small touch of color.

ANGELA
HN 2389
☐ White gown, flowing skirt with elbow length sleeves, dark brown hair highlighted with golden color, height 7⅜", designer M. Davies .... | 1982–1986 | 95.00 | 115.00

ANN
HN 2739
☐ Young lady dressed in a sleeveless white gown with wide skirt, white ribbon in her hair, height unknown, designer M. Davies .... | 1984–1985 | 95.00 | 115.00

BARBARA
HN 2962
☐ White gown, white hat hanging at the neckline tied in front with white ribbons, auburn hair, height 8", designer P. Parsons .... | 1982–1984 | 95.00 | 115.00

CAROL
HN 2961
☐ Regal figure with white gown accented with pale pink, embroidering in hand with design on work of red flowers, green stems and leaves, reddish hair, height 7½", designer P. Parsons ...... | 1982– | 130.00 |

Denise, HN 2477, 115.00

	Date	Price Range
DENISE		
HN 2477		
☐ White gown with highlights of pink and beige, frilled on bottom with slipper showing, blond hair, height 7 3/4 ", designer P. Davies	1986–	**170.00**
DONNA		
HN 2939		
☐ White gown with shades of lemon, hand raises her skirt as if she is ready to dance, height 7 3/4 ", designer P. Gee ..	1986–	**130.00**

	Date	Price Range

GAIL
HN 2937

☐ Young lady wearing ermine-trimmed white jacket over beautiful, red full skirt with slight showing of white petticoat, a small pill-box hat over her brown hair is being held with one hand, height 7½″, designer P. Gee 1986–   230.00

HEATHER
HN 2956

☐ Seated figure, white gown, white purse on arm, blonde hair, height 6″, designer P. Parsons 1982–   130.00

JEAN
HN 2710

☐ Victorian lady in white gown putting the finishing touches to her hair, hair brush and ribbon lie on her gown, height unknown, designer M. Davies   1984–1986   95.00   115.00

JOANNE
HN 2373

☐ Seated figure with legs tucked up revealing ruffled petticoats, gown is white, hair blonde, height 5¼″, designer E. Griffiths 1982–   130.00

LINDA
HN 2758

☐ Young lady dressed in white ball gown, gown is close fitting, draped to a bow in the back. Attractive frilled neckline, dark hair, height unknown, designer E. Griffiths 1984–   130.00

MARGARET
HN 2397

☐ Gown is white accented at waistline with blue ribbon, hat is white with blue ribbon, dark hair, height 7½″, designer M. Davies 1982–   130.00

MARY
HN 2374

☐ Blonde lady out for a walk in her white afternoon dress, her dress flares at the bottom revealing a tiered petticoat, her blonde tresses are covered by a perky

	Date	Price Range	

white hat tied with a bow under her chin, height unknown, designer E. Griffiths 1984–1986   **95.00**   **115.00**

MAUREEN
HN 2481
☐ Figure is dressed in white, full-skirted gown with purple flowers adapted from the Royal Albert tableware design, "Sweet Violets." One hand is raised to her beautiful, brown wavy hair, other hand clutches gown, height 7½", designer P. Davies 1987–   **170.00**

NANCY
HN 2955
☐ White gown, white flower in light brown hair, height 7½", designer P. Parsons 1982–   **130.00**

PAMELA
HN 2479
☐ Young lady in white gown with light shades of blue; slipper shows as she is poised to step forward with hands holding gown up from floor, light auburn hair, height 7", designer P. Gee 1986–   **130.00**

PATRICIA
HN 2715
☐ Beautiful dark haired figure with ball gown of white satin, height 7½", designer J. Bromley 1982–1985   **95.00**   **115.00**

SAMANTHA
HN 2954
☐ Beautiful blonde lady, white gown, white hat, height 7", designer P. Parsons 1982–1984   **95.00**   **115.00**

TRACY
HN 2736
☐ Gown white with tight fitting bodice and plunging neckline with flowing skirt, rose in the folds of the skirt, blonde hair, height 7⅜", designer D. Tootle 1983–   **130.00**

VANITY FAIR CHILDREN

These seven figures of children represent the fashions of the late nineteenth century. They wear a gown exactly as their mothers that are in the Vanity Fair Ladies Collection.

	Date	Price Range
AMANDA **HN 2996** ☐ Height 5¼″, designer R. Tabbenor ..	1986–	**80.00**
ANDREA **HN 3058** ☐ Height 5¼″, designer A. Hughes	1985–	**80.00**
CATHERINE **HN 3044** ☐ Height 5″, designer P. Parsons	1985–	**80.00**
HELEN **HN 2994** ☐ Height 5″, designer R. Tabbenor	1985–	**80.00**
JULIE **HN 2995** ☐ Height 5″, design R. Tabbenor	1985–	**80.00**
KERRY **HN 3036** ☐ Height 5¼″, designer A. Hughes	1986–	**80.00**
LYNSEY **HN 3043** ☐ Height 4¾″, designer P. Parsons	1985–	**80.00**

DOLLS

KATE GREENAWAY HEIRLOOM SERIES

	Date	Price Range
LITTLE MODEL		
☐ Gown is light beige with blue ribbon at waist, hat is blue matching ribbon on dress with deep maroon ties, cape is maroon. Limited edition of 5,000, height 12″	1981–	175.00
VERA		
☐ Beautiful deep beige dress with matching color overdress, hat matches dress, light auburn hair, carrying basket of pink flowers. Limited edition of 5,000, height 12″	1981–	175.00
WINTER		
☐ Costume is scarlet red trimmed with black fur, carrying fur muff, beautiful black hat, showing underneath is her red hair, black shoes. Limited edition of 5,000, height 12″	1981–	175.00
BIG SISTER		
☐ Beautiful white dress with lacy underskirt, royal blue ribbon at the waist, hat is white trimmed in same color blue, slippers white, carrying dark brown basket with white and red flowers. Limited edition of 5,000, height 12″ ..	1981–	175.00
SMALL SISTER		
☐ Small child has all white dress with white shoes tied with pink ribbons, bonnet is white with pink bows over dark blonde hair. Limited edition of 5,000, height 8″	1981–	125.00
PINK RIBBON		
☐ Dress is white taffeta lined with pink underskirt, hat white with pink satin ribbon and white feathers, carrying a miniature bouquet of silk rosebuds. Limited edition of 5,000, height 12″ ..	1982–	195.00

	Date	Price Range

WAITING

☐ Simple white gown of silk with frilled neckline and cuff. Wide sash of orange satin ribbon at waistline, matching the lining of her dark brown lace and feather hat, under the hat is a white linen cap trimmed in lace. Limited edition of 5,000, height 12″ 1982– **195.00**

THE MUFF

☐ Dressed in tailored full length coat with a fur cape collar and carrying a fur muff, the coat has a pink lining, dress is maroon satin, hat is plum colored and trimmed with chocolate and pink feathers, hair is auburn. Limited edition of 5,000, height 12″ 1982– **195.00**

SWANSDOWN

☐ Dressed in a white figured satin fur trimmed coat over a white satin dress, she carries a white fur muff and wears a lace trimmed hat over her blonde curly hair, decorated with Swansdown and yellow ribbons. Limited edition of 5,000, height 12″ 1982– **195.00**

PINK SASH

☐ Dressed in white taffeta over a pink underskirt, wearing white hat decorated with feathers and pink ribbon, over blonde hair, carrying a miniature bouquet of silk rosebuds. Limited edition of 5,000, height 10″ 1982– **150.00**

OTHER HEIRLOOM DOLLS

WEDDING DAY

☐ Bride wears a wedding dress of ivory silk which is almost entirely covered with ivory lace, the veil is matching lace and pink and cream flowers accentuate her brunette real hair, she carries a miniature bouquet of yellow, orange and white flowers, height 14″ 1982– **225.00**

Swansdown, 195.00

	Date	Price Range

LITTLE BRIDESMAID
☐ Dressed in cream satin, trimmed with cream lace, which matches the lace on the bride (Wedding Day), flowers are yellow, orange and white, hair is light auburn, and headdress is a ringlet of similar flowers 175.00

ROYAL BABY DOLL
☐ To commemorate the birth of His

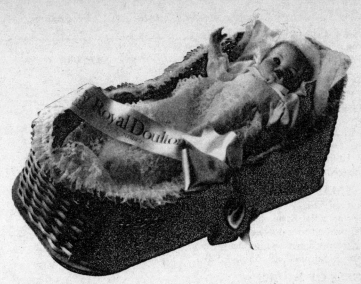

First Born, 195.00

	Date	Price Range
Royal Highness Prince William of Wales, born June 21, 1982. Baby wears a dress and bonnet of cream lace and net over taffeta, underneath are cream cotton bloomers. Bonnet is cream trimmed in matching lace and ribbons, the canopied crib is draped with a white and cream figured cotton, trimmed with baby blue, the face, hands and feet are a delicate baby tone. Limited edition of 2,500	1982–	295.00

FIRST BORN

	Date	Price Range
☐ This baby doll is a beautiful blue-eyed infant in a basket crib trimmed in lace, the infant is dressed in a traditional christening robe of white figured cotton with a lace front panel, bonnet is of white satin and lace	1982–	195.00

HRH PRINCE WILLIAM OF WALES

☐ Toddler doll dressed in a blue and white striped sailor suit trimmed with navy blue. Wearing a white cap with a navy blue bill, cap has embroidered in gold

	Date	Price Range

"H.R.H. Prince William." Baby is holding a light brown teddy bear. Limited edition of 2,500 .... **175.00**

CHRISTMAS-HOLLY
☐ First in a series. Bright red costume trimmed in white fur, red hat trimmed in white fur. She is carrying a green box with Royal Doulton printed in gold on the box. It is a miniature of the green Heirloom doll box in which she is packaged. Limited edition of 3,500   **195.00**

CHRISTMAS-EVERGREEN
☐ Second in the Heirloom Series of Christmas dolls. Bone china head and hands, dressed in a hooded cape of red velvet trimmed with white lace over a green dress, limited edition of 3,500 ..   1985–   **195.00**

PRINCESS OF WALES
☐ The Princess is dressed in her wedding dress of ivory colored taffeta with puffed sleeves, ruffles and a long train, trimmed with white lace. Her bouquet is of cream colored flowers, her outfit is held in place by a tiara. Limited edition of 3,500 ....   **250.00**

CINDERS/CINDERELLA
☐ First transformation doll depicting Cinderella as a poor little girl dressed in a brown patched jumper with tight fitting bodice over a white blouse, brown hair, holding a broom. Other side is Cinderella in pink ball gown trimmed in lace and sequins, holding a tiny glass slipper, blond hair, limited edition of 1,500   1985–   **295.00**

OLD COUNTRY ROSE
☐ Dressed in a beautiful cream colored gown trimmed with roses and wearing a bonnet of the same cream color, carrying a miniature wicker basket filled with roses, limited to 2,500   1985–   **195.00**

EDWARDIAN SOCIAL SEASON DOLLS
(Limited edition of 3500)

	Date	Price Range

PRESENTATION AT COURT
☐ A young debutante ready to be presented at court; her gown is white, trimmed in embroidered yellow flowers, also trimmed with very pastel yellow flowers on her bodice and sleeves   **195.00**

ASCOT
☐ Black and white striped satin gown with lace sleeves, beautiful black straw hat trimmed with violets. She carries a black and white lace parasol **195.00**

HENLEY REGATTA
☐ Dressed in blue, skirt, jacket and hat all matching. Crepe material with gold threads. Chiffon blouse trimmed with embroidery **195.00**

LORDS
☐ Light green gown with long sleeves, green wide brimmed hat trimmed with yellow roses. She carries a matching parasol **195.00**

VICTORIAN BIRTHDAY DOLLS

The well-remembered nursery rhyme inspired this charming collection. While each day's child is represented by a boy and girl doll, each girl has a hairpiece while the boy's hair is sculptured in the ceramic. Their costumes follow the nineteenth-century tradition. This is a non-limited edition. Victorian Birthday dolls were discontinued as of January 1, 1984.

☐ **Monday's Child** is fair of face **125.00**
☐ **Tuesday's Child** is full of grace **125.00**
☐ **Wednesday's Child** is full of woe **125.00**
☐ **Thursday's Child** has far to go **125.00**
☐ **Friday's Child** is loving and giving ...   **125.00**
☐ **Saturday's Child** works hard for a living **125.00**
☐ **Sunday's Child,** a child that is born on the Sabbath Day is bonny and blithe and good and gay **125.00**

LIMITED EDITIONS

The Royal Doulton Company has, on numerous occasions, issued a series in a limited edition. Limited edition, of course, being a pre-determined number of a given item. Each piece, generally, is sequentially numbered, accompanied with a certificate of authenticity, and beautifully boxed.

DANCERS OF THE WORLD. This series, started in 1977, was created by Royal Doulton's premier modeler of feminine figurines, Peggy Davies. The concept is to show folk dancers from various parts of the world, dressed in native costume. The series is noteworthy for the attention given to small detailing and coloration. As the costumes are "traditional," they cannot be assigned to any given time period. Many other porcelain makers have attempted works of this kind, but the Royal Doulton Dancers of the World is generally acknowledged to be the outstanding series of the type.

FEMME FATALE SERIES. A new series begun in 1979. Each figure is limited to 750 pieces. These are large and rather elaborate works. To date only six have been issued, all on historical themes, but it would seem as though the "femme fatale" concept could lend itself to inclusion of fictional or modern types as well—these may be added in the future.

HEIRLOOM DOLLS. In 1981 Royal Doulton, combined with the talents of the House of Nisbet, introduced their first limited edition dolls. The heads and hands are fine bone china, hand painted, with each doll having a different face. The costumes are created to perfection through the skills of the House of Nisbet, whose dolls have long been collected throughout the world. Each carries the Royal Doulton stamp on the nape of the neck, the costumes have a sewn-in label bearing the wording "Royal Doulton and Nisbet."

LADY MUSICIANS. Instituted in 1970. Each has been limited to 750 pieces and, at this writing, all are entirely sold out (that is, obtainable now only from retail dealers—not obtainable from the factory). Each figure shows a female musician playing a different instrument. Some collectors like to group them together as a "band," in the spirit of early porcelain sets that were intended to be displayed in that manner (Staffordshire put out many "bands").

MISCELLANEOUS FIGURINES. These are individually issued Limited Editions, not part of any sub-series. All carry numbering in the standard HN prefix series for Fancy and Character figures. These very desirable works have all been completely sold out and have definite investment appeal. The variety in subject matter adds to their interest.

MYTHS AND MAIDENS. A new collection introduced in 1982 these fine bone china figures have been inspired by ancient myths and legends. Each figure will be limited to 300, and a subject will be offered each year until 1986.

SHIPS' FIGUREHEADS. This series, introduced in 1980, has limited figures of 950 each. These are ceramic reproductions of colorful ship figureheads from the days of sailing vessels. The originals were made of sculptured wood, but porcelain faithfully captures their line and color.

SOLDIERS OF THE REVOLUTION. This limited edition series was issued in conjunction with the U.S. Bicentennial. Most of the figures were released in 1975, on the eve of the celebration, but an additional figure (George Washington at Prayer), appeared two years later.

AGE OF CHIVALRY

A set of three knights issued in a limited edition of 500. Series is now closed. Most are sold as sets only, ranging from $1000 to $1250 per set.

	Date	Price Range

SIR EDWARD
HN 2370
☐ Blue and gold base, blue and gold shield. Red cloak trimmed in silver, height 10¾", designer J. Bromley 1979–

SIR RALPH
HN 2371
☐ Red and gold base, red and blue shield, light blue cloak, silver armor, height 10½", designer J. Bromley 1979–

SIR THOMAS
HN 2372
☐ Green and gold base, black armor, height 10¾", designer J. Bromley 1979–

CARNIVAL OF CLOWNS

Created by the well-known artist Ben Black, this series of four figurines was introduced in 1983, and is a limited edition of 3,500 worldwide. This series has now been closed and is no longer available.

☐ **Final Touches** 100.00
☐ **Between Acts** 100.00
☐ **Three Ring Picnic** 100.00
☐ **Breathtaking Performance** 100.00

Dancers of the World, LE of 750. Spanish Flamenco Dancer, HN 283, 1500.00–1800.00; Philippine Dancer, HN 2439, 850.00–1000.00; Kurdish Dancer, HN 2867, 800.00–900.00; Indian Temple Dancer, HN 2830, 1200.00–1400.00; Scottish Highland Dancer, HN 2436, 900.00–1100.00; Mexican Dancer, HN 2866, 600.00–750.00

DANCERS OF THE WORLD

The Dancers of the World Series was fully subscribed as of January 1, 1984, and is no longer available.

	Date	Price Range	

BALINESE DANCER
HN 2808

☐ Delicate in her gown of green with gold design, overskirts of yellow and pink, sleeveless bodice of multicolors, highlighted with a beautiful black belt. Gold necklace, gold and jeweled crown. Limited edition of 750, height 8¾″, designer M. Davies 1982–   650.00   750.00

BRETON DANCER
HN 2383

☐ Cream colored headdress in lace, black and green bodice over royal blue striped full dress, creamy pink apron, decoration on cuffs and skirt hem are as lace, matte finish. Limited edition of 750, height 8¾″, designer M. Davies 1981–   850.00

	Date	Price Range

CHINESE DANCER
HN 2840
☐ Costume is of blue with overblouse of orange and blue, green skirt, purple sash that is long and extending almost to feet, base is white, height 9″, designer M. Davies 1980– 750.00 850.00

INDIAN TEMPLE DANCER
HN 2830
☐ Costume of yellow with trim of green and gold design. Limited edition of 750, figure on white base, height 9¼″, designer M. Davies 1977– 1200.00 1400.00

KURDISH DANCER
HN 2867
☐ Base is light blue, costume is purple trousers, gown of dark blue with trim of white with black design and red and yellow dots, purple head covering trimmed with gold dots, gold necklace. Limited edition of 750, height 8¼″, designer M. Davies 1979– 800.00 900.00

MEXICAN DANCER
HN 2866
☐ Light brown base, group of orange with shaded browns, trimmed at hemline in designs of black on yellow, waistband of dark brown, hat light yellow with very light red/blue ribbons, long white cloth falls from under hat, figure base footed. Limited edition of 750, height 8¼″, designer M. Davies 1979– 600.00 750.00

NORTH AMERICAN INDIAN DANCER
HN 2809
☐ Beautiful young Indian maiden in traditional dress, holding a bouquet of wildflowers. Hair is raven black with headband of white with red design and white feather. Limited edition of 750, height 8¼″, designer M. Davies 1982– 650.00 750.00

PHILIPPINE DANCER
HN 2439
☐ Skirt of light blue with red shading with darker blue and yellow trim, blouse

	Date	Price Range	

peach with leaf design of red and green, open fan of white in each hand, head-covering is yellow with white trim with long light blue cloth, red shoes, base is blue with cream. Limited edition of 750, height 9½″, designer M. Davies   **1978–**   **850.00**   **1000.00**

POLISH DANCER
HN 2836

☐ Green base, red boots, skirt white with blue design and colored flowers, white apron with red flowers, black and gold bodice, blue/white blouse, headdress of red, blue and yellow flowers, several strands of colored beads, height 9½″, designer M. Davies **1980–**   **850.00**   **950.00**

SCOTTISH HIGHLAND DANCER
HN 2436

☐ Green base, skirt of red with black stripes and squares, red vest trimmed in yellow, white blouse, red and white checkered stockings, black shoes. Limited edition of 750, height 9½″, designer M. Davies **1978–**   **900.00**   **1100.00**

SPANISH FLAMENCO DANCER
HN 2831

☐ Gown of red with large blue/white ruffles trimmed in black, single red flower in hair, red shoes on white/blue base. Limited edition of 750, height 9½″, designer M. Davies **1977–**   **1500.00**   **1800.00**

WEST INDIAN DANCER
HN 2384

☐ Costume is a long sleeved dress of butter-cup yellow decorated with a reddish design, a long white petticoat decorated around hem, figure is brown color on multicolored base, semi-matte finish. Limited edition of 750, height 9″, designer M. Davies **1981–**   **700.00**   **750.00**

Cleopatra and Slave, HN 2868, 1200.00–1400.00

FEMME FATALE SERIES

	Date	Price Range

CLEOPATRA AND SLAVE
HN 2868
☐ Large light brown base, blue chair, gown of white with shaded blues and reds, necklace of blue, red, black and gold, head band gold and blue, mirror blue and gold, black slave holding gold and red bowl, fan is white feathers and red design with blue/red handle, chest of white and black, two bowls, one of gold and blue, the other gold and black. Limited edition of 750, height 7¼", designer M. Davies 1979–   1200.00   1400.00

HELEN OF TROY
HN 2387
☐ Figure is standing on base which

	Date	Price Range	

contains a marble pillar that holds a peacock, his tail flows to base, costume of figure is pale pink dress and sage green cloak. Limited edition of 750, height 12″, designer M. Davies 1981– 975.00 1150.00

QUEEN OF SHEBA
HN 2328
☐ Regal lady she is. Tall in stature, gown is gold and blue with yellow draping sash at waist, lilac cloak draped over her shoulder trimmed in gold, gold neckband, gold crown over her auburn hair. Cheetah at her side. Both figures on a green base, height 9″, designer M. Davies 1982– 975.00 1150.00

TZ'U-HSI EMPRESS DOWAGER
HN 2391
☐ Beautiful figure sitting on a dragon throne green in color with a marble like effect. The Empress Dowager is cooling herself with a fan. Pekinese dog stands on a black lacquered stool. Figure is dressed in red cloak with a deep blue dragon decorated cloak, height 8″, designer M. Davies 1983– 975.00 1150.00

EVE
HN 2466
☐ Nude figure standing on a base with long golden blonde hair flowing almost to her knees. In her hand she is holding an apple. She is standing in front of an apple tree, tree has cloud like foliage with a serpent swirling up through the tree to the top of the tree as if to whisper in her ear, height 9¼″, designer M. Davies 1984– 800.00 850.00

LUCREZIA BORGIA
HN 2342
☐ Gown is lemon color with a crimson scroll design. Cape is red and blue. She is holding a gold goblet. Table holds wine carafe and fruit basket, height 8″, designer M. Davies 1985– 975.00 1150.00

LADY MUSICIANS

	Date	Price Range	

CELLO
HN 2331
☐ Seated lady in gown of yellow with white bow trim, darker brown bodice, white ribbon in hair, playing brown cello. Limited edition of 750, now sold out, height 6″, designer M. Davies 1970– **1100.00** **1200.00**

CHITARRONE
HN 2700
☐ Standing figure in gown of dark blue and light blue with trim of roses on bodice, holding very long neck instrument. Limited edition of 750, now sold out, height 7½″, designer M. Davies 1974– **750.00** **900.00**

CYMBALS
HN 2699
☐ Green and orange gown, standing figure holding cymbals. Limited edition of 750, now sold out, height 7½″, designer M. Davies 1974– **500.00** **600.00**

DULCIMER
HN 2798
☐ Seated lady at table holding instrument, round box at side, gown of lavenders and white. Limited edition of 750, now sold out, height 6½″, designer M. Davies 1975– **550.00** **650.00**

FLUTE
HN 2483
☐ Seated figure in red and white gown playing flute. Limited edition of 750, now sold out, height 6¼″, designer M. Davies 1973– **975.00** **1075.00**

FRENCH HORN
HN 2795
☐ Seated lady holding French horn, gown of light green with darker green design, overlay of purple with white design. Limited edition of 750, now sold out, height 6″, designer M. Davies 1976– **500.00** **600.00**

	Date	Price Range	

HARP
HN 2482

□ Lady seated in chair with hands on golden harp, blue gown with purple overlay. Limited edition of 750, now sold out, height 8¾", designer M. Davies 1973– 1400.00 1675.00

HURDY GURDY
HN 2796

□ Lady seated in chair with instrument on lap, white gown with blue overlay, roses as trim on skirt, red hair. Limited edition of 750, which is now sold out, height 6", designer M. Davies 1975– 750.00 900.00

LUTE
HN 2431

□ Figure seated before a marble top table, holding lute on table, gown of blue and white, white ribbon in hair, open book on table. Limited edition of 750, now sold out, height 6½", designer M. Davies 1972– 500.00 600.00

VIOLA D'AMORE
HN 2797

□ Seated figure on brown and green chair, gown of yellow with red roses around hemline, overdress is blue with flower designs of red and green, holding viola under chin (viola is brown). Limited edition of 750, which is now sold out, height 6", designer M. Davies 1976– 500.00 600.00

VIOLIN
HN 2432

□ Figure seated, gown of yellow with shaded brown overdress holding brown violin under chin. Limited edition of 750, which is now sold out, height 6½", designer M. Davies 1972– 1000.00 1200.00

VIRGINALS
HN 2427

□ Figure seated at brown and white top table with instrument of brown color, gown of yellow with white bows,

	Date	Price Range

overdress of green with white bows, open book on instrument top. Limited edition of 750, which is now sold out, height 6½″, designer M. Davies 1971– 1500.00 2000.00

DANBURY MINT VICTORIAN LADIES

Four Seasons Series

The Danbury Mint commissioned the Royal Doulton Company to create a series of figurines, representing the Victorian era, to be released as a time limited edition. Introduced in 1986, they could be purchased, if desired, one every four months. Prices on the secondary market are ranging from $1200 to $1500 for the set of four figures.

LILIAN IN SUMMER
HN 3003
☐ Victorian lady dressed in long white gown with blue ribbon around waist, blue trim on sleeves and around neck. Wearing pink beads and holding a white parasol, trimmed in pink, over her head. Time limited series, height 8½″, designer P. Gee 1986– 300.00 375.00

EMILY IN AUTUMN
HN 3005
☐ Tall Victorian lady. Gown is white, floor length, highlighted with gold. Hat is white with gold touches over her lovely coiffured red hair. She is carrying a basket of fruit. Time limited series, height 8¼″, designer P. Gee 1986– 300.00 375.00

SARAH IN WINTER
HN 3005
☐ Tall Victorian lady wearing floor-length white coat with blue bodice. Light blue scarf tied over a medium blue hat. She is carrying a white muff. One blue slipper shows as she gaily walks along. Time limited series, height 8″, designer P. Gee 1986– 300.00 375.00

CATHERINE IN SPRING
HN 3006
☐ Victorian lady with long white gown overlaid with shades of pink. Large white hat with brown feather. She is

	Date	Price Range	
carrying a closed parasol. Time limited series, height 8½", designer P. Gee ..	1986–	300.00	375.00

MISCELLANEOUS FIGURINES

BEETHOVEN
HN 1778

☐ Bust style of Beethoven with figures of women around what appears to be hair, matte ivory glaze. Limited edition of 25, sold out, height 22", designer R. Garbe 1933–1939 6000.00 6500.00

DUCHESS OF YORK
HN 3086

☐ This figure was commissioned by Lawley's to celebrate the wedding of Miss Sarah Ferguson to H.R.H. Prince Andrew on July 23, 1986. Figure is wearing the design of Miss Ferguson's wedding dress. Limited edition of 1,500, height 8¼", designer E. Griffiths 1986– 475.00 750.00

HENRY VIII
HN 1792

☐ Robe of red, blue and black trimmed in fur, beige colored stockings, red shoes, standing on small base which has his name on it. Limited edition of 200, sold out, height unknown, designer C.J. Noke 1933–1939 3500.00 4000.00

HER MAJESTY QUEEN ELIZABETH II
HN 2878

☐ Designed as a tribute to Her Majesty, Queen of England, to commemorate the 30th Anniversary of her Coronation. Figure has gown of white over which is blue and crimson robe, badge of order is worn on the left, chain has the initials of the order in 22 kt. gold, trimmed with white crosses, white ribbons on the shoulder. Limited edition of 2,500, height 10½", designer E. Griffiths 1983– 450.00

	Date	Price Range	

HIS HOLINESS POPE JOHN PAUL II
HN 2888
☐ Beautiful likeness of His Holiness inspired by his visit to the United Kingdom, height 10″, designer E. Griffiths — 1982– — 185.00

H.R.H. THE PRINCE OF WALES
HN 2883
☐ Beautiful figure in black suit with red trim, cloak is purple and white with gold trim, gold sword in hand. Limited edition of 1,500, height 8″, designer E. Griffiths .... — 1982– — 600.00 — 750.00
HN 2884
☐ Depicts H.R.H. wearing the uniform of the Welsh Guards (second version). Limited edition of 1,500, height 8″, designer E. Griffiths .... — 1982– — 750.00 — 800.00

H.R.H. PRINCESS OF WALES
HN 2887
☐ Depicts Diana Spencer in her wedding dress. Limited edition of 1,500, height 7¾″, designer E. Griffiths .... — 1982– — 750.00 — 800.00

INDIAN BRAVE
HN 2376
☐ Indian mounted on black and white horse, costume of beige, dark blue, red and white, holding lance and shield of light brown with darker brown figures, headdress has yellow feathers. Limited edition of 500, which is now sold out, height 15½″, designer M. Davies ..... — 1967– — 6500.00 — 8000.00

LADY DIANA SPENCER
HN 2885
☐ Sleeveless gown of blue with white polka dots, white ruffle at bust line, white shawl over her bare shoulders, carrying beautiful bouquet of flowers, blonde hair. Limited edition of 1,500, height 7¾″, designer E. Griffiths ...... — 1982– — 650.00 — 900.00

MARRIAGE OF ART AND INDUSTRY
HN 2261
☐ Two bronze colored figures on base of

	Date	Price Range	

bronze with tints of green, base has figures of birds, flowers, etc. Limited edition of 12—was never put on sale, height 18″, designer M. Davies 1958– 9000.00 10,000.00

PALIO, The
HN 2428
☐ Knight mounted on horse on walnut base, armor of dark blue and light blue with gold design, light brown footwear, horse costume of light blue with gold design, light blue with white design, black, gold and red stripes, dark brown color for animal. Limited edition of 500, height 18″, designer M. Davies 1971–1973 6500.00 8000.00

PRINCE PHILIP, DUKE OF EDINBURG
HN 2386
☐ Limited edition of 750, height 8¼″, designer M. Davies 1981– 450.00 500.00

QUEEN ELIZABETH II
HN 2502
☐ Gown of light blue with blue designs, purple ribbon over shoulder and front. Limited edition of 750, now sold out, height 7¾″, designer M. Davies 1973– 1900.00 2300.00

QUEEN ELIZABETH, THE QUEEN MOTHER
HN 2882
☐ Figure is mounted on dark wooden base, gown is pink with white designs, dark blue ribbons across shoulder down to waist, wearing crown and necklace, holding white gloves. Limited edition of 1500, height 11¾″, designer unknown 1980– 1200.00 1400.00

ROYAL CANADIAN MOUNTED POLICE
HN 2547
☐ Bust figure of a Royal Canadian Policeman showing red coat uniform of 1973 and brown hat mounted on a black base. Limited edition of 1,500, height 8″, designer D. Tootle, sold only in Canada 1973– 1250.00 1550.00

Royal Canadian Mounted Police, HN 2547, 1250.00–1500.00

	Date	Price Range	
HN 2555			
□ Same bust figure but in uniform of 1873. Limited edition of 1,500, height 8″, designer D. Tootle, sold only in Canada	1973–	**1250.00**	**1500.00**
SALOME **HN 1775**			
□ Matte ivory finish. Limited edition of 100, sold out by 1939, height unknown, designer R. Garbe	1933–	**6500.00**	**8000.00**
SPIRIT OF THE WIND **HN 1777**			
□ HN 1825, matte ivory finish. Limited edition of 40, sold out in 1939, height 14½″, designer R. Garbe	1933–	**6500.00**	**8000.00**
SPRING **HN 1774**			
□ As 1827 but with matte ivory finish. Limited edition of 100, sold out by 1939, height 21″, designer R. Garbe	1933–	**5000.00**	**6000.00**

	Date	Price Range	

WEST WIND
HN 1776
☐ Large figure (14½″) of two, head and shoulders only, each has wings, matte ivory finish. Limited edition of 25 sold out in 1939, height 14½″, designer R. Garbe 1933– 4500.00 5000.00

SIR WINSTON CHURCHILL
HN 3057
☐ A white suit with black bow tie, white Homburg hat, leaning slightly on a black cane, traditional cigar in mouth, height 10½″, designer A. Hughes 1985– 185.00

LORD OLIVIER AS RICHARD III
HN 2881
☐ Portrays Lord Olivier in his most famous role . . . Richard of Gloucester. Richard is in battle dress gray and black armor with a tabard bearing the Royal Coat of Arms in colors of red, blue and gold. Standing on a base of gray, he is holding a sword. Limited edition of 750, height 11½″, designer E. Griffiths 1985– 750.00

MYTHS AND MAIDENS

LADY AND THE UNICORN
HN 2825
☐ White unicorn lying on a blue and gold base, lady's dress blue, gold flowers, red bodice with white ties, she is holding a gold mirror to reflect the unicorn to itself, beautiful fleurs-de-lis emphasis on the base, height 8¾″, designer R. Jefferson 1982– 2500.00

LEDA AND THE SWAN
HN 2826
☐ Seated figure within the wingspan of a white swan, barefooted, gown is pale and gold, trimming is black and white, dark brown hair with red headband, base is decorated in blues, greens and reds, banded in blue and gold, height 9¾″, designer R. Jefferson 1983– 2500.00

Juno, HN 2827, 2500.00

	Date	Price Range

JUNO AND THE PEACOCK
HN 2827

☐ Juno, the wife of Jupiter, greatest of the Roman gods, is beautiful in her soft yellow gown, with a soft lavender accentuated with purple draping over her gown. Standing at her side a beautiful peacock. Figures are on an aquamarine base with flowers, gold acorn leaves as trim, height 11″, designer R. Jefferson

1984–   2500.00

EUROPA AND THE BULL
HN 2828

☐ White bull shaded with light browns, garland of blue flowers, each handmade, on the bull's horns. Europa has gown of coral draped over her shoulders, extending to the bull's feet is a gold draping, figure mounted on mauve base

	Date	Price Range
with green trim, height 10½", designer R. Jefferson	1985–	2500.00

DIANA THE HUNTRESS
HN 2829
☐ Dressed in flowing gown of lemon yellow and pale green with an overdrape of olive green, she carries her brass bow which is strung with stainless steel wire. Walking along with her is a panther. Mounted on a yellow base trimmed in white, purple and gold. Limited edition of 300. Height 11¼", designer R. Jefferson 1986–   **2500.00**

GENTLE ARTS SERIES

A new limited edition series of eighteenth-century ladies, each depicting their creative talents. Each figure is created in a vellum color bone china and is accompanied by a metal accessory associated with their skill. Limited to 750 pieces. Introduced in late 1984, there are seven figures in the collection.

SPINNING
HN 2390
☐ Designer M. Davies 1984–   **1250.00**

TAPESTRY WEAVING
HN 3048
☐ Height 11½", designer P. Parsons 1985–   **1250.00**

WRITING
HN 3049
☐ Height 7¾", designer P. Parsons 1986–   **1250.00**

PAINTING
HN 3012
☐ Height 6", designer P. Parsons 1987–   **1250.00**

LES SAISONS SERIES

Introduced in 1986, this series of four figurines represents the four seasons. This series was modelled by Robert Jefferson. It should be most interesting and worth considering for one's collection. Limited edition of 300 worldwide.

AUTOMNE
☐ Standing on a richly colored base with decorative flowers and leaves completely surrounding the base, the figure

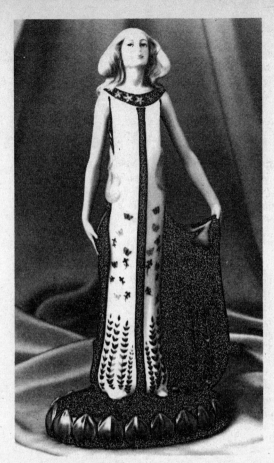

Printemps, HN 3066, 795.00

	Date	Price Range
stands eloquently dressed in a lemon-colored gown, lilac shoes, long flowing light brown hair, mauve cloak, inside of cloak is painted a sycamore tree richly and colorfully decorated with fall colors of oranges, browns, and reds, height 11½″, designer R. Jefferson ...	1986–	795.00

PRINTEMPS
HN 3066
☐ An exceptional figure depicting spring. Tall and slender, with long gown

	Date	Price Range

decorated with sprigs of spring and butterflies. Long blond hair. Figure stands on a dark blue base decorated with green leaves, height 11½, designer R. Jefferson 1987– 795.00

QUEENS OF THE REALM

Royal Doulton, from time to time, has introduced bone china figures of British Royalty. In 1987 they introduced the first of four queen figures created for a series to be called "Queens of the Realm." Each figure will be limited to 5,000. A full-color brochure, historically detailed, will accompany each figurine.

QUEEN ELIZABETH I
HN 3099
☐ First in this new series. Gown is a traditional state of coral red over gold. She is holding a gold mask. Pearl necklace, wearing jeweled tiara in her hair. Elizabeth I, born in 1533, became Queen in 1588, height 9″, designer P. Parsons   1987–   495.00

QUEEN VICTORIA
HN 3125
☐ Second in the "Queen of the Realm" series. Depicts the longest reigning monarch in British history, height 8″, designer P. Parsons   1988–   495.00

SHIPS' FIGUREHEADS

All are Limited Editions of 950. Designed by Sharon Keenan. Ships' Figureheads fully subscribed and no longer available as of January 1, 1984.

AJAX
☐ **HN 2908**   1980–   750.00

BENMORE
☐ **HN 2909**   1980–   750.00

CHIEFTAN
☐ **HN 2929**   1982–   950.00

HIBERNIA
☐ **HN 2932**   1983–   1150.00

	Date	Price Range	

LALLA ROOKH
☐ HN 2910 .... 1981– 950.00

MARY QUEEN OF SCOTS
☐ HN 2931 .... 1983– 1500.00

NELSON
☐ HN 2928 .... 1981– 950.00

POCAHONTAS
☐ HN 2930 .... 1982– 950.00

SOLDIERS OF THE REVOLUTION

CAPTAIN, 2ND NEW YORK REGIMENT
HN 2755
☐ Brown base, beige trousers, darker beige coat with blue trim, holding lance. Limited edition of 350 .... 1975–1980 900.00 1100.00

CORPORAL, 1st NEW HAMPSHIRE REGIMENT 1778
HN 2780
☐ Brown base, green trousers, lighter green coat with red trim, white cross straps, green vest, black hat, white stockings, brown shoes. Limited edition of 350 .... 1975–1980 900.00 1100.00

GEORGE WASHINGTON AT PRAYER
HN 2861
☐ George Washington in full uniform, kneeling on white base. Limited edition of 750, created by Laszlo Ispansky and available by subscription only from Limited Editions Collectors Society of America 1977– 2000.00 2500.00

MAJOR, 3rd NEW JERSEY REGIMENT 1776
HN 2752
☐ Brown base, seated on wooden fence, light blue costume with darker blue trim, hat black with white trim. Limited edition of 350 .... 1975–1980 1750.00 2100.00

	Date	Price Range	

PRIVATE, CONNECTICUT REGIMENT 1777
HN 2845

☐ Yellow/green base, beige trousers, brown coat, white cross straps, red trim on coat, black hat with blue/white trim, small cannon on base. Limited edition of 350 1975–1980   750.00   900.00

PRIVATE, DELAWARE REGIMENT 1776
HN 2761

☐ Yellow/green base, beige trousers, coat dark blue with red and white trim, cross strap of white, hat dark blue with white trim, small black box at waist, white vest. Limited edition of 350 1975–1980   750.00   900.00

PRIVATE, 1st GEORGIA REGIMENT 1777
HN 2779

☐ Brown base, white leggings, brown long coat, white shirt, white cross straps, has a tomahawk attached to base. Limited edition of 350 1975–1980   900.00   1000.00

PRIVATE, MASSACHUSETTS REGIMENT 1778
HN 2760

☐ Dark colored figure in blue/white uniform, dark blue hat, cross straps of dark blue, base contains blue/black barrel, brown box and cream colored box, base is yellow/green. Limited edition of 350   1975–1980   750.00   900.00

PRIVATE, PENNSYLVANIA RIFLE BATTALION 1776
HN 2846

☐ Kneeling figure on yellow/green base, costume of blue/gray, large brimmed hat of same color, powder horn, knife holder and small pouch of brown. Limited edition of 350 1975–1980   750.00   900.00

PRIVATE, RHODE ISLAND REGIMENT 1781
HN 2759

☐ Costume of beige trousers, white stockings, black shoes, blue coat with red

	Date	Price Range	

trim, white crossed straps, black hat with yellow trim, holding ram pole for cannon. Limited edition of 350   1975–1980   750.00   900.00

PRIVATE, 2nd SOUTH CAROLINA REGIMENT 1781
HN 2717

☐ Brown base, light colored trousers, blue coat with red lining, dark brown hat. Limited edition of 350   1975–1980   1000.00   1200.00

PRIVATE, 3rd NORTH CAROLINA REGIMENT 1778
HN 2754

☐ Brown base, costume of beige with green rolled bundle around shoulder. Limited edition of 350   1975–1980   950.00   1250.00

SERGEANT, 6th MARYLAND REGIMENT 1777
HN 2815

☐ Brown base, blue trousers, lighter blue coat and vest trimmed in green, waistband blue with red trim, hat black with white trim. Limited edition of 350   1975–1980   800.00   975.00

SERGEANT, VIRGINIA 1st REGIMENT CONTINENTAL LIGHT DRAGOON 1777
HN 2844

☐ Light yellow/green base which contains tree trunk with posted white sign, horse is brown and black, trappings on horse are green and yellow, costume of soldier is white trousers, brown coat with green trim, blue/white gloves, black hat with green ribbon trim. Limited edition of 350   1975–1980   2500.00   3200.00

MISCELLANEOUS ITEMS

CHERUB BELLS. Royal Doulton instituted its still-young series of Cherub Bells in 1979. To date, one has been issued each year in an edition limited to 5,000 specimens. The name derives from the fact that cherubs (youthful angels) are always included in the motif.

CIGARETTE LIGHTERS. This series was introduced in 1958 when 11 designs were placed on the market, some of which were manufactured in that year only. The last year in which new additions were made was 1964. Royal Doulton's cigarette lighters feature "character" portraits, similar to those on its jugs. A number of the types are taken from Dickens' novels but Shakespeare is also represented (Falstaff) as well as the creation of an American author (Rip Van Winkle, a character of Washington Irving). The scarcest are Musketeer and Rip Van Winkle, made in 1958 only.

EGG SERIES. In 1980 the factors began issuing decorative porcelain eggs in editions of 3,500. The tradition for decorative porcelain eggs is very old, as they were a favorite at European royal courts and especially at St. Petersburg in Russia more than 100 years ago.

GOBLET SERIES.

JUG SERIES. This series goes back to the 1930s and includes some highly sought-after items.

JUGS. These include the "Cliff Cornell Jugs," made in the 1950s for an American business executive as a special order. Royal Doulton has very seldom, in modern times, created "special order" items. Thus the Cliff Cornell jugs have a definite collector appeal.

LIQUOR CONTAINERS. Apparently made for a commercial liquor dealer.

LOVING CUPS. The company began issuing limited edition Loving Cups in 1933 and has added periodically to the series. Originally, loving cups were awarded as prizes in British sporting events, usually made of silver. The Royal Doulton versions are in porcelain with attractive enameling.

MUSICAL JUGS.

NAPKIN RINGS.

NATIVITY CUP AND SAUCER SERIES.

TABLE LAMPS. These have never been a really significant part of the factory line, but some are quite old (from the 1930s) and very attractive. They probably suffered destruction at a heavier rate than figurines and may be scarcer than many collectors realize.

TANKARD SERIES. Begun in 1971, this consists of decorative tankards with motifs from Dickens' "A Christmas Carol." Editions have run from 13,000 to 15,000 pieces.

TEAPOTS.

TOBACCO JARS.

WALL MASKS. Porcelain portraits in small size, to mount on the wall.

"Speech of Angels" Cherub Bell Series
(Limited Edition)

	Number	Year	Edition Size	Issue Price
☐ Glad Tidings (Clarion)	No. 1	1979–	5000	95.00
☐ Peace (Harp)	No. 2	1980–	5000	95.00
☐ Joy (Cymbals)	No. 3	1981–	5000	100.00
☐ Glory	No. 4	1982–	5000	100.00
☐ Harmony	No. 5	1983–	5000	100.00

"Twelve Days of Christmas" Goblet Series
(Limited Edition)

☐ Partridge in a Pear Tree	No. 1	1980–	10,000	55.00
☐ Two Turtle Doves	No. 2	1981–	10,000	60.00
☐ Three French Hens	No. 3	1982–	10,000	60.00
☐ Four Colly Birds	No. 4	1983–	10,000	60.00
☐ Five Golden Rings	No. 5	1984–	10,000	60.00
☐ Six Geese a Laying	No. 6	1985–	10,000	60.00
☐ Seven Swans A-Swimming	No. 7	1986–	10,000	60.00
☐ Eight Maids A-Milking	No. 8	1987–	10,000	60.00

"Joy to the World" Nativity Cup and Saucer Series
(Limited Edition)

☐ The Annunciation	No. 1	1980–	10,000	55.00
☐ Journey to Bethlehem	No. 2	1981–	10,000	60.00
☐ Shepherds in the Fields	No. 3	1982–	10,000	60.00
☐ We Three Kings	No. 4	1983–	10,000	60.00
☐ The Adoration	No. 5	1984–	10,000	60.00
☐ Noel	No. 6	1985–	10,000	60.00

1985 represents the final issue in this very beautiful cup and saucer series.

Egg Series

	Date	Edition Size	Issue Price
☐ Rouge Flambé Egg	1980–	3500	100.00
☐ Royal Crown Derby Paradise Cobalt	1981–	3500	175.00
☐ Minton 19th Century Egg	1979–	3500	75.00
☐ Minton Emperors Garden Egg	1982–	3500	95.00

Nativity Cup and Saucer, Shepherds in the Fields, 60.00

Cigarette Lighters

	Date	Price Range	
☐ Bacchus	1964–1973	150.00	175.00
☐ Beefeater	1958–1973	125.00	150.00
☐ Buz Fuz	1958 only	225.00	325.00
☐ Captain Ahab	1964–1973	200.00	250.00
☐ Cap 'N Cuttle	1958 only	350.00	450.00
☐ Falstaff	1958–1973	125.00	150.00
☐ Lawyer	1962–1973	225.00	275.00

Left to Right: Bacchus, 1964–1973, 150.00–175.00; Lawyer, 1962–1973, 225.00–275.00

	Date	Price Range	
☐ Long John Silver	1958–1973	150.00	200.00
☐ Mr. Micawber	1958 only	350.00	450.00
☐ Mr. Pickwick	1958–1961	250.00	350.00
☐ Musketeer (Porthos)	1958 only	750.00	1000.00
☐ Old Charley	1958 only	275.00	325.00
☐ Poacher	1958–1973	150.00	200.00
☐ Rip Van Winkle	1958 only	600.00	900.00

Ashtrays

DICK TURPIN

☐ D 5601	1936–1960	125.00	160.00

JOHN BARLEYCORN

☐ D 5602	1936–1960	125.00	160.00

OLD CHARLEY

☐ D 5599	1936–1960	130.00	165.00

PARSON BROWN

☐ D 5600	1936–1960	125.00	160.00

Ash Bowls

AULD MAC

☐ D 6006	1939–1960	125.00	150.00

FARMER JOHN

☐ D 6007	1939–1960	130.00	155.00

OLD CHARLEY

☐ D 5925	1938–1960	135.00	160.00

PADDY

☐ D 5926	1938–1960	125.00	150.00

Left to Right: Sairey Gamp, D 6009, 150.00–200.00; Parson Brown, D 6008, 125.00–150.00

	Date	Price Range	
PARSON BROWN			
☐ D 6008	1939–1960	125.00	150.00
SAIREY GAMP			
☐ D 6009	1939–1960	150.00	200.00

Bookends

	Date	Price Range	
MICAWBER			
☐ HN 1615		2000.00	2500.00
TONY WELLER			
☐ HN 1616		2000.00	2500.00
MR. PICKWICK			
☐ HN 1623		2000.00	2500.00
SAIREY GAMP			
☐ HN 1625		2000.00	2500.00

Busts

	Date	Price Range	
BUZ FUZ			
☐ D 6048	1939–1960	90.00	115.00
MR. MICAWBER			
☐ D 6050	1939–1960	90.00	115.00
MR. PICKWICK			
☐ D 6049	1939–1960	90.00	115.00
SAIREY GAMP			
☐ D 6047	1939–1960	100.00	125.00
SAM WELLER			
☐ D 6052	1939–1960	90.00	115.00
TONY WELLER			
☐ D 6051	1939–1960	90.00	115.00

Sugar Bowls

Standing 2½" in height. Produced only one year, 1939.

	Date	Price Range	
SAIREY GAMP			
☐ D 6011		350.00	400.00
OLD CHARLEY			
☐ D 6012		350.00	400.00
TONY WELLER			
☐ D 6013		350.00	400.00

Miniature Sugars

Produced during the years 1940 and 1941. Because they are small (slightly larger than the tinies), they are often referred to as toothpick holders.

	Price Range	
SAIREY GAMP		
☐ D 6150	300.00	350.00
PADDY		
☐ D 6151	300.00	350.00
OLD CHARLEY		
☐ D 6152	300.00	350.00

Limited Edition Jugs

	Date	Edition Size	Price Range	
☐ Captain Cook Jug	1933–	350	3000.00	3500.00
☐ Captain Phillip Jug	1938–	350	3000.00	3500.00
☐ Charles Dickens Jug	1936–	1000	700.00	800.00
☐ Dickens Dream Jug, unlimited but rare			850.00	950.00
☐ George Washington Jug, Rare	1932–	150	7000.00	9000.00
☐ Guy Fawkes Jug	1934–	600	700.00	850.00
☐ Master of Fox Hounds MFH Presentation Jug	1930–	500	650.00	850.00
☐ Pied Piper Jug	1934–	600	800.00	900.00
☐ Regency Coach Jug	1931–	500	750.00	850.00
☐ Sir Frances Drake Jug	1933–	500	800.00	900.00
☐ Tower of London Jug	1933–	500	800.00	900.00
☐ Treasure Island Jug	1934–	600	550.00	650.00
☐ Village Blacksmith Jug	1936–	600	750.00	850.00
☐ William Shakespeare Jug	1933–	1000	700.00	800.00

Charrington Toby, reads "TOBY ALES," 325.00–425.00

Seated Tobies

	Date	Price Range	

CHARRINGTON TOBY

☐ Made in the mid to late 1950s this jug, which is about 9 1/4" high, was produced for Charrington, well known brewers, for advertising purposes. One version reads "Toby Ales," and the second version reads "One Toby Leads to Another." 400.00 500.00

☐ Toby Ale 325.00 425.00

☐ Charringtons, third version 650.00 850.00

CLIFF CORNELL

☐ Special design produced · in the late 1950s for Cliff Cornell, an American

Cliff Cornell, blue suit, 275.00–375.00

	Date	Price Range	
businessman, for presentation to friends and as gifts. Jug depicts Mr. Cornell.			
☐ Large size, 9″, brown suit		250.00	300.00
☐ Large size, 9″, blue suit		275.00	375.00
☐ Large size, 9″, tan suit		400.00	500.00
☐ Medium size, 5½″, brown suit		225.00	250.00
☐ Medium size, 5½″, blue suit	1939–	275.00	325.00
☐ Medium size, 5½″, tan suit	RARE	1500.00	2000.00

CHARLIE CHAPLIN
| ☐ Seated Toby .... | | 4500.00 | 6000.00 |

GEORGE ROBEY
| ☐ Seated Toby .... | | 4500.00 | 6000.00 |

Inscription on base of Cliff Cornell Toby Jug

Liquor Containers

	Price Range	
☐ Falstaff	100.00	150.00
☐ Poacher	100.00	150.00
☐ Rip Van Winkle	100.00	150.00

Limited Edition Loving Cups

	Date	Edition Size	Price Range	
☐ Admiral Lord Nelson	1935–	600	875.00	1000.00
☐ The Apothecary	1934–	600	550.00	650.00
☐ Blacksmith	1934–	600	600.00	700.00
☐ Queen Elizabeth II Coronation	1953–	1000	400.00	500.00
☐ Jan Van Riebeeck	1935–	300	3000.00	3600.00
☐ John Peel	1933–	500	750.00	950.00
☐ King Edward VIII Coronation (large)	1937–	1080	550.00	650.00
☐ King Edward VIII Coronation (small)	1937–	464	500.00	650.00

Charlie Chaplin, 3750.00–4500.00

	Date	Edition Size	Price Range	
☐ King George VI and Queen Elizabeth Coronation (large) ..	1937–	2000	450.00	550.00
☐ King George VI and Queen Elizabeth Coronation (small)	1937–	2000	500.00	650.00
☐ King George and Queen Mary Silver Wedding	1935–	1000	500.00	650.00
☐ Queen Elizabeth II Silver Jubilee	1977–	250	900.00	1200.00
☐ Robin Hood	1938–	600	700.00	850.00
☐ The Wandering Minstrel	1934–	600	550.00	650.00
☐ Three Musketeers	1936–	600	750.00	950.00
☐ Wm. Wordsworth, unlimited but rare			2000.00	2500.00

Musical Jugs

	Price Range	
☐ Paddy	900.00	1100.00
☐ Auld Mac	900.00	1100.00

	Price Range	
☐ Tony Weller	750.00	850.00
☐ Old Charley	1000.00	1200.00
☐ Old King Cole	4500.00	5500.00
☐ Old King Cole, yellow crown	8000.00	10,000.00

Napkin Rings

☐ Mr. Pickwick M 57	400.00	500.00
☐ Mr. Micawber M 58	400.00	500.00
☐ Fat Boy M 59	400.00	500.00
☐ Tony Weller M 60	400.00	500.00
☐ Sam Weller M 61	400.00	500.00
☐ Sairey Gamp M 62	400.00	500.00
☐ Set of six with original box	3000.00	3600.00

These came in a set and were given numbers for record purposes; however, the numbers do not always appear on the napkin rings. Introduced about 1939 and withdrawn in 1960.

Table Lamps

☐ Arabian Horse	450.00	500.00
☐ Autumn Breezes	175.00	225.00
☐ Alice	125.00	175.00
☐ Balloon Man	175.00	225.00
☐ Barnaby	375.00	425.00
☐ Captain, The	250.00	300.00
☐ Carmen	200.00	250.00
☐ Celeste	250.00	275.00
☐ Clotilde	575.00	650.00
☐ Fair Lady	250.00	300.00
☐ Falstaff	200.00	250.00
☐ Foaming Quart	175.00	225.00
☐ Friar Tuck	525.00	600.00
☐ Gay Morning	250.00	300.00
☐ Good Catch	175.00	225.00
☐ Huntsman Fox	150.00	200.00
☐ Immortal (The), sitting green mandarin, 12″	2000.00	2500.00
☐ Jemima Puddleduck	250.00	300.00
☐ Judge, The	200.00	300.00
☐ Lady Fayre	350.00	450.00
☐ Old Balloon Seller	250.00	300.00
☐ Peter Rabbit	250.00	300.00
☐ Polly Peachum	275.00	325.00
☐ Top of the Hill	200.00	250.00
☐ Town Crier	300.00	400.00
☐ Uriah Heep	375.00	425.00
☐ Winston Churchill	250.00	300.00

"Beswick" Christmas Tankards Series

	Date	Edition Size	Issue Price
☐ Bob Crachit and Scrooge	1971–	13,000	50.00
☐ Christmas Carolers at Scrooge's Door	1972–	13,000	40.00
☐ Ghost of Christmas Future	1979–	15,000	60.00
☐ Marley's Ghost Visits Scrooge	1974–	15,000	45.00
☐ Scrooge is Asked to Aid the Poor	1973–	13,000	40.00
☐ Scrooge is Visited by Ghost of Christmas Past	1975–	15,000	50.00
☐ Scrooge is Visited by Ghost of Christmas Present	1976–	15,000	60.00
☐ Scrooge with Ghost of Christmas Present ..	1977–	15,000	50.00
☐ Scrooge with Ghost of Christmas Present ..	1978–	15,000	55.00
☐ Scrooge Going to Church	1981–	15,000	70.00
☐ Scrooge Visits His Own Grave	1980–	15,000	65.00
☐ Christmas at Bob Crachits	1982–	15,000	65.00

Tobacco Jars

	Price Range	
☐ Paddy	2000.00	2500.00
☐ Old Charley	2000.00	2500.00
☐ Dogs (5 or 6 encircling jar)	450.00	500.00

Teapots

☐ Sairey Gamp	2250.00	2750.00
☐ Old Charley	2500.00	3000.00
☐ Tony Weller	2250.00	2750.00
☐ Polar Bears on blue or green band, circling pot	150.00	200.00

Wall Masks

☐ Baby	800.00	1000.00
☐ Blue Lady, mini	350.00	450.00
☐ Fate	1000.00	1200.00
☐ Friar of Orders	800.00	900.00
☐ Green Lady, mini	300.00	350.00
☐ Greta Garbo	700.00	800.00
☐ Jester, large	350.00	450.00
☐ Jester, small	375.00	450.00
☐ Jester, mini	375.00	450.00
☐ Marlene Dietrich	700.00	800.00
☐ Pink Lady, mini	350.00	450.00
☐ Pompadour, large	1200.00	1500.00
☐ Pompadour, small	750.00	850.00

Jesters, 300.00–450.00; Jester, 300.00–450.00

	Price Range	
☐ St. Agnes	1000.00	1200.00
☐ Sweet Anne, pink	450.00	550.00
☐ Sweet Anne, green	600.00	700.00
☐ Sweet Anne, blue	600.00	700.00

Wall Pockets

☐ Jester	2500.00	3000.00
☐ Old Charley	2500.00	3000.00
☐ Crow	200.00	300.00

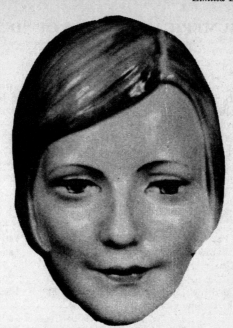

Marlene Dietrich, 700.00–800.00

NUMERICAL LISTINGS OF "D" MODEL NUMBERS

The following is a *numerical* listing of all Royal Doulton products bearing the prefix letter *D*. Mostly these are Character or Toby Jugs, for which the D prefix was instituted. However, over the years the factory has occasionally issued other items bearing the D prefix. In all cases, these non-jug articles with D prefix are directly associated with the company's jugs, as the motifs they carry are adapted from Character or Toby Jugs. Since this is a *numerical* listing, all objects bearing the same motif are not necessarily grouped together. Missing numbers were mostly used for miscellaneous items bearing jug-type motifs. See next section.

	Date	Price Range	
☐ D 5327, John Barleycorn, large	1934–1960	140.00	175.00
☐ D 5327, John Barleycorn, large	1978–	125.00	150.00
☐ D 5420, Old Charley, large	1934–1983	75.00	100.00
☐ D 5451, Sairey Gamp, large	1935–1986	75.00	100.00
☐ D 5486, Parson Brown, large	1935–1960	140.00	175.00
☐ D 5495, Dick Turpin (1st version), large	1935–1960	140.00	175.00
☐ D 5504, Simon the Cellarer, large	1935–1960	140.00	175.00
☐ D 5521, Granny, large	1935–1983	70.00	90.00
☐ D 5527, Old Charley, small	1935–1983	35.00	50.00
☐ D 5528, Sairey Gamp, small	1935–1986	45.00	65.00
☐ D 5529, Parson Brown, small	1935–1960	60.00	80.00
☐ D 5530, Tony Weller, small	1936–1960	60.00	75.00
☐ D 5531, Tony Weller, large	1936–1960	150.00	175.00
☐ D 5556, Jester, small	1936–	125.00	175.00
☐ D 5584, Old Curiosity Shop Jug (Miscellaneous, Dickens Jug)	1935–1960	175.00	225.00
☐ D 5599, Old Charley (Ashtray)	1936–1960	130.00	165.00
☐ D 5600, Parson Brown (Ashtray)	1936–1960	125.00	160.00
☐ D 5601, Dick Turpin (Ashtray)	1936–1960	125.00	160.00
☐ D 5602, John Barleycorn (Ashtray) ...	1936–1960	125.00	160.00
☐ D 5610, Clown, red hair	1937–1942	5500.00	6500.00
☐ D 5610, Clown, brown hair	RARE		
☐ D 5612, John Peel, large	1936–1960	140.00	185.00
☐ D 5613, Touchstone, large	1936–1960	275.00	325.00
☐ D 5614, Cardinal, large	1936–1960	140.00	165.00
☐ D 5615, The Vicar of Bray, large	1936–1960	250.00	300.00
☐ D 5616, Simon the Cellarer, small	1936–1960	75.00	100.00
☐ D 5617, Oliver Twist Jug (Miscellaneous Dickens Jugs)	1937–1960	150.00	200.00

	Date	Price Range	
☐**D 5618**, Dick Turpin (1st version), small	1935–1960	70.00	90.00
☐**D 5731**, John Peel, small	1937–1960	65.00	85.00
☐**D 5735**, John Barleycorn, small	1937–1960	75.00	100.00
☐**D 5736**, Toby Philpots, large	1937–1969	135.00	160.00
☐**D 5737**, Toby Philpots, small	1937–1969	55.00	70.00
☐**D 5753**, Paddy, large	1937–1960	135.00	165.00
☐**D 5756**, Pickwick Papers Jug (Miscellaneous Dickens Jugs)	1937–1960	200.00	250.00
☐**D 5757**, Mephistopheles, large	1937–1948	1750.00	2250.00
☐**D 5758**, Mephistopheles, small	1937–1948	1000.00	1250.00
☐**D 5768**, Paddy, small	1937–1960	50.00	70.00
☐**D 5788**, Farmer John, large	1938–1960	150.00	180.00
☐**D 5789**, Farmer John, small	1938–1960	80.00	110.00
☐**D 5823**, Owd Mac, large	1938–1945	150.00	200.00
☐**D 5823**, Auld Mac, large	1938–1985	60.00	85.00
☐**D 5824**, Auld Mac, small	1938–1985	35.00	50.00
☐**D 5838**, Buz Fuz, intermediate size	1938–1948	200.00	250.00
☐**D 5838**, Buz Fuz, small size	1948–1960	100.00	135.00
☐**D 5839**, Mr. Pickwick, special size	1938–1948	180.00	220.00
☐**D 5839**, Mr. Pickwick, small	1948–1960	90.00	125.00
☐**D 5840**, Fat Boy, special size	1938–1948	200.00	250.00
☐**D 5840**, Fat Boy, small	1948–1960	100.00	125.00
☐**D 5841**, Sam Weller, special size	1938–1948	200.00	250.00
☐**D 5841**, Sam Weller, small	1948–1960	100.00	125.00
☐**D 5842**, Cap'n Cuttle, special size	1938–1949	185.00	220.00
☐**D 5842**, Cap'n Cuttle, small size	1948–1960	90.00	125.00
☐**D 5843**, Mr. Micawber, special size	1938–1948	185.00	225.00
☐**D 5843**, Mr. Micawber, small	1948–1960	90.00	125.00
☐**D 5925**, Old Charley (Ash Bowl)	1938–1960	135.00	160.00
☐**D 5926**, Paddy (Ash Bowl)	1938–1960	125.00	150.00
☐**D 6006**, Auld Mac (Ash Bowl)	1939–1960	125.00	150.00
☐**D 6007**, Farmer John (Ash Bowl)	1939–1960	130.00	155.00
☐**D 6008**, Parson Brown (Ash Bowl)	1939–1960	125.00	150.00
☐**D 6009**, Sairey Gamp (Ash Bowl)	1939–1960	150.00	200.00
☐**D 6011**, Sairey Gamp (Sugar Bowl)	1939–	350.00	400.00
☐**D 6012**, Old Charley (Sugar Bowl)	1939–	350.00	400.00
☐**D 6013**, Tony Weller (Sugar Bowl)	1939–	350.00	400.00
☐**D 6030**, Old Charley (Toby Jug)	1939–1960	200.00	275.00
☐**D 6031**, Happy John (Toby Jug)	1939–	115.00	
☐**D 6033**, Cardinal, small	1939–1960	65.00	85.00
☐**D 6036**, Old King Cole, large	1939–1960	275.00	350.00
☐**D 6036**, Old King Cole, yellow crown, large	1938–	9000.00	11,000.00
☐**D 6037**, Old King Cole, small	1939–1960	100.00	140.00
☐**D 6041**, John Barleycorn, miniature	1939–1960	65.00	85.00
☐**D 6042**, Paddy, miniature	1939–1960	50.00	65.00

	Date	Price Range	
☐ D 6043, Toby Philpots, miniature	1939–1969	40.00	60.00
☐ D 6044, Tony Weller, miniature	1939–1960	40.00	50.00
☐ D 6045, Sairey Gamp, miniature	1939–1986	35.00	50.00
☐ D 6046, Old Charley, miniature	1939–1983	25.00	40.00
☐ D 6047, Sairey Gamp (Bust)	1939–1960	100.00	125.00
☐ D 6048, Buz Fuz (Bust)	1939–1960	90.00	115.00
☐ D 6049, Mr. Pickwick (Bust)	1939–1960	90.00	115.00
☐ D 6050, Mr. Micawber (Bust)	1939–1960	90.00	115.00
☐ D 6051, Tony Weller (Bust)	1939–1960	90.00	115.00
☐ D 6052, Sam Weller (Bust)	1939–1960	90.00	115.00
☐ D 6060, Mr. Pickwick, large	1940–1960	145.00	185.00
☐ D 6062, Falstaff (Toby Jug)	1939–	115.00	
☐ D 6063, Falstaff (Toby Jug)	1939–	60.00	
☐ D 6064, Sam Weller, large	1940–1960	140.00	170.00
☐ D 6069, Old Charley (Toby Jug)	1939–1960	200.00	250.00
☐ D 6070, Happy John (Toby Jug)	1939–	60.00	
☐ D 6088, Double XX or The Man on the Barrel (Toby Jug)	1939–1969	375.00	475.00
☐ D 6107, The Best is Not Too Good (Toby Jug)	1939–1960	300.00	400.00
☐ D 6108, Honest Measure (Toby Jug)	1939–	60.00	
☐ D 6109, Jolly Toby (Toby Jug)	1939–	75.00	
☐ D 6114, The Cavalier, large	1940–1960	150.00	175.00
☐ D 6114 The Cavalier with Goatee, large		6000.00	7500.00
☐ D 6115, Drake (2nd version), large ...	1940–1960	150.00	180.00
☐ D 6128, Dick Turpin (1st version), miniature	1940–1960	50.00	75.00
☐ D 6129, Cardinal, miniature	1940–1960	45.00	65.00
☐ D 6130, John Peel, miniature	1940–1960	50.00	60.00
☐ D 6138, Mr. Micawber, miniature ...	1940–1960	55.00	65.00
☐ D 6139, Fat Boy, miniature	1940–1960	65.00	90.00
☐ D 6140, Sam Weller, miniature	1940–1960	55.00	65.00
☐ D 6142, Fat Boy, tiny	1940–1960	100.00	140.00
☐ D 6143, Mr. Micawber, tiny	—	100.00	140.00
☐ D 6144, Old Charley, tiny	1940–1960	110.00	140.00
☐ D 6145, Paddy, tiny	1940–1960	100.00	140.00
☐ D 6146, Sairey Gamp, tiny	1940–1960	95.00	125.00
☐ D 6147, Sam Weller, tiny	1940–1960	100.00	140.00
☐ D 6150, Sairey Gamp, miniature (Sugar Bowl)	1940–1941	300.00	350.00
☐ D 6151, Paddy, miniature (Sugar Bowl)	1940–1941	300.00	350.00
☐ D 6152, Old Charley, miniature (Sugar Bowl)	1940–1941	300.00	350.00
☐ D 6170, Churchill, large	1940–	7500.00	9000.00

	Date	Price Range	
☐ **D 6171**, Sir Winston Churchill, large (Toby Jug)	1941–	115.00	
☐ **D 6172**, Sir Winston Churchill, small (Toby Jug)	1941–	75.00	
☐ **D 6173**, The Cavalier, small	1940–1960	75.00	90.00
☐ **D 6174**, Drake (2nd version), small ...	1941–1960	75.00	90.00
☐ **D 6175**, Sir Winston Churchill, miniature (Toby Jug)	1941–	60.00	
☐ **D 6198**, Smuts, large	1946–1948	1700.00	2200.00
☐ **D 6202**, Monty, large	1946–	95.00	
☐ **D 6205**, Robin Hood (1st version), large	1947–1960	150.00	175.00
☐ **D 6206**, Beefeater, large	1947–	95.00	
☐ **D 6207**, 'Arry, large	1947–1960	185.00	225.00
☐ **D 6207**, Pearly Boy, large, see alphabetical listing	—	—	
☐ **D 6208**, 'Arriet, large	1947–1960	175.00	200.00
☐ **D 6208**, 'Arriet, large	1947–1960	175.00	225.00
☐ **D 6208**, Pearly Girl, large	—	12,000.00	15,000.00
☐ **D 6233**, Beefeater, small	1947–	50.00	
☐ **D 6234**, Robin Hood (1st version), small	1947–1960	75.00	85.00
☐ **D 6235**, 'Arry, small	1947–1960	100.00	125.00
☐ **D 6235**, Pearly Boy, small, see alphabetical listing	—	—	
☐ **D 6236**, 'Arriet, small	1947–1960	100.00	125.00
☐ **D 6236**, Pearly Girl, small	11	5000.00	7500.00
☐ **D 6245**, Mr. Pickwick, miniature	1947–1960	60.00	75.00
☐ **D 6249**, 'Arry, miniature	1947–1960	80.00	100.00
☐ **D 6250**, 'Arriet, miniature	1947–1960	80.00	100.00
☐ **D 6249**, Pearly Boy, miniature, see alphabetical listing	—	—	
☐ **D 6250**, Pearly Girl, miniature	—	Not known to exist	
☐ **D 6251**, Beefeater, miniature	1947–	40.00	
☐ **D 6252**, Robin Hood (1st version), miniature	1947–1960	60.00	75.00
☐ **D 6253**, Auld Mac, miniature	1946–1985	25.00	35.00
☐ **D 6255**, 'Arry, tiny	1947–1960	200.00	250.00
☐ **D 6256**, 'Arriet, tiny	1947–1960	200.00	250.00
☐ **D 6257**, Auld Mac, tiny	1946–1960	225.00	275.00
☐ **D 6258**, Cardinal, tiny	1947–1960	225.00	275.00
☐ **D 6259**, John Peel, tiny	1947–1960	250.00	300.00
☐ **D 6260**, Mr. Pickwick, tiny	1947–1960	225.00	275.00
☐ **D 6261**, Mr. Pickwick (Toby Jug)	1948–1960	200.00	250.00
☐ **D 6262**, Mr. Micawber (Toby Jug) ...	1948–1960	175.00	225.00
☐ **D 6263**, Sairey Gamp (Toby Jug)	1948–1960	200.00	250.00
☐ **D 6264**, The Fat Boy (Toby Jug)	1948–1960	200.00	225.00

	Date	Price Range	
☐ **D 6265**, Sam Weller (Toby Jug)	1948–1960	200.00	250.00
☐ **D 6266**, Cap'n Cuttle (Toby Jug)	1948–1960	175.00	225.00
☐ **D 6285**, Oliver Twist Jug (Miscellaneous Dickens Jugs)	1936–1960	250.00	325.00
☐ **D 6286**, Oliver Twist Tankard	1949–1960	250.00	325.00
☐ **D 6287**, Falstaff, large	1950–	95.00	
☐ **D 6288**, Jarge, large	1950–1960	375.00	450.00
☐ **D 6289**, Samuel Johnson, large	1950–1960	300.00	400.00
☐ **D 6291**, Old London Jug (Miscellaneous Dickens Jugs)	1949–1960	250.00	325.00
☐ **D 6292**, Peggotty Jug (Miscellaneous Dickens Jugs)	1949–1960	300.00	400.00
☐ **D 6295**, Jarge, small	1950–1960	200.00	250.00
☐ **D 6296**, Samuel Johnson, small	1950–1960	185.00	225.00
☐ **D 6319**, The Squire (Toby Jug)	1950–1969	375.00	475.00
☐ **D 6320**, The Huntsman (Toby Jug) ..	1950–	115.00	
☐ **D 6321**, Friar Tuck, large	1951–1960	375.00	450.00
☐ **D 6322**, Clown, white hair, large	1951–1955	1200.00	1500.00
☐ **D 6335**, Long John Silver, large	1952–	95.00	
☐ **D 6336**, Lord Nelson, large	1952–1969	325.00	375.00
☐ **D 6337**, Uncle Tom Cobbleigh, large	1952–1960	475.00	550.00
☐ **D 6372**, Johnny Appleseed, large	1935–1969	325.00	400.00
☐ **D 6374**, Simple Simon, large	1953–1960	550.00	650.00
☐ **D 6375**, Dick Whittington, large	1953–1960	400.00	500.00
☐ **D 6384**, Granny, small	1953–1983	40.00	50.00
☐ **D 6385**, Falstaff, small	1950–	50.00	
☐ **D 6386**, Long John Silver, small	1952–	50.00	
☐ **D 6403**, The Pied Piper, large	1954–1980	75.00	90.00
☐ **D 6404**, Issac Walton, large	1953–	110.00	125.00
☐ **D 6429**, Poacher, large	1955–	95.00	
☐ **D 6438**, Rip Van Winkle, large	1955–	95.00	
☐ **D 6439**, Athos, large	1956–	95.00	
☐ **D 6440**, Porthos, large	1956–	95.00	
☐ **D 6441**, Aramis, large	1956–	95.00	
☐ **D 6452**, Athos, small	1956–	50.00	
☐ **D 6453**, Porthos, small	1956–	50.00	
☐ **D 6454**, Aramis, small	1956–	50.00	
☐ **D 6455**, Don Quixote, large	1957–	95.00	
☐ **D 6456**, Sancho Panza, large	1960–1982	75.00	100.00
☐ **D 6460**, Don Quixote, small	1957–	50.00	
☐ **D 6461**, Sancho Panza, small	1960–1982	50.00	75.00
☐ **D 6462**, The Pied Piper, small	1957–1980	40.00	50.00
☐ **D 6463**, Rip Van Winkle, small	1957–	50.00	
☐ **D 6464**, Poacher, small	1957–	50.00	
☐ **D 6467**, Captain Henry Morgan, large	1958–1981	75.00	100.00
☐ **D 6469**, Captain Henry Morgan, small	1958–1981	40.00	55.00
☐ **D 6470**, Mine Host, small	1958–1981	40.00	60.00

	Date	Price Range	
☐ **D 6488**, Mine Host, large	1958–1981	75.00	90.00
☐ **D 6496**, Viking, large	1959–1975	175.00	225.00
☐ **D 6497**, The Fortune Teller, large	1959–1967	500.00	600.00
☐ **D 6498**, The Lawyer, large	1959–	95.00	
☐ **D 6499**, Bacchus, large	1959–	95.00	
☐ **D 6500**, Captain Ahab, large	1959–1984	75.00	100.00
☐ **D 6501**, The Mikado, large	1959–1969	550.00	650.00
☐ **D 6502**, Viking, small	1959–1975	125.00	150.00
☐ **D 6503**, The Fortune Teller, small ...	1959–1967	300.00	375.00
☐ **D 6504**, The Lawyer, small	1959–	50.00	
☐ **D 6505**, Bacchus, small	1959–	50.00	
☐ **D 6506**, Captain Ahab, small	1959–1984	35.00	50.00
☐ **D 6507**, The Mikado, small	1959–1969	300.00	375.00
☐ **D 6508**, Aramis, miniature	1960–	40.00	
☐ **D 6509**, Athos, miniature	1960–	40.00	
☐ **D 6510**, Captain Henry Morgan	1960–1981	25.00	40.00
☐ **D 6511**, Don Quixote, miniature	1960–	40.00	
☐ **D 6512**, Long John Silver	1960–	40.00	
☐ **D 6513**, Mine Host, miniature	1960–1981	25.00	35.00
☐ **D 6514**, The Pied Piper, miniature ...	1960–1980	25.00	35.00
☐ **D 6515**, Poacher, miniature	1960–	40.00	
☐ **D 6516**, Porthos, miniature	1960–	40.00	
☐ **D 6517**, Rip Van Winkle, miniature	1960–	40.00	
☐ **D 6518**, Sancho Panza, miniature	1960–1982	40.00	65.00
☐ **D 6519**, Falstaff, miniature	1960–	40.00	
☐ **D 6520**, Granny, miniature	1960–1983	25.00	35.00
☐ **D 6521**, Bacchus, miniature	1960–	40.00	
☐ **D 6522**, Captain Ahab, miniature	1960–1984	30.00	45.00
☐ **D 6523**, The Fortune Teller, miniature	1960–1967	350.00	400.00
☐ **D 6524**, The Lawyer, miniature	1960–	40.00	
☐ **D 6525**, The Mikado, miniature	1960–1969	375.00	450.00
☐ **D 6526**, Viking, miniature	1960–1975	125.00	150.00
☐ **D 6527**, Robin Hood (2nd version), large	1960–	95.00	
☐ **D 6528**, Dick Turpin (2nd version), large	1960–1980	65.00	85.00
☐ **D 6529**, Merlin, large	1960–	95.00	
☐ **D 6530**, Town Crier, large	1960–1973	200.00	275.00
☐ **D 6531**, Gone Away, large	1960–1981	65.00	85.00
☐ **D 6532**, Robinson Crusoe, large	1960–1982	60.00	85.00
☐ **D 6533**, Falconer, larger	1960–	95.00	
☐ **D 6534**, Robin Hood (2nd version), small	1960–	50.00	
☐ **D 6535**, Dick Turpin (2nd version), small	1960–1980	45.00	65.00
☐ **D 6536**, Merlin, small	1960–	50.00	
☐ **D 6537**, Town Crier, small	1960–1973	100.00	160.00

	Date	Price Range	
☐ **D 6538**, Gone Away, small	1960–	40.00	55.00
☐ **D 6539**, Robinson Crusoe, small	1960–1982	35.00	50.00
☐ **D 6540**, Falconer, small	1960–	50.00	
☐ **D 6541**, Robin Hood (2nd version), miniature	1960–	40.00	
☐ **D 6542**, Dick Turpin (2nd version), miniature	1960–1980	40.00	50.00
☐ **D 6543**, Merlin, miniature	1960–	40.00	
☐ **D 6544**, Town Crier, miniature	1960–1973	110.00	160.00
☐ **D 6545**, Gone Away, miniature	1960–	30.00	45.00
☐ **D 6546**, Robinson Crusoe, miniature	1960–	25.00	40.00
☐ **D 6547**, Falconer, miniature	1960–	40.00	
☐ **D 6548**, Neptune, large	1961–	95.00	
☐ **D 6550**, Gladiator, large	1961–1967	575.00	650.00
☐ **D 6551**, Old Salt, large	1961–	95.00	
☐ **D 6552**, Neptune, small	1961–	50.00	
☐ **D 6553**, Gladiator, small	1952–	425.00	500.00
☐ **D 6554**, Old Salt, small	1961–	50.00	
☐ **D 6555**, Neptune, miniature	1961–	40.00	
☐ **D 6556**, Gladiator, miniature	1961–1967	400.00	475.00
☐ **D 6557**, Old Salt, miniature	1984–	40.00	
☐ **D 6558**, Scaramouche, large	1962–1967	675.00	750.00
☐ **D 6559**, Regency Beau, large	1962–1967	1100.00	1300.00
☐ **D 6560**, Gulliver, large	1962–1967	600.00	700.00
☐ **D 6561**, Scaramouche, small	1962–1967	500.00	600.00
☐ **D 6562**, Regency Beau, small	1962–1967	600.00	700.00
☐ **D 6563**, Gulliver, small	1962–1967	425.00	475.00
☐ **D 6564**, Scaramouche, miniature	1962–1967	500.00	600.00
☐ **D 6565**, Regency Beau, miniature	1962–1967	775.00	950.00
☐ **D 6566**, Gulliver, miniature	1962–1967	375.00	425.00
☐ **D 6567**, The Apothecary, large	1963–1983	75.00	100.00
☐ **D 6568**, Guardsman, large	1963–1983	60.00	80.00
☐ **D 6569**, Night Watchman, large	1963–1983	60.00	80.00
☐ **D 6570**, Gaoler, large	1963–1983	75.00	100.00
☐ **D 6571**, Blacksmith, large	1963–1983	60.00	80.00
☐ **D 6572**, Bootmaker, large	1963–1983	60.00	80.00
☐ **D 6573**, Gunsmith, large	1963–1983	60.00	80.00
☐ **D 6574**, The Apothecary, small	1963–1983	40.00	60.00
☐ **D 6575**, Guardsman, small	1963–1983	45.00	60.00
☐ **D 6576**, Night Watchman, small	1963–1983	45.00	60.00
☐ **D 6577**, Gaoler, small	1963–1983	50.00	75.00
☐ **D 6578**, Blacksmith, small	1963–1983	45.00	60.00
☐ **D 6579**, Bootmaker, small	1963–1983	45.00	60.00
☐ **D 6580**, Gunsmith, small	1963–1983	45.00	60.00
☐ **D 6581**, The Apothecary, miniature ..	1963–1983	30.00	40.00
☐ **D 6582**, Guardsman, miniature	1963–1983	35.00	50.00
☐ **D 6583**, Night Watchman, miniature	1963–1983	35.00	50.00

	Date	Price Range	
☐ **D 6584,** Gaoler, miniature	1963–1983	45.00	60.00
☐ **D 6585,** Blacksmith, miniature	1963–1983	40.00	60.00
☐ **D 6586,** Bootmaker, miniature	1963–1983	40.00	50.00
☐ **D 6587,** Gunsmith, miniature	1963–1983	35.00	50.00
☐ **D 6588,** 'Ard of 'Earing, large	1964–1967	1100.00	1300.00
☐ **D 6589,** Gondolier, large	1964–1969	600.00	700.00
☐ **D 6590,** Punch and Judy Man, large	1964–1969	600.00	675.00
☐ **D 6591,** 'Ard of 'Earing, small	1964–1967	650.00	800.00
☐ **D 6592,** Gondolier, small	1964–1969	450.00	550.00
☐ **D 6593,** Punch and Judy Man, small	1964–1969	425.00	500.00
☐ **D 6594,** 'Ard of 'Earing, miniature ...	1964–1967	1200.00	1400.00
☐ **D 6595,** Gondolier, miniature	1964–1969	400.00	500.00
☐ **D 6596,** Punch and Judy Man, miniature	1964–1969	400.00	475.00
☐ **D 6597,** Captain Hook, large	1965–1971	450.00	500.00
☐ **D 6598,** Mad Hatter, large	1965–1983	70.00	85.00
☐ **D 6599,** Ugly Duchess, large	1965–1973	400.00	500.00
☐ **D 6600,** Walrus and Carpenter, large	1965–1979	90.00	125.00
☐ **D 6601,** Captain Hook, small	1965–1971	300.00	350.00
☐ **D 6602,** Mad Hatter, small	1965–1983	40.00	50.00
☐ **D 6603,** Ugly Duchess, small	1965–1973	275.00	350.00
☐ **D 6604,** Walrus and Carpenter, small	1965–1969	60.00	75.00
☐ **D 6605,** Captain Hook, miniature	1965–1971	325.00	375.00
☐ **D 6606,** Mad Hatter, miniature	1965–1983	35.00	45.00
☐ **D 6607,** Ugly Duchess, miniature	1965–1973	275.00	350.00
☐ **D 6608,** Walrus and Carpenter, miniature	1965–1979	40.00	55.00
☐ **D 6609,** Trapper, large	1967–1983	80.00	100.00
☐ **D 6610,** Lumberjack, large	1967–1982	60.00	80.00
☐ **D 6611,** North American Indian, large	1967–	95.00	
☐ **D 6612,** Trapper, small	1967–1983	45.00	65.00
☐ **D 6613,** Lumberjack, small	1967–1982	35.00	55.00
☐ **D 6614,** North American Indian, small	1967–	50.00	
☐ **D 6616,** Smuggler, large	1968–1980	85.00	110.00
☐ **D 6617,** Lobster Man, large	1968–	95.00	
☐ **D 6618,** St. George, large	1968–1975	225.00	275.00
☐ **D 6619,** Smuggler, small	1968–1980	50.00	75.00
☐ **D 6620,** Lobster Man, small	1968–	50.00	
☐ **D 6621,** St. George, small	1968–1975	100.00	140.00
☐ **D 6622,** Yachtsman, large	1971–1979	100.00	150.00
☐ **D 6623,** Golfer, large	1971–	95.00	
☐ **D 6625,** Jockey, large	1971–1975	325.00	375.00
☐ **D 6630,** Gardener, large	1973–1980	125.00	175.00
☐ **D 6631,** Sleuth, large	1973–	95.00	
☐ **D 6632,** Tam O'Shanter, large	1975–1979	100.00	140.00
☐ **D 6633,** Veteran Motorist, large	1973–1983	65.00	85.00
☐ **D 6634,** Gardener, small	1973–1980	60.00	85.00

	Date	Price Range	
☐ **D 6635,** Sleuth, small	1973–	50.00	
☐ **D 6636,** Tam O'Shanter, small	1973–1979	50.00	70.00
☐ **D 6637,** Veteran Motorist, small	1973–1983	50.00	60.00
☐ **D 6638,** Gardener, miniature	1973–1980	50.00	65.00
☐ **D 6639,** Sleuth, miniature	1973–	40.00	
☐ **D 6640,** Tam O'Shanter, miniature ..	1973–1979	40.00	50.00
☐ **D 6641,** Veteran Motorist, miniature	1973–1983	40.00	50.00
☐ **D 6642,** Henry VIII, large	1975–	95.00	
☐ **D 6643,** Catherine of Aragon, large ..	1975–	95.00	
☐ **D 6644,** Anne Boleyn, large	1975–	95.00	
☐ **D 6645,** Catherine Howard, large	1978–	95.00	
☐ **D 6646,** Jane Seymour, large	1979–	95.00	
☐ **D 6647,** Henry VIII, small	1979–	50.00	
☐ **D 6648,** Henry VIII, miniature	1979–	40.00	
☐ **D 6650,** Anne Boleyn, small	1975–	50.00	
☐ **D 6651,** Anne Boleyn, miniature	1980–	40.00	
☐ **D 6652,** Lobster Man, miniature	1981–	40.00	
☐ **D 6653,** Anne of Cleves, large	1980–	95.00	
☐ **D 6654,** Mark Twain, large	1980–	95.00	
☐ **D 6657,** Catherine of Aragon, small ..	1981–	50.00	
☐ **D 6658,** Catherine of Aragon, miniature	1981–	40.00	
☐ **D 6659,** The Cabinetmaker, large	1981–	Piloted only none sold	
☐ **D 6660,** Sir Frances Drake (Toby Jug)	1981–	115.00	
☐ **D 6661,** Sherlock Holmes (Toby Jug)	1981–	115.00	
☐ **D 6664,** Catherine Parr, large	1981–	95.00	
☐ **D 6665,** North American Indian, miniature	1981–	40.00	
☐ **D 6667,** Macbeth, large	1982–1988	95.00	
☐ **D 6668,** Santa Claus, large	1981 only	90.00	110.00
☐ **D 6669,** George Washington, large ...	1982–	95.00	
☐ **D 6670,** Romeo, large	1983–1988	95.00	
☐ **D 6671,** Henry V, large	1982–1988	95.00	
☐ **D 6672,** Hamlet, large	1982–1988	95.00	
☐ **D 6673,** Othello, large	1982–1988	95.00	
☐ **D 6674,** W. C. Fields, large	1983–1985	95.00	125.00
☐ **D 6675,** Santa Claus, large	1982–	90.00	115.00
☐ **D 6676,** Charles Dickens, small	1984–	30.00	40.00
☐ **D 6677,** Oliver Twist, small	1984–	30.00	40.00
☐ **D 6678,** Artful Dodger, small	1984–	30.00	40.00
☐ **D 6679,** Fagen, small	1984–	30.00	40.00
☐ **D 6680,** David Copperfield, small	1984–	30.00	40.00
☐ **D 6681,** Little Nell, small	1984–	30.00	40.00
☐ **D 6682,** Uriah Heep, small	1984–	30.00	40.00
☐ **D 6683,** Scrooge, small	1984–	30.00	40.00
☐ **D 6684,** Bill Sykes, small	1984–	30.00	40.00
☐ **D 6685,** Betsy Trotwood, small	1984–	30.00	40.00

	Date	Price Range	
☐ **D 6686**, Mr. Bumble, small	1984–	30.00	40.00
☐ **D 6687**, Mrs. Bardell, small	1984–	30.00	40.00
☐ **D 6688**, Mae West, large	1983–1985	85.00	115.00
☐ **D 6689**, Shakespeare, large	1983–	95.00	
☐ **D 6690**, Santa Claus, large	1983 only	75.00	95.00
☐ **D 6691**, D'Artagnan, large	1983–	95.00	
☐ **D 6692**, Catherine Howard, small	1984–	50.00	
☐ **D 6693**, Catherine Howard, miniature	1984–	40.00	
☐ **D 6694**, Mark Twain, small	1983–	50.00	
☐ **D 6695**, Benjamin Franklin, small	1983–1988	50.00	
☐ **D 6696**, Loving Cup, Pottery of the Past	1984–	250.00	300.00
☐ **D 6697**, Fireman, large	1983–	95.00	
☐ **D 6698**, U.S. Civil War/Grant and Lee, large (limited edition)	1983–	200.00	250.00
☐ **D 6699**, Mr. Litigate, The Lawyer ...	1983–	45.00	
☐ **D 6700**, Miss Nostrum, The Nurse ...	1983–	45.00	
☐ **D 6701**, Mr. Furrow, The Farmer	1983–	45.00	
☐ **D 6702**, Rev. Cassock, The Clergyman	1983–	45.00	
☐ **D 6703**, Sir Henry Doulton (Collectors Club exclusive)	1984–	100.00	125.00
☐ **D 6704**, Santa Claus, large	1984–	95.00	
☐ **D 6705**, Santa Claus, small	1984–	50.00	
☐ **D 6706**, Santa Claus, miniature	1984–	40.00	
☐ **D 6707**, Louis Armstrong, large	1984–1986	60.00	85.00
☐ **D 6708**, Jimmy Durante, large	1984–1986	60.00	85.00
☐ **D 6709**, Clark Gable, large	1984–	4000.00	5000.00
☐ **D 6710**, Groucho Marx, large	1984–1986	60.00	85.00
☐ **D 6711**, Wyatt Earp, medium	1985–1988	70.00	
☐ **D 6712**, General Custer and Sitting Bull (limited edition)	1984–	95.00	125.00
☐ **D 6713**, Mr. Tonsil, The Town Crier	1984–	45.00	
☐ **D 6714**, Madame Crystal, The Clairvoyant	1984–	45.00	
☐ **D 6715**, Mrs. Loan, The Librarian ...	1984–	45.00	
☐ **D 6716**, Betty Bitters, The Barmaid ..	1984–	45.00	
☐ **D 6717**, Toby Gillette, limited edition of three	1984–	**VERY RARE**	
☐ **D 6718**, Ronald Reagan, limited edition of 2,000	1985–	375.00	500.00
☐ **D 6720**, Sgt. Peeler, The Policeman ..	1985–	45.00	
☐ **D 6721**, Captain Salt, Sea Captain ...	1985–	45.00	
☐ **D 6722**, Miss Studious, The Teacher	1985–	45.00	
☐ **D 6723**, Dr. Pulse, The Physician	1985–	45.00	
☐ **D 6724**, Paul McCartney, The Beatles, 4½"	1984–	40.00	50.00

	Date	Price Range	
☐ **D 6725**, John Lennon, The Beatles, 4½"	1984–	40.00	50.00
☐ **D 6726**, Ringo Starr, The Beatles, 4½"	1984–	40.00	50.00
☐ **D 6727**, George Harrison, The Beatles, 4½"	1984–	40.00	50.00
☐ **D 6728**, Antony and Cleopatra, large (limited edition)	1985–	125.00	
☐ **D 6729**, Davy Crockett and Santa Anna, large (limited edition)	1985–	125.00	
☐ **D 6731**, Doc Holliday, medium	1985–1988	70.00	
☐ **D 6732**, Annie Oakley, medium	1985–1988	70.00	
☐ **D 6733**, Geronimo, medium	1985–1988	70.00	
☐ **D 6735**, Buffalo Bill, medium	1985–1988	70.00	
☐ **D 6736**, Wild Bill Hickock, medium	1985–1988	70.00	
☐ **D 6738**, Mr. Quaker, large (limited edition)	1985–	550.00	650.00
☐ **D 6739**, Hampshire Cricketer	1985–	75.00	100.00
☐ **D 6740**, Major Green, The Golfer	1986–	45.00	
☐ **D 6741**, Mike Mineral, The Miner	1986–	45.00	
☐ **D 6742**, Fred Fly, The Fisherman	1986–	45.00	
☐ **D 6743**, Mr. Brisket, The Butcher	1986–	45.00	
☐ **D 6744**, London Bobby, large	1986–	85.00	
☐ **D 6745**, Albert Sagger, The Potter (Collectors Club exclusive)	1986–	40.00	60.00
☐ **D 6746**, Jane Seymour, small	1986–	50.00	
☐ **D 6747**, Jane Seymour, miniature	1986–	40.00	
☐ **D 6748**, Mad Hatter, second version (limited edition 250)	1985 only	625.00	700.00
☐ **D 6749**, George III/George Washington (limited edition), large	1986–	125.00	
☐ **D 6750**, Napoleon and Josephine, large	1986–	125.00	
☐ **D 6751**, Catherine Parr, small	1987–	45.00	
☐ **D 6752**, Catherine Parr, miniature	1987–	35.00	
☐ **D 6753**, Anne of Cleves, small	1986–	45.00	
☐ **D 6754**, Anne of Cleves, miniature	1986–	35.00	
☐ **D 6755**, Guardsman, large	1986–	85.00	
☐ **D 6756**, Golfer, small	1986–	45.00	
☐ **D 6757**, Golfer, miniature	1986–	35.00	
☐ **D 6758**, Mark Twain, miniature	1986–	35.00	
☐ **D 6759**, Pearly Queen, large	1987–	85.00	
☐ **D 6760**, Pearly King, large	1987–	85.00	
☐ **D 6762**, London Bobby, small	1987–	45.00	
☐ **D 6763**, London Bobby, miniature	1987–	35.00	
☐ **D 6764**, D'Artagnan, small	1987–	45.00	
☐ **D 6765**, D'Artagnan, miniature	1987–	35.00	
☐ **D 6766**, Alderman Mace, The Mayor	1987–	45.00	

	Date	Price Range	
☐ **D 6767,** Flora Fuchsia, The Florist ...	1987–	45.00	
☐ **D 6768,** Charlie Cheer, The Clown ..	1987–	45.00	
☐ **D 6769,** Monsieur Chasseur, The Chef	1987–	45.00	
☐ **D 6771,** Guardsman, small	1987–	45.00	
☐ **D 6772,** Guardsman, miniature	1987–	35.00	
☐ **D 6733,** The Sleuth, small (limited edition of 5,000)	1987–	45.00	
☐ **D 6774,** Scaramouche, large, LE 1,500	1987–	150.00	250.00
☐ **D 6781,** Poacher, large	1987–	95.00	
☐ **D 6782,** Old Salt, large	1987–	95.00	
☐ **D 6783,** Lobster Man, large	1987–	95.00	
☐ **D 6785,** Rip Van Winkle, large (limited edition of 1,000)	1987–	150.00	250.00
☐ **D 6786,** North American Indian, large (limited edition of 1,000)	1987–	150.00	250.00
☐ **D 6787,** Golfer, large (limited edition of 1,000)	1987–	150.00	250.00
☐ **D 6790,** Mad Hatter, small, Higbee's (limited edition of 500)	1987–	125.00	225.00
☐ **D 6791,** Old Charley, small, Higbee's (limited edition of 500)	1987–	125.00	225.00

CHARACTER AND TOBY JUGS

It is thought by most persons who are collectors of "Toby Jugs" and "Character Jugs" that the idea of a pitcher or jug depicting either a full figure or head was first designed and made early in the eighteenth century by some potter believed to be a Staffordshire potter. These drinking vessels and flasks soon became very popular, spreading from England to all parts of the world. We know, from museums around the world, that there are various forms of pitchers, jugs, flasks, etc., although very crude in form, that do resemble a living being. However, it was not until the eighteenth century that there began to appear a series of jugs in a more decorative and distinctive design pattern.

The Toby jug, which over the years has become one of the more popular items for collectors, usually depicts a seated character with a peculiar type hat with three points, one of which is used for the pouring spout. It is believed that this jug gets the name "Toby" from a song popular in the mid-eighteenth century in which there was a character called "Toby Fillpot."

It was not until the early 1930s that Charles J. Noke, then Art Director for the Royal Doulton Company, decided to model a design he had been working on for some time in the form of a pitcher with a face. This was titled "John Barleycorn," an imaginary being representing whiskey. Secondly, there was Old Charley, a night watchman . . . Sairey Gamp, a Dickens character . . . Dick Turpin, a notorious highwayman, and Parson Brown, all accepted with widespread popularity. Some of the other Doulton modellers for the character jugs were Leslie Harradine (who also modelled a number of figurines), Max Henk, Harry Fenton and David Brian Biggs.

From the artist's mind comes the sketch, and from this sketch a master mold is made. The master mold is then taken and a "working" mold is made from it . . . from this working mold there might be as many as thirty molds made for pouring. These are plaster of Paris and when the liquid is poured into them it is allowed to sit for a while as the plaster of Paris will absorb the liquid and the mixture becomes a hardened clay molded figure. After the figure is removed from the mold it is cleaned up, any seams erased and the handle, which is cast separately, is then applied. The figure is then fired at a very high degree causing a great deal of shrinkage. When removed and carefully inspected it is sent to the decorating studios where specially prepared paints are used in colors selected from the original design. It is then fired a second time for the hardening of the colors. The third firing is for the glossy finish which appears on most all of the figurines and mugs. There was a span of a few years in the late 1960s and 1970s when the character jugs were made of fine china instead of earthenware, and these figures have the translucent appearance of fine china.

Each character jug is titled and the name appears on the bottom along with the Royal Doulton trademark and a "D" number. The name also is embedded into the back of the jug. It is widely recognized among collectors that a jug bearing an "A" mark is of more value because of this mark, which supposedly signified an earlier issue. However, it appears there is no basis to this as this mark was apparently used for factory identification purposes. Nevertheless, the jugs bearing the "A" mark command a higher price.

As with the figurines, a few prototype jugs are made but, to the author's knowledge, were never marketed. Sometimes prototypes are made as samples for the factory's use in determining if the subject is a saleable item or, perhaps to test market in areas through the world. Quite often or probably most often these figures are never available to the public or to the collector, such as the character jugs titled Buffalo Bill, Maori and the Baseball Player. It has been reported that these jugs do exist in collections, although to my knowledge they were not marketed in any manner. Perhaps a few escaped from the factory in an unexplained manner. Since it is not known how many truly exist one cannot put a dollar value on them.

A few jugs have experienced some design changes over the years of production. Auld Mac was "Owd Mac" during production years of 1938 through 1945; Beefeater appears with both "GR" and "ER" on the handles . . . from 1947 through 1953 the handle bears "GR" for George Rex and in 1953 the initials "ER" for Elizabeth Regina were used and are still in current production. Cavalier experienced a color change (though very slight) and a change in the collar in 1950; Dick Turpin in the earlier version has a mask on his hat but was changed in 1960 to a mask covering his eyes, a horse for a handle and a completely different color version . . . a total reconstruction of this figure; Drake, the very early version did not have a hat . . . this figure was test marketed but never put into general production . . . a few do exist in collections today and are known as the "Hatless Drake" . . . the second version redesigned with a hat and different coloring was introduced in 1940; John Barleycorn jugs in the early versions bear a different handle than the later pieces. The handle is molded down into the pitcher itself rather than leaving the appearance of an attached handle; earlier versions of Lumberjack, North American Indian and The Trapper bear the words "Canadian Centennial Series 1867–1967" and were produced for sale in Canada in 1967, however, in 1968 they were issued for sale worldwide without the backstamp; four Dickens characters were changed to a smaller size in 1949 with styling remaining the same . . . they were Buz Fuz, Cap'n Cuttle, Fat Boy, Mr. Micawber, Mr. Pickwick and Sam Weller; an earlier version of Old King Cole shows the character with a yellow crown.

On the bottom of the jug may appear a copyright date, register number and a Royal Doulton trademark . . . sometimes one, two or all three may be on the jug, however, the date that appears does not necessarily mean the date the jug was placed in production, it is merely the date of copyright for that particular piece. Normally release is sometime within a twelve month period of the copyright date.

CHARACTER JUGS

Character jugs were first introduced to the Royal Doulton line of products in 1933. They were made from regular earthenware dinnerware body and fired in coal-burning bottle kilns that were in use at the time. The factory experienced some difficulty in the firing, and to cut down the loss, started to experiment with other earthenware bodies.

In 1939, a new earthenware body called Georgian was adopted for the making of character jugs and other earthenware dinnerware pieces. To identify those items made of the new Georgia earthenware bodies, the capital letter "A" was imprinted alongside the trademark.

In 1952, the factory installed electric tunnel kilns. After extensive tests, it was discovered that character jugs and other earthenware dinnerware pieces made of the Georgian body could be fired in the electric kilns using the regular earthenware dinnerware body.

Starting in 1955, the special earthenware body called Georgian was discontinued and the letter "A" next to the trademark eliminated. Therefore, all character jugs that were produced prior to 1939 and after 1954 were made from the factory's regular earthenware dinnerware body which do not carry the "A" mark.

Prior to 1966, the United Kingdom did not have a copyright law but did have a design registration act that in part corresponded to the copyright law in effect in the United States. To protect their new products from plagiarism, the Royal Doulton management in England registered all new products under England's design registration act. This registration also involved the countries of Australia, New Zealand, and South Africa.

Because the United States had a copyright law, the American company copyrighted new products in the United States. Since approximately 1950, all new products carry the copyright notice of the United States with the date and four registration numbers of the United Kingdom, Australia, New Zealand, and South Africa.

When the copyright act in the United Kingdom became law in 1966, it extended copyright protection to articles previously registered under the design registration act. As the periods of registration ran out, the relevant registration numbers disappeared from the respective article.

	Date	Price Range	
ANNE BOLEYN			
Second wife of Henry VIII.			
☐ **D 6644**, large	1975–	95.00	
☐ **D 6650**, small	1975–	50.00	
☐ **D 6651**, miniature	1980–	40.00	
ANNE OF CLEVES			
Fourth wife of Henry VIII.			
☐ **D 6653**, horse-head handle, ears down,			
large	1980–	95.00	
☐ **D 6753**, small	1986–	50.00	
☐ **D 6754**, miniature	1986–	40.00	
☐ Horse head handle with ears up	1980 only	250.00	350.00

APOTHECARY, THE
  A character from the Williamsburg series. Apothecary was the forerunner of

Anne of Cleves, horse-head handle with ears up, D 6653, 250.00–350.00

	Date	Price Range	
what today is our drug store. The person who owned an apothecary was allowed to dispense drugs for medicinal purposes, even going as far as treating a patient.			
☐ **D 6567**, large	1963–1983	75.00	100.00
☐ **D 6574**, small	1963–1983	40.00	60.00
☐ **D 6581**, miniature	1963–1983	30.00	40.00

ARAMIS
A character from the book *The Three Musketeers*.

	Date	Price Range	
☐ **D 6441**, large	1956–	95.00	
☐ **D 6454**, small	1956–	50.00	
☐ **D 6508**, miniature	1960–	40.00	

	Date	Price Range	

'ARD OF 'EARING

A character with hand cupped to his ear indicating he is partially deaf.

	Date	Price Range	
☐ **D 6588**, large	1964–1967	1100.00	1300.00
☐ **D 6591**, small	1964–1967	650.00	800.00
☐ **D 6594**, miniature	1964–1967	1200.00	1400.00

'ARRIET

Depicts a London Cockney street trader or costermonger, as they are called in England. A color change was made on this jug in 1951.

☐ **D 6208**, large	1947–1960	175.00	225.00
☐ **D 6236**, small	1947–1960	100.00	125.00
☐ **same jug with an "A" mark**		110.00	140.00
☐ **D 6250**, miniature	1947–1960	80.00	100.00
☐ **same jug with an "A" mark**		90.00	110.00
☐ **D 6256**, tiny	1947–1960	200.00	250.00

'Arry, D 6207, large, 185.00–225.00

	Date	Price Range	

'ARRY

Companion to 'Arriet; also depicts a London Cockney street trader or costermonger. A color change was made on this jug in 1951.

	Date	Price Range	
☐ **D 6207**, large	1947–1960	185.00	225.00
☐ **D 6235**, small	1947–1960	100.00	125.00
☐ same jug with an "A" mark		110.00	140.00
☐ **D 6249**, miniature	1947–1960	80.00	100.00
☐ same jug with an "A" mark		90.00	110.00
☐ **D 6255**, tiny	1947–1960	200.00	250.00

ATHOS

A character from the book *The Three Musketeers.*

☐ **D 6439**, large	1956–	95.00	
☐ **D 6452**, small	1956–	50.00	
☐ **D 6509**, miniature	1960–	40.00	

AULD MAC

Depicts a thrift Scotsman. Also known as "Owd Mac," note listing under that title.

☐ **D 5823**, large	1938–1985	60.00	85.00
☐ same jug with an "A" mark		85.00	95.00
☐ **D 5824**, small	1938–1985	35.00	50.00
☐ same jug with an "A" mark		40.00	55.00
☐ **D 6253**, miniature	1946–1985	25.00	35.00
☐ same jug with an "A" mark		45.00	60.00
☐ **D 6257**, tiny	1946–1960	225.00	275.00

BACCHUS

The Greek "god of wine," this character has a wreath of greenery and grapes representing the grape harvest.

☐ **D 6499**, large	1959–	95.00	
☐ **D 6505**, small	1959–	50.00	
☐ **D 6521**, miniature	1960–	40.00	

BASEBALL PLAYER

Large size only. Piloted but never produced. Portrays a character in gray shirt with pink-red sleeves and pink-red baseball cap. The handle is a bat and ball.

☐		**RARE**	

THE BEATLES

Issued in a set of four, these are the first in a new "POP" Collecting

Bacchus, D 6499, large, 95.00

	Date	Price Range	
Series. This collection will not be available for distribution in the United States.			
☐ **D 6724,** Paul McCartney, size 4½″ ..	1984–	40.00	50.00
☐ **D 6725,** John Lennon, size 4½″	1984–	40.00	50.00
☐ **D 6726,** Ringo Starr, size 4½″	1984–	40.00	50.00
☐ **D 6727,** George Harrison, size 4½″	1984–	40.00	50.00

BEEFEATER

A popular name for a member of the Yeoman of the Guard, bodyguards for the Queen. Beefeater jugs with GR on the handle are more desirable for the collector, as the initials were changed to ER in 1953. The value of the GR jug is determined to be approximately

Beefeater, D 6206, large, 95.00

	Date	Price Range	
50 percent higher than the jugs with ER embossed on the handle.			
☐ **D 6206, large**	1947–	**95.00**	
☐ **same jug with an "A" mark**		**85.00**	**115.00**
☐ **D 6233, small**	1947–	**50.00**	
☐ **same jug with an "A" mark**		**55.00**	**65.00**
☐ **D 6251, miniature**	1947–	**40.00**	

BENJAMIN FRANKLIN

Depicting one of America's most famous statesmen in his famous experiment of flying a kite in a thunderstorm to demonstrate that lightning was a form of electricity. Handle is a kite in the clouds with a key at the base of the handle.

☐ **D 6695, small**	1983–1988	**50.00**	

BLACKSMITH

A character from the Williamsburg series. A blacksmith was an eighteenth

	Date	Price Range	

century ironworker. These characters have been recreated in the restoration of the town of Williamsburg, the original capital of Virginia.

	Date	Price Range	
☐ D 6571, large	1963–1983	60.00	80.00
☐ D 6578, small	1963–1983	45.00	60.00
☐ D 6585, miniature	1963–1983	40.00	60.00

BOOTMAKER

A character from the Williamsburg series. A bootmaker was the gentleman who made shoes and boots in the eighteenth century.

☐ D 6572, large	1963–1983	60.00	80.00
☐ D 6579, small	1963–1983	45.00	60.00
☐ D 6586, miniature	1963–1983	40.00	50.00

BUFFALO BILL

Piloted but never produced. On the right shoulder in raised letters is "W.F. Cody Buffalo Bill." Shoulders and hat are brown; hair, mustache, and goatee are gray. Handle is buffalo head and rifle. One known example is in an American collection.

☐..		RARE	

BUZ FUZ

A character from the book *Pickwick Papers* by Charles Dickens. Also note listing under Sergeant Buz Fuz.

☐ D 5838, intermediate size	1938–1948	200.00	250.00
☐ D 5838, small size	1948–1960	100.00	135.00
☐ same jug with an "A" mark		135.00	160.00
☐ Limited Edition 2000	1982–	100.00	120.00

CABINETMAKER, THE

A character from the Williamsburg series. Marketing was delayed and eventually cancelled. A number of the jugs are reported to be stored at the factory.

☐ D 6659, large	1981–		

CAPTAIN AHAB

A character from the book *Moby Dick*.

☐ D 6500, large	1959–1984	75.00	100.00
☐ D 6506, small	1959–1984	35.00	50.00
☐ D 6522, miniature	1960–1984	30.00	45.00

Buz Fuz, D 5838, intermediate size, 200.00–250.00

	Date	Price Range	
CAP'N CUTTLE			
A character from the novel by Charles Dickens titled *Dombey and Sons*.			
☐ **D 5842**, special size	1938–1948	200.00	250.00
☐ **D 5842**, small size	1948–1960	100.00	125.00
☐ **same jug with an "A" mark**		100.00	125.00
CAPTAIN HENRY MORGAN			
Probably the most famous British Buccaneer of his time. Born in 1635, died in 1688.			
☐ **D 6467**, large	1958–1981	75.00	100.00
☐ **D 6469**, small	1958–1981	40.00	55.00
☐ **D 6510**, miniature	1960–1981	25.00	40.00
CAPTAIN HOOK			
A villainous pirate in James M. Barrie's book titled *Peter Pan*.			

Captain Hook, D 6597, large, 450.00–500.00

	Date	Price Range	
☐ **D 6597**, large	1965–1971	**450.00**	**500.00**
☐ **D 6601**, small	1965–1971	**300.00**	**350.00**
☐ **D 6605**, miniature	1965–1971	**325.00**	**375.00**

CARDINAL
A dignitary in the Catholic Church. This jug may represent a character from Shakespeare's Henry VIII, known as Cardinal Wolsey.

	Date	Price Range	
☐ **D 5614**, large	1936–1960	**140.00**	**165.00**
☐ same jug with an "A" mark		**150.00**	**165.00**
☐ **D 6033**, small	1939–1960	**65.00**	**85.00**
☐ same jug with an "A" mark		**75.00**	**90.00**
☐ **D 6129**, miniature	1940–1960	**45.00**	**65.00**
☐ same jug with an "A" mark		**50.00**	**65.00**
☐ **D 6258**, tiny	1947–1960	**225.00**	**275.00**

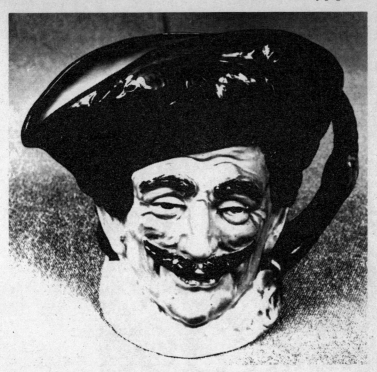

The Cavalier, D 6114, large, 150.00–175.00

	Date	Price Range
CATHERINE HOWARD		
Fifth wife of Henry VIII.		
☐ **D 6645**, large	1978–	**95.00**
☐ **D 6692**, small	1984–	**50.00**
☐ **D 6693**, miniature	1984–	**40.00**
CATHERINE OF ARAGON		
First wife of Henry VIII.		
☐ **D 6643**, large	1975–	**95.00**
☐ **D 6657**, small	1981–	**50.00**
☐ **D 6658**, miniature	1981–	**40.00**
CATHERINE PARR		
Sixth and final wife of Henry VIII.		
☐ **D 6664**, large	1981–	**95.00**
☐ **D 6751**, small	1987–	**50.00**
☐ **D 6752**, miniature	1987–	**40.00**

CAVALIER, THE
During the reign of King Charles I his

Churchill, D 6170, large, 7500.00–9000.00

	Date	Price Range	
staunch supporters were given a title of honor and were known as "The Cavaliers."			
☐ D 6114, large	1940–1960	150.00	175.00
☐ same jug with an "A" mark		160.00	185.00
☐ D 6173, small	1941–1960	75.00	90.00
☐ same jug with an "A" mark		75.00	90.00

CAVALIER WITH GOATEE
This character jug is different from the regular version. Although there are other distinctions, the most notable is a very prominent goatee. Considered rare.

☐ D 6114, large		6000.00	7500.00

CHURCHILL
Depicting the distinguished statesman

Inscription on base of Churchill Jug

	Date	Price Range	
	Date	Price Range	

Winston Churchill, this jug is believed to have been in production for a short time only. It is not known the exact date it was withdrawn from the market. Considered extremely rare.

☐ **D 6170**, large	1940–	**7500.00**	**9000.00**

CLOWN, RED HAIR
Depicting a character from the circus. Considered rare.

☐ **D 5610**, large	1937–1942	**5500.00**	**6500.00**

CLOWN, WHITE HAIR

☐ **D 6322**, large	1951–1955	**1200.00**	**1500.00**

CLOWN, BROWN HAIR
In March 1982 a third version of the clown was sold at Phillips in London, thus making known another variation.

☐ **D 5610**, large, produced briefly	1937–	**2750.00**	**3250.00**

DAVY CROCKETT AND SANTA ANNA
Third in the Antagonists series depicts

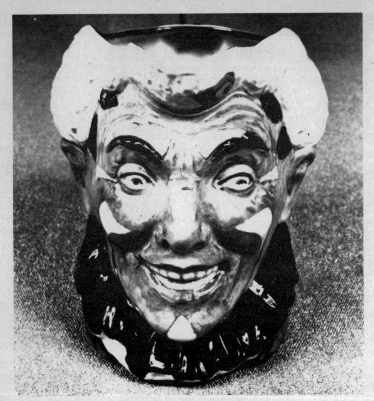

White Hair Clown, D 6322, large, 1200.00–1500.00

	Date	Price Range
the two persons most prominent in the Battle of the Alamo. Davy Crockett with coonskin cap and musket resting on the arch of the fort at Alamo. Santa Anna is dressed in the uniform of a general in the Mexican Army.		
☐ **D 6729**, large	1985–	**125.00**
D'ARTAGNAN Depicting one of the colorful Dumas characters. Attired in costume of the period, plumed hat, lace trimmed collar.		
☐ **D 6691**, large	1983–	**95.00**
☐ **D 6764**, small	1987–	**50.00**
☐ **D 6765**, miniature	1987–	**40.00**

	Date	Price Range	

DICK TURPIN

A notorious highwayman who was eventually hanged. Released in two versions. **First version**—mask up on hat

	Date	Price Range	
□ **D 5495,** large	1935–1960	140.00	175.00
□ **same jug with an "A" mark**		140.00	180.00
□ **D 5618,** small	1935–1960	70.00	90.00
□ **same jug with an "A" mark**		70.00	90.00
□ **D 6128,** miniature	1940–1960	50.00	75.00
□ **same jug with an "A" mark**		60.00	75.00

Second version—mask on face, horse handle

□ **D 6528,** large	1960–1980	65.00	85.00
□ **D 6535,** small	1960–1980	45.00	65.00
□ **D 6542,** miniature	1960–1980	40.00	50.00

DICK WHITTINGTON

Lord Mayor of London three times during the fifteenth century.

□ **D 6375,** large	1953–1960	400.00	500.00

DON QUIXOTE

A character from the novel by Miguel de Cervantes titled *Don Quixote.*

□ **D 6455,** large	1957–	95.00	
□ **D 6460,** small	1957–	50.00	
□ **D 6511,** miniature	1960–	40.00	

DRAKE

Depicting Sir Frances Drake, a distinguished figure in British sea power in the sixteenth century.

First version—hatless Drake		8000.00	10,000.00

Second version—with hat and different collar

□ **D 6115,** large	1940–1960	150.00	180.00
□ **same jug with an "A" mark**		150.00	180.00
□ **D 6174,** small	1941–1960	75.00	90.00
□ **same jug with an "A" mark**		75.00	100.00

FALCONER

Depicting a man who is trainer of birds. A falcon is the handle of this jug.

□ **D 6533,** large	1960–	95.00	
□ **D 6540,** small	1960–	50.00	
□ **D 6547,** miniature	1960–	40.00	

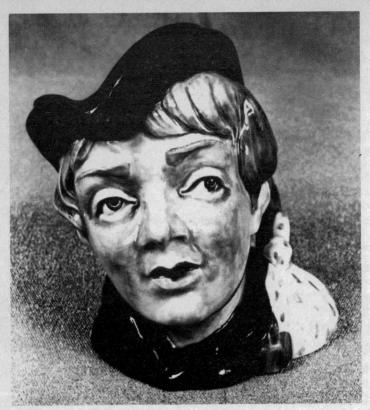

Dick Whittington, D 6375, large, 400.00–500.00

	Date	Price Range	
FALSTAFF			
A character in the Shakespeare play *Henry IV*, Sir John Falstaff, a fat and jolly character particularly liked for his wit and laughter.			
☐ **D 6287**, large	1950–	**95.00**	
☐ **D 6385**, small	1950–	**50.00**	
☐ **D 6519**, miniature	1960–	**40.00**	
FARMER JOHN			
Depicts the typical English farmer.			
☐ **D 5788**, large	1938–1960	**150.00**	**180.00**
☐ **same jug with an "A" mark**		**160.00**	**185.00**
☐ **D 5789**, small	1938–1960	**80.00**	**110.00**
☐ **same jug with an "A" mark**		**80.00**	**110.00**

Drake, D 6115, large, 150.00–180.00

	Date	Price Range	
FAT BOY			
Depicting a character from the Charles Dickens' novel *Pickwick Papers*.			
☐ **D 5840**, special size	1938–1948	**200.00**	**250.00**
☐ **D 5840**, small	1948–1960	**100.00**	**125.00**
☐ same jug with an "A" mark		**100.00**	**1325.00**
☐ **D 6139**, miniature	1940–1960	**65.00**	**90.00**
☐ same jug with an "A" mark		**65.00**	**90.00**
☐ **D 6142**, tiny	1940–1960	**100.00**	**140.00**

FIREMAN, THE
Created for the Griffith Pottery House, a company that sells gifts related to the fire fighting industry, this jug depicts a fireman in an authentic antique fireman outfit. Antique helmet with #1 appearing on the badge. Outfit has gold buckles and rivets. Fire hose is the handle.

☐ **D 6697**, large	1983–	**95.00**	

Fat Boy, D 5840, special size, 200.00–250.00

	Date	Price Range	
FORTUNE TELLER, THE			
Depicts a gypsy woman who roams the countryside and for a "piece of silver" will reveal the future for you.			
☐ D 6497, large	1959–1967	500.00	600.00
☐ D 6503, small	1959–1967	300.00	375.00
☐ D 6523, miniature	1960–1967	350.00	400.00
FRIAR TUCK			
A member of Robin Hood's band, he was the chaplain. Also a character in Sir Walter Scott's book titled *Ivanhoe*.			
☐ D 6321, large	1951–1960	375.00	450.00

**GENERAL CUSTER AND
SITTING BULL**

The second in The Antagonists Series.
Each double-faced jug in the series
portrays two personalities involved in

Chief Sitting Bull, D 6712, large, 95.00–125.00

	Date	Price Range
well-known conflicts. Chief Sitting Bull, Teton Dakota Indian Chief and General George Armstrong Custer are depicted on this jug. Limited edition of 9,500.		
☐ **D 6712**, large	1984–	**125.00**

GEORGE WASHINGTON
Issued to commemorate the 250th anniversary of his birth. Designed by Stan Taylor, this mug depicts the first President of the United States.

☐ **D 6669**, large size 1982– **95.00**

GEORGE III/GEORGE WASHINGTON
Fourth in the Antagonist series. This double-faced jug issued in a limited edition of 9,500.

☐ **D 6749**, large size 1986– **125.00**

GARDENER
A character jug depicting the typical

General Custer, D 6712, large, 125.00

	Date	Price Range	
man who can be found working with the earth with the handle being a shovel and some vegetables.			
☐ D 6630, large	1973–1980	125.00	175.00
☐ D 6634, small	1973–1980	60.00	85.00
☐ D 6638, miniature	1973–1980	50.00	65.00
GLADIATOR Depicting a warrior of the Roman Empire.			
☐ D 6550, large	1961–1967	575.00	650.00
☐ D 6553, small	1961–1967	425.00	500.00
☐ D 6556, miniature	1961–1967	400.00	475.00
GAOLER A character from the Williamsburg series.			
☐ D 6570, large	1963–1983	75.00	100.00
☐ D 6577, small	1963–1983	50.00	75.00
☐ D 6584, miniature	1963–1983	45.00	60.00

Gaoler, D 6570, large, 75.00–100.00

	Date	Price Range	

GOLFER
Depicting an English gentleman out for a game of golf.

	Date	Price Range	
☐ **D 6623**, large	1971–	95.00	
☐ **D 6756**, small	1986–	50.00	
☐ **D 6757**, miniature	1986–	40.00	
☐ **D 6787**, large, new colorway special edition of 1,000, commissioned by John Sinclair, Sheffield, England	1987–	150.00	250.00

GONDOLIER
Depicts the romantic singing boat-man, who guides his boat through the

	Date	Price Range	

narrow canals of Venice singing his romantic songs.

☐ D 6589, large	1964–1969	600.00	700.00
☐ D 6592, small	1964–1969	450.00	550.00
☐ D 6595, miniature	1964–1969	400.00	500.00

GONE AWAY

Depicts an English huntsman with his typical red coat and black silk hat. Handle is a fox.

☐ D 6531, large	1960–1981	65.00	85.00
☐ D 6538, small	1960–1981	40.00	55.00
☐ D 6545, miniature	1960–1981	30.00	45.00

GRANNY

Depicts an aged woman.

☐ D 5521, large	1935–1983	70.00	90.00
☐ same jug with an "A" mark		85.00	100.00
☐ D 6384, small	1953–1983	40.00	50.00
☐ same jug with an "A" mark		50.00	80.00
☐ D 6520, miniature	1960–1983	25.00	35.00

An early version of Granny shows the character's face without the front tooth which appears on the currently produced jugs. Usually found on older "A" marked pieces.

| ☐ Granny, jug without tooth | 1934–1940 | 1150.00 | 1400.00 |

GRANT AND LEE—THE CIVIL WAR

The first in a series titled "The Antagonists Collection," this mug represents the first double-faced character jug since 1937. Both men wear the uniforms of their sides, navy blue for the Union and gray for the Confederacy. Their collars are embellished with bright golden stars of rank and the handle is their colorful flags. Limited edition of 9,500.

| ☐ D 6698, large | 1983– | 200.00 | 250.00 |

GUARDSMAN

A character from the Williamsburg series.

☐ D 6568, large	1963–1983	60.00	80.00
☐ D 6575, small	1963–1983	45.00	60.00
☐ D 6582, miniature	1963–1983	35.00	50.00

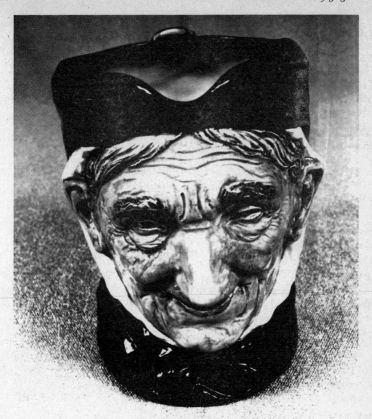

Granny, without tooth, 1150.00–1400.00

	Date	Price Range

GUARDSMAN

One of the London character jugs, this jug depicts one of the famous Grenadier Guardsman of Buckingham Palace. Uniform is very colorful with red jacket and black collar. Pompous black hat with chin strap of gold. Handle is bayonet with flag of his regiment wrapped around the bayonet.

	Date	Price Range
☐ **D 6755,** large	1986–	**95.00**
☐ **D 6771,** small	1987–	**50.00**
☐ **D 6772,** miniature	1987–	**40.00**

	Date	Price Range	

GULLIVER
Depicting a character from the book
Gulliver's Travels, the handle is a castle
with two Lilliputians on top.

	Date	Price Range	
☐ **D 6560,** large	1962–1967	600.00	700.00
☐ **D 6563,** small	1962–1967	425.00	475.00
☐ **D 6566,** miniature	1962–1967	375.00	425.00

GUNSMITH
A character from the Williamsburg series.

☐ **D 6573,** large	1963–1983	60.00	80.00
☐ **D 6580,** small	1963–1983	45.00	60.00
☐ **D 6587,** miniature	1963–1983	35.00	50.00

HAMLET
Depicting one of the characters from a
Shakespearian play.

☐ **D 6672,** large size	1982–1988	95.00	

HENRY V
Depicting one of the famous kings of
England.

☐ **D 6671,** large size with decal-type han- dle	1982–1988	95.00	
☐ **D 6671,** large size with embossed han- dle	1982–1988	200.00	250.00
☐ **D 6671,** large with yellow crown. Fac- tory second with gold and red colors missing		**VERY RARE**	

HENRY VIII
Second Son of Henry VII . . . he ruled
England from 1509 to 1547.

☐ **D 6642,** large	1975–	90.00	
☐ **D 6647,** small	1979–	50.00	
☐ **D 6648,** miniature	1979–	45.00	

IZAAC WALTON
An author who has endeared himself to
many . . . probably best known for his
work titled *The Compleat Angler.*

☐ **D 6404,** large	1953–1982	110.00	125.00

JANE SEYMOUR
Third wife of Henry VIII.

☐ **D 6646,** large	1979–	95.00	
☐ **D 6746,** small	1986–	50.00	
☐ **D 6747,** miniature	1986–	40.00	

Henry V, D 6671, large with embossed handle, 200.00–250.00

	Date	Price Range	
JARGE			
Depicts the original country boy, by no means handsome and often ridiculed.			
☐ **D 6288**, large	1950–1960	**375.00**	**450.00**
☐ **D 6295**, small	1950–1960	**200.00**	**250.00**
JESTER			
A character known for his wit, he was often one who was instructed to use his wit to entertain nobility.			
☐ **D 5556**, small	1936-	**125.00**	**175.00**
☐ **same jug with an "A" mark**		**135.00**	**185.00**
JOCKEY			
Depicting a character who rides thoroughbred horses.			
☐ **D 6625**, large	1971–1975	**325.00**	**375.00**

Jarge, D 6288, large, 375.00–450.00

	Date	Price Range	
Small and miniature sizes were test marketed but not produced.			
☐ Small pilot jug known to exist		4000.00	5000.00

JOHN BARLEYCORN
Depicting a character in Old English ballads, familiar to many as the personification of whiskey or malt liquors. This jug was re-issued in 1978 as a limited edition of 7,500 for distribution in North America.

☐ **D 5327, large**	1934–1960	140.00	175.00
☐ **same jug with an "A" mark**		140.00	185.00
☐ **D 5327, large, signed by Doulton**	1978–	125.00	150.00
☐ **D 5735, small**	1937–1960	75.00	100.00
☐ **same jug with an "A" mark**		85.00	100.00

Jockey, D 6625, large, 325.00–375.00

	Date	Price Range	
☐ **D 6041**, miniature	1939–1960	**65.00**	**85.00**
☐ same jug with an "A" mark		**75.00**	**95.00**

JOHN PEEL

Immortalized by John Woodcock Graves in a song titled "D'ye ken John Peel," a man who had a passion for fox-hunting.

	Date	Price Range	
☐ **D 5612**, large	1936–1960	**140.00**	**185.00**
☐ same jug with an "A" mark		**140.00**	**185.00**
☐ **D 5731**, small	1937–1960	**65.00**	**85.00**
☐ same jug with an "A" mark		**65.00**	**85.00**
☐ **D 6130**, miniature	1940–1960	**50.00**	**60.00**
☐ same jug with an "A" mark		**70.00**	**80.00**
☐ **D 6259**, tiny	1947–1960	**250.00**	**300.00**

	Date	Price Range	

JOHNNY APPLESEED

Depicts the man John Chapman, whose
nickname was "Johnny Appleseed,"
because he traveled on foot all across
the Midwestern United States planting
apple seeds near the cabins of early set-
tlers.

☐ D 6372, large	1935–1969	325.00	400.00

LAWYER, The

Depicts an English lawyer with a quill
for a handle.

☐ D 6498, large	1959–	95.00	
☐ D 6504, small	1959–	50.00	
☐ D 6524, miniature	1960–	40.00	

LOBSTER MAN

Depicts a seaman, a jolly one, who sets
out at night to set his pots for a lobster
catch. Handle is a lobster.

☐ D 6617, large	1968–	95.00	
☐ D 6620, small	1968–	50.00	
☐ D 6652, miniature	1981–	40.00	
☐ D 6783, large, new colorway	1987–	95.00	

LONDON BOBBY

☐ D 6744, large size. Depicts one of England's most famous guardians of law
and order. Handle is the famous Tower
of London and the Bobby's whistle. ...

	1986–	95.00	
☐ D 6762, small	1987–	50.00	
☐ D 6763, miniature	1987–	40.00	

LONG JOHN SILVER

Depicts one of the most famous fictional buccaneers. A character from the
book *Treasure Island* by Robert Louis
Stevenson. Handle is a parrot.

☐ D 6335, large	1952–	95.00	
☐ D 6386, small	1952–	50.00	
☐ D 6512, miniature	1960–	40.00	

LORD NELSON

Depicts Admiral Lord Nelson, one of
England's great naval heroes.

☐ D 6336, large	1952–1969	325.00	375.00

LUMBERJACK

Depicts the typical fellow who works in

Lumberjack, D 6610, large, 60.00–80.00

	Date	Price Range	
a lumber camp. His work was hard and often his only tool was an axe. Handle is a tree with an axe.			
☐ **D 6610**, large	1967–1982	**60.00**	**80.00**
☐ **D 6613**, small	1967–1982	**35.00**	**55.00**
Miniature piloted examples have surfaced within the past few years.		**2250.00**	**2750.00**

MACBETH
Depicting one of the characters from a Shakespearian play.

| ☐ **D 6667**, large .... | 1982– | **95.00** | |

MAD HATTER
Depicts a character from the book *Alice's Adventures in Wonderland* by Lewis Carroll. Handle is a mouse and a clock.

| ☐ **D 6598**, large .... | 1965–1983 | **70.00** | **85.00** |

☐ **D 6598**, large, recently discovered with

Mad Hatter, D 6598, large, 70.00–85.00

	Date	Price Range	
red hat, worth several thousand dollars		—	—
☐ **D 6602**, small	1965–1983	40.00	50.00
☐ **D 6606**, miniature	1965–1983	35.00	45.00
☐ **D 6748**, second version (limited edition 250)	1985 only	625.00	700.00

MAD HATTER
Dressed in black suit, black hat, and yellow bow tie. Brown rat for the handle. Issued to commemorate the second anniversary of the opening of the first Royal Doulton room at Higbee's, Cleveland, OH. Limited edition of 500.

☐ **D 6790**, small, new colorway	1987–	125.00	225.00

	Date	Price Range	

MAORI
Piloted in large size only. There are two known versions. One has bluish gray hair with a friendly expression, the other has dark hair with two white tipped feathers in the hair, very serious expression and piercing eyes. ....

EXTREMELY RARE

MARK TWAIN
Depicts the author of such well known classics as *The Adventures of Tom Sawyer* and *The Adventures of Huck Finn*. His real name was Samuel Clemens, Mark Twain being a pen name.

	Date	Price Range	
☐ D 6654, large	1980-	95.00	
☐ D 6694, small	1983–	50.00	
☐ D 6758, miniature	1986–	40.00	

McCALLUM
Large size only. Made for D.J. McCallum, whiskey distillers, and was made in several versions. Probably produced in the '30s and '40s. Kingsware version and white version. ....

		3500.00	4500.00

MEPHISTOPHELES
A two-faced jug showing a happy face and the sad face of the legendary figure most people associate with the devil to whom Faust sold his soul. It carries a verse on the bottom as shown in an illustration of this jug. Considered extremely rare.

	Date	Price Range	
☐ D 5757, large	1937–1948	1750.00	2250.00
☐ same jug with an "A" mark		1750.00	2250.00
☐ D 5758, small	1937–1948	1000.00	1250.00

MERLIN
Depicting the magician from the tales of King Arthur and The Knights of the Round Table. Has an owl for a handle.

	Date	Price Range	
☐ D 6529, large	1960–	95.00	
☐ D 6536, small	1960–	50.00	
☐ D 6543, miniature	1960–	40.00	

MIKADO, The
Depicts a Japanese Emperor. Probably

Mephistopheles, D 5757, large, 2500.00–3000.00

	Date	Price Range	
most well remembered as a character in the opera *The Mikado* by Gilbert & Sullivan. Handle is a fan.			
☐ **D 6501**, large	1959–1969	550.00	650.00
☐ **D 6507**, small	1959–1969	300.00	375.00
☐ **D 6525**, miniature	1960–1969	375.00	450.00

MINE HOST
Depicting a jovial and hospitable character from the nineteenth century.

☐ **D 6488**, large	1958–1981	75.00	90.00
☐ **D 6470**, small	1958–1981	40.00	60.00
☐ **D 6513**, miniature	1960–1981	25.00	35.00

MONTY
Depicting the popular Field Marshal Montgomery, commander of the British forces, who achieved great respect for his command of the 8th Army in

Mephistopheles, **D 5757**, large, 2500.00–3000.00

	Date	Price Range	
North Africa and during the Allied invasion of Europe.			
☐ **D 6202**, large	1946–	**95.00**	
☐ same jug with an "A" mark		**85.00**	**100.00**

MR. MICAWBER
Depicting a character from the Charles Dickens classic tale "David Copperfield."

☐ **D 5843**, special size	1938–1948	**185.00**	**225.00**
☐ same jug with an "A" mark		**190.00**	**240.00**
☐ **D 5843**, small	1948–1960	**90.00**	**125.00**
☐ same jug with an "A" mark		**90.00**	**125.00**
☐ **D 6138**, miniature	1940–1960	**55.00**	**65.00**
☐ same jug with an "A" mark		**60.00**	**70.00**
☐ **D 6143**, tiny		**100.00**	**140.00**

MR. PICKWICK
Depicting a character from another of

The Mikado, D 6501, large, 475.00–575.00

	Date	Price Range	
Charles Dickens classics, "Pickwick Papers."			
☐ **D 6060, large**	1940–1960	**145.00**	**185.00**
☐ **same jug with an "A" mark**		**145.00**	**185.00**
☐ **D 5839, special size**	1938–1948	**180.00**	**220.00**
☐ **same jug with an "A" mark**		**190.00**	**230.00**
☐ **D 5839, small**	1948–1960	**90.00**	**125.00**
☐ **same jug with an "A" mark**		**90.00**	**125.00**
☐ **D 6245, miniature**	1947–1960	**60.00**	**75.00**
☐ **same jug with an "A" mark**		**65.00**	**85.00**
☐ **D 6260, tiny**	1947–1960	**225.00**	**275.00**

MR. QUAKER

Depicts the trademark of the Quaker Oats Company, issued in a limited edition of 3,500, of which 1,000 were designated for the United States.

	Date	Price Range	
☐ **D 6738, large**	1985–	**550.00**	**650.00**

Mine Host. D 6488, large, 75.00–90.00

	Date	Price Range	
NEPTUNE			
Depicting the Roman God of the seas and rivers. Handle is a fish.			
☐D 6548, large	1961–	95.00	
☐D 6552, small	1961–	50.00	
☐D 6555, miniature	1961–	40.00	
NIGHT WATCHMAN			
A character from the Williamsburg series.			
☐D 6569, large	1963–1983	60.00	80.00
☐D 6576, small	1963–1983	45.00	60.00
☐D 6583, miniature	1963–1983	35.00	50.00

NORTH AMERICAN INDIAN

Depicting the Chief of the Blackfoot tribe. Handle is a totem pole representing the thunderbird and bear mother.

Mr. Pickwick, D 6060, large, 145.00–185.00

	Date	Price Range	
☐ **D 6611**, large	1967–	**95.00**	
☐ **D 6614**, small	1967–	**50.00**	
☐ **D 6665**, miniature	1981–	**40.00**	
☐ **D 6786**, large, new colorway special edition of 1,000, commissioned by John Sinclair, Sheffield, England	1987–	**150.00**	**250.00**
OLD CHARLEY Depicting a night watchman of the eighteenth century.			
☐ **D 5420**, large	1934–1983	**75.00**	**100.00**
☐ **same jug with an "A" mark**		**85.00**	**110.00**
☐ **D 5527**, small	1935–1983	**35.00**	**50.00**
☐ **same jug with an "A" mark**		**40.00**	**55.00**
☐ **D 6046**, miniature	1939–1983	**25.00**	**40.00**
☐ **same jug with an "A" mark**		**30.00**	**45.00**
☐ **D 6144**, tiny	1940–1960	**110.00**	**140.00**

Old King Cole, D 6036, large, 275.00–350.00

	Date	Price Range

OLD CHARLEY

Dressed in maroon coat, black hat, and white bow tie with black dots. Issued to commemorate the second anniversary of the opening of the first Royal Doulton room at Higbee's, Cleveland, OH. Limited edition of 500.

	Date	Price Range	
☐ **D 6791**, small, new colorway	1987–	**125.00**	**225.00**

OLD KING COLE

Depicting the "merry old soul" from the familiar nursery rhyme Old King Cole. This jug is known to exist with a yellow crown instead of orange. It is also believed to have been made in both large and small size.

	Date	Price Range	
☐ **D 6036**, large	1939–1960	**275.00**	**350.00**
☐ **yellow**, large	1938 only	**9000.00**	**11,000.00**
☐ **D 6037**, small	1939–1960	**100.00**	**140.00**
☐ **yellow**, small	1939–	**4000.00**	**5000.00**

OLD SALT
Depicting an old sailor whose face shows the many years he spent at sea, but smiling as he recalls the days he spent sailing. Handle is a mermaid.

☐ **D 6551**, large	1961–	**95.00**	
☐ **D 6554**, small	1961–	**50.00**	
☐ **D 6557**, miniature	1984–	**40.00**	
☐ **D 6782**, large, new colorway	1987–	**95.00**	

OTHELLO
The Moor who murdered his beautiful wife Desdemona in a jealous rage, having been convinced she was an adultress.

☐ **D 6673**, large	1982–1988	**95.00**	

OWD MAC
The earlier version of Auld Mac. This jug depicts a thrifty Scotsman.

☐ **D 5823**, large	1938–1945	**150.00**	**200.00**

PADDY
Depicting a jolly Irish character. Paddy is the familiar nickname for Patrick, St. Patrick being the Patron Saint of Ireland.

☐ **D 5753**, large	1937–1960	**135.00**	**165.00**
☐ **same jug with an "A" mark**		**135.00**	**165.00**
☐ **D 5768**, small	1937–1960	**50.00**	**70.00**
☐ **same jug with an "A" mark**		**60.00**	**70.00**
☐ **D 6042**, miniature	1939–1960	**50.00**	**65.00**
☐ **same jug with an "A" mark**		**50.00**	**65.00**
☐ **D 6145**, tiny ....:......	1940–1960	**100.00**	**140.00**

PARSON BROWN
Depicting a typical Anglican parson of the eighteenth and nineteenth century.

☐ **D 5486**, large	1935–1960	**140.00**	**175.00**
☐ **same jug with an "A" mark**		**140.00**	**175.00**
☐ **D 5529**, small	1935–1960	**60.00**	**80.00**
☐ **same jug with an "A" mark**		**60.00**	**80.00**

PEARLY BOY
An early version of 'Arry except

Pearly Boy, D 6207, large, 1700.00–2200.00

	Date	Price Range	
buttons are on the cap and around the collar. Known to be made in two color variations. Blue variety considered rare.			
☐ **D 6207,** brown with brown buttons, large	—	1200.00	1500.00
☐ **D 6235,** brown with brown buttons, small	—	650.00	750.00
☐ **D 6249,** brown with brown buttons, miniature	—	400.00	500.00
☐ **D 6207,** brown with pearl buttons, large	—	8000.00	10,000.00
☐ **D 6235,** brown with pearl buttons, small	—	3500.00	4500.00
☐ **D 6249,** brown with pearl buttons, miniature	—	2000.00	2500.00

Pearly King, D 6760, large, 85.00

	Date	Price Range	
□ **D 6207**, blue, large	—	7500.00	9000.00
□ **D 6235**, blue, small	—	3000.00	4000.00

PEARLY GIRL
An early version of 'Arriet. Known to be made in blue coat instead of brown.

□ **D 6208**, large		12,000.00	15,000.00
□ **D 6236**, small		5000.00	7500.00
□ **D 6250**, miniature		not known to exist	

PEARLY KING
Depicting a cockney in a costume loaded with buttons. His black cap is also covered with buttons; handle is bells and buttons.

□ **D 6760**, large	1987–	95.00	

	Date	Price Range	

PEARLY QUEEN

Depicting a ''donah'' or Queen of the cockneys; dress is covered with buttons. Wearing black hat covered with colorful ostrich feathers; handle is bells and ostrich feathers.

☐ **D 6759**, large	1987–	95.00	

PIED PIPER, The

Immortalized by Robert Browning, the Pied Piper of Hamelin was a figure of medieval legend.

☐ **D 6403**, large	1954–1980	75.00	90.00
☐ **D 6462**, small	1957–1980	40.00	50.00
☐ **D 6514**, miniature	1960–1980	25.00	35.00

POACHER

Depicts a person who trespasses on other people's property illegally, taking fish or game or personal property. Handle is a fish.

☐ **D 6429**, large	1955–	95.00	
☐ **D 6464**, small	1957–	50.00	
☐ **D 6515**, miniature	1960–	40.00	
☐ **D 6781**, large, new colorway	1987–	95.00	

PORTHOS

A character from *The Three Musketeers* by Alexandre Dumas.

☐ **D 6440**, large	1956–	95.00	
☐ **D 6453**, small	1956–	50.00	
☐ **D 6516**, miniature	1960–	40.00	

PUNCH AND JUDY MAN

Depicts the man who might resemble the original puppet showman. Handle is a puppet and the curtain.

☐ **D 6590**, large	1964–1969	600.00	675.00
☐ **D 6593**, small	1964–1969	425.00	500.00
☐ **D 6596**, miniature	1964–1969	400.00	475.00

REGENCY BEAU

Depicts a gentleman of the early nineteenth century who was instantly recognized for his fashionable clothes and elegant living.

☐ **D 6559**, large	1962–1967	1100.00	1300.00
☐ **D 6562**, small	1962–1967	600.00	700.00
☐ **D 6565**, miniature	1962–1967	775.00	950.00

Regency Beau, D 6559, large, 1100.00–1300.00

	Date	Price Range	
RIP VAN WINKLE			
Depicts a character from Washington Irving's *Sketch Book*.			
☐ **D 6438**, large	1955–	95.00	
☐ **D 6463**, small	1957–	50.00	
☐ **D 6517**, miniature	1960–	40.00	
☐ **D 6785**, large, new colorway (special edition of 1,000 commissioned by John Sinclair, Sheffield, England)	1987–	150.00	250.00
ROBIN HOOD			
Depicts the notorious outlaw who robbed the rich to feed the poor.			
First Version			
☐ **D 6205**, large	1947–1960	150.00	175.00
☐ **D 6234**, small	1947–1960	75.00	85.00
☐ same jug with an "A" mark		75.00	85.00

	Date	Price Range	
☐ **D 6252**, miniature	1947–1960	60.00	75.00
☐ same jug with an "A" mark		65.00	75.00
Second Version			
Different jug than the first version. Shows acorns and oak leaves on the hat and bow/arrow for the handle.			
☐ **D 6527**, large	1960–	95.00	
☐ **D 6534**, small	1960–	50.00	
☐ **D 6541**, miniature	1960–	40.00	

ROBINSON CRUSOE
Depicts a character from the book *Robinson Crusoe* by Daniel Defoe.

☐ **D 6532**, large	1960–1982	60.00	85.00
☐ **D 6539**, small	1960–1982	35.00	50.00
☐ **D 6546**, miniature	1960–1982	25.00	40.00

ROMEO
Depicting the popular hero of centuries ago. Handle is the dagger that Juliet uses to stab herself on discovering her loved one's death.

☐ **D 6670**, large	1983–1988	95.00	

RONALD REAGAN
First in the President's Signature Edition, numbered, limited edition of 5,000 but only 2,000 were actually produced. Portion of the original cost donated to the James Brady Foundation.

☐ **D 6718**, large	1985–	375.00	500.00

ST. GEORGE
Depicting the legendary character who saved the king's daughter by slaying the dragon. Handle is a dragon.

☐ **D 6618**, large	1968–1975	225.00	275.00
☐ **D 6621**, small	1968–1975	100.00	140.00

SAIREY GAMP
Depicts the fat mid-wife from the Charles Dickens book titled *The Life and Adventures of Martin Chuzzlewit.*

☐ **D 5451**, large	1935–1986	75.00	100.00
☐ same jug with an "A" mark		80.00	100.00
☐ **D 5528**, small	1935–1986	45.00	65.00
☐ same jug with an "A" mark		60.00	75.00
☐ **D 6045**, miniature	1939–1986	35.00	50.00
☐ same jug with an "A" mark		45.00	60.00
☐ **D 6146**, tiny	1940–1960	95.00	125.00

	Date	Price Range	

SAMUEL JOHNSON

Depicting the great English writer, most widely recognized for writing *Dictionary of the English Language*.

	Date	Price Range	
□ **D 6289**, large	1950–1960	300.00	400.00
□ **D 6296**, small	1950–1960	185.00	225.00
□ same jug with an "A" mark		200.00	225.00

SAM WELLER

Depicting a character from Charles Dickens' *Pickwick Papers*.

	Date	Price Range	
□ **D 6064**, large	1940–1960	140.00	170.00
□ same jug with an "A" mark		140.00	170.00
□ **D 5841**, special size	1938–1948	185.00	220.00
□ **D 5841**, small	1948–1960	75.00	100.00
□ same jug with an "A" mark		75.00	100.00
□ **D 6140**, miniature	1940–1960	55.00	65.00
□ same jug with an "A" mark		55.00	65.00
□ **D 6147**, tiny	1940–1960	100.00	140.00

SANCHO PANZA

Depicting a character from Miguel de Cervantes' book *Don Quixote*.

	Date	Price Range	
□ **D 6456**, large	1960–1982	75.00	100.00
□ **D 6461**, small	1960–1982	50.00	75.00
□ **D 6518**, miniature	1960–1982	40.00	65.00

SANTA CLAUS

Depicting the jovial character with his twinkling eyes and jolly expression. Handle is rag doll.

	Date	Price Range	
□ **D 6668**, large	1981 only	90.00	110.00
□ **D 6675**, large, handle is reindeer	1982 only	90.00	115.00
□ **D 6690**, large, handle is Christmas stocking filled with toys	1983 only	75.00	90.00

SANTA CLAUS

A perfect interpretation of the character Santa Claus. He has a ruddy, wrinkled complexion, long white hair and full white beard. Scarlet red cap with matching red plain jug handle.

	Date	Price Range	
□ **D 6704**, large	1984–	95.00	
□ **D 6705**, small	1984–	50.00	
□ **D 6706**, miniature	1984–	40.00	

SCARAMOUCHE

Depicting a character probably from an Italian comedy, a buffoon.

Scaramouche, D 6558, large, 675.00–750.00

	Date	Price Range	
☐ **D 6558,** large	1962–1967	675.00	750.00
☐ **D 6561,** small	1962–1967	500.00	600.00
☐ **D 6564,** miniature	1962–1967	500.00	600.00
☐ **D 6774,** large, new colorway (limited edition of 1,500 commissioned by the Guild of Specialists China & Glass Retailers of England)	1987–	150.00	200.00

SIMON THE CELLARER
Depicting the man who was in charge of the wine cellar. Shown in Elizabethan costume, he was an expert on wines.

	Date	Price Range	
☐ **D 5504,** large	1935–1960	140.00	175.00
☐ same jug with an "A" mark		140.00	180.00
☐ **D 5616,** small	1936–1960	75.00	100.00
☐ same jug with an "A" mark		85.00	110.00

	Date	Price Range	

SIMPLE SIMON

Depicting the character in the well-known nursery rhyme "Simple Simon."

☐ **D 6374**, large 1953–1960   550.00   650.00

SLEUTH

Depicting a character similar to the famous detective "Sherlock Holmes" from the book by Sir Arthur Conan Doyle. Handle is a pipe and magnifying glass.

☐ **D 6631**, large 1973–   95.00

☐ **D 6635**, small 1973–   50.00

☐ **D 6639**, miniature 1973–   40.00

☐ **D 6639**, small, limited edition of 5,000. Issued to commemorate the Centenary of the publication of the first Sherlock Holmes story *A Study in Scarlet.* 1987–   45.00   60.00

SMUGGLER

Depicting a member of a gang who smuggled goods into the country without paying duty, and whom dwellers along the coast feared.

☐ **D 6616**, large 1968–1980   85.00   110.00

☐ **D 6619**, small 1968–1980   50.00   75.00

SMUTS

Depicting Field Marshal Jan Christian Smuts.

☐ **D 6198**, large 1946–1948   1700.00   2200.00

TAM O'SHANTER

Depicting the character from the Robert Burns poem "Tam O'Shanter." He was a farmer who barely escaped the witches.

☐ **D 6632**, large 1975–1979   100.00   140.00

☐ **D 6636**, small 1973–1979   50.00   70.00

☐ **D 6640**, miniature 1973–1979   40.00   50.00

TOBY GILLETTE

Modelled by Eric Griffiths in response to a twelve year old boy's dream of having a character jug of himself. With the assistance of a very popular British television personality, this was accomplished and the three jugs were made. One was presented to the young man,

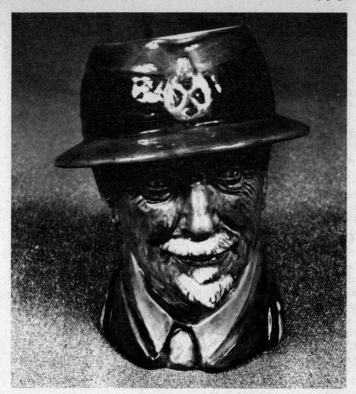

Smuts, D 6198, large, 2200.00–2600.00

	Date	Price Range	
Toby Gillette, one went to Sir Henry Doulton Gallery and the third was auctioned at Sotheby's in London. Extremely rare.			
□ **D 6717**, large	1984 only		
TOBY PHILPOTS			
Depicting the familiar character from a mid-eighteenth century song. He has always been pictured as a seated male with a three-cornered hat, with the points being used as pouring spouts.			
□ **D 5736**, large	1937–1969	135.00	160.00
□ same jug with an "A" mark		140.00	170.00
□ **D 5737**, small	1937–1969	55.00	70.00
□ same jug with an "A" mark		60.00	75.00
□ **D 6043**, miniature	1939–1969	40.00	60.00

	Date	Price Range	
☐ same jug with an "A" mark		50.00	65.00

TONY WELLER
The father of Sam Weller, he was a coach driver.

	Date	Price Range	
☐ D 5531, large	1936–1960	150.00	175.00
☐ same jug with an "A" mark		150.00	175.00
☐ D 5530, small	1936–1960	60.00	75.00
☐ same jug with an "A" mark		60.00	75.00
☐ D 6044, miniature	1939–1960	40.00	50.00
☐ same jug with an "A" mark		50.00	60.00

TOUCHSTONE
Depicting the clown in Shakespeare's play *As You Like It.*

	Date	Price Range	
☐ D 5613, large	1936–1960	275.00	325.00

TOWN CRIER
Depicts the eighteenth century man who called to the townspeople all the latest news, coming events, and meetings taking place, plus many other important events, before the advent of newspapers.

	Date	Price Range	
☐ D 6530, large	1960–1973	200.00	275.00
☐ D 6537, small	1960–1973	100.00	160.00
☐ D 6544, miniature	1960–1973	110.00	160.00

TRAPPER
Depicting the northwoodsman of North America who trapped for fur bearing animals. Handle is a horn and snowshoes.

	Date	Price Range	
☐ D 6609, large	1967–83	80.00	100.00
☐ D 6612, small	1967–83	45.00	65.00
☐ miniature sizes are known to exist ...		1200.00	1500.00

UGLY DUCHESS
A character from the Lewis Carroll book *Alice in Wonderland.* Handle is a flamingo.

	Date	Price Range	
☐ D 6599, large	1965–1973	400.00	500.00
☐ D 6603, small	1965–1973	275.00	350.00
☐ D 6607, miniature	1965–1973	275.00	350.00

UNCLE TOM COBBLEIGH
Depicting a character from a nineteenth century song. Uncle Tom and others rode a horse to the Widdecombe Fair.

Veteran Motorist, D 6633, large, 65.00–85.00

	Date	Price Range	
☐ **D 6337**, large	1952–1960	475.00	550.00

VETERAN MOTORIST
Depicting a driver in the Veteran Car Run held each year from London to Brighton.

☐ **D 6633**, large	1973–1983	65.00	85.00
☐ **D 6637**, small	1973–1983	50.00	60.00
☐ **D 6641**, miniature	1973–1983	40.00	50.00

VICAR OF BRAY, The
Depicting a country parson from an eighteenth century song.

☐ **D 5615**, large	1936–1960	250.00	300.00
☐ **same jug with an "A" mark**		250.00	300.00

	Date	Price Range	

VIKING

Depicting one of a band of Scandina-
vian seafarers and explorers.

☐ D 6496, large	1959–1975	175.00	225.00
☐ D 6502, small	1959–1975	125.00	150.00
☐ D 6526, miniature	1960–1975	125.00	150.00

WALRUS AND CARPENTER

A character from the Lewis Carroll
classic *Through The Looking Glass*. Handle is a walrus.

☐ D 6600, large	1965–1979	90.00	125.00
☐ D 6604, small	1965–1979	60.00	75.00
☐ D 6608, miniature	1965–1979	40.00	55.00

WILLIAM SHAKESPEARE

Very recognizable with his Vandyke
beard and bald head. Collar has the
masks of comedy and tragedy. Handle
is pen and quill.

☐ D 6689, large	1983–	95.00	

YACHTSMAN

Depicting a modern, English sailing
man. Handle is a sailboat.

☐ D 6622, large	1971–1979	100.00	150.00
☐ Small and miniature sizes are known to exist.			

The Celebrity Collection

The Celebrity Collection, introduced in the United States in 1983, consists
of well-known personalities from the entertainment field. Available in large size
only.

W. C. FIELDS

An excellent portrayal of the well-
known personality. Black suit with pink
carnation. Gray top hat, and the handle is the familiar black cane with silver
top. Jug bears the inscription, "I was
in love with a beautiful blonde once.
She drove me to drink—it's the one
thing I am indebted to her for." This
was introduced as a Premier Edition for
American Express, which is stated on
the base.

☐ D 6674, large	1983–1985	95.00	125.00
☐ D 6674, large, American Express	—	100.00	150.00

	Date	Price Range	

MAE WEST
  Depicts the great platinum blonde with her liberal makeup and her silver fox wrap. This was introduced as a Premier Edition for American Express, which is stated on the base.

☐ **D 6688**, large	1983–1985	85.00	115.00
☐ **D 6688**, large, American Express	—	150.00	200.00

LOUIS ARMSTRONG
  A welcome addition to the Celebrity Collection. His familiar face with his typical smile. Black suit, white shirt, bow tie, and of course, the handle is his trumpet.

☐ **D 6707**, large	1985–1986	60.00	85.00

JIMMY DURANTE
  With his traditional gray hat, flashing a smile, and long nose, this jug is truly Jimmy. Piano keyboard is the handle. Bottom bears inscription ''Good night Mrs. Calabash wherever you are.''

☐ **D 6708**, large	1984–1986	60.00	85.00

ELVIS PRESLEY
  American Rock & Roll singer, born 1935, died 1977, was never marketed but does exist as a pilot jug.

☐...	—	—	

HUMPHREY BOGART
  An American movie tough guy. This was never approved although a pilot jug does exist.

☐...	—	—	

GROUCHO MARX
  A good likeness of the popular comedian with his side glance at a pretty lady, his typical bow tie, sloppy suit and a cigar for a handle.

☐ **D 6710**, large	1985–1986	60.00	85.00

CLARK GABLE
  Produced in 1984, the jug was marketed for a brief period and then recalled. It had a grayish green shirt with light brown tie. The handle was a movie camera and film.

☐ **D 6709**	—	4000.00	5000.00

Antony and Cleopatra, D 6728, large, 125.00

Star-Crossed Lovers

A new series of double-faced character jugs introduced in 1985 in a limited edition of 9,500.

	Date	Price Range
ANTONY AND CLEOPATRA		
☐ **D 6728**, first in a series, limited edition of 9,500	1985–	**125.00**
NAPOLEON AND JOSEPHINE		
☐ **D 6750**, second in a series, limited edition of 9,500	1986–	**125.00**

The Wild West Collection

A collection of character jugs consisting of six pieces, this series was introduced in late 1985. The fame of these Wild West characters has spread worldwide due to the popularity of western movies. All jugs are 5½″ high.

WYATT EARP		
☐ **D 6711**, medium size	1985–1988	**70.00**

	Date	Price Range
ANNIE OAKLEY		
☐ **D 6732**, medium size	1985–1988	**70.00**
BUFFALO BILL		
☐ **D 6735**, medium size	1985–1988	**70.00**
DOC HOLLIDAY		
☐ **D 6731**, medium size	1985–1988	**70.00**
WILD BILL HICKOCK		
☐ **D 6736**, medium size	1985–1988	**70.00**
GERONIMO		
☐ **D 6733**, medium size	1985–1988	**70.00**

New Tiny Character Jug Collection

Introduced in the United States in 1984, this collection consists of the following twelve tinies.

CHARLES DICKENS			
☐ **D 6676**	1984–	**30.00**	**40.00**
OLIVER TWIST			
☐ **D 6677**	1984–	**30.00**	**40.00**
ARTFUL DODGER			
☐ **D 6678**	1984–	**30.00**	**40.00**
FAGEN			
☐ **D 6679**	1984–	**30.00**	**40.00**
DAVID COPPERFIELD			
☐ **D 6680**	1984–	**30.00**	**40.00**
LITTLE NELL			
☐ **D 6681**	1984–	**30.00**	**40.00**
URIAH HEEP			
☐ **D 6682**	1984–	**30.00**	**40.00**
SCROOGE			
☐ **D 6683**	1984–	**30.00**	**40.00**
BILL SYKES			
☐ **D 6684**	1984–	**30.00**	**40.00**
BETSY TROTWOOD			
☐ **D 6685**	1984–	**30.00**	**40.00**
MR. BUMBLE			
☐ **D 6686**	1984–	**30.00**	**40.00**

	Date	Price Range	

MRS. BARDELL

☐ D 6687 1984–   30.00   40.00

TOBY JUGS

THE BEST IS NOT TOO GOOD
Depicts a jovial character who loves his brew.

☐ D 6107 1939–1960   300.00   400.00

CAP'N CUTTLE
A character from the Charles Dickens book *Dombey and Son*.

☐ D 6266 1948–1960   175.00   225.00

DOUBLE XX or THE MAN ON THE BARREL
Depicts a person astride a barrel of brew yet still demanding another drink.

☐ D 6088 1939–1969   300.00   400.00

FALSTAFF
Depicts a character in the Shakespearean plays *Henry VIII* and *The Merry Wives of Windsor*.

☐ D 6062 1939–   115.00

☐ D 6063 1939–   60.00

FAT BOY, The
Depicts a character from Charles Dicken's *Pickwick Papers*.

☐ D 6264 1948–1960   175.00   225.00

HAPPY JOHN
Depicts a seated character with a pitcher of ale in one hand and a glass full of ale in the other.

☐ D 6031 1939–   115.00

☐ D 6070 1939–   60.00

HONEST MEASURE
Inscription reads "Honest Measure: Drink at Leisure." Sitting on the base and approximate 4½″ tall, this character is doing just that, "taking it easy."

☐ D 6108 1939–   60.00

THE HUNTSMAN
Depicts an English huntsman.

☐ D 6320 1950–   115.00

Double XX or The Man on the Barrel, 375.00–475.00

	Date	Price Range	
JOLLY TOBY			
Seated toby with a warm smile.			
☐ D 6109	1939–	**75.00**	
MR. MICAWBER			
Depicts a character from Charles Dickens' book *David Copperfield*.			
☐ D 6262	1948–1960	**175.00**	**225.00**
MR. PICKWICK			
A character from Charles Dickens' book *Pickwick Papers*.			
☐ D 6261	1948–1960	**175.00**	**225.00**

Honest Measure, D 6108, 60.00

	Date	Price Range	
OLD CHARLEY			
Seated character depicting an early nineteenth century nightwatchman.			
☐ D 6030	1939–1960	200.00	275.00
☐ D 6069	1939–1960	200.00	250.00
SAIREY GAMP			
A character from Charles Dickens' book *Martin Chuzzlewit.*			
☐ D 6263	1948–1960	175.00	225.00
SAM WELLER			
Depicts a character from Charles Dickens' *Pickwick Papers.*			
☐ D 6265	1948–1960	200.00	250.00
SHERLOCK HOLMES			
Depicting the famous sleuth from Sir Arthur Conan Doyle's many mystery			

	Date	Price Range

books. Released to commemorate the fiftieth anniversary of the death of Sir Arthur.

		Date	Price Range	
☐ **D 6661**		1981–	**115.00**	

THE SQUIRE
Depicts a character known to exist in early medieval times. He was all-around assistant to a knight and often accompanied him into battle. In later years this title was given to young men of good family training who would later become knights themselves.

☐ **D 6319**	1950–1969	**325.00**	**400.00**

SIR FRANCES DRAKE
Depicts this famous nobleman kneeling as if to bow before the queen. Released to commemorate the 400th anniversary of the arrival of Sir Francis Drake and his ship's landing at Plymouth.

☐ **D 6660**	1981–	**115.00**

SIR WINSTON CHURCHILL
Depicting the statesman and Prime Minister of Great Britain. Earlier models bear the inscription "Winston Churchill Prime Minister of Great Britain 1940."

☐ **D 6171**, large	1941–	**115.00**
☐ **D 6172**, small	1941–	**75.00**
☐ **D 6175**, miniature	1941–	**60.00**

New Doultonville Toby Jugs

Introduced in 1983, these Tobies are all 4″ high. All figures are created from a fictitious town called "Doultonville." Designer W.K. Harper.

MR. FURROW, THE FARMER
Depicting a man with weatherbeaten face indicating much time spent in the outdoors. Wears an old battered hat. He carries in one hand a riding crop and in the other corn. Coat is brown, his waistcoat yellow, green bow tie.

☐ **D 6701**	1983–1988	**45.00**

Sir Winston Churchill, D 6171, large, 95.00

	Date	Price Range

MR. LITIGATE, THE LAWYER
Figure has long black coat, gray trousers, yellow vest. Gold watch chain. Traditional powdered wig.
☐ **D 6699** 1983– **45.00**

MISS NOSTRUM, THE NURSE
Jolly lady with rosy cheeks. Wearing blue/black uniform with white apron. Hat same color as uniform, gray hair. Fob watch on the bib of her apron.
☐ **D 6723** 1983– **45.00**

REV. CASSOCK, THE CLERGYMAN
Dressed in a black jacket, wearing a clerical collar, gray uniform under jacket. Carrying an open Bible.
☐ **D 6702** 1983– **45.00**

	Date	Price Range

MR. TONSIL, THE TOWN CRIER
Cries of "Hear Ye Hear Ye" can almost be heard as he rings his golden bell. Character is dressed in silver gray wig, plumed hat and purple coat.

☐ D 6713 1984–   45.00

MADAME CRYSTAL, THE CLAIRVOYANT
Character is wearing a purple skirt with pink shawl, green turban wrapped around her head.

☐ D 6714 1984–1988   45.00

MRS. LOAN, THE LIBRARIAN
Green skirt with light green blouse, brown hair. Character is sternly watching to keep the silence in the library.

☐ D 6715 1984–   45.00

BETTY BITTERS, THE BARMAID
Gaily dressed in purple skirt with green blouse. Accenting her blouse is a string of pearls.

☐ D 6716 1984–   45.00

SGT. PEELER, THE POLICEMAN
☐ D 6720 1985–   45.00

CAPTAIN SALT, SEA CAPTAIN
☐ D 6721 1985–   45.00

MISS STUDIOUS, THE TEACHER
☐ D 6722 1985–1988   45.00

DR. PULSE, THE PHYSICIAN
☐ D 6723 1985–   45.00

MIKE MINERAL, THE MINER
Middle-aged man in miner's outfit, wearing safety helmet. Lamp and explosive in hand.

☐ D 6741 1986–   45.00

MR. BRISKET, THE BUTCHER
Gentleman with a wry look, wearing a butcher's apron over his white shirt. Wearing a straw hat and holding a steel cleaver.

☐ D 6743 1986–   45.00

Doultonville Tobies. Alderman Mace; Flora Fuchsia, Charlie Cheer; Monsieur Chasseur

	Date	Price Range
MAJOR GREEN, THE GOLFER Elderly gentleman dressed in sleeveless cardigan and yellow shirt, holding putter in his hand.		
☐ D 6740	1986–	45.00
FRED FLY, THE FISHERMAN Elderly gentleman wearing a heavy jacket, wool tie, and gold fishing cap decorated with fishing flies. Fish and fishing net in hands.		
☐ D 6742	1986–	45.00
FLORA FUCHSIA, THE FLORIST Lady with red hair, dressed in a fashionable but modest gray dress, holding a vase with flowers.		
☐ D 6767	1987–	45.00
MONSIEUR CHASSEUR, THE CHEF Typically dressed for his job, he wears a tall white hat, white coat, blue		

	Date	Price Range

neckerchief, and in his hand he holds a spoon.

☐ **D 6769** 1987– **45.00**

ALDERMAN MACE, THE MAYOR
Dressed in red robe with white fancy collar, black, three-cornered hat, holding speech in his hand as if ready to address a crowd.

☐ **D 6766** 1987– **45.00**

CHARLIE CHEER, THE CLOWN
Dressed in brown coat, white shirt with wide, blue tie. Yellow hat, yellow hair. Holding scissors in one hand, clipping his tie, and some weiners in the other hand.

☐ **D 6768** 1987– **45.00**

MISCELLANEOUS ITEMS

Royal Doulton has produced a number of miscellaneous items that do not fall into any of the major categories. All the works listed in this section are out of production and have acquired solid collector status.

DEWARS WHISKEY FLASKS

	Date	Price Range	
BEN JOHNSON □D		225.00	275.00
BONNIE PRINCE CHARLIE □D		200.00	250.00
FALSTAFF □D		200.00	255.00
GEORGE THE GUARD □D		200.00	250.00
JOVIAL MONK □D		250.00	300.00
MICAWBER □D		200.00	250.00
MR. MICAWBER □D	1983–	65.00	
MacNABB □D		250.00	275.00
JOHN DEWARS & SON □D Stoneware Egyptian design		175.00	225.00
OYEZ, OYEZ □D		275.00	325.00
PIED PIPER □D		200.00	250.00
SPORTING SQUIRE □D		225.00	250.00
WATCHMAN □D		250.00	325.00
TONY WELLER □D		200.00	250.00

Mr. Pickwick, Jim Beam handle, 85.00–110.00; Sergeant Buz Fuz, 75.00–125.00; Mr. Pickwick, old bottle handle, 125.00–175.00

PICKWICK WHISKEY DECANTERS

These decanters were made by Royal Doulton and sold only in the United Kingdom from Pick-Kwik Shops and Harrods Ltd., London. Some are finding their way into the United States and are being advertised by various dealers.

	Date	Price Range	
MR. PICKWICK ☐ With old bottle handle. 3¾″, limited edition of 2,000, now sold out	1982–	**125.00**	**175.00**
SERGEANT BUZ FUZ ☐ With Dewars White Label whiskey bottle handle, 3¾″ high, limited edition of 2,000	1983–	**75.00**	**125.00**
MR. PICKWICK ☐ With Jim Beam bottle handle, 3¾″ high, limited edition of 2,000, now sold out	1984–	**85.00**	**110.00**
MR. PICKWICK ☐ With Jim Beam bourbon whiskey bottle handle, 3¾″ high, limited edition of 1,000	1984–1987	**50.00**	

MR. PICKWICK
☐ With Jim Beam Black Label bottle

Uncle Sam, American Bald Eagle on handle, Beam whiskey, 85.00–100.00; Uncle Sam, Jim Beam bottle handle 85.00–100.00

	Date	Price Range	
handle, 5¾" high, limited edition of 1,000	1984–1987	50.00	
MR. MICAWBER ☐ With Pickwick Whiskey bottle handle, 5¾" high, only 2,000 made, now discontinued	1983–1987	55.00	
MR. MICAWBER ☐ With Dewars Whiskey bottle handle, 5¾" high, unlimited, now discontinued	1983–	55.00	
UNCLE SAM ☐ With eagle handle, 5¾" high, only 500 made for promotional purpose	1986 only	85.00	100.00
UNCLE SAM ☐ With Jim Beam bottle handle, 5¾" high, only 2,000 made, now discontinued	1984–1987	85.00	100.00
MR. PICKWICK/SAM WELLER ☐ Two headed decanter, Mr. Pickwick, Charles Dickens' most famous character, with his faithful valet and aide, Sam Weller, 5¼", unlimited	1985–	85.00	100.00

JOHN BULL
☐ This decanter represents the national symbol for England. Symbol was originated in the 1600s. The popular idea was established in 1712 and has carried on to this date. The handle is his cane

Mr. Pickwick/Sam Weller, two-headed decanter, 85.00–100.00

	Date	Price Range	
with the famous British "bulldog," which is Great Britain's national dog, top.	1985	70.00	90.00
CAPTAIN COOK ☐ Captain James Cook R.M.F.R.S., born in 1723 and died in 1770, was a very famous English explorer and circumnavigator of the globe. Handle is a scroll, naming his three famous discoveries, New Zealand, Australia, and Canada	1985–	70.00	90.00
SAMURAI WARRIOR ☐ Samurai was the hereditary warrior in Japan, whose ancestors were farmers who had taken up arms to fight in the army, now discontinued	1986–	70.00	90.00
OLD MR. TURVEYDROP ☐ A fat, old gentleman with false teeth, false whiskers, and a wig. Handle is a Jim Beam bottle. Only 2,000 made, now discontinued	1985–	70.00	90.00
TOWN CRIER OF EATONSWILL ☐ In the early nineteenth century, each village and town in England had its own town crier who read all the important news. Handle is a Jim Beam bottle. Only 2,000 made, now sold out ...	1985–	70.00	90.00

DICKENS JUGS AND TANKARDS

	Date	Price Range	
OLD CURIOSITY SHOP JUG Figures in relief of Little Nell and her grandfather on one side, and the Marchioness on the other.			
☐ D 5584	1935–1960	175.00	225.00
OLD LONDON JUG Depicts London during the time of Charles Dickens with Old Charley on one side and Sairey Gamp on the other.			
☐ D 6291	1949–1960	250.00	325.00
OLIVER TWIST JUG			
☐ D 5617	1937–1960	150.00	200.00
OLIVER TWIST JUG Oliver asking for more.			
☐ D 6285	1936–1960	150.00	200.00
OLIVER TWIST TANKARD Oliver watching the Artful Dodger picking a pocket.			
☐ D 6286	1949–1960	200.00	250.00
PEGGOTTY JUG Depicting a scene from *David Copperfield*.			
☐ D 6292	1949–1960	250.00	325.00
PICKWICK PAPERS JUGS Depicts the characters from Dickens' book *The Pickwick Papers* outside the White Hart Inn.			
☐ D 5756	1937–1960	200.00	250.00

PLATES

This terminology is strictly British and is often misunderstood by Americans. A "head rack plate" is a plate designed to be displayed on a wall or in a cabinet ("rack"), rather than used as tableware. Head rack means that the plate carries a human likeness. Royal Doulton's Head Rack Plates have borne portraits of characters from the novels of Charles Dickens, as well as miscellaneous types, both historical and fictional. In addition to Head Rack Plates, the factory has also made Scenic Rack Plates, which have landscape views, often including colorful wildlife.

Though we live in an age of plate collecting and might think decorative plates to be something new, the concept of Head Rack and Scenic Rack Plates dates back very far. Beautifully enameled majolica plates, with painted scenes, were made in Italy in the fifteenth century. English porcelain factories began putting them out in the 1700s for use on elegant tables. But many were, in fact, purchased to use as wall decorations. In the early Victorian era (1840s), a vogue developed in England for encircling rooms with these plates, on walls near the ceiling. This gave further impetus to the manufacturers. Royal Doulton has been making decorative plates for many years. Interested collectors might want to seek out some of the early issues, in addition to the modern ones listed here.

These plates are issued without serial numbers.

Back in the early 1970s when the collector plate market was in somewhat of a turmoil, plaques with poor examples of what was supposed to be quality plates at high prices, and a seemingly get-rich quick attitude of many persons, the Doulton Company conceived the idea of transferring quality works of art by good artists, some well-known, some not, to plates of highest quality with great emphasis on the finished product being as near the artists' original work as possible.

After considerable thought, the Collectors International was established to issue products of Fine Art on Fine China. The first plate was introduced in 1973 with a series of Mother's Day plates by artist Edna Hibel. Following is the entire series offered since 1973, bearing the secondary market prices as of the current date.

HEAD RACK PLATES

Charles Dickens Series

	Size	Price Range	
☐ Artful Dodger	10¼"	65.00	85.00
☐ Barkis	10¼"	80.00	100.00
☐ Cap'n Cuttle	10¼"	80.00	100.00
☐ Fagin	9½"	55.00	75.00

	Size	Price Range	
☐ Fat Boy	10¼″	65.00	85.00
☐ Mr. Micawber	10¼″	65.00	85.00
☐ Mr. Pickwick	10¼″	80.00	100.00
☐ Old Peggoty	10¼″	80.00	100.00
☐ Poor Jo	10¼″	65.00	85.00
☐ Sairey Gamp	10 ¼″	80.00	100.00
☐ Sam Weller	10¼″	65.00	85.00
☐ Sergeant Buz Fuz	10¼″	80.00	100.00
☐ Tony Weller	10¼″	65.00	85.00

HISTORICAL BRITAIN SERIES

English Translucent China plates:

	Size	Price Range	
☐ Anne Hathaway's Cottage, Shottery, Near Stratford-on-Avon	10½″	60.00	75.00
☐ Clovelly, North Devon	10½″	45.00	65.00
☐ House of Parliament, London	10½″	45.00	65.00
☒ Tower of London	10½″	55.00	75.00
☒ Tudor Mansion	10½″	60.00	80.00

MISCELLANEOUS

	Size	Price Range	
☐ A Company of Odd Looking Persons Playing at Nine Pins	10¼″	85.00	100.00
☐ The Admiral	10¼″	55.00	70.00
☐ Arabian Knights	10¼″	70.00	85.00
☐ Bradley Golfers, pictures of men golfing, with sayings printed around the plate, very early 1900s era	10¼″	175.00	225.00
☐ Charles Dickens	10¼″	85.00	125.00
☐ The Cobbler	10¼″	65.00	85.00
☐ The Doctor	10¼″	65.00	85.00
☐ Don Quixote	10¼″	65.00	85.00
☐ The Falconer	10¼″	65.00	85.00
☐ Falstaff	10¼″	65.00	85.00
☐ Gaffers	10¼″	65.00	85.00
☐ The Hunting Man	10¼″	85.00	110.00
☐ Jackdaw of Reims	10¼″	65.00	85.00
☐ The Jester	10¼″	75.00	125.00
☐ The Mayor	10¼″	85.00	110.00
☐ Night Watchman, with pike and lantern	10¼″	65.00	85.00
☐ Old English Coaching Scene	10¼″	75.00	90.00
☐ Omar Khayyam	10¼″	80.00	100.00
☐ Ophelia, Shakespeare	10¼″	80.00	100.00
☐ Othelo, The Moor of Venice, Act IV	10¼″	85.00	110.00

	Size	Price Range	
☐ The Parson	10¼″	65.00	85.00
☐ Rip Van Winkle	10¼″	100.00	150.00
☐ Robert Burns	10¼″	65.00	85.00
☐ Shakespeare	10¼″	65.00	85.00
☐ The Squire	10¼″	55.00	75.00

SCENIC RACK PLATES

	Size	Price Range	
☐ African Elephants	10¼″	25.00	35.00
☐ Australian Aborigine	10¼″	20.00	25.00
☐ Bow Valley	10¼″	30.00	40.00
☐ Giraffes	10¼″	25.00	35.00
☐ Koala Bears	10¼″	25.00	35.00
☐ Lake Louise and Victoria Glacier	10¼″	22.50	35.00
☐ Lioness	10¼″	35.00	45.00
☐ Maritime Provinces	10¼″	25.00	35.00
☐ Mother Kangaroo with Joey	10¼″	30.00	40.00
☐ Mount Egmont	10¼″	20.00	30.00
☐ Murray River Gums	10¼″	20.00	30.00
☐ Niagara Falls	10¼″	25.00	35.00
☐ Vermilion Lake and Mount Rundle	10¼″	20.00	30.00
☐ Young Kookaburras	10¼″	35.00	45.00

ANIMAL PLATES

A dozen 10¼″ plates bearing one or more full-body dogs were produced; also one signed Cecil Aldin. There was a series of 7½″ plates with head studies. Collectors have been able to find five breeds that are known; however, it has been suggested probably a dozen were made all prior to 1944.

	Size	Price Range	
☐ Dogs, signed Cecil Aldin	10¼″	110.00	125.00
☐ Dogs, Cocker Spaniel	10¼″	40.00	60.00
☐ Dogs, Cocker Spaniel Head Study	7½″	65.00	85.00
☐ Dogs, English Setter	10½″	60.00	80.00
☐ Dogs, Hounds	10¼″	60.00	80.00
☐ Dogs, Irish Setter Head Study	7½″	75.00	100.00
☐ Dogs, Labrador Retriever Head Study	7½″	75.00	100.00
☐ Dogs, Pointer	10¼″	60.00	80.00
☐ Dogs, Scottish Terrier	10¼″	50.00	75.00
☐ Dogs, Sealyham Terrier Head Study	7½″	75.00	100.00

Painted Feelings, Artist: Ben Black, 95.00

SERIES PLATES

Title	Date	Edition Size	Issue Price
"BEHIND THE PAINTED MASQUE" by Ben Black			
☐ Painted Feelings	1982	10,000	**95.00**
☐ Make Me Laugh	1983	10,000	**95.00**
☐ Minstrel Serenade	1984	10,000	**95.00**
☐ Pleasing Performance	1985	10,000	**95.00**
"AMERICAN TAPESTRIES" by C.A. Brown			
☐ Sleigh Bells	1978	15,000	**70.00**
☐ Pumpkin Patch	1979	15,000	**70.00**
☐ General Store	1981	10,000	**95.00**
☐ Fourth of July	1982	10,000	**95.00**
"FESTIVAL CHILDREN OF THE WORLD" by Brenda Burke			
☐ Mariana (Balinese)	1983	15,000	**65.00**
☐ Magdalena (Mexico)	1984	15,000	**65.00**
☐ Michiko (Japanese)	1985	15,000	**65.00**
"REFLECTIONS OF CHINA" by Chen Chi			
☐ Garden of Tranquility	1976	15,000	**90.00**

Pumpkin Patch, Artist: C.A. Brown, 70.00

Title	Date	Edition Size	Issue Price
☐ Imperial Palace	1977	15,000	80.00
☐ Temple of Heaven	1978	15,000	75.00
☐ Lake of Mists	1980	15,000	85.00
"ALL GOD'S CHILDREN" by Lisette DeWinne			
☐ A Brighter Day	1978	10,000	75.00
☐ Village Children	1980	10,000	65.00
☐ Noble Heritage	1981	10,000	85.00
☐ Buddies	1982	10,000	85.00
☐ My Little Brother	1983	10,000	95.00
"MOTHER AND CHILD" by Edna Hibel			
☐ Colette and Child	1973	15,000	500.00
☐ Sayuri and Child	1974	15,000	175.00
☐ Kristina and Child	1975	15,000	125.00

Mariana, Artist: Brenda Burke, 65.00

Title	Date	Edition Size	Issue Price
☐ Marilyn and Child	1976	15,000	110.00
☐ Lucia and Child	1977	15,000	90.00
☐ Kathleen and Child	1981	15,000	85.00
"CHILDREN OF THE PUEBLO" by Mimi Jungbluth			
☐ Apple Flower	1983	15,000	60.00
☐ Morning Star	1984	15,000	60.00
"PORTS OF CALL" by Doug Kingman			
☐ San Francisco, Fisherman's Wharf	1975	15,000	90.00
☐ New Orleans, Royal Street	1976	15,000	80.00
☐ Venice, Grand Canal	1977	15,000	65.00
☐ Paris, Montmartre	1978	15,000	70.00
"PORTRAITS OF INNOCENCE" by Francisco Masseria			
☐ Panchito	1980	15,000	300.00
☐ Adrien	1981	15,000	85.00
☐ Angelica	1982	15,000	95.00

Venice, Grand Canal, Artist: Doug Kingman, 65.00

Title	Date	Edition Size	Issue Price
☐ Juliana	1983	15,000	95.00
☐ Gabriella	1985	15,000	95.00
☐ Francesca	1986	15,000	95.00
"THE GRANDEST GIFT" by Mago			
☐ Reunion	1985	10,000	75.00
☐ Storytime	1985	10,000	75.00
"GRANDPARENTS" by Mago			
☐ Grandfather and Children	1984	15,000	95.00
"COMMEDIA DELL'ARTE" by LeRoy Neiman			
☐ Harlequin	1974	15,000	100.00
☐ Pierrot	1975	15,000	90.00
☐ Columbine	1977	15,000	80.00
☐ Punchinello	1978	15,000	75.00

Angelica, Artist: Francisco Masseria, 95.00

Title	Date	Edition Size	Issue Price
☐ **Winning Colors.** Although not part of the Commedia Dell'arte Series, this plate was offered in recognition of the vast popularity of LeRoy Neiman's most notable subject matter	1980	10,000	**85.00**
"JUNGLE FANTASY" by Gustavo Novoa			
☐ The Ark	1979	10,000	**75.00**
☐ Compassion	1981	10,000	**95.00**
☐ Patience	1982	10,000	**95.00**
☐ Refuge	1983	10,000	**95.00**
"I REMEMBER AMERICA" by Eric Sloane			
☐ Pennsylvania Pastorale	1977	15,000	**90.00**
☐ Lovejoy Bridge	1978	15,000	**80.00**
☐ Four Corners	1979	15,000	**75.00**
☐ Marshlands	1981	15,000	**95.00**
"LOG OF THE DASHING WAVE" by John Stobart			
☐ Sailing with the Tide	1976	15,000	**115.00**
☐ Running Free	1977	15,000	**110.00**

Columbine, Artist: Leroy Nieman, 80.00

Title	Date	Edition Size	Issue Price
☐ Rounding the Horn	1978	15,000	85.00
☐ Hong Kong	1979	15,000	75.00
☐ Bora Bora	1981	15,000	95.00
☐ Journey's End	1982	15,000	95.00
"FLOWER GARDEN" by Hahn Vidal			
☐ Spring Harmony	1975	15,000	80.00
☐ Dreaming Lotus	1976	15,000	90.00
☐ From the Poet's Garden	1977	15,000	75.00
☐ Country Bouquet	1978	15,000	75.00
☐ From My Mother's Garden	1980	15,000	85.00
"CELEBRATION OF FAITH" by James Woods			
☐ Rosh Hashanah	1982	7,500	250.00
☐ Yom Kippur	1983	7,500	250.00
☐ Passover	1984	7,500	250.00
☐ Chanukah	1985	7,500	250.00

Kathleen and Child, Artist: Edna Hibel, 85.00

"CHARACTER" PLATES
Series limited to the period of issue each year. Entire series discontinued as of January 1, 1984.

	Date	Price Range	
☐ Old Balloon Seller	1979	100.00	150.00
☐ Balloon Man	1980	125.00	175.00
☐ Silk and Ribbons	1981	125.00	175.00
☐ Biddy Penny Farthing	1982	125.00	175.00

"AROUND THE WORLD SERIES"
Beswick Christmas Plates

Title	Date	Edition Size	Issue Price
☐ Christmas in Old England	1972	15,000	35.00
☐ Christmas in Mexico	1973	15,000	37.50
☐ Christmas in Bulgaria	1974	15,000	37.50
☐ Christmas in Norway	1975	15,000	45.00
☐ Christmas in Holland	1976	15,000	50.00
☐ Christmas in Poland	1977	15,000	50.00

Morning Star, Artist: Mimi Jungbluth, 60.00

Title	Date	Edition Size	Issue Price
☐ Christmas in America	1978	15,000	**55.00**

"VICTORIAN ERA" CHRISTMAS PLATES
Series limited to the period of issue each year.

☐ Winter Fun	1977		**55.00**
☐ Christmas Day	1978		**25.00**
☐ Christmas	1979		**30.00**
☐ Santa's Visit	1980		**33.00**
☐ Christmas Carolers	1981		**37.50**
☐ Santa on Bicycle	1982		**39.95**

"VICTORIAN ERA" VALENTINE PLATES
Series limited to the period of issue each year.

☐ Victorian Boy and Girl	1976		**65.00**
☐ My Sweetest Friend	1977		**40.00**
☐ If I Loved You	1978		**40.00**
☐ My Valentine	1979		**35.00**

Gabriella, Artist: Francisco Masseria, 95.00

Title	Date	Edition Size	Issue Price
☐ Valentine	1980		33.00
☐ Valentine Boy and Girl	1981		35.00
☐ Angel with Mandolin	1982		39.95
☐ My Valentine	1985		39.95

"CHILDHOOD SERIES" CHRISTMAS PLATES
Series will consist of six plates, each featuring a young child. Series limited to the period of issue each year.

☐ Silent Night	1983		35.00
☐ While Shepherds Watched	1984		39.95
☐ Oh Little Town of Bethlehem	1985		39.95
☐ We Saw Three Ships A Sailing	1986		39.95
☐ The Holly and the Ivy	1987		39.95

The Ark, Artist: Gustavo Novoa, 75.00

Four Corners, Artist: Eric Sloane, 75.00

Sailing with the Tide, Artist: John Stobart, 115.00

Spring Harmony, Artist: Hahn Vidal, 80.00

Rosh Hashanah, Artist: James Woods, 250.00

Old Balloon Seller, 100.00–150.00

Balloon Man, 125.00–175.00

Silk and Ribbons, 125.00–175.00

Biddy Penny Farthing, 125.00–175.00

Christmas in Old England, 35.00

Christmas in Mexico, 37.00

Christmas in Bulgaria, 37.50

Christmas in Norway, 45.00

Christmas in America, 55.00

Winter Fun, 55.00

Christmas Day, 25.00

Christmas Sleigh Ride, 30.00

Santa's Visit, 33.00

Christmas Carolers, 37.50

Santa on Bicycle, 39.95

Christmas Carols, 39.95

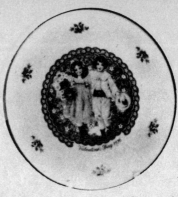

Victorian Boy and Girl, 65.00

My Valentine, 35.00

Valentine Boy and Girl, 35.00

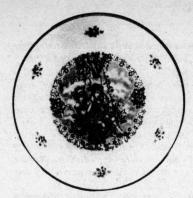

Valentine, 33.00

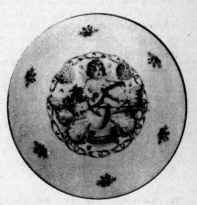

Angel with Mandolin, 39.95

To My Sweet Valentine, 39.95

FLAMBÉ

This article is excerpted from the Royal Doulton International Collectors Club Magazine with permission of Royal Doulton Tableware, Limited, Stoke-on-Trent, England.

Royal Doulton are justifiably proud of their famous flambé glazes. They were the first British firm to achieve consistent success with these exotic Oriental glaze effects and consequently to put them into commercial production. Experimentation began in the 1890s and since that date their discoveries have remained a closely guarded secret. According to C. J. Noke, the only outsider ever to have had the technique explained to him was King George V and he was certain it would be safe with him! Flambé artists have a gentlemen's agreement never to divulge details of the process and even today, visitors are never shown round the studio which specializes in this ware.

Why all this cloak and dagger intrigue? It dates back to the late nineteenth century when leading European ceramicists vied with each other to emulate the rich ruby glazes perfected by the Chinese. No recipes existed and each potter and chemist went through long periods of trial and error. At Doulton's the art director John Slater and the young Charles Noke had put their heads together and by 1900 had succeeded in producing the occasional good specimen. That year the manager's son Cuthbert Bailey joined the firm and he immediately became fascinated by the research. He set up a camp bed in his studio and stayed there day and night when a firing was going on. Essential ingredients of the flambé glaze, such as copper, had been established but the most important factor to gain control of was the kiln and how much and when to reduce the oxygen levels in order to make the copper turn red. Consistency in this field eluded them until they commissioned the help of Bernard Moore, a local consultant potter. He had already achieved some measure of success independently and so before long their combined expertise and resources came to fruition. Royal Doulton were able to launch their new flambé wares at the St. Louis Exhibition in 1904 and the reception was overwhelming. Even from the outset, they were considered to be collectors items, worthy of a place in the finest museums. Over the years, flambé glaze has been applied to hundreds of different Oriental style vases, bowls and plaques, as well as to a host of animal models and occasional figures.

When Cuthbert Bailey, who had been the driving force in the rediscovery of flambé left Doulton in 1907, Charles Noke took on the responsibility for the further development of the transmutation glazes. During the first World War, when his modelling skills were less in demand, he evolved the *Sung* wares which are distinguished by more pronounced veinings in bright yellows, blues and greens. The scope of this new glaze, which was publicly launched in 1920, was vast. Artists such as Harry Nixon, Arthur Eaton and Fred Moore now had a wider color palette with which to create appropriate images of birds of paradise, fantastic dragons and tropical fish.

As well as the hand painted variety, there were many *Sung* wares which relied for their appeal on form and glaze alone. Texture also preoccupied Noke and by 1925 he had developed the most tactile of the transmutation glazes, the *Chang* Wares. The shapes were fashioned in a coarse refractory marl, often with the throwing rings left for effect. Over this trickled thick, viscous glazes in a myriad of colors. Collector interest in the distinctive *Chang* wares is enormous, so much so that unusual pieces have been selling at the rate of $200 per inch.

As well as the prestige wares such as *Sung* and *Chang* there were also less expensive flambé glazes. Mottled flambé, where the different metallic oxides were daubed on to create splashes of bright color when fired, were quicker and therefore less expensive to produce. Also very much in vogue since the thirties, has been landscape flambé in which pastoral scenes are part printed and part painted to form a silhouette under a deep red glaze. A more recent development of this style is the woodcut flambé which features the romantic landscapes of Thomas Beswick, the famous 18th century engraver. Woodcut flambé was introduced by art director Jo Ledger shortly after he joined Royal Doulton in 1955 and the flambé experimentation continues to flourish under his direction.

Alongside all the continuing research into the reduction fired flambé glazes, other experimental glaze effects were being developed. Lustre glazes also require a reducing atmosphere to create their metallic sheen from oxides of gold, silver, platinum and copper, so it is not surprising to find a wide range of effects dating from the same time as the flambé developments. Examples of 'peach blow,' 'haricot,' iridescent peacock hues, and silvery mother of pearl will all be included in the displays.

Royal Doulton's preoccupation with experimental glazes reflected the activities of many European and American potteries. All admired the crystalline glazes pioneered in Scandinavia which featured random groups of frost-like crystals. Bailey and Noke succeeded in controlling the cooling of a special glaze to create this effect in 1907. Most crystalline wares are in pastel shades but the technique was also occasionally used in conjunction with flambe and *Titanian* glazes.

The development of the latter in 1915 was yet another string to Mr. Noke's bow. Titanium was an essential component of the glaze, responsible for the ethereal blue coloring which formed an ideal background for evocative painting of birds, insects or fairy revels by artists such as Harry Nixon or Harry Tittensor. A much deeper ultramarine blue was also developed to simulate the semi-precious stone Lapis Lazuli, but very little of this turns up today, so production must have been limited. Equally hard to find is *Chinese Jade,* a white glazed ware with green veins imitating the translucent stone much venerated by the Chinese. Figure and animal models, as well as vases and bowls based on chinese bronze prototypes, were decorated with Noke's new glaze which was introduced in 1920.

Flambé ware has always been a desirable collectible; however, not many pieces surfaced to collect. In the past ten years more pieces seem to be appearing on the market. Articles and books including material on these pieces and collector interest is increasing. The following prices reflect what the author has seen at auctions, antique sales, and pieces in private collections which have been valued by their owners. These prices are shown in order that a prospective buyer would have an idea of the price range should a similar piece become available for purchase, and should not be construed as firm prices.

FLAMBÉ LISTINGS

Price Range

ALLIGATOR

☐ Rouge 1400.00   1500.00

	Price Range	

ALSATIAN, SITTING UP
☐ 5½″ x 9″ 800.00 900.00

BEAR, SITTING UP
☐ Rouge 500.00 600.00
☐ Bottle Vase, 12″ high, signed Noke 200.00 250.00

BEAR, STANDING
☐ Sung, 1¾″ × 5″ 700.00 800.00

BIRDS, TWO ON AN IVORY BASE
☐ Rouge 350.00 400.00

BIRD WITH BABIES
☐ Rouge 225.00 275.00

BOWL
☐ Veined Sung, 8″ round 700.00 750.00
☐ Sung, 5″ round 200.00 300.00

BUDDHA
☐ Veined Sung, 7″ 1100.00 1200.00

BULL
☐ Signed Noke, 10½″ × 6″ 1800.00 2000.00

BULLDOG, SITTING WITH FRONT LEGS APART
☐ 4″ × 4″ 500.00 600.00

CAT, CURLED UP SLEEPING
☐ 3¾″ × 1½″ 700.00 800.00

CAT
☐ Rouge, No. 9, 4¾″ 75.00 85.00
☐ Rouge, No. 2259, 12″ 300.00 350.00

CREAM
☐ Covered sugar landscape 200.00 300.00

DEMITASSE
☐ Cup and saucer 135.00 175.00

DOG
☐ Rouge, Airedale, 5½″ 600.00 700.00
☐ Rouge, Alsatian, 4″ 350.00 400.00
☐ Rouge, Daschund, same as HN 970 .... 750.00 850.00

DOG, PEKE SITTING AND LOOKING OVER SHOULDER
☐ 4¾″ × 3½″ 600.00 700.00

DOUBLE PENGUIN, MOTHER WITH WING AROUND BABY
☐ 3½″ × 5¾″ 500.00 600.00

DRAGON
☐ Veined Sung, No. 2085, 8″ 500.00 550.00

DRAKE
☐ Rouge, No. 137, 6″ 110.00 95.00

	Price Range	
☐ Rouge, No. 806, 6″	500.00	550.00
DUCK		
☐ Rouge, No. 112, 1½″	55.00	60.00
☐ Rouge, No. 395, 2½″	55.00	60.00
DUCK, SITTING		
☐ Rouge, 7½″	500.00	600.00
DUCK, WINGS FOLDED		
☐ Modelled as floating on water, signed Noke, 7″ × 4″	500.00	600.00
ELEPHANT		
☐ Rouge, 9″, tusks down	300.00	350.00
☐ Rouge, No. 489, white tusks, 7″	300.00	350.00
☐ Rouge, No. 489A, 5½″	115.00	150.00
☐ Elephant Head ashtray, Sung, four heads	300.00	350.00
FISH		
☐ Veined Sung, 12″	1000.00	1100.00
FOX ASHTRAY		
☐	600.00	650.00
FOX, LYING		
☐ Rouge, No. 29, 12″	550.00	600.00
☐ Rouge 29B, 1″	60.00	75.00
☐ Rouge 2593	250.00	300.00
FOX, SITTING		
☐ Rouge, No. 12 (Head pointed down), 5″	75.00	100.00
☐ Rouge, No. 14, 4″	85.00	100.00
FROG		
☐ 2″	135.00	175.00
GIFT OF LIFE		
☐ Mare and Foal, same figure as HN 3524	600.00	750.00
HARE, LYING		
☐ Rouge, No. 656A, 1¾″	60.00	75.00
☐ Rouge, No. 1157, 2¾″	85.00	100.00
HIPPO		
☐ 6¾″ × 3¼″	1100.00	1300.00
IMAGES (Probably prototypes)		
☐ Rouge, double	300.00	350.00
☐ Rouge, single	250.00	300.00
LADY SEATED WITH FLOWING CLOAK		
☐ Veined, rare, 5½″	1200.00	1300.00
☐ Lamp Base Woodcut, house on lake, 7″ high	100.00	150.00

Leaping Salmon, Rouge, 450.00–550.00

	Price Range	
LAUGHING CAVALIER SUNG PLATE		
☐ 10″	150.00	200.00
LEAPING SALMON		
☐ Rouge, No. 666, 12″	450.00	550.00
LION, WITH HEAD ON PAWS		
☐ 7″ × 2½″	1100.00	1400.00
MADONNA AND CHILD		
☐ Sung, signed Noke, 4½″	500.00	600.00
MONKEY		
☐ Seated, arms folded, HN 118, 2¾″	200.00	250.00
MONKEY, LISTENING, SUNG		
☐ 3½″ × 3½″	300.00	400.00

Price Range

MONKEYS
☐ Rouge, No. 486, two in embrace 300.00 350.00

MOUSE ON A CUBE
☐ Rouge, HN 255 .... 500.00 750.00

NUDE ON A ROCK
☐ HN 604, 4½″ (considered rare) 700.00 800.00

OWL
☐ Veined, No. 2249, 12″ 300.00 350.00

OWL WITH BABY UNDER WING
☐ Rouge 500.00 600.00

PENGUIN
☐ Character study on flambé base, signed Noke, 4″ ×
  6″ 600.00 700.00

PENGUIN, WINGS SLIGHTLY AWAY FROM BODY
☐ Signed Noke, 2½″ x 6¾″ 450.00 550.00

PENGUIN
☐ Rouge, No. 84, 6″ 95.00 115.00
☐ Rouge, No. 585, 9″ 700.00 800.00

PIG PLANTER
☐ With silver rim, Rouge, 8″ long, 4½″ high 600.00 700.00

PIPER MINSTREL
☐ 16″ 1350.00 1500.00

PUPPY SITTING
☐ Rouge, HN 128, 4″ 250.00 300.00

RABBIT, EAR UP
☐ Rouge, No. 113, 2½″ 85.00 100.00
☐ Memo Holder 175.00 225.00

RHINOCEROS
☐ Veined, No. 615, 12″ 1200.00 1400.00

SCOTCH TERRIER, STANDING
☐ 7″ × 4″ 700.00 800.00

SOW
☐ 2½″ 300.00 350.00

SQUIRREL
☐ 1¾″ × 1″ 550.00 650.00

TIGER
☐ Rouge, No. 809, 6″ 650.00 700.00

	Price Range	

TORTOISE

□ 3″ × 1″	500.00	550.00

TRAY

□ Veined, No. 1620, 4″	45.00	60.00
□ Veined, No. 1621, 6″	75.00	85.00
□ Woodcut, No. 1620, 4⅛″	45.00	60.00
□ Woodcut, No. 1621, 7½″	85.00	125.00

VASE

□ Landscape, 14″ high, 7″ round, old mark	750.00	900.00
□ Landscape, 1½″ across base, tiny long neck	65.00	75.00
□ Landscape, No. 3879, 5¼″, signed O.C.K.	175.00	225.00
□ No. 1622, large size	1100.00	1200.00
□ No. 1623, large size	1100.00	1200.00
□ No. 1624, large size	1100.00	1200.00
□ Veined, No. 1606, 4¼″	85.00	100.00
□ Veined, No. 1612, 8″	125.00	150.00
□ Veined, No. 1614, 5¾″	75.00	85.00
□ Veined, No. 1616, 8¾″	300.00	350.00
□ Veined, No. 1618, 13¼″	300.00	350.00
□ Veined, No. 7798, artist signed, 11″	550.00	600.00
□ Veined, flamed design with aurene highlights, artist signed, 10½″	350.00	450.00
□ Veined Sung, fish design, artist signed, 8½″	1000.00	1250.00
□ Veined Sung, Pumpkin shape, 6″	550.00	600.00
□ Veined Sung, No. 925, 7″	125.00	150.00
□ Woodcut, Deer Scene, old mark, 11″	600.00	700.00
□ Woodcut, Desert Scene, 8½″	500.00	550.00
□ Woodcut, No. 1603, 7¼″	85.00	
□ Woodcut, No. 1606, 4¼″	70.00	
□ Woodcut, No. 1613, 6½″	110.00	
□ Woodcut, No. 1617, 13¼″	350.00	
□ Woodcut, No. 1619, 11″	350.00	
□ Woodcut, boat scene, No. 7203, 7½″	225.00	275.00
□ Woodcut, landscape, No. 7754, 8″	275.00	325.00
□ Woodcut, scenic landscape miniature, 2½″ high	100.00	125.00

Left to Right: "Veined Sung," No. 1618, No. 1619, 300.00–350.00 each

Left to Right: Woodcut Flambéware, No. 1618, No. 1619, 300.00-350.00 each

ABOUT THE AUTHOR

Mrs. Pollard has been a dealer in limited editions and collectibles for over thirty years. She was owner of Beru's, Inc., a store designed with the collector in mind, for eleven years, but sold it in order to devote more time to writing and traveling. She was the editor of the American Artist Print Price Trends for a national magazine now out of production.

She is a past charter member of the National Association of Limited Edition Dealers and President of the Irvington Businessmen's Association in Indianapolis, for two terms.

Mrs. Pollard was awarded Dealer of the Year award by Frame House Gallery for outstanding sales and advertisements in 1973; and the President's Cup in 1977 for her continuing efforts on behalf of both dealer and collector in the limited edition print field.

Ruth M. Pollard

The author welcomes any comments, corrections, or additions which will either be answered personally or used in any future updating of this price guide. Please write:
> *Ruth M. Pollard*
> *8229 60th St.*
> *Circle East, #501*
> *Sarasota, FL 34243*

The HOUSE OF COLLECTIBLES Series

☐ Please send me the following price guides—
☐ I would like the most current edition of the books listed below.

THE OFFICIAL PRICE GUIDES TO:

☐ 199-3	American Silver & Silver Plate 5th Ed.	$11.95
☐ 513-1	Antique Clocks 3rd Ed.	10.95
☐ 283-3	Antique & Modern Dolls 3rd Ed.	10.95
☐ 287-6	Antique & Modern Firearms 6th Ed.	11.95
☐ 755-X	Antiques & Collectibles 9th Ed.	11.95
☐ 289-2	Antique Jewelry 5th Ed.	11.95
☐ 447-X	Arts and Crafts: American Decorative Arts, 1894–1923 (ID) 1st Ed.	12.95
☐ 539-5	Beer Cans & Collectibles 4th Ed.	7.95
☐ 521-2	Bottles Old & New 10th Ed.	10.95
☐ 532-8	Carnival Glass 2nd Ed.	10.95
☐ 295-7	Collectible Cameras 2nd Ed.	10.95
☐ 548-4	Collectibles of the '50s & '60s 1st Ed.	9.95
☐ 740-1	Collectible Toys 4th Ed.	10.95
☐ 531-X	Collector Cars 7th Ed.	12.95
☐ 538-7	Collector Handguns 4th Ed.	14.95
☐ 748-7	Collector Knives 9th Ed.	12.95
☐ 361-9	Collector Plates 5th Ed.	11.95
☐ 296-5	Collector Prints 7th Ed.	12.95
☐ 001-6	Depression Glass 2nd Ed.	9.95
☐ 589-1	Fine Art 1st Ed.	19.95
☐ 311-2	Glassware 3rd Ed.	10.95
☐ 243-4	Hummel Figurines & Plates 6th Ed.	10.95
☐ 523-9	Kitchen Collectibles 2nd Ed.	10.95
☐ 291-4	Military Collectibles 5th Ed.	11.95
☐ 525-5	Music Collectibles 6th Ed.	11.95
☐ 313-9	Old Books & Autographs 7th Ed.	11.95
☐ 298-1	Oriental Collectibles 3rd Ed.	11.95
☐ 761-4	Overstreet Comic Book 18th Ed.	12.95
☐ 522-0	Paperbacks & Magazines 1st Ed.	10.95
☐ 297-3	Paper Collectibles 5th Ed.	10.95
☐ 744-4	Political Memorabilia 1st Ed.	10.95
☐ 529-8	Pottery & Porcelain 6th Ed.	11.95
☐ 524-7	Radio, TV & Movie Memorabilia 3rd Ed.	11.95
☐ 081-4	Records 8th Ed.	16.95
☐ 247-7	Royal Doulton 5th Ed.	11.95
☐ 280-9	Science Fiction & Fantasy Collectibles 2nd Ed.	10.95
☐ 747-9	Sewing Collectibles 1st Ed.	8.95
☐ 358-9	Star Trek/Star Wars Collectibles 2nd Ed.	8.95
☐ 086-5	Watches 8th Ed.	12.95
☐ 248-5	Wicker 3rd Ed.	10.95

THE OFFICIAL:

☐ 760-6	Directory to U.S. Flea Markets 2nd Ed.	5.95
☐ 365-1	Encyclopedia of Antiques 1st Ed.	9.95
☐ 369-4	Guide to Buying and Selling Antiques 1st Ed.	9.95
☐ 414-3	Identification Guide to Early American Furniture 1st Ed.	9.95
☐ 413-5	Identification Guide to Glassware 1st Ed.	9.95
☐ 448-8	Identification Guide to Gunmarks 2nd Ed.	9.95
☐ 412-7	Identification Guide to Pottery & Porcelain 1st Ed.	$9.95
☐ 415-1	Identification Guide to Victorian Furniture 1st Ed.	9.95

THE OFFICIAL (SMALL SIZE) PRICE GUIDES TO:

☐ 309-0	Antiques & Flea Markets 4th Ed.	4.95
☐ 269-8	Antique Jewelry 3rd Ed.	4.95
☐ 085-7	Baseball Cards 8th Ed.	4.95
☐ 647-2	Bottles 3rd Ed.	4.95
☐ 544-1	Cars & Trucks 3rd Ed.	5.95
☐ 519-0	Collectible Americana 2nd Ed.	4.95
☐ 294-9	Collectible Records 3rd Ed.	4.95
☐ 306-6	Dolls 4th Ed.	4.95
☐ 359-7	Football Cards 7th Ed.	4.95
☐ 540-9	Glassware 3rd Ed.	4.95
☐ 526-3	Hummels 4th Ed.	4.95
☐ 279-5	Military Collectibles 3rd Ed.	4.95
☐ 745-2	Overstreet Comic Book Companion 1st Ed.	4.95
☐ 278-7	Pocket Knives 3rd Ed.	4.95
☐ 527-1	Scouting Collectibles 4th Ed.	4.95
☐ 494-1	Star Trek/Star Wars Collectibles 3rd Ed.	3.95
☐ 088-1	Toys 5th Ed.	4.95

THE OFFICIAL BLACKBOOK PRICE GUIDES OF:

☐ 092-X	U.S. Coins 27th Ed.	4.95
☐ 095-4	U.S. Paper Money 21st Ed.	4.95
☐ 098-9	U.S. Postage Stamps 11th Ed.	4.95

THE OFFICIAL INVESTORS GUIDE TO BUYING & SELLING:

☐ 534-4	Gold, Silver & Diamonds 2nd Ed.	12.95
☐ 535-2	Gold Coins 2nd Ed.	12.95
☐ 536-0	Silver Coins 2nd Ed.	12.95
☐ 537-9	Silver Dollars 2nd Ed.	12.95

THE OFFICIAL NUMISMATIC GUIDE SERIES:

☐ 254-X	The Official Guide to Detecting Counterfeit Money 2nd Ed.	7.95
☐ 257-4	The Official Guide to Mint Errors 4th Ed.	7.95

SPECIAL INTEREST SERIES:

☐ 506-9	From Hearth to Cookstove 3rd Ed.	17.95
☐ 530-1	Lucky Number Lottery Guide 1st Ed.	4.95
☐ 504-2	On Method Acting 8th Printing	6.95

TOTAL

SEE REVERSE SIDE FOR ORDERING INSTRUCTIONS